# Modified Theories of Gravity and Cosmological Applications

# Modified Theories of Gravity and Cosmological Applications

Editors

**Panayiotis Stavrinos**
**Emmanuel Saridakis**

MDPI • Basel • Beijing • Wuhan • Barcelona • Belgrade • Manchester • Tokyo • Cluj • Tianjin

*Editors*
Panayiotis Stavrinos
National and Kapodistrian
University of Athens
Athens, Greece

Emmanuel Saridakis
National Observatory of
Athens
Athens, Greece

*Editorial Office*
MDPI
St. Alban-Anlage 66
4052 Basel, Switzerland

This is a reprint of articles from the Special Issue published online in the open access journal *Universe* (ISSN 2218-1997) (available at: https://www.mdpi.com/journal/universe/special_issues/MTGCA).

For citation purposes, cite each article independently as indicated on the article page online and as indicated below:

LastName, A.A.; LastName, B.B.; LastName, C.C. Article Title. *Journal Name* **Year**, *Volume Number*, Page Range.

**ISBN 978-3-0365-5829-5 (Hbk)**
**ISBN 978-3-0365-5830-1 (PDF)**

# Contents

**About the Editors** . . . . . . . . . . . . . . . . . . . . . . . . . . . . . . . . . . . . . . . . . . . . . **vii**

**Preface to "Modified Theories of Gravity and Cosmological Applications"** . . . . . . . . . . . . **ix**

**Panayiotis Stavrinos and Emmanuel Saridakis**
Editorial of *Modified Theories of Gravity and Cosmological Applications*
Reprinted from: *Universe* **2022**, *8*, 415, doi:10.3390/universe8080415 . . . . . . . . . . . . . . . . . . **1**

**Yu-Peng Zhang, Shao-Wen Wei and Yu-Xiao Liu**
Spinning Test Particle in Four-Dimensional Einstein–Gauss–Bonnet Black Holes
Reprinted from: *Universe* **2020**, *6*, 103, doi:10.3390/universe6080103 . . . . . . . . . . . . . . . . . . **5**

**Jianhui Qiu and Changjun Gao**
Constructing Higher-Dimensional Exact Black Holes in Einstein-Maxwell-Scalar Theory
Reprinted from: *Universe* **2020**, *6*, 148, doi:10.3390/universe6090148 . . . . . . . . . . . . . . . . . . **19**

**Thomas Berry, Alex Simpson, and Matt Visser**
Photon Spheres, ISCOs, and OSCOs: Astrophysical Observables for Regular Black Holes with Asymptotically Minkowski Cores
Reprinted from: *Universe* **2021**, *7*, 2, doi:10.3390/universe7010002 . . . . . . . . . . . . . . . . . . . **29**

**Panayiotis Stavrinos and Sergiu I. Vacaru**
Broken Scale Invariance, Gravity Mass, and Dark Energy inModified Einstein Gravity with Two Measure Finsler like Variables
Reprinted from: *Universe* **2021**, *7*, 89, doi:10.3390/universe7040089 . . . . . . . . . . . . . . . . . . . **47**

**Sergey Il'ich Kruglov**
New Model of 4D Einstein–Gauss–Bonnet Gravity Coupled with Nonlinear Electrodynamics
Reprinted from: *Universe* **2021**, *7*, 249, doi:10.3390/universe7070249 . . . . . . . . . . . . . . . . . . **79**

**Damianos Iosifidis, Nurgissa Myrzakulov and Ratbay Myrzakulov**
Metric-Affine Version of Myrzakulov $F(R,T,Q,\mathcal{T})$ Gravity and Cosmological Applications
Reprinted from: *Universe* **2021**, *7*, 262, doi:10.3390/universe7080262 . . . . . . . . . . . . . . . . . . **91**

**Andronikos Paliathanasis**
New Anisotropic Exact Solution in Multifield Cosmology
Reprinted from: *Universe* **2021**, *7*, 323, doi:10.3390/universe7090323 . . . . . . . . . . . . . . . . . . **103**

**Felipe J. Llanes-Estrada**
Elongated Gravity Sources as an Analytical Limit for Flat Galaxy Rotation Curves
Reprinted from: *Universe* **2021**, *7*, 346, doi:10.3390/universe7090346 . . . . . . . . . . . . . . . . . . **111**

**John W. Moffat and Viktor Toth**
Scalar–Tensor–Vector Modified Gravity in Light of the Planck 2018 Data
Reprinted from: *Universe* **2021**, *7*, 358, doi:10.3390/universe7100358 . . . . . . . . . . . . . . . . . . **131**

**Gabriele U. Varieschi**
Relativistic Fractional-Dimension Gravity
Reprinted from: *Universe* **2021**, *7*, 387, doi:10.3390/universe7100387 . . . . . . . . . . . . . . . . . . **139**

**Andronikos Paliathanasis**
Dynamical Analysis and Cosmological Evolution in Weyl Integrable Gravity
Reprinted from: *Universe* **2021**, *7*, 468, doi:10.3390/universe7120468 . . . . . . . . . . . . . . . . . . **159**

# About the Editors

**Panayiotis Stavrinos**

I am an organizer of International Conferences and Seminars and Editorial Board Member of international journals. I have published four monographs in the English language. I am a founding member of the Balkan Society of Geometers and served as its Vice-President from 2000 to 2004. I am also a founding member of the Hellenic Relativity, Gravitation and Cosmology Society. I am referee in many international journals and an invited speaker at Universities and Workshops worldwide. I contributed in the development of the research topic of Finslerian Gravitation and Finslerian Cosmology, with more than 90 research papers published in international journals and proceedings in international conferences since 1991. I am a member of the Scientific and Organizing Committees of more than 20 Conferences.

**Emmanuel Saridakis**

I am the author of 240 publications, with a total of 17.000 citations and an h-index of 75 (Google Scholar). I am a representative of Greece and a Working Group Leader at COST Action "Addressing observational tensions in cosmology with systematics and fundamental physics" (CosmoVerse),a member of the "Hellenic Relativity, Gravitation and Cosmology Society" (HSRGC), and a member of the management board. I am on the review boards of various journals and have performed more than 850 reviews of scientific works. I have given 70 talks at internationally established conferences, among which 50 were invited talks. I am also a member of the Organizing Committee of 15 Conferences.

# Preface to "Modified Theories of Gravity and Cosmological Applications"

The recent data release by the Planck satellite collaboration presents a renewed challenge for modified theories of gravitation.

Modified gravity theories and their consequences in cosmology, motivated by rapid progress in the field of observational cosmology, allow for precision tests which are of fundamental significance for the development of new gravitational theories in the framework of the observational Universe.

The purpose of this book edition of this Special Issue is to provide some recent results of investigations in the field of gravitation and cosmology with interesting published works in the corresponding research areas.

**Panayiotis Stavrinos and Emmanuel Saridakis**
*Editors*

universe

MDPI

*Editorial*

# Editorial of *Modified Theories of Gravity and Cosmological Applications*

Panayiotis Stavrinos [1,*] and Emmanuel Saridakis [2,3,4]

1 Department of Mathematics, National and Kapodistrian University of Athens, 15784 Athens, Greece
2 National Observatory of Athens, 11852 Athens, Greece
3 Department of Astronomy, School of Physical Sciences, University of Science and Technology of China, Hefei 230026, China
4 CAS Key Laboratory for Research in Galaxies and Cosmology, University of Science and Technology of China, Hefei 230026, China
* Correspondence: pstavrin@math.uoa.gr

General Relativity is a theory of gravity that describes some of the effects of gravity with high accuracy, such as solar system tests, gravitational lensing, gravitational waves, black holes, deflection angle, etc., in a definite framework of an homogeneous and isotropic space–time.

However, taking into account the abundance and nature of dark energy and dark matter, the nature of inflation, cosmological tensions such as the H0 and S8, the possible values of local anisotropy in the evolution of the universe, as well as the theoretical problems of the cosmological constant and of nonrenormalizability, the validity range of general relativity might be restricted.

Modified theories of gravity extend the framework of general relativity through various methods, leading to different field equations and thus to different cosmological implications. They play an essential role in and contribute to modern cosmology, providing a foundation for the current understanding of physical phenomena of the Universe.

We would like to thank all the valued authors, who contributed to the success of this Special Issue, *"Modified Theories of Gravity and Cosmological Applications"*. Their research has promoted the topics of Modified Theories of Gravity, General Relativity and Cosmology. Here, we will briefly cite the main results of the contributors.

Yu-Peng Zhang, Shao-Wen Wei and Yu-Xiao Liu, in their paper *"Spinning Test Particle in Four-Dimensional Einstein-Gauss-Bonnet Black Holes"* [1], investigated the motion of a spinning test particle in a background of a spherically symmetric black hole based on the novel four-dimensional Einstein–Gauss–Bonnet gravity. They successfully found an interesting result: that the innermost stable circular orbit (ISCO) of the spinning test particle has similar behavior as the case of a spinning test particle in GR.

Jianhui Qiu and Changjun Gao, in the paper *"Constructing Higher-Dimensional Exact Black Holes in Einstein-Maxwell-Scalar Theory* [2], constructed higher-dimensional and exact black holes in Einstein–Maxwell–scalar theory. They investigated black hole thermodynamics in connection with the generalized Smarr formula and the first law of thermodynamics. They also provided interesting results for the transition from small black holes to medium and finally to large black holes, by using Hawking temperature.

Thomas Berry, Alex Simpson and Matt Visser, in their paper *Photon Spheres, ISCOs, and OSCOs: Astrophysical Observables for Regular Black Holes with Asymptotically Minkowski Cores* [3], calculated physically observable quantities for a recently proposed regular black hole with an asymptotically Minkowski core. They studied the manner in which the photon sphere and the extremal stable timelike circular orbit (ESCO) relate to the presence (or absence) of horizons. The authors also investigated different situations of photon spheres and ESCO, which is extended to horizonless compact massive objects providing interesting results.

Citation: Stavrinos, P.; Saridakis, E. Editorial of *Modified Theories of Gravity and Cosmological Applications*. *Universe* **2022**, *8*, 415. https://doi.org/10.3390/universe8080415

Received: 4 August 2022
Accepted: 5 August 2022
Published: 9 August 2022

Panayiotis Stavrinos and Sergiu I. Vacaru, in the paper *Broken Scale Invariance, Gravity Mass, and Dark Energy in Modified Einstein Gravity with Two Measure Finsler-Like Variables* [4], studied new classes of generic off-diagonal and diagonal cosmological solutions for effective Einstein equations in modified gravity theories (MGTs), with modified dispersion relations (MDRs), and encoding possible violations of (local) Lorentz invariance (LIVs). Effective potentials for the scalar field provide an interesting unified description of locally anisotropic and/or isotropic early universe inflation related to acceleration cosmology and dark energy. The authors also describe "emergent universes" by off-diagonal and diagonal solutions for certain nonholonomic phases and parametric cosmological evolution resulting in various inflationary phases.

Sergey Il'ich Kruglov, in his paper *New Model of 4D Einstein-Gauss-Bonnet Gravity Coupled with Nonlinear Electrodynamics* [5], obtained an exact spherically symmetric and magnetized Black Hole solution in 4D Einstein–Gauss–Bonnet gravity coupled with nonlinear electrodynamics. He also investigated the black hole thermodynamics, entropy, shadow, energy emission rate and quasinormal modes of black holes, providing interesting results.

Damianos Iosifidis, Nurgissa Myrzakulov and Ratbay Myrzakulov, in their paper *Metric-Affine Version of Myrzakulov* $F(R,T,\mathcal{Q},\mathcal{T})$ *Gravity and Cosmological Applications* [6], derived the full set of field equations of the class of theories whose gravitational part of the Lagrangian is given by $F(R,T,\mathcal{Q},\mathcal{T},\mathcal{D})$. They generalized the family of theories to those also including the divergence of the dilation current obtaining interesting results. In their theory, they also derived the Friedmann equations and examined under what circumstances the presence of torsion can have an accelerating affect on cosmological evolution.

Andronikos Paliathanasis, in his paper *New Anisotropic Exact Solution in Multifield Cosmology* [7], investigated the existence of inflationary solutions on multifield cosmology with a homogeneous locally rotational spacetimes (LRS) anisotropic background space. He also provided an interesting exact solution to describe anisotropic inflation with a Kantowski–Sachs geometry.

Felipe J. Llanes-Estrada, in the paper *Elongated Gravity Sources as an Analytical Limit for Flat Galaxy Rotation Curves* [8], showed that galactic rotation curves are natural in the analytic limit in which the gravitational source is cylindrical, receiving interesting results.

John W. Moffat and Viktor Toth, in the paper *Scalar-Tensor-Vector Modified Gravity in Light of the Planck 2018 Data* [9], extended a calculation that was used previously to demonstrate compatibility between the Scalar–Tensor–Vector–Gravity (STVG) theory. They also found the very interesting result that within the limits of this approximation, the theory accurately reproduces the features of the angular power spectrum.

Gabriele U. Varieschi in the paper *Relativistic Fractional-Dimension Gravity* [10], showed that a relativistic version can be derived from the mathematical theory for spaces with non-integer dimensions, the extended Euler–Lagrange equations for scalar fields, and the existing methods for scalar–tensor models of gravity, multi-scale spacetimes and fractional gravity theories with applications to the FLRW metric of standard cosmology. It was also shown that it is straightforward to extend the standard Friedmann equations and to solve them numerically for different choices of parameters.

Andronikos Paliathanasis, in the paper *Dynamical Analysis and Cosmological Evolution in Weyl Integrable Gravity* [11], investigated the cosmological evolution for the physical parameters in Weyl integrable gravity in a Friedmann–Lemaître–Robertson–Walker universe with zero spatial curvature. He calculated the stationary points for the field equations and he studied their stability properties. He also successfully solved the inverse problem for the case of an ideal gas and proved that the gravitational field equations can follow from the variation of a Lagrangian function.

Joshua Baines, Thomas Berry, Alex Simpson and Matt Visser, in the paper *Killing Tensor and Carter Constant for Painlevé-Gullstrand Form of Lense-Thirring Spacetime* [12], showed that the Painlevé–Gullstrand variant of the Lense–Thirring spacetime possesses a nontrivial Killing tensor, implying separability of the Hamilton–Jacobi equation. They also successfully proved that the Klein–Gordon equation is also separable on this spacetime and they extracted the Carter constant which allowed the geodesic equations to become integrable.

Sergey Paston and Taisiia Zaitseva, in the paper *Nontrivial Isometric Embeddings for Flat Spaces* [13], used an interesting method of sequential surface deformations for the construction of unfolded embeddings to successfully construct such embeddings of flat Euclidean three-dimensional space and Minkowski space, which can be used to analyze the equations of motion of embedding gravity. This method can also be used to build new multidimensional embeddings based on already known embeddings with a small value of the embedding class.

Hongxing Zhang, Naying Zhou, Wenfang Liu and Xin Wu in their paper, *Charged Particle Motions near Non-Schwarzschild Black Holes with External Magnetic Fields in Modified Theories of Gravity* [14], introduced a metric deformation to the Schwarzschild spacetime. They also discussed orbital dynamical properties and successfully proved that the deformation perturbation metric can be changed into a Kerr-like black hole metric via some appropriate coordinate transformation. Finally, they used one of the obtained time-transformed explicit symplectic integrators combined with the techniques of Poincaré sections and FLIs to show how small changes of the parameters affect the dynamical transitions from order to chaos.

Stanislav Alexeyev, Daniil Krichevskiy and Boris Latosh, in the paper *Gravity Models with Nonlinear Symmetry Realization* [15], studied three interesting models with particular non-linear conformal symmetry realizations. Two models are found to be equivalent up to a change of coset coordinates. It was found that models contain ghost degrees of freedom that may be excluded by an introduction of an additional symmetry to the target space. One model was also found to be safe in the early universe.

Aleksander Kozak and Aneta Wojnar, in their paper *Interiors of Terrestrial Planets in Metric-Affine Gravity* [16], used modified gravity theory and showed that it affects the internal properties of terrestrial planets, such as the physical characteristics of their core, mantle and core–mantle boundary. They successfully applied these results for modeling a two-layer exoplanet in Palatini $f(R)$ gravity.

Alexei M. Frolov, in his paper *On Maxwell Electrodynamics in Multi-Dimensional Spaces* [17], derived the equations of Maxwell electrodynamics in multi-dimensional spaces from the variational principle of least action, which is applied to the action function of the electromagnetic field, providing interesting results. He also successfully applied methods of scalar electrodynamics to analyze Maxwell equations in the two- and one-dimensional spaces.

Yuri Shtanov, in the paper *On the Conformal Frames in $f(R)$ Gravity* [18], pointed out that the effect of "running units" in the Einstein frame is related to the fact that the explicit and implicit quantum parameters of the Standard Model, such as the Higgs vacuum expectation value and the parameter $\Lambda_{QCD}$, are modified by the conformal transformation of the metric and matter fields and become scalaron-dependent. Considering the scalaron of $f(R)$ gravity describing dark matter, he showed that the effect of running units in this case is extremely weak, making two frames practically equivalent. He also focused on the interesting situation that arises in a late-time universe in which the oscillating scalaron plays the role of dark matter.

Dusko Borka, Vesna Borka Jovanovic, Violeta N. Nikolic, Nenad D. Lazarov and Predrag Jovanovic, in their paper *Estimating the Parameters of the Hybrid Palatini Gravity Model with the Schwarzschild Precession of S2, S38 and S55 Stars: Case of Bulk Mass Distribution* [19], estimated the parameters of the Hybrid Palatini gravity model with the Schwarzschild precession of S-stars, specifically of the S2, S38 and S55 stars. They took into account the case of bulk mass distribution near the Galactic Center. Based on this observational fact, they successfully evaluated the parameters of the Hybrid Palatini Gravity model with the Schwarzschild precession of the S2, S38 and S55 stars, and they estimated the range of parameters of the Hybrid Palatini gravity model for which the orbital precession is as in GR for all three stars. They also evaluated the parameters of the Hybrid Palatini Gravity model in the case of different values of bulk mass density distribution of extended matter.

Mahmoud AlHallak, Amer AlRakik, Nidal Chamoun and Moustafa Sayem El-Daher, in their paper *Palatini $f(R)$ Gravity and Variants of k-/Constant Roll/Warm Inflation within Variation of Strong Coupling Scenario* [20], showed that upon applying Palatini $f(R)$ method, characterized by an $\alpha R^2$, one obtains a quadratic kinetic energy. They investigated in Palatini formalism two extreme cases corresponding first to $(\alpha >> 1)$, which represents a highly non-canonical k-inflation, and second to $(\alpha << 1)$, where they kept terms to the first order and examined a specific type of the k-inflation, namely the constant-roll inflation. They also successfully showed the viability of the model for some choices of the free parameters in regards to the spectral parameters $(n_s, r)$ when compared to the results of Planck 2018.

**Conflicts of Interest:** The authors declare no conflict of interest.

## References


1. Zhang, Y.-P.; Wei, S.-W.; Liu, Y.-X. Spinning Test Particle in Four-Dimensional Einstein–Gauss–Bonnet Black Holes. *Universe* **2020**, *6*, 103. [CrossRef]
2. Qiu, J.; Gao, C. Constructing Higher-Dimensional Exact Black Holes in Einstein-Maxwell-Scalar Theory. *Universe* **2020**, *6*, 148. [CrossRef]
3. Berry, T.; Simpson, A.; Visser, M. Photon Spheres, ISCOs, and OSCOs: Astrophysical Observables for Regular Black Holes with Asymptotically Minkowski Cores. *Universe* **2021**, *7*, 2. [CrossRef]
4. Stavrinos, P.; Vacaru, S.I. Broken Scale Invariance, Gravity Mass, and Dark Energy in Modified Einstein Gravity with Two Measure Finsler-like Variables. *Universe* **2021**, *7*, 89. [CrossRef]
5. Kruglov, S.I. New Model of 4D Einstein-Gauss-Bonnet Gravity Coupled with Nonlinear Electrodynamics. *Universe* **2021**, *7*, 249. [CrossRef]
6. Iosifidis, D.; Myrzakulov, N.; Myrzakulov, R. MetricAffine Version of Myrzakulov F (R; T; Q; T ) Gravity and Cosmological Applications. *Universe* **2021**, *7*, 262. [CrossRef]
7. Paliathanasis, A. New Anisotropic Exact Solution in Multifield Cosmology. *Universe* **2021**, *7*, 323. [CrossRef]
8. Llanes-Estrada, F.L. Elongated Gravity Sources as an Analytical Limit for Flat Galaxy Rotation Curves. *Universe* **2021**, *7*, 346. [CrossRef]
9. Moffat, J.W.; Toth, V. Scalar-Tensor-Vector Modified Gravity in Light of the Planck 2018 Data. *Universe* **2021**, *7*, 358. [CrossRef]
10. Varieschi, G.U. Relativistic Fractional-Dimension Gravity. *Universe* **2021**, *7*, 387. [CrossRef]
11. Paliathanasis, A. Dynamical Analysis and Cosmological Evolution in Weyl Integrable Gravity. *Universe* **2021**, *7*, 468. [CrossRef]
12. Baines, J.; Berry, T.; Simpson, A.; Visser, M. Killing Tensor and Carter Constant for Painlevé–Gullstrand Form of Lense–Thirring Spacetime. *Universe* **2021**, *7*, 473. [CrossRef]
13. Paston, S.; Zaitseva, T. Nontrivial Isometric Embeddings for Flat Spaces. *Universe* **2021**, *7*, 477. [CrossRef]
14. Zhang, H.; Zhou, N.; Liu, W.; Wu, X. Charged Particle Motions near Non-Schwarzschild Black Holes with External Magnetic Fields in Modified Theories of Gravity. *Universe* **2021**, *7*, 488. [CrossRef]
15. Alexeyev, S.; Krichevskiy, D.; Latosh, B. Gravity Models with Nonlinear Symmetry Realization. *Universe* **2021**, *7*, 501. [CrossRef]
16. Kozak, A.; Wojnar, A. Interiors of Terrestrial Planets in Metric-Affine Gravity. *Universe* **2021**, *8*, 3. [CrossRef]
17. Frolov, A.M. On Maxwell Electrodynamics in Multi-Dimensional Spaces. *Universe* **2021**, *8*, 20. [CrossRef]
18. Shtanov, Y. On the Conformal Frames in $f(R)$ Gravity. *Universe* **2021**, *8*, 69. [CrossRef]
19. Borka, D.; Jovanović, V.B.; Nikolic, V.N.; Lazarov, N.Đ.; Jovanovic, P. Estimating the Parameters of the Hybrid Palatini Gravity Model with the Schwarzschild Precession of S2, S38 and S55 Stars: Case of Bulk Mass Distribution. *Universe* **2021**, *8*, 70. [CrossRef]
20. AlHallak, M.; AlRakik, A.; Chamoun, N.; El-Daher, M.S. Palatini f(R) Gravity and Variants of k-/Constant Roll/Warm Inflation within Variation of Strong Coupling Scenario. *Universe* **2021**, *8*, 126. [CrossRef]

universe

MDPI

Communication

# Spinning Test Particle in Four-Dimensional Einstein–Gauss–Bonnet Black Holes

**Yu-Peng Zhang [1,2], Shao-Wen Wei [1,2] and Yu-Xiao Liu [1,2,3,*]**

1 Joint Research Center for Physics, Lanzhou University and Qinghai Normal University, Lanzhou 730000 and Xining 810000, China; zhangyupeng14@lzu.edu.cn (Y.-P.Z.); weishw@lzu.edu.cn (S.-W.W.)
2 Institute of Theoretical Physics & Research Center of Gravitation, Lanzhou University, Lanzhou 730000, China
3 Key Laboratory for Magnetism and Magnetic of the Ministry of Education, Lanzhou University, Lanzhou 730000, China
* Correspondence: liuyx@lzu.edu.cn

Received: 27 June 2020; Accepted: 27 July 2020; Published: 28 July 2020

**Abstract:** In this paper, we investigate the motion of a classical spinning test particle in a background of a spherically symmetric black hole based on the novel four-dimensional Einstein–Gauss–Bonnet gravity [D. Glavan and C. Lin, Phys. Rev. Lett. 124, 081301 (2020)]. We find that the effective potential of a spinning test particle in this background could have two minima when the Gauss–Bonnet coupling parameter $\alpha$ is nearly in a special range $-8 < \alpha/M^2 < -2$ ($M$ is the mass of the black hole), which means a particle can be in two separate orbits with the same spin-angular momentum and orbital angular momentum, and the accretion disc could have discrete structures. We also investigate the innermost stable circular orbits of the spinning test particle and find that the corresponding radius could be smaller than the cases in general relativity.

**Keywords:** Gauss–Bonnet; innermost stable circular orbits; spinning test particle

## 1. Introduction

As the most successful gravitational theory, general relativity (GR) can explain the relation between geometry and matter. One of the most impressive results derived from GR is black hole solutions. As vacuum solutions of strong gravitational systems, black holes have lots of interesting characters, for examples, a binary black hole system can produce gravitational waves [1–5], and a black hole can act as an accelerator of particles [6,7]. However, we should note that, even though GR is so powerful and can be used to explain many phenomena, there are still some problems that cannot be interpreted by GR. Therefore, it is believed that there should be a more fundamental theory beyond GR.

It is well-known that the existence of a singularity located inside a black hole leads to geodesics incompleteness [8,9]. To overcome the problem of singularity, several quantum theories of gravity have been proposed, like the superstring/M theory and the extension of such theories. With the help of the perturbation approximation of these theories, the Gauss–Bonnet (GB) term was found as the next leading order term [10–12], and this term has ghost-free combinations and does not add higher derivative terms into the gravitational field equations [13]. The GB term appears in $D$-dimensional spacetime as follows

$$S_{[\mathrm{GB}]}[g_{\mu\nu}] = \int d^D x \sqrt{-g}\alpha\mathcal{G}, \tag{1}$$

where $D$ is the number of the spacetime dimensions, $\alpha$ is the GB coupling parameter with mass dimension $D-4$, and the GB invariant $\mathcal{G}$ is defined as

$$\mathcal{G} = R^{\mu\nu\rho\sigma}R_{\mu\nu\rho\sigma} - 4R^{\mu\nu}R_{\mu\nu} + R^2. \tag{2}$$

Many black hole solutions of GB gravity in $D \geq 5$ have been derived, such as the vacuum case [14], Einstein-Maxwell fields with a GB term [15,16], and anti-de Sitter (AdS) case [17]. In four-dimensional spacetime, the GB term does not make contributions to the gravitational dynamics, which makes the four-dimensional minimally coupled GB gravity is hard to obtain. However, very recently, D. Glavan and C. Lin [18] proposed a novel four-dimensional Einstein–Gauss–Bonnet (EGB) gravity that bypasses the Lovelock theorem by adopting an artful coupling constant $\alpha \to \frac{\alpha}{D-4}$. It takes the contributions from the Gauss–Bonnet term into the dynamics of the four-dimensional spcaetime. The same idea about rescaling the coupling constant $\alpha$ has been already introduced in Ref. [19].

In this novel four-dimensional EGB gravity, the GB invariant term does not affect the properties of the massless graviton and a four-dimensional static and spherically symmetric black hole solution was obtained. The stability and shadow of this four-dimensional EGB black hole have been studied in Ref. [20], where the quasinormal modes of a scalar, electromagnetic, and gravitational perturbations were studied. The solutions of a charged black hole [21] and spinning black hole [22] have also been obtained, and a constraint to the GB parameter $\alpha$ was first given in Ref. [22] in terms of the shadow of the rotating black hole. Inspired by the novel four-dimensional EGB gravity, the novel four-dimensional Einstein–Lovelock gravities are also proposed [23,24]. Note that the way of rescaling coupling constant is based on the limit of $D \to 4$ in a higher $D$-dimensional spacetime, where the limit is not continuous due to the parameter $D$—the number of dimensions—a new way for the dimensional-regularization is proposed [25]. Apart from the discontinuousness of the dimension, there are also several works [26–36] pointing out that this novel four-dimensional EGB gravity [18] will cause problems at the level of action and equation of motion and give the improved four-dimensional EGB gravity. However, the Schwarzchild black hole solution in this novel four-dimensional EGB gravity [18] is the same as the result in the improved four-dimensional EGB gravity, which means the properties of the black hole still deserve to be investigated.

It is known that a massless or massive particle can orbit around a central black hole and the motion depends on the geometry of the central black hole. The innermost stable circular orbit (ISCO) of the test particle is the last stable circular orbit, and when a particle is in the location with a radius less than the ISCO, it will plunge into the black hole. Therefore the information of the ISCO and the motion of the test particle in the background black hole could give us some properties of the accretion disc and the corresponding radiation spectrum [37]. In Ref. [38], the authors extended the range of the GB coupling parameter for the black hole solution to $-8 \leq \alpha/M^2 \leq 1$ ($M$ is the mass of the black hole) and investigated the shadow and ISCO of a spinless test particle. They found that a positive (or negative) GB coupling parameter $\alpha$ will reduce (or increase) the ISCO radius. It is shown that the spin of a test particle can also reduce or increase the ISCO radius of a test particle in the background of a black hole in GR [39]. Inspired by the effects of the four-dimensional GB term and the non-vanishing spin on the motion of the test particle, it is necessary to investigate the motion of a spinning test particle and the corresponding ISCO in this novel four-dimensional EGB black hole. In this paper, we will investigate the motion of a spinning test particle in the background of the novel four-dimensional EGB black hole and show how the ISCO of the spinning test particle is changed. For simplicity, we only consider the motion of a spinning test particle in the equatorial plane.

This paper is organized as follows. In Section 2, we use the MPD equation to obtain the four-momentum and four-velocity of a spinning test particle in the novel four-dimensional EGB black hole background. In Section 2.2, we study the motion of the spinning test particle and give the relations between the motion of the spinning test particle and the properties of the four-dimensional EGB black hole. Finally, a brief summary and conclusion are given in Section 3.

## 2. Motion of a Spinning Test Particle in a Four-Dimensional EGB Black Hole

### 2.1. Four-Momentum and Four-Velocity of the Spinning Test Particle

In this part, we will solve the equations of motion for a spinning test particle in the novel four-dimensional EGB black hole background. Firstly, let us review the solution of the four-dimensional EGB black hole. The action of the $D$-dimensional EGB gravity is described by

$$S = \int d^D x \sqrt{-g} \left[ \frac{1}{2\kappa^2} R + \alpha \mathcal{G} \right], \tag{3}$$

where $\kappa$ is the gravitational constant and will be set as $\kappa^2 = 1/2$ in this paper. The GB term does not contribute to the dynamics of the four-dimensional spacetime because it is a total derivative. Recently, by rescaling the coupling parameter as

$$\alpha \rightarrow \frac{\alpha}{D-4}, \tag{4}$$

and taking the limit $D \rightarrow 4$, Glaan and Lin [18] obtained the four-dimensional novel EGB gravity. The four-dimensional static spherically symmetric black hole solution was found [18]

$$ds^2 = -f(r)dt^2 + \frac{dr^2}{f(r)} + r^2 d\Omega^2, \tag{5}$$

$$f(r) = 1 + \frac{r^2}{2\alpha}\left(1 - \sqrt{1 + \frac{8\alpha M}{r^3}}\right), \tag{6}$$

where $M$ is the mass of the black hole and the coupling parameter $-8 \leq \frac{\alpha}{M^2} \leq 1$ [38]. Solving $f(r) = 0$, one can get two black hole horizons

$$r_\pm = M \pm \sqrt{M^2 - \alpha}. \tag{7}$$

In fact, the above solution (5)–(7) was also found in gravity with a conformal anomaly in Ref. [40] and was extended to the case with a cosmological in Ref. [41].

For a spinning test particle, its motion will not follow the geodesics because of the spin-curvature force $-\frac{1}{2}R^{\mu}{}_{\nu\alpha\beta}u^\nu S^{\alpha\beta}$. The equations of motion for the spinning test particle are described by the Mathisson-Papapetrou-Dixon (MPD) equations [42–50] under the "pole–dipole" approximation, and the four-velocity $u^\mu$ and the four-momentum $P^\mu$ are not parallel [46,51] due to the spin-curvature force. The MPD equations are

$$\frac{DP^\mu}{D\lambda} = -\frac{1}{2}R^{\mu}{}_{\nu\alpha\beta}u^\nu S^{\alpha\beta}, \tag{8}$$

$$\frac{DS^{\mu\nu}}{D\lambda} = P^\mu u^\nu - u^\mu P^\nu, \tag{9}$$

where $P^\mu$, $S^{\mu\nu}$, and $u^\mu$ are the four-momentum, spin tensor, and tangent vector of the spinning test particle along the trajectory, respectively. Note that the MPD equations are not uniquely specified and we should use a spin-supplementary condition to determine them. This spin-supplementary condition is related to the center of mass of the spinning test particle with different observers [52–56]. In this paper, we choose the Tulczyjew spin-supplementary condition [57]

$$P_\mu S^{\mu\nu} = 0, \tag{10}$$

and the four-momentum $P^\mu$ satisfies

$$P^\mu P_\mu = -m^2, \tag{11}$$

which makes sure that the spinning test particle stays timelike along the trajectory, where $m$ is the mass of the test particle. On the contrary, the four-velocity would be superluminal [46,51] when the spin of the test particle is too large. Actually, this superluminal behavior comes from the ignorance of the "multi-pole" effects. When such effects are considered, the superluminal problem can be avoided [58–62]. For the properties of the spinning test particle in different black hole backgrounds, see Refs. [39,55,63–84].

For the equatorial motion of the spinning test particle with spin-aligned or anti-aligned orbits, the four-momentum and spin tensor should satisfy $P^\theta = 0$ and $S^{\theta\mu} = 0$. The non-vanishing independent variables for the equatorial orbits are $P^t$, $P^r$, $P^\phi$, and $S^{r\phi}$. After adopting the spin-supplementary condition (10), we have [47]

$$S^{rt} = -S^{r\phi}\frac{P_\phi}{P_t}, \quad S^{\phi t} = S^{r\phi}\frac{P_r}{P_t}. \tag{12}$$

Substituting Equation (12) into the following equation

$$s^2 = \frac{1}{2}S^{\mu\nu}S_{\mu\nu} = S^{\phi r}S_{\phi r} + S^{tr}S_{tr} + S^{t\phi}S_{t\phi}, \tag{13}$$

and using Equation (11), we get the $r-\phi$ component of spin tensor

$$S^{r\phi} = -\frac{s}{r}\frac{P_t}{m}. \tag{14}$$

The non-vanishing components of the spin tensor $S^{\mu\nu}$ in the four-dimensional EGB black hole background are

$$\begin{aligned} S^{r\phi} &= -S^{\phi r} = -\frac{s}{r}\frac{P_t}{m}, \\ S^{rt} &= -S^{tr} = -S^{r\phi}\frac{P_\phi}{P_t} = \frac{s}{r}\frac{P_\phi}{m}, \\ S^{\phi t} &= -S^{t\phi} = S^{r\phi}\frac{P_r}{P_t} = -\frac{s}{r}\frac{P_r}{m}, \end{aligned} \tag{15}$$

where the parameter $s$ is the spin angular momentum of the test particle and the spin direction is perpendicular to the equatorial plane.

Due to the existence of the spin-curvature coupling term, the conserved quantities of the spinning test particle are modified. The relation between a killing vector field $\mathcal{K}^\mu$ and the conserved quantity is [46,47]

$$\mathcal{C} = \mathcal{K}^\mu P_\mu - \frac{1}{2}S^{\mu\nu}\mathcal{K}_{\mu;\nu}, \tag{16}$$

where the semicolon denotes the covariant derivative. For simplicity, we only consider the motion in the equatorial plane. Then in the spherically-symmetric EGB black hole with the metric (5), we have the conserved energy with a timelike killing vector $\xi^\mu = (\partial_t)^\mu$ and the conserved total angular momentum with a spacelike killing vector $\eta^\mu = (\partial_\phi)^\mu$ [47], they are

$$m\bar{e} = -\mathcal{C}_t = -\xi^\mu P_\mu + \frac{1}{2}S^{\mu\nu}\xi_{\mu;\nu} = -P_t - \frac{1}{2}\frac{\bar{s}}{r}P_\phi\partial_r g_{tt}, \tag{17}$$

$$m\bar{j} = \mathcal{C}_\phi = \eta^\mu P_\mu - \frac{1}{2}S^{\mu\nu}\eta_{\mu;\nu} = P_\phi - \frac{1}{2}\frac{\bar{s}}{r}P_t\partial_r g_{\phi\phi}. \tag{18}$$

Here, the parameters are defined as $\bar{e} = \frac{e}{m}$, $\bar{j} = \frac{j}{Mm}$, and $\bar{s} = \frac{s}{Mm}$ (we set $M = 1$), where $e$, $m$, and $j$ are the energy, mass, and total angular momentum of the spinning test particle, respectively. Note that we have used the relations $S^{\mu\nu}\xi_{\mu;\nu} = S^{\mu\nu}\xi^\beta\partial_\nu g_{\beta\mu}$ and $S^{\mu\nu}\eta_{\mu;\nu} = S^{\mu\nu}\eta^\beta\partial_\nu g_{\beta\mu}$ for the two Killing vectors.

Solving Equations (11), (17) and (18), we get the non-vanishing components of the four-momentum:

$$P_t = -\frac{m^2\left(\alpha\left(2\bar{e}r^3\Delta + 2\bar{j}\bar{s}\right) - \bar{j}r^3\bar{s}\left(\Delta-1\right)\right)}{\alpha\left(2r^3\Delta + 2\bar{s}^2\right) - r^3\bar{s}^2\left(\Delta - 1\right)}, \tag{19}$$

$$P_\phi = \frac{2\alpha m^2 r^3 \Delta(\bar{j} - \bar{e}\bar{s})}{\alpha\left(2r^3\Delta + 2\bar{s}^2\right) - r^3\bar{s}^2\left(\Delta-1\right)}, \tag{20}$$

and

$$(P^r)^2 = -\frac{m^2 + g^{\phi\phi}P_\phi^2 + g^{tt}P_t^2}{g_{rr}}, \tag{21}$$

where the function $\Delta = \sqrt{1 + \frac{8\alpha}{r^3}}$. We can solve the four-velocity $u^\mu$ by using the equations of motion (8) and (9) and the components of $S^{\mu\nu}$ in (15) [82,85]

$$\frac{DS^{tr}}{D\lambda} = P^t\dot{r} - P^r = \frac{\bar{s}}{2r}g_{\phi\mu}R^\mu_{\ \nu\alpha\beta}u^\nu S^{\alpha\beta} + \frac{\bar{s}}{r^2}P_\phi\dot{r}, \tag{22}$$

$$\frac{DS^{t\phi}}{D\lambda} = P^t\dot{\phi} - P^\phi = -\frac{\bar{s}}{2r}g_{r\mu}R^\mu_{\ \nu\alpha\beta}u^\nu S^{\alpha\beta} - \frac{\bar{s}}{r^2}P_r\dot{r}. \tag{23}$$

Finally, the non-vanishing components of the four-velocity are

$$\dot{r} = \frac{b_2c_1 - b_1c_2}{a_2b_1 - a_1b_2}, \tag{24}$$

$$\dot{\phi} = \frac{a_2c_1 - a_1c_2}{a_1b_2 - a_2b_1}, \tag{25}$$

where the functions $a_1$, $b_1$, $c_1$, $a_2$, $b_2$, and $c_2$ are defined as

$$a_1 = P^t - \frac{\bar{s}}{r^2}P_\phi + \frac{\bar{s}}{2r}R_{\phi r\mu\nu}S^{\nu\mu}, \tag{26}$$

$$b_1 = \frac{\bar{s}}{2r}R_{\phi\phi\mu\nu}S^{\nu\mu}, \tag{27}$$

$$c_1 = -P^r + \frac{\bar{s}}{2r}R_{\phi t\mu\nu}S^{\nu\mu}, \tag{28}$$

$$a_2 = \frac{\bar{s}P_r}{r^2} - \frac{\bar{s}}{2r}R_{rr\mu\nu}S^{\nu\mu}, \tag{29}$$

$$b_2 = P^t - \frac{\bar{s}}{2r}R_{r\phi\mu\nu}S^{\nu\mu}, \tag{30}$$

$$c_2 = -P^\phi - \frac{\bar{s}}{2r}R_{rt\mu\nu}S^{\nu\mu}. \tag{31}$$

We can set the affine parameter $\lambda$ as coordinate time and choose $u^t = 1$ because the trajectories of the test particle are independent of the affine parameter $\lambda$ [45,56]. Then the orbital frequency parameter $\Omega$ of the test particle is

$$\Omega \equiv \frac{u^\phi}{u^t} = \dot{\phi}, \tag{32}$$

where the dot means $\dot{} = d/dt$.

### 2.2. Circular Orbits of Spinning Test Particle

The motion of a test particle in a central field can be determined with the help of the effective potential in the Newtonian dynamics [86,87]. We can use the same method to solve the motion of a test particle in the black hole background in GR. We can prove that the radial velocity $u^r$ is parallel to the radial momentum $P^r$ [88], therefore the effective potential of the spinning test particle can be solved by using the form of $P^r$ (21) [79]. We decompose the $(P^r)^2$ (21) as [68,79]

$$\frac{(P^r)^2}{m^2} = \left(A\bar{e}^2 + B\bar{e} + C\right) \propto \left(\bar{e} - \frac{-B + \sqrt{B^2 - 4AC}}{2A}\right)\left(\bar{e} + \frac{B + \sqrt{B^2 - 4AC}}{2A}\right), \tag{33}$$

where the functions $A$, $B$, and $C$ are

$$A = 2\mathcal{E}^{-1}\alpha m^2 r\left(8\alpha + r^3\right)\left(r^2\bar{s}^2(\Delta - 1) + 2\alpha\left(r^2 - \bar{s}^2\right)\right), \tag{34}$$

$$B = 8\mathcal{E}^{-1}\alpha^2\bar{j}m^2 r\bar{s}\left(-3r^2\Delta + 8\alpha + r^3\right), \tag{35}$$

and

$$\begin{aligned} C = & -2m^2(\alpha\mathcal{E})^{-1}\Big\{16\alpha^4 r\left(\bar{j}^2 + r^2\right) + \alpha^3\Big[2\bar{j}^2(4r^3(1-\Delta) - \bar{s}^2 + r^4) + 4r^3\bar{s}^2(\Delta - 4) \\ & + r^5(8 - 8\Delta) + 2\bar{s}^2\left(\bar{s}^2 - 8r^2\right) + 2r^6\Big] + \alpha^2\Big[\bar{j}^2 r^3\left(2\bar{s}^2(\Delta - 3) + r^3(1 - \Delta)\right) \\ & - r^2\bar{s}^4(\Delta - 9) - 2r^3\bar{s}^4(\Delta - 3) + r^8(1 - \Delta) + 2r^6\bar{s}^2(\Delta - 1) + 2r^5\bar{s}^2(5\Delta - 9)\Big] \\ & + \alpha r^5\bar{s}^2\Big[\bar{j}^2 r(\Delta - 1) + r\bar{s}^2(1 - \Delta) - 4\bar{s}^2(\Delta - 2) + r^3(2\Delta - 2)\Big] + r^8\bar{s}^4((1 - \Delta))\Big\}, \end{aligned} \tag{36}$$

where the function $\mathcal{E}$ is

$$\mathcal{E} = \left[r^3\bar{s}^2(\Delta - 1) - 2\alpha\left(r^3\Delta + \bar{s}^2\right)\right]^2. \tag{37}$$

The effective potential of the test particle is defined by the positive square root of Equation (33)

$$V_{\rm eff}^{\rm spin} = \frac{-B + \sqrt{B^2 - 4AC}}{2A}. \tag{38}$$

The positive square root corresponds to the four-momentum pointing toward future, while the negative one corresponds to the past-pointing four-momentum [89]. When the spin of the test particle is zero, it reduces to

$$V_{\rm eff} = \sqrt{1 + \frac{r^2}{2\alpha}\left(1 - \sqrt{1 + \frac{8\alpha}{r^3}}\right)}\sqrt{1 + \frac{\bar{j}^2}{r^2}} = \sqrt{f(r)\left(1 + \frac{\bar{j}^2}{r^2}\right)}. \tag{39}$$

Note that for the four-dimensional Schwarzchild black hole in GR, the function $f(r) = 1 - \frac{2M}{r}$.

The properties of a test particle in a central field are mainly determined by the effective potential. Thus, the effects on the motion of a spinning test particle can be derived based on how the effective potential depends on the GB coupling parameter $\alpha$ and the spin angular momentum $\bar{s}$. We plot some shapes of the effective potential (38) in Figure 1. We can see that the radii of the extreme points become smaller when the coupling parameter $\alpha > 0$ and become larger when the parameter $\alpha < 0$. The extreme points of the effective potential mean a test particle could move in circular orbits, noting that the orbit at the maximum (minimum) point is unstable (stable). These phenomena mean that a positive GB coupling parameter induces the attractive effect and a negative one results in the repulsive effect on the motion of the test particle.

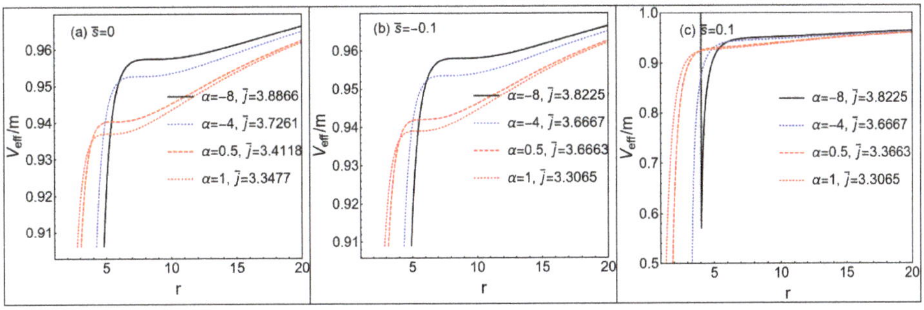


**Figure 1.** The effective potential for a spinning test particle in the four-dimensional Einstein–Gauss–Bonnet (EGB) black hole background. The parameters are set as $M = 1$ and $m = 1$.

In addition to the attractive or repulsive effects on the motion of the test particle, some more interesting results are found when we check the shapes of the effective potential in the parameter space $(\bar{s} - \bar{j})$. We find that the effective potential has two minima when the GB coupling parameter $\alpha$ is in a special range. When the test particle moves in stable circular orbits [79], the radial velocity should be zero

$$\frac{dr}{d\lambda} = 0, \tag{40}$$

and the the radial acceleration vanishes

$$\frac{d^2r}{d\lambda^2} = 0, \left(\frac{dV_{\rm eff}}{dr} = 0 \text{ and } \frac{d^2V_{\rm eff}}{dr^2} > 0\right). \tag{41}$$

The conditions $\frac{dV_{\rm eff}}{dr} = 0$ and $\frac{d^2V_{\rm eff}}{dr^2} > 0$ mean that the energy of the particle should equal to the minimum of the effective potential.

Therefore, when the effective potential of a spinning test particle has two minima, there will be two stable circular orbits for the particle with a spin angular momentum and an orbital angular momentum. This is a new feature for the motion of a spinning test particle in four-dimensional EGB black hole background. We plot the effective potential with two minima in Figure 2, where the corresponding two separate orbits of the spinning test particle with $\bar{s} = 0.3$ and $\bar{j} = 5$ are still given. The case of a spinning test particle can posses two stable circular orbits only happens when $\alpha < 0$ with a special range for $\alpha$. We give the numerical results in Figure 3 and find that the range of $\alpha/M^2$ is nearly in $(-8, -2)$.

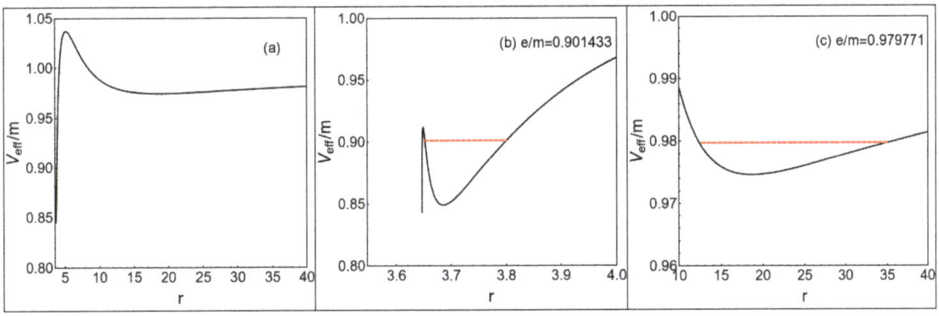


**Figure 2.** *Cont.*

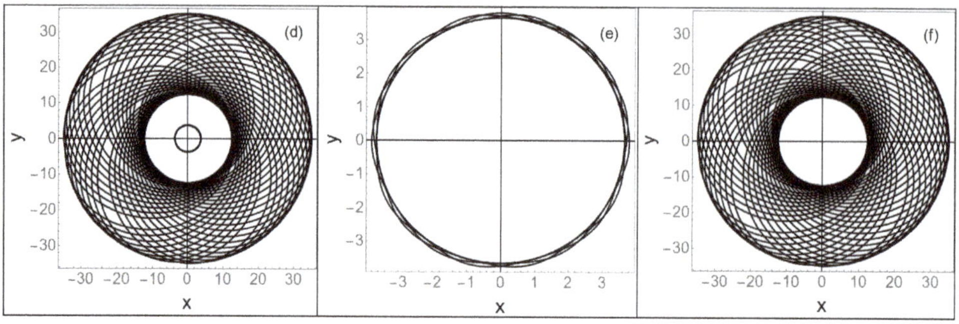


**Figure 2.** Plots of the effective potential and orbits for a spinning test particle with $\bar{s} = 0.3$, $\bar{j} = 5$, and $\alpha = -6$. Here $r^2 = x^2 + y^2$. Subfigures (**b**,**c**) are the two minima of the effective potential shown in subfigure (**a**). Subfigures (**e**,**f**) are two separate orbits around the two minima of the effective potential shown in subfigure (**d**), and they are related to the effective potential in subfigures (**b**,**c**). The values of the red dashed line in subfigures (**b**,**c**) stand for the energy of the test particle. The range of the red dashes in the radial direction stands for the radial range that the test particle can move in, see the corresponding orbits in subfigures (**e**,**f**). The test particles on the two orbits have the same spin and orbital angular momentum. The parameters are set as $M = 1$ and $m = 1$.

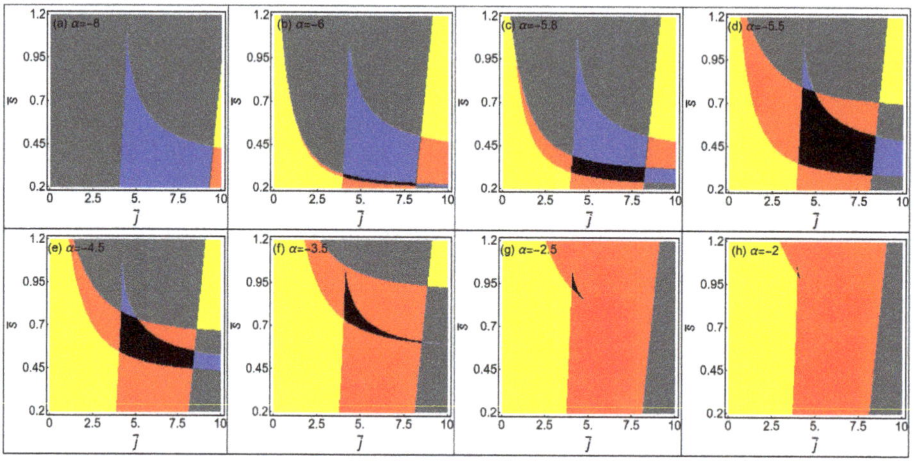


**Figure 3.** Plots of the parameter space ($\bar{s} - \bar{j}$) describing whether a spinning test particle have two stable circular orbits with the same spin $\bar{s}$ and the same total angular momentum $\bar{j}$. The parameters are set as $M = 1$ and $m = 1$. In the black and blue regions, the effective potential has two minima corresponds two stable circular orbits. In the red region the effective potential has one minimum and the test particle has one stable circular orbit. In the gray and yellow regions, the test particle has no stable circular orbits.

We have mentioned that the MPD equations of the spinning test particle is obtained under the "pole–dipole" approximation, which will lead the four-velocity transform from timelike to spacelike if the particle spin is too large. In order to make sure the motion of the spinning test particle is timelike, we adopt the superluminal constraint [68]

$$\frac{u^{\mu}u_{\mu}}{(u^t)^2} = g_{tt} + g_{rr}\dot{r}^2 + g_{\phi\phi}\dot{\phi}^2 < 0. \tag{42}$$

By using the superluminal constraint and circular orbit conditions (40) and (41) of the spinning test particle, we obtain the parameter space ($\bar{s} - l$) in Figure 4, which describes whether the motion on a circular orbit is timelike or spacelike. By comparing the results in Figure 3 and in Figure 4, we confirm that the motion of the particle in the two separate stable orbits is timelike. We know that the effects from the GB term on the motion of the test particle can be attractive or repulsive, where a positive (or negative) GB coupling parameter $\alpha$ leads to an attractive (or repulsive) force. The spin–curvature force can also be attractive or repulsive. When the effects induced by the GB term and the spin–curvature force exist simultaneously, the total attractive or negative force will be enhanced or weakened. It will change the shapes of the regions in $(\bar{l}-\bar{j})$.

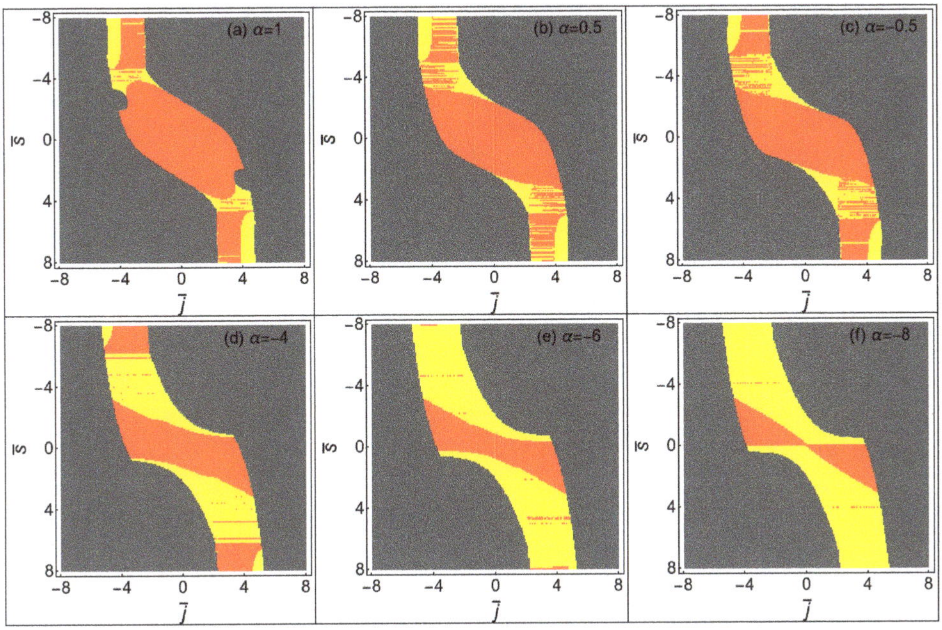


**Figure 4.** Properties of circular orbits for the spinning test particle in the four-dimensional GB black hole background. Here $\bar{l} = \bar{j} - \bar{s}$ is the orbital angular momentum. The parameters are set as $M = 1$ and $m = 1$. In the gray region, the test particle can have timelike circular orbits. In the red and yellow regions, the test particle does not have stable timelike circular orbits. In the yellow region, the motion of the test particle is spacelike and unphysical.

Next, we will investigate the ISCO of the spinning test particle. The ISCO of the test particle locates at the position where the maximum and minimum of the effective potential merge. Thus, the effective potential of the test particle at the ISCO should satisfy

$$\frac{d^2V_{\text{eff}}}{dr^2} = 0. \tag{43}$$

By using Equations (40), (41) and (43), we can derive the ISCO of the test particle. In Ref. [38], the authors showed that the radius of the ISCO for a spinless test particle varies in the form of

$$r_{ISCO} = 6 - \frac{11}{18}\alpha + \mathcal{O}(\alpha). \tag{44}$$

This result was derived under the linear approach with a small $\alpha$ around 0. Obviously, the ISCO of a spinless test particle can be larger or smaller due to the existence of the GB term. This phenomenon is consistent with the behavior of the effective potential, see the subfigure (a) in Figure 1.

When the test particle possesses a non-vanishing spin, the contribution of the spin-curvature force should affect the properties of the motion. The relation between the effective potential and the spin of the test particle is still shown in Figure 1. We give the numerical results of the ISCO in Figure 5.

Note that there is a jump behavior for the ISCO parameters in the subfigure (e) in Figure 5, which is induced by the fact that the effective potential has two minima. Because we use the position where the maximum and minimum of the effective potential merge to locate the ISCO and our step length of spin is not small enough to cover the change of the ISCO parameters. We summarize how the ISCO of the spinning test particle depends on the spin $\bar{s}$ and GB coupling parameter $\alpha$ as follows:

- For the ISCO of the spinning test particle in four-dimensional EGB black hole, the corresponding radius and angular momentum decrease with the spin $\bar{s}$ when the GB coupling parameter $\alpha$ is fixed. When the effect from the GB term is considered, the radius of the ISCO will be smaller than the case of the Schwarzchild black hole in GR, and the Gauss–Bonnet term does not change the laws of the ISCO with spin.
- When the spin of the test particle is fixed, the radius and angular momentum of the ISCO decrease with the GB coupling parameter and this behavior is almost the same as the results of the spinless case in Ref. [38].

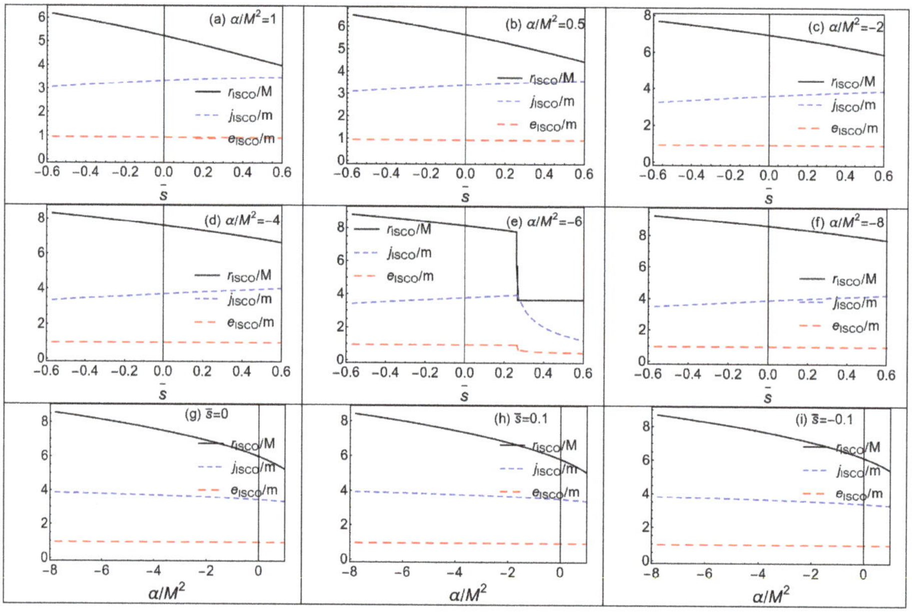


**Figure 5.** The ISCO parameters of the spinning test particle with different values of $\alpha$. The parameters are set as $M = 1$ and $m = 1$.

## 3. Summary

In this paper, we investigated the motion of a spinning test particle in the equatorial plane of the four-dimensional novel EGB black hole. We solved the four-momentum and four-velocity of the spinning test particle and investigated the properties the ISCO. We found that the ISCO of the spinning test particle has similar behavior as the case of a spinning test particle in GR. The GB term and spin parameter $\bar{s}$ can reduce or increase the radius of the ISCO. The new feature for the spinning test particle in the four-dimensional EGB black hole is that the test particle could have two separate stable orbits with the same spin $\bar{s}$ and same total angular momentum $\bar{j}$ when the GB coupling parameter $\alpha$ is in a special range $-8 < \alpha/M^2 < -2$. Due to the fact that the motion of the spinning test particle will be superluminal when the spinning is too large, we also gave the superluminal constraint on the four-velocity of the spinning test particle in the circular orbits and confirmed that the motion of the spinning test particle that can move at two seperate orbits is timelike. It means that there will be a discrete gravitational radiation spectrum when a spinning test particle is inspiraling into a four-dimensional EGB black hole, and the corresponding accretion disc could have discrete structures, which provides a possible way to test and constraint the four-dimensional EGB gravity.

**Author Contributions:** The authors have contributed equally to this work. All authors have read and agreed to the published version of the manuscript.

**Funding:** This work was supported in part by the National Natural Science Foundation of China (Grants No. 11875151, No. 11705070, No. 11522541, and No. 11675064). Y.P. Zhang was supported by a scholarship granted by the Chinese Scholarship Council (CSC: 201806180036).

**Conflicts of Interest:** The authors declare no conflict of interest.

## References

1. Abbott, B.; Jawahar, S.; Lockerbie, N.; Tokmakov, K. [LIGO Scientific Collaboration and Virgo Collaboration]. Observation of Gravitational Waves from a Binary Black Hole Merger. *Phys. Rev. Lett.* **2016**, *116*, 061102. [CrossRef] [PubMed]
2. Abbott, B.; Jawahar, S.; Lockerbie, N.; Tokmakov, K. [LIGO Scientific Collaboration and Virgo Collaboration]. GW151226: Observation of Gravitational Waves from a 22-Solar-Mass Binary Black Hole Coalescence. *Phys. Rev. Lett.* **2016**, *116*, 241103. [CrossRef]
3. Abbott, B.P.; Abbott, R.; Abbott, T.D.; Acernese, F.; Ackley, K.; Adams, C.; Adams, T.; Addesso, P.; Adhikari, R.X.; Adya, V.B. [LIGO Scientific Collaboration and Virgo Collaboration]. GW170104: Observation of a 50-Solar-Mass Binary Black Hole Coalescence at Redshift 0.2. *Phys. Rev. Lett.* **2017**, *118*, 221101. [CrossRef] [PubMed]
4. Abbott, B.P.; Abbott, R.; Abbott, T.D.; Acernese, F.; Ackley, K.; Adams, C.; Adams, T.; Addesso, P.; Adhikari, R.X.; Adya, V.B.; et al. [LIGO Scientific Collaboration and Virgo Collaboration]. GW170814: A Three-Detector Observation of Gravitational Waves from a Binary Black Hole Coalescence. *Phys. Rev. Lett.* **2017**, *119*, 141101. [CrossRef] [PubMed]
5. Abbott, B.; Jawahar, S.; Lockerbie, N.; Tokmakov, K. [LIGO Scientific Collaboration and Virgo Collaboration]. GW170817: Observation of Gravitational Waves from a Binary Neutron Star Inspiral. *Phys. Rev. Lett.* **2017**, *119*, 161101. [CrossRef]
6. Banados, M.; Silk, J.; West, S.M. Kerr Black Holes as Particle Accelerators to Arbitrarily High Energy. *Phys. Rev. Lett.* **2009**, *103*, 111102. [CrossRef]
7. Wei, S.-W.; Liu, Y.-X.; Guo, H.; Fu, C.-E. Charged spinning black holes as Particle Accelerators. *Phys. Rev. D* **2010**, *82*, 103005. [CrossRef]
8. Penrose, R. Gravitational collapse and space-time singularities. *Phys. Rev. Lett.* **1965**, *14*, 57. [CrossRef]
9. Hawking, S.W.; Penrose, R. The Singularities of gravitational collapse and cosmology. *Proc. R. Soc. Lond. A* **1970**, *314*, 529–548.
10. Gross, D.J.; Witten, E. Superstring Modifications of Einstein's Equations. *Nucl. Phys. B* **1986**, *277*, 1–10. [CrossRef]
11. Gross, D.J.; Sloan, J.H. The Quartic Effective Action for the Heterotic String. *Nucl. Phys. B* **1987**, *291*, 41–89. [CrossRef]
12. Bento, M.C.; Bertolami, O. Maximally Symmetric Cosmological Solutions of higher curvature string effective theories with dilatons. *Phys. Lett. B* **1996**, *368*, 198–201. [CrossRef]
13. Zwiebach, B. Curvature Squared Terms and String Theories. *Phys. Lett. B* **1985**, *156*, 315–317. [CrossRef]
14. Boulware, D.G.; Deser, S. String-generated gravity models. *Phys. Rev. Lett.* **1985**, *55*, 2656–2660. [CrossRef]
15. Wiltshire, D.L. Spherically symmetric solutions of Einstein-Maxwell theory with a Gauss-Bonnet term. *Phys. Lett. B* **1986**, *169*, 36–40. [CrossRef]
16. Wiltshire, D.L. Black holes in string-generated gravity models. *Phys. Rev. D* **1988**, *38*, 2445. [CrossRef] [PubMed]
17. Cai, R.-G. Gauss-Bonnet black holes in AdS spaces. *Phys. Rev. D* **2002**, *65*, 084014. [CrossRef]
18. Glavan, D.; Lin, C. Einstein-Gauss-Bonnet Gravity in Four-Dimensional Spacetime. *Phys. Rev. Lett.* **2020**, *124*, 081301. [CrossRef]
19. Cognola, G.; Myrzakulov, R.; Sebastiani, L.; Zerbini, S. Einstein gravity with Gauss-Bonnet entropic corrections. *Phys. Rev. D* **2013**, *88*, 024006. [CrossRef]
20. Konoplya, R.A.; Zinhailo, A.F. Quasinormal modes, stability and shadows of a black hole in the novel 4D Einstein-Gauss-Bonnet gravity. *arXiv* **2020**, arXiv:2003.01188.

21. Fernandes, P.G.S. Charged Black Holes in AdS Spaces in 4D Einstein Gauss-Bonnet Gravity. *Phys. Lett. B* **2020**, *805*, 135468. [CrossRef]
22. Wei, S.-W.; Liu, Y.-X. Testing the nature of Gauss-Bonnet gravity by four-dimensional rotating black hole shadow. *arXiv* **2020**, arXiv:2003.07769.
23. Konoplya, R.A.; Zhidenko, A. Black holes in the four-dimensional Einstein-Lovelock gravity. *arXiv* **2020**, arXiv:2003.07788.
24. Casalino, A.; Colleaux, A.; Rinaldi, M.; Vicentini, S. Regularized Lovelock gravity. *arXiv* **2020**, arXiv:2003.07068.
25. Ai, W.-Y. A note on the novel 4D Einstein-Gauss-Bonnet gravity. *arXiv* **2020**, arXiv:2004.02858.
26. Bonifacio, J.; Hinterbichler, K.; Johnson, L.A. Amplitudes and 4D Gauss-Bonnet Theory. *Phys. Rev. D* **2020**, *102*, 024029. [CrossRef]
27. Metin, G.; Sisman, T.C.; Tekin, B. Is there a novel Einstein-Gauss-Bonnet theory in four dimensions? *arXiv* **2020**, arXiv:2004.03390.
28. Hennigar, R.A.; Kubiznak, D.; Mann, R.B.; Pollack, C. On Taking the $D \to 4$ limit of Gauss-Bonnet Gravity: Theory and Solutions. *J. High Energy Phys.* **2020**, *2020*, 27. [CrossRef]
29. Aoki, K.; Gorji, M.A.; Mukohyama, S. A consistent theory of $D \to 4$ Einstein-Gauss-Bonnet gravity. *arXiv* **2020**, arXiv:2005.03859.
30. Shu, F.-W. Vacua in novel 4D Einstein-Gauss-Bonnet Gravity: Pathology and instability? *arXiv* **2020**, arXiv:2004.09339.
31. Mahapatra, S. A note on the total action of 4*D* Gauss-Bonnet theory. *arXiv* **2020**, arXiv:2004.09214.
32. Tian, S.-X.; Zhu, Z.-H. Comment on "Einstein-Gauss-Bonnet Gravity in Four-Dimensional Spacetime". *arXiv* **2020**, arXiv:2004.09954.
33. Arrechea, J.; Delhom, A.; Jiménez-Cano, A. Yet another comment on four-dimensional Einstein-Gauss-Bonnet gravity. *arXiv* **2020**, arXiv:2004.12998.
34. Lu, H.; Pang, Y. Horndeski Gravity as $D \to 4$ Limit of Gauss-Bonnet. *arXiv* **2020**, arXiv:2003.11552.
35. Kobayashi, T. Effective scalar-tensor description of regularized Lovelock gravity in four dimensions. *J. Cosmol. Astropart. Phys.* **2020**, *2020*, 013. [CrossRef]
36. Fernandes, P.G.S.; Carrilho, P.; Clifton, T.; Mulryne, D.J. Derivation of Regularized Field Equations for the Einstein-Gauss-Bonnet Theory in Four Dimensions. *Phys. Rev. D* **2020**, *102*, 024025. [CrossRef]
37. Page, D.N.; Thorne, K.S. Disk-accretion onto a black hole. Time-averaged structure of accretion disk. *Astrophys. J.* **1974**, *191*, 499–506. [CrossRef]
38. Guo, M.-Y.; Li, P.-C. The innermost stable circular orbit and shadow in the novel 4D Einstein-Gauss-Bonnet gravity. *Eur. Phys. J. C* **2020**, *80*, 588. [CrossRef]
39. Suzuki, S.; Maeda, K. Innermost stable circular orbit of a spinning particle in Kerr space-time. *Phys. Rev. D* **1998**, *58*, 023005. [CrossRef]
40. Cai, R.-G.; Cao, L.-M.; Ohta, N. Black Holes in Gravity with Conformal Anomaly and Logarithmic Term in Black Hole Entropy. *J. High Energy Phys.* **2010**, *2010*, 082. [CrossRef]
41. Cai, R.-G. Thermodynamics of Conformal Anomaly Corrected Black Holes in AdS Space. *Phys. Lett. B* **2014**, *733*, 183–189. [CrossRef]
42. Mathisson, M. New mechanics of material systems. *Acta Phys. Pol.* **1937**, *6*, 163.
43. Papapetrou, A. Spinning test-particles in general relativity. I. *Proc. R. Soc. Lond. A* **1951**, *209*, 248–258.
44. Corinaldesi, E.; Papapetrou, A. Spinning test-particles in general relativity. II. *Proc. R. Soc. Lond. A* **1951**, *209*, 259–268.
45. Dixon, W.G. Dynamics of extended bodies in general relativity II. Moments of the charge-current vector. *Proc. R. Soc. Lond. A* **1970**, *319*, 509–547.
46. Hojman, S.A. Electromagnetic and Gravitational Interactions of a Spherical Relativistic Top. Unpublished Ph.D. Thesis, Princeton University, Princeton, NJ, USA, 1975.
47. Hojman, R.; Hojman, S. Spinning Charged Test Particles in a Kerr-Newman Background. *Phys. Rev. D* **1977**, *15*, 2724. [CrossRef]
48. Mashhoon, B.; Singh, D. Dynamics of Extended Spinning Masses in a Gravitational Field. *Phys. Rev. D* **2006**, *74*, 124006. [CrossRef]
49. Zalaquett, N.; Hojman, S.A.; Asenjo, F.A. Spinning massive test particles in cosmological and general static spherically symmetric spacetimes. *Class. Quant. Grav.* **2014**, *31*, 085011. [CrossRef]

50. Uchupol, R.; Sarah, J.V.; Scott, A.H. Gyroscopes orbiting black holes: A frequency-domain approach to precession and spin-curvature coupling for spinning bodies on generic Kerr orbits. *Phys. Rev. D* **2016**, *94*, 044008.
51. Armaza, C.; Banados, M.; Koch, B. Collisions of spinning massive particles in a Schwarzschild background. *Class. Quantum Gravity* **2016**, *33*, 105014. [CrossRef]
52. Wald, R.M. Gravitational spin interaction. *Phys. Rev. D* **1972**, *6*, 406–413. [CrossRef]
53. Lukes-Gerakopoulos, G.; Seyrich, J.; Kunst, D. Investigating spinning test particles: Spin supplementary conditions and the Hamiltonian formalism. *Phys. Rev. D* **2014**, *90*, 104019. [CrossRef]
54. Filipe, L.; Costa, O.; Lukes-Gerakopoulos, G.; Semerák, O. On spinning particles in general relativity: Momentum-velocity relation for the Mathisson-Pirani spin condition. *Phys. Rev. D* **2018**, *97*, 084023.
55. Lukes-Gerakopoulos, G.; Harms, E.; Bernuzzi, S.; Nagar, A. Spinning test-body orbiting around a Kerr black hole: Circular dynamics and gravitational-wave fluxes. *Phys. Rev. D* **2017**, *96*, 064051. [CrossRef]
56. Lukes-Gerakopoulos, G. Time parameterizations and spin supplementary conditions of the Mathisson-Papapetrou-Dixon equations. *Phys. Rev. D* **2017**, *96*, 104023. [CrossRef]
57. Tulczyjew, W. Motion of multipole particles in general relativity theory. *Acta Phys. Pol.* **1959**, *18*, 393.
58. Deriglazov, A.A.; Ramírez, W.G. Mathisson-Papapetrou-Tulczyjew-Dixon (MPTD) equations in ultra-relativistic regime and gravimagnetic moment. *Int. J. Mod. Phys. D* **2016**, *26*, 1750047. [CrossRef]
59. Deriglazov, A.A.; Ramírez, W.G. Ultrarelativistic Spinning Particle and a Rotating Body in External Fields. *Adv. High Energy Phys.* **2016**, *2016*, 1376016. [CrossRef]
60. Ramírez, W.G.; Deriglazov, A.A. Relativistic effects due to gravimagnetic moment of a rotating body. *Phys. Rev. D* **2017**, *96*, 124013. [CrossRef]
61. Deriglazov, A.A.; Ramírez, W.G. Recent progress on the description of relativistic spin: Vector model of spinning particle and rotating body with gravimagnetic moment in General Relativity. *Adv. Math. Phys.* **2017**, *2017*, 7397159. [CrossRef]
62. Steinhoff, J.; Puetzfeld, D. Multipolar equations of motion for extended test bodies in general relativity. *Phys. Rev. D* **2010**, *81*, 044019. [CrossRef]
63. Han, W.-B. Gravitational Radiations from a Spinning Compact Object around a supermassive Kerr black hole in circular orbit. *Phys. Rev. D* **2010**, *82*, 084013. [CrossRef]
64. Harms, E.; Lukes-Gerakopoulos, G.; Bernuzzi, S.; Nagar, A. Spinning test body orbiting around a Schwarzschild black hole: Circular dynamics and gravitational-wave fluxes. *Phys. Rev. D* **2016**, *94*, 104010. [CrossRef]
65. Mukherjee, S.; Nayak, K.R. Off-equatorial stable circular orbits for spinning particles. *Phys. Rev. D* **2018**, *98*, 084023. [CrossRef]
66. Zhang, M.; Liu, W.-B. Innermost stable circular orbits of charged spinning test particles. *Phys. Lett. B* **2019**, *789*, 393. [CrossRef]
67. Pugliese, D.; Quevado, H.; Ruffini, R. Equatorial circular orbits of neutral test particles in the Kerr Newman spacetime. *Phys. Rev. D* **2013**, *88*, 024042. [CrossRef]
68. Zhang, Y.-P.; Wei, S.-W.; Guo, W.-D.; Sui, T.-T.; Liu, Y.-X. Innermost stable circular orbit of spinning particle in charged spinning black hole background. *Phys. Rev. D* **2018**, *97*, 084056. [CrossRef]
69. Stuchlík, Z. Equilibrium of spinning test particles in the Schwarzschild-de Sitter spacetimes. *Acta Phys. Slov.* **1999**, *49*, 319.
70. Stuchlík, Z.; Ková, J. Equilibrium conditions of spinning test particles in Kerr-de Sitter spacetimes. *Class. Quant. Grav.* **2006**, *23*, 3935. [CrossRef]
71. Plyatsko, R.; Fenyk, M.; Panat, V. Highly relativistic spin-gravity-$\Lambda$ coupling. *Phys. Rev. D* **2017**, *96*, 064038. [CrossRef]
72. Plyatsko, R.; Panat, V.; Fenyk, M. Nonequatorial circular orbits of spinning particles in the Schwarzschild-de Sitter background. *Gen. Relat. Grav.* **2018**, *50*, 150. [CrossRef]
73. Han, W.-B. Dynamics of extended bodies with spin-induced quadrupole in Kerr spacetime: Generic orbits. *Gen. Relat. Grav.* **2017**, *49*, 48. [CrossRef]
74. Warburton, N.; Osburn, T.; Evans, C.R. Evolution of small-mass-ratio binaries with a spinning secondary. *Phys. Rev. D* **2017**, *96*, 084057. [CrossRef]
75. Liu, Y.; Liu, W.-B. Energy extraction of a spinning particle via the super Penrose process from an extremal Kerr black hole. *Phys. Rev. D* **2018**, *97*, 064024. [CrossRef]
76. Mukherjee, S. Collisional Penrose process with spinning particles. *Phys. Lett. B* **2018**, *778*, 54–59. [CrossRef]

77. Faye, G.; Blanchet, L.; Buonanno, A. Higher-order spin effects in the dynamics of compact binaries. I. Equations of motion. *Phys. Rev. D* **2006**, *74*, 104033. [CrossRef]
78. Witzany, V.; Steinhoff, J.; Lukes-Gerakopoulos, G. Hamiltonians and canonical coordinates for spinning particles in curved space-time. *Class. Quantum Gravity* **2019**, *36*, 075003. [CrossRef]
79. Jefremov, P.I.; Tsupko, O.Y.; Bisnovatyi-Kogan, G.S. Innermost stable circular orbits of spinning test particles in Schwarzschild and Kerr space-times. *Phys. Rev. D* **2015**, *91*, 124030. [CrossRef]
80. Toshmatov, B.; Malafarina, D. Spinning test particle in the $\gamma$ space-times. *Phys. Rev. D* **2019**, *100*, 104052. [CrossRef]
81. Nucamendi, U.; Becerril, R.; Sheoran, P. Bounds on spinning particles in their innermost stable circular orbits around rotating braneworld black hole. *Eur. Phys. J. C* **2020**, *80*, 35. [CrossRef]
82. Zhang, Y.-P.; Gu, B.-M.; Wei, S.-W.; Yang, J.; Liu, Y.-X. Charged spinning black holes as accelerators of spinning particles. *Phys. Rev. D* **2016**, *94*, 124017. [CrossRef]
83. Conde, C.; Galvis, C. Properties of the Innermost Stable Circular Orbit of a spinning particle moving in a rotating Maxwell-dilaton black hole background. *Phys. Rev. D* **2019**, *99*, 104059. [CrossRef]
84. Liu, Y.-L.; Zhang, X.-D. Maximal efficiency of the collisional Penrose process with spinning particles in Kerr-Sen black hole. *Eur. Phys. J. C* **2020**, *80*, 31. [CrossRef]
85. Hojman, S.A.; Asenjo, F.A. Can gravitation accelerate neutrinos? *Class. Quantum Gravity* **2013**, *30*, 025008. [CrossRef]
86. Kaplan, S.A. On crcular orbits in Einstein's Gravitation Theory. *J. Exp. Theor. Phys.* **1949**, *19*, 951.
87. Landau, L.D.; Lifshitz, E.M. *The Classical Theory of Fields*; Pergamon: Oxford, UK, 1993.
88. Zhang, Y.-P.; Wei, S.-W.; Amaro-Seoane, P.; Yang, J.; Liu, Y.-X. Motion deviation of test body induced by spin and cosmological constant in extreme mass ratio inspiral binary system. *Eur. Phys. J. C* **2019**, *79*, 856. [CrossRef]
89. Misner, C.W.; Thorne, K.S.; Wheeler, J.A. *Gravitation*; Freeman: New York, NY, USA, 1973; p. 911.

universe

MDPI

Communication

# Constructing Higher-Dimensional Exact Black Holes in Einstein-Maxwell-Scalar Theory

**Jianhui Qiu** [1,2,*] **and Changjun Gao** [1,2]

1 Key Laboratory of Computational Astrophysics, National Astronomical Observatories, Chinese Academy of Sciences, Beijing 100101, China; gaocj@bao.ac.cn
2 School of Astronomy and Space Sciences, University of Chinese Academy of Sciences, No. 19A, Yuquan Road, Beijing 100049, China
* Correspondence: jhqiu@nao.cas.cn

Received: 21 July 2020; Accepted: 4 September 2020; Published: 9 September 2020

**Abstract:** We construct higher-dimensional and exact black holes in Einstein-Maxwell-scalar theory. The strategy we adopted is to extend the known, static and spherically symmetric black holes in the Einstein-Maxwell dilaton gravity and Einstein-Maxwell-scalar theory. Then we investigate the black hole thermodynamics. Concretely, the generalized Smarr formula and the first law of thermodynamics are derived.

**Keywords:** Einstein-Maxwell-scalar black holes; modified gravity theory; Hawking-Page phase transition

## 1. Introduction

According to the Lovelock [1,2] and the Ostrogradsky instability [3] theorems, it is uniquely the Einstein gravity that consists of metric and its derivatives and with the equations of motion no more than second order. Therefore, to extend the Einstein gravity, the easiest way is to couple it with a scalar field. On the other hand, string theory is generally considered to be the most promising approach to unify quantum theory and gravity in higher dimensions. The low energy limit of string theory does lead to the Einstein gravity coupled non-minimally to a scalar dilaton field [4]. The dilaton field, coupled in a nontrivial way to other fields such as gauge fields has aroused many interests and many black hole solutions are found [5–8].

These solutions are all asymptotically flat. It has been proved [9,10] that in the presence of one or two Liouville-type potential which is considered to be a generalization of the cosmological constant, neither asymptotically flat nor (anti)-de Sitter solutions exist. However, by combining three Liouville-type dilaton potential, one successfully constructs a higher-dimensional asymptotically (anti)-de Sitter solutions [11]. Then the topological anti-de Sitter black branes with higher dimensions in Einstein-Maxwell dilaton theory were constructed and their properties were investigated [12]. With the same dilaton potential in [11], Sheykhi [13] finds the metric for the n-dimensional charged slowly rotating dilaton black hole in the background of asymptotically (anti)-de Sitter spacetime.

On the other hand, a remarkable phenomenon of spontaneous scalarization of charged black holes is recently discovered [14,15] and vast studies on the scalarization of black holes in various Einstein-Maxwell-scalar (EMS) models (see [16] and references therein) are carried out. Most of these studies are based on numerical calculations. In view of this point, we will construct exact charged black hole solutions in EMS theory. Our strategy is to extend the known, static and spherically symmetric black holes in the Einstein-Maxwell dilaton gravity to EMS theory. Actually, using this method, we have constructed the four-dimensional black holes in EMS in [17]. Thus, the purpose of this paper is to extend it from four dimensions to higher dimensions.

The paper is organized as follows. In Section 2, we derive the equations of motion for the fields and present the metric. In Section 3, we introduce the generalized Smarr formula for this solution and verify the validity of the first law of black hole thermodynamics. In Section 4, we investigate the thermodynamic stability problem and the phase transitions by using heat capacity and Gibbs free energy. In Section 5 we summarize our results.

## 2. Action and the Equations Motion

We start from the action of Einstein-Maxwell-scalar theory

$$S=\int d^n x\sqrt{-g}\left[R-\frac{4}{n-2}\nabla_\mu\phi\nabla^\mu\phi-V(\phi)-K(\phi)F^2\right], \tag{1}$$

where $R$ is the Ricci scalar curvature, $F^2\equiv F_{\mu\nu}F^{\mu\nu}$ comes from the Maxwell field, $K(\phi)$ is the coupling function between scalar field and Maxwell field. $V(\phi)$ is the scalar potential.

Varying the action with respect to the metric, Maxwell and the scalar field, respectively, yields

$$R_{\mu\nu}=\frac{4}{n-2}\nabla_\mu\phi\nabla_\nu\phi+\frac{V}{n-2}g_{\mu\nu}+2KF_{\mu\alpha}F_\nu^\alpha-\frac{K}{n-2}F^2 g_{\mu\nu}), \tag{2}$$

$$\partial_\mu\left(\sqrt{-g}KF^{\mu\nu}\right)=0, \tag{3}$$

$$\nabla_\mu\nabla^\mu\phi-\frac{n-2}{8}\left(\frac{\partial V}{\partial\phi}+\frac{\partial K}{\partial\phi}F^2\right)=0. \tag{4}$$

We choose the most general form of the metric for static black hole as follows

$$ds^2=-U(x)\,dt^2+\frac{1}{U(x)}dx^2+f(x)^2\,d\Omega_{n-2}^2, \tag{5}$$

where $x$ denotes the radial variable. Then the Maxwell Equation (3) can be integrated to give

$$F^{10}=\frac{q}{Kf^{n-2}}, \tag{6}$$

where $q$ is the constant of integration and it has the dimension of $l^{n-3}$. Then the equations of motion (2) to (4) reduce to three independent equations

$$\frac{1}{f^{n-2}}\frac{d}{dx}\left(f^{n-2}U\frac{d\phi}{dx}\right)=\frac{n-2}{8}\left[\frac{\partial V}{\partial\phi}-\frac{2q^2\partial_\phi K}{f^{2n-4}K^2}\right], \tag{7}$$

$$\frac{1}{f}\frac{d^2f}{dx^2}=-\frac{4}{(n-2)^2}\left(\frac{d\phi}{dx}\right)^2, \tag{8}$$

$$\frac{1}{f^{n-2}}\frac{d}{dx}\left(U\frac{d}{dx}f^{n-2}\right)=\frac{(n-2)(n-3)}{f^2}-V-\frac{2q^2}{Kf^{2n-4}}. \tag{9}$$

There are five functions $U$, $f$, $\phi$, $V$ and $K$ in these equations. However, we have only three equations. Therefore, the system of equations is not closed. In general, one usually presumes $V$, $K$ and then solve for $U$, $f$, $\phi$. For example, Reference [11] assumes

$$K(\phi)=e^{\frac{4\alpha\phi}{n-2}}, \tag{10}$$

$$V(\phi)=\frac{\lambda}{3(n-3+\alpha^2)^2}\left[-\alpha^2(n-2)\left(n^2-n\alpha^2-6n+\alpha^2+9\right)e^{\frac{4(n-3)\phi}{(n-2)\alpha}}+(n-2)(n-3)^2\left(n-1-\alpha^2\right)e^{-\frac{4\alpha\phi}{n-2}}+4\alpha^2(n-3)(n-2)^2e^{\frac{2\phi\left(n-3-\alpha^2\right)}{(n-2)\alpha}}\right]. \tag{11}$$

Here $V(\phi)$ is the dilaton potential in higher dimensions. It combines three Liouville-type potential which is considered to be a generalization of the cosmological constant. We have mentioned in the introduction that it has been proved [9–11] that only by combining more than two such potential, can the asymptotically (anti)-de Sitter solution exists.

Then Reference [11] gives the solution as follows

$$\begin{aligned} ds^2 &= -\left\{\left[1-\left(\frac{b}{r}\right)^{n-3}\right]\left[1-\left(\frac{a}{r}\right)^{n-3}\right]^{1-\gamma(n-3)} - \frac{1}{3}\lambda r^2\left[1-\left(\frac{a}{r}\right)^{n-3}\right]^{\gamma}\right\} dt^2 \\ &+\left\{\left[1-\left(\frac{b}{r}\right)^{n-3}\right]\left[1-\left(\frac{a}{r}\right)^{n-3}\right]^{1-\gamma(n-3)} - \frac{1}{3}\lambda r^2\left[1-\left(\frac{a}{r}\right)^{n-3}\right]^{\gamma}\right\}^{-1} \\ &\cdot\left[1-\left(\frac{a}{r}\right)^{n-3}\right]^{-\gamma(n-4)} dr^2 + r^2\left[1-\left(\frac{a}{r}\right)^{n-3}\right]^{\gamma} d\Omega_{n-2}^2, \end{aligned} \tag{12}$$

$$\phi = -\frac{(n-2)\alpha}{2\left(\alpha^2+n-3\right)} \ln\left[1-\left(\frac{a}{r}\right)^{n-3}\right]. \tag{13}$$

Here $a$, $b$ are two integration constants which are related to the black hole mass and electric charge. $\lambda$ is the cosmological constant and $\alpha$ is the coupling constant. $\gamma$ is given by [11]

$$\gamma \equiv \frac{2\alpha^2}{(n-3)\left(n-3+\alpha^2\right)}. \tag{14}$$

In contrast to the above example, here we shall presume $U$, $f$ in advance and then solve for $\phi$, $V$, $K$. To find the desirable expressions for $U$ and $f$, we observe Equation (12) and find that the $\lambda$ term is proportional to $r^2\left[1-\left(\frac{a}{r}\right)^{n-3}\right]^{\gamma}$.

On the other hand, the four-dimensional black hole solution in EMS theory is [17]

$$U = \left(1-\frac{2m}{r}\right)\left(1-\frac{Q^2}{mr}\right)^{\frac{1-\alpha^2}{1+\alpha^2}} + \frac{\beta Q^2}{f^2} - \frac{1}{3}\lambda f^2, \tag{15}$$

$$f = r\left(1-\frac{Q^2}{mr}\right)^{\frac{\alpha^2}{1+\alpha^2}}, \tag{16}$$

$$K = \frac{2e^{2\alpha\phi}}{2+\beta+\beta\alpha^2 e^{2\alpha\phi+2\phi/\alpha}}, \tag{17}$$

$$\begin{aligned} V &= \frac{2\lambda}{3\left(1+\alpha^2\right)^2}\left[\alpha^2\left(3\alpha^2-1\right)e^{2\phi/\alpha} + \left(3-\alpha^2\right)e^{-2\alpha\phi}\right. \\ &\left. +8\alpha^2 e^{-\phi\alpha+\phi/\alpha}\right]. \end{aligned} \tag{18}$$

Equation (18) is the expression of $V(\phi)$ in four dimensions. $K(\phi)$ is the extension of dilaton coupling $e^{2\alpha\phi}$. We [17] have shown that with this extension, the well-known Reissner-Nordstrom-de Sitter solution can be included when $\gamma = 0$.

Therefore, motivated by Equations (12) and (15), we presume a new solution

$$ds^2 = -Udt^2 + \frac{1}{U}\cdot\left[1-\left(\frac{a}{r}\right)^{n-3}\right]^{-\gamma(n-4)} dr^2 + f^2 d\Omega_{n-2}^2, \tag{19}$$

with

$$
\begin{aligned}
U &= \left[1-\left(\frac{b}{r}\right)^{n-3}\right]\left[1-\left(\frac{a}{r}\right)^{n-3}\right]^{1-\gamma(n-3)} - \frac{1}{3}\lambda r^2\left[1-\left(\frac{a}{r}\right)^{n-3}\right]^{\gamma} \\
&\quad +\beta q^2\left\{r^2\left[1-\left(\frac{a}{r}\right)^{n-3}\right]^{\gamma}\right\}^{3-n}, \\
f &= r\left[1-\left(\frac{a}{r}\right)^{n-3}\right]^{\gamma/2}, 
\end{aligned} \tag{20}
$$

where $\beta$ is a constant. If we take the limit of $r \to \infty$, we shall find Equation (19) reduces to the metric describing (anti)-de Sitter metric. Therefore, the metric is asymptotically (anti)-de Sitter. Compared with metric (12), this metric includes a new term of $\beta$ which is related the charge squared. With the introduction of this new term, the higher-dimensional Reissner-Nordstrom-de Sitter black holes can be reduced provided that $a \to 0$ and $\beta = 1$. In fact, the metric is the higher-dimensional extension of the metric found in [17]

$$
\begin{aligned}
U &= \left(1-\tfrac{2m}{r}\right)\left(1+\tfrac{\gamma Q^2}{mr}\right)^{\frac{1-\alpha^2}{1+\alpha^2}} + \tfrac{\beta Q^2}{f} - \tfrac{1}{3}\lambda f\,, \\
f &= r^2\left(1+\tfrac{\gamma Q^2}{mr}\right)^{\frac{2\alpha^2}{1+\alpha^2}}\,.
\end{aligned} \tag{21}
$$

When $\gamma = 0$, we find $U$ and $f$ reduce to the four-dimensional metric describing charged (Anti)-de-Sitter black holes. Therefore, given the Einstein-Maxwell-scalar theory (the extension of dilaton coupling Equation (27) and the dilaton potential Equation (11)), the metric Equation (19) is unique. Now a new term of $\beta$ is inserted in the expression of $U$. Since $q$ has the dimension of $l^{n-3}$, $\beta$ is dimensionless. Given the expressions of $U,\ f$, the expressions of $\phi,\ K,\ V$ are then worked out from the equations of motion. To this end, we transform the equations of motion from $(t,\ x)$ coordinates to $(t,\ r)$ coordinates via the following coordinates transformation

$$
x = \int dr\left[1-\left(\frac{a}{r}\right)^{n-3}\right]^{-\gamma(n-4)/2}, \quad \text{or} \quad r' = \left[1-\left(\frac{a}{r}\right)^{n-3}\right]^{\gamma(n-4)/2}. \tag{22}
$$

Then the equations of motion Equations (7)–(9) turn out to be

$$
\frac{1}{f^{n-2}}r'\frac{d}{dr}\left(f^{n-2}Ur'\frac{d\phi}{dr}\right) = \frac{n-2}{8}\left(\frac{\partial V}{\partial\phi} - \frac{2q^2\partial_\phi K}{f^{2n-4}K^2}\right), \tag{23}
$$

$$
\frac{1}{f}\frac{d}{dr}\left(r'\frac{df}{dr}\right) = -\frac{4}{(n-2)^2}\left(\frac{d\phi}{dr}\right)^2 r', \tag{24}
$$

$$
\frac{1}{f^{n-2}}r'\frac{d}{dr}\left(Ur'\frac{d}{dr}f^{n-2}\right) = \frac{(n-2)(n-3)}{f^2} - V - \frac{2q^2}{Kf^{2n-4}}. \tag{25}
$$

Substituting Equation (20) into above equations of motion, we obtain

$$
\phi = -\frac{(n-2)\alpha}{2\left(\alpha^2+n-3\right)}\ln\left[1-\left(\frac{a}{r}\right)^{n-3}\right], \tag{26}
$$

$$
K(\phi) = \frac{2\left(\alpha^2+n-3\right)e^{\frac{4\alpha\phi}{n-2}}}{2\,\alpha^2+(n-3)\left[2+\left(n^2-5\,n+6\right)\beta\right]+\beta\,\alpha^2\,(n-2)\,(n-3)\,e^{\frac{4\left(\alpha^2+n-3\right)\phi}{\alpha\,(n-2)}}}, \tag{27}
$$

and

$$
q^2 = \tfrac{(n-2)(n-3)^2}{2(n-3+\alpha^2)}a^{n-3}b^{n-3}\,, \tag{28}
$$

with $V$ the exact form of Equation (11). When $n = 4$, $K$ restores to Equation (17). Up to this point, the n-dimensional and exact black hole solution is constructed in EMS theory.

In the next, we calculate the electric charge and mass of the black hole. The electric charge is

$$Q = \frac{1}{4\pi} \lim_{x \to \infty} \int F_{tr} \sqrt{-g} K(\phi)\, d^{n-2}x = \frac{\Omega_{n-2}}{4\pi} q \,. \tag{29}$$

The definition of variable "$x$" is given by Equation (22). $x \to \infty$ means $r \to \infty$. In other words, we take the limit at spatial infinity. The quasilocal mass of the dilaton (anti)de Sitter black hole can be calculated by using the subtraction method of Brown and York (BY) [18,19]. This is an extension of ADM definition of the mass. For asymptotically flat or asymptotically AdS spacetimes, the ADM mass at infinity coincides with the conserved mass in Brown York method. Therefore, following the procedures of [20], we choose the method of Brown and York in this paper. The definition of conserved mass is given by

$$M \equiv \frac{1}{8\pi} \int_{\mathcal{B}} d^2\varphi \sqrt{\sigma} \left\{ (K_{ab} - K h_{ab}) - \left( K^0_{ab} - K^0 h^0_{ab} \right) \right\} n^a \xi^b \,, \tag{30}$$

where $\mathcal{B}$ is the boundary surface of the spacetime, $\xi$ a timelike Killing vector field on $\mathcal{B}$, $\sigma$ the determinant of the metric of the boundary $\mathcal{B}$, $K^0_{ab}$ the extrinsic curvature of the background metric and $n^a$ the timelike unit normal vector to the boundary $\mathcal{B}$. In the context of counterterm method and following the procedure of [20], we get, after a detailed calculation,

$$M = \frac{\Omega_{n-2}}{16\pi} (n-2) \left[ b^{n-3} + (1 - (n-3)\gamma)\, a^{n-3} \right] \,, \tag{31}$$

which is the same as [20].

## 3. Thermodynamics

In this section, we explore the black hole thermodynamics. Concretely, we shall construct the generalized Smarr formula and the first law of thermodynamics. To this end, we start from the calculation of Hawking temperature which is defined as follows:

$$\kappa^2 = -\frac{1}{2} \nabla_a \chi_b \nabla^a \chi^b \,, \tag{32}$$

where $\chi^\mu$ is a Killing vector field which is null on the horizon. Since we are dealing with a static metric and we can choose $\chi^\mu = \frac{\partial}{\partial t}$. Then one can write the expression of temperature for black holes

$$T = \frac{1}{4\pi} \frac{U'(r_+)}{\sqrt{U(r_+) W(r_+)}} \,, \tag{33}$$

with the metric

$$ds^2 = -U(r)dt^2 + W(r)dr^2 + f(r)^2 d\Omega^2_{n-2} \,. \tag{34}$$

The coordinate system used here is singular on the black hole horizon. However, the divergence of coordinate system on the black hole horizon does not mean the thermodynamic quantities are divergent. This is because the thermodynamic quantities, for example, the mass, the temperature, the entropy and so on, evaluated below are all defined and observed by the observers in spatial infinity. Of course, for the observers resting on the horizon, these thermodynamic quantities are all divergent. The technique we adopt in the paper is very traditional in the literature. For example, the Schwarzschild coordinate system used in the Schwarzschild metric is singular on the black hole horizon. However, the corresponding thermodynamic quantities are all regular although they are evaluated in Schwarzschild coordinate system. As for the definition of the temperature, it is divergent on the horizon at first glance. However, it is not the case. Actually, since $W(r) = \frac{1}{U} \cdot \left[ 1 - \left( \frac{a}{r} \right)^{n-3} \right]^{-\gamma(n-4)}$, we conclude that there is no singularity in the temperature.

After substituting the equation of event horizon $U(r_+) = 0$, we get the formula for temperature

$$
\begin{aligned}
T = & \frac{1}{12\pi r_+}\left[-3q^2\beta r_+^{-2n+6}(n-3)\Gamma^{-1+\frac{(-n+2)\gamma}{2}} + (-9+3n)\Gamma^{1+\frac{(-n+2)\gamma}{2}}\right. \\
& \left. + r_+^2\lambda\left(-(n-3)\left(\gamma n - 2\gamma - 1\right)\right)\Gamma^{-1+\frac{\gamma(-2+n)}{2}} + r_+^2\lambda\Gamma^{\frac{\gamma(n-2)}{2}}(n-2)\left(\gamma n - 3\gamma - 2\right)\right],
\end{aligned} \tag{35}
$$

where $\Gamma \equiv 1 - \left(\frac{a}{r_+}\right)^{n-3}$ and $r_+$ represents the radius of black hole event horizon.

The entropy of black holes generally satisfies the area law which states that the entropy is a quarter of the area of black hole event horizon [21–23]. This nearly universal law applies to almost all kinds of black holes, including Einstein-Maxwell-scalar black holes [24–26]. Therefore, we have the entropy

$$
S = \frac{A}{4} = \frac{f(r_+)^{n-2}\Omega_{n-2}}{4}. \tag{36}
$$

The electrical potential is defined by

$$
\begin{aligned}
\Phi = & \int_{x_1}^{\infty} \frac{dA_0}{dx}dx = \int_{r_+}^{\infty} \frac{dA_0}{dx}\frac{dx}{dr}dr = \int_{r_+}^{\infty} -F^{10}\left[1-\left(\frac{a}{r}\right)^{n-3}\right]^{-\frac{\gamma(n-4)}{2}} dr \\
= & \int_{r_+}^{\infty} \frac{-q}{f(r)^{n-2}K(\phi)}\left[1-\left(\frac{a}{r}\right)^{n-3}\right]^{-\frac{\gamma(n-4)}{2}} dr \\
= & \, \eta / \left[2(-3+n)\left(\alpha^2+n-3\right)\left(a^3 r_+^n - a^n r_+^3\right)\right],
\end{aligned} \tag{37}
$$

where $\eta$ is defined by

$$
\begin{aligned}
\eta \equiv q & \left[-a^n\left(n^3\beta - 8n^2\beta + (21\beta+2)n + 2\alpha^2 - 18\alpha - 6\right)r_+^{6-n}\right. \\
& \left. + a^3 r_+^3\left(\alpha^2+n-3\right)\left(n^2\beta - 5\beta n + 6\beta + 2\right)\right].
\end{aligned} \tag{38}
$$

When $\beta = 0$, $\Phi$ reduces to that in [20].

We define the thermal pressure $P$

$$
P = \frac{-1}{8\pi}\frac{(n-1)(n-2)\lambda}{6}. \tag{39}
$$

Given the equation of event horizon, $\lambda$ can be expressed as the functions of $a,\ b,\ r_+$. However, we do not bother to give it here because it is too lengthy.

The conjugate thermal volume is

$$
\begin{aligned}
\mathfrak{V} \equiv & \left(\frac{\partial M}{\partial P}\right)_{S,Q} = \frac{6\Omega_{n-2}}{n-1} r_+^{-1+n}\left(1-\left(\frac{a}{r_+}\right)^{-3+n}\right)^{\frac{2\alpha^2(n-2)}{(-3+n)(\alpha^2+n-3)}} \\
& \cdot \frac{1}{6\left(\alpha^2+n-3\right)}\left[-3+n+\alpha^2-(-3+n)\left(\frac{a}{r_+}\right)^{-3+n}\right]\left[1-\left(\frac{a}{r_+}\right)^{-3+n}\right]^{-1}.
\end{aligned} \tag{40}
$$

Then we find that the generalized Smarr formula

$$
(n-3)M = (n-2)TS + (n-3)\Phi Q - 2P\mathfrak{V}, \tag{41}
$$

is indeed satisfied. It is apparent the formula is related to dimension of spacetime.

Choosing $a, b, r_+$ as independent variables and making the differentiation $M, S, Q, P$ with respect to $a, b, r_+$, we obtain

$$\begin{aligned} dM &= \frac{\partial M}{\partial a}da + \frac{\partial M}{\partial b}db + \frac{\partial M}{\partial r_+}dr_+ \,, \\ dS &= \frac{\partial S}{\partial a}da + \frac{\partial S}{\partial b}db + \frac{\partial S}{\partial r_+}dr_+ \,, \\ dQ &= \frac{\partial Q}{\partial a}da + \frac{\partial Q}{\partial b}db + \frac{\partial Q}{\partial r_i}dr_+ \,, \\ dP &= \frac{\partial P}{\partial a}da + \frac{\partial P}{\partial b}db + \frac{\partial P}{\partial r_+}dr_+ \,. \end{aligned} \tag{42}$$

After straightforward but complicated calculations, the first law of thermodynamics $dU = TdS + \Phi dQ - \mathfrak{V}dP$ is indeed satisfied. In contrast to the Smarr formula, the first law is not related to the dimension of spacetime.

## 4. Heat Capacity and Stability in Canonical Assemble

The local stability of a thermodynamic system in canonical ensemble depends on the sign of the heat capacity. If the sign is positive, the system is thermodynamically stable. On the contrary, if the sign is negative, the system would go under phase transition and then acquires stable state. This phase transition could happen whenever heat capacity meets a root or has a divergency.

In Figure 1a,b, we plot the black hole temperature $T$ and the heat capacity $C_Q$ with respect to the black hole event horizon $r_+$. We consider the parameters as follows $n = 5$, $\alpha = 2$, $a = 0.2$, $\lambda = -0.2$ for different $\beta$. The negative $\lambda$ means we are considering black hole in anti-Sitter universe. Figure 1a shows that when $\beta \leq 0$, there are two phases of black holes, the so-called small black holes and large black holes, respectively. On the other hand, if $\beta > 0$, there would be three phases of black holes, the so-called small, middle and large black holes, respectively. The case with positive $\beta$ has generally two event horizons, namely the inner horizon and the outer event horizon while the negative $\beta$ has only one outer event horizon. Figure 1b shows some points of divergence. According to the viewpoint of Davies [27], the divergence of heat capacity means the second-order phase transition. Comparing it with Figure 1a, we see, for negative $\beta$, the heat capacity of small black hole is negative while the one of large black hole is positive. We conclude that the small black holes with one event horizon is thermodynamically unstable while the large black holes with one event horizon are stable. For positive $\beta$, the heat capacity of middle black hole is negative while the heat capacity of both small and large black holes is positive. Thus, we conclude that the middle black hole with two horizons is unstable while the small and large black holes with two horizons are stable.

We can also identify these phase transitions through the diagram of Gibbs energy with respect to black hole temperature. In Figure 2, we plot the $G(T)$ relations with running $\beta$. It shows that when $\beta < 0$, the black holes make phases transition from small black holes to large black holes with the increasing of Hawking temperature. As is known, the specific heat is $C_{Q,P} = -\partial^2 G/\partial T^2$. Therefore, the thermodynamically stable and unstable phases have the concave downward and upward $G(T)$ curves, respectively. Then we conclude that the large black holes are thermodynamically stable while the small black holes are unstable. Figure 2 also shows that when $\beta > 0$, the system makes phase transitions from small black hole to middle black hole, and finally to large black holes with the increasing of Hawking temperature. In this case, both the phase large and small black holes are thermodynamically stable while the middle black holes are unstable.

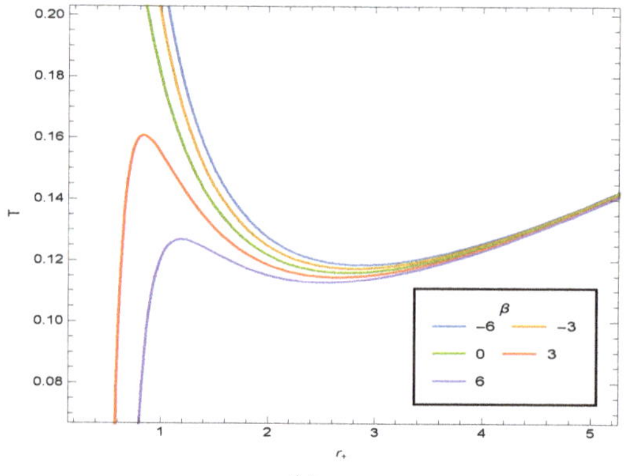


(a)

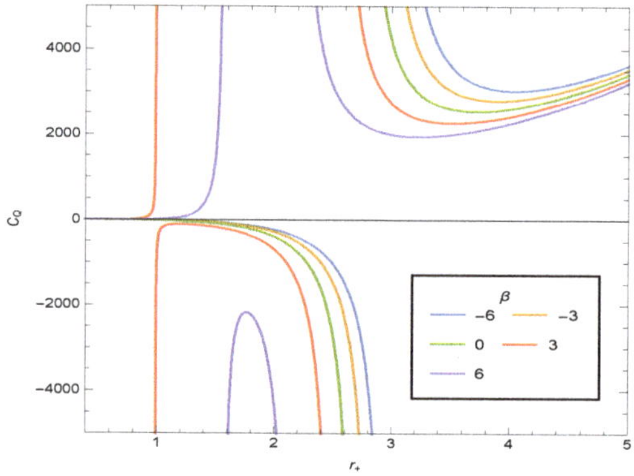


(b)

**Figure 1.** (**a**) The black hole temperature with respect to event horizon $r_+$. (**b**) The black hole heat capacity with respect to the event horizon $r_+$. The parameters are $n = 5$, $\alpha = 2$, $a = 0.2$, $\lambda = -0.2$.

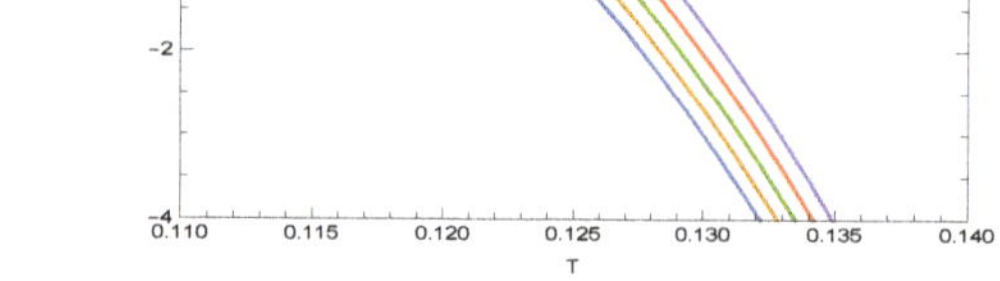

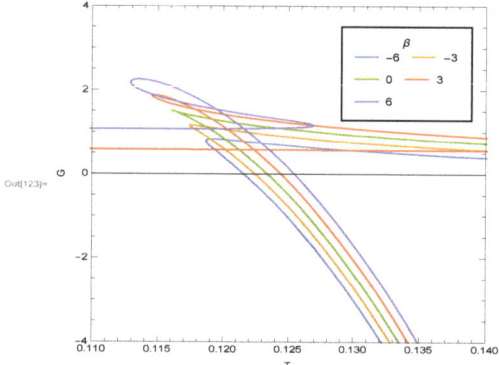

**Figure 2.** The black hole Gibbs free energy with respect to temperature. The parameters are $n = 5$, $\alpha = 2$, $a = 0.2$, $\lambda = -0.2$.

## 5. Conclusions and Discussion

In Section 2 2, starting from the n-dimensional black hole solution in Einstein dilaton gravity and inspired by the four-dimensional black hole solution in Einstein-Maxwell-scalar theory, and the metric is (19), we construct n-dimensional black hole in Einstein-Maxwell-scalar theory. A new coupling function $K(\phi)$(27) between the scalar field and the Maxwell invariant is present. However, the scalar potential $V(\phi)$(11) remains the form in Einstein-Maxwell dilaton gravity.

The black hole is described by physical mass (31), electric charge (29), cosmological constant and two dimensionless coupling constants $\alpha$ and $\beta$. However, in essence, the solution has three hairs, namely the mass $M$, electric charge $Q$ and cosmological constant $\lambda$. There are not any new hairs. Therefore, the solution is not inconsistent with the no-hair theorem.

Then in Section 3, we explore the corresponding thermodynamics. The fundamental thermodynamic functions, namely the enthalpy (31), the temperature (35), the entropy (36) and the thermal volume (40) are derived. Then the generalized Smarr formula (41) which contains the dimension of spacetime is found. By straightforward but complicated calculations, the first law of thermodynamics (42) is satisfied.

Finally, in Section 4, we also study the thermodynamic stability problem and the phase transitions in anti-de Sitter universe. We find, for negative $\beta$, there is generally one event horizon. In this case, According to the figure of black hole temperature with respect to event horizon $r_+$, we find there are two phases of black holes, namely the small black hole phase and large black hole phase, respectively. The small black hole is thermodynamically unstable while the large black hole is stable. With the increasing of Hawking temperature, the system makes phase transitions from small black hole phase to large black hole phase. For positive $\beta$, there are generally two horizons, namely the inner horizon and outer event horizon. In this case, there are three phases corresponding to small, middle and large black holes, respectively (See Figure 1a). The middle black hole is thermodynamically unstable while both the small and large black holes are stable (See Figure 1b). With the increasing of Hawking temperature, the system makes phase transitions from small black hole to middle black hole, and finally to large black holes (See Figure 2).

**Author Contributions:** J.Q.: Conceptualization, validation, writing—original draft preparation, writing—review and editing. C.G.: Conceptualization, validation, supervision, project administration, funding acquisition. All authors have read and agreed to the published version of the manuscript.

**Funding:** This work is partially supported by the Strategic Priority Research Program "Multi-wavelength Gravitational Wave Universe" of the CAS, Grant No. XDB23040100 and the NSFC under grants 11633004, 11773031.

**Conflicts of Interest:** The authors declare no conflict of interest.

## References


1. Lovelock, D. The Einstein tensor and its generalizations. *J. Math. Phys.* **1971**, *12*, 498–501. [CrossRef]
2. Lovelock, D. The four-dimensionality of space and the Einstein tensor. *J. Math. Phys.* **1972**, *13*, 874–876. [CrossRef]
3. Woodard, R.P. The theorem of Ostrogradsky. *arXiv* **2015**, arXiv:1506.02210.
4. Green, M.B.; Schwarz, J.H.; Witten, E. *Superstring Theory: Volume 2, Loop Amplitudes, Anomalies and Phenomenology*; Cambridge University Press: Cambridge, UK, 1987; Volume 2.
5. Gibbons, G.W.; Maeda, K.i. Black holes and membranes in higher-dimensional theories with dilaton fields. *Nucl. Phys. B* **1988**, *298*, 741–775. [CrossRef]
6. Garfinkle, D.; Horowitz, G.T.; Strominger, A. Charged black holes in string theory. *Phys. Rev. D* **1991**, *43*, 3140. [CrossRef]
7. Brill, D.; Horowitz, G.T. Negative energy in string theory. *Phys. Lett. B* **1991**, *262*, 437–443. [CrossRef]
8. Gregory, R.; Harvey, J.A. Black holes with a massive dilaton. *Phys. Rev. D* **1993**, *47*, 2411. [CrossRef]
9. Poletti, S.J.; Wiltshire, D.L. Global properties of static spherically symmetric charged dilaton spacetimes with a Liouville potential. *Phys. Rev. D* **1994**, *50*, 7260. [CrossRef]
10. Poletti, S.J.; Twamley, J.; Wiltshire, D.L. Charged dilaton black holes with a cosmological constant. *Phys. Rev. D* **1995**, *51*, 5720. [CrossRef]
11. Gao, C.J.; Zhang, S.N. Higher-dimensional dilaton black holes with cosmological constant. *Phys. Lett. B* **2005**, *605*, 185–189. [CrossRef]
12. Hendi, S.H.; Sheykhi, A.; Dehghani, M.H. Thermodynamics of higher dimensional topological charged AdS black branes in dilaton gravity. *Eur. Phys. J. C* **2010**, *70*, 703–712. [CrossRef]

13. Sheykhi, A.; Allahverdizadeh, M. Higher dimensional charged rotating dilaton black holes. *Gen. Relativ. Gravit.* **2010**, *42*, 367–379. [CrossRef]
14. Herdeiro, C.A.; Radu, E.; Sanchis-Gual, N.; Font, J.A. Spontaneous scalarization of charged black holes. *Phys. Rev. Lett.* **2018**, *121*, 101102. [CrossRef]
15. Fernandes, P.G.; Herdeiro, C.A.; Pombo, A.M.; Radu, E.; Sanchis-Gual, N. Spontaneous scalarisation of charged black holes: coupling dependence and dynamical features. *Class. Quantum Gravity* **2019**, *36*, 134002. [CrossRef]
16. Blázquez-Salcedo, J.L.; Herdeiro, C.A.; Kunz, J.; Pombo, A.M.; Radu, E. Einstein-Maxwell-scalar black holes: the hot, the cold and the bald. *Phys. Lett. B* **2020**, *806, 135493.*

    [CrossRef]
17. Yu, S.; Qiu, J.; Gao, C. Constructing black holes in Einstein-Maxwell-scalar theory. *arXiv* **2020**, arXiv:2005.14476.
18. Brown, J.D.; York, J.W., Jr. Quasilocal energy and conserved charges derived from the gravitational action. *Phys. Rev. D* **1993**, *47*, 1407. [CrossRef]
19. Brown, J.D.; Creighton, J.; Mann, R.B. Temperature, energy, and heat capacity of asymptotically anti-de Sitter black holes. *Phys. Rev. D* **1994**, *50*, 6394. [CrossRef]
20. Sheykhi, A.; Dehghani, M.; Hendi, S. Thermodynamic instability of charged dilaton black holes in AdS spaces. *Phys. Rev. D* **2010**, *81*, 084040. [CrossRef]
21. Bekenstein, J.D. Black holes and entropy. *Phys. Rev. D* **1973**, *7*, 2333. [CrossRef]
22. Hawking, S. Nature (London) 248, 30; Hawking, SW (1975). *Commun. Math. Phys* **1974**, *43*, 199. [CrossRef]
23. Gibbons, G.W.; Hawking, S.W. Cosmological event horizons, thermodynamics, and particle creation. *Phys. Rev. D* **1977**, *15*, 2738. [CrossRef]
24. Hunter, C. Action of instantons with a nut charge. *Phys. Rev. D* **1998**, *59*, 024009. [CrossRef]
25. Hawking, S.W.; Hunter, C.; Page, D.N. NUT charge, anti-de Sitter space, and entropy. *Phys. Rev. D* **1999**, *59*, 044033. [CrossRef]
26. Mann, R.B. Misner string entropy. *Phys. Rev. D* **1999**, *60*, 104047. [CrossRef]
27. Davies, P.C. The thermodynamic theory of black holes. *Proc. R. Soc. Lond. A* **1977**, *353*, 499–521.

universe

MDPI

Article

# Photon Spheres, ISCOs, and OSCOs: Astrophysical Observables for Regular Black Holes with Asymptotically Minkowski Cores

Thomas Berry *,† Alex Simpson † and Matt Visser †

School of Mathematics and Statistics, Victoria University of Wellington, P.O. Box 600, Wellington 6140, New Zealand; alex.simpson@sms.vuw.ac.nz (A.S.); matt.visser@sms.vuw.ac.nz (M.V.)
* Correspondence: thomas.berry@sms.vuw.ac.nz
† These authors contributed equally to this work.

**Abstract:** Classical black holes contain a singularity at their core. This has prompted various researchers to propose a multitude of modified spacetimes that mimic the physically observable characteristics of classical black holes as best as possible, but that crucially do not contain singularities at their cores. Due to recent advances in near-horizon astronomy, the ability to observationally distinguish between a classical black hole and a potential black hole mimicker is becoming increasingly feasible. Herein, we calculate some physically observable quantities for a recently proposed regular black hole with an asymptotically Minkowski core—the radius of the photon sphere and the extremal stable timelike circular orbit (ESCO). The manner in which the photon sphere and ESCO relate to the presence (or absence) of horizons is much more complex than for the Schwarzschild black hole. We find situations in which photon spheres can approach arbitrarily close to (near extremal) horizons, situations in which some photon spheres become stable, and situations in which the locations of both photon spheres and ESCOs become multi-valued, with both ISCOs (innermost stable circular orbits) and OSCOs (outermost stable circular orbits). This provides an extremely rich phenomenology of potential astrophysical interest.

**Keywords:** regular black hole; Minkowski core; Lambert $W$ function; black hole mimic.

**Citation:** Berry, T.; Simpson, A.; Visser, M. Photon Spheres, ISCOs, and OSCOs: Astrophysical Observables for Regular Black Holes with Asymptotically Minkowski Cores. *Universe* **2021**, 7, 2. https://dx.doi.org/10.3390/universe7010002

Received: 17 November 2020
Accepted: 17 December 2020
Published: 22 December 2020



## 1. Introduction

Karl Schwarzschild first derived the spacetime metric for the region exterior to a static, spherically symmetric source in 1916 [1]; only some 50 years later was it properly understood that this spacetime could be extrapolated inwards to describe a black hole. Without any loss of generality, any static spherically symmetric spacetime can be described by a metric of the form

$$ds^2 = -e^{-2\Phi(r)}\left(1-\frac{2m(r)}{r}\right)dt^2 + \frac{dr^2}{1-\frac{2m(r)}{r}} + r^2\left(d\theta^2 + \sin^2\theta\, d\phi^2\right). \tag{1}$$

For the standard Schwarzschild metric, one sets $\Phi(r) = 0$ and $m(r) = m_0$. Over the past century, a vast host of black hole spacetimes, qualitatively distinct from that of Schwarzschild, have been investigated by multiple researchers [2–14].

Furthermore, the field has now grown to not only include classical black holes, but also quantum-modified black holes [15–18], regular black holes [19–23], and various other exotic spherically symmetric spacetimes that are fundamentally different from black holes but mimic many of their observable phenomena (e.g., traversable wormholes [24–39], gravastars [40–46], ultracompact objects [47,48], etc. [49–51]; see [52] for an in-depth discussion). Herein, we investigate a specific model spacetime representing a regular black hole. That is, a spacetime that has a well-defined horizon structure, but the curvature invariants are everywhere finite.

Investigating black hole mimickers is becoming increasingly relevant due to recent advances in both observational and gravitational wave astronomy. Projects such as the Event Horizon Telescope [53–58], LIGO [59,60], and the planned LISA [61] are and will be continuously probing closer to the horizons of compact massive objects (CMOs), and so there is hope that such projects will eventually be able to distinguish between the near-horizon physics of classical black holes and possible astrophysical mimickers [52]. Herein, we focus on photon rings, ISCOs and OSCOs. Modifications to photon rings would potentially affect the images gathered by the EHT. Modifications to ISCOs would potentially affect both accretion disks and the final inspiral and plunge events detected by LIGO. In contrast, OSCOs (outermost stable circular orbits) do not exist for Schwarzschild or Kerr black holes—so *any* evidence for the existence of an OSCO would be of immediate astrophysical interest.

The model spacetime investigated in this work is a specific regular black hole with an asymptotically Minkowski core, as discussed in [62,63]. This is an example of a metric with an exponential mass suppression, and is described by the line element

$$ds^2 = -\left(1 - \frac{2m\,\mathrm{e}^{-a/r}}{r}\right) dt^2 + \frac{dr^2}{1 - \frac{2m\,\mathrm{e}^{-a/r}}{r}} + r^2\left(d\theta^2 + \sin^2\theta\, d\phi^2\right). \tag{2}$$

A rather different (extremal) version of this model spacetime, based on nonlinear electrodynamics, was previously discussed by Culetu [64], with follow-up on some aspects of the non-extremal case in [65–67] (see also [68,69]).

Most regular black holes have a core that is asymptotically de Sitter (with constant positive curvature) [19–22]. However, the regular black hole described by the metric (2) has an asymptotically Minkowski core (in the sense that the stress-energy tensor asymptotes to zero). Such models have some attractive features compared to the more common de Sitter core regular black holes: the stress–energy tensor vanishes at the core, greatly simplifying the physics in this region; and many messy algebraic expressions are replaced by simpler expressions involving the exponential and Lambert $W$ functions, whilst still allowing for explicit closed form expressions for quantities of physical interest [62]. Additionally, the results obtained in this work reproduce the standard results for the Schwarzschild metric by letting the parameter $a \to 0$. Thus, the value of the parameter $a$ determines the extent of the "deviation" from the Schwarzschild spacetime.

If $0 < a < 2m/\mathrm{e}$, then the spacetime described by the metric (2) has two horizons located at

$$r_{H^-} = 2m\,\mathrm{e}^{W_{-1}(-\frac{a}{2m})}, \qquad \text{and} \qquad r_{H^+} = 2m\,\mathrm{e}^{W_0(-\frac{a}{2m})}. \tag{3}$$

Here, $W_{-1}(x)$ and $W_0(x)$ are the real-valued branches of Lambert $W$ function. We could also write

$$r_{H^-} = \frac{a}{|W_{-1}(-\frac{a}{2m})|}, \qquad \text{and} \qquad r_{H^+} = \frac{a}{|W_0(-\frac{a}{2m})|}. \tag{4}$$

Perturbatively, for small $a$, we have

$$r_{H^+} = 2m - a + \mathcal{O}(a^2), \tag{5}$$

nicely reproducing Schwarzschild in the $a \to 0$ limit. For the inner horizon, since $r_{H_-} < 2m$,

$$r_{H^-} = \frac{a}{\ln(2m/r_{H_-})} \tag{6}$$

implies $r_{H^-} < a$, whence we have a strict upper bound given by the simple analytic expression:

$$r_{H^-} < \frac{a}{\ln(2m/a)}. \tag{7}$$

Certainly, $\lim_{a\to 0} r_{H^-}(m,a) = 0$ as we would expect to recover Schwarzschild; however, the form of $r_{H^-}(m,a)$ is not analytic. This bound can also be viewed as the first term in an asymptotic expansion [70] based on (as $x \to 0^+$)

$$W_{-1}(-x) = \ln(x) + \mathcal{O}(\ln(-\ln(x))) = -\ln(1/x) + \mathcal{O}(\ln(\ln(1/x))). \tag{8}$$

This leads to

$$r_{H^-} = \frac{a}{\ln(2m/a) + \mathcal{O}(\ln(\ln(2m/a)))} = \frac{a}{\ln(2m/a)} + \mathcal{O}\left(\frac{a\ln(\ln(2m/a))}{(\ln(2m/a))^2}\right). \tag{9}$$

More specifically (as $a/m \to 0$ or $m/a \to \infty$),

$$\frac{r_{H^-}}{a} = \frac{1}{\ln(2m/a)} + \mathcal{O}\left(\frac{\ln(\ln(2m/a))}{(\ln(2m/a))^2}\right). \tag{10}$$

If $a = 2m/\mathrm{e}$, then the two horizons merge at $r_H = 2m/\mathrm{e} = a$ and one has an extremal black hole. If $a > 2m/\mathrm{e}$, then there are no horizons, and one is dealing with a regular horizonless extended but compact object (the energy density peaks at $r = a/4$).

This object could either be extended all the way down to $r = 0$, or alternatively be truncated at some finite value of $r$, to be used as the exterior geometry for some static and spherically symmetric mass source that *is not* a black hole. This is potentially useful as a model for planets, stars, etc. Consequently, we also incorporate aspects of the analysis for $a > 2m/\mathrm{e}$ as and when required to generate astrophysical observables in the case when Equation (2) is modeling a compact object other than a black hole.

## 2. Geodesics and the Effective Potential

Continuing the analysis of [62], we now calculate the location of the photon sphere and extremal stable circular orbit (ESCO) for the regular black hole with line element given by equation (2). Photon spheres (or more precisely the closely related black hole silhouettes) have been recently observed for the massive objects M87 and Sgr A* [53–58]. As such, they are, along with the closely related ESCOs, practical and useful quantities to calculate for black hole mimickers.

We begin by considering the affinely parameterized tangent vector to the worldline of a massive or massless particle in our spacetime (2):

$$\begin{aligned} g_{\mu\nu}\frac{\mathrm{d}x^\mu}{\mathrm{d}\lambda}\frac{\mathrm{d}x^\nu}{\mathrm{d}\lambda} &= -\left(1-\frac{2m\,\mathrm{e}^{-a/r}}{r}\right)\left(\frac{\mathrm{d}t}{\mathrm{d}\lambda}\right)^2 + \left(\frac{1}{1-\frac{2m\,\mathrm{e}^{-a/r}}{r}}\right)\left(\frac{\mathrm{d}r}{\mathrm{d}\lambda}\right)^2 \\ &\quad + r^2\left[\left(\frac{\mathrm{d}\theta}{\mathrm{d}\lambda}\right)^2 + \sin^2\theta\left(\frac{\mathrm{d}\phi}{\mathrm{d}\lambda}\right)^2\right] = \epsilon, \end{aligned} \tag{11}$$

where $\epsilon \in \{-1, 0\}$, with $-1$ corresponding to a massive (timelike) particle and 0 corresponding to a massless (null) particle. (The case $\epsilon = +1$ would correspond to tachyonic particles following spacelike geodesics, a situation of no known physical applicability.) Since we are working with a spherically symmetric spacetime, we can set $\theta = \pi/2$ without any loss of generality and reduce Equation (11) to

$$g_{\mu\nu}\frac{\mathrm{d}x^\mu}{\mathrm{d}\lambda}\frac{\mathrm{d}x^\nu}{\mathrm{d}\lambda} = -\left(1-\frac{2m\,\mathrm{e}^{-a/r}}{r}\right)\left(\frac{\mathrm{d}t}{\mathrm{d}\lambda}\right)^2 + \left(\frac{1}{1-\frac{2m\,\mathrm{e}^{-a/r}}{r}}\right)\left(\frac{\mathrm{d}r}{\mathrm{d}\lambda}\right)^2 + r^2\left(\frac{\mathrm{d}\phi}{\mathrm{d}\lambda}\right)^2 = \epsilon. \tag{12}$$

Due to the presence of time-translation and angular Killing vectors, we can now define the conserved quantities

$$E = \left(1-\frac{2m\,\mathrm{e}^{-a/r}}{r}\right)\left(\frac{\mathrm{d}t}{\mathrm{d}\lambda}\right) \quad \text{and} \quad L = r^2\left(\frac{\mathrm{d}\phi}{\mathrm{d}\lambda}\right), \tag{13}$$

corresponding to the energy and angular momentum of the particle, respectively. Thus, Equation (12) implies

$$E^2 = \left(\frac{\mathrm{d}r}{\mathrm{d}\lambda}\right)^2 + \left(1 - \frac{2m\,\mathrm{e}^{-a/r}}{r}\right)\left(\frac{L^2}{r^2} - \epsilon\right). \tag{14}$$

This defines an "effective potential" for geodesic orbits

$$V_\epsilon(r) = \left(1 - \frac{2m\,\mathrm{e}^{-a/r}}{r}\right)\left(\frac{L^2}{r^2} - \epsilon\right), \tag{15}$$

with the circular orbits corresponding to extrema of this potential.

## 3. Photon Spheres

We subdivide the discussion into two topics: First the *existence* of circular photon orbits (photon spheres) and then the *stability* of circular photon orbits. The discussion is considerably more complex than for the Schwarzschild spacetime, where there is only one circular photon orbit, at $r = 3m$, and that circular photon orbit is unstable. Once the extra parameter $a$ is nonzero, and in particular sufficiently large, the set of photon orbits exhibits more diversity.

### 3.1. Existence of Photon Spheres

For null trajectories, we have

$$V_0(r) = \left(1 - \frac{2m\,\mathrm{e}^{-a/r}}{r}\right)\frac{L^2}{r^2}. \tag{16}$$

Thus, for circular photon orbits,

$$V_0'(r_c) = \frac{2L^2}{r_c^5}\left[m\,\mathrm{e}^{-a/r_c}(3r_c - a) - r_c^2\right] = 0. \tag{17}$$

To be explicit about this, the location of a circular photon orbit, $r_c$, is given implicitly by the equation

$$r_c^2 = m\,\mathrm{e}^{-a/r_c}(3r_c - a), \tag{18}$$

where $a$ and $m$ are fixed by the geometry of the spacetime. [1] The curve described by the loci of these circular photon orbits is plotted in two distinct ways in Figure 1.

For clarity, defining $w = r_c/a$ and $z = m/a$, we can re-write the condition for circular photon orbits as

$$w^2 = z\,\mathrm{e}^{-1/w}(3w - 1); \qquad \Longrightarrow \qquad z = \frac{w^2\,\mathrm{e}^{1/w}}{3w - 1}. \tag{19}$$

In Figure 1, we also plot the locations of both inner and outer horizons.

The inner and outer horizons merge at $a/m = 2/\mathrm{e} = 0.7357588824\ldots$, i.e., at $m/a = \mathrm{e}/2 = 1.359140914\ldots$. For $a/m > 2/\mathrm{e}$, i.e., for $m/a < \mathrm{e}/2$, one is dealing with a horizonless compact object and we see that there is a region where there are *two* circular photon orbits. Note that the curve described by the loci of circular photon orbits terminates once one hits a horizon, i.e., at $w = 1$. Sub-horizon curves of constant $r$ are spacelike (tachyonic), and *cannot* be lightlike, so they are explicitly excluded. That is, photon spheres can only *exist* in the region $w \in (1, \infty)$.

1 As $a \to 0$, we have $r_c \to 3m$, as expected for Schwarzschild spacetime.

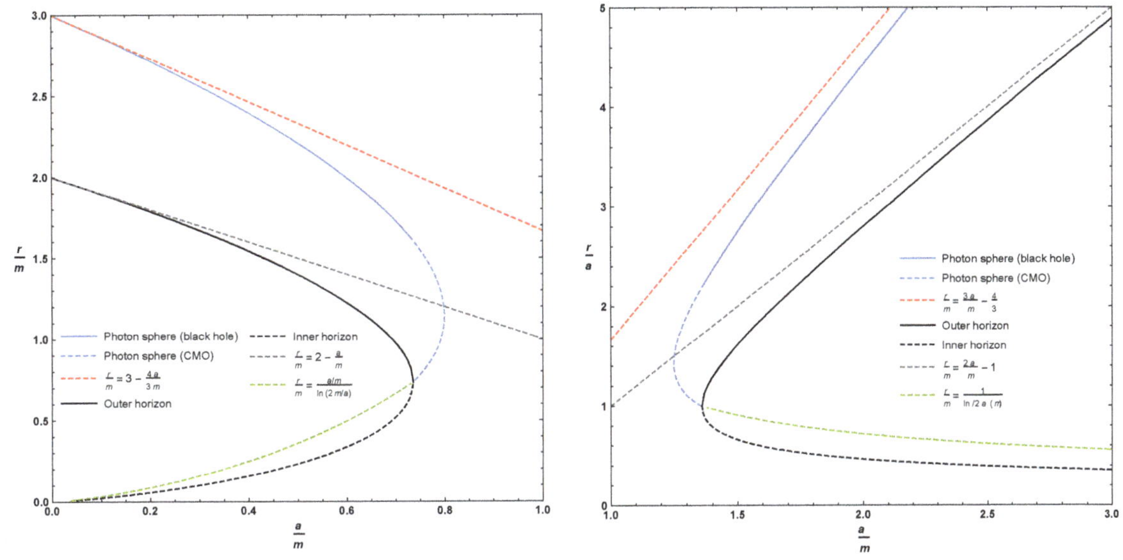


(a) (b)

**Figure 1.** Location of the photon sphere, inner horizon, and outer horizon. Sub-figure (**a**) plots these quantities as a function of the parameter $a$; sub-figure (**b**) plots these quantities as a function of the parameter $m$. The dashed blue line represents the extension of the photon sphere to horizonless compact massive objects (CMOs), whilst the dashed red line is the asymptotic solution for small values of the parameter $a$ (Equation (21)). The dashed grey line is the asymptotic solution to the outer horizon for small values of $a$ (Equation (5)). The dashed green line is the simple analytic bound and asymptotic estimate for the location of the inner horizon (Equations (7) and (10)).

Can we be more explicit about the key qualitative and quantitative features of this plot? Specifically, let us now analyze stability versus instability and find the exact location of the various turning points.

### 3.2. *Stability versus Instability for Circular Photon Orbits*

To check the *stability* of these circular photon orbits, we now need to investigate

$$V_0''(r_c) = \frac{2L^2}{r_c^7}\left[3r_c^3 - m\,\mathrm{e}^{-a/r_c}(6r_c - a)(2r_c - a)\right]. \tag{20}$$

#### 3.2.1. Perturbative Analysis (small $a$)

We note that determining $r_c(m,a)$ from Equation (18) is not analytically feasible, but $r_c(m,a)$ can certainly be estimated perturbatively for small $a$. We have

$$r_c(m,a) = 3m - \frac{4ma}{r_c} + \mathcal{O}(a^2) \quad \Longrightarrow \quad r_c(m,a) = 3m - \frac{4}{3}a + \mathcal{O}(a^2). \tag{21}$$

Thus, for small values of $a$, we recover the standard result for the location of the photon sphere in Schwarzschild spacetime.

Estimating $V_0''(r_c)$ by now substituting the approximate location of the photon sphere as $r_c(m,a) = 3m - 4a/3 + \mathcal{O}(a^2)$, we find

$$V_0''(r_c(m,a)) = -\frac{2L^2}{81m^4}\left(1 + \frac{4}{3}\frac{a}{m} + \mathcal{O}(a^2)\right). \tag{22}$$

This quantity is manifestly negative for small $a$. That is, (within the limits of the current small-$a$ approximation), photons are in an unstable orbit at the small-$a$ photon sphere.

#### 3.2.2. Non-Perturbative Analysis

However, if we rephrase the problem, then we can make some much more explicit exact statements that are no longer perturbative in small $a$: Whereas determining $r_c(m,a)$ is analytically infeasible, it should be noted that in contrast both $a(m,r_c)$ and $m(r_c,a)$ are easily determined analytically:

$$a(m,r_c) = r_c(3 - W(r_c e^3/m)); \qquad m(r_c,a) = \frac{r_c^2\, e^{a/r_c}}{(3r_c - a)}. \tag{23}$$

Consequently, at the peak we can write

$$V_0(r_c,m) = \frac{L^2}{r_c^2}\left(1 - \frac{2}{W(r_c e^3/m)}\right); \qquad V_0(r_c,a) = \frac{L^2}{r_c^2}\,\frac{r_c - a}{3r_c - a}. \tag{24}$$

Regarding stability, in the first case, substituting (23) (left) into (20), we have

$$V_0''(r_c,m) = -\frac{2L^2(W(r_c e^3/m)^2 - W(r_c e^3/m) - 3)}{r_c^4 W(r_c e^3/m)}. \tag{25}$$

Using properties of the Lambert $W$ function, we quickly see that this is negative for $r_c/m > \frac{1}{2}(1+\sqrt{13})\, e^{-5/2+\sqrt{13}/2} = 1.146702958\ldots$, implying instability of the circular photon orbits in this region, (and stability outside this region).

That is, on the curve of circular photon orbits, $V''(r_c) = 0$ at the point

$$(r_c/m, a/m)_* = (1.146702958\ldots, 0.7995092385\ldots). \tag{26}$$

In the second case, substituting (23) (right) into (20), we have

$$V_0''(r_c,a) = -\frac{2L^2}{r_c^5}\,\frac{3r_c^2 - 5ar_c + a^2}{3r_c - a}. \tag{27}$$

This will certainly be negative for $r_c/a > (5+\sqrt{13})/6 = 1.434258546\ldots$, implying instability of the circular photon orbits in this region, (and stability outside this region).

That is, on the curve of circular photon orbits, $V''(r_c) = 0$ at the point

$$(r_c/a, m/a)_* = (1.434258546\ldots, 1.250767286\ldots). \tag{28}$$

Consequently, on the curve of circular photon orbits, we have *existence* and *stability* in the region $w \in (1, 1.434258546\ldots)$ and *existence* and *instability* in the region $w \in (1.434258546\ldots, \infty)$. Precisely at the point $w = 1.434258546\ldots$, the photon sphere exhibits neutral stability.

### 3.3. *Turning Points*

To evaluate the exact location of the turning points on the curve described by the loci of circular photon orbits, recall that using $w = r_c/a$ and $z = m/a$ we can write this curve as

$$w^2 = z\, e^{-1/w}(3w-1) \qquad \Longrightarrow \qquad z = \frac{w^2 e^{1/w}}{(3w-1)}. \tag{29}$$

This allows us to calculate

$$\frac{dz}{dw} = e^{1/w}\,\frac{3w^2 - 5w + 1}{(3w-1)^2}, \tag{30}$$

which has a zero located at $w = (5+\sqrt{13})/6$, where we have already seen that $V_0''(r_c,a) = V_0''(w) = 0$.

At this point, $z$ takes on its maximum value

$$z = e^{6/(5+\sqrt{13})} \frac{(5+\sqrt{13})^2}{18(3+\sqrt{13})} = e^{(5-\sqrt{13})/2} \frac{(2+\sqrt{13})}{9}. \tag{31}$$

Consequently, no photon sphere can exist if

$$\frac{a}{m} > e^{-(5-\sqrt{13})/2} (\sqrt{13}-2) = 0.7995092385...; \tag{32}$$

or equivalently

$$\frac{m}{a} < e^{(5-\sqrt{13})/2} \frac{(2+\sqrt{13})}{9} = 1.250767286.... \tag{33}$$

Note that this happens when

$$\frac{r_c}{m} > \frac{1}{2}(1+\sqrt{13})e^{-(5-\sqrt{13})/2}; \qquad \frac{r_c}{a} > \frac{5+\sqrt{13}}{6}, \tag{34}$$

which is where, as shown above, $V_0''(r_c, m) = 0$.

As can be seen, originally in Figure 1, and now in more detail in the zoomed-in plot in Figure 2, for horizonless compact massive objects, there is a region where there are two possible locations for the photon sphere for fixed values of $m$ and $a$. Furthermore, when this happens, it is the upper branch that corresponds to an unstable photon orbit, while the lower branch is a stable photon orbit.

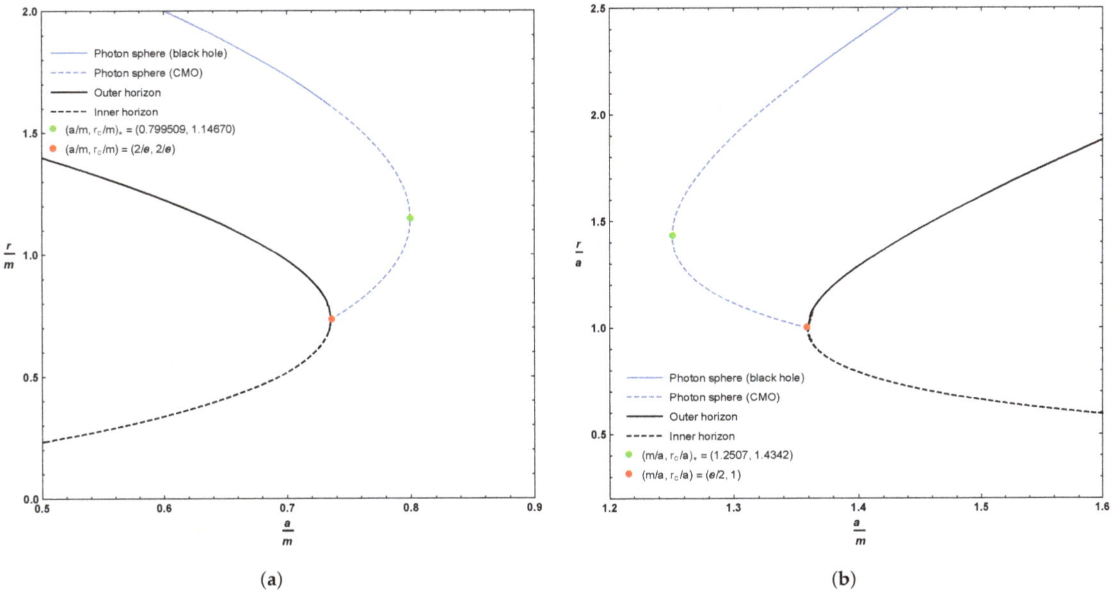


**Figure 2.** Zoomed in plots of the location of the photon sphere, inner horizon, and outer horizon, focusing on the extremal and merger regions. Sub-figure (**a**) plots these quantities as a function of the parameter $a$; sub-figure (**b**) plots these quantities as a function of the parameter $m$. The dashed blue line represents the extension of the photon sphere to horizonless compact massive objects (CMOs). Whenever the location of the photon sphere is double-valued, the upper branch corresponds to an unstable photon orbit while the lower branch corresponds to a stable photon orbit.

## 4. Timelike Circular Orbits

Let us first check the *existence*, and then the *stability*, of timelike circular orbits. Even in Schwarzschild spacetime ($a \to 0$) this is not entirely trivial: Timelike circular orbits *exist* for all $r_c \in (3m, \infty)$; they are unstable for $r_c \in (3m, 6m)$, exhibit neutral stability at $r_c = 6m$, and are stable for $r_c \in (6m, \infty)$. Once the parameter $a$ is non-zero the situation is much more complex.

### 4.1. Existence of Circular Timelike Orbits

For timelike trajectories, the effective potential is given by

$$V_{-1}(r) = \left(1 - \frac{2m\,\mathrm{e}^{-a/r}}{r}\right)\left(1 + \frac{L^2}{r^2}\right), \tag{35}$$

and so the locations of the circular orbits can be found from

$$V'_{-1}(r_c) = -\frac{2}{r_c^5}\left\{L^2 r_c^2 + m\,\mathrm{e}^{-a/r_c}[a(L^2 + r_c^2) - r_c(3L^2 + r_c^2)]\right\} = 0. \tag{36}$$

That is, all timelike circular orbits (there will be infinitely many of them) must satisfy

$$L^2 r_c^2 + m\,\mathrm{e}^{-a/r_c}[a(L^2 + r_c^2) - r_c(3L^2 + r_c^2)] = 0. \tag{37}$$

This is not analytically solvable for $r_c(L, m, a)$, however we *can* solve for the required angular momentum $L_c(r_c, m, a)$ of these circular orbits:

$$L_c(r_c, m, a)^2 = \frac{r_c^2\, m(r_c - a)}{ma - 3mr_c + r_c^2\,\mathrm{e}^{a/r_c}}. \tag{38}$$

Physically, we must demand $0 \le L_c^2 < \infty$, so the boundaries for the *existence* region of circular orbits (whether stable or unstable) are given by

$$r_c = a; \qquad\qquad ma - 3mr_c + r_c^2\,\mathrm{e}^{a/r_c} = 0. \tag{39}$$

The first of these conditions, $r_c = a$, comes from the fact that in this spacetime gravity is effectively repulsive for $r < a$. Remember that $g_{tt} = -(1 - 2m\mathrm{e}^{-a/r}/r)$, and that the pseudo-force due to gravity depends on $\partial_r g_{tt}$. Specifically,

$$\partial_r g_{tt} = -\frac{2m}{r^2}\,\mathrm{e}^{-a/r}\left(1 - \frac{a}{r}\right), \tag{40}$$

and this changes sign at $r = a$. Thus, for $r > a$, gravity attracts you to the center, but for $r < a$ gravity repels you from the center.

If gravity repels you, there is no way to counter-balance it with a centrifugal pseudo-force, and so there is simply no way to get a circular orbit, regardless of whether it is stable or unstable. Precisely at $r = a$, there are stable "orbits" where the test particle just sits there, with zero angular momentum, no sideways motion required. Since by construction $r_c > r_{H^+} \ge a$, this constraint is relevant only for horizonless CMOs.

The second of these conditions is exactly the location of the photon orbits considered in the previous sub-section. (Physically, what is going on is this: At large distances, it is easy to put a massive particle into a circular orbit with $L_c \propto \sqrt{mr_c}$. As one moves inwards and approaches the photon orbit, the massive particle must move more and more rapidly, and the angular momentum per unit mass must diverge when a particle with nonzero invariant mass tries to orbit at the photon orbit.)

Thus, the existence region (rather than just its boundary) for timelike circular orbits is (see Figure 3):

$$r_c > a; \qquad\qquad ma - 3mr_c + r_c^2\,\mathrm{e}^{a/r_c} > 0 \tag{41}$$

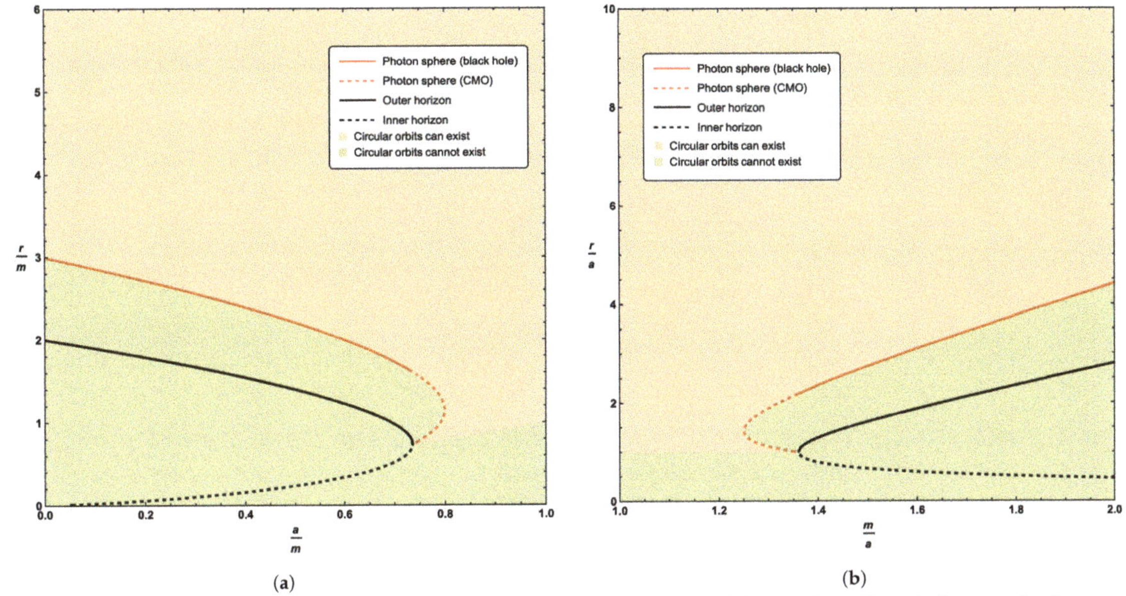


**Figure 3.** Locations of the *existence* region for timelike circular orbits in terms of the circular null geodesics, outer horizon, and inner horizon. Sub-figure (**a**) plots these quantities as a function of the parameter $a$; sub-figure (**b**) plots these quantities as a function of the parameter $m$.

### 4.2. Stability versus Instability for Circular Timelike Orbits

Now, consider the general expression

$$V''_{-1}(r) = \frac{6L^2r^3 - 2m(2r^4 - 4ar^3 + (12L^2 + a^2)r^2 - 8L^2ar + L^2a^2)e^{-a/r}}{r^7}, \tag{42}$$

and substitute the known value of $L \to L_c(r_c)$ for circular orbits (see (38)). Then,

$$V''_{-1}(r_c) = -\frac{2me^{-a/r_c}(2m(3r_c^2 - 3ar_c + a^2)e^{-a/r_c} - r_c(r_c^2 + ar_c - a^2))}{(r_c^2 - m(3r_c - a)e^{-a/r_c})r^4}. \tag{43}$$

Note that $V''_{-1}(r_c) \to \infty$ at the photon orbit (where the denominator has a zero).

To locate the *boundary* of the region of *stable* circular orbits, the ESCO (extremal stable circular orbit), we now need to set $V''_{-1}(r_c) = 0$, leading to the equation

$$2m(3r_c^2 - 3ar_c + a^2)e^{-a/r_c} = r_c(r_c^2 + ar_c - a^2). \tag{44}$$

We note that locating this boundary is equivalent to extremizing $L_c(r_c)$. To see this, consider the quantity $[V'_{-1}(L(r), r)] = 0$ and differentiate:

$$\frac{d\,[V'_{-1}(L(r), r)]}{dr} = \left.\frac{\partial V'_{-1}(L, r)}{\partial L}\right|_{L=L(r)} \times \frac{dL(r)}{dr} + V''_{-1}(L, r)\big|_{L=L(r)}. \tag{45}$$

This implies

$$0 = \left.\frac{\partial V'_{-1}(L, r)}{\partial L}\right|_{L=L(r)} \times \frac{dL(r)}{dr} + V''_{-1}(L, r)\big|_{L=L(r)}. \tag{46}$$

Thence,

$$V''_{-1}(L,r)\big|_{L=L(r)} = -\left.\frac{\partial V'_{-1}(L,r)}{\partial L}\right|_{L=L(r)} \times \frac{\mathrm{d}L(r)}{\mathrm{d}r}. \tag{47}$$

However, it is easily checked that $\partial V'_{-1}(L,r)/\partial L$ is non-zero outside the photon sphere (that is, in the existence region for circular timelike geodesics). Thence,

$$V''_{-1}(L,r)\big|_{L=L(r)} = 0 \quad \Longleftrightarrow \quad \frac{\mathrm{d}L(r)}{\mathrm{d}r} = 0. \tag{48}$$

Thus, one might also extremize $L_c^2(r_c)$, as in Equation (38), and once again find Equation (44).

Defining $w = r_c/a$ and $z = m/a$, the curve describing the boundary of the region of stable timelike circular orbits can be rewritten as

$$2z(3w^2 - 3w + 1)\mathrm{e}^{-1/w} = w(w^2 + w - 1). \tag{49}$$

Plots of the boundary implied by Equation (44), or equivalently (49), can be seen in Figure 4. As for the photon sphere, we have the interesting result that the extension of the ESCO to horizonless compact massive objects results in up to two possible ESCO locations for fixed values of $a$ and $m$. Perhaps unexpectedly, the curve of ESCOs does not terminate at the horizon—it terminates once it hits the curve of circular photon orbits at a very special point. Let us now turn to the detailed analysis of both the qualitative behavior and the various turning points presented in Figures 4 and 5. Note that where the ESCO is single-valued, it is an ISCO (innermost stable circular orbit). Where the ESCO is double-valued, the upper branch is an ISCO and the lower branch is an OSCO (outermost stable circular orbit) [71].

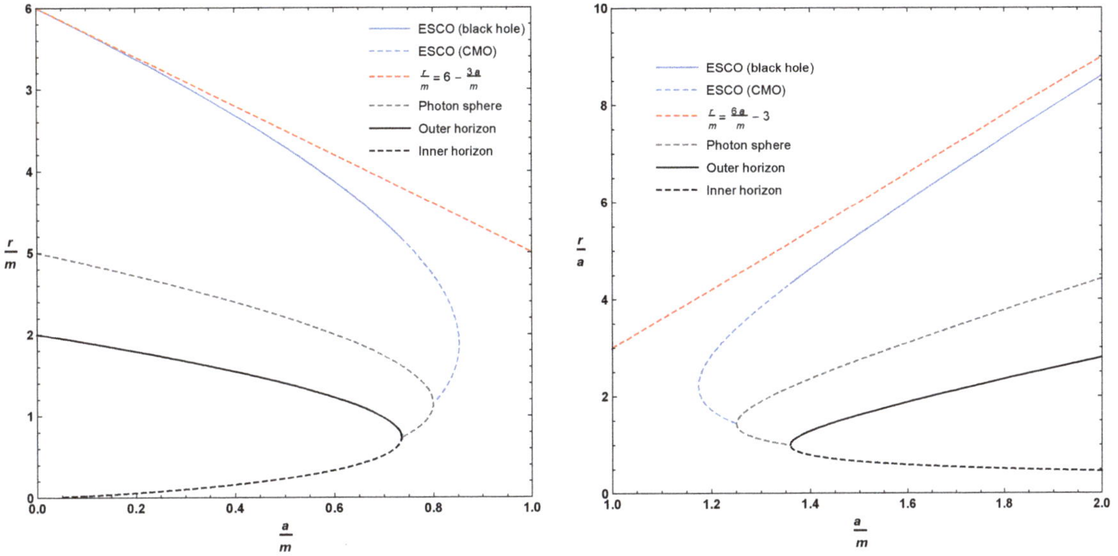


(a) (b)

**Figure 4.** Locations of the ESCO, photon sphere, outer horizon, and inner horizon. Sub-figure (**a**) plots these quantities as a function of the parameter $a$; sub-figure (**b**) plots these quantities as a function of the parameter $m$. The dashed blue line represents the extension of the ESCO to CMOs. The dashed red curves in (a,b) are the asymptotic location of the ISCO for small values of $a$ (approaching the Schwarzschild solution).

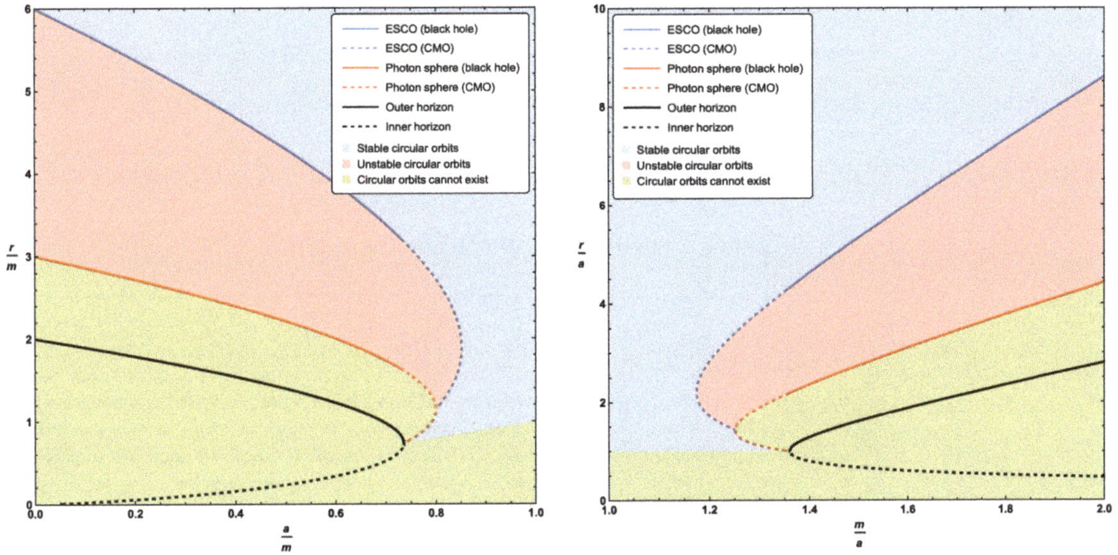


(a) (b)

**Figure 5.** Locations of the ESCO, photon sphere, outer horizon, and inner horizon. Sub-figure (**a**) plots these quantities as a function of the parameter $a$; sub-figure (**b**) plots these quantities as a function of the parameter $m$. The dashed blue line represents the extension of the ESCO to CMOs. The dashed red line represents the extension of the photon sphere to CMOs. The blue region denotes stable timelike circular orbits, while the red region denotes unstable timelike circular orbits, and the green region denotes the non-existence of timelike circular orbits. Where the ESCO is single-valued, it is an ISCO. Where the ESCO is double-valued, the upper branch is an ISCO and the lower branch is an OSCO (outermost stable circular orbit).

#### 4.2.1. Perturbative Analysis (Small $a$)

Let us first investigate the existence region perturbatively for small $a$. We have

$$L_c(r_c, m, a)^2 = \frac{m r_c^2}{r_c - 3m} - \frac{2 m r_c (r_c - m)}{(r_c - 3m)^2}\, a + \mathcal{O}(a^2). \tag{50}$$

Note that this approximation diverges at the Schwarzschild photon sphere $r = 3m$. Thus, for small $a$ the boundary for the region of *existence* of timelike circular orbits is still $r = 3m$.

Now, we investigate the *stability* region perturbatively for small $a$. Rearranging Equation (44), we see

$$r_c = \frac{6m(r_c^2 - a r_c + a^2/3)\mathrm{e}^{-a/r_c}}{r_c^2 + a r_c - a^2} = 6m\left(1 - \frac{3a}{r_c} + \mathcal{O}(a^2)\right). \tag{51}$$

Thence,

$$r_c = 6m - 3a + \mathcal{O}(a^2), \tag{52}$$

which sensibly reproduces the Schwarzschild ISCO to lowest order in $a$, and explains the asymptote in Figure 4b.

Furthermore, for small $a$, substituting $L_c(r_c)$ into $V''_{-1}(L, r_c)$ and expanding

$$V''_{-1}(r_c) = \frac{2m(r_c - 6m)}{r_c^3(r_c - 3m)} + \frac{4m^2(7r_c - 15m)}{r^4(r_c - 3m)^2}\, a + \mathcal{O}(a^2) \tag{53}$$

Demanding that this quantity be zero self-consistently yields $r_c = 6m - 3a + \mathcal{O}(a^2)$.

#### 4.2.2. Non-Perturbative Analysis

We show above that, defining $w = r_c/a$ and $z = m/a$, the curve describing the boundary of the region of stable timelike circular orbits can be rewritten as

$$2z(3w^2 - 3w + 1)\mathrm{e}^{-1/w} = w(w^2 + w - 1). \tag{54}$$

Thence,

$$z = \frac{w(w^2 + w - 1)\mathrm{e}^{1/w}}{2(3w^2 - 3w + 1)}. \tag{55}$$

Let us look for the turning points of $z(w)$. The derivative is

$$\frac{\mathrm{d}z}{\mathrm{d}w} = \frac{(w-1)(3w^4 - 6w^3 - 3w^2 + 4w - 1)\mathrm{e}^{1/w}}{2w(3w^2 - 3w + 1)^2}. \tag{56}$$

There is one obvious local extrema at $w = 1$, corresponding to $z = \mathrm{e}/2$. Physically, this corresponds to the point where inner and outer horizon merge and become extremal—but from inspection of Figure 4, the descriptive plots of Figure 5, and the zoomed-in plots of Figure 6, we see that the curve of ESCOs hits the photon orbit (and becomes unphysical) before getting to this point. In terms of the variables used when plotting Figures 4–6, this unphysical (from the point of view of ESCOs) point corresponds to

$$(r_c/a, m/a)_* = (1, \mathrm{e}/2) \qquad (r_c/m, a/m)_* = (2/\mathrm{e}, 2/\mathrm{e}). \tag{57}$$

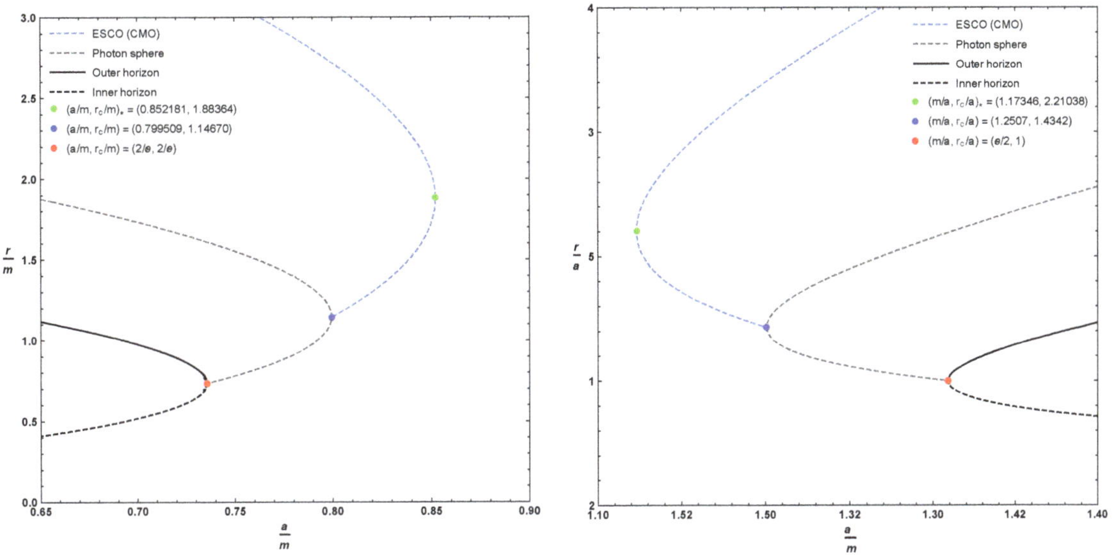


(a) (b)

**Figure 6.** Zoomed in plot of the locations of the ESCO, outer horizon, and inner horizon for various values of the parameters $a$ and $m$, focusing on the turning points. Sub-figure (**a**) plots these quantities as a function of the parameter $a$; sub-figure (**b**) plots these quantities as a function of the parameter $m$. The dashed blue line represents the extension of the ESCO to CMOs. Where the ESCO is single-valued, it is an ISCO. Where the ESCO is double-valued, the upper branch is an ISCO and the lower branch is an OSCO.

The other local extrema is located at the only physical root of the quartic polynomial

$$3w^4 - 6w^3 - 3w^2 + 4w - 1 = 0. \tag{58}$$

While this can be solved analytically, the results are too messy to be enlightening and so we resort to numerics. Two roots are complex, one is negative, and the only physical root is $w = 2.210375896\ldots$, corresponding to $z = 1.173459017\ldots$. Physically, this implies that the ESCO curve should exhibit a non-trivial local extremum—and from inspection of Figure 4 we see that the curve of ESCOs does indeed have a local extremum at this point. In terms of the variables used when plotting Figure 4, this extremal point corresponds to

$$(r_c/a, m/a)_* = (2.210375896, 1.173459017), \tag{59}$$

and

$$(r_c/m, a/m)_* = (1.883641323, 0.8521814444). \tag{60}$$

### 4.3. Intersection of ESCO and Photon Sphere

We can rewrite the curve for the loci of the photon spheres (19) as

$$e^{-1/w} z = \frac{w^2}{(3w-1)}. \tag{61}$$

Similarly, for the loci of ESCOs, we rewrite (55) as

$$e^{-1/w} z = \frac{w(w^2+w-1)}{2(3w^2-3w+1)}. \tag{62}$$

These curves cross at

$$\frac{w}{(3w-1)} = \frac{(w^2+w-1)}{2(3w^2-3w+1)}. \tag{63}$$

That is, at

$$(w-1)(3w^2-5w+1) = 0, \tag{64}$$

with explicit roots at

$$1, \quad \frac{5 \pm \sqrt{13}}{6}. \tag{65}$$

The physically relevant root is $w = \frac{5+\sqrt{13}}{6} = 1.434258546...$, which is where we determine above that the photon sphere became stable and at the point where the curve of photon spheres maximizes the value of $z = m/a$.

### 4.4. Explicit Result for the Angular Momentum

We can rewrite the curve for the angular momentum (38) as

$$L_c^2 = a^2 \left( \frac{e^{-1/w} z\, w^2(w-1)}{w^2 - e^{-1/w} z(3w-1)} \right). \tag{66}$$

Similarly, for the loci of ESCOs, we can rewrite (55) as

$$e^{-1/w} z = \frac{w(w^2+w-1)}{2(3w^2-3w+1)}. \tag{67}$$

We then substitute this into back into $L_c$:

$$L_c^2 = a^2 \frac{w^2(w^2+w-1)}{3w^2-5w+1}. \tag{68}$$

This has a pole at $w = \frac{5+\sqrt{13}}{6} = 1.434258546...$, and is then positive and finite for all $w > \frac{5+\sqrt{13}}{6}$. (Of course, the point $w = \frac{5+\sqrt{13}}{6}$ on the ESCO curve is exactly where the ESCO curve hits the photon curve, so we would expect the angular momentum to go to infinity there.) Asymptotically, for large $r$ (large $w = r_c/a$), we have $L_c^2 \sim a^2 w^2/3$ and $m/a = z \sim w/6$, so $L_c^2 \sim 2mr_c$ as expected from the large-distance Newtonian limit.

### 4.5. Summary

Overall, we see that the boundary of the stability region for timelike circular orbits is rather complicated. In terms of the variable $w = r_c/a$:

- For $w \in (\frac{5+\sqrt{13}}{6}, \infty)$, we have an ESCO.
  This ESCO then subdivides as follows:
  - For $w \in (2.210375896, \infty)$, we have an ISCO.
  - For $w \in (\frac{5+\sqrt{13}}{6}, 2.210375896)$, we have an OSCO.
- For $w \in (1, \frac{5+\sqrt{13}}{6})$, the stability region is bounded by a stable photon orbit.
- The line $w = 1$ bounds the stability and existence region for timelike circular orbits from below.

This is considerably more complicated than might reasonably have been expected.

## 5. Conclusions

In this work, we investigate astrophysically observable quantities of a specific novel regular black hole model based on an asymptotically Minkowski core [62,63]: Specifically, we investigate the photon sphere and ESCO. The spacetime under consideration is an example of a black hole mimicker. For the regular black hole model, both the photon sphere and the ESCO exist and are located outside of the outer horizon, and thus (at least in theory) could be astrophysically observable. The analysis of the photon sphere and ESCO is extended to horizonless compact massive objects, leading to the surprising results that, for fixed values of $m$ and $a$, up to two possible photon sphere and up to two possible ESCO locations exist in our model spacetime; and that the very existence of the photon sphere and ESCO depends explicitly on the ratio $a/m$. Somewhat unexpectedly, due to the effectively repulsive nature of gravity in the region near the core, we find some situations in which the photon orbits are stable and some situations where the ESCOs are OSCOs rather than ISCOs. There is a rich phenomenology here that is significantly more complex than for the Schwarzschild spacetime.

**Author Contributions:** Conceptualization, T.B., A.S. and M.V.; methodology, T.B., A.S. and M.V.; software, T.B., A.S. and M.V.; validation, T.B., A.S. and M.V.; formal analysis, T.B., A.S. and M.V.; resources, M.V.; writing—original draft preparation, T.B., A.S. and M.V.; writing—review and editing, T.B., A.S. and M.V.; visualization, T.B., A.S. and M.V.; supervision, M.V.; project administration, M.V.; and funding acquisition, M.V. All authors have read and agreed to the published version of the manuscript.

**Funding:** TB was supported by a Victoria University of Wellington MSc scholarship and was also indirectly supported by the Marsden Fund, via a grant administered by the Royal Society of New Zealand. AS acknowledges financial support via a PhD Doctoral Scholarship provided by Victoria University of Wellington. AS is also indirectly supported by the Marsden fund, via a grant administered by the Royal Society of New Zealand. MV was directly supported by the Marsden Fund, via a grant administered by the Royal Society of New Zealand.

**Conflicts of Interest:** The authors declare no conflict of interest.

### Abbreviations

The following abbreviations are used in this manuscript:

| | |
|---|---|
| ESCO | Extremal stable circular orbit |
| ISCO | Innermost stable circular orbit |
| OSCO | Outermost stable circular orbit |
| CMO | Compact massive object |

## References


1. Schwarzschild, K. Über das Gravitationsfeld eines Massenpunktes nach der Einsteinschen Theorie. *Sitzungsberichte Der KÖniglich Preuss. Akad. Der Wiss.* **1916**, *7*, 189.
2. Reissner, H. Über die Eigengravitation des elektrischen Feldes nach der Einsteinschen Theorie. *Ann. Der Phys.* **1916**, *50*, 106. [CrossRef]
3. Weyl, H. Zur Gravitationstheorie. *Ann. Der Phys.* **1917**, *54*, 117. [CrossRef]
4. Nordström, G. On the Energy of the Gravitational Field in Einstein's Theory. *Verhandl. Koninkl. Ned. Akad. Wetenschap. Afdel. Natuurk.* **1918**, *24*, 1201.
5. Kerr, R. Gravitational Field of a Spinning Mass as an Example of Algebraically Special Metrics. *Phys. Rev. Lett.* **1963**, *11*, 237. [CrossRef]
6. Newmann, E.; Couch, E.; Chinnapared, K.; Exton, A.; Prakash, A.; Torrence, R. Metric of a Rotating, Charged Mass. *J. Math. Phys.* **1965**, *6*, 918. [CrossRef]
7. Kerr, R.; Schild, A. Republication of: A new class of vacuum solutions of the Einstein field equations. *Gen. Rel. Grav.* **2009**, *41*, 2485. [CrossRef]
8. Visser, M. The Kerr spacetime: A brief introduction. *arXiv* **2007**, arXiv:0706.0622.
9. Wiltshire, D.L.; Visser, M.; Scott, S.M. *The Kerr Spacetime: Rotating Black Holes in General Relativity*; Cambridge University Press: Cambridge, UK, 2009.
10. Baines, J.; Berry, T.; Simpson, A.; Visser, M. Unit-lapse versions of the Kerr spacetime. *arXiv* **2008**, arXiv:2008.03817
11. Baines, J.; Berry, T.; Simpson, A.; Visser, M. Painleve-Gullstrand form of the Lense-Thirring spacetime. *arXiv* **2006**, arXiv:2006.14258
12. Vaidya, P.C. The External Field of a Radiating Star in General Relativity. *Curr. Sci. (India)* **1943**, *12*, 183. [CrossRef]
13. Vaidya, P.C. The external field of a radiating star. *Proc. Indian Acad. Sci.* **1951**, *33*, 264. [CrossRef]
14. Vaidya, P.C. Nonstatic solutions of Einstein's field equations for spheres of fluids radiating energy. *Phys. Rev.* **1951**, *83*, 10. [CrossRef]
15. Calmet, X. *Quantum Aspects of Black Holes*; Springer Int. Pub.: Heidelberg, Germany, 2015.

16. Calmet, X.; El-Menoufi, B.K. Quantum corrections to Schwarzschild black hole. *Eur. Phys. J. C* **2017**, *77*, 243. [CrossRef]
17. Kazakov, D.I.; Solodukhin, S.N. On quantum deformation of the Schwarzschild solution. *Nucl. Phys. B* **1994**, *429*, 153. [CrossRef]
18. Ali, A.F.; Khalil, M.M. Black hole with quantum potential. *Nucl. Phys. B* **2016**, *909*, 173. [CrossRef]
19. Bardeen, J.M. Non-singular general-relativistic gravitational collapse. In Proceedings of the International Conference GR5, Tbilisi, Georgia, USSR, 9–13 September 1968.
20. Hayward, S.A. Formation and Evaporation of Nonsingular Black Holes. *Phys. Rev. Lett.* **2006**, *96*, 031103. [CrossRef]
21. Frolov, V.P. Information loss problem and a 'black hole' model with a closed apparent horizon. *J. High Energy Phys.* **2014**, *2014*, 49. [CrossRef]
22. Ansoldi, S. Spherical black holes with regular center: A review of existing models including a recent realization with Gaussian sources. *arXiv* **2008**, arXiv:0802.0330.
23. Carballo-Rubio, R.; di Filippo, F.; Liberati, S.; Pacilio, C.; Visser, M. On the viability of regular black holes. *J. High Energy Phys.* **2018**, *2018*, 20. [CrossRef]
24. Morris, M.; Thorne, K.S. Wormholes in spacetime and their use for interstellar travel: A tool for teaching General Relativity. *Am. J. Phys.* **1988**, *56*, 395. [CrossRef]
25. Morris, M.S.; Thorne, K.S.; Yurtsever, U. Wormholes, Time Machines, and the Weak Energy Condition? *Phys. Rev. Lett.* **1988**, *61*, 1446. [CrossRef] [PubMed]
26. Visser, M. *Lorentzian Wormholes: From Einstein to Hawking*; Springer: New York, NY, USA, 1995.
27. Visser, M. Traversable wormholes: Some simple examples. *Phys. Rev. D* **1989**, *39*, 3182. [CrossRef] [PubMed]
28. Visser, M. Traversable wormholes from surgically modified Schwarzschild space-times. *Nucl. Phys. B* **1989**, *328*, 203–212, doi:10.1016/0550-3213(89)90100-4. [CrossRef]
29. Visser, M. Wormholes, Baby Universes and Causality. *Phys. Rev. D* **1990**, *41*, 1116. [CrossRef]
30. Visser, M.; Kar, S.; Dadhich, N. Traversable wormholes with arbitrarily small energy condition violations. *Phys. Rev. Lett.* **2003**, *90*, 201102. [CrossRef]
31. Visser, M. From wormhole to time machine: Comments on Hawking's chronology protection conjecture. *Phys. Rev. D* **1993**, *47*, 554–565. [CrossRef]
32. Kar, S.; Dadhich, N.; Visser, M. Quantifying energy condition violations in traversable wormholes. *Pramana* **2004**, *63*, 859–864. [CrossRef]
33. Poisson, E.; Visser, M. Thin shell wormholes: Linearization stability. *Phys. Rev. D* **1995**, *52*, 7318–7321. [CrossRef]
34. Cramer, J.G.; Forward, R.L.; Morris, M.S.; Visser, M.; Benford, G.; Landis, G.A. Natural wormholes as gravitational lenses. *Phys. Rev. D* **1995**, *51*, 3117–3120. [CrossRef]
35. Dadhich, N.; Kar, S.; Mukherji, S.; Visser, M. $R = 0$ space-times and selfdual Lorentzian wormholes. *Phys. Rev. D* **2002**, *65*, 064004. [CrossRef]
36. Boonserm, P.; Ngampitipan, T.; Simpson, A.; Visser, A. The exponential metric represents a traversable wormhole. *Phys. Rev. D* **2018**, *98*, 084048. [CrossRef]
37. Simpson, A.; Visser, M. Black-bounce to traversable wormhole. *JCAP* **2019**, *1902*, 42. [CrossRef]
38. Simpson, A.; Martín-Moruno, P.; Visser, M. Vaidya spacetimes, black-bounces, and traversable wormholes. *Class. Quant. Grav.* **2019**, *36*, 145007. [CrossRef]
39. Lobo, F.S.N.; Simpson, A.; Visser, M. Dynamic thin-shell black-bounce traversable wormholes. *Phys. Rev. D* **2020**, *101*, 124035. [CrossRef]
40. Mazur, P.O.; Mottola, E. Gravitational vacuum condensate stars. *Proc. Natl. Acad. Sci. USA* **2004**, *101*, 9545. [CrossRef]
41. Mazur, P.O.; Mottola, E. Gravitational Condensate Stars: An Alternative to Black Holes. *arXiv* **2001**, arXiv:0109035.
42. Visser, M.; Wiltshire, D. Stable gravastars: An alternative to black holes?. *Class. Quant. Grav.* **2004**, *21*, 1135. [CrossRef]
43. Cattoën, C.; Faber, T.; Visser, M. Gravastars must have anisotropic pressures. *Class. Quant. Grav.* **2005**, *22*, 4189–4202. [CrossRef]
44. Lobo, F.S.N. Stable dark energy stars. *Class. Quant. Grav.* **2006**, *23*, 1525. [CrossRef]
45. Martín-Moruno, P.; Montelongo-García, N.; Lobo, F.S.N.; Visser, M. Generic thin-shell gravastars. *JCAP* **2012**, *3*, 34. [CrossRef]
46. Lobo, F.S.N.; Martín-Moruno, P.; Montelongo-García, N.; Visser, M. Novel stability approach of thin-shell gravastars. *arXiv* **2015**, arXiv:1512.07659.
47. Cunha, P.V.; Berti, E.; Herdeiro, C.A.R. Light-Ring Stability for Ultracompact Objects. *Phys. Rev. Lett.* **2017**, *119*, 251102. [CrossRef] [PubMed]
48. Cunha, P.V.; Herdeiro, C.A.R. Stationary black holes and light rings. *Phys. Rev. Lett.* **2020**, *124*, 181101. [CrossRef] [PubMed]
49. Carballo-Rubio, R.; di Filippo, F.; Liberati, S.; Visser, M. Opening the Pandora's box at the core of black holes. *Class. Quant. Grav.* **2020**, *37*, 145005. [CrossRef]
50. Visser, M.; Barceló, C.; Liberati, S.; Sonego, S. Small, dark, and heavy: But is it a black hole? *PoS BHGRS* **2008**, *17*. [CrossRef]
51. Visser, M. Physical observability of horizons. *Phys. Rev. D* **2014**, *90*, 127502. [CrossRef]
52. Carballo-Rubio, R.; di Filippo, F.; Liberati, S.; Visser, M. Phenomenological aspects of black holes beyond general relativity. *Phys. Rev. D* **2018**, *98*, 124009. [CrossRef]
53. The Event Horizon Telescope Collaboration. First M87 Event Horizon Telescope Results. I. The Shadow of the Supermassive Black Hole. *ApJL* **2019**, *875*, L1. [CrossRef]

4. The Event Horizon Telescope Collaboration. First M87 Event Horizon Telescope Results. II. Array and Instrumentation. *ApJL* **2019**, *875*, L2. [CrossRef]
5. The Event Horizon Telescope Collaboration. First M87 Event Horizon Telescope Results. III. Data Processing and Calibration. *ApJL* **2019**, *875*, L3. [CrossRef]
6. The Event Horizon Telescope Collaboration. First M87 Event Horizon Telescope Results. IV. Imaging the Central Supermassive Black Hole. *ApJL* **2019**, *875*, L4. [CrossRef]
7. The Event Horizon Telescope Collaboration. First M87 Event Horizon Telescope Results. V. Physical Origin of the Asymmetric Ring. *ApJL* **2019**, *875*, L5. [CrossRef]
8. The Event Horizon Telescope Collaboration. First M87 Event Horizon Telescope Results. VI. The Shadow and Mass of the Central Black Hole. *ApJL* **2019**, *875*, L6. [CrossRef]
9. Collection of Detection Papers from LIGO. Publications from the LIGO Scientific Collaboration and Virgo Collaboration. Available online: https://www.ligo.caltech.edu/page/detection-companion-papers (accessed on 20 December 2020).
0. Current Gravitational Wave Observations. Available online: wikipedia.org/List_of_gravitational_wave_observations (accessed on 20 December 2020).
1. Barausse, E.; Berti, E.; Hertog, T.; Hughes, S.A.; Jetzer, P.; Pani, P.; Sotiriou, T.P.; Tamanini, N.; Witek, H.; Yagi, K.; et al. Prospects for Fundamental Physics with LISA. *Gen. Rel. Grav.* **2020**, *52*, 8. [CrossRef]
2. Simpson, A.; Visser, M. Regular black holes with asymptotically Minkowski cores. *Universe* **2020**, *6*, 8. [CrossRef]
3. Berry, T.; Lobo, F.S.; Simpson, A.; Visser, M. Simpson and M. Visser, Thin-shell traversable wormhole crafted from a regular black hole with asymptotically Minkowski core. *Phys. Rev. D* **2020**, *102*, 064054. [CrossRef]
4. Culetu, H. On a regular modified Schwarzschild spacetime. *arXiv* **2013**, arXiv:1305.5964
5. Culetu, H. On a regular charged black hole with a nonlinear electric source. *Int. J. Theor. Phys.* **2015**, *54*, 2855. [CrossRef]
6. Culetu, H. Nonsingular black hole with a nonlinear electric source. *Int. J. Mod. Phys. D* **2015**, *24*, 1542001. [CrossRef]
7. Culetu, H. Screening an extremal black hole with a thin shell of exotic matter. *Phys. Dark Univ.* **2016**, *14*, 1. [CrossRef]
8. Junior, E.L.B.; Rodrigues, M.E.; Houndjo, M.J.S. Regular black holes in $f(T)$ Gravity through a nonlinear electrodynamics source. *JCAP* **2015**, *1510*, 60. [CrossRef]
9. Rodrigues, M.E.; Junior, E.L.B.; Marques, G.T.; Zanchin, V.T. Regular black holes in $f(R)$ gravity coupled to nonlinear electrodynamics. *Phys. Rev. D* **2016**, *94*, 024062. [CrossRef]
0. Corless, R.M.; Gonnet, G.H.; Hare, D.E.G.; Jeffrey, D.J.; Knuth, D.E. On the Lambert *W* function. *Adv. Comput. Math.* **1996**, *5*, 329–359. [CrossRef]
1. Boonserm, P.; Ngampitipan, T.; Simpson, A.; Visser, M. Innermost and outermost stable circular orbits in the presence of a positive cosmological constant. *Phys. Rev. D* **2020**, *101*, 24050. [CrossRef]

*universe*

MDPI

*Article*

# Broken Scale Invariance, Gravity Mass, and Dark Energy in Modified Einstein Gravity with Two Measure Finsler like Variables

**Panayiotis Stavrinos [1] and Sergiu I. Vacaru [2,3,*,†]**

[1] Department of Mathematics, National and Kapodistrian University of Athens, 1584 Athens, Greece; pstavrin@math.uoa.gr
[2] Physics Department, California State University at Fresno, Fresno, CA 93740, USA
[3] Department of Theoretical Physics and Computer Modelling, Yu. Fedkovych Chernivtsi National University, 101 Storozhynetska Street, 58029 Chernivtsi, Ukraine
* Correspondence: sergiu.vacaru@gmail.com
† Current address: Correspondence in 2021 as a Visiting Researcher at YF CNU Ukraine: Yu. Gagarin Street, nr. 37/3, 58008 Chernivtsi, Ukraine.

**Abstract:** We study new classes of generic off-diagonal and diagonal cosmological solutions for effective Einstein equations in modified gravity theories (MGTs), with modified dispersion relations (MDRs), and encoding possible violations of (local) Lorentz invariance (LIVs). Such MGTs are constructed for actions and Lagrange densities with two non-Riemannian volume forms (similar to two measure theories (TMTs)) and associated bimetric and/or biconnection geometric structures. For conventional nonholonomic 2 + 2 splitting, we can always describe such models in Finsler-like variables, which is important for elaborating geometric methods of constructing exact and parametric solutions. Examples of such Finsler two-measure formulations of general relativity (GR) and MGTs are considered for Lorentz manifolds and their (co) tangent bundles and abbreviated as FTMT. Generic off-diagonal metrics solving gravitational field equations in FTMTs are determined by generating functions, effective sources and integration constants, and characterized by nonholonomic frame torsion effects. By restricting the class of integration functions, we can extract torsionless and/or diagonal configurations and model emergent cosmological theories with square scalar curvature, $R^2$, when the global Weyl-scale symmetry is broken via nonlinear dynamical interactions with nonholonomic constraints. In the physical Einstein–Finsler frame, the constructions involve: (i) nonlinear re-parametrization symmetries of the generating functions and effective sources; (ii) effective potentials for the scalar field with possible two flat regions, which allows for a unified description of locally anisotropic and/or isotropic early universe inflation related to acceleration cosmology and dark energy; (iii) there are "emergent universes" described by off-diagonal and diagonal solutions for certain nonholonomic phases and parametric cosmological evolution resulting in various inflationary phases; (iv) we can reproduce massive gravity effects in two-measure theories. Finally, we study a reconstructing procedure for reproducing off-diagonal FTMT and massive gravity cosmological models as effective Einstein gravity or Einstein–Finsler theories.

**Keywords:** modified and massive gravity; two measure theories; Einstein and Finsler gravity; off-diagonal cosmological solutions; nonholonomic dynamical Weyl-scale symmetry breaking; (anisotropic) inflation; dark energy; reconstructing procedure

**Citation:** Stavrinos, P.; Vacaru, S.I. Broken Scale Invariance, Gravity Mass, and Dark Energy in Modified Einstein Gravity with Two Measure Finsler like Variables. *Universe* **2021**, *7*, 89. https://doi.org/10.3390/universe7040089

Academic Editor: Lorenzo Iorio

Received: 17 March 2021
Accepted: 31 March 2021
Published: 3 April 2021



## 1. Introduction

Modern cosmology has the very important task of providing a theoretical description of many aspects of the observable universe with exponential expansion (inflation), particle creation, and radiation. We cite books [1–5] on standard cosmology [6–8] and further developments. Then, regarding acceleration cosmology [9,10] and related dark energy and dark matter physics, one a series of works on modified gravity theories, MGTs, and cosmology [11–16] can be considered. Another direction of research is devoted t nonholonomic and Finsler-like, locally anisotropic cosmological models [17–23]; see [24,2 for an axiomatic approach to Finsler–Lagrange–Hamilton gravity theories. The physic community almost accepted the idea that the Einstein gravity and standard particle physic have to be modified in order to elaborate self-consistent quantum gravity theories an describe existing experimental and observational data in modern cosmology. As a resul a number of MGTs and cosmological scenarios have been elaborated in the last 20 years.

In a series of works [26–33]—see also references therein—a geometric approach (th so-called anholonomic frame deformation method (AFDM)) was developed for the co struction of exact and parametric solutions in MGTs, general relativity (GR) and the theor of nonholonomic geometric and classical/quantum information flows. Such solution use generic off-diagonal metrics (such metrics can not be diagonalized via coordinat transforms in a finite spacetime region; the solutions, in general, have non zero torsio configurations; the Levi-Civita connection can be extracted by imposing additional noni tegrable constraints (in the physics and mathematical literature, two equivalent terms a also used: nonholonomic and/or anholonomic conditions)) and generalized connectior when their coefficients depend on all spacetime coordinates via generating and integratio functions, for vacuum and non-vacuum configurations. Effective and matter field source can be considered for possible Killing and non-Killing symmetries, various types of con mutative and noncommutative parameters, etc. For Finsler-like modified-gravity theorie (FMGTs), the coefficients of geometric and physical objects depend, in general, on (co)fibe velocity (momentum) type coordinates. Following the AFDM, the geometric constru tions and variational calculus are preformed with respect to certain classes of (adapte nonholonomic frames for a formal splitting of spacetime dimension in the form 2(3) + 2 ... + and a well-defined, geometrically "auxiliary" linear connection which is convenier for performing, for instance, a deformation quantization procedure, or for constructin exact and/or parametric solutions. This allows for the gravitational field equations i MGTs, FMGTs, and GR, and geometric/information flow equations to be decoupled. Suc nonholonomic deformations of fundamental geometric objects determined by distortior of nonlinear and linear connection structures were not considered in other approache with vierbeins (tetrads), 2 + 2 and/or 3 + 1 splitting; see standard textbooks on gener relativity and exact solutions [34–38]. The methods elaborated by other authors were on successful in the generation of exact solutions with two and three Killing symmetries, b do not provide a geometric/analytic formalism for a general decoupling of gravitation and matter field equations. The surprising result is that such a decoupling is possible fc various classes of effective/modified Einstein equations and matter fields, which can b derived for certain physically motivated general assumptions in MGTs.

Let us summarize most of the important ideas and methods developed i References [16,24–33]:

(a) The (modified) Einstein equations with some effective and/or matter field source consist of very sophisticated systems of nonlinear partial derivative equations (PDEs The bulk of most known and important physical applications (of black hole, cosm logical and other type solutions) were elaborated for the ansatz of metrics whic can be diagonalized by certain frame/coordinate transforms, and when physicall important systems of nonlinear PDEs can be reduced to systems of decoupled no linear ordinary differential equations (ODEs). In such cases, the generated exact c parametric solutions (i.e., integrals, with possible non-trivial topology, singularitie of different smooth classes, etc.) depend on one space, or time, like the coord nate, being determined by certain imposed symmetries (for instance, spherical/axi ones, which are invariant on some rotations, with Lie algebras symmetries, etc The integration constants can be found in an explicit form by considering certai symmetry/Cauchy/boundary/asymptotic conditions. In this way, tvarious classe of black/worm hole and isotropic and anisotropic cosmological solutions were co structed;

(b) The AFDM allows us to decouple and integrate physically important systems of nonlinear PDEs in more general forms than (a) when the integral varieties are parameterized not only by integration constants but also by generating and integration functions subjected to nonholonomic constraints and functional/nonlinear dependence on sources and data for certain classes of "prime metrics and connections". The resulting "target" off-diagonal metrics and generalized connections depend, in general, on all space–time coordinates. It is important to note that, at the end, we can impose additional nonholonomic constraints and consider "smooth" limits or various type non-trivial topology and/or parametric transitions to Levi–Civita configurations (with zero torsion) and/or diagonal metrics. In this way, we can reproduce well-known black hole/cosmological solutions, which can have deformed horizons (for instance, ellipsoid/toroid symmetries), anisotropic polarized physical constants, for instance, imbedding into nontrivial gravitational vacuum configurations. These new classes of solutions cannot be constructed if we impose particular types of ansatz for diagonalizable metrics, frames of references and/or sources at the beginning, depending on only one spacetime coordinate. This is an important property of nonlinear parametric physical systems subjected to certain nonholonomic constraints. More general solutions with geometric rich structure and various applications for a nonlinear gravitational and matter field dynamics can be found if we succeed in directly solving certain generic nonlinear systems of PDEs which are not transformed into systems of ODEs. Having constructed such general classes of solutions, one might analyze the limits to diagonal configurations and possible perturbative effects. We "loose" the bulk of generic nonlinear solutions with multi-variables if we consider certain "simplified" ansatz for "higher-symmetries", resulting in ODEs, from the beginning.

Applying the AFDM as explained in paragraph (b), and choosing corresponding types of generating functions and integration functions and constants, it is possible to model various MGTs and accelerating cosmology effects by considering generic off-diagonal interactions and re-parameterizations of generating functions and sources in effective Einstein gravity. In the present paper, we shall elaborate on a unified cosmological scenario for MGTs and GR with nonholonomic off-diagonal interactions when effective Finsler-like variables can be considered for a 2 + 2 splitting. In such an approach, both inflation and slowly accelerated universe models are reproduced by exact solutions constructed following the AFDM. In general, such solutions are inhomogeneous and have local anisotropy. For a corresponding class of generating and integration functions, and for necessary type of effective sources, we can model effective scalar field potentials with anisotropy and limits to two flat regions. We shall construct and study nonlinear parametric cosmological theories by generalizing the standard models based on Friedman–Lamaître–Robertson–Walker (FLRW), with diagonalizable configurations derived for ODEs. The goal is to address the initial singularity problem and to explain how two periods of exponential expansion with widely different scales can be described via solutions to effective gravitational equations.

A well-known mechanism for generating accelerated expansion as a consequence of vacuum energy can be performed in the context of the scalar field theory paradigm, which is described by an effective potential ${}^{ef}U$ with flat regions. For such "slow roll" configurations of the vacuum field, the kinetic energy terms are small and the resulting energy-momentum tensor is of type $T_{\mu\nu} \simeq g_{\mu\nu}\, {}^{ef}U$. If the potential ${}^{ef}U$ contains contributions of some modified gravity terms (two measures, massive gravity, etc.), we can analyse the possible effects of such terms in the inflationary phase. However, this is not enough to elaborate a theory of modern cosmology with acceleration and dark energy and dark matter contributions. Theoreticians developed different quintessential, $k$-essence and "variable gravity" inflation scenarios [39–46] and $f(R)$ modified models, with contributions from massive gravity, Finsler-like theories, bi-metrics and bi-connections and/or generic off-diagonal interactions; see [14,15,17,18,24,25,30,47,48] and references therein.

The solutions with anisotropies and flat regions can be used for speculations on the phase that proceeds the inflation, and may explain both the non-singular origin of universe and the early universe evolution. This is similar to the concept of "emergent universe which was considered with the aim of solving the problem of initial singularity, includir the singularity theorems for inflationary cosmology driven by scalar field [49–54]. In o approach, with solutions constructed following the AFDM, the universe does not start as static Einstein universe but as a parametric effective one, when the scalar field rolls with a almost constant speed for a non-singular configuration with small anisotropies.

Let us briefly explain the origins of and motivations for the present work. The ma ideas and methods for constructing generic off-diagonal solutions in MGTs come fro Refs. [26–31]. In articles [11–19], various examples were given of instances where th gravitational and matter field equations in MGTs can be re-defined and solved as certai effective/generalized Einstein equations or their Finsler-like modifications. A series papers [55–59] is devoted to a new class of modified-measure gravity-matter theori containing different terms in the pertinent Lagrangian action, for instance, one with non-Riemannian integration measure and another with standard Riemannian integratic measure. We shall call such models two measure theories (TMTs) of gravity. In a mo general case, two non-metric densities [60] are considered. An important feature of suc theories is that the constructions are with global Weyl-scale invariance and further dynam breaking. In particular, the second action term is the standard Riemannian integratic measure containing a Weyl-scale symmetry, preserving $R^2$, or more general $f(R)$ terr which, in this work, may encode modifications from massive gravity, bi-metric and b connection theories. The latter formalism and geometrization of such TMTs allows for th representation of the corresponding gravitational field equations as certain effective Ei stein equations in nonholonomic variables; see various applications in modern cosmolog (super) string/brane theories, non-Abelian confinement, etc. [61,62]. The main goal of th article is to develop the AFDM for generating exact solutions in TMTs formulated in no holonomic and Einstein–Finsler variables—see also a partner work [63]—and analyze i possible implications in modern cosmology and for dark energy and dark matter physic

The work is organized as follows. Geometric preliminaries on nonholonomic Loren manifolds and relativistic Lagrange–Finsler spaces are provided in Section 2. The in Section 3, we formulate a geometric approach to MGT cosmology in the framewo of TMT with nonholonomic variables and effective Einstein–Finsler gravity theories. W apply the AFDM for the construction of generic off-diagonal cosmological solutions i various MGTs in Section 4. Cosmological models with locally anisotropic effective scal potentials and two flat regions are studied in Section 5. We devote Section 6 to the form lation of certain conditions when modified massive gravity can be reproduced as TM and effective GR theories, with nonholonomic Finsler-like variables, and speculate on potential reconstructing procedure for such massive gravity cosmological models. Final we provide a discussion and conclusions in Section 7.

## 2. Nonholonomic Variables and (Modified) Einstein and Lagrange–Finsler Equations

In this section, we outline some necessary results from the geometry of four dime sional (4D) Lorentz manifolds with so-called canonical nonholonomic variables, whic can be transformed into Finsler–Lagrange-like variables. The motivation for considerir canonical variables is that they can prove certain general decoupling and integration pro erties of gravitational field equations in MGTs and GR. However, Finsler–Lagrange-lik variables and the associated almost-symplectic structures can be used for deformation an other types of quantization procedure in gravity theories. Proofs and details can be foun for instance, in [24,25].

### 2.1. Geometric Objects and GR and MGTs in Nonholonomic Variables

Let us consider a 4D pseudo-Riemannian manifold $V$, defined by a metric structure

$$g = g_{\alpha\beta}(u^{\gamma})du^{\alpha} \otimes du^{\beta} \quad (\text{:}$$

of signature $(+,+,+-)$, with local coordinates $u = \{u^\gamma\}$, where indices $\alpha, \beta, \gamma, \ldots$ run values $1, 2, 3$ and (for the time-like coordinate) 4. The Einstein summation rule on up/low repeating indices is applied if the contrary is not stated. For a corresponding causality structure, the postulates of the special relativity theory, the principle of equivalence, etc, are locally combined (see a review of axiomatic appraoches in GR- and Finsler-like modified theories in [17,24,25]); such a curved space–time is called a Lorentz manifold. In this work, we study generalizations of geometric and gravitational and cosmological models when certain nonholonomic (nonintegrable, anholonomic) distributions and related bimeasure structures, and Lagrangians for MGTs, are considered on $\mathbf{V}$.

On a curved spacetime $\mathbf{V}$, we can always introduce a nonholonomic $2+2$ splitting, which is determined by a non-integrable distribution

$$\mathbf{N} : T\mathbf{V} = h\mathbf{V} \oplus v\mathbf{V},$$

where $T\mathbf{V}$ is the tangent bundle of $\mathbf{V}$, the Withney sum $\oplus$ defines a conventional splitting into horizontal (h), $h\mathbf{V}$, and vertical (v), $v\mathbf{V}$, subspaces. In local cooridnates

$$\mathbf{N} = N_i^a(x^k, y^b) dx^i \otimes \partial/\partial y^a, \tag{2}$$

states a nonlinear connection, N–connection structure. For such a N–connection decomposition, the indices and coordinates split in the form $u = (x, y)$, or $u^\alpha = (x^i, y^a)$, for $x = \{x^i\}$ and $y = \{y^a\}$, with $i, j, k, \cdots = 1, 2$ and $a, b, c, \cdots = 3, 4$, which is respectively adapted to a nonholonomic $2+2$ splitting. The data $(\mathbf{V}, \mathbf{N})$ define a nonholonomic manifold with a prescribed fibered structure described locally by fiber-like coordinates $y^a$.

In our works, "boldface" symbols are used to emphasize that certain geometric/physical objects are defined for spaces enabled with a 2 + 2 splitting determined by an N-connection structure. On pseudo-Riemannian manifolds, introducing an N-connection with a 2 + 2 splitting is equivalent to the convention that there are used certain subclasses of local (N-adapted) bases $\mathbf{e}_\mu = (\mathbf{e}_i, e_a)$ and their duals $\mathbf{e}^\nu = (e^j, \mathbf{e}^b)$, where

$$\mathbf{e}_i = \frac{\partial}{\partial x^i} - N_i^c \frac{\partial}{\partial y^c}, e_a = \partial_a = \frac{\partial}{\partial y^a} \text{ and } e^j = dx^j, \mathbf{e}^b = dy^b + N_k^b dx^k. \tag{3}$$

Such frames are called nonholonomic because they generally satisfy the relations

$$[\mathbf{e}_\alpha, \mathbf{e}_\beta] = \mathbf{e}_\alpha \mathbf{e}_\beta - \mathbf{e}_\beta \mathbf{e}_\alpha = W_{\alpha\beta}^\gamma \mathbf{e}_\beta,$$

with nontrivial anholonomy coefficients $W_{ia}^b = \partial_a N_i^b, W_{ji}^b = \Omega_{ij}^b = \mathbf{e}_j(N_i^b) - \mathbf{e}_i(N_j^b)$. For zero $W$–coefficients, we obtain holonomic bases, which allow us to consider coordinate transforms $\mathbf{e}_\alpha \to \partial_\alpha$ and $\mathbf{e}^\beta \to du^\beta$.

On any manifold $V$ and its tangent and cotangent bundle, there are also possible general vierbein (tetradic) transformations $e_\alpha = e_\alpha^{\underline{\alpha}}(u)\partial/\partial u^{\underline{\alpha}}$ and $e^\beta = e^\beta_{\ \underline{\beta}}(u) du^{\underline{\beta}}$, where the coordinate indices are underlined in order to distinguish them from arbitrary abstract ones and the matrix $e^\beta_{\ \underline{\beta}}$ is inverse to $e_\alpha^{\underline{\alpha}}$ for orthonormalized bases. We do not use boldface symbols for such transformations because an arbitrary decomposition (we can consider certain diadic 2 + 2 splitting as particular cases) is not adapted to an N-connection structure.

With respect to N-adapted bases, we shall say that a vector, a tensor and other geometric objects are represented as a distinguished vector (d-vector), a distinguished tensor (d-tensor) and distinguished objects (d–object), respectively. Using frame transforms $\mathbf{g}_{\alpha\beta} = e^{\alpha'}_{\ \alpha} e^{\beta'}_{\ \beta} g_{\alpha'\beta'}$, any metric $g$ (1) on $\mathbf{V}$ can be written in N-adapted form as a distinguished metric (in brief, d-metric)

$$\mathbf{g} = \mathbf{g}_{\alpha\beta} \mathbf{e}^\alpha \otimes \mathbf{e}^\beta = g_{ij}(u) dx^i \otimes dx^j + g_{ab}(u) \mathbf{e}^a \otimes \mathbf{e}^b. \tag{4}$$

In brief, such an h–v decomposition of a metric structure is parameterized in the for[m] $\mathbf{g} = (h\mathbf{g} = \{g_{ij}\}, v\mathbf{g} = \{g_{ab}\})$.

On nonholonomic manifolds, we can work with a subclass of linear connection[s] $\mathbf{D} = (h\mathbf{D}, v\mathbf{D})$, called distinguished connections, d–connections, preservingm under pa[r]allelism, the N–connection splitting. A d-connection is determined by its coefficien[ts] $\mathbf{\Gamma}^{\alpha}_{\ \beta\gamma} = \{L^{i}_{\ jk}, \acute{L}^{a}_{\ bk}, \acute{C}^{i}_{\ jc}, C^{a}_{\ bc}\}$, computed with respect to an N-adapted base (3). Linear co[n]nections structures which are not adapted to N-connections can also be considered, b[ut] they are not preserved under parallelism (2), and satisfy other types of transformation la[ws] under frame/coordinate transforms.

For any d-vectors $\mathbf{X}$ and $\mathbf{Y}$,, we can define, in standard form, the torsion d–tensor, $\mathcal{T}$, the nonmetricity d–tensor, $\mathcal{Q}$, and the curvature d–tensor, $\mathcal{R}$, of a $\mathbf{D}$, respectively, whic[h] generally do not depend on $\mathbf{g}$ and/or $\mathbf{N}$. The formulas are

$$\mathcal{T}(\mathbf{X},\mathbf{Y}) := \mathbf{D}_{\mathbf{X}}\mathbf{Y} - \mathbf{D}_{\mathbf{Y}}\mathbf{X} - [\mathbf{X},\mathbf{Y}], \mathcal{Q}(\mathbf{X}) := \mathbf{D}_{\mathbf{X}}\mathbf{g}, \mathcal{R}(\mathbf{X},\mathbf{Y}) := \mathbf{D}_{\mathbf{X}}\mathbf{D}_{\mathbf{Y}} - \mathbf{D}_{\mathbf{Y}}\mathbf{D}_{\mathbf{X}} - \mathbf{D}_{[\mathbf{X},\mathbf{Y}]}. \quad (5)$$

In N-adapted coefficients labeled by h- and v-indices, such geometric d-objects ar[e] parameterized, respectively, as

$$\begin{aligned} \mathcal{T} &= \{\mathbf{T}^{\gamma}_{\ \alpha\beta} = \left(T^{i}_{\ jk}, T^{i}_{\ ja}, T^{a}_{\ ji}, T^{a}_{\ bi}, T^{a}_{\ bc}\right)\}, \mathcal{Q} = \{\mathbf{Q}^{\gamma}_{\ \alpha\beta}\}, \\ \mathcal{R} &= \{\mathbf{R}^{\alpha}_{\ \beta\gamma\delta} = \left(R^{i}_{\ hjk}, R^{a}_{\ bjk}, R^{i}_{\ hja}, R^{c}_{\ bja}, R^{i}_{\ hba}, R^{c}_{\ bea}\right)\}. \end{aligned}$$

Such coefficients can be computed in explicit form by introducing $\mathbf{X} = \mathbf{e}_{\alpha}$ and $\mathbf{Y} = \mathbf{e}$[$_\beta$], see (3), and coefficients of a D-connection $\mathbf{D} = \{\mathbf{\Gamma}^{\gamma}_{\ \alpha\beta}\}$ into formulas (5).

The AFDM is easy to work with two "preferred" linear connections: the Levi–Civit[a] connection $\nabla$ and the canonical d-connection $\widehat{\mathbf{D}}$. Both connections are completely define[d] by a metric structure $\mathbf{g}$, following the conditions

$$\mathbf{g} \rightarrow \left\{ \begin{array}{ll} \nabla: & {}^{\nabla}\mathcal{Q} = 0 \text{ and } {}^{\nabla}\mathcal{T} = 0; \\ \widehat{\mathbf{D}}: & \widehat{\mathcal{Q}} = 0 \text{ and } h\widehat{\mathcal{T}} = 0, v\widehat{\mathcal{T}} = 0, \end{array} \right. \quad (6)$$

where the left label $\nabla$ is used for the geometric objects determined by the Levi–Civita (LC) connection. It should be noted here that the N-adapted coefficients of the torsion $\widehat{\mathcal{T}}$ ar[e] not zero for the case of mixed $h$- and $v$-coefficients computed with respect to N-adapte[d] frames (conventionally, we can write this as $hv\widehat{\mathcal{T}} \neq 0$, with some nontrivial N-adapte[d] coefficients from the subset $\{T^{i}_{\ ja}, T^{a}_{\ ji}, T^{a}_{\ bi}\}$). Such a torsion $\widehat{\mathcal{T}}$ is completely determined b[y] the coefficients of $\mathbf{N}$ and $\mathbf{g}$ (in coordinate frames, such values determine certain generi[c] off-diagonal terms $g_{\alpha\beta}$ which cannot be diagonalized in a finite space–time region $U \subset$ [...] by coordinate transforms). We can consider a distortion relation

$$\widehat{\mathbf{D}} = \nabla + \widehat{\mathbf{Z}},$$

when both linear connections and the distortion tensors $\widehat{\mathbf{Z}}$ are completely defined by th[e] geometric data $(\mathbf{g}, \nabla)$, or (in nonholonomic variables) by $(\mathbf{g}, \mathbf{N}, \widehat{\mathbf{D}})$.

Contracting the indices of a canonical Riemann d-tensor of $\widehat{\mathbf{D}}$, $\widehat{\mathcal{R}}=\{\widehat{\mathbf{R}}^{\alpha}_{\ \beta\gamma\delta}\}$, we co[n]struct a respective canonical Ricci d-tensor, $\widehat{\mathcal{R}ic} = \{\widehat{\mathbf{R}}_{\alpha\beta} := \widehat{\mathbf{R}}^{\gamma}_{\ \alpha\beta\gamma}\}$. The correspondin[g] nontrivial N-adapted coefficients are

$$\widehat{\mathbf{R}}_{\alpha\beta} = \{\widehat{R}_{ij} := \widehat{R}^{k}_{\ ijk}, \ \widehat{R}_{ia} := -\widehat{R}^{k}_{\ ika}, \ \widehat{R}_{ai} := \widehat{R}^{b}_{\ aib}, \ \widehat{R}_{ab} := \widehat{R}^{c}_{\ abc}\}, \quad (7)$$

when the scalar curvature is computed

$$\widehat{R} := \mathbf{g}^{\alpha\beta}\widehat{\mathbf{R}}_{\alpha\beta} = g^{ij}\widehat{R}_{ij} + g^{ab}\widehat{R}_{ab}.$$

It should be noted that, generally, $\widehat{\mathbf{R}}_{\alpha\beta} \neq \widehat{\mathbf{R}}_{\beta\alpha}$, even this type of tensor is symmetric to the LC-connection, $R_{\alpha\beta} = R_{\beta\alpha}$. This a nonholonomic deformation and nonholonomic frame effect.

We can introduce the Einstein d-tensor

$$\widehat{\mathbf{E}}_{\alpha\beta} := \widehat{\mathbf{R}}_{\alpha\beta} - \frac{1}{2}\mathbf{g}_{\alpha\beta}\,\widehat{R}$$

and consider an effective Lagrangian $\widehat{L}$, for which the stress–energy momentum tensor, $\widehat{\mathbf{T}}_{\alpha\beta}$, is defined by an N-adapted (with respect to $\mathbf{e}_\beta$ and $\mathbf{e}^\alpha$) variational calculus on a nonholonomic manifold $(\mathbf{g}, \mathbf{N}, \widehat{\mathbf{D}})$,

$$\widehat{\mathbf{T}}_{\alpha\beta} = -\frac{2}{\sqrt{|\mathbf{g}_{\mu\nu}|}}\frac{\delta(\sqrt{|\mathbf{g}_{\mu\nu}|}\,\widehat{\mathcal{L}})}{\delta\mathbf{g}^{\alpha\beta}}. \tag{8}$$

Following geometric principles, we can postulate the Einstein equations in GR for the data $(\mathbf{g},\widehat{\mathbf{D}})$, and/or re-write them equivalently for the data $(\mathbf{g}, \nabla)$ if additional nonholonomic constraints for zero torsion are imposed

$$\widehat{\mathbf{R}}_{\beta\gamma} = \widehat{\Upsilon}_{\beta\gamma}, \tag{9}$$

$$\text{and} \quad \widehat{\mathcal{T}} = 0, \text{ additional condition for } \nabla. \tag{10}$$

In general, the condition $\widehat{\mathbf{D}}_{|\widehat{\mathcal{T}}=0} = \nabla$ may not have a smooth limit, and such an equation can be considered as a nonholonomic or parametric constraint. Here, we note that the source

$$\widehat{\Upsilon}_{\beta\gamma} := \varkappa(\widehat{\mathbf{T}}_{\alpha\beta} - \frac{1}{2}\mathbf{g}_{\alpha\beta}\widehat{T})$$

is computed with the trace $\widehat{T} := \mathbf{g}^{\alpha\beta}\widehat{\mathbf{T}}_{\alpha\beta}$, and $\varkappa$ should be determined by the Newton constant ${}^{New}G$, as in GR, if we want to study the limits to the Einstein gravity theory. In this work, we shall use the units when ${}^{New}G = 1/16\pi$ and the Planck mass ${}^{Pl}M = (8\pi\,{}^{New}G)^{-1/2} = \sqrt{2}$. If we do not impose the LC-conditions (10), the system of nonholonomic nonlinear PDEs (9), and similar higher dimension ones, for instance, those with noncommutative and/or supersymmetric variables, can be considered in various classes of MGTs, Finsler–Lagrange gravity, etc.

The values $\widehat{\mathcal{R}}, \widehat{\mathcal{R}ic}$ and $\widehat{R}$ for the canonical d-connection $\widehat{\mathbf{D}}$ are different from the similar ones, $\mathcal{R}, \mathcal{R}ic$ and $R$, computed for the LC-connection $\nabla$. Nevertheless, both classes of such fundamental geometric objects are related via distorting relations derived in a unique form for a given metric structure and N-connection splitting. There are at least two priorities that work with $\widehat{\mathbf{D}}$, instead of $\nabla$. The first one is ensuring that we can find solutions for generalized gravity theories with nontrivial torsion. The second priority is that the equations (9) decouple in very general forms with respect to certain classes of N-adapted frames. The basic idea of the AFDM is to write the Lagrange densities and the resulting fundamental gravitational and matter field equations in terms of such nonholonomic variables, which allows us to decouple and solve nonlinear systems of PDEs. This cannot be done if we use the LC-connection $\nabla$ from the beginning. It is not a d-connection, does not preserve the $h$- and $v$-splitting and the condition of zero torsion, ${}^{\nabla}\mathcal{T} = 0$, under general transformations, and does not allow the equations in general forms to be decoupled. Working with $\widehat{\mathbf{D}}$, we introduce certain "flexibility" in order to apply corresponding geometric techniques for integration PDEs. In such cases, we do not make additional assumptions regarding particular cases for ansatz and connections transforming the fundamental field equations into nonlinear systems of ODEs. Having defined a quite general class of solutions, expressed via generating functions and integration functions and constants, we can impose additional nonholonomic constraints (10), which allows the extraction of LC–configurations. In this way, we can construct an explicit form of ne classes of exact solutions in GR and MGTs, both in $(\mathbf{g}, \nabla)$ and $(\mathbf{g}, \mathbf{N}, \widehat{\mathbf{D}})$ variables.

## 2.2. Finsler–Lagrange Variables in GR and MGTs

On a 4D/Lorentz manifold $V$, we can introduce Finsler-like variables considering conventional 2 + 2 splitting of coordinates $u^\alpha = (x^i, y^a)$ for a nonholonmic fiber structu where $y = \{y^a\}$, for $a = 3, 4$, are treated as effective fiber coordinates (which are analogo to velocity ones in theories on tangent bundles). In this way, we elaborate a toy mod of relativistic Finsler–Lagrange geometry. Let us explain how such constructions provic examples of the above-formulated nonholonomic models of (pseudo) Riemannian geomet A fundamental function (equivalently, generating function) $V \ni (x, y) \to L(x, y) \in$ i.e., a real valued function (an effective Lagrangian, or a Lagrange density) which differentiable on $\widetilde{V} := V/\{0\}$, with $\{0\}$ being the null section of $V$, and continuous on th null section of $\pi : V \to hV$. A relativistic 4D model of a fibered effective Lagrange spac $L^{3,1} = (V, L(x, y))$ is determined by a prescribed regular Hessian metric (equivalently, th v-metric)

$$\widetilde{g}_{ab}(x, y) := \frac{1}{2}\frac{\partial^2 L}{\partial y^a \partial y^b} \quad (1$$

is non-degenerate, i.e., det $|\widetilde{g}_{ab}| \neq 0$, and of constant signature. Non-regular configuratio can be studied as special cases.

The non-Riemannian total phase space geometries are characterized by nonline quadratic line elements

$$ds^2_L = L(x, y). \quad (1$$

We can elaborate on geometric and physical theories with a spacetime enabled wi a nonholonomic frame and metric, and (non)linear connection structures determined b a nonlinear quadratic line element (12) and related v-metric (11). The geometric objec on $L^{3,1}$ will be labeled by a tilde "~" (for instance, $\widetilde{g}_{ab}$) if they are defined canonical by an effective Lagrange generating function. We write $\widetilde{L}^{3,1}$ with tilde in order to er phasize that $V$ is enabled with an effective relativistic Lagrange structure and respecti nondegenerate Hessian.

The dynamics of a probing point particle in $\widetilde{L}^{3,1}$ are described by Euler–Lagran equations,

$$\frac{d}{d\tau}\frac{\partial \widetilde{L}}{\partial y^i} - \frac{\partial \widetilde{L}}{\partial x^i} = 0.$$

These equations are equivalent to the *nonlinear geodesic (semi-spray) equations*

$$\begin{aligned} \frac{d^2 x^i}{d\tau^2} + 2\widetilde{G}^i(x, y) &= 0, \\ \text{for } \widetilde{G}^i &= \frac{1}{2}\widetilde{g}^{ij}\Big(\frac{\partial^2 \widetilde{L}}{\partial y^i}y^k - \frac{\partial \widetilde{L}}{\partial x^i}\Big), \end{aligned} \quad (1$$

where $\widetilde{g}^{ij}$ is inverse to $\widetilde{g}_{ab}$ (11). In this way, we define a canonical Lagrange N-connectio structure

$$\widetilde{\mathbf{N}} = \left\{ \widetilde{N}^a_i := \frac{\partial \widetilde{G}}{\partial y^i} \right\}, \quad (1$$

determining an effective Lagrange N-splitting $\widetilde{\mathbf{N}} : TV = hV \oplus vV$, similar to (2). Using $\widetilde{N}$ from (14), we define effective Lagrange N-adapted (co)frames

$$\widetilde{\mathbf{e}}_\alpha = (\widetilde{\mathbf{e}}_i = \frac{\partial}{\partial x^i} - \widetilde{N}^a_i(x, y)\frac{\partial}{\partial y^a}, e_b = \frac{\partial}{\partial y^b}) \text{ and } \widetilde{\mathbf{e}}^\alpha = (\widetilde{e}^i = dx^i, \widetilde{\mathbf{e}}^a = dy^a + \widetilde{N}^a_i(x, y)dx^i). \quad (1$$

Such $\widetilde{N}$-adapted frames can be considered as results of certain vierbein (frame, for 4 tetradic) transforms of type $e_\alpha = e^{\underline{\alpha}}_{\ \alpha}(u)\partial/\partial u^{\underline{\alpha}}$ and $e^\beta = e^\beta_{\ \underline{\beta}}(u)du^{\underline{\beta}}$. (We can underline th local coordinate indices in order to distinguish them from arbitrary abstract ones; the matrix $e^{\beta}_{\ \underline{\beta}}$ is inverse to $e^{\underline{\alpha}}_{\ \alpha}$ for orthonormalized bases.).

We can also consider frame transforms $e_{\alpha} = e^{\alpha'}_{\ \alpha}(u)e_{\alpha'}$, when $\widetilde{g}_{ij} = e^{i'}_{\ i}e^{j'}_{\ k}\widetilde{g}_{i'j'}$ and $\widetilde{g}_{ab} = e^{a'}_{\ a}e^{b'}_{\ b}\widetilde{g}_{a'b'}$ for $\widetilde{g}_{i'j'}$ and $\widetilde{g}_{a'b'}$ being of type (11), define the respective h- and v-components of a d-metric of signature $(+++-)$. As a result, we can construct a relativistic Sasaki type d-metric structure

$$\widetilde{\mathbf{g}} = \widetilde{\mathbf{g}}_{\alpha\beta}(x,y)\widetilde{\mathbf{e}}^{\alpha}\otimes\widetilde{\mathbf{e}}^{\beta} = \widetilde{g}_{ij}(x,y)e^{i}\otimes e^{j} + \widetilde{g}_{ab}(x,y)\widetilde{\mathbf{e}}^{a}\otimes\widetilde{\mathbf{e}}^{a}. \tag{16}$$

Using respective frame transforms $\mathbf{g}_{\alpha'\beta'} = e^{\alpha}_{\ \alpha'}e^{\beta}_{\ \beta'}\widetilde{\mathbf{g}}_{\alpha\beta}$ and $\mathbf{g}_{\alpha'\beta'} = e^{\underline{\alpha}}_{\ \alpha'}e^{\underline{\beta}}_{\ \beta'}g_{\underline{\alpha}\underline{\beta}}$, such an effective Lagrange–Sasaki can be represented as a general d-metric (4), or equivalently, as a off-diagonal metric (1),

$$\mathbf{g} = \mathbf{g}_{\alpha'\beta'}(x,y)\mathbf{e}^{\alpha'}\otimes\mathbf{e}^{\beta'} = g_{\underline{\alpha}\underline{\beta}}(x,y)du^{\underline{\alpha}}\otimes du^{\underline{\beta}},$$

where

$$g_{\underline{\alpha}\underline{\beta}} = \begin{bmatrix} g_{ij}(x) + g_{ab}(x,y)N^{a}_{i}(x,y)N^{b}_{j}(x,y) & g_{ae}(x,y)N^{e}_{j}(x,y) \\ g_{be}(x,y)N^{e}_{i}(x,y) & g_{ab}(x,y) \end{bmatrix}. \tag{17}$$

Parameterizations of type (17) for metrics are considered in Kaluza–Klein theories, but, in our approach, the N-coefficients are determined by a general or Lagrange N-connection structure.

The Lagrange N-connections $\widetilde{\mathbf{N}}$ define an almost complex structure $\widetilde{\mathbf{J}}$. Such a linear operator $\widetilde{\mathbf{J}}$ acts on $\mathbf{e}_{\alpha} = (\mathbf{e}_i, e_b)$ using formulas $\widetilde{\mathbf{J}}(\mathbf{e}_i) = -e_{n+i}$ and $\widetilde{\mathbf{J}}(e_{n+i}) = \mathbf{e}_i$, and globally defines an almost complex structure $\widetilde{\mathbf{J}}\circ\widetilde{\mathbf{J}} = -\mathbf{I}$, where $\mathbf{I}$ is the unity matrix. We note that $\widetilde{\mathbf{J}}$ is only a (pseudo) almost complex structure for a (pseudo) Euclidean signature. There are omitted tildes written, for instance, $\mathbf{J}$ for arbitrary frame/coordinate transforms.

A Lagrange Neijenhuis tensor field is determined by a Lagrange-generating function introduced as the curvatures of a respective N-connection,

$$\widetilde{\mathbf{\Omega}}(\widetilde{\mathbf{X}},\widetilde{\mathbf{Y}}) := -[\widetilde{\mathbf{X}},\widetilde{\mathbf{Y}}] + [\widetilde{\mathbf{J}}\widetilde{\mathbf{X}},\widetilde{\mathbf{J}}\widetilde{\mathbf{Y}}] - \widetilde{\mathbf{J}}[\widetilde{\mathbf{J}}\widetilde{\mathbf{X}},\widetilde{\mathbf{Y}}] - \widetilde{\mathbf{J}}[\widetilde{\mathbf{X}},\widetilde{\mathbf{J}}\widetilde{\mathbf{Y}}], \tag{18}$$

for any d–vectors $\mathbf{X}$, $\mathbf{Y}$. Such formulas can be written without tilde values if arbitrary frame transforms are considered. In local form, an N-connection is characterized by such coefficients of (18) (i.e., the coefficients of an N-connection curvature):

$$\Omega^{a}_{ij} = \frac{\partial N^{a}_{i}}{\partial x^{j}} - \frac{\partial N^{a}_{j}}{\partial x^{i}} + N^{b}_{i}\frac{\partial N^{a}_{j}}{\partial y^{b}} - N^{b}_{j}\frac{\partial N^{a}_{i}}{\partial y^{b}}. \tag{19}$$

An almost complex structure $\mathbf{J}$ transforms into a standard complex structure for the Euclidean signature if $\mathbf{\Omega} = 0$.

Using the Lagrange d-metric $\widetilde{\mathbf{g}}$ and d-operator $\widetilde{\mathbf{J}}$, we can define the almost symplectic structure $\widetilde{\theta} := \widetilde{\mathbf{g}}(\widetilde{\mathbf{J}}\cdot,\cdot)$. Then, we can construct canonical d-tensor fields defined by $L(x,y)$ and N-adapted, respectively, to $\widetilde{N}^{a}_{i}$ (14) and $\widetilde{\mathbf{e}}_{\alpha} = (\widetilde{\mathbf{e}}_i, e_b)$ (15):

$$\begin{aligned} \widetilde{\mathbf{J}} &= -\delta^{a}_{i}e_{a}\otimes e^{i} + \delta^{i}_{a}\widetilde{\mathbf{e}}_{i}\otimes\widetilde{\mathbf{e}}^{a} \text{ the almost complex structure;} \\ \widetilde{\mathbf{P}} &= \widetilde{\mathbf{e}}_{i}\otimes e^{i} - e_{a}\otimes\widetilde{\mathbf{e}}^{a} \text{ almost product structure;} \\ \widetilde{\theta} &= \widetilde{g}_{aj}(x,y)\widetilde{\mathbf{e}}^{a}\wedge e^{i} \text{ almost symplectic structure.} \end{aligned} \tag{20}$$

We can define the Cartan–Lagrange d-connection $\widetilde{\mathbf{D}} = (h\widetilde{\mathbf{D}}, v\widetilde{\mathbf{D}})$ which, by definition, satisfies the conditions (compare with (6)),

$$\widetilde{\mathbf{D}}\widetilde{\theta} = 0, \widetilde{\mathcal{Q}} = 0 \text{ and } h\widetilde{\mathcal{T}} = 0, v\widetilde{\mathcal{T}} = 0. \tag{21}$$

The geometric d-objects (16), (20) and (4) can be subjected to arbitrary frame transforn on a Lorentz nonholonomic manifold $\mathbf{V}$, when we can omit tilde on symbols, for instanc by writing geometric data in the form $(\mathbf{g}, \mathbf{J}, \mathbf{P},)$, but we have to preserve the notation $\widetilde{\mathbf{D}}$ i all systems of frames/coordinates because such a d-connection is different, for instanc from the LC-connection $\nabla$.

We can elaborate a relativistic 4D model of Finsler space on a Lorentz manifold as an example of Lagrange space when a regular $L = F^2$ is defined by a fundament (generating) Finsler function $F(x,y)$, also called a Finsler metric, when the nonlinea quadratic element (12) is changed into

$$ds_F^2 = F^2(x,y)$$

and when the following conditions are satisfied: (1) $F$ is a real positive valued functio which is differential on $\widetilde{TV}$ and continuous on the null section of the projection $\pi : TV \rightarrow$ (2) a homogeneity condition, $F(x,\lambda y) = |\lambda|\ F(x,y)$, is imposed for a nonzero real value (3) the Hessian (11) is defined by $F^2$ in such a form that in any point $(x_{(0)}, y_{(0)})$, the v-metri is of signature $(+-)$. The conditions (1)–(3) allow the construction of various types of ge metric models with homogenenous fiber coordinates, with local anisotropy distinguishe on directions. Nevertheless, to extend, for instance, the GR theory in a relativistic covariar form, we need additional assumptions and physical motivations on the type of nonlinea and linear connections we take consideration, as well as how to extract effective quadrati elements, etc.; see details and references in [24,25]. In this work, we consider that we ca always prescribe a respective nonholonomic geometric modeling to a Lorentz manifold $V$ Finsler, or Lagrange, type function using canonical data $(\widetilde{L},\ \widetilde{\mathbf{N}}; \widetilde{\mathbf{e}}_\alpha, \widetilde{\mathbf{e}}^\alpha; \widetilde{g}_{jk}, \widetilde{g}_{ab})$, when certai homogeneity conditions can be satisfied for Finsler configurations. For general fram transforms and modified dispersion relations, we do not consider Lagrange- or Finsler-lik nonholonomic variables, but can preserve a conventional h- and v-splitting adapted to N-connection structure with geometric data $(\mathbf{V},\ \mathbf{N}; \mathbf{e}_\alpha, \mathbf{e}^\alpha; g_{jk}, g_{ab})$. To elaborate physicall realistic gravity models, we need further conventions on the type of linear connectio structure (covariant derivative) we shall use for our geometric constructions.

We can always consider distortion relations

$$\widehat{\mathbf{D}} = \nabla + \widehat{\mathbf{Z}}, \widetilde{\mathbf{D}} = \nabla + \widetilde{\mathbf{Z}}, \text{ and } \widehat{\mathbf{D}} = \widetilde{\mathbf{D}} + \mathbf{Z}, \text{ all determined by } (\mathbf{g}, \mathbf{N}) \sim (\widetilde{\mathbf{g}}, \widetilde{\mathbf{N}}), \quad (22)$$

with distortion d-tensors $\widehat{\mathbf{Z}}, \widetilde{\mathbf{Z}}$, and $\mathbf{Z}$, and postulate the (modified) Einstein Equations ( in various forms

$$\widetilde{\mathbf{R}}_{\ \beta\gamma} = \widetilde{\Upsilon}_{\ \beta\gamma}[\widetilde{\mathbf{Z}}, \widehat{\mathbf{T}}_{\alpha\beta}], \text{ or} \quad (23)$$

$$R_{\ \beta\gamma}[\nabla] = \Upsilon_{\ \beta\gamma}[\widehat{\mathbf{Z}}, \widehat{\mathbf{T}}_{\alpha\beta}], \quad (24)$$

where the (effective) matter sources are respective functionals on distortions and energ momentum tensors for matter fields. Such systems of nonlinear PDEs are different an characterized by different types of Bianchi identities, local conservation laws and associate symmetries. Nevertheless, we can establish such classes of nonholonomic frame an distortion structures, with respective equivalence relations

$$(\mathbf{g}, \mathbf{N}, \widehat{\mathbf{D}}) \leftrightarrows (L : \widetilde{\mathbf{g}}, \widetilde{\mathbf{N}}, \widetilde{\mathbf{D}}) \leftrightarrow (\widetilde{\theta}, \widetilde{\mathbf{P}}, \widetilde{\mathbf{J}}, \widetilde{\mathbf{D}}) \leftrightarrow [(\mathbf{g}, \nabla)]$$

when the Equations (9), (23) and (24) describe equivalent gravitational and matter fiel models. Different geometric data have their priorities in constructing explicit differer classes of exact/parametric/approximate solutions or for performing certain procedures quantization and further generalizations of physical theories. If we work with a respectiv canonical d-connection structure $\widehat{\mathbf{D}}$, we can prove a general decoupling property of ( and construct exact solutions with generic off-diagonal metrics $g_{\underline{\alpha}\underline{\beta}}(u^\gamma)$ (17) represented a d-metrics $\mathbf{g}_{\alpha'\beta'}(x,y)$ (4), when the coefficients of such metrics and associated nonlinear an linear connection structures depend, in principle, on all space–time coordinates $u^\gamma$. We can not decouple the systems of nonlinear PDEs (23), in Lagrange–Finsler variables in general form, and (24), in local coordinates and for the LC-connection. In MGTs with modifications of (23) or (24), even in GR, we are able to find exact solutions for some "special" ansatz of metrics, which, for instance, are diagonalizable and depend only on a radial or time-like coordinate (for instance, for black hole and/or cosmological solutions). In this work, we shall apply the AFDM in order to construct cosmological locally anisotropic solutions in MGTs with (in general, generic off-diagonal) metrics of type $\mathbf{g}_{\alpha'\beta'}(x^i, y^4 = t)$. In geometric and analytic form, this is possible if we work with nontrivial N-connection structures and certain variables which are similar to those in Lagrange–Finsler geometry but on Lorentz manifolds. The almost symplectic Lagrange–Finsler variables $(\widetilde{\theta}, \widetilde{\mathbf{P}}, \widetilde{\mathbf{J}}, \widetilde{\mathbf{D}})$ allow for the elaboration of deformation quantization and, together with $(\mathbf{g}, \mathbf{N}, \widehat{\mathbf{D}})$, allow the introduction of nonholonomic and Finsler-like spinors and, for instance, nonholonomic Einstein–Finsler–Dirac systems. This is not possible if the so-called Berwald– or Chern–Finsler connections are used, because they are not metric-compatible, and self-consistent definitions of locally anisotropic versions of the Dirac equation are a problem.

## 3. TMTs and Other MGTs in Canonical Nonholonomic Variables

The goal of this section is to show how various classes of MGTs can be extracted from certain effective Einstein gravity theories using nonholonomic or Finsler-like variables. This allows to decouple the gravitational field equations and to generate exact solutions in very general forms, with generic off-diagonal metrics and generalized connections, and with constraints to zero-torsion configurations; see details in [26–33].

In [14–16,26–33,63], different possibilities for modelling different MGTs by imposing corresponding nonholonomic constraints on the metric and canonical d-connection structures and source in (9) were considered. One of the main goals of this work is to prove that, by using corresponding type parameterizations of the effective Lagrangian $\widehat{\mathcal{L}}$ in (8), the so-called modified massive gravity theories (in general, with bi-connection and bi-metric structures) can be modeled at TMTs with effective Einstein equations for $\widehat{\mathbf{D}}$ when additional constraints $\widehat{\mathbf{D}}_{|\widehat{\mathcal{T}}=0} = \nabla$ have to be imposed in order to extract LC–configurations.

The actions for equivalent TMT, MGT and nonholonomically deformed Einstein models are postulated

$$\mathcal{S} = ({}^{Pl}M)^2 \int d^4u \sqrt{|\mathbf{g}|}[\widehat{R} + \widehat{\mathcal{L}}] = \quad (25)$$

$$\begin{aligned} {}^{\Phi}\mathcal{S} + {}^{m}\mathcal{S} &= \int d^4u\, {}^{1}\Phi(\mathbf{A})\Big[\widehat{R} + {}^{1}L\Big] + \quad (26)\\ &\int d^4u\, {}^{2}\Phi(\mathbf{B})\Big[{}^{2}L + \epsilon \mathbf{f}(\widetilde{\mathbf{R}}) + (\sqrt{|\mathbf{g}|})^{-1}\,\Phi(\mathbf{H})\Big] + \int d^4u \sqrt{|\widehat{\mathbf{g}}|}\, {}^{m}\mathcal{L} = \end{aligned}$$

$${}^{F,\mu}\mathcal{S} + {}^{m}\mathcal{S} = ({}^{Pl}M)^2 \int d^4u[\sqrt{|\widehat{\mathbf{g}}|}\, {}^{F,\mu}\mathcal{L} + \sqrt{|\widehat{\mathbf{g}}|}\, {}^{m}\mathcal{L}], \quad (27)$$

where $|\widehat{\mathbf{g}}| = \det|\widehat{\mathbf{g}}_{\alpha\beta}|$ for a d-metric, $\widehat{\mathbf{g}}_{\alpha\beta}$, constructed effectively by a conformal transform of a TMT reference one, $\mathbf{g}_{\alpha\beta}$, (see below, Formula (34)); ${}^{\Phi}L$ defines a class of theories with two independent non-Riemannian volume-forms ${}^{1}\Phi(A)$ and ${}^{2}\Phi(B)$ as in [61,62] but with a more general functional for modification, of type $\epsilon\mathbf{f}(\check{\mathbf{R}})$, than $\epsilon R^2$ if $\widehat{\mathbf{D}} \to \nabla$; the Lagrange density functional ${}^{f,\mu}\mathcal{L} = \mathbf{F}(\widetilde{\mathbf{R}})$ is determined similarly to a modified massive gravity, by a mass-deformed scalar curvature [14,15,64–66], (there are various ambiguities and controversies in different approaches to massive gravity when modifications by mass terms are postulated for different Lagrange densities; in this paper, we consider a "toy model" when terms of type $\mathbf{f}(\check{\mathbf{R}}, \mu)$ and/or $\mathbf{f}(\mathbf{R}) + \mu \ldots$ can modeled by the same MGT, but for different classes of nonholonomic constraint and different classes of solution)

$$\check{\mathbf{R}} := \widehat{\mathbf{R}} + 2\,\mu^2(3 - tr\sqrt{\mathbf{g}^{-1}\mathbf{q}} - \det\sqrt{\mathbf{g}^{-1}\mathbf{q}}), \quad (28)$$

where $\mu$ is the graviton's mass and $\mathbf{q} = \{\mathbf{q}_{\alpha\beta}\}$ is the so–called non-dynamical referen metric; ${}^{m}\mathcal{L}$ is the Lagrangian for matter fields.

### 3.1. Nonholonomic Ghost–Free Massive Configurations

The term $\epsilon\mathbf{f}(\check{\mathbf{R}})$ in (26) contains possible contributions from a nontrivial gravit mass. Such a theory can be constructed to be ghost-free for very special conditions [14,1 see explicit results and discussions on possible applications in modern cosmology Refs [64–66]. In this section, we show how prescribing necessary type nonholonom configurations such a theory can equivalently be realized as a TMT one (taking equ actions (26) and (27)). For any $(\widehat{\mathbf{g}}, \mathbf{N}, \widehat{\mathbf{D}})$, we consider the d-tensor $(\sqrt{\widehat{\mathbf{g}}^{-1}\mathbf{q}})^{\mu}_{\ \nu}$ computed the square root of $\widehat{\mathbf{g}}^{\mu\rho}\mathbf{q}_{\rho\nu}$, where

$$(\sqrt{\widehat{\mathbf{g}}^{-1}\mathbf{q}})^{\mu}_{\ \rho}(\sqrt{\widehat{\mathbf{g}}^{-1}\mathbf{q}})^{\rho}_{\ \nu} = \widehat{\mathbf{g}}^{\mu\rho}\mathbf{q}_{\rho\nu}, \text{ and } \sum_{k=0}^{4} {}^{k}\beta\, e_k(\sqrt{\widehat{\mathbf{g}}^{-1}\mathbf{q}}) = 3 - tr\sqrt{\widehat{\mathbf{g}}^{-1}\mathbf{q}} - \det\sqrt{\widehat{\mathbf{g}}^{-1}\mathbf{q}}$$

for some coefficients ${}^{k}\beta$. The values $e_k(\mathbf{Y})$ are defined for a d-tensor $\mathbf{Y}^{\mu}_{\ \rho}$ and $Y = [Y]$ : $tr(\mathbf{Y}) = \mathbf{Y}^{\mu}_{\ \mu}$, where

$$\begin{aligned} e_0(Y) &= 1, e_1(Y) = Y, 2e_2(Y) = Y^2 - [Y^2],\ 6e_3(Y) = Y^3 - 3Y[Y^2] + 2[Y^3], \\ 24e_4(Y) &= Y^4 - 6Y^2[Y^2] + 3[Y^2]^2 + 8Y[Y^3] - 6[Y^4];\ e_k(Y) = 0 \text{ for } k > 4. \end{aligned}$$

We chose the functional for Lagrange density in (27) in the form ${}^{F,\mu}\mathcal{L} = \mathbf{F}(\widetilde{\mathbf{R}})$, whe the functional dependence $\mathbf{F}$ is different (in general) from $\mathbf{f}(\widetilde{\mathbf{R}})$. For simplicity, we consid Lagrange densities for matter, ${}^{m}\mathcal{L}$, which only depend on the coefficients of a metr field and not on their derivatives. The energy–momentum d-tensor can be computed v N-adapted variational calculus,

$$ {}^{m}\widehat{\mathbf{T}}_{\alpha\beta} := -\frac{2}{\sqrt{|\widehat{\mathbf{g}}_{\mu\nu}|}}\frac{\delta(\sqrt{|\widehat{\mathbf{g}}_{\mu\nu}|}\ {}^{m}\mathcal{L})}{\delta\widehat{\mathbf{g}}^{\alpha\beta}} = {}^{m}\mathcal{L}\widehat{\mathbf{g}}^{\alpha\beta} + 2\frac{\delta({}^{m}\mathcal{L})}{\delta\widehat{\mathbf{g}}_{\alpha\beta}}. \quad (2$$

Applying such a calculus to ${}^{F,\mu}\mathcal{S} + {}^{m}\mathcal{S}$, with ${}^{1}\mathbf{F}(\check{\mathbf{R}}) := d\mathbf{F}(\check{\mathbf{R}})/d\check{\mathbf{R}}$, see detai in [14,15,64–66], we obtain the modified gravitational field equations

$$\widehat{\mathbf{R}}_{\mu\nu} = {}^{F,\mu}\widehat{\mathbf{Y}}_{\mu\nu}, \quad (3$$

where ${}^{F,\mu}\widehat{\mathbf{Y}}_{\mu\nu} = {}^{m}\widehat{\mathbf{Y}}_{\mu\nu} + {}^{f}\widehat{\mathbf{Y}}_{\mu\nu} + {}^{\mu}\widehat{\mathbf{Y}}_{\mu\nu}$, for

$$\begin{aligned} {}^{m}\widehat{\mathbf{Y}}_{\mu\nu} &= \frac{1}{2M_P^2}\,{}^{m}\widehat{\mathbf{T}}_{\alpha\beta},\ {}^{f}\widehat{\mathbf{Y}}_{\mu\nu} = (\frac{\mathbf{F}}{2\,{}^{1}\mathbf{F}} - \frac{\widehat{\mathbf{D}}^2\,{}^{1}\mathbf{F}}{{}^{1}\mathbf{F}})\widehat{\mathbf{g}}_{\mu\nu} + \frac{\widehat{\mathbf{D}}_{\mu}\widehat{\mathbf{D}}_{\nu}\,{}^{1}\mathbf{F}}{{}^{1}\mathbf{F}}, \quad (3 \\ {}^{\mu}\widehat{\mathbf{Y}}_{\mu\nu} &= -2\mu^2[(3 - tr\sqrt{\widehat{\mathbf{g}}^{-1}\mathbf{q}} - \det\sqrt{\widehat{\mathbf{g}}^{-1}\mathbf{q}}) - \frac{1}{2}\det\sqrt{\widehat{\mathbf{g}}^{-1}\mathbf{q}})]\widehat{\mathbf{g}}_{\mu\nu} + \\ & \frac{\mu^2}{2}\{\mathbf{q}_{\mu\rho}[(\sqrt{\widehat{\mathbf{g}}^{-1}\mathbf{q}})^{-1}]^{\rho}_{\ \nu} + \mathbf{q}_{\nu\rho}[(\sqrt{\widehat{\mathbf{g}}^{-1}\mathbf{q}})^{-1}]^{\rho}_{\ \mu}\}. \end{aligned}$$

The field equations for massive gravity (30) are constructed as nonholonomic defo mations of the Einstein Equations (9) when the source $\widehat{Y}_{\beta\gamma} \rightarrow {}^{F,\mu}\widehat{\mathbf{Y}}_{\mu\nu}$.

### 3.2. Tmt Massive Configurations with (Broken) Global Scaling Invariance

Let us explain the notations and terms used in the above actions, chosen in such form that a TMT (26) is equivalent to a massive MGT model (27) when both classes of suc theories are encoded via corresponding nonholonomic structures into a nonholonomical deformed Einstein gravity model (25). The non-Riemannian volume-forms (integratio measures on nonholonomic manifold $(\mathbf{g}, \mathbf{N}, \widehat{\mathbf{D}}))$ in (26) are determined by two auxiliary 3-index antisymmetric d-tensor fields $\mathbf{A}_{\alpha\beta\gamma}$ and $\mathbf{B}_{\alpha\beta\gamma}$, when

$$^1\Phi(\mathbf{A}) := \frac{1}{3!}\varepsilon^{\mu\alpha\beta\gamma}\mathbf{e}_\mu\mathbf{A}_{\alpha\beta\gamma} \text{ and } {}^2\Phi(\mathbf{B}) := \frac{1}{3!}\varepsilon^{\mu\alpha\beta\gamma}\mathbf{e}_\mu\mathbf{B}_{\alpha\beta\gamma}.$$

Nevertheless, for non-triviality of the TMT model, the presence of the 3D auxiliary antisymmetric d-tensor gauge field $\mathbf{H}_{\alpha\beta\gamma}$, when $\Phi(\mathbf{H}) := \frac{1}{3!}\varepsilon^{\mu\alpha\beta\gamma}\mathbf{e}_\mu\mathbf{H}_{\alpha\beta\gamma}$ *is crucial*. In order to model two flat regions for the inflationary and accelerating universe in some limits, we consider two Lagrange densities for a scalar field

$$\begin{aligned} {}^1L &= -\frac{1}{2}\mathbf{g}^{\mu\rho}(\mathbf{e}_\mu\varphi)(\mathbf{e}_\rho\varphi) - {}^1U(\varphi),\ {}^1U(\varphi) = {}^1ae^{-q\varphi}; \\ {}^2L &= -\frac{{}^2b}{2}e^{-q\varphi}\mathbf{g}^{\mu\rho}(\mathbf{e}_\mu\varphi)(\mathbf{e}_\rho\varphi) + {}^2U(\varphi),\ {}^2U(\varphi) = {}^2ae^{-2q\varphi}, \end{aligned} \tag{32}$$

with dimensional positive parameters $q$, ${}^1a$, ${}^2a$ and a dimensionless one ${}^2b$. The action (26) is invariant under global N-adapted Weyl-scale transforms with a positive scale parameter $\lambda$, $\mathbf{g}_{\alpha\beta} \to \lambda\mathbf{g}_{\alpha\beta}$, $\varphi \to \varphi + q^{-1}\ln\lambda$, $\mathbf{A}_{\alpha\beta\gamma} \to \lambda\mathbf{A}_{\alpha\beta\gamma}$, $\mathbf{B}_{\alpha\beta\gamma} \to \lambda^2\mathbf{B}_{\alpha\beta\gamma}$ and $\mathbf{H}_{\alpha\beta\gamma} \to \mathbf{H}_{\alpha\beta\gamma}$. For holonomic configurations and quadratic functionals on LC-scalar $\mathbf{f}(\check{\mathbf{R}}) \to R^2$, such a theory is equivalent to that elaborated in [55–57,61,62]. In a more general context, the developments in this work involve non-quadratic nonlinear and nonholonomic functionals and mass gravity deformations via $\check{\mathbf{R}}$ (28), and generic off-diagonal interactions encoded in $\widehat{\mathbf{R}}$.

A variational N-adapted calculus on form fields $\mathbf{A}, \mathbf{B}, \mathbf{H}$ and on d-metric $\mathbf{g}$ (with respect to coordinate bases and for $\nabla$, being similar to that presented in Section 2 of [61,62]), results in effective gravitational field equations

$$\widehat{\mathbf{R}}_{\mu\nu}[\widehat{\mathbf{g}}_{\alpha\beta}] = {}^{ef}\widehat{\Upsilon}_{\mu\nu} + {}^{F,\mu}\widehat{\Upsilon}_{\mu\nu}, \tag{33}$$

where ${}^{F,\mu}\widehat{\Upsilon}_{\mu\nu}$ is determined by (31) and ${}^{ef}\widehat{\Upsilon}_{\beta\gamma} := \varkappa({}^{ef}\widehat{\mathbf{T}}_{\alpha\beta} - \frac{1}{2}\widehat{\mathbf{g}}_{\alpha\beta}\,{}^{ef}\widehat{T})$ is computed using Formulas (8) and (29) for $\mathbf{g}_{\alpha\beta} \to \widehat{\mathbf{g}}_{\alpha\beta}$ and $\widehat{\mathcal{L}} \to {}^{ef}\mathcal{L}$, where

$$\begin{aligned} \widehat{\mathbf{g}}_{\alpha\beta} &= \Theta\mathbf{g}_{\alpha\beta},\ \text{for } \Theta = {}^1\chi - {}^2\chi\epsilon\,{}^1\mathbf{f}({}^1L + {}^1M, \mu); \\ {}^{ef}L &= \Theta^{-1}\Big\{{}^1L + {}^1M + {}^2\chi\Theta^{-1}\Big[{}^2L + {}^1M + \epsilon\,{}^1\mathbf{f}({}^1L + {}^1M, \mu)\Big]\Big\}, \end{aligned} \tag{34}$$

when the conformal factor $\Theta$ for the Weyl re-scaling of d-metric is induced by the nonlinear functional in the action

$${}^1\mathbf{f}({}^1L + {}^1M, \mu) = \frac{d\mathbf{f}(\widehat{\mathbf{R}}, \mu)}{d\widehat{\mathbf{R}}}\,|_{\widehat{\mathbf{R}} = {}^1L + {}^1M} \tag{35}$$

and the two measure functionals ${}^1\chi = {}^1\Phi(\mathbf{A})/\sqrt{|\widehat{\mathbf{g}}_{\mu\nu}|}$ and ${}^2\chi = {}^2\Phi(\mathbf{B})/\sqrt{|\widehat{\mathbf{g}}_{\mu\nu}|}$.

The variations in auxiliary anti-symmetric form fields impose certain constants

$$\mathbf{e}_\mu(\widehat{R} + {}^1L) = 0, \mathbf{e}_\mu[{}^2L + \epsilon\mathbf{f}(\check{\mathbf{R}}) + \Phi(\mathbf{H})/\sqrt{|\mathbf{g}|}] = 0, \mathbf{e}_\mu[{}^2\Phi(\mathbf{B})/\sqrt{|\widehat{\mathbf{g}}_{\mu\nu}|}] = 0.$$

The nonconstant solutions of such nonholonomic constraints allow to preserve the global Weyl-scale invariance for certain configurations. If we take constant values

$$\widehat{R} + {}^1L = -\,{}^1M = const \text{ and } {}^2L + \epsilon\mathbf{f}(\check{\mathbf{R}}) + \Phi(\mathbf{H})/\sqrt{|\mathbf{g}|} = -\,{}^2M = const \tag{36}$$

we select configuration with a nonholonomic dynamical spontaneous breakdown of global Weyl-scale invariance when the condition

$${}^2\Phi(\mathbf{B})/\sqrt{|\widehat{\mathbf{g}}|} = {}^2\chi = const \tag{37}$$

preserves the scale invariance. There are certain constraints on the scale factc $^1\chi = {}^1\Phi(\mathbf{A})/\sqrt{|\mathbf{g}|}$, which can be derived from variations in (26) on $\mathbf{g}_{\mu\nu}$ in N-adapted forı The conditions (36) relate $^1\chi$ and $^2\chi$, i.e., the integration measures, to traces ${}^{1,2}\mathbf{T} := \mathbf{g}^{\alpha}$ ${}^{1,2}\mathbf{T}_{\alpha\beta}$ of the energy momentum tensors

$$ {}^{1,2}\mathbf{T}_{\alpha\beta} = \mathbf{g}_{\alpha\beta}\ {}^{1,2}L - 2\partial(\ {}^{1,2}L)/\partial\mathbf{g}^{\alpha\beta} $$

of Lagrangians for scalar fields (32). (For simplicity, we consider matter actions which onl depend on the coefficients of certain effective metric fields and not on their derivatives This follows from the N-adapted variation on $\mathbf{g}_{\alpha\beta}$ of the action (26), taken, for simplicit with zero ${}^m\mathcal{L}$., which results in

$$ 2\ {}^1\chi\left[\widehat{\mathbf{R}}_{\mu\nu}(\mathbf{g}_{\alpha\beta}) + \mathbf{g}_{\mu\nu}\ {}^1L - \ {}^1\mathbf{T}_{\mu\nu}\right] - {}^2\chi\left[\ {}^2\mathbf{T}_{\mu\nu} + \mathbf{g}_{\mu\nu}\left(\epsilon\mathbf{f}(\widetilde{\mathbf{R}}) + {}^2M\right) - \ {}^1\mathbf{f}\ \widehat{\mathbf{R}}_{\mu\nu}(\mathbf{g}_{\alpha\beta})\right] = 0. \quad (38) $$

Taking the trace of these equations and using (36), we obtain the formul $^1\chi = {}^2\chi\frac{{}^2\mathbf{T}+2\ {}^2M}{2\ {}^1L-\ {}^2\mathbf{T}-2\ {}^1M}$, which does not depend on the type of $f$-modifications containin possible $\mu$-terms. We conclude that the non-Riemannian integration measures considere above, and the interactions of scalar fields (32), can be modelled as additional distributior on nonholonomic manifold $(\mathbf{g}, \mathbf{N}, \widehat{\mathbf{D}})$. They modify the conformal factor $\Theta$ (34) and ca express the field Equations (38) in Einstein like form (33), where ${}^{F,\mu}\widehat{\mathbf{Y}}_{\mu\nu}$ is added as a additional effective matter contribution to the source of scalar fields ${}^{1,2}\mathbf{T}_{\alpha\beta}$.

It should be noted that, using the canonical d-connection, we obtain $\widehat{\mathbf{D}}_\alpha\mathbf{T}^{\alpha\beta} = \mathbf{Q}^\beta \neq$ when $\mathbf{Q}_\beta[\mathbf{g}, \mathbf{N}]$ is completely defined by the d-metric and chosen N-connection structur Considering nonholonomic distortions with $\nabla = \widehat{\mathbf{D}} - \widehat{\mathbf{Z}}$, we obtain standard relations

$$ \nabla^\alpha(R_{\alpha\beta} - \frac{1}{2}g_{\alpha\beta}R) = 0 \text{ and } \nabla^\alpha \Upsilon_{\alpha\beta} = 0. $$

A similar property exists in Lagrange mechanics with non-integrable constraints whe the standard conservation laws do not hold true. A new class of effective variables an new types of conservation laws can be introduced and, respectively, constructed usin Lagrange multiples.

The main conclusion of this section is that various MGTs with two integration me sures, possible deformations by mass graviton terms, bi-connection and bi-metric structure can be expressed as nonholonomic deformations of the Einstein equations in the form (9 Different theories are characterized by respective sources (in explicit form, ${}^{F,\mu}\widehat{\mathbf{Y}}_{\mu\nu}$ in (30 or ${}^{ef}\widehat{\mathbf{Y}}_{\mu\nu} + {}^{F,\mu}\widehat{\mathbf{Y}}_{\mu\nu}$ in (33)). Our next goal is to prove that such effective Einstein equation can be integrated in certain general forms for $\widehat{\mathbf{D}}$ and possible constraints (10) for LC configurations.

## 4. Cosmological Solutions in Effective Einstein Gravity and Fmgts

We can generate explicit integral varieties of systems of PDEs of type (9) for d-metric $\widehat{\mathbf{g}}$ (34) and sources $\widehat{\Upsilon}_{\beta\gamma} = {}^{ef}\widehat{\mathbf{Y}}_{\mu\nu} + {}^{F,\mu}\widehat{\mathbf{Y}}_{\mu\nu}$ as in (33) which, via frame and coordinat transforms,

$$ \widehat{\mathbf{g}}_{\alpha\beta} = e^{\alpha'}_{\ \alpha}(x^i, y^a)e^{\beta'}_{\ \beta}(x^i, y^a)\widehat{\mathbf{g}}_{\alpha'\beta'}(x^i, t) \text{ and } \widehat{\Upsilon}_{\alpha\beta} = e^{\alpha'}_{\ \alpha}(x^i, y^a)e^{\beta'}_{\ \beta}(x^i, y^a)\widehat{\Upsilon}_{\alpha'\beta'}(x^i, t), $$

for a time like coordinate $y^4 = t$ $(i', i, k, k', \cdots = 1, 2$ and $a, a', b, b', \cdots = 3, 4)$, can b parameterized in the form

$$ \begin{aligned} \widehat{\mathbf{g}} &= \widehat{\mathbf{g}}_{\alpha'\beta'}\mathbf{e}^{\alpha'} \otimes \mathbf{e}^{\beta'} = g_i(x^k)dx^i \otimes dx^j + \omega^2(x^k, y^3, t)h_a(x^k, t)\mathbf{e}^a \otimes \mathbf{e}^a, \quad (39) \\ \mathbf{e}^3 &= dy^3 + n_i(x^k, t)dx^i, \mathbf{e}^4 = dt + w_i(x^k, t)dx^i, \end{aligned} $$

for nontrivial

$$\{g_{i'j'}\} = diag[g_i], g_1 = g_2 = e^{\psi(x^k)}; \{g_{a'b'}\} = diag[h_a], h_a = h_a(x^k, t);$$
$$N_i^3 = n_i(x^k, t);\ N_i^4 = w_i(x^k, t);$$

and

$$\begin{aligned} \widehat{Y}_{\alpha'\beta'} &= diag[Y_i; Y_a], \text{ for } Y_1 = Y_2 = \widetilde{Y}(x^k) = {}^{ef}\widetilde{Y}(x^k) + {}^{m}\widetilde{Y}(x^k) + {}^{f}\widetilde{Y}(x^k) + {}^{\mu}\widetilde{Y}(x^k), \\ Y_3 &= Y_4 = Y(x^k, t) = {}^{ef}Y(x^k, t) + {}^{m}Y(x^k, t) + {}^{f}Y(x^k, t) + {}^{\mu}Y(x^k, t). \end{aligned} \quad (40)$$

These ansatz for the d-metric and sources are very general, but for an assumption that there are N-adapted frames with respect to which the MGTs interactions have Killing symmetry on $\partial/\partial y^3$ when geometric and physical values do not depend on coordinate $y^3$. (It should be noted that it is possible to construct very general classes of generic off-diagonal solutions depending on all spacetime variables in arbitrary finite dimensions; see details and examples in [26–29] for more "non-Killing" configurations. For simplicity, we shall study nonhomogeneous and locally anisotropic cosmological solutions in this work, depending on variables $(x^k, t)$, with smooth limits to cosmological diagonal configurations depending only on $t$ and very small off-diagonal contributions characterized by a small parameter $\varepsilon$, $0 \leq \varepsilon \ll 1$.). We use parameterizations $g_1 = g_2 = e^{\psi(x^i)}$ and $h_a(x^k, t)$ for $i, j, \cdots = 1, 2$ and $a, b, \cdots = 3, 4$; and N-connection coefficients $\mathbf{N}_i^3 = n_i(x^k, t)$ and $\mathbf{N}_i^4 = w_i(x^k, t)$. Introducing brief denotations for partial derivatives, like $a^\bullet = \partial_1 a, b' = \partial_2 b, h^* = \partial_4 h = \partial_t h$ and defining the values $\alpha_i = h_3^* \partial_i \varpi, \beta = h_3^*\, \varpi^*, \gamma = \left(\ln |h_3|^{3/2}/|h_4|\right)^*$ for a generating function

$$\varpi := \ln |h_3^*/\sqrt{|h_3 h_4|}|, \text{ we shall also use the value } \Psi := e^{\varpi}, \quad (41)$$

we transform (33) into a nonlinear system of PDEs with decoupling properties for the unknown functions $\psi(x^i), h_a(x^k, t), w_i(x^k, t)$ and $n_i(x^k, t)$,

$$\psi^{\bullet\bullet} + \psi'' = 2\,\widetilde{Y},\ \varpi^* h_3^* = 2h_3 h_4 Y,\ n_i^{**} + \gamma n_i^* = 0,\ \beta w_i - \alpha_i = 0. \quad (42)$$

This system possesses another very important property, which allows us to redefine the generating function, $\Psi \longleftrightarrow \widetilde{\Psi}$, when $\Lambda(\Psi^2)^* = |Y|(\widetilde{\Psi}^2)^*$ and

$$\Lambda \Psi^2 = \widetilde{\Psi}^2 |Y| + \int dt \widetilde{\Psi}^2 |Y|^* \quad (43)$$

for $\widetilde{\Psi} := \exp \widetilde{\varpi}$ and any prescribed values of effective (for different types of contribution $ef, m, f, \mu$) cosmological constants in $\Lambda = {}^{ef}\Lambda + {}^{m}\Lambda + {}^{f}\Lambda + {}^{\mu}\Lambda$ associated, respectively, with

$$Y(x^k, t) = {}^{ef}Y(x^k, t) + {}^{m}Y(x^k, t) + {}^{f}Y(x^k, t) + {}^{\mu}Y(x^k, t).$$

For generating off-diagonal cosmological solutions depending on $t$, we have to consider generating functions, for which $\Psi^* \neq 0$. The Equations (42) for ansatz (39) transform, respectively, into a system of nonlinear PDEs

$$\psi^{\bullet\bullet} + \psi' = 2\,\widetilde{Y},\ \widetilde{\varpi}^* h_3^* = 2h_3 h_4 \Lambda,\ n_i^{**} + \gamma n_i^* = 0,\ \varpi^* w_i - \partial_i \varpi = 0 \quad (44)$$
$$\text{and } \varpi^* \partial_i \omega - \omega^* \partial_i \varpi = 0, \text{ for the vertical conformal factor.}$$

We have to subject the d-metric and N-connection coefficients to additional constraints (10) in order to satisfy the torsionless conditions, which for the ansatz (39) are written

$$w_i^* = (\partial_i - w_i \partial_4) \ln \sqrt{|h_4|}, (\partial_i - w_i \partial_4) \ln \sqrt{|h_3|} = 0, \partial_i w_j = \partial_j w_i, n_i^* = 0, \partial_i n_j = \partial_j n_i. \quad (45)$$

We can generate exact solutions in TMT, MGT and nonholonomically deforme Einstein theories with respective actions (25), (26) and (27) using integral varieties (Th term "integral variety" is used in the theory of differential equations for certain "classes solutions", determined by corresponding classes of parameters, generating and integratic functions, etc. In GR, we search for an integral variety of solutions of associated systen of PDEs determining, for instance, Einstein spacetimes, black holes, and cosmologic solutions. In modified gravity theories, we can establish an analogy for GR if we consid effective models.) of the system of PDEs (44), which can be found in very general form Let us briefly explain this geometric formalism elaborated in the framework of the AFD (see details in [30–33]):

1. The first equation for $\psi$ is the 2D Laplace/d' Alambert equation which can be solve for any given $\widetilde{\Upsilon}$, which allows us to find $g_1 = g_2 = e^{\psi(x^k)}$.
2. Using the second equation in (44) and (41), the coefficients $h_a$ can be expressed functionals on $(\Psi, \Upsilon)$. We redefine the generating function as in (43) and consider a effective source
$$\Xi := \int dt \Upsilon(\widetilde{\Psi}^2)^* = {}^{ef}\Xi + {}^{m}\Xi + {}^{f}\Xi + {}^{\mu}\Xi,$$
when ${}^{ef}\Xi := \int dt\, {}^{ef}\Upsilon(\widetilde{\Psi}^2)^*$, ${}^{m}\Xi := \int dt\, {}^{m}\Upsilon(\widetilde{\Psi}^2)^*$, ${}^{f}\Xi := \int dt\, {}^{f}\Upsilon(\widetilde{\Psi}^2)^*$, and write
$$h_3 = \frac{\widetilde{\Psi}^2}{4({}^{ef}\Lambda + {}^{m}\Lambda + {}^{f}\Lambda + {}^{\mu}\Lambda)} \text{ and } h_4 = \frac{(\widetilde{\Psi}^*)^2}{({}^{ef}\Xi + {}^{m}\Xi + {}^{f}\Xi + {}^{\mu}\Xi)}.$$
3. We have to integrate $t$ twice in order to find it in the 3D subset of equations in (44)
$$n_i = {}_1n_i + {}_2n_i \int dt \frac{(\widetilde{\Psi}^*)^2}{\widetilde{\Psi}^3({}^{ef}\Xi + {}^{m}\Xi + {}^{f}\Xi + {}^{\mu}\Xi)}$$
for some integration functions ${}_1n_i(x^k)$ and ${}_2n_i(x^k)$.
4. The 4th set of equations in (44) are algebraic ones, which allows us to compute
$$w_i = [\varpi^*]^{-1}\partial_i\varpi = [\Psi^*]^{-1}\partial_i\Psi = [(\Psi^2)^*]^{-1}\partial_i(\Psi)^2 = [\Xi^*]^{-1}\partial_i\Xi.$$
5. We can satisfy the conditions for $\omega$ in the second line in (44) if we keep the Killir symmetry on $\partial_i$ and take, for instance, $\omega^2 = |h_4|^{-1}$.
Different types of inhomogeneous cosmological solutions of the system (33) ar determined by corresponding classes of effective sources

| | |
|---|---|
| generating functions: | $\psi(x^k), \widetilde{\Psi}(x^k,t), \omega(x^k,y^3,t)$ |
| effective sources: | $\widetilde{\Upsilon}(x^k)$; ${}^{ef}\Xi(x^k,t)$, ${}^{m}\Xi(x^k,t)$, ${}^{f}\Xi(x^k,t)$, ${}^{\mu}\Xi(x^k,t)$, |
| | or ${}^{ef}\Upsilon(x^k,t)$, ${}^{m}\Upsilon(x^k,t)$, ${}^{f}\Upsilon(x^k,t)$, ${}^{\mu}\Upsilon(x^k,t)$ |
| integration cosm. constants: | ${}^{ef}\Lambda$, ${}^{m}\Lambda$, ${}^{f}\Lambda$, ${}^{\mu}\Lambda$ |
| integration functions: | ${}_1n_i(x^k)$ and ${}_2n_i(x^k)$ |

We can generate solutions with any nontrivial ${}^{ef}\Lambda$, ${}^{m}\Lambda$, ${}^{f}\Lambda$, ${}^{\mu}\Lambda$ even any, or a effective source ${}^{ef}\Upsilon$, ${}^{m}\Upsilon$, ${}^{f}\Upsilon$, ${}^{\mu}\Upsilon$ can be zero.

### 4.1. Inhomogeneous FTMT and MGT Configurations with Induced Nonholonomic Torsion

The solutions with coefficients computed above in 1–5 can be parametrized to describ nonholonomic deformations, $\widehat{\mathbf{g}}_{\alpha\beta} = \mathbf{e}^{\alpha'}_{\ \alpha}\mathbf{e}^{\beta'}_{\ \beta}\mathring{g}_{\alpha'\beta'}$, of the Friedman–Lemaître–Robertsor Walker (FLRW) diagonal quadratic element (we can consider spherical symmetry coo dinates $u^{\alpha'} = (x^{1'} = r, x^{2'} = \theta, y^{3'} = \varphi, y^{4'} = t)$, or Cartesian ones, $u^{\alpha'} = (x^{1'} = x, x^{2'} = y, y^{3'} = z, y^{4'} = t)$, for a scale factor $\mathring{a}(t)$ determining the Hubble constant $H := \mathring{a}^*/\mathring{a}$.)

$$d\mathring{s}^2 = \mathring{g}_{\alpha'\beta'}du^{\alpha'}du^{\beta'} = \mathring{a}^2(t)[dr^2 + r^2d\theta^2 + r^2\sin^2\theta d\varphi^2] - dt^2 \quad (46)$$

into a generic off-diagonal inhomogeneous cosmological metric of type (39) with $g_i = \eta_i e^{\psi}$ and $h_a = \eta_a \mathring{g}_a$ with effective polarization functions $\eta_1 = \eta_2 = a^{-2}e^{\psi}, \eta_3 = \mathring{a}^{-2}h_3, \eta_4 = 1$ and $\widehat{h}_3 = h_3/a^2|h_4|$, when

$$\begin{aligned} ds^2 &= a^2(x^k,t)[\eta_1(x^k,t)(dx^1)^2 + \eta_2(x^k,t)(dx^2)^2] \\ &+ a^2(x^k,t)\widehat{h}_3(x^k,t)[dy^3 + ({}_1n_i + {}_2n_i\int dt \frac{(\widetilde{\Psi}^*)^2}{\widetilde{\Psi}^3({}^{ef}\Xi + {}^{m}\Xi + {}^{f}\Xi + {}^{\mu}\Xi)})dx^i]^2 \\ &- [dt + \frac{\partial_i({}^{ef}\Xi + {}^{m}\Xi + {}^{f}\Xi + {}^{\mu}\Xi)}{({}^{ef}\Xi + {}^{m}\Xi + {}^{f}\Xi + {}^{\mu}\Xi)^*}dx^i]^2. \end{aligned} \quad (47)$$

The inhomogeneous scaling factor $a(x^k,t)$ in (47) is related to the generating function $\widetilde{\Psi}$ via formula

$$a^2\widehat{h}_3 = \omega^2 h_3 = \frac{h_3}{|h_4|} = \frac{\widetilde{\Psi}^2|{}^{ef}\Xi + {}^{m}\Xi + {}^{f}\Xi + {}^{\mu}\Xi|}{4({}^{ef}\Lambda + {}^{m}\Lambda + {}^{f}\Lambda + {}^{\mu}\Lambda)(\widetilde{\Psi}^*)^2}.$$

In general, such target metrics $\widehat{\mathbf{g}}_{\alpha\beta}(x^k,t)$ determine new classes of cosmological metrics with nontrivial nonholonomically induced torsion computed for $\widehat{\mathbf{D}}$. Such modified spacetimes cannot be diagonalized by coordinate transforms if the anholonomy coefficients $W^{\gamma}_{\alpha\beta}$ are not zero. For trivial gravitational polarizations, $\eta_\alpha = 1$, trivial N-connection coefficients, $N^3_i = n_i = 0$ and $N^4_i = w_i = 0$, and for $a(x^k,t) \to \mathring{a}(t)$, we obtain torsionless FLRW metrics. We emphasize that one could not have smooth limits $\widehat{\mathbf{g}}_{\alpha\beta} \to \mathring{g}_{\alpha\beta}$ for the arbitrary generating function $\widetilde{\Psi}$ and any nontrivial effective cosmological constant ${}^{ef}\Lambda$, ${}^{m}\Lambda$, ${}^{f}\Lambda$, or ${}^{\mu}\Lambda$, associated with respective mater fields.

We can generate off-diagonal cosmological configurations as "small" deformations with $\eta_\alpha = 1 + \epsilon_\alpha, n_i = {}^{\epsilon}n_i$ and $w_i = {}^{\epsilon}w_i$, with $|\epsilon_\alpha|, |{}^{\epsilon}n_i|, |{}^{\epsilon}w_i| \ll 1$. In particular, we can only study TMT models if ${}^{m}\Xi = {}^{f}\Xi = {}^{\mu}\Xi = 0$ and ${}^{m}\Lambda = {}^{f}\Lambda = {}^{\mu}\Lambda = 0$ but ${}^{ef}\Upsilon(x^k,t) \neq 0$ and ${}^{ef}\Lambda \neq 0$. off-diagonal cosmological scenarios in massive and bi-metric gravity with nontrivial ${}^{\mu}\Xi$ and ${}^{\mu}\Lambda$ were studied in our recent works [14,15]. Other classes of MGTs and cosmological models with off-diagonal configurations when $f$-modified gravity effects, modelled in GR, were studied in [26–33]. The goal of Section 6 is to show how TMT gravity and cosmological models can be associated with certain nonholonomic off-diagonal de Sitter configurations with nontrivial ${}^{ef}\Lambda$ for an effective Einstein–Lagrange spacetime, and such constructions can be generalized to reproduce MGTs and massive gravity.

### 4.2. Extracting Levi–Civita Cosmological Configurations

Let us show how we can generate, in explicit form, solutions to the system (45) for nonholonomic, generic, off-diagonal configurations with zero torsion. We have to consider certain special classes of generating and integration functions. By straightforward computations, we can check that such conditions are satisfied if we state such conditions for a metric (47) that

$$\begin{aligned} {}_2n_i &= 0 \text{ and } {}_1n_i = \partial_i n(x^k), \text{ for any } n(x^k) \\ \Psi &= \check{\Psi}, \text{ for } (\partial_i\check{\Psi})^* = \partial_i(\check{\Psi}^*) \text{ and find a function } \check{A}(x^k,t) \text{ when} \\ \partial_i w_j &= \partial_j w_i \text{ for } w_i = \check{w}_i = \partial_i\check{\Psi}/\check{\Psi}^* = \partial_i\widehat{\Xi}/\widehat{\Xi}^* = \partial_i\check{A} \end{aligned} \quad (48)$$

when

$$\Lambda\check{\Psi}^2 = \widehat{\Psi}^2|\Upsilon| + \int dt\widehat{\Psi}^2|\Upsilon|^* \text{ and } \widehat{\Xi} := \int dt\Upsilon(\widehat{\Psi}^2)^*$$

are computed with the following formulas (43), except for $\Psi(\widetilde{\Psi}) \to \check{\Psi}(\widehat{\Psi})$ and $\widetilde{\Psi} \to$ For certain configurations, we can consider functional dependencies $\widehat{\Psi} = \widehat{\Psi}(\ln\sqrt{|h_3|})$ an invertible functional dependencies $h_3[\widehat{\Psi}[\check{\Psi}]]$. In such cases, we take $h_3(x^k,t)$ as a generatin function and consider necessary type functionals $\check{\Psi}[h_3]$ with the property $(\partial_i\check{\Psi})^* = \partial_i(\check{\Psi}^*$ which are used for defining $\check{w}_i[h_3] = \partial_i\check{\Psi}/\check{\Psi}^* = \partial_i\check{A}[h_3]$.

Putting together the conditions (48), we generate nonhomogeneous cosmologica LC–configurations with quadratic linear elements

$$\begin{aligned} ds^2 &= \check{a}^2(x^k,t)[\eta_1(x^k,t)(dx^1)^2 + \eta_2(x^k,t)(dx^2)^2] + \check{a}^2(x^k,t)\widehat{h}_3(x^k,t)[dy^3 + (\partial_i n)dx^i]^2 \\ &\quad -[dt + (\partial_i\check{A})dx^i]^2 \\ &= e^{\psi(x^k)}[(dx^1)^2 + (dx^2)^2] + \frac{\widehat{\Psi}^2}{4(\,^{ef}\Lambda + \,^{m}\Lambda + \,^{f}\Lambda + \,^{\mu}\Lambda)}[dy^3 + (\partial_i n)dx^i]^2 \\ &\quad - \frac{(\widehat{\Psi}^*)^2}{\widehat{\Xi}}[dt + (\partial_i\check{A})dx^i]^2. \end{aligned} \quad (4$$

The inhomogeneous scaling factor $\check{a}(x^k,t)$ is computed similarly to (47), but using th generating function $\widehat{\Psi}$,

$$\check{a}^2\widehat{h}_3 = \frac{\widehat{\Psi}^2|\,\widehat{\Xi}|}{4(\,^{ef}\Lambda + \,^{m}\Lambda + \,^{f}\Lambda + \,^{\mu}\Lambda)(\widehat{\Psi}^*)^2} \text{ for } \check{\Psi} := e^{\check{\varpi}}.$$

Having constructed a class of generic off-diagonal solutions (49), we can impos additional constraints on the generating/integration functions and constants and source i order to explain certain observational cosmological data. For instance, we can fix subclasse of functions $\widehat{\Psi} \to \widehat{\Psi}(t), (\partial_i\check{A}) \to w_i(t)$ etc., describing small deformations of an FLRV metric (46) in a nonlinear parametric way, as well as redefined generating functions (4 and different types of effective source in TMT, MGT and/or massive gravity models.

## 5. Locally Anisotropic Effective Scalar Potentials and Flat Regions

We study three examples of off-diagonal cosmological solutions reproducing the TM model with two flat regions of the effective scalar potental studied in [60], than analys how massive gravity can be modelled as a TMT theory and effective GR, and (in the la subsection) we speculate on non-singular emergent anisotropic universes. The solutions i this section will be constructed to contain nontrivial nonholonomically induced torsion, a for quadratic elements (47). For certain important limits, LC-configurations of type (4 will also be examined.

### 5.1. Off-Diagonal Interactions and Associated Tmt Models with Two Flat Regions

We chose the nontrivial off-diagonal data in (47) for $\,^{m}\Lambda = \,^{f}\Lambda = \,^{\mu}\Lambda = 0$ an $\,^{m}\Upsilon = \,^{f}\Upsilon = \,^{\mu}\Upsilon = 0$ resulting in $\,^{m}\Xi = \,^{f}\Xi = \,^{\mu}\Xi = 0$,, but considering nonzero $\,^{ef}\Lambda$ an $\,^{ef}\Upsilon$ is taken as a one-Killing configuration, not depending on $y^3$ in

$$\,^{ef}\widehat{\Upsilon}_{\beta\gamma} := \varkappa(\,^{ef}\widehat{\mathbf{T}}_{\alpha\beta} - \frac{1}{2}\widehat{\mathbf{g}}_{\alpha\beta}\,^{ef}\widehat{T})$$

is computed using formula (8) and (29) for $\mathbf{g}_{\alpha\beta} \to \widehat{\mathbf{g}}_{\alpha\beta}$ and $\widehat{\mathcal{L}} \to {}^{ef}\mathcal{L}$ for two scalar densities (32) as in (34). We generate solutions of $\widehat{\mathbf{R}}_{\mu\nu}[\widehat{\mathbf{g}}_{\alpha\beta}] = {}^{ef}\widehat{\mathbf{Y}}_{\mu\nu}$ (in a particular case of (33)) for $\widehat{\mathbf{g}}_{\alpha\beta}(x^k,t) = \widehat{\Theta}(x^k,t)\mathbf{g}_{\alpha\beta}(x^k,t)$, parameterized in the form

$$\begin{aligned} ds^2 &= \widehat{\mathbf{g}}_{\alpha\beta}\mathbf{e}^{\alpha}\mathbf{e}^{\beta} = \widetilde{a}^2(x^k,t)[\eta_1(x^k,t)(dx^1)^2 + \eta_2(x^k,t)(dx^2)^2] \\ &+ \widetilde{a}^2(x^k,t)\widehat{h}_3(x^k,t)[dy^3 + ({}_1n_i + {}_2n_i \int dt \frac{(\widetilde{\Psi}^*)^2}{\widetilde{\Psi}^3\ {}^{ef}\Xi})dx^i]^2 - [dt + \frac{\partial_i({}^{ef}\Xi)}{({}^{ef}\Xi)^*}dx^i]^2. \end{aligned} \tag{50}$$

The inhomogeneous scaling factor $\widetilde{a}(x^k,t)$ is related to the generating function $\widetilde{\Psi}$ via formula

$$\widetilde{a}^2\widehat{h}_3 = \omega^2 h_3 = \frac{h_3}{|h_4|} = \frac{\widetilde{\Psi}^2|\ {}^{ef}\Xi|}{4({}^{ef}\Lambda)(\widetilde{\Psi}^*)^2}. \tag{51}$$

Choosing a function $\widetilde{\Psi}$, we prescribe a corresponding dependence for $\widehat{\Theta}(x^k,t)$ and, respectively, $\widetilde{a}(x^k,t)$ as follows from the above formulas. Let us speculate on the structure of $\widehat{\Theta}$, which describes off-diagonal generalizations of the model given by Formulas (18)–(23) in [60] on the assumption that the relation (35) for zero-graviton mass and quadratic Ricci scalar curvature has the limit

$${}^1\mathbf{f}({}^1L + {}^1M, \mu = 0) = \frac{d\mathbf{f}(\widehat{\mathbf{R}}, \mu = 0)}{d\widehat{\mathbf{R}}}\ |_{\widehat{\mathbf{R}} = {}^1L + {}^1M} \to\ {}^1U - {}^1M.$$

In this subsection, we consider ${}^1\mathbf{f} \approx {}^1U - {}^1M$ for a nonhomogeneous $\varphi(x^k,t) \approx \varphi(t)$ in order to construct cosmological TMT models with limits to diagonal two flat regions.

We consider $\widehat{\Theta}$ as a conformal factor $\Theta$ in (34) not depending on $y^3$, written in explicit form for an Einstein N-adapted frame with effective scalar Lagrangian

$$\begin{aligned} {}^{ef}\widehat{L} &= \widehat{\Theta}^{-1}\{{}^1\widehat{L} + {}^1M + {}^2\chi\widehat{\Theta}^{-1}[{}^2\widehat{L} + {}^1M + \epsilon({}^1\mathbf{f})^2]\} \\ &= A(\varphi)X + B(\varphi)X^2 - {}^{ef}U(\varphi), \end{aligned} \tag{52}$$

where we omit cumbersome formulas for $A(\varphi)$ and $B(\varphi)$ in the second line (see similar ones given by Formulas (24) and (25) in [60]), but present

$$\begin{aligned} {}^1\widehat{L} &= \widehat{\Theta}\,X - {}^1U \text{ for } {}^2\widehat{L} = \frac{{}^2b}{{}^1a}\widehat{\Theta}\ {}^1U\widehat{X} + {}^2U \text{ for } \widehat{X} = -\frac{1}{2}\widehat{\mathbf{g}}^{\alpha\beta}\mathbf{e}_{\alpha}\varphi\mathbf{e}_{\beta}\varphi, \\ {}^{ef}U &= \frac{({}^1\mathbf{f})^2}{4\,{}^2\chi[{}^2U + {}^2M + \epsilon({}^1\mathbf{f})^2]}. \end{aligned} \tag{53}$$

For simplicity, we can construct off-diagonal configurations with $\widehat{h}_3 \simeq 1$ in (51), prescribing a value ${}^{ef}\Lambda$ corresponding to observational data in the accelerating Universe, and computing ${}^{ef}\Xi$ for ${}^{ef}\widehat{L}$ using formulas

$${}^{ef}\widehat{\mathbf{T}}_{\alpha\beta} := {}^{ef}\widehat{L}\widehat{\mathbf{g}}^{\alpha\beta} + 2\frac{\delta({}^{ef}\widehat{L})}{\delta\widehat{\mathbf{g}}_{\alpha\beta}} \text{ and } {}^{ef}\widehat{\Upsilon}_{\beta\gamma} := \varkappa({}^{ef}\widehat{\mathbf{T}}_{\alpha\beta} - \frac{1}{2}\widehat{\mathbf{g}}_{\alpha\beta}\ {}^{ef}\widehat{T})$$

and constraints of type (40),

$${}^{ef}\widehat{\Upsilon}_{\alpha'\beta'} = diag[\widehat{\Upsilon}_i; \widehat{\Upsilon}_a], \text{ for } \widehat{\Upsilon}_1 = \widehat{\Upsilon}_2 = {}^{ef}\widetilde{\Upsilon}(x^k), \widehat{\Upsilon}_3 = \widehat{\Upsilon}_4 = {}^{ef}\widehat{\Upsilon}(x^k,t).$$

Then, we can compute ${}^{ef}\Xi := \int dt\ {}^{ef}\widehat{\Upsilon}(\widetilde{\Psi}^2)^*$. Such a problem can be also solved in inverse form for a given $\widetilde{a}(x^k,t)$, when $\widetilde{\Psi}$ has to be defined from an integro-differential Equation (51), $\widetilde{a}^2 = \frac{\widetilde{\Psi}^2|\int dt\ {}^{ef}\widehat{\Upsilon}(t)(\widetilde{\Psi}^2)^*|}{4({}^{ef}\Lambda)(\widetilde{\Psi}^*)^2}$. For cosmological solutions, we can consider $\widetilde{a}(x^k,t) \simeq \widetilde{a}(t)$ and $\widetilde{\Psi}(x^k,t) \simeq \widetilde{\Psi}(t)$, when the generation function $\widetilde{\Psi}(t)$ is prescribed to depend only on time-like coordinate $t$. The observable effective scaling factor $\widetilde{a}(t)$ is expressed as a functional on constant ${}^{ef}\Lambda$, on TMT source ${}^{ef}\widehat{\Upsilon}(t)$ and generating functic $\widetilde{\Psi}(t)$. For instance, variations in ${}^{ef}\widehat{\Upsilon}(t)$ are determined by the variation in the secor auxiliary 3-index antisymmetric d-tensor field $\mathbf{B}_{\alpha\beta\gamma}$ in ${}^{2}\Phi(\mathbf{B})$ in the Formula (37). W adapt and write a similar formula with "tilde" values, in order to emphasize that the valu are computed for a prescribed value $\widetilde{a}(t)$,

$$ {}^{2}\Phi(\widetilde{\mathbf{B}})/\sqrt{|\widehat{\mathbf{g}}|} = {}^{2}\widetilde{\chi} = const. \quad (5 $$

There are two options to fix a constant ${}^{2}\widetilde{\chi}$ : the first one is to choose a function and/or to modify $\widetilde{\mathbf{B}}$ in the second measure. In general, this is a nonlinear effect of the r definition of generation functions (43), which holds for generic off-diagonal configuratior We can finally prescribe some small off-diagonal corrections but the diagonal values wi be re-scaled (we shall maintain "tilde " in order to distinguish such values from simil ones computed from the very beginning, using diagonalized equations).

The main conclusion of this subsection is that by working with generic off-diagon solutions for effective Einstein Equations (33)—see equivalent Formulas (38)—we ca choose generating functions and effective sources that allow us to reproduce, in genera ized forms, the properties of TMT gravity theories determined by action (26) and scal Lagrangians (32). In the next subsection, we prove that such models may be generated have limits to diagonal two flat regions reproducing accelerating cosmology scenarios.

### 5.2. Limits to Diagonal Two Flat Regions

Let us consider in ${}^{ef}\widehat{L}$ (52) the approximation

$$ {}^{1}\mathbf{f}({}^{1}L + {}^{1}M, \mu = 0) = \frac{d\mathbf{f}(\widehat{\mathbf{R}}, \mu = 0)}{d\widehat{\mathbf{R}}} |_{\widehat{\mathbf{R}} = {}^{1}L + {}^{1}M} \rightarrow {}^{1}U - {}^{1}M \quad (5 $$

with $\widetilde{\Psi}(t)$ and $\widetilde{a}(t)$ resulting in diagonal cosmological solutions with effective FLR metrics. We approximate the effective potential ${}^{ef}U$ (53) for a prescribed constant ${}^{2}\widetilde{\chi}$ by relation (54),

$$ \begin{aligned} {}^{ef}U &= \frac{({}^{1}U - {}^{1}M)^2}{4\,{}^{2}\widetilde{\chi}[{}^{2}U + {}^{2}M + ({}^{1}U - {}^{1}M)^2]} \simeq \\ {}^{ef}\widetilde{U} &= \left\{ \begin{array}{cc} {}^{[-]}\widetilde{U} = \frac{({}^{1}a)^2}{4\,{}^{2}\widetilde{\chi}[{}^{2}a + \epsilon({}^{1}a)^2]} & \text{for } \varphi \rightarrow -\infty \\ {}^{[+]}\widetilde{U} = \frac{({}^{1}M)^2}{4\,{}^{2}\widetilde{\chi}[{}^{2}M + \epsilon({}^{1}M)^2]} & \text{for } \varphi \rightarrow +\infty \end{array} \right| . \end{aligned} $$

For such diagonal approximations, the $A$– and $B$–functions can be computed explicit form

$$ \widetilde{A} \simeq \left\{ \begin{array}{c} {}^{[-]}\widetilde{A} = \frac{{}^{2}a + \frac{1}{2}\,{}^{2}b\,{}^{1}a}{{}^{2}a + \epsilon({}^{1}a)^2} \\ {}^{[+]}\widetilde{A} = \frac{{}^{2}M}{{}^{2}M + \epsilon({}^{1}M)^2} \end{array} \right| \text{ and } \widetilde{B} \simeq \left\{ \begin{array}{c} {}^{[-]}\widetilde{B} = -\,{}^{2}\widetilde{\chi}\frac{{}^{2}b/4 - \epsilon({}^{2}a + {}^{2}b\,{}^{1}a)}{{}^{2}a + \epsilon({}^{1}a)^2} \\ {}^{[+]}\widetilde{B} = \epsilon\,{}^{2}\widetilde{\chi}\frac{{}^{2}M}{{}^{2}M + \epsilon({}^{1}M)^2} \end{array} \right| . $$

Such values reproduce the results of Section 3 in [60] with two flat regions of the effectiv potential ${}^{ef}\widetilde{U}$, but in our approach, the effective diagonalized metric is of type (49) wi $\breve{a} \simeq \widetilde{a}(t)$ for $\eta_\alpha \simeq 1$. This class of diagonalized solutions determined by generating functior contain explicit solutions with an effective scalar field, evolving on the first flat region fc large negative $\varphi$ and describing non-singular "emergent universes" [49–54].

## 6. Reproducing Modified Massive Gravity as TMTS and Effective GR

The goal of this section is to study solutions to effective Einstein Equations (33) when the source (40) is taken for ${}^{m}\widetilde{\Upsilon} = {}^{f}\widetilde{\Upsilon} = 0$ and ${}^{m}\Upsilon = {}^{f}\Upsilon = 0$, i.e.,

$$\begin{aligned} \widehat{\Upsilon}_{\alpha'\beta'} &= diag[\Upsilon_i; \Upsilon_a], \text{ for} \\ \Upsilon_1 &= \Upsilon_2 = {}^{e\mu}\widetilde{\Upsilon}(x^k) = {}^{ef}\widetilde{\Upsilon}(x^k) + {}^{\mu}\widetilde{\Upsilon}(x^k), \\ \Upsilon_3 &= \Upsilon_4 = {}^{e\mu}\Upsilon(x^k,t) = {}^{ef}\Upsilon(x^k,t) + {}^{\mu}\Upsilon(x^k,t), \end{aligned}$$

with a left label "$e\mu$" emphasizing that such sources are considered for TMT configurations with a nontrivial mass term $\mu$ but zero-matter field configurations and for a possible quadratic $\epsilon R^2$ cosmological term. We shall chose such N-adapted frames of reference and generating functions when the TMT gravity model describes modifications to $\mu^2$ terms for nonholonomic ghost-free configurations and corrections to scalar curvature (28) of type $\check{\mathbf{R}} \simeq \widehat{\mathbf{R}} + \widetilde{\mu}^2$, where

$$\widetilde{\mu}^2 \simeq 2\,\mu^2(3 - tr\sqrt{\mathbf{g}^{-1}\mathbf{q}} - \det\sqrt{\mathbf{g}^{-1}\mathbf{q}})$$

is determined by the graviton's mass $\mu$ and $\mathbf{q} = \{\mathbf{q}_{\alpha\beta}\}$ is the so-called non-dynamical reference metric. For simplicity, we make the assumption that such values can be redefined as constant for certain choices of the generating functions, effective sources ${}^{ef}\Upsilon(x^k,t)$, ${}^{\mu}\Upsilon(x^k,t)$ and respective nontrivial constants ${}^{e\mu}\Lambda = {}^{ef}\Lambda + {}^{\mu}\Lambda$.

### 6.1. Massive Gravity Modifications of Flat Regions

We can integraten generic, off-diagonal forms of TMT systems that are subclasses of solutions (47) when

$$\begin{aligned} ds^2 &= \overline{a}^2(x^k,t)[\eta_1(x^k,t)(dx^1)^2 + \eta_2(x^k,t)(dx^2)^2] + \\ & \overline{a}^2(x^k,t)\widehat{h}_3(x^k,t)[dy^3 + ({}_1n_i + {}_2n_i \int dt \frac{(\widetilde{\Psi}^*)^2}{\widetilde{\Psi}^3({}^{ef}\Xi + {}^{\mu}\Xi)})dx^i]^2 - \\ & [dt + \frac{\partial_i({}^{ef}\Xi + {}^{\mu}\Xi)}{({}^{ef}\Xi + {}^{\mu}\Xi)^*}dx^i]^2, \end{aligned} \tag{56}$$

for

$${}^{ef}\Xi := \int dt\, {}^{ef}\Upsilon(\widetilde{\Psi}^2)^*, \ {}^{\mu}\Xi := \int dt\ {}^{\mu}\Upsilon(\widetilde{\Psi}^2)^*.$$

We write $\widetilde{\Psi} \to \overline{\Psi}$ when the generating function is chosen to satisfy the conditions

$$\overline{a}^2\widehat{h}_3 = \omega^2 h_3 = \frac{h_3}{|h_4|} = \frac{\overline{\Psi}^2|\,{}^{ef}\Xi + {}^{\mu}\Xi|}{4({}^{e\mu}\Lambda)(\overline{\Psi}^*)^2}.$$

In general, such nonhomogeneous locally anisotropic configurations contain nontrivial, nonholonomically induced, canonical d-torsion, which can be constrained to zero for corresponding subclasses of generating functions and sources.

We study off-cosmological solutions depending only on time-like coordinates when $\widetilde{a}(x^k,t) \simeq \widetilde{a}(t)$ and $\widetilde{\Psi}(x^k,t) \simeq \widetilde{\Psi}(t)$ and the generation function $\widetilde{\Psi}(t)$. The formula relating variations in ${}^{e\mu}\Upsilon(t)$ to the variation in the second auxiliary 3-index antisymmetric d-tensor field $\mathbf{B}_{\alpha\beta\gamma}$ in ${}^{2}\Phi(\mathbf{B})$, a particular case of (37), is given by

$${}^{2}\Phi(\overline{\mathbf{B}})/\sqrt{|\mathbf{g}|} = {}^{2}\overline{\chi} = {}^{2}\widetilde{\chi} + {}^{\mu}\chi = const,$$

where the constant ${}^{\mu}\chi$ is zero for $\mu = 0$ and $|{}^{\mu}\chi| \ll |{}^{2}\widetilde{\chi}|$. Another assumption is that w can formulate a TMT theory corresponding to "pure" $\mu$–deformations of GR, even $\epsilon =$ The formula (55) has to be generalized for nontrivial $\mu$ when

$$ {}^{1}\mathbf{f}({}^{1}L + {}^{1}M + {}^{\mu}M, \mu) = \frac{d\mathbf{f}(\widehat{\mathbf{R}}, \mu)}{d\widehat{\mathbf{R}}} |_{\widehat{\mathbf{R}} = {}^{1}L + {}^{1}M} \rightarrow {}^{1}U - {}^{1}M - {}^{\mu}M $$

is a version of generalized Starobinsky relation (35), Formulas (36) and (28) and approx mation of type $\tilde{\mathbf{R}} \simeq \widehat{\mathbf{R}} + \widetilde{\mu}^{2}$.

The resulting formulas for effective potential (53) contain additional $\mu$–terms

$$ \begin{aligned} {}^{e\mu}U &= \frac{({}^{1}U - {}^{1}M - {}^{\mu}M)^{2}}{4\,{}^{2}\widetilde{\chi}[\,{}^{2}U + {}^{2}M + ({}^{1}U - {}^{1}M - {}^{\mu}M)^{2}]} \\ &\simeq {}^{e\mu}\overline{U} = \left\{ \begin{array}{ll} {}^{[-]}\overline{U} = \frac{({}^{1}a)^{2}}{4({}^{2}\widetilde{\chi} + {}^{\mu}\chi)\,[\,{}^{2}a + \epsilon({}^{1}a)^{2}]} & \text{for } \varphi \rightarrow -\infty \\ {}^{[+]}\overline{U} = \frac{({}^{1}M + {}^{\mu}M)^{2}}{4({}^{2}\widetilde{\chi} + {}^{\mu}\chi)[\,{}^{2}M + \epsilon({}^{1}M)^{2}]} & \text{for } \varphi \rightarrow +\infty \end{array} \right| . \end{aligned} $$

The $A$– and $B$–functions can also contain contributions of $\mu$–terms,

$$ \begin{aligned} \overline{A} &\simeq \left\{ \begin{array}{l} {}^{[-]}\overline{A} = \frac{{}^{2}a + \frac{1}{2}\,{}^{2}b\,{}^{1}a}{{}^{2}a + \epsilon({}^{1}a)^{2}} \\ {}^{[+]}\widetilde{A} = \frac{{}^{2}M}{{}^{2}M + \epsilon({}^{1}M + {}^{\mu}M)^{2}} \end{array} \right| \text{ and } \\ \overline{B} &\simeq \left\{ \begin{array}{l} {}^{[-]}\overline{B} = -\,({}^{2}\widetilde{\chi} + {}^{\mu}\chi)\frac{{}^{2}b/4 - \epsilon({}^{2}a + {}^{2}b\,{}^{1}a)}{{}^{2}a + \epsilon({}^{1}a)^{2}} \\ {}^{[+]}\overline{B} = \epsilon\,({}^{2}\widetilde{\chi} + {}^{\mu}\chi)\frac{{}^{2}M}{{}^{2}M + \epsilon({}^{1}M + {}^{\mu}M)^{2}} \end{array} \right| , \end{aligned} $$

when ${}^{[-]}\overline{A}$ is not modified. We conclude that solutions with nontrivial generating functior for nontrivial massive gravity terms modelled as effective TMT theories may also describ non-singular "emergent universes" [49–54] with corresponding modifications.

### 6.2. Reconstructing Off-Diagonal Tmt and Massive Gravity Cosmological Models

For the class of solutions (56), we show how we can perform a reconstruction proc dure. We introduce a new time coordinate $\widehat{t}$ for $t = t(x^{i}, \widehat{t})$ and $\sqrt{|h_{4}|}\partial t/\partial\widehat{t}$, and redefine the scale factor, $\overline{a} \rightarrow \widehat{a}(x^{i}, \widehat{t})$, representing the quadratic elements in the form

$$ \begin{aligned} ds^{2} &= \widehat{a}^{2}(x^{i}, \widehat{t})[\eta_{i}(x^{k}, \widehat{t})(dx^{i})^{2} + \widehat{h}_{3}(x^{k}, \widehat{t})(\mathbf{e}^{3})^{2} - (\widehat{\mathbf{e}}^{4})^{2}], \quad (57) \\ \text{for } \eta_{i} &= \widehat{a}^{-2}e^{\psi}, \widehat{a}^{2}\widehat{h}_{3} = h_{3}, \mathbf{e}^{3} = dy^{3} + \partial_{k}n\,dx^{k}, \widehat{\mathbf{e}}^{4} = d\widehat{t} + \sqrt{|h_{4}|}(\partial_{i}t + w_{i}). \end{aligned} $$

To model small off-diagonal deformations, we use a small parameter $\varepsilon$, $0 \leq \varepsilon <$ when

$$ \eta_{i} \simeq 1 + \varepsilon\chi_{i}(x^{k}, \widehat{t}), \partial_{k}n \simeq \varepsilon\widehat{n}_{i}(x^{k}), \sqrt{|h_{4}|}(\partial_{i}t + w_{i}) \simeq \varepsilon\widehat{w}_{i}(x^{k}, \widehat{t}) \quad (58) $$

and there are subclasses of generating functions and sources for which $\widehat{a}(x^{i}, \widehat{t}) \rightarrow \widehat{a}(t), \widehat{h}_{3}(x^{i}, \widehat{t})$ – $\widehat{h}_{3}(\widehat{t})$ etc., see details for such a procedure from Section 5 of [67] (see references therein The analogous TMT massive gravity theory is taken with a source ${}^{\mu}\widehat{\mathbf{Y}}_{\mu\nu}$ (31) and parametri tion $\mathbf{f}(\check{\mathbf{R}}) = \widehat{\mathbf{R}} + \mathbf{S}({}^{\mu}\mathbf{T})$, for any N-adapted value

$$ {}^{\mu}\mathbf{T} := \mathbf{T} + 2\,\mu^{2}(3 - tr\sqrt{\mathbf{g}^{-1}\mathbf{q}} - \det\sqrt{\mathbf{g}^{-1}\mathbf{q}}). $$

Introducing values ${}^{1}\mathbf{S} := \mathbf{dS}/\mathbf{d}\,{}^{\mu}\mathbf{T}$ and $\widehat{H} := \widehat{a}^{*}/\widehat{a}$ for a limit $\widehat{a}(x^{i}, \widehat{t}) \rightarrow \widehat{a}(t)$ wit $N_{i}^{a} = \{n_{i}, w_{i}(t)\}$ and effective polarizations $\eta_{\alpha}(t)$.

In order to test cosmological scenarios, we consider a redshift $1 + z = \widehat{a}^{-1}(t)$ fc ${}^{\mu}T = {}^{\mu}T(z)$ by introducing a new "shift" derivative. For instance, for a function $s(t$

$s^* = -(1+z)H\partial_z$. We can derive TMT massive, modified, off-diagonal, deformed FLRW equations using Formulas (63) and (64) in [67], when

$$\begin{aligned} 3\widehat{H}^2 + \frac{1}{2}[\mathbf{f}(z) + \mathbf{S}(z)] - \kappa^2\rho(z) &= 0, \\ -3\widehat{H}^2 + (1+z)\widehat{H}(\partial_z\widehat{H}) - \frac{1}{2}\{\mathbf{f}(z) + \mathbf{S}(z) + 3(1+z)\widehat{H}^2 &= 0, \end{aligned} \quad (59)$$

for $\rho(z)\,\partial_z\,\mathbf{f} = 0$. We can fix the condition $\partial_z\,{}^1\mathbf{S}(z) = 0$, and rescale the generating function in order to satisfy the condition $\partial_z\,\mathbf{f} = 0$. We have nonzero densities in certain adapted frames of reference. Here, we note that the functional $\mathbf{S}(\,{}^{\mu}\mathbf{T})$ encodes effects of mass gravity for the evolution of the energy-density when $\rho = \rho_0 a^{-3(1+\varpi)} = \rho_0(1+z)a^{3(1+\varpi)}$, when, for the dust matter approximation, $\varpi$ and $\rho \sim (1+z)^3$. Any FLRW cosmology can be realized in a corresponding class of $f$-gravity models, which can be re-encoded as a TMT theories using actions of type (25)–(27). Let us introduce $\zeta := \ln a/a_0 = -\ln(1+z)$ as the "e-folding" variable to be used instead of the cosmological time $t$, and consider

$$\widehat{\mathbf{Y}}(x^i,\zeta) = \,{}^{f}\mathrm{Y}(x^i,\zeta) + \,{}^{\mu}\mathrm{Y}(x^i,\zeta)$$

with dependencies on $(x^i,\zeta)$ of generating functions $\partial_\zeta = \partial/\partial\zeta$ with $q^* = \widehat{H}\partial_\zeta q$ for any function $q$.

Repeating all computations leading to Equations (2)–(7) in [68], in our approach for $\mathbf{f}(\check{\mathbf{R}})$, we construct an FLRW-like cosmological model with nonholonomic field equation corresponding to the first FLRW equation

$$\mathbf{f}(\check{\mathbf{R}}) = (\widehat{H}^2 + \widehat{H}\,\partial_\zeta\widehat{H})\partial_\zeta[\mathbf{f}(\check{\mathbf{R}})] - 36\widehat{H}^2\left[4\widehat{H} + (\partial_\zeta\widehat{H})^2 + \widehat{H}\partial^2_{\zeta\zeta}\widehat{H}\right]\partial^2_{\zeta\zeta}\mathbf{f}(\check{\mathbf{R}})] + \kappa^2\rho.$$

We consider an effective quadratic Hubble rate, $\tilde{\kappa}(\zeta) := \widehat{H}^2(\zeta)$, where $\zeta = \zeta(\check{\mathbf{R}})$, we write this equation in the form

$$\mathbf{f} = -18\tilde{\kappa}(\zeta)[\partial^2_{\zeta\zeta}\tilde{\kappa}(\zeta) + 4\partial_\zeta\tilde{\kappa}(\zeta)]\frac{d^2\mathbf{f}}{d\check{\mathbf{R}}^2} + 6\left[\tilde{\kappa}(\zeta) + \frac{1}{2}\partial_\zeta\tilde{\kappa}(\zeta)\right]\frac{d\mathbf{f}}{d\check{\mathbf{R}}} + 2\rho_0 a_0^{-3(1+\varpi)} a^{-3(1+\varpi)\zeta(\widehat{\mathbf{R}})}. \quad (60)$$

For any off-diagonal cosmological models with quadratic metric elements of type (57) for redefined $t \to \zeta$ when a functional $\mathbf{f}(\check{\mathbf{R}})$ is used for computing $\widehat{\mathbf{Y}}$, the generating function and respective d-metric and N-connection coefficients as solutions of certain effective Einstein spaces for auxiliary connections and effective cosmological constant ${}^{e\mu}\Lambda$. The value $d\mathbf{f}/d\check{\mathbf{R}}$ and higher derivatives vanish for any functional dependence $\mathbf{f}(\,{}^{e\mu}\Lambda)$ because $\partial_\zeta\,{}^{e\mu}\Lambda = 0$. We conclude that the recovering procedure simplifies substantially, even in TMT theories, by re-scaling the generating function and sources following formulas of type (43).

Now, we speculate on how we can reproduce *the* $\Lambda$*CDM era*. Using values $\widehat{a}(\zeta)$ and $\widehat{H}(\zeta)$ determined by an off-diagonal quadratic element (57) and writing analogs of the FLRW equations for $\Lambda$CDM cosmology in the form

$$3\kappa^{-2}\widehat{H}^2 = 3\kappa^{-2}H_0^2 + \rho_0\widehat{a}^{-3} = 3\kappa^{-2}H_0^2 + \rho_0 a_0^{-3}e^{-3\zeta},$$

for fixed constant values $H_0$ and $\rho_0$. The second term in this formula describes an inhomogeneous distribution of cold dark mater (CDM). This allows for computation of the effective quadratic Hubble rate and the modified scalar curvature, $\check{\mathbf{R}}$, in the forms $\tilde{\kappa}(\zeta) := H_0^2 + \kappa^2\rho_0 a_0^{-3}e^{-3\zeta}$ and

$$\check{\mathbf{R}} = 3\partial_\zeta\tilde{\kappa}(\zeta) + 12\tilde{\kappa}(\zeta) = 12H_0^2 + \kappa^2\rho_0 a_0^{-3}e^{-3\zeta}.$$

The solutions of (60) can be found by following [67,68] as Gauss hypergeomet functions. We might denote $\mathbf{f} = F(X) := F(\chi_1, \chi_2, \chi_3; X)$, where, for some constants, and $B$,

$$F(X) = AF(\chi_1, \chi_2, \chi_3; X) + BX^{1-\chi_3}F(\chi_1 - \chi_3 + 1, \chi_2 - \chi_3 + 1, 2 - \chi_3; X).$$

This is the proof that MGTs and various TMT models can indeed describe $\Lambda$CD scenarios without the need for an effective cosmological constant, because we have fective sources, and this follows from the re-scaling property (43) of generic off-diagor configurations. The Equation (60) transforms into

$$X(1-X)\frac{d^2\mathbf{f}}{dX^2} + [\chi_3 - (\chi_1 + \chi_2 + 1)X]\frac{d\mathbf{f}}{dX} - \chi_1\chi_2\mathbf{f} = 0, \quad (6$$

for certain constants, for which $\chi_1 + \chi_2 = \chi_1\chi_2 = -1/6$ and $\chi_3 = -1/2$ where $3\zeta$ $- \ln[\kappa^{-2}\rho_0^{-1}a_0^3(\check{\mathbf{R}} - 12H_0^2)]$ and $X := -3 + \check{\mathbf{R}}/3H_0^2$.

Finally, we note that the reconstruction procedure can be performed in a similar for for any MGTs and TMT ones which can modeled, for well-defined conditions, by effecti nonholonomic Einstein spaces.

## 7. Results and Conclusions

### *7.1. Modified Gravity and Cosmology Theories with Metric Finsler Connections on (Co) Tange Lorentz Bundles or for Nonholonmic Einstein Manifolds*

In the present paper and partner works [26–33], we follow an orthodox point of vie that inflation and accelerating cosmological models can be elaborated in the framewo of effective Einstein theories via off—diagonal and diagonal solutions for nonholonor vacuum and non–vacuum configurations determined by generating functions and in gration functions and constants. Fixing respective classes of such functions and constan we can extract various types of modified gravity–matter theories defined in terms of no Riemannian volume–forms (for instance, in a manifestly globally Weyl-scale invaria form) and with certain modified Lagrange densities of type $f(\check{\mathbf{R}})$ including contributio from the Einstein–Hilbert term $R$, its square $R^2$, possible massive gravity $\mu$ parametr terms, nonholonomic deformations etc. The principal results are as follows:

1. We defined nonholonomic geometric variables for which various classes of moc fied gravity theories (MGTs), (generally with nontrivial gravitational mass) can l modelled equivalently as respective two-measure (TMT) [55–57,60–62], bi-connectic and/or bi-metric theories. For well-defined nonholonomic constraint conditior the corresponding gravitational and matter field equations are equivalent to certa classes of generalized Einstein equations with nonminimal connection to effecti matter sources and nontrivial nonholonomic vacuum configurations;
2. We stated the conditions when nonholonomic TMT models encode ghost-free massi configurations with (broken) scale invariance and such interactions can modelled l generic off-diagonal metrics in effective general relativity (GR) and generalizatio with induced torsion. Such a nonholonomic geometric technique was elaborated Finsler geometry in gravity theories and, for a corresponding 2 + 2 splitting, we ca consider Finsler-like variables and work with so-called FTMT models;
3. We developed the anholonomic frame deformation method [30–33], AFDM, in ord to generate off-diagonal, generally inhomogeneous and locally anisotropic cosmolog cal solutions in TMT snd MGTs. It was proven that the effective Einstein equations f such gravity and cosmological models can be decoupled in general form, which a lows for the construction of various classes of exact solution depending on generatir functions and integration functions and constants;
4. We analysed a very important re-scaling property of generating functions with asso ation of effective cosmological constants for different types of modified gravity ar matter field interactions, which allow for the definition of nonholonomic variables in

which the associated systems of nonlinear partial differential equations (PDEs) can be integrated in explicit form when the coefficients of generic off-diagonal metrics and (generalized) nonlinear and linear connections depend on all space–time coordinates;
5. There were stated conditions for generating functions and effective sources when zero-torsion (Levi–Civita, LC) configurations can be extracted in general form, with possible nontrivial limits to diagonal configurations in $\Lambda$CDM cosmological scenarios, encoding dark energy and dark matter effects, possible nontrivial zero mass contributions, effective cosmological constants induced by off-diagonal interactions and constrained nonholonomically, to result in nonlinear diagonal effects;
6. Special attention was devoted to subclasses of generic off-diagonal cosmological solution with effective scalar potentials and two flat regions and limits to the diagonal cosmological TMT scenarios investigated in [61,62] were studied;
7. We studied possible massive gravity modifications of flat regions and the possible reconstruction of off-diagonal TMT and massive gravity cosmological models. Through corresponding frame transforms and the re-definition of generating functions and nonholonomic variables, we proved that the same geometric techniques are applicable in all such MGTs.

Let us explain why it is important to study exact solutions for off-diagonal and nonlinear gravitational interactions in different MGTs, depending on 2–4 spacetime coordinates, and consider possible the implications for modern cosmology. The gravitational and matter field equations in such theories consist of very sophisticated systems of nonlinear PDEs. It was possible to construct, for instance physically important black hole and cosmological solutions to certain diagonal ansatz, depending on one space/time-like variable modelling (generalized) Einstein spacetimes with two and three Killing symmetries or other types of high-symmetry and asymptotic condition. There were two kinds of motivation for such assumptions: the technical one was that, for diagonalizable ansatz, the systems of nonlinear PDEs transform in "more simple" systems of nonlinear ordinary differential equations (ODEs), which can be integrated in general form. The physical interpretation of such solutions determined by integration constants is more intuitive and natural. Nevertheless, a series of problems arise in modern acceleration cosmology with dark energy and dark matter effects. It became clear that standard diagonal cosmological solutions in GR, together with standard scenarios from particle physics and former elaborated cosmological models, cannot be appliedrto explain observational cosmological data. A number of MGTs and new cosmological theories have been proposed and developed.

After mathematically selecting some special diagonalizable ansatz with prescribed symmetries, we eliminate other, more general classes of solution, which seem to be important for explaining nonlinear parametric and nonholonomic off-diagonal interactions. This could be related to a new nonlinear physics in gravity and particle field theory which has not been yet investigated. In the past, there were a number of technical restrictions to the construction of such solutions and study of their applications but, at present, there are accessible, advanced numerical, analytic and geometric methods. In this work, we follow a geometric approach developed in [14–16,26–33,63], which allows us to construct exact solutions in different classes of gravity and cosmology theories. Even observational data in modern cosmology can be explained by almost diagonal and homogeneous models; when possible off-diagonal effects and anisotropies are very small, we are not constrained to studying only the solutions to associated systems' ODEs. For nonlinear gravitational and matter field systems, a well-defined mathematical approach is to generate (if possible, exact) solutions in the most general form, and then to impose additional constraints for diagonal configurations. In result, a number of MGT effects and accelerating cosmology can be explained as standard, except for off-diagonal nonlinear ones in effective GR. Alternative interpretations in the framework of TMT and other type theories are also possible.

### 7.2. Alternative Finsler Gravity Theories with Metric Non-Compatible Connections

The referee of this work requested "minimal modification" in order to cite and discus papers [69–74] where some alternative Finsler gravity and geometry models are considere This is a good opportunity for authors, which allows them to explain their approac geometric methods, and new results for the construction of new classes of generic, of diagonal cosmological solutions in more detail, as well as elaborating on application in non-standard particle physics and modified gravity. To comment on key ideas an constructions in the authors' works, and compare them to similar ones from the mentione alternative geometric and cosmological theories, we have to additionally cite [75–79 and references therein. We note that readers should pay attention to reference [24], wit respective Introduction and Conclusion sections, and Appendix B (in that work), containin historical remarks and a review of 20 directions on modern generalized Finsler geometr and applications in modern particle physics, modified gravity, and cosmology, mechanic and thermodynamics, information theory, etc. to [24] a number of historical remark and a review of the last 80 years of research activity are provided, as well as the mai achievements in Finsler–Lagrange–Hamilton geometry and its applications in moder physics, gravity, cosmology, mechanics and information theory. The axiomatic part wa published in [25]. In the mentioned works, a study of evolution of main research groups c "Finsler geometry and physics" in different countries, and the international collaboratior formed is included. The results and bibliography of the conventional 20 directions, an more than 100 sub-directions of research and publications, were reviewed, by the preser and other authors, related to Finsler geometry and applications. We also cite the paper [7 and the monograph [79], (for a collection of works on (non-)commutative metric-affin generalized Finsler geometries and nonholonomic supergravity and string theories, locall anisotropic kinetic and diffusion processes, Finsler spinors, etc.), and articles [77,78]. Her we summarize and discuss such issues:

1. In the abstract and introduction, as well as Section 2.2 of this article, it is emphasize that we do not elaborate a typical work on Finsler gravity and cosmology, but rathe provide a cosmological work on Einstein gravity and MGTs, TMTs ones, with tw measures/two connections and/or bi-metrics, mass terms, etc., when the constru tions are modelled on a Lorentz manifold $V$ of signature $(+++-)$ with convention nonholonomic 2 + 2 splitting. For such theories, the spacetime metrics $g_{\alpha\beta}(x^i, y^a$ (with $i, j, \cdots = 1, 2$ and $a, b, \cdots = 3, 4$) are generic off-diagonal and, together wit the coefficients of other fundamental geometric objects, depend on all space–tim conventional fibred coordinates. Lagrange–Finsler-like variables are introduced to for "toy" models, when $y^a$ are treated similarly to (co) fiber coordinates on a (co) ta gent manifold $(T^*V)$ $TV$, for a prescribed a fundamental Lagrange, $L(x, y)$ (or Finsle for certain homogeneity conditions $F(x, \beta y) = \beta F(x, y), x = \{x^i\}$ etc., for a real co stant $\beta > 0$, when $L = F^2$). This states, for $V$, a canonical Finsler-like N-connectio and nonholonomic (co-)frames structure, which can also be described in coordinat bases, using additional constraints to extract the LC-connection or distorting it to othe linear connections determined by the same metric structures. In dual form, we ca consider momentum, like $p_a$-dependencies in $g_{\alpha\beta}(x^i, p_a)$, for a conventional Hamilt nian $H(x, p)$, which can be related to an $L$ via corresponding Legendre transform The reason for introducing Finsler-like and other types of nonholonomic variable to manifold $V$, or on a tangent bundle $TV$ is that, in so-called nonholonomic canonica variables (with hats on geometric objects), the modified Einstein Equation (9) can b decoupled and integrated in vary general forms. We have to consider some additiona nonholonomic constraints (10) in order to extract LC-configurations. This is the mai idea of the AFDM [30–33], which was applied in a series of works for construc ing a locally anisotropic black hole and cosmological solutions defied by generi off-diagonal metrics and (generalized) connections in Lagrange–Finsler–Hamilto gravity in various limits of (non-)commutative/supersymmetric string/brain theorie massive gravity, TMT models, etc., as we consider in partner works [26–33].

2. One of the formal difficulties in modern Finsler geometry and gravity is that some authors (usually mathematicians) use a different terminology compared to that elaborated by physicists in GR, MGTs, TMTs etc. For instance, a theory of "standard static Finsler spaces", with a time like Killing field and/or for static solutions of a type of filed equation in Finsler gravity is elaborated in [69–71]. Of course, it is possible to prescribe a class of static and a corresponding smooth class of Finsler-generating functions, $F(x,y)$, when semi-spray, N-connections and d-connections, and certain Finsler–Ricci generalized tensors, etc., can be computed for static configurations embedded in locally anisotropic backgrounds. Such constructions can be chosen to have spherical symmetry. However, by introducing and computing corresponding "standard static" Sasaki type metrics of type (16), and their off-diagonal coordinate base equivalents, involving N-coefficients (see the total (phase) space–time metric (17)), we can check that such geometric d-objects (and their corresponding canonical d-connection, or LC-connection) do not solve the (modified) Einstein Equation (9) if the data are the general ones considered in [69–71]. If the d-metric coefficients $g_{\alpha\beta}(x^i, y^a)$ are generic off-diagonal with nontrivial N-connection coefficients, such metrics can be only quasi-stationary following the standard terminology in mathematical relativity and MGTs (when coefficients do not depend on time-like variable, i.e., $\partial_t$ is a Killing symmetry d-vector), but there are nontrivial off-diagonal metric terms because of rotation, N-connections, etc. Stationary metrics of type (16) and/or (17) can be prescribed to describe, for instance, black ellipsoids, which are different from the solutions for Kerr black holes, BHs, because of their more general Finsler local anisotropy. Static configurations with diagonal metrics of Schwarzschild type BHs can be introduced for some trivial N-connection structures (but, in Finsler geometry, this is a cornerstone geometric object). For Finsler-like gravity theories, there are no proofs of BH uniqueness theorems, and it is not clear if such static configurations (for instance, with spherical symmetry) can be stable. Such proofs are sketched for black ellipsoids; see details in [26–33]. Therefore, the existing concepts, definitions, and proofs of "standard" static/stationary/cosmological /stable/nonlinear evolution models, etc., depend on the type of postulated principles for respective concepts and theories of Finsler spacetime.
3. In [72,73,75], certain attempts to elaborate models of Finsler spacetime, geometry and gravity are considered for some types of N-connection and chosen classes of Finsler metric compatible and non-compatible d-connections. In many cases, the Berwald–Finsler d-connection is considered, which is generally noncompatible but can be subjected to certain metrization procedures. Different geometric constructions, with a non-fixed signature for Hessians and sophisticate causality conditions via semi-sprays and generalized nonlinear geodesic configurations, have been proposed and analyzed. In such approaches, there are a series of fundamental unsolved physical and geometric problems in the development of such Finsler theories in self-consistent and viable physical forms. Here, we focus only on the most important issues (for details, critiques, discussions, and motivation regarding Finsler gravity principles, we cite [17,24,25,76,79]):
    - For theories with metric noncompatible connections, for instance, of Chern or Berwald type, there are no unique and simple possibilities to define spinors, conservation laws of type $D_i T^{jk}$, elaborate on supersymmetric and/or noncommutative/nonassociative generalizations, or to consider generalized type classical and quantum symmetries, considering only Finsler type d-connections proposed by some prominent geometers like E. Cartan, S. Chern, B. Berwald etc., and physically un-motivated (effective) energy-momentum tensors with local anisotropy;
    - Physical principles and nonlinear causality schemes elaborated on a base manifold with undetermined lifts, without geometric and physical motivations, on total bundles, depend on the type of Finsler-generating function. Hessians

and nonlinear and linear connections are chosen for elaborating geometr and physical models. A Finsler geometry is not a (pseudo/semi-) Riema nian geometry, where all constructions are determined by the metric and L connection structures. For instance, certain constructions with cosmologic kinetic/statistical Finsler spacetime in [73,75] are subjected to very complex typ conservation laws and nonlinear kinetic/diffusion equations. Those autho have not cited and or applied earlier, locally anisotropic, generalized Finsl kinetic/diffusion/statistical constructions performed for the metric compatib connections studied in [77–79] (N. Voicu was at S. Vacaru's seminars in Brashc in 2012, on Finsler kinetics, diffusion and applications in modern physics an information theory; see also [33], but, together with her co-authors, do n cite, discuss, or apply such locally anisotropic, metric, compatible and solvab geometric flow, kinetic and geometric thermodynamic theories);

- Various variational principles and certain versions of Finsler modified Einste equations were proposed and developed in [72,73,75], but such theories hav been not elaborated on total bundle spaces, for certain metric compatible Finsl connections. Usually, metric non-compatible Finsler connections were use when it is not possible to elaborate on certain general methods for the constru tion of exact and parametric solutions to nonlinear systems of PDEs; for instanc describing locally anisortopic interactions of modified Finsler–Einstein–Dira Yang–Mills–Higgs systems. In S. Vacaru and co-authors' axiomatic approach relativistic Finsler–Lagrange–Hamilton theories [17,24,25,76], such generalize systems can be studied—for instance, on (co) tangent Lorentz bundles (an on Lorentz manifolds with conventional nonhlonomic fibred splitting)—whe the AFDM was applied to generate exact and parametric solutions, and certai deformation quantization, gauge-like, etc., schemes were developed;

4. As a result, the authors of [74] concluded their work in a pessimistic fashion: "Finsl geometry is a very natural generalisation of pseudo-Riemannian geometry and the are good physical motivations for considering Finsler spacetime theories. We hav mentioned the Ehlers-Pirani-Schild axiomatic and also the fact that a Finsler modific tion of GR might serve as an effective theory of gravity that captures some aspec of a (yet unknown) theory of Quantum Gravity. We have addressed the somewh embarrassing fact that there is not yet a general consensus on fundamental Finsl equations, in particular on Finslerian generalisations of the Dirac equation and the Einstein equation, and not even on the question of which precise mathematic definition of a Finsler spacetime is most appropriate in view of physics. We have see that the observational bounds on Finsler deviations at the laboratory scale are qui tight. By contrast, at the moment we do not have so strong limits on Finsler deviatior at astronomical or cosmological scales." In that work, there was no discussion analysis of the approach developed for Lorentz–Finsler–Lagrange–Hamilton, and th nonholonomic manifolds developed by authors of this paper, beginning in 1994 an published in more than 150 papers in prestigious mathematical and physical journa as well as summarized in three monographs (for reviews, see [24,25,79]).

S. Vacaru's research group was more optimistic regarding their obtained results an perspectives of Finsler geometry in physics. Having obtained 10 NATO, CERN an DAAD research grants, the group elaborated an axiomatic approach to Finsler–Lagrang Hamilton gravity theories, using constructions on nonholonomic (co-)tangent Loren bundles and Lorentz manifolds, with an N-connection structure and Finsler-like metr compatible connections. They began their activity almost 40 years ago—see the historic remarks, summaries of results and discussions in [17,24,25,76,79], with recent developmen in [26–33]. P. Stavrinos (with more than 40 years research experience on Finsler geometr and applications), and his co-authors also published a series of works on modified Finsl gravity and cosmology theorise involving tangent Lorentz bundles [18,22,79]. For suc classes of modified Finsler geometric flow and gravity theories, a general geometric metho can be used for constructing exact and parametric solutions: the AFDM, with self-consistent extensions to noncommutative and nonassociative, supestring and supergravity, Clifford–Finsler, etc., theories. Together with papers on deformation and other type quantum Finsler–Einstein-gauge gravity theories, which were elaborated and developed in more than 20 research directions for Finsler geometry and applications, this article belongs to an axiomatized and self-consistent direction of mathematical and acceleration cosmology, dark matter and dark energy physics, involving Finsler geometry methods.

**Author Contributions:** Both authors contributed equally to this work. Both authors have read and agreed to the published version of the manuscript.

**Funding:** No funding but a volunteer work.

**Institutional Review Board Statement:** Not applicable.

**Informed Consent Statement:** Not applicable.

**Data Availability Statement:** Not applicable.

**Acknowledgments:** S. V. research develops former programs partially supported by CERN and DAAD senior fellowships and extended to collaborations with the California State University at Fresno, the USA, and Yu. Fedkovych Chernivtsi National University, Ukraine. The main ideas and results of this work and a respective series of partner papers were communicated at MG13 Meeting on General Relativity (Stockholm University, Sweden, 2012), the Particle and Fields Seminar at Physics Department of Ben-Gurion University of the Negev (Beer Sheva, Israel, 2015) and the IUCSS Workshop "Finsler Geometry and Lorentz Violation" (Indiana University, Bloomington, IL, USA, 2017). Authors are grateful to professors E. Guendelman, A. Kostelecky, N. Mavromatos, Yu. O. Seti, D. Singleton, and M. V. Tkach for respective support and collaboration.

**Conflicts of Interest:** The authors declare no conflict of interest.

## References

1. Linde, A. *Particle Physics and Inflationary Cosmology;* Harwood: Chur, Switzerland, 1990.
2. Kolb, E.W.; Turner, M.S. *The Early Universe;* Addison Wesley: Boston, MA, USA, 1990.
3. Guth, A. *The Inflationary Universe;* Vintage, Random House: London, UK, 1998.
4. Weinber, S. *Cosmology;* Oxford University Press: Oxford, UK, 2008.
5. Liddle, A.R.; Lyth, D.H. *The Primordial Density Perturbanions-Cosmology, Inflation and Origin of Structure;* Cambridge University Press: Cambridge, UK, 2009.
6. Starobinsky, A. A new type of isotropic cosmological models without singularity. *Phys. Lett. B* **1980**, *91*, 99–102. [CrossRef]
7. Linde, A. A new inflationary universe scenario: A possible solution of the horizon, flatness, homogeneity, isotropy an primordial monopole problems. *Phys. Lett. B* **1982**, *108*, 389–393. [CrossRef]
8. Albrecht, A.; Steinhardt, P. Cosmology for grand unified theories with radiatively induced symmetry breaking. *Phys. Rev. Lett.* **1982**, *48*, 1220–1223. [CrossRef]
9. Riess, A. Supernova Search Team Collaboration. *Astron. J.* **1998**, *116*, 1009–1038. [CrossRef]
10. Perlmutter, S. Supernova Cosmology Project Collaboration. *Astron. J.* **1999**, *517*, 565–586. [CrossRef]
11. Capozziello, S.; Faraoni, V. *Beyond Einstein Gravity: A Survey of Gravitional Theories for Cosmology and Astrophysics;* Springer: Berlin/Heidelberg, Germany, 2010.
12. Nojiri, S.; Odintsov, S.D.; Oikonomou, V.K. Modified gravity theories in nutshell: Inflation, bounce and late-time evolution. *Phys. Rep.* **2017**, *692*, 1–104. [CrossRef]
13. Elghozi, T.; Mavromatos, N.E.; Sakellariadou, M.; Yusaf, M.F. The D-material univese. *JCAP* **2016**, *1602*, 60. [CrossRef]
14. Vacaru, S. Ghost-free massive f(R) theories modelled as effective Einstein spaces and cosmic acceleration. *Eur. Phys. J. C* **2014**, *74*, 3132. [CrossRef]
15. Vacaru, S. Cosmological Solutions in Biconnection and Bimetric Gravity Theories. In Proceedings of the MG13 Meeting on General Relativity, Stockholm University, Stockholm, Sweden, 1–7 July 2012.
16. Vacaru, S. Space-time quasicrystal structures and inflationary and late time evolution dynamics in accelerating cosmology. *Class. Quant. Grav.* **2018**, *35*, 245009. [CrossRef]
17. Vacaru, S. Principles of Einstein-Finsler gravity and perspectives in modern cosmology. *Int. J. Mod. Phys. D* **2012**, *21*, 1250072. [CrossRef]
18. Stavrinos, P.; Vacaru, S. Cyclic and ekpyrotic universes in modified Finsler osculating gravity on tangent Lorentz bundles. *Class. Quant. Grav.* **2013**, *30*, 055012. [CrossRef]

19. Basilakos, S.; Kouretsis, A.; Saridakis, E.; Stavrinos, P. Resembling dark energy and modified gravity with Finsler-Rande cosmology. *Phys. Rev. D* **2013**, *88*, 123510. [CrossRef]
20. Stavrinos, C.; Savvopoulos, C. Dark Gravitational Field on Riemannian and Sasaki Spacetime. *Universe* **2020**, *6*, 138. [CrossRef]
21. Papagiannopoulos, G.; Basilakos, S.; Paliathanasis, A.; Pan, S.; Stavrinos, P.C. Dynamics in Varying Vacuum Finsler-Rande Cosmology. *Eur. Phys. J. C* **2020**, *80*, 16. [CrossRef]
22. Ikeda, S.; Saridakis, E.; Stavrinos, P.C.; Triantafyllopoulos, A. Cosmology of Lorentz fiber-bundle induced scalar-tensor theorie *Phys. Rev. D* **2019**, *100*, 124035. [CrossRef]
23. Minas, G.; Saridakis, E.N.; Stavrinos, P.C.; Triantafyllopoulos, A. Bounce cosmology in generalized modified gravities. *Univer* **2019**, *5*, 74. [CrossRef]
24. Vacaru, S. On axiomatic formulation of gravity and matter field theories with MDRs and Finsler-Lagrange-Hamilton geometr on (co) tangent Lorentz bundles. *arXiv* **2018**, arXiv:1801.06444.
25. Bubuianu, L.; Vacaru, S. Axiomatic formulations of modified gravity theories with nonlinear dispersion relations and Finsle Lagrange-Hamilton geometry. *Eur. Phys. J. C* **2018**, *78*, 969. [CrossRef]
26. Vacaru, S. Anholonomic soliton-dilaton and black hole solutions in general relativity. *J. High Energy Phys.* **2001**, *4*, 9. [CrossRef]
27. Stavrinos, P.; Vacaru, O.; Vacaru, S. Off-diagonal solutions in modified Einstein and Finsler theories on tangent Lorentz bundle *Int. J. Mod. Phys. D* **2014**, *23*, 1450094. [CrossRef]
28. Gheorghiu, T.; Vacaru, O.; Vacaru, S. Modified Dynamical Supergravity Breaking and Off-Diagonal Super-Higgs Effects. *Clas Quant. Grav.* **2015**, *32*, 065004. [CrossRef]
29. Gheorghiu, T.; Vacaru, O.; Vacaru, S. Off-Diagonal Deformations of Kerr Black Holes in Einstein and Modified Massive Gravi and Higher Dimensions. *Eur. Phys. J. C* **2014**, *74*, 3152. [CrossRef]
30. Bubuianu, L.; Vacaru, S. Deforming black hole and cosmological solutions by quasiperiodic and/or pattern forming structures i modified and Einstein gravity. *Eur. Phys. J. C* **2018**, *78*, 393. [CrossRef]
31. Bubuianu, L.; Vacaru, S. Black holes with MDRs and Bekenstein-Hawking and Perelman entropies for Finsler-Lagrange-Hamilto spaces. *Ann. Phys. N. Y.* **2019**, *404*, 10–38. [CrossRef]
32. Bubuianu, L.; Vacaru, S. Quasi-Stationary Solutions in Gravity Theories with Modified Dispersion Relations and Finsler-Lagrang Hamilton Geometry. *Eur. Phys. J. P* **2020**, *135*, 148. [CrossRef]
33. Vacaru, S. Geometric information flows and G. Perelman entropy for relativistic classical and quantum mechanical systems. *Eu Phys. J. C* **2020**, *80*, 639. [CrossRef]
34. Hawking, S.W.; Ellis, G.F.R. *The Large Scale Structure of Space–Time*; Cambridge University Press: Cambridge, UK, 1973.
35. Misner, C.W.; Thorne, K.S.; Wheeler, J.A. *Gravitation*; Freeman: Hong Kong, China, 1973.
36. Wald, R.M. *General Relativity*; The University of Chicago Press: Chicago, IL, USA; London, UK, 1984.
37. Kramer, D.; Stephani, H.; Herdlt, E.; MacCallum, M.A.H. *Exact Soutions of Einstein's Field Equations*, 2nd ed.; Cambridge Universi Press: Cambridge, UK, 2003.
38. Griffith, J.B.; Podolsky, J. Exact Space—Times in Einstein's General Relativity. In *Cambfidge Monographs on Mathematical Physic* Cambridge University Press: Cambridge, UK, 2009.
39. Peebles, P.J.E.; Vilenkin, A. Quintessential inflation. *Phys. Rev. D* **1999**, *59*, 063505. [CrossRef]
40. Appleby, S.A.; Battye, R.A.; Starobinsly, A.A. Curing singularities in cosmological evoluiton of F(R) gravity. *J. Cosmol. Astropar Phys.* **2010**, *1006*, 005. [CrossRef]
41. Chiba, T.; Okabe, T.; Yamaguchi, M. Kinetically driven quintessence. *Phys. Rev. D* **2000**, *62*, 023511. [CrossRef]
42. Armendariz-Picon, C.; Mukhanov, V.; Steinhardt, P.J. A dynamical solution to the problem of a small cosmological constant an late-time cosmic acceleration. *Phys. Rev. Lett.* **2000**, *85*, 4438. [CrossRef]
43. Chiba, T. Tracking kinetically quintessence. *Phys. Rev. D* **2002**, *66*, 063514. [CrossRef]
44. Saitou, R.; Nojiri, S. The unification of inflation and late-time acceleration in the frame of k-essence. *Eur. Phys. J. C* **2011**, *71*, 171 [CrossRef]
45. Wetterich, C. Variable gravity Universe. *Phys. Rev. D* **2014**, *89*, 024005. [CrossRef]
46. Hossain, M.W.; Myrzakulov, R.; Sami, M.; Saridakis, E.N. Variable gravity: A suitable frameork for quintessential inflation. *Phy Rev. D* **2014**, *90*, 023512. [CrossRef]
47. Rham, C.D.; Gabadadze, G.; Tolley, A.J. Resummation of massive gravity. *Phys. Rev. Lett.* **2011**, *106*, 231101. [CrossRef]
48. Hassan, S.; Rosen, R.A. Resolving the ghost problem in non-linear massive gravity. *Phys. Rev. Lett.* **2012**, *108*, 041101. [CrossRe
49. Ellis, C.F.R.; Murugan, J.; Tsagas, C.G. The emergent universe: An explicit construction. *Class. Quant. Grav.* **2004**, *21*, 23 [CrossRef]
50. Lidsey, J.E.; Mulryne, D.J. A graceful entrance to branworld inflation. *Phys. Rev. D* **2006**, *73*, 083508. [CrossRef]
51. Mukherjee, S.; Paul, B.C.; Dahich, N.K.; Beesham, S.D.M.A. Emergent universe with exotic matter. *Class. Quant. Grav.* **200** *23*, 6927. [CrossRef]
52. Penrose, R.; Hawking, S.W. The singularities of gravitational collapse and cosmology. *Proc. Roy. Soc. A* **1970**, *314*, 529.
53. Geroch, R.P. Singularities in closed universes. *Phys. Rev. Lett.* **1966**, *17*, 445. [CrossRef]
54. Brode, A.; Vilenkin, A. Eternal inflation and the initial singularity. *Phys. Rev. Lett.* **1994**, *72*, 3305–3309. [CrossRef]
55. Guendelman, E. Scale invariance, new inflation and decaying Lambda terms. *Mod. Phys. Lett. A* **1999**, *14*, 1043–1052. [CrossRe

56. Guendelman, E.; Kaganovich, A. Dynamical measure and field theory models free of the cosmological constant problem. *Phys. Rev. D* **1999**, *60*, 065004. [CrossRef]
57. Guendelman, E.; Katz, O. Inflation and transition to a slowly accelerating phase from S. S. B. of scale invariance. *Class. Quant. Grav.* **2003**, *20*, 1715–1728. [CrossRef]
58. Guendelman, E.; Singleton, D.; Yongram, N. A two measure model of dark energy and dark matter. *J. Cosmol. Astropart. Phys.* **2012**, *1211*, 044. [CrossRef]
59. Guendelman, E.; Nishino, H.; Rajpoot, S. Scale symmetry breaking from total derivative densities and the cosmological constant problem. *Phys. Lett. B* **2014**, *732*, 156. [CrossRef]
60. Guendelman, E.; Kaganovich, A.; Nissimov, E.; Pacheva, S. Emergent cosmology, inflation and dark energy. *arXiv* **2015**, arXiv:1408.5344.
61. Guendelman, E.; Kaganovich, A.; Nissimov, E.; Pacheva, S. String and brane models with spontaneously/dynamically induced tension. *Phys. Rev. D* **2002**, *66*, 046003. [CrossRef]
62. Guendelman, E.; Nissimov, E.; Pacheva, S.; Vasihoun, M. Dynamical volume element in scale-invariant and supergravity theories. *Bulg. J. Phys.* **2013**, *40*, 121–126.
63. Rajpoot, S.; Vacaru, S. Cosmological Attractors and Anisotropies in two Measure Theories, Effective EYMH systems, and Off-diagonal Inflation Models. *Eur. Phys. J. C* **2017**, *77*, 313. [CrossRef]
64. Cai, Y.F.; Duplessis, F.; Saridakis, E.N. F(R) nonlinear massive theories of gravity and their cosmological implications. *Phys. Rev. D* **2014**, *90*, 064051. [CrossRef]
65. Klusoň, J.; Nojiri, S.; Odintsov, S.D. New proposal for non-linear ghost-free massive F(R) gravity: Cosmic acceleartion and Hamilton analysis. *Phys. Lett. B* **2013**, *726*, 918–925. [CrossRef]
66. Nojiri, S.; Odintsov, S.D.; Schirai, N. Variety of cosmic acceleration models from massive F(R) bigravity. *J. Cosmol. Astropart. Phys.* **2013**, *1305*, 020. [CrossRef]
67. Elizalde, E.; Vacaru, S. Effective Einstein Cosmological Spaces for Non-Minimal Modified Gravity. *Gen. Relativ. Grav.* **2015**, *47*, 64. [CrossRef]
68. Nojiri, S.; Odintsov, S.D.; Saez-Gomez, D. Cosmological reconstruction of realistic modified F(R) gravities. *Phys. Lett. B* **2009**, *681*, 74–80. [CrossRef]
69. Caponio, E.; Stancarone, G. Standard static Finser spacetimes. *Int. J. Geom. Methods Mod. Phys.* **2018**, *13*, 1650040. [CrossRef]
70. Caponio, E.; Stancarone, G. On Finsler spacetime with a timelike Killing vector field. *Class. Quant. Grav.* **2018**, *35*, 085007. [CrossRef]
71. Caponio, E.; Masiello, A. On the analicity of static solutions of a field equation in Finsler graivty. *Universe* **2020**, *6*, 59. [CrossRef]
72. Pfeifer, C. Finsler spacetime geometry in physics. *Int. J. Geom. Methods Mod. Phys.* **2019**, *16*, 1941004. [CrossRef]
73. Hohmann, M.; Pfeifer, C.; Voicu, N. Cosmological Finsler spacetimes. *Universe* **2020**, *6*, 65. [CrossRef]
74. Laammerzahl, C.; Perlick, V. Finsler geometry as a model for relativistic gravity. *Int. J. Geom. Methods Mod. Phys.* **2018**, *15*, 1850166. [CrossRef]
75. Hohmann, M.; Pfeifer, C.; Voicu, N. Relativistic kinetic gases as direct sources of gravity. *Phys. Rev. D* **2020**, *101*, 024062. [CrossRef]
76. Vacaru, S. Critical remarks on Finsler modifications of gravity and cosmology by Zhe Chang and Xin Li. *Phys. Lett. B* **2010**, *690*, 224–228. [CrossRef]
77. Vacaru, S. Locally anisotropic kinetic processes and thermodynamics in curved spaces. *Ann. Phys. (N. Y.)* **2001**, *290*, 83–123. [CrossRef]
78. Vacaru, S. Nonholonomic relativistic diffusion and exact solutions for stochastic Einstein spaces. *Eur. Phys. Plus* **2012**, *127*, 32. [CrossRef]
79. Vacaru, S.; Stavrinos, P.; Gaburov, E.; Gonta, D. Clifford and Riemann-Finsler Structures in Geometric Mechanics and Gravity, Selected Works. In *Differential Geometry-Dynamical Systems, Monograph 7*; Geometry Balkan Press: Bucharest, Romania, 2006.

*universe*

MDPI

*Article*

# New Model of 4D Einstein–Gauss–Bonnet Gravity Coupled with Nonlinear Electrodynamics

Sergey Il'ich Kruglov [1,2]

[1] Department of Physics, University of Toronto, 60 St. Georges St., Toronto, ON M5S 1A7, Canada; serguei.krouglov@utoronto.ca
[2] Department of Chemical and Physical Sciences, University of Toronto, 3359 Mississauga Road North, Mississauga, ON L5L 1C6, Canada

**Abstract:** New spherically symmetric solution in 4D Einstein–Gauss–Bonnet gravity coupled with nonlinear electrodynamics is obtained. At infinity, this solution has the Reissner–Nordström behavior of the charged black hole. The black hole thermodynamics, entropy, shadow, energy emission rate, and quasinormal modes of black holes are investigated.

**Keywords:** Einstein–Gauss–Bonnet gravity; nonlinear electrodynamics; hawking temperature; entropy; heat capacity; black hole shadow; energy emission rate; quasinormal modes

**Citation:** Kruglov, S.I. New Model of 4D Einstein–Gauss–Bonnet Gravity Coupled with Nonlinear Electrodynamics. *Universe* **2021**, *7*, 249. https://doi.org/10.3390/universe7070249

Academic Editors: Panayiotis Stavrinos and Emmanuel N. Saridakis

Received: 5 June 2021
Accepted: 12 July 2021
Published: 19 July 2021



## 1. Introduction

The heterotic string theory at the low energy limit gives the action including higher order curvature terms [1–5]. Glavan and Lin proposed a new theory of gravity in four dimensions, 4D Einstein–Gauss–Bonnet gravity (4D EGB) [6], with higher-order curvature corrections. The action of the 4D EGB theory consists of the Einstein–Hilbert action and the Gauss–Bonnet (GB) term, which is a case of the Lovelock theory. The Lovelock gravity represents the generalization of Einstein's general relativity in higher dimensions that leads to covariant second-order field equations. The Einstein–Gauss–Bonnet gravity in 5D and higher dimensions was studied in [7]. Recently, 4D EGB gravity has received much attention [8–27]. Glavan and Lin showed [6] that the GB term, which is a topological invariant before regularization, while rescaling the coupling constant after regularization, contributes to the equation of motion. The authors of [12,13] found a solution of the semiclassical Einstein equations with conformal anomaly, which is also a solution in the 4D EGB gravity. The approach of Glavan and Lin was recently debated in [28–33]. It was shown by [34,35] that solutions in the 4D EGB theory are different from GR solutions as they are due to extra infinitely strongly coupled scalars. The authors of [36–38] proposed a consistent theory of 4D EGB gravity with two dynamical degrees of freedom that breaks the temporal diffeomorphism invariance, in agreement with the Lovelock theorem. In accordance with the Lovelock theorem [11], for a novel 4D theory with two degrees of freedom, the 4D diffeomorphism invariance has to be broken. In the theory of [36–38], the invariance under the 3D spatial diffeomorphism holds. The authors considered EGB gravity in arbitrary D-dimensions with the Arnowitt–Deser–Misner decomposition. Then, they regularized the Hamiltonian with counterterms, where $D-1$ diffeomorphism invariance holds and taking the limit $D \to 4$. It should be noted that the theory of [36–38], in the spherically symmetric metrics, represents the solution that is a solution in the scheme of [6] (see [39]). In this work, we obtain a black hole (BH) solution in the 4D EGB gravity coupled with nonlinear electrodynamics (NED) proposed in [40] in the framework of [36–38] theory. Quasinormal modes, deflection angle, shadows of BHs, and Hawking radiation were studied in [41–47]. The image of the M87* BH, observed by collaboration with the Event Horizon Telescope [48], confirms the existence of BHs in the universe. The BH shadow is the closed curve that separates capture orbits and scattering orbits. For a review on BH shadows, see, for example, [49].

The paper is organized as follows. In Section 2, we find BH spherically symmetric solution in the 4D EGB gravity. It is shown that at infinity, we have the Reissner–Nordström behavior of the charged BH. We study the BH thermodynamics in Section 3. The Hawking temperature and the heat capacity are calculated showing the possibility of second-order phase transitions. The entropy of BHs is obtained, which includes the area law and the logarithmic correction. In Section 4, the BH shadow is studied. The photon sphere radii, the event horizon radii, and the shadow radii are calculated. We investigate the BH energy emission rate in Section 5. In Section 6, quasinormal modes are studied, and we obtain the complex frequencies. In Section 7, we draw our conclusions.

## 2. The Model

The action of the EGB gravity in D-dimensions coupled with nonlinear electrodynamics (NED) is given by

$$I = \int d^D x\sqrt{-g}\left[\frac{1}{16\pi G}(R+\alpha\mathcal{L}_{GB}) + \mathcal{L}_{NED}\right], \tag{1}$$

where $\alpha$ has the dimension of (length)$^2$, and the Lagrangian of NED, proposed in [40], is

$$\mathcal{L}_{NED} = -\frac{\mathcal{F}}{\cosh\left(\sqrt[4]{|\beta\mathcal{F}|}\right)}, \tag{2}$$

with the parameter $\beta$ ($\beta \geq 0$) having the dimension of (length)$^4$, $\mathcal{F} = (1/4)F_{\mu\nu}F^{\mu\nu} = (B^2 - E^2)/2$, $F_{\mu\nu} = \partial_\mu A_\nu - \partial_\nu A_\mu$ is the field strength tensor. The GB Lagrangian reads

$$\mathcal{L}_{GB} = R^{\mu\nu\alpha\beta}R_{\mu\nu\alpha\beta} - 4R^{\mu\nu}R_{\mu\nu} + R^2. \tag{3}$$

The variation of action (1) with respect to the metric results in field equations

$$R_{\mu\nu} - \frac{1}{2}g_{\mu\nu}R + \alpha H_{\mu\nu} = -8\pi G T_{\mu\nu}, \tag{4}$$

where

$$H_{\mu\nu} = 2\left(RR_{\mu\nu} - 2R_{\mu\alpha}R^{\alpha}_{\ \nu} - 2R_{\mu\alpha\nu\beta}R^{\alpha\beta} - R_{\mu\alpha\beta\gamma}R^{\alpha\beta\gamma}_{\ \ \ \ \nu}\right) - \frac{1}{2}\mathcal{L}_{GB}g_{\mu\nu}. \tag{5}$$

In the following we consider a magnetic BH with the spherically symmetric field. The static and spherically symmetric metric in $D$ dimension is given by

$$ds^2 = -f(r)dt^2 + \frac{dr^2}{f(r)} + r^2 d\Omega^2_{D-2}, \tag{6}$$

where $d\Omega^2_{D-2}$ is the line element of the unit $(D-2)$-dimensional sphere. Equations (1) and (3)–(5) are valid in $D$ dimensions, and we will consider rescaled $\alpha$ as $\alpha \to \alpha/(D-4)$ and then the limit $D \to 4$. Taking into account that the electric charge $q_e = 0$, $\mathcal{F} = q^2/(2r^4)$ ($q$ is a magnetic charge), one obtains the magnetic energy density [40]

$$\rho = T_0^{\ 0} = -\mathcal{L} = \frac{\mathcal{F}}{\cosh\left(\sqrt[4]{|\beta\mathcal{F}|}\right)} = \frac{1}{\beta x^4\cosh(1/x)}, \tag{7}$$

where we introduced the dimensionless variable $x = 2^{1/4}r/(\beta^{1/4}\sqrt{q})$. We consider the limit $D \to 4$ and at $\mu = \nu = t$ field Equation (4) gives

$$r(2\alpha f(r) - r^2 - 2\alpha)f'(r) - (r^2 + \alpha f(r) - 2\alpha)f(r) + r^2 - \alpha = 2r^4 G\rho. \tag{8}$$

Making use of Equation (7), we obtain

$$\int_0^r r^2 \rho dr = m_M - \frac{2^{1/4} q^{3/2}}{\beta^{1/4}} \arctan\left(\tanh\left(\frac{\beta^{1/4}\sqrt{q}}{2^{5/4} r}\right)\right), \quad (9)$$

where the magnetic mass of the black hole reads

$$m_M = \int_0^\infty r^2 \rho dr = \frac{\pi q^{3/2}}{2^{7/4}\beta^{1/4}}. \quad (10)$$

Then, the solution to Equation (8) is

$$f(r) = 1 + \frac{r^2}{2\alpha}\left(1 \pm \sqrt{1 + \frac{8\alpha G}{r^3}(m + h(r))}\right),$$

$$h(r) = m_M - \frac{2^{1/4} q^{3/2}}{\beta^{1/4}} \arctan\left(\tanh\left(\frac{\beta^{1/4}\sqrt{q}}{2^{5/4} r}\right)\right), \quad (11)$$

where $m$ is the Schwarzschild mass (the constant of integration), and $M = m + m_M$ is the total mass of the BH. One can verify that the Weyl tensor for the $D$-dimensional spatial part of the spherically symmetric $D$-dimensional line element (6) vanishes [39]. As a result, the new solution (11) obtained in the framework of [6] is also a solution for the consistent theory [36–38]. For Maxwell electrodynamics, the energy density is $\rho = q^2/(2r^4)$, and Equation (8) leads to the metric function obtained in [15]. In the dimensionless form, Equation (11) becomes

$$f(x) = 1 + Cx^2 \pm C\sqrt{x^4 + x(A - Bg(x))}, \quad (12)$$

where

$$A = \frac{2^{15/4}(m + m_M)\alpha G}{\beta^{3/4} q^{3/2}}, \quad B = \frac{16\alpha G}{\beta}, \quad C = \frac{\sqrt{\beta} q}{2\sqrt{2}\alpha},$$

$$g(x) = \arctan\left(\tanh\left(\frac{1}{2x}\right)\right). \quad (13)$$

We will use the sign minus of the square root in Equations (11) and (12) (the negative branch) because, in this case, the BH is stable and without ghosts [8]. The asymptotic of the metric function $f(r)$ (11) for the negative branch is given by

$$f(r) = 1 - \frac{2MG}{r} + \frac{Gq^2}{r^2} + \mathcal{O}(r^{-3}) \quad r \to \infty, \quad (14)$$

where the total mass of the BH $M = m + m_M$ includes the Schwarzschild mass $m$ and the electromagnetic mass $m_M$. According to Equation (14), the Reissner–Nordström behavior of the charged BH holds at infinity. It is worth noting that the limit $\beta \to 0$ has been in Equation (8) before the integration. In this case, the solution to Equation (8) at $\beta = 0$ is given by [15]. The plot of the function (12) is given in Figure 1.

In accordance with Figure 1,we have two horizons—one (the extreme) horizon and no horizons—depending on the model parameters.

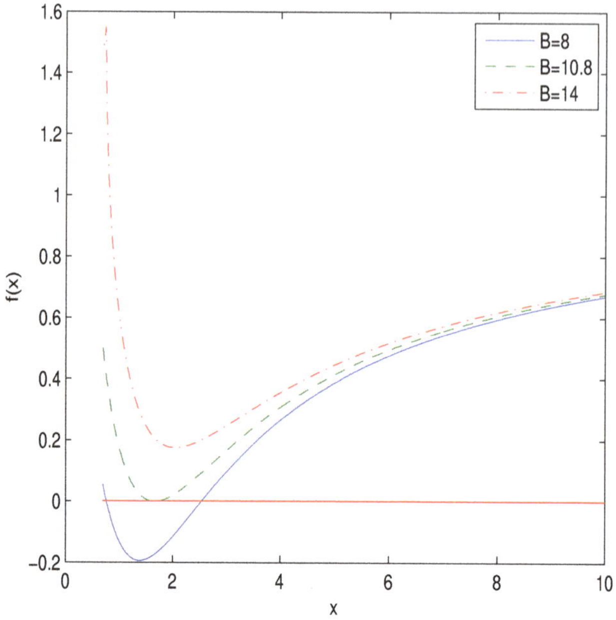


**Figure 1.** The plot of the function $f(x)$ for $A = 7, C = 1$.

### 3. The BH Thermodynamics

Consider the BH thermodynamics and the thermal stability of the BH. The Hawking temperature is given by

$$T_H(r_+) = \frac{f'(r)\mid_{r=r_+}}{4\pi}, \tag{15}$$

where $r_+$ is the event horizon radius defined by the biggest root of the equation $f(r_h) = 0$. Making use of Equations (12) and (15), with the variable $x = 2^{1/4}r/\sqrt[4]{\beta q^2}$, we obtain the Hawking temperature

$$T_H(x_+) = \frac{2^{1/4}}{4\pi\sqrt[4]{\beta q^2}}\left(\frac{2cx_+^2 - 1 + BC^2x_+^2 g'(x_+)}{2x_+(1+cx_+^2)}\right), \tag{16}$$

$$g'(x_+) = -\frac{1}{2x_+^2\cosh^2(1/(2x_+))(\tanh^2(1/(2x_+))+1)},$$

where we substituted parameter $A$ from equation $f(x_+) = 0$. The plot of the dimensionless function $T_H(x_+)\sqrt[4]{\beta q^2}$ versus $x_+$ is depicted in Figure 2.

According to Figure 2, the Hawking temperature is positive in some range of $x_+$. To study the local stability of the BH, we calculate the heat capacity, making use of the expression

$$C_q(x_+) = T_H\left(\frac{\partial S}{\partial T_H}\right)_q = \frac{\partial M(x_+)}{\partial T_H(x_+)} = \frac{\partial M(x_+)/\partial x_+}{\partial T_H(x_+)/\partial x_+}, \tag{17}$$

where $M(x_+)$ is the BH gravitational mass depending on the event horizon radius. From equation $f(x_+) = 0$, one obtains the BH gravitational mass

$$M(x_+) = \frac{\beta^{3/4}q^{3/2}}{2^{15/4}\alpha G}\left(\frac{1+2Cx_+^2}{C^2x_+} + Bg(x_+)\right). \tag{18}$$

With the aid of Equations (16) and (18), we find

$$\frac{\partial M(x_+)}{\partial x_+} = \frac{\beta^{3/4}q^{3/2}}{2^{15/4}\alpha G}\left(\frac{2Cx_+^2-1}{C^2x_+^2}+Bg'(x_+)\right), \tag{19}$$

$$\frac{\partial T_H(x_+)}{\partial x_+} = \frac{1}{4\pi 2^{3/4}\sqrt[4]{\beta q^2}}\left(\frac{5Cx_+^2-2C^2x_+^4+1}{x_+^2(1+Cx_+^2)^2}\right.$$
$$\left.+\frac{BC^2[g'(x_+)(1-Cx_+^2)+x_+g''(x_+)(1+Cx_+^2)]}{(1+Cx_+^2)^2}\right), \tag{20}$$

$$g''(x_+) = \frac{(\tanh^2(1/(2x_+))+1)(2x_+-\tanh(1/(2x_+)))}{2x_+^4\cosh^2(1/(2x_+))(\tanh^2(1/(2x_+))+1)^2}$$
$$-\frac{\tanh(1/(2x_+))}{2x_+^4\cosh^4(1/(2x_+))(\tanh^2(1/(2x_+))+1)^2}.$$

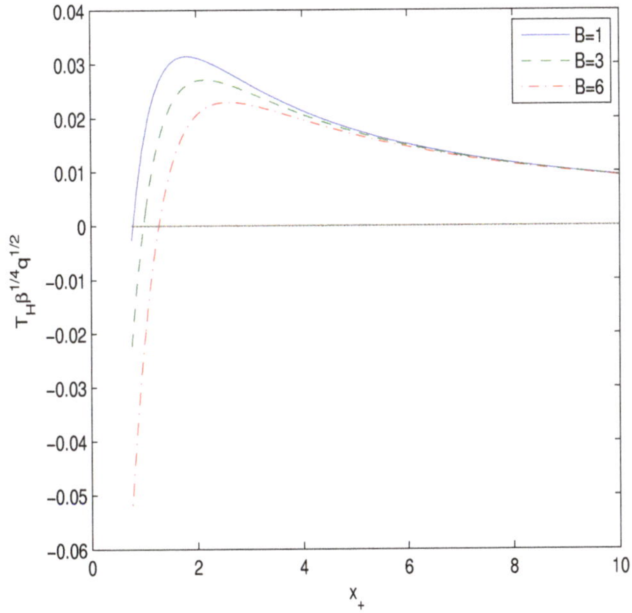


**Figure 2.** The plot of the function $T_H(x_+)\sqrt[4]{\beta q^2}$ at $C=1$.

According to Equation (17), the heat capacity possesses a singularity when the Hawking temperature has an extremum, $\partial T_H(x_+)/\partial x_+ = 0$. It follows from Equations (16) and (17) that at some point, $x_+ = x_1$, the Hawking temperature and heat capacity are zero where a first-order phase transition occurs. In this point, $x_1$, the BH remnant with nonzero BH mass is formed, but the Hawking temperature and heat capacity become zero. In the point $x = x_2$, $\partial T_H(x_+)/\partial x_+ = 0$, the heat capacity has a discontinuity, and the second-order phase transition occurs. In the interval $x_2 > x_+ > x_1$, BHs are locally stable, and at $x_+ > x_2$, the BH becomes unstable. By using Equations (17), (19), and (20), we represented the heat capacity in Figure 3.

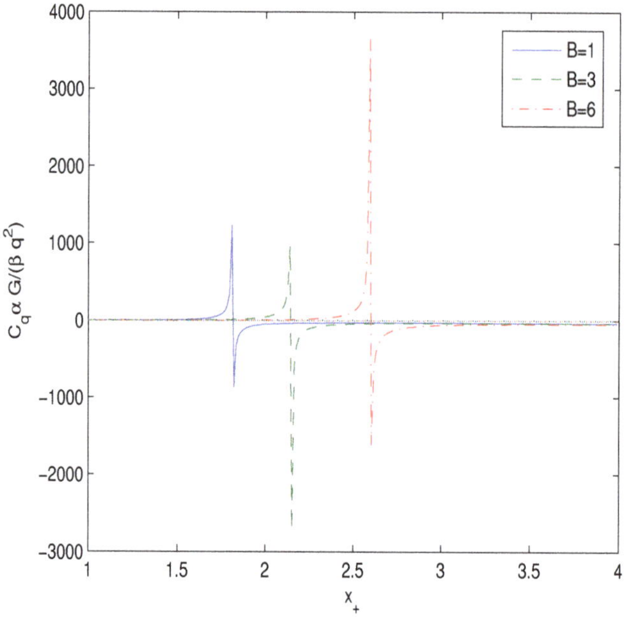


**Figure 3.** The plot of the function $C_q(x_+)\alpha G/(\beta q^2)$ at $C = 1$.

In accordance with Figure 3, the BH is locally stable in the range $x_2 > x_+ > x_1$ with a positive Hawking temperature and heat capacity. The entropy $S$ at the constant charge $q$ could be calculated from the first law of BH thermodynamics $dM(x_+) = T_H(x_+)dS + \phi dq$,

$$S = \int \frac{dM(x_+)}{T_H(x_+)} = \int \frac{1}{T_H(x_+)} \frac{\partial M(x_+)}{\partial x_+} dx_+. \tag{21}$$

It should be noted that the entropy in this expression is defined as a constant of integration. Making use of Equations (16), (19) and (21), we obtain the entropy

$$S = \frac{\pi \beta q^2}{8C^2 \alpha G} \int \frac{1 + Cx_+^2}{x_+} dx_+ = \frac{\pi r_+^2}{G} + \frac{4\pi\alpha}{G} \ln\left(\frac{\sqrt[4]{2}r_+}{\sqrt[4]{\beta q^2}}\right) + Constant, \tag{22}$$

where *Constant* is the integration constant. One can see the discussion of integration constants in [50]. We choose the integration constant as

$$Constant = \frac{2\pi\alpha}{G} \ln\left(\frac{\pi q \sqrt{\beta}}{\sqrt{2}G}\right). \tag{23}$$

From Equations (22) and (23), we find the BH entropy

$$S = S_0 + \frac{2\pi\alpha}{G} \ln(S_0), \tag{24}$$

where $S_0 = \pi r_+^2/G$ is the Bekenstein–Hawking entropy. According to Equation (24), there is a logarithmic correction to area law. The entropy (24) does not contain the NED parameter $\beta$. The entropy (24) was obtained in 4D EGB gravity coupled with other NED models in [51–53]. Thus, entropy (24) does not depend on NED, which is due to the GB term in action, and the logarithmic correction vanishes when $\alpha = 0$. At big $r_+$ (event horizon radii), the Bekenstein–Hawking entropy is dominant, and for small $r_+$, the logarithmic correction is important. It is worth noting that at some event horizon radius $r_0$, the entropy vanishes, and when $r_+ < r_0$, the entropy becomes negative. The negative entropy of BHs was discussed in [7].

## 4. The Shadow of Black Holes

The shadow of the BH is due to the light gravitational lensing and is a black circular disk. The image of the super-massive M87* BH was observed by collaboration with the Event Horizon Telescope [48]. The shadow of a neutral Schwarzschild BH was investigated in [54]. The photons moving in the equatorial plane with $\vartheta = \pi/2$ will be considered. Making use of the Hamilton–Jacobi method, the photon motion in null curves is described by the Equation (see, for example, [55])

$$H = \frac{1}{2}g^{\mu\nu}p_\mu p_\nu = \frac{1}{2}\left(\frac{L^2}{r^2} - \frac{E^2}{f(r)} + \frac{\dot{r}^2}{f(r)}\right) = 0, \tag{25}$$

where $p_\mu$ is the photon momentum, $\dot{r} = \partial H/\partial p_r$, and the energy and angular momentum of a photon, which are constants of motion, are defined by $E = -p_t$ and $L = p_\phi$ . Equation (25) can be represented in the form

$$V + \dot{r}^2 = 0, \quad V = f(r)\left(\frac{L^2}{r^2} - \frac{E^2}{f(r)}\right). \tag{26}$$

The radius of the photon circular orbit $r_p$ obeys the equation $V(r_p) = V'(r)_{|r=r_p} = 0$. From Equation (26), one obtains

$$\xi \equiv \frac{L}{E} = \frac{r_p}{\sqrt{f(r_p)}}, \quad f'(r_p)r_p - 2f(r_p) = 0, \tag{27}$$

where $\xi$ is the impact parameter. The shadow radius $r_s$ for a distant observer, $r_0 \to \infty$, reads $r_s = r_p/\sqrt{f(r_p)}$. Note that the impact parameter is $\xi = r_s$. The event horizon radius $r_+$ is the biggest root of the equation $f(r_h) = 0$. Making use of Equation (12) and $f(r_h) = 0$, one finds the parameters $A$, $B$ and $C$ versus $x_h$

$$A = \frac{1 + 2Cx_h^2 + C^2x_hBg(x_h))}{C^2x_h}, \quad B = \frac{-1 - 2Cx_h^2 + C^2x_hA}{C^2x_hg(x_h))},$$

$$C = \frac{x_h^2 + \sqrt{x_h^4 + x_h(A - Bg(x_h))}}{x_h(A - Bg(x_h))}, \tag{28}$$

where $x_h = r_h/\sqrt[4]{\beta q^2}$. The plots of functions (28) are given in Figure 4.

According to Figure 4 (Subplot 1), if parameter $A$ increases, the event horizon radius $x_+$ also increases. Figure 4 (Subplot 2) shows that when parameter $B$ increases, the event horizon radius decreases. According to Figure 4 (Subplot 3), if $C$ increasing the event horizon radius $x_+$ also increasing.

In Table 1, we presents the photon sphere radii ($x_p$), the event horizon radii ($x_+$), and the shadow radii ($x_s$) for $A = 7$ and $C = 1$. The null geodesics radii $x_p$ belong to unstable orbits and correspond to the maximum of the potential $V(r)$ ($V'' \leq 0$).

According to Table 1, when the parameter $B$ increasing the shadow radius $x_s$ decreases. Because $x_s > x_+$, the BH shadow radius is given by the radius $r_s = x_s\sqrt[4]{\beta q^2}/2^{1/4}$.

It is worth noting that nonlinear interaction of fields in the framework of NED leads to self-interaction, and photons propagate along null geodesics of the effective metric [56,57]. However, corrections in radii of photon spheres and impact parameters (due to the self-interaction of electromagnetic fields) are small [58].

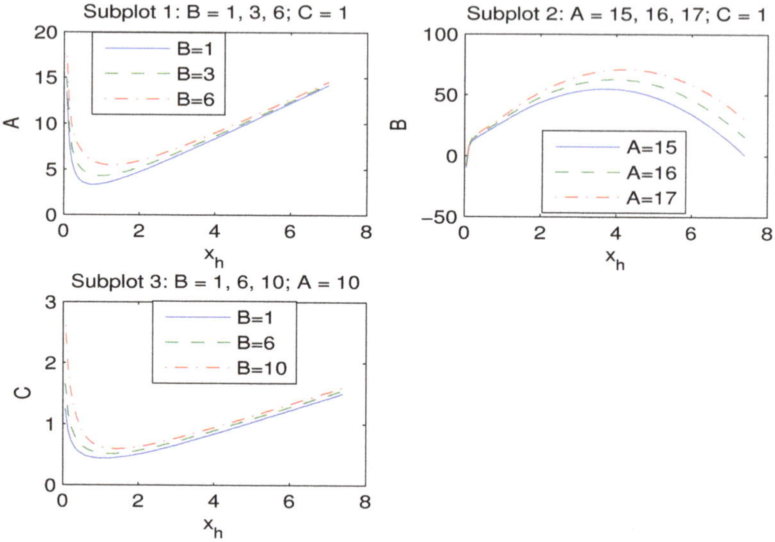


**Figure 4.** The plot of the functions $A(x_h)$, $B(x_h)$, $C(x_h)$. (**A**) Subplot 1: B = 1, 3, 6; C = 1; (**B**) Subplot 2: A = 15, 16, 17; C = 1; (**C**) Subplot 3: B = 1, 6, 10; A = 10.

**Table 1.** The event horizon, photon sphere and shadow dimensionless radii for $A = 7, C = 1$.

| $B$ | 0.1 | 0.5 | 1 | 2 | 3 | 4 | 5 | 6 |
|---|---|---|---|---|---|---|---|---|
| $x_+$ | 3.34 | 3.31 | 3.27 | 3.19 | 3.10 | 3.01 | 2.91 | 2.80 |
| $x_p$ | 5.11 | 5.07 | 5.02 | 4.91 | 4.80 | 4.68 | 4.55 | 4.42 |
| $x_s$ | 8.97 | 8.92 | 8.85 | 8.71 | 8.57 | 8.43 | 8.27 | 8.11 |

## 5. The Energy Emission Rate of Black Holes

For the observer at infinity, the BH shadow is linked with the high energy absorption cross section [43,59]. The absorption cross section, at very high energies, oscillates around the photon sphere $\sigma \approx \pi r_s^2$, and the BH energy emission rate is expressed as

$$\frac{d^2E(\omega)}{dtd\omega} = \frac{2\pi^3\omega^3 r_s^2}{\exp(\omega/T_H(r_+)) - 1}, \tag{29}$$

where $\omega$ is the emission frequency. From Equations (16) and (29), we obtain the BH energy emission rate in terms of the dimensionless variable $x_+ = 2^{1/4} r_+ / \sqrt[4]{\beta q^2}$

$$\beta^{1/4}\sqrt{q}\frac{d^2E(\omega)}{dtd\omega} = \frac{2\pi^3\varpi^3 x_s^2}{\exp(\varpi/\bar{T}_H(x_+)) - 1}, \tag{30}$$

where $\bar{T}_H(x_+) = \beta^{1/4}\sqrt{q}T_H(x_+)$, and $\varpi = \beta^{1/4}\sqrt{q}\omega$. The radiation rate, as a function of the dimensionless emission frequency $\bar{\omega}$ for $C = 1$, $A = 7$ and $B = 0.1, 3, 6$, is plotted in Figure 5.

According to Figure 5, we have a peak of the BH energy emission rate. If the parameter $B$ increases, the peak of the energy emission rate becomes smaller and is in the low frequency. At a bigger parameter $B$, the BH possesses a bigger lifetime.

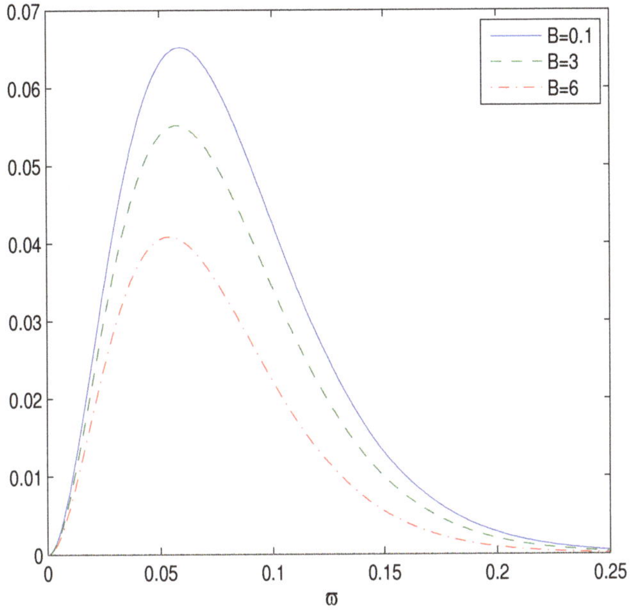


**Figure 5.** The plot of the function $\beta^{1/4}\sqrt{q}\frac{d^2E(\omega)}{dtd\omega}$ vs. $\varpi$ for $B = 0.1, 3, 6$, $A = 7$, $C = 1$.

## 6. Quasinormal Modes

Information about the stability of BHs under small perturbations can be obtained by studying quasinormal modes (QNMs), which are characterized by complex frequencies $\omega$. The mode is stable when Im $\omega < 0$ otherwise it is unstable. In the eikonal limit Re, $\omega$ is connected with the radius of the BH shadow [60,61]. The perturbations by a scalar massless field around BHs are described by the effective potential barrier

$$V(r) = f(r)\left(\frac{f'(r)}{r} + \frac{l(l+1)}{r^2}\right), \quad (31)$$

where $l$ is the multipole number $l = 0, 1, 2 \ldots$. Equation (27) can be represented as

$$V(x)\sqrt{\beta q} = \sqrt{2}f(x)\left(\frac{f'(x)}{x} + \frac{l(l+1)}{x^2}\right). \quad (32)$$

The dimensionless potential $V(x)\sqrt{\beta q}$ is given in Figure 6 for $A = 7, B = 1, C = 1$ (Subplot 1), and $l = 3, 4, 5$ and for $A = 7, C = 1, l = 5$, and $B = 1, 3, 6$ (Subplot 2).

Figure 6, Subplot 1, shows that the potential barriers of effective potentials have the maxima. When the $l$ increases, the height of the potential increases. According to Figure 6, Subplot 2, if the parameter $B$ increases, the height of the potential increases. The quasinormal frequencies can be found by [60,61]

$$\text{Re}\,\omega = \frac{l}{r_s} = \frac{l\sqrt{f(r_p)}}{r_p}, \quad \text{Im}\,\omega = -\frac{2n+1}{2\sqrt{2}r_s}\sqrt{2f(r_p) - r_p^2 f''(r_p)}, \quad (33)$$

where $r_s$ is the BH shadow radius, $r_p$ is the BH photon sphere radius, and $n = 0, 1, 2, \ldots$ is the overtone number. The frequencies, depending on parameter $B$ (at $A = 7, C = 1, n = 1$, $l = 5$), are represented in Table 2.

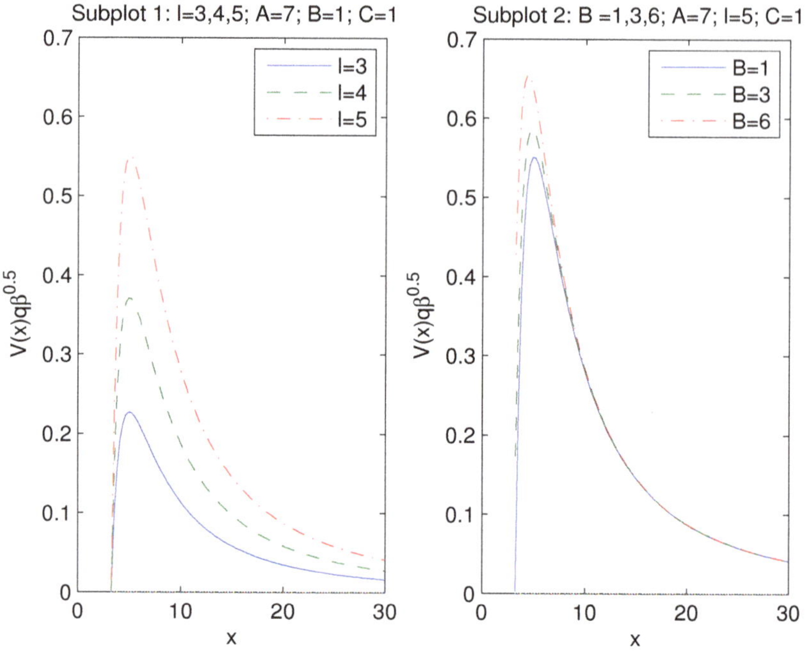


**Figure 6.** The plot of the function $V(x)\sqrt{\beta q}$ for $A = 7, C = 1$.

**Table 2.** The real and the imaginary parts of the frequencies vs. the parameter $B$ at $n = 1, l = 5$, $A = 7, C = 1$.

| $B$ | 0.1 | 0.5 | 1 | 2 | 3 | 4 | 5 | 6 |
|---|---|---|---|---|---|---|---|---|
| $\sqrt[4]{\beta q^2}\mathrm{Re}\ \omega$ | 0.557 | 0.561 | 0.565 | 0.574 | 0.583 | 0.593 | 0.605 | 0.617 |
| $-\sqrt[4]{\beta q^2}\mathrm{Im}\ \omega$ | 0.3212 | 0.3215 | 0.3221 | 0.3229 | 0.3234 | 0.3232 | 0.3230 | 0.3220 |

The modes are stable (the real part represents the frequency of oscillations) because the imaginary parts of the frequencies in Table 2 are negative. Table 2 shows that when parameter $B$ increases the real part of the frequency $\sqrt[4]{\beta q^2}\mathrm{Re},\ \omega$ increases, and the absolute value of the imaginary part of the frequency $\mid \sqrt[4]{\beta q^2}\mathrm{Im}\ \omega \mid$ increases. Therefore, when parameter $B$ is increased, the scalar perturbations oscillate with greater frequency and decay fast.

## 7. Conclusions

We obtained the exact spherically symmetric and magnetized BH solution in 4D EGB gravity coupled with NED. The thermodynamics and the thermal stability of magnetically charged BHs were studied by calculating the Hawking temperature and the heat capacity. The phase transitions occur in the points where the Hawking temperature possesses the extremum. It is shown that BHs are thermodynamically stable at some interval of event horizon radii when the heat capacity and the Hawking temperature are positive. The heat capacity possesses a singularity in some event horizon radii where the second-order phase transitions occur. The entropy of BHs is calculated, including the Hawking entropy and the logarithmic correction. The photon sphere radii, the event horizon radii, and the shadow radii are calculated. We show that with increasing the model parameter $B$, the BH energy emission rate decreases and, as a result, the BH has a longer lifetime. The quasinormal modes are investigated and it is shown that increasing the parameter $B$ the scalar perturbations oscillate with greater frequency and decay fast. It is worth noting that other solutions in 4D EGB gravity coupled with some NED were obtained in [51–53]. It is of interest to study solutions of BHs in 4D EGB gravity coupled with different NED because astrophysical characteristics depend on them.

**Funding:** This research received no external funding.

**Conflicts of Interest:** The author declares no conflict of interest.

## References

1. Gross, D.J.; Witten, E. Superstring modifications of Einstein's equations. *Nucl. Phys. B* **1986**, *277*, 1–10. [CrossRef]
2. Gross, D.J.; Sloan, J.H. The quartic effective action for the heterotic string. *Nucl. Phys. B* **1987**, *291*, 41–89. [CrossRef]
3. Metsaev, R.R.; Tseytlin, A.A. Two-loop $\beta$-function for the generalized bosonic sigma model. *Phys. Lett. B* **1987**, *191*, 354–362. [CrossRef]
4. Zwiebach, B. Curvature squared terms and string theories. *Phys. Lett. B* **1985**, *156*, 315–317. [CrossRef]
5. Metsaev, R.R.; Tseytlin, A.A. Order $\alpha'$ (two-loop) equivalence of the string equations of motion and the $\sigma$-model Weyl invariance conditions: Dependence on the dilaton and the antisymmetric tensor. *Nucl. Phys. B* **1987**, *293*, 385–419. [CrossRef]
6. Glavan, D.; Lin, C. Einstein-Gauss-Bonnet gravity in four-dimensional spacetime. *Phys. Rev. Lett.* **2020**, *124*, 081301. [CrossRef] [PubMed]
7. Cvetic, M.; Nojiri, S.I.; Odintsov, S.D. Black hole thermodynamics and negative entropy in de Sitter and anti-de Sitter Einstein–Gauss–Bonnet gravity. *Nucl. Phys. B* **2002**, *628*, 295–330. [CrossRef]
8. Boulware, D.G.; Deser, S. String-generated gravity models. *Phys. Rev. Lett.* **1985**, *55*, 2656–2660. [CrossRef]
9. Wheeler, J.T. Symmetric solutions to the Gauss–Bonnet extended Einstein equations. *Nucl. Phys. B* **1986**, *268*, 737–746. [CrossRef]
10. Myers, R.C.; Simon, J.Z. Black-hole thermodynamics in Lovelock gravity. *Phys. Rev. D* **1988**, *38*, 2434–2444. [CrossRef]
11. Lovelock, D.J. The Einstein tensor and its generalizations. *Math. Phys.* **1971**, *12*, 498–501. [CrossRef]
12. Cai, R.G.; Cao, L.M.; Ohta, N. Black holes in gravity with conformal anomaly and logarithmic term in black hole entropy. *J. High Energy Phys.* **2010**, *1004*, 82. [CrossRef]
13. Cai, R.-G. Thermodynamics of conformal anomaly corrected black holes in AdS space. *Phys. Lett. B* **2014**, *733*, 183–189. [CrossRef]
14. Cognola, G.; Myrzakulov, R.; Sebastiani, L.; Zerbini, S. Einstein gravity with Gauss-Bonnet entropic corrections. *Phys. Rev. D* **2013**, *88*, 024006. [CrossRef]
15. Fernandes, P.G.S. Charged black holes in AdS spaces in 4D Einstein Gauss–Bonnet gravity. *Phys. Lett. B* **2020**, *805* 135468. [CrossRef]
16. Jusufi, K. Nonlinear magnetically charged black holes in 4D Einstein—Gauss—Bonnet gravity. *Ann. Phys.* **2020**, *421*, 168285. [CrossRef]
17. Ghosh, S.G.; Singh, D.V.; Kumar, R.; Maharaj, S.D. Phase transition of AdS black holes in 4D EGB gravity coupled to nonlinear electrodynamics. *Ann. Phys.* **2021**, *424*, 168347. [CrossRef]
18. Ghosh, S.G.; Maharaj, S.D. Radiating black holes in the novel 4D Einstein—Gauss—Bonnet gravity. *Phys. Dark Univ.* **2020**, *30*, 100687. [CrossRef]
19. Kumar, R.; Ghosh, S.G. Rotating black holes in 4D Einstein-Gauss-Bonnet gravity and its shadow. *J. Cosmol. Astro. Phys* **2020**, *7*, 53. [CrossRef]
20. Jin, X.H.; Gao, Y.X.; Liu, D.J. Strong gravitational lensing of a 4D Einstein—Gauss—Bonnet black hole in homogeneous plasma. *Int. J. Mod. Phys. D* **2020**, *29*, 2050065. [CrossRef]
21. Jusufi, K.; Banerjee, A.; Ghosh, S.G. Wormholes in 4D Einstein—Gauss—Bonnet gravity. *Eur. Phys. J. C* **2020**, *80*, 698. [CrossRef]
22. Guo, M.; Li, P. Innermost stable circular orbit and shadow of the 4D Einstein—Gauss—Bonnet black hole. *Eur. Phys. J. C* **2020**, *80*, 588. [CrossRef]
23. Zhang, C.; Zhang, S.; Li, P.; Guo, M. Superradiance and stability of the regularized 4D charged Einstein–Gauss–Bonnet black hole. *J. High Energy Phys.* **2020**, *8*, 105. [CrossRef]
24. Odintsov, S.; Oikonomou, V.; Fronimos, F. Rectifying Einstein–Gauss–Bonnet inflation in view of GW170817. *Nucl. Phys. B* **2020**, *958*, 115135. [CrossRef]
25. Ai, W. A note on the novel 4D Einstein–Gauss–Bonnet gravity. *Commun. Theor. Phys.* **2020**, *72*, 095402. [CrossRef]
26. Fernandes, P.G.; Carrilho, P.; Clifton, T.; Mulryne, D.J. Derivation of regularized field equations for the Einstein–Gauss–Bonnet theory in four dimensions. *Phys. Rev. D* **2020**, *102*, 024025. [CrossRef]
27. Hennigar, R.A.; Kubiznak, D.; Mann, R.B.; Pollack, C. On taking the $D \to 4$ limit of Gauss–Bonnet gravity: Theory and solutions. *J. High Energy Phys.* **2020**, *2020*, 27. [CrossRef]
28. Gurses, M.; Sisman, T.C.; Tekin, B. Comment on "Einstein–Gauss–Bonnet Gravity in 4-Dimensional Space-Time". *Phys. Rev. Lett.* **2020**, *125*, 149001. [CrossRef]
29. Gurses, M.; Sisman, T.C.; Tekin, B. Is there a novel Einstein–Gauss–Bonnet theory in four dimensions? *Eur. Phys. J. C* **2020**, *80*, 647. [CrossRef]
30. Mahapatra, S. A note on the total action of 4D Gauss–Bonnet theory. *Eur. Phys. J. C* **2020**, *80*, 992. [CrossRef]

31. Arrechea, J.; Delhom, A.; Jiménez-Cano, A. Inconsistencies in four-dimensional Einstein–Gauss–Bonnet gravity gravity. *Chin. Phys. C* **2021**, *45*, 013107. [CrossRef]
32. Arrechea, J.; Delhom, A.; Jiménez-Cano, A. Comment on "Einstein–Gauss–Bonnet Gravity in Four-Dimensional Spacetime". *Phys. Rev. Lett.* **2020**, *125*, 149002. [CrossRef]
33. Hohmann, M.; Pfeifer, C. Canonical variational completion and 4D Einstein–Gauss–Bonnet gravity. *Eur. Phys. J. Plus* **2021**, *136*, 180. [CrossRef]
34. Kobayashi, T. Effective scalar-tensor description of regularized Lovelock gravity in four dimensions. *J. Cosmol. Astro. Phys.* **2020**, *7*, 13. [CrossRef]
35. Bonifacio, J.; Hinterbichler, K.; Johnson, L.A. Amplitudes and 4D Gauss–Bonnet Theory. *Phys. Rev. D* **2020**, *102*, 024029. [CrossRef]
36. Aoki, K.; Gorji, M.A.; Mukohyama, S. A consistent theory of $D \to 4$ Einstein-Gauss-Bonnet gravity. *Phys. Lett. B* **2020**, *810*, 135843. [CrossRef]
37. Aoki, K.; Gorji, M.A.; Mukohyama, S. A consistent theory of $D \to 4$ Einstein–Gauss–Bonnet gravity. *J. Cosmol. Astro. Phys.* **2020**, *2009*, 14. [CrossRef]
38. Aoki, K.; Gorji, M.A.; Mizuno, S.; Mukohyama, S. Cosmology and gravitational waves in consistent $D \to 4$ Einstein–Gauss–Bonnet gravity, *J. Cosmol. Astro. Phys.* **2021**, *2101*, 54. [CrossRef]
39. Jafarzade, K.; Zangeneh, M.K.; Lobo, F.S.N. hadow, deflection angle and quasinormal modes of Born-Infeld charged black holes. *J. Cosmol. Astro. Phys.* **2021**, *4*, 8. [CrossRef]
40. Kruglov, S.I. Magnetically charged black hole in frameworkof nonlinear electrodynamics model . *Int. J. Mod. Phys. A* **2018**, *33*, 1850023. [CrossRef]
41. Konoplya, R.A.; Zinhailo, A.F. Quasinormal modes, stability and shadows of a black hole in the 4D Einstein–Gauss–Bonnet gravity. *Eur. Phys. J. C* **2020**, *80*, 1049. [CrossRef]
42. Konoplya, R.A.; Zinhailo, A.F. 4D Einstein–Lovelock black holes: Hierarchy of orders in curvature. *Phys. Lett. B* **2020**, *807*, 135607. [CrossRef]
43. Belhaj, A.; Benali, M.; Balali, A.E.; Moumni, H.E.; Ennadifi, S.E. Deflection Angle and Shadow Behaviors of Quintessential Black Holes in arbitrary Dimensions. *Class. Quant. Grav.* **2020**, *37*, 215004. [CrossRef]
44. Konoplya, R.A.; Stuchlik, Z. Are eikonal quasinormal modes linked to the unstable circular null geodesics? *Phys. Lett. B* **2017**, *771*, 597. [CrossRef]
45. Stefanov, I.Z.; Yazadjiev, S.S.; Gyulchev, G.G. Connection between black-hole quasinormal modes and lensing in the strong deflection limit. *Phys. Rev. Lett.* **2010**, *104*, 251103. [CrossRef]
46. Guo, Y.; Miao, Y.G. Null geodesics, quasinormal modes and the correspondence with shadows in high-dimensional Einstein–Yang–Mills spacetimes. *Phys. Rev. D* **2020**, *102*, 084057. [CrossRef]
47. Wei, S.W.; Liu, Y.X. Null geodesics, quasinormal modes, and thermodynamic phase transition for charged black holes in asymptotically flat and dS spacetimes. *Chin. Phys. C* **2020**, *44*, 115103. [CrossRef]
48. Event Horizon Telescope Collaboration; Akiyama, K. First M87 event horizon telescope results. V. Physical origin of the asymmetric ring. *Astrophys. J.* **2019**, *875*, L5.
49. Dokuchaev, V.I.; Nazarova, N.O. Silhouettes of invisible black holes. *Usp. Fiz. Nauk* **2020**, *190*, 627. [CrossRef]
50. Medved, A.J.M.; Vagenas, E.C. When conceptual worlds collide: The GUP and the BH entropy. *Phys. Rev. D* **2004**, *70*, 124021. [CrossRef]
51. Kruglov, S.I. Einstein–Gauss–Bonnet gravity with nonlinear electrodynamics. *Ann. Phys.* **2021**, *428*, 168449. [CrossRef]
52. Kruglov, S.I. Einstein–Gauss–Bonnet Gravity with Nonlinear Electrodynamics: Entropy, Energy Emission, Quasinormal Modes and Deflection Angle. *Symmetry* **2021**, *13*, 944. [CrossRef]
53. Kruglov, S.I. Einstein–Gauss–Bonnet gravity with rational nonlinear electrodynamics. *EPL* **2021**, *133*, 69001. [CrossRef]
54. Synge, J.L. The escape of photons from gravitationally intense stars. *Mon. Not. Roy. Astron. Soc.* **1966**, *131*, 463. [CrossRef]
55. Kruglov, S.I. 4D Einstein–Gauss–Bonnet Gravity Coupled with Nonlinear Electrodynamics. *Symmetry* **2021**, *13*, 204. [CrossRef]
56. Novello, M.; Lorenci, V.A.D.; Salim, J.M.; Klippert, R. Geometrical aspects of light propagation in nonlinear electrodynamics. *Phys. Rev. D* **2000**, *61*, 045001. [CrossRef]
57. Novello, M.; Bergliaffa, S.E.P.; Salim, J.M. Singularities in general relativity coupled to nonlinear electrodynamics. *Class. Quant. Grav.* **2000**, *17*, 3821. [CrossRef]
58. Kocherlakota, P.; Rezzolla, L. Accurate mapping of spherically symmetric black holes in a parametrized framework. *Phys. Rev. D* **2020**, *6*, 064058. [CrossRef]
59. Wei, S.W.; Liu, Y.X. Observing the shadow of Einstein–Maxwell-Dilaton-Axion black hole. *J. Cosmol. Astropart. Phys.* **2013**, *11*, 63. [CrossRef]
60. Jusufi, K. Quasinormal Modes of Black Holes Surrounded by Dark Matter and Their Connection with the Shadow Radius. *Phys. Rev. D* **2020**, *101*, 084055. [CrossRef]
61. Jusufi, K. Connection Between the Shadow Radius and Quasinormal Modes in Rotating Spacetimes. *Phys. Rev. D* **2020**, *101*, 124063. [CrossRef]

*universe*

MDPI

*Article*

# Metric-Affine Version of Myrzakulov $F(R,T,Q,\mathcal{T})$ Gravity and Cosmological Applications

**Damianos Iosifidis *, Nurgissa Myrzakulov † and Ratbay Myrzakulov †**

Institute of Theoretical Physics, Department of Physics, Aristotle University of Thessaloniki, 54124 Thessaloniki, Greece; myrzakulov_na@enu.kz (N.M.); myrzakulov_r@enu.kz (R.M.)
* Correspondence: diosifid@auth.gr
† Ratbay Myrzakulov International Centre for Theoretical Physics, Nur-Sultan 010009, Kazakhstan.

**Abstract:** We derive the full set of field equations for the metric-affine version of the Myrzakulov gravity model and also extend this family of theories to a broader one. More specifically, we consider theories whose gravitational Lagrangian is given by $F(R,T,Q,\mathcal{T},\mathcal{D})$ where $T$, $Q$ are the torsion and non-metricity scalars, $\mathcal{T}$ is the trace of the energy-momentum tensor and $\mathcal{D}$ the divergence of the dilation current. We then consider the linear case of the aforementioned theory and, assuming a cosmological setup, we obtain the modified Friedmann equations. In addition, focusing on the vanishing non-metricity sector and considering matter coupled to torsion, we obtain the complete set of equations describing the cosmological behavior of this model along with solutions.

**Keywords:** cosmology; torsion

check for updates

**Citation:** Iosifidis, D.; Myrzakulov, N.; Myrzakulov, R. Metric-Affine Version of Myrzakulov $F(R,T,Q,\mathcal{T})$ Gravity and Cosmological Applications. *Universe* **2021**, *7*, 262. https://doi.org/10.3390/universe7080262

Academic Editors: Panayiotis Stavrinos and Emmanuel N. Saridakis

Received: 17 June 2021
Accepted: 21 July 2021
Published: 23 July 2021



## 1. Introduction

Even though general relativity (GR) is undeniably one of the most beautiful and successful theories of physics, recent observational data have challenged its status [1]. Probably the most important observations that cannot be explained within the realm of GR are the early time as well as the late time accelerated expansion of our universe. This contradiction between theory and observations has lead to the development of a fairly large number of alternative theories to GR which collectively go by the name of modified gravity [2]. The search for a successful alternative has been proven to be both fruitful as well as constructive in regard to our understanding of gravity.

Among this plethora of modified gravities, let us mention the metric $f(R)$ theories, the metric-affine (Palatini) $f(R)$ gravity [3–5], the teleparallel $f(T)$ gravities [6,7], the symmetric teleparallel $f(Q)$ [8,9], scalar–tensor theories [10,11], etc., and also certain extensions of them (see discussion in Section $IV$). Of course, the kind of modifications one chooses to adopt is a matter of personal taste. From our point of view, interesting and well-motivated alternatives are those which extend the underlying geometry of spacetime by allowing a connection that is more general than the usual Levi-Civita one. In generic settings, when no a priori restriction is imposed on the connection and the latter is regarded as another fundamental field on top of the metric, the space will be non-Riemannian [12] and possess both torsion and non-metricity. These last geometric quantities can then be computed once the affine connection is found. The theories formulated on this non-Riemannian manifold are known as metric-affine theories of gravity [13,14].

In recent years, there has been an ever-increasing interest in the metric-affine approach [5,15–29] and especially in its cosmological applications [30–41]. This interest is possibly due to the fact that the additional effects (compared to GR) that come into play in this framework have a direct geometrical interpretation. That is, the modifications are solely due to spacetime torsion and non-metricity. Furthermore, these geometric notions are excited by matter that has intrinsic structure [32,42–45]. This inner structure-generalized geometry interrelation adds another positive characteristic to the MAG scheme. This is the framework we consider in this study.

The paper is organized as follows. Firstly, we fix conventions and briefly review some of the basic elements of non-Riemannian geometry and the physics of metric-affine gravity. We then consider an extended version of the $F(R, T, Q, \mathcal{T}, \mathcal{D})$ theory [46]. To be more specific, working in a metric-affine setup, we consider the class of theories with gravitational Lagrangians of the form $F(R, T, Q, \mathcal{T}, \mathcal{D})$, where $\mathcal{D}$ is the divergence of the dilation current, the new add-on we are establishing here. Then, we obtain the field equations for this family of theories by varying with respect to the metric and the independent affine connection. Considering a linear function $F$ we then present a cosmological application for this model and, finally, switching off non-metricity and considering a scalar field coupled to torsion, we obtain the modified Friedmann equations and also provide solutions for this simple case.

## 2. Conventions/Notation

Let us now briefly go over the basic geometric as well as physical setup we are going to use and also fix notation. We consider a 4-dim non-Riemannian manifold endowed with a metric and an affine connection $(\mathcal{M}, g, \nabla)$. Our definition for the covariant derivative, for example, of a vector, will be

$$\nabla_\alpha u^\lambda = \partial_\alpha u^\lambda + \Gamma^\lambda{}_{\beta\alpha} u^\beta \tag{1}$$

We also define the (Cartan) torsion tensor by

$$S_{\mu\nu}{}^\lambda := \Gamma^\lambda{}_{[\mu\nu]} \tag{2}$$

and the non-metricity tensor as

$$Q_{\alpha\mu\nu} := -\nabla_\alpha g_{\alpha\beta} \tag{3}$$

Contracting these with the metric tensor, we obtain the associated torsion and non-metricity vectors

$$S_\mu := S_{\mu\nu}{}^\nu \tag{4}$$

$$Q_\mu := Q_{\mu\alpha\beta} g^{\alpha\beta} \ , \ q_\mu := Q_{\alpha\beta\mu} g^{\alpha\beta}, \tag{5}$$

respectively. In addition, since we are in four dimensions, we can also form the torsion pseudo-vector according to

$$t^\mu := \varepsilon^{\mu\alpha\beta\gamma} S_{\alpha\beta\gamma} \tag{6}$$

Given the above definitions for torsion and non-metricity, one can easily show (see, for instance, [14]) the affine connection decomposition [1]

$$\Gamma^\lambda{}_{\mu\nu} = N^\lambda{}_{\mu\nu} + \tilde{\Gamma}^\lambda{}_{\mu\nu} = \frac{1}{2} g^{\alpha\lambda}(Q_{\mu\nu\alpha} + Q_{\nu\alpha\mu} - Q_{\alpha\mu\nu}) - g^{\alpha\lambda}(S_{\alpha\mu\nu} + S_{\alpha\nu\mu} - S_{\mu\nu\alpha}) + \tilde{\Gamma}^\lambda{}_{\mu\nu} \tag{7}$$

where $N^\lambda{}_{\mu\nu}$ is known as the distortion tensor. Continuing, we define the curvature tensor as usual

$$R^\mu{}_{\nu\alpha\beta} := 2\partial_{[\alpha}\Gamma^\mu{}_{|\nu|\beta]} + 2\Gamma^\mu{}_{\rho[\alpha}\Gamma^\rho{}_{|\nu|\beta]} \tag{8}$$

and by a double contraction of the latter, we get the Ricci scalar

$$R := R^\mu{}_{\nu\mu\beta} g^{\nu\beta} \tag{9}$$

Then, by using decomposition (7), we obtain the post-Riemannian expansion for the Ricci scalar [14]

$$R = \tilde{R} + T + Q + 2Q_{\alpha\mu\nu}S^{\alpha\mu\nu} + 2S_\mu(q^\mu - Q^\mu) + \tilde{\nabla}_\mu(q^\mu - Q^\mu - 4S^\mu) \tag{10}$$

where $\tilde{R}$ is the Riemannian Ricci tensor (i.e., computed with respect to the Levi-Civita connection) and we have also defined the torsion and non-metricity scalars as [2]

$$T := S_{\mu\nu\alpha}S^{\mu\nu\alpha} - 2S_{\mu\nu\alpha}S^{\alpha\mu\nu} - 4S_{\mu}S^{\mu} \tag{11}$$

and

$$Q := \frac{1}{4}Q_{\alpha\mu\nu}Q^{\alpha\mu\nu} - \frac{1}{2}Q_{\alpha\mu\nu}Q^{\mu\nu\alpha} - \frac{1}{4}Q_{\mu}Q^{\mu} + \frac{1}{2}Q_{\mu}q^{\mu}, \tag{12}$$

respectively. Note that with the introduction of the superpotentials [3]

$$\Omega^{\alpha\mu\nu} := \frac{1}{4}Q^{\alpha\mu\nu} - \frac{1}{2}Q^{\mu\nu\alpha} - \frac{1}{4}g^{\mu\nu}Q^{\alpha} + \frac{1}{2}g^{\alpha\mu}Q^{\nu} \tag{13}$$

$$\Sigma^{\alpha\mu\nu} := S^{\alpha\mu\nu} - 2S^{\mu\nu\alpha} - 4g^{\mu\nu}S^{\alpha} \tag{14}$$

these can be expressed more compactly as

$$T = S_{\alpha\mu\nu}\Sigma^{\alpha\mu\nu} \tag{15}$$

$$Q = Q_{\alpha\mu\nu}\Omega^{\alpha\mu\nu} \tag{16}$$

Equation (8) is of key importance in teleparallel formulations. For instance, by imposing vanishing curvature (which also implies $R = 0$) and metric compatibility ($Q_{\alpha\mu\nu} = 0$), one obtains from (7)

$$\tilde{R} = -T + 4\hat{\nabla}_{\mu}S^{\mu} \tag{17}$$

which is the basis of the metric teleparallel formulation. In a similar manner, the symmetric teleparallel (vanishing curvature and torsion) and also the generalized teleparallelism (only vanishing curvature) are obtained [48].

Let us now turn our attention to the matter content. In metric-affine gravity, apart from the energy-momentum tensor, which we define as usual,

$$T_{\mu\nu} := -\frac{2}{\sqrt{-g}}\frac{\delta(\sqrt{-g}\mathcal{L}_M)}{\delta g^{\mu\nu}}, \tag{18}$$

one also has to vary the matter part with respect to the affine connection. This new object, which is defined by

$$\Delta_{\lambda}{}^{\mu\nu} := -\frac{2}{\sqrt{-g}}\frac{\delta(\sqrt{-g}\mathcal{L}_M)}{\delta\Gamma^{\lambda}{}_{\mu\nu}}, \tag{19}$$

is called hypermomentum [42] and encodes the microscopic characteristics of matter such as spin, dilation and shear. In the same way that the energy-momentum tensor sources spacetime curvature by means of the metric field equations, the hypermomentum is the source of spacetime torsion and non-metricity (through the connection field equations). Note that these energy-related tensors are not quite independent and are subject to the conservation law

$$\sqrt{-g}(2\tilde{\nabla}_{\mu}T^{\mu}{}_{\alpha} - \Delta^{\lambda\mu\nu}R_{\lambda\mu\nu\alpha}) + \hat{\nabla}_{\mu}\hat{\nabla}_{\nu}(\sqrt{-g}\Delta_{\alpha}{}^{\mu\nu}) + 2S_{\mu\alpha}{}^{\lambda}\hat{\nabla}_{\nu}(\sqrt{-g}\Delta_{\lambda}{}^{\mu\nu}) = 0 \tag{20}$$

$$\hat{\nabla}_{\mu} := 2S_{\mu} - \nabla_{\mu} \tag{21}$$

which comes from the diffeomorphism invariance of the matter sector of the action (see [32]). In the above discussion, we have briefly developed the geometric and physical setup needed for the rest of our study. Let us focus on the cosmological aspects of theories with torsion and non-metricity (i.e., non-Riemannian extensions).

## 3. Cosmology with Torsion and Non-Metricity

Let us consider a homogeneous flat FLRW cosmology, with the usual Robertson–Walker line element

$$ds^2 = -dt^2 + a^2(t)\delta_{ij}dx^i dx^j \tag{22}$$

where $i, j = 1, 2, 3$ and $a(t)$ are as usual the scale factor of the universe. As usual, the Hubble parameter is defined as $H := \dot{a}/a$. Now, let $u^\mu$ be the normalized 4-velocity field and

$$h_{\mu\nu} := g_{\mu\nu} + u_\mu u_\nu \tag{23}$$

be the projection tensor projecting objects on the space orthogonal to $u^\mu$. The affine connection of the non-Riemannian FLRW spacetime reads [32]

$$\Gamma^\lambda{}_{\mu\nu} = \tilde{\Gamma}^\lambda{}_{\mu\nu} + X(t)u^\lambda h_{\mu\nu} + Y(t)u_\mu h^\lambda{}_\nu + Z(t)u_\nu h^\lambda{}_\mu + V(t)u^\lambda u_\mu u_\nu + \epsilon^\lambda{}_{\mu\nu\rho}u^\rho W(t)\delta_{n,4} \tag{24}$$

where the non-vanishing components of the Levi-Civita connection are, in this case,

$$\tilde{\Gamma}^0{}_{ij} = \tilde{\Gamma}^0{}_{ji} = \dot{a}a\delta_{ij} = Hg_{ij}\,, \quad \tilde{\Gamma}^i{}_{j0} = \tilde{\Gamma}^i{}_{0j} = \frac{\dot{a}}{a}\delta^i{}_j = H\delta^i_j \tag{25}$$

Continuing with the rest of the geometric objects, in this highly symmetric spacetime, the torsion and non-metricity tensors take the forms [32]

$$S^{(n)}_{\mu\nu\alpha} = 2u_{[\mu}h_{\nu]\alpha}\Phi(t) + \epsilon_{\mu\nu\alpha\rho}u^\rho P(t) \tag{26}$$

$$Q_{\alpha\mu\nu} = A(t)u_\alpha h_{\mu\nu} + B(t)h_{\alpha(\mu}u_{\nu)} + C(t)u_\alpha u_\mu u_\nu, \tag{27}$$

respectively. The five functions $\Phi, P, A, B, C$ describe the non-Riemannian cosmological effects. These, along with the scale factor, give the cosmic evolution of non-Riemannian geometries. Let us note that, using the relations of the torsion and non-metricity tensors with the distortion tensor, it is trivial to show that the functions $X(t), Y(t), Z(t), V(t), W(t)$ are linearly related to $\Phi(t), P(t), A(t), B(t), C(t)$ as [32]

$$2(X+Y) = B\,, \quad 2Z = A\,, \quad 2V = C\,, \quad 2\Phi = Y - Z\,, \quad P = W \tag{28}$$

or inverting them

$$W = P\,, \quad V = C/2\,, \quad Z = A/2 \tag{29}$$

$$Y = 2\Phi + \frac{A}{2}\,, \quad X = \frac{B}{2} - 2\Phi - \frac{A}{2}. \tag{30}$$

Now, using the Equations (11) and (12) for the torsion and non-metricity scalars and the above cosmological forms for torsion and non-metricity, we find for the former

$$T = 24\Phi^2 - 6P^2 \tag{31}$$

$$Q = \frac{3}{4}\Big[2A^2 + B(C-A)\Big], \tag{32}$$

respectively. These are the expressions for the torsion and non-metricity scalars in a homogeneous cosmological setup when no teleparallelism is imposed.

Finally, using the post-Riemannian decomposition of the Ricci scalar and the above forms of the torsion and non-metricity scalars, we find

$$R = \tilde{R} + 6\left[\frac{1}{4}A^2 + 4\Phi^2 + \Phi(2A - B)\right] + \frac{3}{4}B(C-A) - 6P^2$$
$$+3\left(\frac{\dot{B}}{2} - \dot{A} - 4\dot{\Phi}\right) + 9H\left(\frac{B}{2} - A - 4\Phi\right) \tag{33}$$

where

$$\tilde{R} = 6\left[\frac{\ddot{a}}{a} + \left(\frac{\dot{a}}{a}\right)^2\right] \tag{34}$$

is the usual Riemannian part. The last decomposition will be very useful in our subsequent discussion.

## 4. MG-VIII Model and Extension: The $F(R, T, Q, \mathcal{T}, \mathcal{D})$ Theories

In this paper, we study the Myrzakulov gravity [46] VIII (MG-VIII) [4]. Its action is given by [46]

$$S[g, \Gamma, \phi] = S_g + S_m = \frac{1}{2\kappa}\int \sqrt{-g}d^4x[F(R, T, Q, \mathcal{T}) + 2\kappa\mathcal{L}_m], \tag{35}$$

where $R$ stands for the Ricci scalar (curvature scalar), $T$ is the torsion scalar, $Q$ is the non-metricity scalar and $\mathcal{T}$ is trace of the energy-momentum tensor of matter Lagrangian $L_m$. The MG-VIII can be seen as some kind of unification of $F(R), F(T), F(Q)$ or $F(R, \mathcal{T}), F(T, \mathcal{T})$, $F(Q, \mathcal{T})$ theories (see [51–53], respectively). For instance, if one imposes flatness (i.e., $R^{\lambda}{}_{\alpha\mu\nu} \equiv 0$) and metric compatibility ($Q_{\alpha\mu\nu} \equiv 0$), one arrives at the $f(T)$ gravity [7,54]. Demanding flatness and a torsionless connection, we get symmetric teleparallel $f(Q)$ gravity [8,9]. More generally, imposing only teleparallelism, we arrive at the recently developed generalized teleparallel scheme of f(G) [48,55] theories. If no restriction on the connection is assumed, then (35) serves as a specific generalization of metric-affine $f(R)$ gravity where the energy-momentum trace $\mathcal{T}$ and certain quadratic combinations of torsion and non-metricity are added as well. In fact, in this generalized metric-affine setup, one could also consider the presence of the hypermomentum analogue of the (metrical) energy-momentum trace. Giving it a little thought, we observe that the divergence of the dilation current is similar to the trace $\mathcal{T}$, as they appear in the trace of the canonical [5] energy-momentum tensor (see, for instance, [32])

$$t = \mathcal{T} + \frac{1}{2\sqrt{-g}}\partial_\nu(\sqrt{-g}\Delta^\nu)\ , \quad \Delta^\nu := \Delta_\mu{}^{\mu\nu}. \tag{36}$$

In this sense, $\mathcal{T}$ and the divergence of $\Delta^\nu$ are placed on equal footing as is obvious from the above equation. Therefore, the scalar obtained by the divergence of the dilation current

$$\mathcal{D} = \frac{1}{\sqrt{-g}}\partial_\nu(\sqrt{-g}\Delta^\nu) \tag{37}$$

would be a trace analogue for the hypermomentum. With this inclusion, we may generalize the class of theories (35) to

$$S[g, \Gamma, \phi] = S_g + S_m = \frac{1}{2\kappa}\int \sqrt{-g}d^4x[F(R, T, Q, \mathcal{T}, \mathcal{D}) + 2\kappa\mathcal{L}_m], \tag{38}$$

The field equations of the family of theories given by the the above action read as follows:

**g-Variation:**

$$\begin{aligned}-\frac{1}{2}g_{\mu\nu}F + F_R R_{(\mu\nu)} + F_T\left(2S_{\nu\alpha\beta}S_\mu{}^{\alpha\beta} - S_{\alpha\beta\mu}S^{\alpha\beta}{}_\nu + 2S_{\nu\alpha\beta}S_\mu{}^{\beta\alpha} - 4S_\mu S_\nu\right) + F_Q L_{(\mu\nu)}\\ +\hat{\nabla}_\lambda(F_Q J^\lambda{}_{(\mu\nu)}) + g_{\mu\nu}\hat{\nabla}_\lambda(F_Q\zeta^\lambda) + F_{\mathcal{T}}(\Theta_{\mu\nu} + T_{\mu\nu}) + F_{\mathcal{D}}M_{\mu\nu} = \kappa T_{\mu\nu}\end{aligned} \tag{39}$$

where

$$\hat{\nabla}_\lambda := \frac{1}{\sqrt{-g}}(2S_\lambda - \nabla_\lambda) \tag{40}$$

$$\Omega^{\alpha\mu\nu} = \frac{1}{4}Q^{\alpha\mu\nu} - \frac{1}{2}Q^{\mu\nu\alpha} - \frac{1}{4}g^{\mu\nu}Q^{\alpha} + \frac{1}{2}g^{\alpha\mu}Q^{\nu} \tag{41}$$

$$4L_{\mu\nu} = (Q_{\mu\alpha\beta} - 2Q_{\alpha\beta\mu})Q_{\nu}{}^{\alpha\beta} + (Q_{\mu} + 2q_{\mu})Q_{\nu} + (2Q_{\mu\nu\alpha} - Q_{\alpha\mu\nu})Q^{\alpha}) \\ -4\Omega^{\alpha\beta}{}_{\nu}Q_{\alpha\beta\mu} - 4\Omega_{\alpha\mu\beta}Q^{\alpha\beta}{}_{\nu} \tag{42}$$

$$\Theta_{\mu\nu} := g^{\alpha\beta}\frac{\delta T_{\alpha\beta}}{\delta g^{\mu\nu}} \tag{43}$$

$$M_{\mu\nu} := \frac{\delta D}{\delta g^{\mu\nu}} \tag{44}$$

and we also define the densities

$$J^{\lambda}{}_{\mu\nu} := \sqrt{-g}\Big(\frac{1}{4}Q^{\lambda}{}_{\mu\nu} - \frac{1}{2}Q_{\mu\nu}{}^{\lambda} + \Omega^{\lambda}{}_{\mu\nu}\Big) \tag{45}$$

$$\zeta^{\lambda} = \sqrt{-g}\Big(-\frac{1}{4}Q^{\lambda} + \frac{1}{2}q^{\lambda}\Big) \tag{46}$$

**Γ-Variation:**

$$P_{\lambda}{}^{\mu\nu}(F_R) + 2F_T\Big(S^{\mu\nu}{}_{\lambda} - 2S_{\lambda}{}^{[\mu\nu]} - 4S^{[\mu}\delta^{\nu]}_{\lambda}\Big) - M_{\lambda}{}^{\mu\nu\alpha}\partial_{\alpha}F_D \\ +F_Q\Big(2Q^{[\nu\mu]}{}_{\lambda} - Q_{\lambda}{}^{\mu\nu} + (q^{\nu} - Q^{\nu})\delta^{\mu}_{\lambda} + Q_{\lambda}g^{\mu\nu} + \frac{1}{2}Q^{\mu}\delta^{\nu}_{\lambda}\Big) = F_{\mathcal{T}}\Theta_{\lambda}{}^{\mu\nu} + \kappa\Delta_{\lambda}{}^{\mu\nu} \tag{47}$$

where

$$P_{\lambda}{}^{\mu\nu}(F_R) = -\frac{\nabla_{\lambda}(\sqrt{-g}F_R g^{\mu\nu})}{\sqrt{-g}} + \frac{\nabla_{\alpha}(\sqrt{-g}F_R g^{\mu\alpha}\delta^{\nu}_{\lambda})}{\sqrt{-g}} + \\ 2F_R(S_{\lambda}g^{\mu\nu} - S^{\mu}\delta^{\nu}_{\lambda} - S_{\lambda}{}^{\mu\nu}) \tag{48}$$

is the modified Palatini tensor and

$$\Theta_{\lambda}{}^{\mu\nu} := -\frac{\delta\mathcal{T}}{\delta\Gamma^{\lambda}{}_{\mu\nu}} \;, \quad M_{\lambda}{}^{\mu\nu\alpha} := \frac{\delta\Delta^{\alpha}}{\delta\Gamma^{\lambda}{}_{\mu\nu}}. \tag{49}$$

Note: if matter does not couple to the connection (e.g., classical perfect fluid with no inner structure) we have that $\Theta_{\lambda}{}^{\mu\nu} = 0$ as well as $\Delta_{\lambda}{}^{\mu\nu} = 0$ and $M_{\lambda}{}^{\mu\nu\alpha}$. The above set of field equations constitutes an extended (with the divergence of dilation included) metric-affine version of the Myrzakulov gravities [46]. Here, we derive the field equations with no restriction on the connection and also for the extended case $F(R,T,Q,\mathcal{T},D)$. In the next section, we further analyze the linear case $F = R + \beta T + \gamma Q + \mu\mathcal{T} + \nu\mathcal{D}$ and also touch upon cosmological applications.

## 5. Cosmological Applications

### *5.1. The Cosmology of $F = R + \beta T + \gamma Q + \mu\mathcal{T}$ Theory*

Let us now analyze in more detail the linear case $F = R + \beta T + \gamma Q + \mu\mathcal{T}$ and also obtain the associated cosmological equations. To start with, let us note that even if we consider the theory $F = R + \beta T + \gamma Q + \mu\mathcal{T} + \nu\mathcal{D}$, since $\sqrt{-g}\mathcal{D}$ is a total divergence, the dilation current would not contribute to the field equations when included linearly [6].

Therefore we can safely set $\nu = 0$ for the rest of our discussion. In addition, in this linear case, the metric field equations take the form

$$-\frac{1}{2}g_{\mu\nu}F + R_{(\mu\nu)} + \beta\Big(2S_{\nu\alpha\beta}S_{\mu}{}^{\alpha\beta} - S_{\alpha\beta\mu}S^{\alpha\beta}{}_{\nu} + 2S_{\nu\alpha\beta}S_{\mu}{}^{\beta\alpha} - 4S_{\mu}S_{\nu}\Big) + \gamma L_{(\mu\nu)} + \hat{\nabla}_{\lambda}(\gamma J^{\lambda}{}_{(\mu\nu)}) + g_{\mu\nu}\hat{\nabla}_{\lambda}(\gamma\zeta^{\lambda}) + \mu(\Theta_{\mu\nu} + T_{\mu\nu}) = \kappa T_{\mu\nu} \tag{50}$$

Taking the trace of the last equation, using the post-Riemannian expansion (33) and also employing (26) along with (27) and after some long calculations, we finally arrive at

$$\frac{\ddot{a}}{a} + \left(\frac{\dot{a}}{a}\right)^2 + (1+\beta)(4\Phi^2 - P^2) + \frac{1}{8}\Big(2A^2 + B(C-A)\Big) + \Phi(2A - B) + \dot{f} + 3Hf = -\mu(\Theta + \mathcal{T}) + \kappa\mathcal{T} \tag{51}$$

where

$$f := \frac{1}{2}\left[(1-\gamma)\left(\frac{B}{2} - A\right) - 4\Phi\right], \quad \Theta := \Theta_{\mu\nu}g^{\mu\nu} \tag{52}$$

which is a variant of the modified Friedmann equation. As for the second Friedmann (acceleration) equation, its general form was derived in [31] for general non-Riemannian cosmological setups. It reads

$$\frac{\ddot{a}}{a} = -\frac{1}{3}R_{\mu\nu}u^{\mu}u^{\nu} + 2\left(\frac{\dot{a}}{a}\right)\Phi + 2\dot{\Phi} + \left(\frac{\dot{a}}{a}\right)\left(A + \frac{C}{2}\right) + \frac{\dot{A}}{2} - \frac{A^2}{2} - \frac{1}{2}AC - 2A\Phi - 2C\Phi \tag{53}$$

One could then proceed by contracting (50) with $u^{\mu}u^{\nu}$ in order to eliminate the first term ($R_{\mu\nu}u^{\mu}u^{\nu}$) and express everything in terms of the scale factor and the torsion and non-metricity variables. This results in a fairly complicated expression which we refrain from presenting here since it goes beyond the scope of the present study. As a final note, let us mention that in order to analyze the above cosmological model in depth, one should consider an appropriate form of matter for which both the metrical energy-momentum and hypermomentum tensors respect the cosmological principle. The fluid with such characteristics was constructed in [32] (also see, for a generalized version, [45]) and goes by the name perfect cosmological hyperfluid. The hypermomentum part of this fluid will then source the torsion and non-metricity variables $\Phi, P, A, \ldots$, etc. by virtue of the connection field equations. We note that scalar fields coupled to the connection belong (are certain subcases) to the aforementioned fluid description. For the sake of illustration, below we present such an example with a scalar field non-minimally coupled to the connection in the case of vanishing non-metricity and also study some of the cosmological implications of this theory.

### *5.2. Scalar Field Coupled to Torsion*

We now focus on the vanishing non-metricity sector and also set $\gamma = 0$, that is, we concentrate on the case $F = R + \beta T$. As for the matter part, let us consider a scalar field. In the usual (i.e., purely Riemannian) case, one would have the usual Lagrangian

$$\mathcal{L}_m^{(0)} = -\frac{1}{2}g^{\mu\nu}\nabla_{\mu}\phi\nabla_{\nu}\phi - V(\phi), \tag{54}$$

for the scalar field $\phi$. However, in the presence of torsion, nothing prevents us from considering direct couplings of the scalar field with torsion. The most straightforward form of such a coupling is a torsion vector-scalar field derivative interaction of the form $\lambda_0 S^{\mu}\nabla_{\mu}\phi$, where $\lambda_0$ is the coupling constant measuring the strength of the interaction. Including this term, our full matter Lagrangian now reads

$$\mathcal{L}_m = -\frac{1}{2}g^{\mu\nu}\nabla_{\mu}\phi\nabla_{\nu}\phi - V(\phi) + \lambda_0 S^{\mu}\nabla_{\mu}\phi \tag{55}$$

Then, substituting this into (35) and varying the latter with respect to the scalar field, we obtain

$$\frac{1}{\sqrt{-g}}\partial_\mu\left[\sqrt{-g}(\partial^\mu\phi - \lambda_0 S^\mu)\right] = \frac{\partial V}{\partial\phi} \tag{56}$$

which is the evolution equation for the scalar field under the influence of torsion. In addition, the very presence of the interaction term $\lambda_0 S^\mu \nabla_\mu \phi$ produces a non-vanishing hypermomentum which is trivially computed to be

$$\Delta_\lambda{}^{\mu\nu} = 2\lambda_0 \delta_\lambda^{[\mu}\nabla^{\nu]}\phi \tag{57}$$

With this result, starting from the connection field Equation (47) which, in our case, reads

$$P_\lambda{}^{\mu\nu} + 2\beta\left(S^{\mu\nu}{}_\lambda - 2S_\lambda{}^{[\mu\nu]} - 4S^{[\mu}\delta_\lambda^{\nu]}\right) = \kappa\Delta_\lambda{}^{\mu\nu} \tag{58}$$

and contracting in $\mu = \lambda$, we find

$$S^\mu = \frac{3\kappa\lambda_0}{8\beta}\partial^\mu\phi \tag{59}$$

that in the presence of a scalar field produces spacetime torsion [7]. In addition, contracting (58) with $\varepsilon^\lambda{}_{\mu\nu\alpha}$, it follows that

$$t_\alpha = 0 \tag{60}$$

Note that we can now plug back into (55) the above form of the torsion tensor to end up with

$$\mathcal{L}_m = -\frac{1}{2}\left(1 - \frac{3\kappa\lambda_0^2}{4\beta}\right)g^{\mu\nu}\nabla_\mu\phi\nabla_\nu\phi - V(\phi) \tag{61}$$

Interestingly, from the last equation, we conclude that the scalar–torsion interaction changes the factor of the kinetic term for the scalar field. We also see that this is a crucial value for the coupling $|\lambda_0| = 2\sqrt{\frac{\beta}{3\kappa}}$ above which the kinetic term changes sign and, for exactly this value, vanishes identically. Since this last case would require severe fine tuning, we disregard it and we also assume that $\lambda_0$ is under this bound so that the kinetic term keeps its original sign.

Up to this point, the above considerations have been general. Let us now focus on the homogeneous FLRW cosmology of this theory. In this case, Equation (60) implies that $p = 0$ and, as a result, upon using (59), the full torsion tensor is given by

$$S_{\mu\nu\alpha} = 2u_{[\mu}h_{\nu]\alpha}\Phi(t), \tag{62a}$$

$$\Phi = -\frac{\kappa\lambda_0}{8\beta}\dot{\phi} \tag{62b}$$

In the case of a free scalar field (i.e., $V(\phi) = 0$) [8] inserting (59) into (56), we obtain

$$\left(1 - \frac{3\kappa\lambda_0^2}{8\beta}\right)\partial_\mu\left[\sqrt{-g}\partial^\mu\phi\right] = 0 \tag{63}$$

which for $|\lambda_0| \neq 2\sqrt{\frac{\beta}{3\kappa}}$ implies that

$$\dot{\phi} = \frac{c_0}{a^3} \tag{64}$$

On the other hand, the metric field equations in this case read

$$-\frac{1}{2}g_{\mu\nu}F + R_{(\mu\nu)} + \beta\Big(2S_{\nu\alpha\beta}S_{\mu}{}^{\alpha\beta} - S_{\alpha\beta\mu}S^{\alpha\beta}{}_{\nu} + 2S_{\nu\alpha\beta}S_{\mu}{}^{\beta\alpha} - 4S_{\mu}S_{\nu}\Big) = \kappa T_{\mu\nu} \tag{65}$$

and by taking the trace, using the same procedure we outlined previously, we finally obtain

$$\frac{\ddot{a}}{a} + \left(\frac{\dot{a}}{a}\right)^2 = \left[-\frac{\kappa}{6} + (1-\beta)\left(\frac{\kappa\lambda_0}{4\beta}\right)^2\right]\dot{\phi}^2 \tag{66}$$

which is again a variant of the modified Friedmann equation. Let us now derive the acceleration equation for this case. First, we contract the above field equations with $u^\mu u^\nu$ to obtain

$$R_{\mu\nu}u^\mu u^\nu = 24\beta\Phi^2 + \frac{\kappa}{2}(\rho + 3p) \tag{67}$$

which when substituted in (53) for vanishing non-metricity and the given scalar matter results in the acceleration equation

$$\frac{\ddot{a}}{a} = -8\beta\Phi^2 - \frac{\kappa}{6}(\rho + 3p) + 2H\Phi + 2\dot{\Phi} \tag{68}$$

where $\rho$ and $p$ are the density and pressure associated with the scalar field Lagrangian (61). It is interesting to note that the first term on the right-hand side of the acceleration equation has a fixed sign depending on the value of $\beta$. Intriguingly, for $\beta < 0$, the contribution from this term always has a fixed positive sign producing an accelerated expansion regardless of the sign of $\Phi$ (or equivalently $\dot{\phi}$). As for the last two terms, combining (62b) and (64), we observe that $\dot{\Phi} = -3H\Phi$ which, when substituted into the above acceleration equation, yields

$$\frac{\ddot{a}}{a} = -8\beta\Phi^2 - \frac{\kappa}{6}(\rho + 3p) + \frac{4}{3}\dot{\Phi} \tag{69}$$

We can conclude, therefore, that the last term aids acceleration when $\dot{\Phi} > 0$ and slows it down whenever $\dot{\Phi} < 0$. From the above analysis, we see that the non-Riemannian degrees of freedom play a crucial role in the cosmological evolution, providing new interesting phenomena. Now, using the latter form of the acceleration equation, we can obtain the first Friedmann equation from (66) by eliminating the double derivative of the scale factor. For the simple case $V(\phi) = 0$, we find

$$\left(\frac{\dot{a}}{a}\right)^2 = \left[\frac{\kappa}{6} + (1+\beta)\left(\frac{\kappa\lambda_0}{4\beta}\right)^2\right]\dot{\phi}^2 - \frac{4}{3}\dot{\Phi} \tag{70}$$

as the modified first Friedmann equation. Note that on substituting (62b) in the above and completing the square in the resulting expression, we easily find the power-law solution

$$a(t) \propto t^{1/3} \tag{71}$$

which is the stiff matter solution. We see that in the simplified case of a zero potential for the scalar, we arrive at a known solution. However, we should remark that the situation changes drastically when one considers a non-vanishing potential. Note also that the torsion tensor in this case goes like $1/t$ and therefore its effect diminishes with time.

Needless to say, when non-metricity is also included, one obtains more complicated expressions with a much richer phenomenology. It would be quite interesting to see exactly to what degree the simultaneous presence of torsion and non-metricity alters the cosmological evolution in such models. This will be the theme of a separate work.

## 6. Conclusions

By working in a metric-affine approach (i.e., considering the metric and the connection as independent variables) we have considered a generalized version of the theory proposed in [46]. In particular, we derived the full set of field equations of the class of theories whose gravitational part of the Lagrangian is given by $F(R, T, Q, \mathcal{T}, \mathcal{D})$, where $T$, $Q$ are the torsion and non-metricity scalars, $\mathcal{T}$ is the trace of the energy-momentum tensor and $\mathcal{D}$ is the divergence of the dilation current (one of the hypermomentum sources). The family of theories contained in our Lagrangian is fairly large since all metric and Palatini $f(R)$ theories, teleparallel $f(T)$, symmetric teleparallel $f(Q)$ or even generalized teleparallel $f(G)$ and generalizations of them such as $f(R, \mathcal{T})$, $f(T, \mathcal{T})$, $f(Q, \mathcal{T})$ can be seen as special cases of our theory.

Our contribution was two-fold. Firstly, we generalized the family of theories to those also including the divergence of the dilation current (which is the analogue of the energy-momentum trace for hypermomentum). Furthermore, as already mentioned above, we worked in a metric-affine framework, considering an independent affine connection as a fundamental variable along with the metric. This allows one not only to study the aforementioned theories (by restricting the connection one way or another), but also to analyze them in this general metric-affine scheme. Having derived the complete set of metric-affine $F(R, T, Q, \mathcal{T}, \mathcal{D})$ theories, we then concentrated our attention on the linear case $F = R + \beta T + \gamma Q + \mu \mathcal{T} + \nu \mathcal{D}$ and obtained a variant version of the modified Friedmann equation. Finally, we focused on the vanishing non-metricity sector and also considered a scalar field coupled to torsion as our matter sector. In this case, we derived both the first and second (acceleration) Friedmann equations and examined under what circumstances the presence of torsion can have an accelerating affect on the cosmological evolution. For this simple case, we were also able to provide an exact power-law solution for the scale factor.

In closing, let us note some further applications and additional developments of our study here. Firstly, it would be interesting to study in more detail the linear case, especially in regard to its cosmological implications in the presence of the cosmological hyperfluid [32,45]. In addition, as we have already mentioned, it would be worth elaborating more on the coupled scalar field we presented when both torsion and non-metricity are allowed and direct couplings of the latter with the scalar field occur. Finally, it would be quite interesting to go beyond linear functions $F$ of the new dilation current term we considered. In this way, we will be able to investigate what exactly is the effect of this new addition/extension as well as its phenomenology, especially with regard to its energy-momentum trace counterpart.

**Author Contributions:** Writing—original draft preparation, D.I.; writing—review and editing, N.M. and R.M. All authors have read and agreed to the published version of the manuscript.

**Funding:** This research received no external funding.

**Institutional Review Board Statement:** Not applicable.

**Informed Consent Statement:** Not applicable.

**Data Availability Statement:** Not applicable.

**Acknowledgments:** The work was supported by the Ministry of Education and Science of the Republic of Kazakhstan, Grant AP09058240. We would like to thank Lucrezia Ravera for useful discussions.

**Conflicts of Interest:** The authors declare no conflict of interest.

## Notes

1 From here onwards, we shall use the tilde notation in order to denote Riemannian objects, that is, objects computed with respect to the Levi-Civita connection $\tilde{\Gamma}^{\lambda}{}_{\mu\nu}$.

Note that we define the combination of the torsion scalar in the usual way so as to obtain the usual teleparallel equivalent of GR. As a generalization, one could consider an arbitrary linear combination of the three independent torsion scalars connected with the three irreducible components of the torsion (see, for instance, [47]).

Here, we are using the conventions of [16].

See also [49,50] for some observational implications of this theory.

Here $t = t^{\mu\nu} g_{\mu\nu}$ is the trace of the canonical energy-momentum tensor $t^{\mu\nu}$.

If we considered a quadratic contribution $\nu \mathcal{D}^2$, we would have the additional terms $-\frac{\nu}{2} D^2 g_{\mu\nu} + 2\nu \frac{g_{\mu\nu}}{\sqrt{-g}} \partial_\alpha (\sqrt{-g} D \Delta^\alpha)$ on the right-hand side of the metric field equations. These terms would then have an interesting impact in the cosmological setup we consider below, however, a detailed discussion goes beyond the purpose of this study and will be pursued elsewhere.

Of course, this is so because of the connection coupling which yields a non-vanishing hypermomentum. If no such coupling is included, the scalar field can neither feel nor produce torsion.

One can investigate the case of a non-vanishing potential by making use of reconstruction techniques developed in [56] (see also [57]).

## References


1. Will, C.M. The confrontation between general relativity and experiment. *Living Rev. Relativ.* **2014**, *17*, 1–117. [CrossRef]
2. Saridakis, E.N.; Lazkoz, R.; Salzano, V.; Moniz, P.V.; Capozziello, S.; Jiménez, J.B.; De Laurentis, M.; Olmo, G.J.; Akrami, Y.; Bahamonde, S.; et al. Modified Gravity and Cosmology: An Update by the CANTATA Network. *arXiv* **2021**, arXiv:2105.12582.
3. Sotiriou, T.P.; Faraoni, V. f (R) theories of gravity. *arXiv* **2008**, arXiv:0805.1726.
4. Iosifidis, D.; Petkou, A.C.; Tsagas, C.G. Torsion/nonmetricity duality in f (R) gravity. *Gen. Relativ. Gravit.* **2019**, *51*, 66. [CrossRef]
5. Capozziello, S.; Vignolo, S. Metric-affine f (R)-gravity with torsion: An overview. *Ann. Der Phys.* **2010**, *19*, 238–248. [CrossRef]
6. Aldrovandi, R.; Pereira, J.G. *Teleparallel Gravity: An Introduction*; Springer Science & Business Media: Berlin/Heidelberg, Germany, 2012; Volume 173.
7. Myrzakulov, R. Accelerating universe from F (T) gravity. *Eur. Phys. J. C* **2011**, *71*, 1–8. [CrossRef]
8. Nester, J.M.; Yo, H.J. Symmetric teleparallel general relativity. *arXiv* **1998**, arXiv:gr-qc/9809049.
9. Jiménez, J.B.; Heisenberg, L.; Koivisto, T.S. Teleparallel palatini theories. *J. Cosmol. Astropart. Phys.* **2018**, *2018*, 039. [CrossRef]
10. Bartolo, N.; Pietroni, M. Scalar-tensor gravity and quintessence. *Phys. Rev. D* **1999**, *61*, 023518. [CrossRef]
11. Charmousis, C.; Copeland, E.J.; Padilla, A.; Saffin, P.M. General second-order scalar-tensor theory and self-tuning. *Phys. Rev. Lett.* **2012**, *108*, 051101. [CrossRef]
12. Eisenhart, L.P. *Non-Riemannian Geometry*; Courier Corporation: Chelmsford, England 2012.
13. Hehl, F.W.; McCrea, J.D.; Mielke, E.W.; Ne'eman, Y. Metric-affine gauge theory of gravity: field equations, Noether identities, world spinors, and breaking of dilation invariance. *Phys. Rep.* **1995**, *258*, 1–171. [CrossRef]
14. Iosifidis, D. Metric-Affine Gravity and Cosmology/Aspects of Torsion and non-Metricity in Gravity Theories. *arXiv* **2019**, arXiv:1902.09643.
15. Iosifidis, D. Exactly solvable connections in metric-affine gravity. *Class. Quantum Gravity* **2019**, *36*, 085001. [CrossRef]
16. Iosifidis, D.; Koivisto, T. Scale transformations in metric-affine geometry. *Universe* **2019**, *5*, 82. [CrossRef]
17. Vitagliano, V.; Sotiriou, T.P.; Liberati, S. The dynamics of metric-affine gravity. *Ann. Phys.* **2011**, *326*, 1259–1273. [CrossRef]
18. Sotiriou, T.P.; Liberati, S. Metric-affine f (R) theories of gravity. *Ann. Phys.* **2007**, *322*, 935–966. [CrossRef]
19. Percacci, R.; Sezgin, E. New class of ghost-and tachyon-free metric affine gravities. *Phys. Rev. D* **2020**, *101*, 084040. [CrossRef]
20. Jiménez, J.B.; Delhom, A. Instabilities in metric-affine theories of gravity with higher order curvature terms. *Eur. Phys. J. C* **2020**, *80*, 585. [CrossRef]
21. Beltrán Jiménez, J.; Delhom, A. Ghosts in metric-affine higher order curvature gravity. *Eur. Phys. J. C* **2019**, *79*, 656. [CrossRef]
22. Olmo, G.J. Palatini Approach to Modified Gravity: F(R) Theories and Beyond. *Int. J. Mod. Phys. D* **2011**, *20*, 413–462. [CrossRef]
23. Aoki, K.; Shimada, K. Scalar-metric-affine theories: Can we get ghost-free theories from symmetry? *Phys. Rev. D* **2019**, *100*, 044037. [CrossRef]
24. Cabral, F.; Lobo, F.S.N.; Rubiera-Garcia, D. Fundamental Symmetries and Spacetime Geometries in Gauge Theories of Gravity—Prospects for Unified Field Theories. *Universe* **2020**, *6*, 238. [CrossRef]
25. Ariwahjoedi, S.; Suroso, A.; Zen, F.P. (3 + 1)-Formulation for Gravity with Torsion and Non-Metricity: The Stress-Energy-Momentum Equation. *Class. Quantum Gravity* **2020**. [CrossRef]
26. Yang, J.Z.; Shahidi, S.; Harko, T.; Liang, S.D. Geodesic deviation, Raychaudhuri equation, Newtonian limit, and tidal forces in Weyl-type $f(Q,T)$ gravity. *Eur. Phys. J. C* **2021**, *81*, 111. [CrossRef]
27. Helpin, T.; Volkov, M.S. A metric-affine version of the Horndeski theory. *Int. J. Mod. Phys. A* **2020**, *35*, 2040010. [CrossRef]
28. Bahamonde, S.; Valcarcel, J.G. New models with independent dynamical torsion and nonmetricity fields. *J. Cosmol. Astropart. Phys.* **2020**, *2020*, 57. [CrossRef]
29. Iosifidis, D.; Ravera, L. Parity violating metric-affine gravity theories. *Class. Quantum Gravity* **2021**, *38*, 115003. [CrossRef]
30. Iosifidis, D. Riemann Tensor and Gauss-Bonnet density in Metric-Affine Cosmology. *arXiv* **2021**, arXiv:2104.10192.
31. Iosifidis, D. Cosmic acceleration with torsion and non-metricity in Friedmann-like Universes. *Class. Quantum Gravity* **2020**, *38*, 015015. [CrossRef]

32. Iosifidis, D. Cosmological Hyperfluids, Torsion and Non-metricity. *Eur. Phys. J. C* **2020**, *80*, 1042. [CrossRef]
33. Iosifidis, D.; Ravera, L. The Cosmology of Quadratic Torsionful Gravity. *arXiv* **2021**, arXiv:2101.10339.
34. Jiménez, J.B.; Koivisto, T.S. Spacetimes with vector distortion: Inflation from generalised Weyl geometry. *Phys. Lett. B* **2016**, *756*, 400–404. [CrossRef]
35. Beltrán Jiménez, J.; Koivisto, T. Modified gravity with vector distortion and cosmological applications. *Universe* **2017**, *3*, 47. [CrossRef]
36. Kranas, D.; Tsagas, C.G.; Barrow, J.D.; Iosifidis, D. Friedmann-like universes with torsion. *Eur. Phys. J. C* **2019**, *79*, 341. [CrossRef]
37. Barragán, C.; Olmo, G.J.; Sanchis-Alepuz, H. Bouncing cosmologies in Palatini f (R) gravity. *Phys. Rev. D* **2009**, *80*, 024016. [CrossRef]
38. Shimada, K.; Aoki, K.; Maeda, K.i. Metric-affine gravity and inflation. *Phys. Rev. D* **2019**, *99*, 104020. [CrossRef]
39. Kubota, M.; Oda, K.y.; Shimada, K.; Yamaguchi, M. Cosmological perturbations in Palatini formalism. *J. Cosmol. Astropart. Phys.* **2021**, *2021*, 6. [CrossRef]
40. Mikura, Y.; Tada, Y.; Yokoyama, S. Conformal inflation in the metric-affine geometry. *EPL* **2020**, *132*, 39001. [CrossRef]
41. Mikura, Y.; Tada, Y.; Yokoyama, S. Minimal *k*-inflation in light of the conformal metric-affine geometry. *arXiv* **2021**, arXiv:2103.13045.
42. Hehl, F.W.; Kerlick, G.D.; von der Heyde, P. On hypermomentum in general relativity I. The notion of hypermomentum. *Z. Fuer Naturforschung A* **1976**, *31*, 111–114. [CrossRef]
43. Babourova, O.; Frolov, B. The variational theory of perfect fluid with intrinsic hypermomentum in space-time with nonmetricity. *arXiv* **1995**, arXiv:gr-qc/9509013.
44. Obukhov, Y.N.; Tresguerres, R. Hyperfluid—A model of classical matter with hypermomentum. *Phys. Lett. A* **1993**, *184*, 17–22. [CrossRef]
45. Iosifidis, D. The Perfect Hyperfluid of Metric-Affine Gravity: The Foundation. *JCAP* **2021**, *04*, 72. [CrossRef]
46. Myrzakulov, R. Dark energy in F (R, T) gravity. *arXiv* **2012**, arXiv:1205.5266.
47. Fabbri, L.; Vignolo, S. A modified theory of gravity with torsion and its applications to cosmology and particle physics. *Int. J. Theor. Phys.* **2012**, *51*, 3186–3207. [CrossRef]
48. Jiménez, J.B.; Heisenberg, L.; Iosifidis, D.; Jiménez-Cano, A.; Koivisto, T.S. General Teleparallel Quadratic Gravity. *arXiv* **2019**, arXiv:1909.09045.
49. Anagnostopoulos, F.K.; Basilakos, S.; Saridakis, E.N. Observational constraints on Myrzakulov gravity. *Phys. Rev. D* **2021**, *103*, 104013. [CrossRef]
50. Saridakis, E.N.; Myrzakul, S.; Myrzakulov, K.; Yerzhanov, K. Cosmological applications of $F(R,T)$ gravity with dynamical curvature and torsion. *Phys. Rev. D* **2020**, *102*, 023525. [CrossRef]
51. Harko, T.; Lobo, F.S.N.; Nojiri, S.; Odintsov, S.D. $f(R,T)$ gravity. *Phys. Rev. D* **2011**, *84*, 024020. [CrossRef]
52. Harko, T.; Lobo, F.S.; Saridakis, E.N.; Otalora, G. $f(T,\mathcal{T})$ gravity and cosmology. *JCAP* **2014**, *12*, 21. [CrossRef]
53. Xu, Y.; Li, G.; Harko, T.; Liang, S.D. f (Q, T) gravity. *Eur. Phys. J. C* **2019**, *79*, 1–19. [CrossRef]
54. Krššák, M.; Saridakis, E.N. The covariant formulation of f (T) gravity. *Class. Quantum Gravity* **2016**, *33*, 115009. [CrossRef]
55. Beltrán Jiménez, J.; Koivisto, T.S. Accidental gauge symmetries of Minkowski spacetime in Teleparallel theories. *Universe* **2021**, *7*, 143. [CrossRef]
56. Ellis, G.F.R.; Madsen, M.S. Exact scalar field cosmologies. *Class. Quant. Grav.* **1991**, *8*, 667–676. [CrossRef]
57. Carloni, S.; Goswami, R.; Dunsby, P.K.S. A new approach to reconstruction methods in $f(R)$ gravity. *Class. Quant. Grav.* **2012**, *29*, 135012. [CrossRef]

universe

MDPI

Communication

# New Anisotropic Exact Solution in Multifield Cosmology

Andronikos Paliathanasis [1,2]

1 Institute of Systems Science, Durban University of Technology, P.O. Box 1334, Durban 4000, South Africa; anpaliat@phys.uoa.gr
2 Instituto de Ciencias Físicas y Matemáticas, Universidad Austral de Chile, Valdivia 5090000, Chile

**Abstract:** In the case of two-scalar field cosmology, and specifically for the Chiral model, we determine an exact solution for the field equations with an anisotropic background space. The exact solution can describe anisotropic inflation with a Kantowski–Sachs geometry and can be seen as the anisotropic analogue of the hyperbolic inflation. Finally, we investigate the stability conditions for the exact solution.

**Keywords:** multifield cosmology; anisotropic spacetimes; Kantowski–Sachs; anisotropic inflation

## 1. Introduction

The early acceleration epoch of the universe is the inflationary era [1], to which the isotropy and homogeneity of the observed universe are due [2]. The origin of the inflation is unknown. However, the introduction of a minimally coupled scalar field, the inflation, into the cosmological dynamics of Einstein's General Relativity provides an acceleration when the scalar field potential dominates. Hence, the scalar field drives the spacetime towards a locally isotropic and homogeneous space form that leaves only very small residual anisotropies, which are left from the pre-inflationary era [3,4]. Therefore, anisotropies may have been important for the evolution of the universe. Thus, the investigation of exact solutions in anisotropic inflationary models is a subject of special interest.

Exact and analytic solutions are important for the study of the evolution and of the viability of a given cosmological model. In one scalar field cosmology, exact and analytic solutions in a homogeneous and isotropic background space can be found in [5–14]. On the other hand, there are few known anisotropic exact solutions with one scalar field [15–21].

Multiscalar field models have been proposed as alternative models for the description of the whole cosmological history [22,23]. In the multiscalar field model the additional degrees of freedom provide new dynamical behaviours in the cosmological dynamics [24–30]. Some anisotropic exact solutions in multifield cosmology can be found in [20,31,32].

A multiscalar field model that has drawn the attention of cosmologists in recent years is the Chiral model. The Lagrangian function of the Chiral model is inspired by the $\sigma$-model [33] and is composed of two scalar fields, and the kinetic energy is defined on a two-dimensional hyperbolic space [34]. The Chiral model with an exponential potential provides a new inflationary solution known as hyperbolic inflation [35,36]. Hyperinflation solves various problems of inflationary physics. In hyperbolic inflation, the dynamics are driven by all of the matter components of the field equations, that is, by the scalar field potential and the kinetic parts of the two scalar fields. Moreover, the initial conditions in the start and in the end of the inflation can be different in the Chiral model, which means that the curvature perturbations depend upon the number of the e-fold [37]. Furthermore, detectable non-Gaussianities in the power spectrum are supported by the multifield inflation [38].

In this study we investigate the existence of a new exact solution in Chiral cosmology with an anisotropic background space. As far as isotropic and homogeneous models are concerned, Chiral theory has been widely studied previously with many interesting

Citation: Paliathanasis, A. New Anisotropic Exact Solution in Multifield Cosmology. *Universe* **2021**, 7, 323. https://doi.org/10.3390/universe7090323

Academic Editor: Lorenzo Iorio

Received: 16 August 2021
Accepted: 27 August 2021
Published: 30 August 2021

results—see for instance [39–42]—while recently, extensions of Chiral cosmology were considered by assuming one of the two scalar fields to be a phantom field [43]. In our consideration for the background space we consider locally rotational spacetimes (LRS) with two scale factors that belong to the family of Bianchi I, Bianchi III and Kantowski–Sachs spacetimes. These anisotropic spacetimes have the property that they fall into the spatially flat, closed and open Friedmann–Lemaître–Robertson–Walker (FLRW) spacetime when they reach isotropy. The plan of the paper is as follows.

In Section 2 we present the cosmological model of our consideration and we derive the gravitational field equations. In Section 3 we present the new solution of our analysis, which is that of anisotropic hyperbolic inflation. The analysis of homogeneous perturbations is presented in Section 4, where we discuss the stability properties of the new exact solution. Finally, in Section 5 we draw our conclusions.

## 2. Chiral Cosmology

We consider the gravitational Action Integral

$$S = \int \sqrt{-g} dx^4 \left( R + L_C(\phi, \nabla_\mu \phi, \psi, \nabla_\mu \psi) \right) \tag{1}$$

in which $R(x^\kappa)$ is the Ricci scalar of the metric tensor $g_{\mu\nu}(x^\kappa)$, and $L_C(\phi, \nabla_\mu\phi, \psi, \nabla_\mu\psi)$ is the Lagrangian function for the Chiral model, which describes the dynamics for the two scalar fields $\phi(x^\kappa)$ and $\psi(x^\kappa)$, that is:

$$L_C(\phi, \nabla_\mu \phi, \psi, \nabla_\mu \psi) = -\frac{1}{2} g^{\mu\nu}(x^\kappa) \left( \nabla_\mu \phi(x^\kappa) \nabla_\nu \phi(x^\kappa) + e^{-2\kappa\phi(x^\kappa)} \nabla_\mu \psi(x^\kappa) \nabla_\nu \psi(x^\kappa) \right) + V(\phi(x^\kappa)). \tag{2}$$

From the kinetic term of Equation (2) we observe that the scalar field lies on two geometries: The physical space with metric tensor $g_{\mu\nu}(x^\kappa)$ and the two-dimensional space of constant curvature with metric $h_{AB} = diag(1, e^{-2\kappa\phi})$ and curvature $R_h \simeq -\kappa^2$, $A, B = 1, 2$. The parameter $\kappa$ is assumed to be a nonzero constant, otherwise the line element $h_{AB}$ reduces to the two-dimensional flat space and the Lagrangian Equation (2) is reduced to that of multiquintessence theory. In general, the potential function (Equation (2)) has been assumed to also be a function of the second field $\psi\left(x^k\right)$. However, hyperbolic inflation in the case of FLRW space follows for the exponential potential [35] $V(\phi(x^\kappa)) = V_0 \exp(-\lambda\phi(x^\kappa))$, which we shall consider in this analysis.

*Anisotropic Spacetime*

In this study for the physical space we consider the LRS anisotropic line element in the Milne variables

$$ds^2 = -dt^2 + e^{2\alpha(t)} \left( e^{2\beta(t)} dx^2 + e^{-\beta(t)} \left( dy^2 + f^2(y) dz^2 \right) \right) \tag{3}$$

in which the function $f(y)$ has one of the following forms, $f_A(y) = 1$, and the line element describes a Bianchi I spacetime, $f_B(y) = \sinh\left(\sqrt{|K|}y\right)$, where $g_{\mu\nu}(x^\kappa)$ is that of Bianchi III spacetime and $f_C(y) = \sin\left(\sqrt{|K|}y\right)$, where $g_{\mu\nu}$ takes the form of Kantowski–Sachs space. Variable $\beta(t)$ indicates the existence of anisotropy. When $\dot{\beta}(t) = 0$, the background space is that of the FLRW universe.

For the line element (Equation (3)) and the Action Integral (Equation (1)) it follows that the equations of motions that drive the dynamics for the variables $\alpha(t)$, $\beta(t)$, $\phi(t)$ and $\psi(t)$ are

$$e^{3\alpha} \left( 3\dot{\alpha}^2 - \frac{3}{4}\dot{\beta}^2 - \frac{1}{2}\left( \dot{\phi}^2 + e^{-2\kappa\phi}\dot{\psi}^2 \right) - V(\phi) \right) - e^{\alpha-\beta}K = 0, \tag{4}$$

$$2\ddot{\alpha} + 3\dot{\alpha}^2 + \frac{3}{4}\dot{\beta}^2 + \frac{1}{2}\left( \dot{\phi}^2 + e^{-2\kappa\phi}\dot{\psi} \right) - V(\phi) - \frac{1}{3}e^{-2\alpha-\beta}K = 0, \tag{5}$$

$$\ddot{\beta} + 3\dot{\alpha}\dot{\beta} + \frac{2}{3}e^{-2\alpha-\beta}K = 0, \tag{6}$$

$$\ddot{\phi} + \kappa e^{-2\kappa\phi}\dot{\psi}^2 + 3\dot{\alpha}\dot{\phi} + V_{,\phi} = 0, \tag{7}$$

$$\ddot{\psi} - 2\kappa\dot{\phi}\dot{\psi} + 3\dot{\alpha}\dot{\psi} = 0, \tag{8}$$

where $K = \frac{f(y)_{,yy}}{f(y)}$ is the spatial curvature of the three-dimensional hypersurface of Equation (3). For Bianchi I spacetime, $K = 0$, for Bianchi III space, $K > 0$, and for the Kantowski–Sachs spacetime, $K < 0$.

## 3. Exact Solution

We assume the exponential potential $V(\phi) = V_0 \exp(-\lambda\phi)$. Moreover, we observe that Equation (8) is total derivative, i.e., $\frac{d}{dt}\left(\dot{\psi}e^{3\alpha-2\kappa\phi}\right) = 0$. Hence, the conservation law for the field equations is

$$I_0 = \dot{\psi}e^{3\alpha-2\kappa\phi}. \tag{9}$$

Equation (5) can be seen as a second conservation law for the dynamical system. In the case of a spatially flat FLRW universe, i.e., $\dot{\beta} = 0$ and $K = 0$, the analytic solution of the field equation was presented recently in [28] using the Lie symmetry approach.

Hence, in order to investigate the existence of additional conservation laws, we apply the theory of Lie symmetries. For a review on applications of the Lie symmetry analysis in cosmology we refer the reader to [44]. We omit the presentation of the calculations and we directly present the results.

The dynamical system consisting of the second-order differential Equations (5)–(8) for the exponential potential admits the symmetry vectors

$$X_1 = \partial_\psi \ , \ X_2 = 2t\partial_t + \frac{2}{3}(\partial_\alpha + \partial_\beta) + \frac{4}{\lambda}(\partial_\phi + \kappa\psi\partial_\psi) \ , \text{ for } \lambda \neq 0 \tag{10}$$

with the corresponding conservation laws $I_0$ and

$$I_1 = e^{3\alpha}\left(\dot{\beta} - 4\dot{\alpha} + \frac{4}{\lambda}\left(\dot{\phi} + \kappa e^{-2\kappa\phi}\dot{\psi}\right)\right). \tag{11}$$

For $\lambda = 0$, that is $V(\phi) = V_0$, the admitted symmetry vectors are the elements of the $so(3)$ algebra for the metric tensor $h_{AB}$. They are

$$Z_1 = \partial_\psi, \ Z_2 = \left(\partial_\phi + \kappa\psi\partial_\psi\right), \tag{12}$$

$$Z_3 = \psi\partial_\phi + \kappa\left(\frac{\psi^2}{2} + \psi - \frac{1}{2\kappa}e^{2\kappa\phi}\right), \tag{13}$$

with conservation laws $I_0$ and

$$\bar{I}_2 = \left(\dot{\phi} + \kappa e^{-2\kappa\phi}\dot{\psi}\right) \tag{14}$$

and

$$\bar{I}_3 = \psi\dot{\phi} + \kappa\left(\left(\frac{\psi^2}{2} + \psi\right)e^{-2\kappa\phi} - \frac{1}{2\kappa}\right)\dot{\psi}. \tag{15}$$

We focus on the case for which $\lambda \neq 0$. We observe that the two conservation laws $I_0, I_1$ are not in involution, that is, $\{I_0, I_1\} \neq 0$, where $\{,\}$ is the Poisson Bracket. Consequently we cannot infer the Liouville integrability of the field equations. However, the existence of the symmetry vector $X_2$ indicates the existence of invariant functions. We follow [44] and we search for the exact solution of the form

$$a(t) = p_1 \ln t \ , \ \beta(t) = p_2 \ln t \ , \ \phi(t) = p_3 \ln t. \tag{16}$$

We substitute into the conservation law $I_0$, which gives $I_0 = t^{3p_1 - 2\kappa p_3}\dot{\psi}$, that is,

$$\psi(t) = \frac{I_0}{1 - 3p_1 + 2\kappa p_3} t^{1-3p_1+2\kappa p_3}\ , \ 3p_1 - 2\kappa p_3 \neq 1 \tag{17}$$

$$\psi(t) = I_0 \ln t\ , \ 3p_1 - 2\kappa p_3 = 1. \tag{18}$$

In addition, we assume that $I_0 \neq 0$, otherwise we reduce to the case of anisotropic spaces with a quintessence field [15].

Let us assume now that $3p_1 - 2\kappa p_3 \neq 1$, then by replacing Equations (16) and (17) in the field Equations (4)–(7) we arrive at the exact solution

$$\alpha(t) = \frac{1}{3}\left(1 + 2\frac{\kappa}{\lambda}\right)\ln t\ , \ \beta(t) = \frac{4}{3}\left(1 - \frac{\kappa}{\lambda}\right)\ln t\ , \ \phi(t) = \frac{2}{\lambda}\ln t\ , \tag{19}$$

$$\psi(t) = \frac{\lambda I_0}{2\kappa} t^{2\frac{\kappa}{\lambda}}\ , \ V_0 = \frac{\kappa}{\lambda}\left(4 + I_0^2\lambda^2\right)\ , \ K = 4\frac{\kappa}{\lambda}\left(1 - \frac{\kappa}{\lambda}\right) \tag{20}$$

with the constraint equation

$$\left(4(1 - \kappa\lambda) + \left(2 + I_0^2\right)\lambda^2\right) = 0. \tag{21}$$

Hence, $3p_1 - 2\kappa p_3 = \frac{2\kappa}{\lambda}$, which means that $2\kappa - \lambda \neq 0$.

This is a new anisotropic exact solution with two scalar fields. For $K = 0$, it follows that $\lambda = \kappa$. Thus, $\beta(t) = 0$, which means we end with the spatially flat FLRW spacetime. The background spacetime is that of Bianchi III spacetime when $\kappa(\lambda - \kappa) > 0$, while the Kantowski–Sachs metric is recovered when $\kappa(\lambda - \kappa) < 0$.

The anisotropic scale factor can be written as $\beta(t) = \frac{\lambda}{\kappa}K\ln t$, which means that the existence of a spatial curvature indicates the existence of anisotropy. Thus, the isotropic open or closed FLRW spacetimes, similarly to Kasner-like universes, are not provided by this exact solution.

Indeed, this solution is the analogue of the hyperbolic inflation in the anisotropic background space. The deceleration parameter is defined as $q = -1 - \frac{\ddot{a}}{\dot{a}^2}$, that is, $q(t) = -\frac{2(\kappa-\lambda)}{2\kappa+\lambda}$. Consequently, when the acceleration parameter is negative, $q(t) < 0$, the exact solution describes an accelerated solution. Thus, when $-\frac{2(\kappa-\lambda)}{2\kappa+\lambda} < 0$, we observe that $K < 0$. Hence acceleration exists only for the Kantowski–Sachs background space. This inflationary solution is an extension of the inflationary solution found before for the inflation field in Kantowski–Sachs geometry [45].

Finally, for the case $3p_1 - 2\kappa p_3 = 1$, by replacing Equations (16) and (18) in the field equations, from Equation (6) we find $p_2 = 2(1 - p_1)$ and $K = -3(1 - 4p_1 + 3p_1^2)$. Thus, from Equation (7) it follows that

$$2I_0^2\kappa^2 + (1 - 3p_1)t^{-1+3p_1} - 2t^{1+3p_1+\frac{\lambda-3p_1\lambda}{2\kappa}}V_0\kappa\lambda = 0. \tag{22}$$

Because we are interested in solutions with two scalar fields, we study cases with $I_0 \neq 0$ and $p_1 \neq \frac{1}{3}$. Thus, the polynomial Equation (22) can not be solved, which means that there is no anisotropic solution of the form of Equation (16) for $2p_1 - 2\kappa p_3 = 1$.

## 4. Stability Analysis

We continue our analysis with the study of the stability properties for the new anisotropic inflationary solution. We define the new variable $H = \dot{a}$, and we substitute into Equations (4)–(7)

$$H = \frac{\left(1 + 2\frac{\kappa}{\lambda}\right)}{3t} + \delta H(t)\ , \ \beta(t) = \frac{4}{3}\left(1 - \frac{\kappa}{\lambda}\right)\ln t + \delta\beta(t)\ , \tag{23}$$

$$\phi(t) = \frac{2}{\lambda}\ln t + \delta\phi\ , \ \dot{\psi} = I_0 e^{-3\alpha+2\kappa\phi}\ , \ V_0 = \frac{\kappa}{\lambda}\left(4 + I_0^2\lambda^2\right)\ , \ K = 4\frac{\kappa}{\lambda}\left(1 - \frac{\kappa}{\lambda}\right) \tag{24}$$

and we linearize. Moreover, we perform the new change of variable, this time for the dependent variable $t = e^s$. Hence we obtain the system of two linear second-order differential equations

$$0 = 3\lambda\left(\lambda(2\kappa+\lambda)\delta\beta'' + \left(8\kappa^2 - 6\kappa\lambda + 4\lambda^2\right)\delta\beta' + 4(\lambda-\kappa)\delta\phi'\right) - 8\kappa(5\kappa - 2\lambda)(\kappa-\lambda)\delta\beta + 24\kappa(\kappa-\lambda)\delta\phi \tag{25}$$

and

$$0 = \lambda(6(\lambda-\kappa)\delta\beta' + \lambda(2\kappa+\lambda)\delta\phi'' + 2(\kappa(2\kappa+\lambda)+3)\delta\phi') + 12\kappa(\kappa-\lambda)\delta\beta + 2\kappa\left((2\kappa+\lambda)\left(4\kappa^2\lambda - 4\kappa - \lambda^3\right) - 6\right)\delta\phi \tag{26}$$

with the constraint

$$\delta H(s) = \frac{e^{-s}(\lambda((\lambda-\kappa)\delta\beta' + \delta\phi') + 2\kappa(\kappa-\lambda)\delta\beta - 2\kappa\delta\phi)}{\lambda(2\kappa+\lambda)} \tag{27}$$

and $\delta\beta' = \frac{d\delta\beta}{ds}$.

The solutions of the perturbations are expressed as

$$(\delta\beta, \delta\phi)^T = \begin{pmatrix} \zeta_1 & \zeta_2 \\ \zeta_3 & \zeta_4 \end{pmatrix} (\exp(\mu_1(\lambda,\kappa)s), \exp(\mu_2(\lambda,\kappa)s))^T, \tag{28}$$

where $\mu_1(\lambda,\kappa)$, $\mu_2(\lambda,\kappa)$ are the eigenvalues for the linearized system. The asymptotic solution is stable, when $\mathrm{Re}(\mu_1 < 0)$ and $\mathrm{Re}(\mu_2 < 0)$.

In Figure 1 we present the region plots for the parameters $\mu_1$ and $\mu_2$ is the space $(\lambda,\kappa)$, where the perturbations decay.

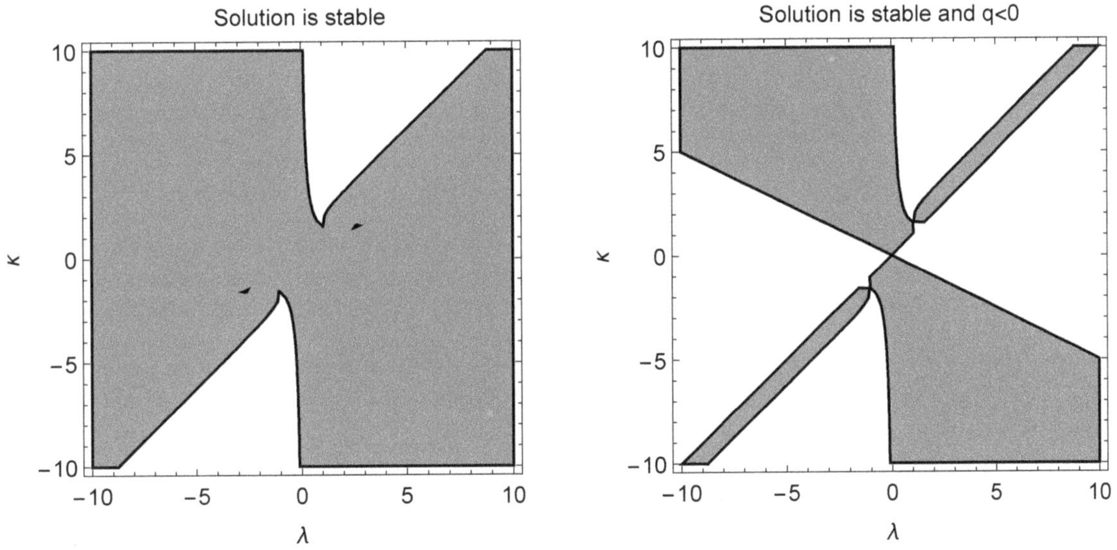


**Figure 1.** Region plot for the eigenvalues $\mu_1(\lambda,\kappa)$, $\mu_2(\lambda,\kappa)$, where the perturbations around the new anistropic solution decay (**left**), and the perturbations around the new anistropic solution decay and the new anisotropic solution describes an anisotopic inflationary universe (**right**).

## 5. Conclusions

In this work we investigated the existence of inflationary solutions on multifield cosmology with a homogeneous LRS anisotropic background space. In the context of Chiral cosmology and for the model that describes the hyperbolic inflation in an FLRW background space, we found an anisotropic exact solution that provides anisotropic inflation when the background spacetime has a negative spatial curvature, that is, the physical space is described by the Kantowski–Sachs spacetime.

For the exact solution, the anisotropic parameter and the spatial curvature are analogues. Therefore, when the curvature term vanishes, the physical space becomes isotropic. The method that we applied for the derivation of the exact solution is based upon the investigation of Lie invariant functions, by calculating the Lie symmetries for the cosmological field equations. Finally, the stability properties for these exact solutions were studied. We found that the inflationary anisotropic solution can be a stable solution.

In contrary to the slow-roll inflationary solution for the single scalar field [1], in which $\dot{\psi}=0$, and $3\dot{\alpha}\dot{\phi}\simeq -V_{,\phi}$, in the hyperinflation the following expressions are true [35]:

$$\dot{\phi}\simeq\frac{6}{2\kappa+\lambda}\dot{\alpha}\,, \tag{29}$$

which means that the evolution of the scalar field is independent on the derivative of the potential. Hence, by replacing the new anisotropic solution in Equation (29) we find that it is true, while for the second field $\psi(t)$ it holds that

$$e^{-2\kappa\phi}\dot{\psi}^2=6\left(1-\frac{6}{2\kappa+\lambda}\right)\dot{\alpha}^2-\dot{\alpha}-\frac{3}{2}\dot{\beta}^2--2V(\phi)-2e^{-2\alpha-\beta}K \tag{30}$$

where we conclude that we have derived the analogue for the hyperinflation in an anisotropic background space.

At this point it is important to mention that the exact solution that we found does not provide the limit of the cosmological constant [46]. Indeed, the declaration parameter is $q(t)=-\frac{2(\kappa-\lambda)}{2\kappa+\lambda}$ and the limit for the cosmological constant is recovered when $q(t)=1$, that is $\lambda=0$. However, in our analysis we considered $\lambda\neq 0$. For other forms of the scalar field potential, it is possible that there exist exact solutions that provide the limit of the cosmological constant. Such an analysis is outside the scope of this work, since we focused on the exponential potential. From this result we can infer that the Chiral model provides inflationary anisotropic solutions that can be used as a toy model for the study of the very early universe.

Let us assume now the new anisotropic exact solution in the limit where $\frac{\kappa}{\lambda}\simeq 1+\varepsilon$, then $\alpha(t)=\left(1+\frac{2}{3}\varepsilon\right)\ln t$ and $\beta(t)=\frac{4}{3}\varepsilon\ln t$. Hence, for $\varepsilon^2=0$ the anisotropies are small, and inflation can be described by the Hubble slow roll parameters [47] $\varepsilon_H=-\frac{\dot{H}}{H^2}$, $\eta_H=\frac{\dot{\varepsilon}_H}{H\dot{\varepsilon}_H}$, from where we calculate $\varepsilon_H\simeq 1-\frac{2}{3}\varepsilon$ and $\eta_H=0$. However, these slow-roll parameters are similar to those of the exponential potential for the inflation field. However, because of the additional degrees of freedom, the solution may not be always stable, and thus the actual solution will be different from the exact solution.

In a future study we plan to investigate the stability properties for the general model and also to investigate the behaviour of the inflationary parameters with initial conditions near the region of the exact solution.

**Funding:** This work is based on research supported in part by the National Research Foundation ofSouth Africa (Grant Numbers 131604).

**Institutional Review Board Statement:** Not applicable.

**Informed Consent Statement:** Not applicable.

**Data Availability Statement:** Not applicable.

Conflicts of Interest: The author declares no conflict of interest.

## References


1. Guth, A. Inflationary universe: A possible solution to the horizon and flatness problems. *Phys. Rev. D* **1981**, *23*, 347–356. [CrossRef]
2. Saadeh, D.; Feeney, S.; Pontzen, A.; Peiris, H.; McEwen, J.D. How isotropic is the Universe? *Phys. Rev. Lett.* **2016**, *117*, 131302. [CrossRef]
3. Goldwirth, D.S. Inhomogeneous initial conditions for inflation. *Phys. Rev. D* **1991**, *43*, 3204–3213. [CrossRef]
4. Clough, K.; Lim, E.A.; Di Nunno, B.S.; Fischler, W.; Flauger, R.; Paban, S. Robustness of Inflation to Inhomogeneous Initial Conditions. *J. Cosmol. Astropart. Phys.* **2017**, *2017*, 025. [CrossRef]
5. Ellis, G.F.R.; Madsen, M.S. Exact scalar field cosmologies. *Class. Quantum Gravity* **1991**, *8*, 667–676. [CrossRef]
6. Ram, B. Infinitely many solutions of Einstein cosmology in 'slow roll'. *Phys. Lett. A* **1993**, *172*, 404–406. [CrossRef]
7. Barrow, J.D.; Saich, P. Scalar field cosmologies. *Class. Quantum Gravity* **1993**, *10*, 297. [CrossRef]
8. Maartens, R.; Taylor, D.R.; Roussos, N. Exact inflationary cosmologies with exit. *Phys. Rev. D* **1995**, *52*, 3358. [CrossRef]
9. Barrow, J.D.; Paliathanasis, A. Observational Constraints on New Exact Inflationary Scalar-field Solutions. *Phys. Rev. D* **2016**, *94*, 083518. [CrossRef]
10. Chimento, L.P.; Jakubi, A.S. Scalar field cosmologies with perfect fluid in robertson-walker metric. *Int. J. Mod. Phys. D* **1996**, *5*, 71. [CrossRef]
11. Banerjee, N.; Sen, S. Power law inflation and scalar field cosmology with a causal viscous fluid. *Phys. Rev. D* **1998**, *57*, 4614–4619. [CrossRef]
12. Chimento, L.P.; Mendez, V.; Zuccala, N. Cosmological models arising from generalized scalar field potentials. *Class. Quantum Gravity* **1999**, *16*, 3749–3763. [CrossRef]
13. Kruger, A.T.; Norburry, J.W. Another exact inflationary solution. *Phys. Rev. D* **2000**, *61*, 087303. [CrossRef]
14. Andrianov, A.A.; Cannata, F.; Kamenshchik, A.Y. General solution of scalar field cosmology with a (piecewise) exponential potential. *J. Cosmol. Astropart. Phys.* **2011**, *10*, 004. [CrossRef]
15. Demianski, M.; de Ritis, R.; Rubano, C.; Scudellaro, P. Scalar fields and anisotropy in cosmological models. *Phys. Rev. D* **1992**, *46*, 1391–1398. [CrossRef]
16. Chimento, L.P.; Cossarini, A.E.; Zuccala, N.A. Isotropic and anisotropic N-dimensional cosmologies with exponential potentials. *Class. Quantum Gravity* **1998**, *15*, 57–74. [CrossRef]
17. Fadragas, C.R.; Leon, G.; Saridakis, E.N. Dynamical analysis of anisotropic scalar-field cosmologies for a wide range of potentials. *Class. Quantum Gravity* **2014**, *31*, 075018. [CrossRef]
18. Tsamparlis, M.; Paliathanasis, A. The geometric nature of Lie and Noether symmetries. *Gen. Relativ. Gravit.* **2011**, *43*, 1861. [CrossRef]
19. Christodoulakis, T.; Grammenos, T.; Helias, C.; Kevrekidis, P.G.; Spanou, A. Decoupling of the general scalar field mode and the solution space for Bianchi type I and V cosmologies coupled to perfect fluid sources. *J. Math. Phys.* **2006**, *47*, 042505. [CrossRef]
20. Do, T.Q.; Kao, W.F. Anisotropic power-law inflation for a model of two scalar and two vector fields. *Eur. Phys. J. C* **2021**, *81*, 525. [CrossRef]
21. Faraoni, V.; Jose, S.; Dussault, S. Multi-fluid cosmology in Einstein gravity: Analytical solutions. *arXiv* **2021**, arXiv:2107.12488.
22. Di Valentino, E.; Mena, O.; Pan, S.; Visinelli, L.; Yang, W.; Melchiorri, A.; Mota, D.F.; Riess, A.G.; Silk, J. In the Realm of the Hubble tension—A Review of Solutions. *Class. Quantum Gravity* **2021**, *38*, 153001. [CrossRef]
23. Cai, Y.-F.; Saridakis, E.; Setare, M.R.; Xia, J.-Q. Quintom Cosmology: Theoretical implications and observations. *Phys. Rep.* **2010**, *493*, 1–60. [CrossRef]
24. Coley, A.A.; Hoogen, R.V.D. The Dynamics of Multi-Scalar Field Cosmological Models and Assisted Inflation. *Phys. Rev. D* **2000**, *92*, 023517. [CrossRef]
25. Calcagni, G.; Liddle, A.R. Stability of multifield cosmological solutions. *Phys. Rev. D* **2008**, *77*, 023522. [CrossRef]
26. Collinucci, A.; Nielsen, M.; Van Riet, T. Scalar cosmology with multi-exponential potentials. *Class. Quantum Gravity* **2005**, *22*, 1269–1287. [CrossRef]
27. Paliathanasis, A. Dynamics of Chiral Cosmology. *Class. Quantum Gravity* **2020** *37*, 195014. [CrossRef]
28. Christodoulidis, P.; Paliathanasis, A. N-field cosmology in hyperbolic field space: Stability and general solutions. *J. Cosmol. Astropart. Phys.* **2021**, *5*, 038. [CrossRef]
29. Christodoulidis, P. General solutions to N-field cosmology with exponential potentials. *Eur. Phys. J. C* **2021**, *81*, 471. [CrossRef]
30. Socorro, J.; Pérez-Payán, S.; Hernández, R.; Espinoza-García, A.; Díaz-Barrón, L.R. Classical and quantum exact solutions for a FRW in chiral like cosmology. *Class. Quantum Gravity* **2021**, *38*, 135027. [CrossRef]
31. Socorro, J.; Nuñez, O.E. Scalar potentials with multi-scalar fields from quantum cosmology and supersymmetric quantum mechanics. *Eur. Phys. J. Plus* **2017**, *132*, 168. [CrossRef]
32. Díaz-Barrón, L.R.; Espinoza-García, A.; Pérez-Payán, S.; Socorro, J. Anisotropic chiral cosmology: Exact solutions. *Int. J. Mod. Phys. D.* **2021**, in press. [CrossRef]
33. Ketov, S.V. *Quantum Non-linear Sigma Models*; Springer: Berlin, Germany, 2000.
34. Chervon, S.V. Chiral Cosmological Models: Dark Sector Fields Description. *Quantum Matter* **2013**, *2*, 71–82. [CrossRef]
35. Brown, A.R. Hyperbolic Inflation. *Phys. Rev. Lett.* **2018**, *121*, 251601. [CrossRef]

36. Mizuno, S.; Mukohyama, S. Primordial perturbations from inflation with a hyperbolic field-space. *Phys. Rev. D* **2017**, *96*, 103533. [CrossRef]
37. Lyth, D.H. A numerical study of non-gaussianity in the curvaton scenario. *J. Cosmol. Astropart. Phys.* **2006**, *2006*, 008.
38. Langlois, D.; Renaux-Peterl, S. Perturbations in generalized multi-field inflation. *J. Cosmol. Astropart. Phys.* **2008**, *2008*, 017. [CrossRef]
39. Christodoulidis, P.; Roest, D.; Sfakianakis, E.I. Scaling attractors in multi-field inflation. *J. Cosmol. Astropart. Phys.* **2019**, *2019*, 059. [CrossRef]
40. Christodoulidis, P.; Roest, D.; Sfakianakis, E.I. Angular inflation in multi-field $\alpha$-attractors. *J. Cosmol. Astropart. Phys.* **2019**, *2019*, 002. [CrossRef]
41. Paliathanasis, A.; Tsamparlis, M. Two scalar field cosmology: Conservation laws and exact solutions. *Phys. Rev. D* **2014**, *90*, 103524. [CrossRef]
42. Giacomini, A.; Gonzalez, E.; Leon, G.; Paliathanasis, A. Variational symmetries and superintegrability in multifield cosmology. *arXiv* **2021**, arXiv:2104.13649.
43. Paliathanasis, A.; Leon, G. Dynamics of a two scalar field cosmological model with phantom terms. *Class. Quantum Gravity* **2021**, *38*, 075013. [CrossRef]
44. Tsamparlis, M.; Paliathanasis, A. Symmetries of Differential Equations in Cosmology. *Symmetry* **2018**, *10*, 233. [CrossRef]
45. Mendes, L.E.; Henriques, A. Inflation in a simple Kantowski–Sachs model. *Phys. Lett. B* **1991**, *254*, 44–48. [CrossRef]
46. Gron, O. Expansion isotropization during the inflationary era. *Phys. Rev. D* **1985**, *32*, 2522–2527. [CrossRef] [PubMed]
47. Liddle, A.R.; Parson, P.; Barrow, J.D. Formalising the Slow-Roll Approximation in Inflation. *Phys. Rev. D* **1994**, *50*, 7222–7232. [CrossRef]

*universe*

MDPI

*Article*

# Elongated Gravity Sources as an Analytical Limit for Flat Galaxy Rotation Curves

**Felipe J. Llanes-Estrada**

Departamento de Física Teórica and IPARCOS, Institute for Particle and Cosmological Physics, Universidad Complutense de Madrid, 28040 Madrid, Spain; fllanes@fis.ucm.es; Tel.: +34-913-944-460

**Abstract:** The flattening of spiral-galaxy rotation curves is unnatural in view of the expectations from Kepler's third law and a central mass. It is interesting, however, that the radius-independence velocity is what one expects in one less dimension. In our three-dimensional space, the rotation curve is natural if, outside the galaxy's center, the gravitational potential corresponds to that of a very prolate ellipsoid, filament, string, or otherwise cylindrical structure perpendicular to the galactic plane. While there is observational evidence (and numerical simulations) for filamentary structure at large scales, this has not been discussed at scales commensurable with galactic sizes. If, nevertheless, the hypothesis is tentatively adopted, the scaling exponent of the baryonic Tully–Fisher relation due to accretion of visible matter by the halo comes out to reasonably be 4. At a minimum, this analytical limit would suggest that simulations yielding prolate haloes would provide a better overall fit to small-scale galaxy data.

**Keywords:** galactic rotation; nonspherical gravitational sources; modified gravity

**Citation:** Llanes-Estrada, F.J. Elongated Gravity Sources as an Analytical Limit for Flat Galaxy Rotation Curves. *Universe* **2021**, *7*, 346. https://doi.org/10.3390/universe7090346

Academic Editors: Panayiotis Stavrinos and Emmanuel N. Saridakis

Received: 14 August 2021
Accepted: 11 September 2021
Published: 14 September 2021



## 1. Introduction

With decades of effort [1], it has been established that the rotation speed of spiral galaxies is largely independent of the distance to their center, $v \sim$ constant, even well beyond the end of the luminous matter distribution, whereas Kepler's third law applied to a point-like mass or spherical source yields $v \sim 1/\sqrt{r}$. This unexpected result (see Figure 1 for a small sample of the SPARC data) is usually interpreted by (a) there being non-luminous matter spherically distributed with a very specific radial dependence, which is actively searched for in the laboratory (Dark Matter), or (b) Newton's law of gravitation is failing for small centripetal acceleration (Modified Newtonian Dynamics), and the force law is different, yielding to a modified Kepler's first law.

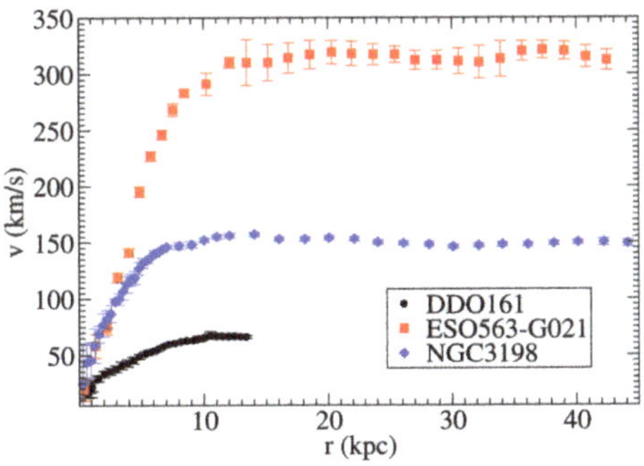


**Figure 1.** Galactic rotation curves show a flat (distance-independent) rotation velocity at large distances to the galactic center (data sample from Reference [2], SPARC collaboration).

Investigations on the first possibility have concentrated on spherical galactic haloes. However, much evidence of dark matter in present-day cosmology seems consistent with it having filamentary structure at large scales. Thus, it is reasonable to ask oneself down to what scale is that filamentary organization meaningful.

At least for scales commensurable with those galaxy-sized ones, statistical gravitational lensing analysis (stacking galaxy pairs) [3] is an interesting indication that there actually are matter filaments extending between galaxies, though no actual filament has been individually resolved, to my knowledge.

Figure 2 sketches the point of this article that there may be merit in allowing dark matter at the galactic scale (~10–100 kpc) to be organized in a cylindrical or otherwise elongated, rather than spherical, geometry. A difference between spherical and elongated gravitational-source distributions is the local density of dark matter at a given point in the galactic equator, where elongated sources would assign a smaller density, concentrating it instead along the polar regions.

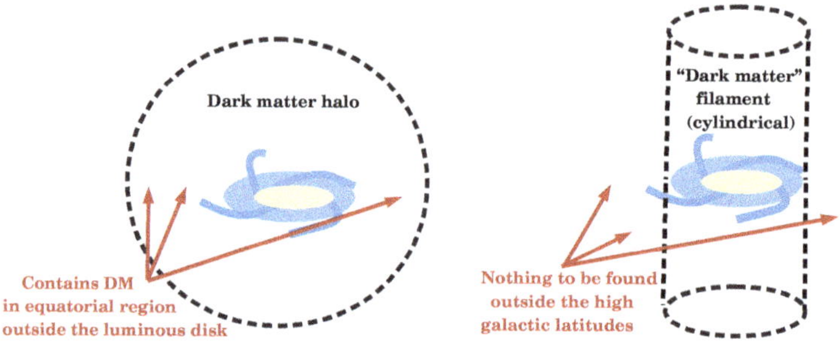


**Figure 2.** (**Left**): A spherical halo of dark matter extending much beyond the disk of spiral galaxies. The radial dependence of that mass distribution that yields a flat rotation curve is the quite unique $\rho_{DM} \propto r^{-2}$. This can be obtained from hydrostatic equilibrium with an isothermal distribution, but requires that dark matter is thermalized, involving some heat transfer mechanism (at odds with dark matter particles being very weakly interacting). (**Right**): A cylindrical distribution extending from the galactic polar regions explains flat rotation curves without any fine tuning: they are the natural consequence of such gravitational source independently of its nature (whether dark matter or otherwise) without having to abandon Newtonian mechanics for MOND or other modifications. An immediate consequence of such geometry is that dark matter searches (by lensing or otherwise) at low galactic latitudes have less scope.

## 2. Most Common Explanations for Flat Rotation Curves

### *2.1. Kepler's Problem*

The solar system responds mostly to the concentration of mass at its center in the sun. Circular orbit equilibrium, together with Newton's gravitation law, demands that

$$m\frac{v^2}{r} = \frac{GM_\odot m}{r^2}, \tag{1}$$

that is the simplest illustration of Kepler's third law ($T^2 \propto r^3$). Solving for the rotation velocity $v$, one finds a velocity falling with the square root of the distance to the center

$$v = \frac{\sqrt{GM}}{\sqrt{r}} . \tag{2}$$

This simple law works flawlessly in the solar system down to a precision of $10^{-3}$–$10^{-4}$, at which level perturbations, largely due to Jupiter and other planets, become important (see Section 5.2 below).

However, extrapolating the law to galactic rotation curves, as seen in Figure 1, becomes a startling failure, which has been a driver of much research in astrophysics: rotation curves reach a plateau with an approximately constant velocity $v_\infty \sim 30$–300 km/s for tens of kiloparsec, very much unlike Equation (2). Sometimes, modifications of General Relativity are invoked as an explanation of the discrepancy, but a nonrelativistic, Newtonian treatment should suffice to a reasonable precision since

$$\frac{v_{\text{galaxy}}}{c} = \frac{(30-300)\ \text{km/s}}{(3\times 10^5\ \text{km/s})} = O(10^{-3}) \tag{3}$$

or less. A much explored possibility is to modify Newton's laws, as recalled later in Section 2.3.

Alternatively, since luminous matter in galaxies stops being dense enough well before that flatness sets in, a dark matter halo that produces no light is most often postulated, that I briefly recall in the next section, Section 2.2.

Indeed, if the orbit is inside the mass distribution, the mass in Equation (2) refers to that of the inner sphere with the orbit as equator (from Gauss's law), $M(r)$. For example, a constant density cloud would yield $M(r) = \frac{4\pi}{3}r^3\rho$ and a linearly-growing velocity field

$$v = \sqrt{\frac{4}{3}\pi G\rho}\, r, \tag{4}$$

not unlike what is observed for small $r$ in usual rotation curves, such as the example in Figure 1.

To obtain a constant velocity $v \simeq v_\infty$, independent of $r$, the density in the square root of Equation (4) needs to cancel the $r$ outside and, therefore, behave as $\rho \propto \frac{1}{r^2}$.

### 2.2. Standard Isothermal, Spherical Dark Matter Halo

Hydrostatic, nonrelativistic, equilibrium in a standard spherical halo made of fluid-like matter dictates

$$\frac{dP}{dr} = -\frac{G\rho(r)}{r^2}\int_0^r 4\pi r'^2\rho(r')dr', \tag{5}$$

so that inner layers of the halo, at a higher pressure, can support the weight of the outer ones.

The ideal gas law is usually employed to eliminate the pressure, so that

$$P(r) = \frac{k_B}{m}T(r)\rho(r)\,, \tag{6}$$

with $m$ the typical "particle" matter, and $T(r)$ the temperature field.

Taking a derivative of Equation (5) with respect to $r$, to convert it into a pure differential equation, one finds [4]

$$\frac{k_B}{m}\frac{d}{dr}\left(\frac{r^2}{\rho(r)}\frac{d}{dr}(T(r)\rho(r))\right) = -4\pi G r^2\rho(r)\,. \tag{7}$$

Under the hypothesis that the dark matter halo has reached a uniform temperature (and it is not known how this happens, as it depends on the dark matter interactions, but requires some sort of heat conduction between different spherical shells), one finds easily that the equation admits the power-law solution

$$\rho \propto \frac{1}{r^2}\,. \tag{8}$$

This behavior is exactly what is needed to produce the observed flat rotation curves.

On the contrary, experimental searches for particulate dark matter at colliders [5] (through production of dark matter particles), at underground laboratories [6,7] (through direct detection by collisions with nuclei), or at gamma-ray or other particle observatories [8] (through indirect detection of presumed decay products) have all come up empty-handed.

Searches for macroscopic-sized dark matter constituents, such as Massive Compact Halo Objects, by gravitational lensing and by binary star disruption [9], have yielded stringent constraints that leave little space for the existence of large dark matter chunks in the halo. An exception that is still standing is the possibility of $O(100M_\odot)$ black holes [10].

### 2.3. Modified Newtonian Dynamics

An alternative to dark matter that naturally explains galaxy rotation curves is Modified Newtonian Dynamics (MOND) [11]. The basic idea is to postulate a new scale $a_0 \sim 1.2 \times 10^{-10}$ m/s$^2$ such that the acceleration caused by a force depends on its size respective to this scale,

$$\begin{array}{ll} a > a_0 & a_{\rm Newton} = \frac{MG}{r^2} \\ a < a_0 & a = \sqrt{a_0 a_{\rm Newton}} \end{array} . \tag{9}$$

This recipe was thereafter formulated as an Effective Field Theory in the gravitational potential and given shape as a bimetric theory of gravity [12].

A key prediction of MOND that is observationally a reasonable success is that the exponent of the baryonic Tully–Fisher relation (discussed below in Section 5) is exactly equal to 4, so that $M_{\rm luminous} \propto v_\infty^4$. The intensity of the second peak of the cosmic microwave background was also successfully predicted.

Another modification of the theory of gravity has been applied to the explanation of galactic data by Varieschi in a series of articles contemporary to the present manuscript [13–15]. The idea is that of so-called "Newtonian Fractional-Dimension Gravity" (NFDG). If the space dimension is generalized from the integer 3 to a real number $D$, while demanding Gauss's law, the Newtonian potential becomes

$$\begin{array}{rcl} \tilde{\phi}(\mathbf{r}/\mathbf{l_0}) & = & -\frac{2\pi^{1-D/2}\Gamma(D/2)}{l_0(D-2)} \int_{\Omega_D} d^D(\mathbf{r}'/l_0) \frac{\rho(\mathbf{r}')l_0^3}{|\mathbf{r}/l_0 - \mathbf{r}'/l_0|^{D/2}} \quad D \neq 2 \\ \tilde{\phi}(\mathbf{r}/\mathbf{l_0}) & = & \int_{\Omega_2} d^2(\mathbf{r}'/l_0) \frac{2G}{l_0} \rho(\mathbf{r}') l_0^3 \ln|\mathbf{r}/l_0 - \mathbf{r}'/l_0| \quad D = 2\,. \end{array} \tag{10}$$

For $D = 2$, this modified-gravity theory achieves the asymptotic flatness that is thoroughly compared with MOND predictions in those works (additionally, MOND can be directly derived from fractional gravity [16,17]). Moreover, it can also reproduce a non-flat behavior of the galactic rotation curves by being able to smoothly interpolating between $D = 3$ (conventional gravity) and $D = 2$. In this aspect, the approach is akin to those with dark matter distributions controlled by one parameter. It will be interesting to see what its implications are for yet larger scales: if it stabilizes in $D = 2$ or it continues decreasing into distances relevant for cosmology. Substituting the factor 3 in the Friedmann-Robertson-Walker equations by $D$ must lead to a very different cosmological model.

Problems with large scale data are already an issue for MOND: the intensity of the 3rd peak in the cosmic microwave background, the galaxy power spectrum, the gravitational lensing in galactic cumuli, and, generically, observables at scales much larger than the 100 kpc one for which MOND was conceived, have turned out to be disappointing [18]. To bring MOND into broad agreement with data, various authors typically supplement it with additional matter [11] (such as sterile neutrinos, vector fields as in the TeVeS formulation, etc.). Its advantages over dark matter-based formulations are then blurred.

Even more so, the claimed evidence for galaxies without dark matter [19] and the analysis of the bullet cluster [20], where dark and conventional matter would be separated, plays against MOND as therein no effect beyond what luminous matter suggests is visible: whereas dark matter is contingent on accretion, modified gravity cannot be taken away from conventional matter.

Finally, adoption of MOND would force us to abandon the theoretically compelling nonrelativistic Newtonian theory, in which the flux of the gravitational field is conserved, so that its spreading in our three-dimensional world dilutes it over a $4\pi r^2$ sphere yielding the $1/r^2$ law of gravity, and translational invariance implies Newton's second law with the conventional acceleration. MOND is unconvincing for most theorists.

However, the working recipe of Equation (9) to obtain the right galaxy rotation curves can be obtained in a different, simple way.

## 3. Cylindrical Symmetry of the Gravitational Source

What MOND achieves by taking the square root of a constant times the $1/r^2$ force is to moderate its falloff to $1/r$, the geometric mean.

However, Gauss's law suggests that $F \propto 1/r$ is the natural one in a two-dimensional world. This is achieved routinely in electrostatics with a cylindrical/filamentary source running from $-\infty$ to $\infty$, yielding translational invariance along the $OZ$ axis and effectively leaving a two-dimensional theory in the perpendicular directions. Thus, while, in three-dimension, $F \propto 1/r^2$ implies $v^2 \propto 1/r$ (Kepler's law), in two-dimension, $F \propto 1/r$ brings the desired $v^2 \propto$ constant about.

To see it, recall that the gravitational acceleration around a cylindrical mass distribution, in cylindrical coordinates $(r, \phi, z)$, takes the form $\vec{g} = g(r)\hat{r}$ by symmetry. Its flux outwards of a pillbox of height $a$ surrounding the cylinder is

$$\Phi = \int_0^a dz \int_0^{2\pi} r d\phi \hat{r} \cdot \vec{g} = (2\pi a) r g(r) \tag{11}$$

through its side, and zero through its lids. Because of Gauss's law, the flux is also

$$\Phi = -2\pi a \int_0^r \rho \Delta V(\rho) d\rho = -(4\pi G) m \tag{12}$$

in terms of the gravitational potential, with $\vec{g} = -\nabla V$ and with $m$ the mass contained by the pillbox. If the linear mass density of the cylinder is

$$\lambda = \frac{dm}{dz}, \tag{13}$$

combining Equations (11) and (12) yields

$$\vec{g} = \frac{-2G\lambda\hat{r}}{r}, \tag{14}$$

that, of course, stems from a potential

$$V(r) = 2G\lambda \ln\left(\frac{r}{r_0}\right). \tag{15}$$

As it diverges at large $r$, its zero needs to be arbitrarily chosen at a certain $r_0$.

This is a staple discussion of any textbook covering electrostatics, and the potential is the natural one conserving the integrated flux out of the source in a reduced 2-dimensional problem. However, it is not often discussed in the context of gravitational interactions because of the scarcity of known large cylindrical sources of gravity.

The extraction of the rotation velocity mirroring that of Section 2.1 proceeds by again equating the gravitational and centripetal forces for a circular orbit

$$mg = \frac{2mG\lambda}{r}. \tag{16}$$

This indeed yields a distance-independent rotation velocity,

$$v^2 = 2G\lambda. \tag{17}$$

This formula contains one independent parameter, $\lambda = m/L$, the linear mass–density of the cylindrical source, and notably absent is $R$, the radius of the cylinder in the transverse direction to be discussed shortly.

Let me put some figures to Equation (17). Conveniently, take the velocity in terms of a dimensionless parameter of order 1, $v = v_{100}$ (100 km/s), and substitute Cavendish's constant $G$ so that

$$\lambda = 1.16 v_{100}^2 \times 10^{12} M_{\odot}/\mathrm{Mpc}\,. \tag{18}$$

For the Andromeda galaxy, $v_{100} \simeq 2.2$; therefore, $\lambda = 5.6 \times 10^{12} M_{\odot}/$ Mpc. To understand this number, we need to think that a Megaparsec of such filament (the typical galaxy–galaxy separation) contains about 7 times the stellar mass of Andromeda, $M^{\mathrm{stellar}} \simeq 8 \times 10^{11} M_{\odot}$ This means that such filamentary structure is compatible with the overall dark matter fraction needed for the cosmic sum rule $\Omega_\Lambda + \Omega_{DM} + \Omega_b = 1$ in present day's cosmology, with $\Omega_b \sim 4\%$ and $\Omega_{DM} \sim 23\%$.

### 3.1. Corrections to a Basic Filamentary Geometry

Next, let us relax the assumption of an infinitely long cylinder of unspecified radius and see the corrections brought about by various geometrical modifications.

#### 3.1.1. Finite-Length Cylinder

First, consider a finite cylinder that, instead of extending over the entire OZ axis $(-\infty, \infty)$, does so only over the interval $(-a, a)$.

Matter naturally accretes to the horizontal plane by the center of the cylinder where the gravitational potential is minimum, and, there, Equation (17) is replaced by

$$v_{\mathrm{equator}} \simeq \sqrt{2G\lambda(1 - \frac{r^2}{2a^2})}\,. \tag{19}$$

Thus, the end of the filament threading, the galaxy is reflected in the velocity field starting to falloff at sufficient distance.

There is scarce data suggesting such fall for most galaxies in the SPARC catalogue. However, it can be accommodated within the uncertainty bands of the velocity measured. With typical error of 10 km/s in $v = 200$ km/s, we can propagate the error backwards and find

$$a \geq 1.6\, r_{\mathrm{break}}, \tag{20}$$

with $r_{\mathrm{break}}$ being the point at which the constant velocity law might start breaking down.

Data for our neighboring Andromeda galaxy has been reported, suggesting that, at 100 kpc, the velocity field starts diminishing in modulus [21]. Taking that data at face value, for Andromeda $r_{\mathrm{break}} \sim 0.1$ Mpc) implies an elongated source out to at most a similar length.

#### 3.1.2. Finite-Width Cylinder

If the density of a finite-sized cylinder of radius $R$ is uniform, $\rho =$ constant, the linear density becomes quadratic $\lambda(r) = 2\pi \int_0^r r' dr' \rho(r') \propto r^2$, and the velocity field inside the cylinder shows a linear rise,

$$v = \sqrt{2G\lambda}\frac{r}{R}\,. \tag{21}$$

Matching this to the flat rotation curve of Equation (17) yields a reasonable first-order explanation of typical spiral rotation, as shown in Figure 3.

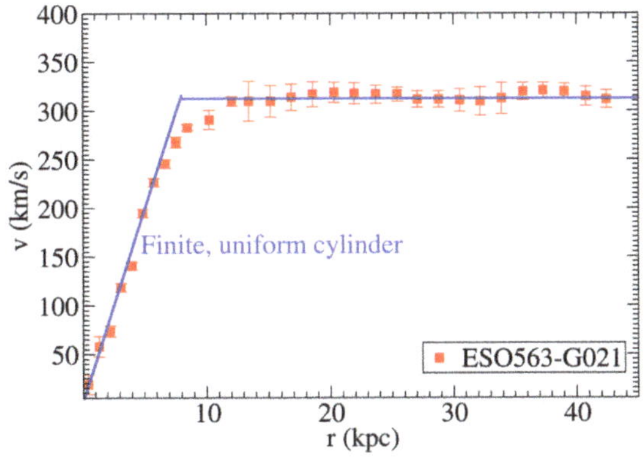


**Figure 3.** A linear rise out to a radius $R$ given by Equation (21), followed by a flat $v_\infty = \sqrt{2G\lambda}$, is a reasonable first approximation to numerous spiral galaxy rotation curves, and follows from a finite-sized cylinder of uniform density. Of course, edge effects or other density profiles could be included in extensive studies.

With a power law density profile, one would obtain an additional factor of $(1 - \frac{2}{\alpha+2}(r/R)^\alpha)$ that I have not yet attempted to match to the data (An extended study of the entire SPARC database with several different geometries is underway [22], and the resulting $\chi^2$ distributions will be reported elsewhere.).

### 3.1.3. Rotation Curve Outside a Sphere + Filament Distribution Arrangement

One can combine the leading cylindrical mass distribution with a smaller spherical one that can represent the visible matter bulge (and only very crudely, the monopole contribution of the galactic disk).

In terms of the cylinder's linear mass density and of the sphere's mass, the velocity field takes the form

$$v = \sqrt{2G\lambda + \frac{GM}{r}}, \tag{22}$$

that converges $v \to v_\infty = \sqrt{2G\lambda}$ at large radii. The SPARC data file offers examples of rotation curves where this effect might be visible, and one of them is plotted in Figure 4.

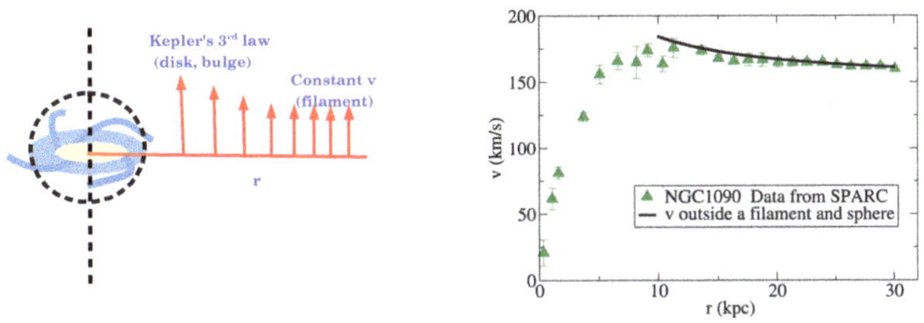


**Figure 4. Left**: Scheme showing how the velocity falls towards the asymptotic limit given by the filament alone, as the contribution of the sphere becomes smaller as per Kepler's third law. **Right**: An example galaxy curve extracted off the SPARC database where the effect might be visible.

## 4. Classical Equations of Motion Outside the Filament

The cylindrical symmetry and the conservative gravitational potential provide us with two constants of motion: the energy $E_0$ and angular momentum along the cylinder's axis $L_z$. This means that, out of the three second-order differential equations for the cylindrical coordinates $(r, \varphi, z)$, two can be integrated once. If these are chosen to be that for $\varphi$ and that for $r$, Newton's equations become

$$\dot{\varphi} = \frac{L_z}{mr^2} \tag{23}$$
$$\ddot{z} = \frac{-GMz}{(z^2+r^2)^{3/2}}$$
$$\dot{r} = \sqrt{\frac{2E_0}{m} - \frac{L_z^2}{2m^2r^2} - \dot{z}^2 + \frac{2GM}{\sqrt{r^2+z^2}} - 4G\lambda\ln(r)},$$

in which the potential due to the cylinder appears in the square root,

$$V(r) = 4G\lambda\ln(r)\,. \tag{24}$$

The first two of Equation (23) are the same as in the planar Kepler problem. It is the third one that shows a difference due to the presence of the cylinder. We next explore a few consequences of these equations.

### 4.1. Helicoidal Motion along the Filament

The first kind of motion is helicoidal along a filament, sketched in Figure 5, with $r$ constant, $\dot{r} = 0$, $\dot{z}$, and $\dot{\varphi}$ also constant.

Though, in late-time cosmology, the voids around the filaments have little matter to accrete, matter can still hop from galaxy to galaxy along the cylinders in a helicoidal manner. This costs only the gravitational energy needed to escape the field of the luminous matter in the galaxy disk, while the displacement along the filament, because of Equation (23), takes place with constant $v_z$, or $\frac{dv_z}{dt} = 0$ far from the galaxy.

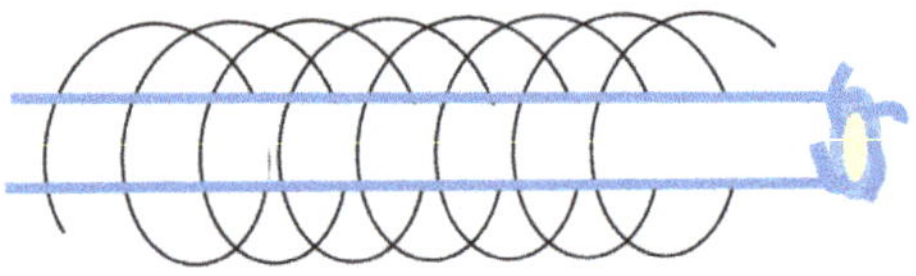

**Figure 5.** At large distance from any galaxy, movement along cosmic web filaments is helicoidal. This is well known from the movement along a $B$ field in electrodynamics; the difference here is that not only charged particles, but also neutral objects (whether gas or any sort of aggregate), by the equivalence principle, follow the helix. The trajectory is stretched by the galaxy upon approaching it when the acceleration due to the extra mass at the end is felt.

#### 4.1.1. Cyclotron/Synchrotron Radiation

When charged particles follow such helicoidal trajectory, they radiate. The phenomenon is analogous to circular trajectories in a magnetic field, but there are several curious differences that I now expose.

Unlike in conventional magnetic synchrotrons, the rotation around the filament, by construction (after all, that is what yields flat galaxy rotation curves) occurs with constant perpendicular velocity

$$v_\perp^2 = \frac{2G\lambda}{\gamma}, \tag{25}$$

where, if the motion is relativistic, the Lorentz time-dilation factor $\gamma > 1$ has to be taken into account. The gyration period then grows with distance, so that the angular frequency falls with $r$,

$$\omega = \frac{\sqrt{2G\lambda}}{\sqrt{\gamma}r} \tag{26}$$

(compare this with the equivalent $(eB)/(\gamma m_e c)$, an $r$-independent constant, in a $B$ field).

The characteristic frequency can then be read off the conventional synchrotron theory but substituting for the $\omega$ in Equation (26) as

$$\nu_{\text{char}} = 0.29\frac{3}{2}\gamma^{2.5}\frac{\sqrt{2G\lambda}}{r}, \tag{27}$$

and the total power emitted as

$$P = \frac{2}{3}\frac{e^2}{c^3}\gamma^4\left(\frac{2G\lambda}{\gamma r}\right)^2. \tag{28}$$

A first remarkable property of these expressions is the dependence in $e^2\lambda$ as opposed to the $e^4$ dependence of conventional radiation (the $e^2$ from emitting photons is common to both, but the force to turn the trajectory is $\propto e^2$ in the Lorentz force case, $\propto \lambda$ in the gravitational one). A second difference is the inverse-$r$ dependence that distinguishes it from radiation in a uniform $B$-field. The integrated emission is dominated by the inner electrons in the radial distribution, since $\int_R n(r)dr/r^2 \simeq n/R$ diverges for small $R$.

These observables serve to distinguish between an infinitely thin filament (such as a cosmic string) and a cylinder of more or less uniform density. In the first case, electrons near the filament ($R \to 0$) strongly radiate synchrotron power, which should be observable. In that case, additionally, a clear prediction is that this polar synchrotron radiation is correlated with the galactic rotation parameter $\sqrt{2G\lambda}$.

In the second case, a finite cylinder with $\lambda_{\text{inside}}(r) \propto r^2$, the maximum emission happens at the filament's edge; however, $R$ being now of galactic $\sim$ 10 kpc scale, the frequency and power are very suppressed, and the radiation is negligible.

It is known that numerous elliptical galaxies, for example, M87, radiate synchrotron-like along a filament (likely due to jet emission). There seem to be only four known spiral galaxies that radiate in the same way: J1352+3126, J1159+5820, J1649+2635, and J083+0532. These sources are not found in the SPARC database, so that I cannot presently answer whether their synchrotron radiation is or not correlated with their rotation velocity. We really should not expect this, but that would be a fun observation.

4.1.2. Galactic Aurora

It is well known that matter being pushed in jets out of an active galactic nucleus, for example, can heat up the medium and radiate. However, the situation is symmetric, and there can be matter propagating along the filament that falls into a galaxy from the poles. The produced radiation would be totally analogous to the phenomenon of the Aurora when charged particles fall on Earth following its magnetic field. Except, once more, neutral gas and matter chunks moving along the filament can now also cause it.

The effect could be similar to known axial structures, for example, the $\gamma$-ray bubbles of Fermi/LAT (respectively, the X-ray emission of ROSAT) over the north and under the south poles of the Milky Way [23].

*4.2. Radial Motion towards the Filament*

The purely radial motion towards the cylinder, far from the galaxy (large $z$) and with vanishing angular momentum $L_z = 0$, is interesting by itself, to evaluate the time that it takes for a filament to empty its environment by accreting all available matter.

The resulting one-dimensional radial equation from Equation (23) yields a time for moving a parcel of matter from distance $d$ into the cylinder radius $R$ given by

$$t = \int_d^R \frac{dr}{\sqrt{4G\lambda}\log^{1/2}\left(\frac{d}{r}\right)}. \tag{29}$$

Upon substituting a typical value for $\sqrt{4G\lambda} \simeq 10^{-3}c \simeq 0.307$ Mpc/Myr, one obtains

$$t = 3.26\text{Gyr} \times \int_d^R \frac{dr(\text{Mpc})}{\log^{1/2}(d/r)}. \tag{30}$$

To clean up a distance out to $d = 1$ Mpc, and bring the material into $R = 0.1$ Mpc, the value of the integral (numerically evaluated) is 1.7, yielding $t = 5.7$ Gyr. This is, of course, the standard formation of empty bubbles seen in SDSS, as well as computer simulations. All matter has had time to accrete to nearby filaments during a Hubble time.

### *4.3. Precession of Orbits Outside but near the Galactic Plane*

Motion in the disk of the galaxy, supposed nearly perpendicular to the dark filament, is planar. However, perturbations above or below this plane put satellites in a precessing motion whose instantaneous plane is rotating around the axis (see Figure 6).

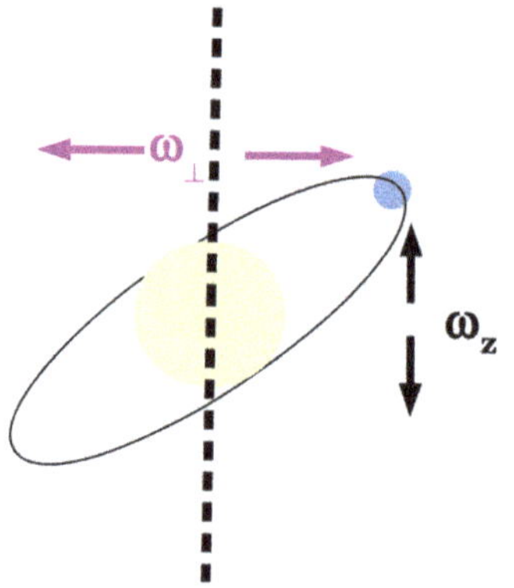


**Figure 6.** The generic motion of a satellite bound to the galaxy but off its disk's plane is not planar: the instantaneous orbital plane precesses around the cylinder. It can be seen by noting that the angular frequency of vertical motion $\omega_z$ coincides with that of the Newtonian problem, consistently with the translational invariance of the filament, but the oscillation angular frequency $\omega_\perp$ in the orbital plane differs due to the part of the force caused by $G\lambda$.

This comes about because vertical oscillation are unaffected by the cylinder and remain as in the two-body Keplerian problem: around $z = 0$,

$$\omega_z = \sqrt{\frac{GM}{r^3}} \tag{31}$$

(Kepler's third law), as can be seen from the second of Equation (23) corresponding to vertical motion.

Horizontal motion, however, returns to the same position with an angular frequency

$$\omega_\perp = \sqrt{\omega_z^2 + \frac{2G\lambda}{r^2}} = \sqrt{\omega_z^2 + \frac{v_{\perp\infty}^2}{r^2}} . \quad (32)$$

This is modified by the presence of the cylinder.

At certain radial distances, the resonance condition (that yields closed orbits) is met, and the ratio $\omega_z/\omega_\perp$ is a rational number, a quotient of two integers. These $r$s may be written as

$$r = \frac{GM}{v_{\perp\infty}^2}\left(\left(\frac{n}{m}\right)^2 - 1\right) . \quad (33)$$

Such distances would yield less chaotic, less collisional orbits around the cylinder+galaxy mass distribution. For integer $n/m$, the orbital times are too large [24]: with the Andromeda numbers, $GM/v_\infty^2 \simeq 166$ kpc. The smallest integer $n^2 - 1 = 3$ then yields about half a Mpc, which amounts to a 10 M lightyear circumference. Because $v_\perp \simeq 10^{-3}c$, the orbital time is of order $1/H$, commensurable with the entire lifetime of the universe. However, for rational (smaller) $n/m$, perhaps some regularity in the satellite distribution can be found which correlates with the galactic rotation velocity, as in Equation (33).

In truth, it is not strictly necessary to require dark matter structures perpendicular to the galactic plane; if the angle between the disk and the cylinder- or cigar-like distribution was notably less than 90 degrees, the movement on the plane of the disk itself would be similar, except for a projection factor between the radius $r$ on the disk and $r_\perp$, its projection over the plane perpendicular to the filament, now different enough to require different variables. This projection factor being constant, it would not be directly measurable in the disk motion but shifted to the linear mass density in Equation (17) through the velocity,

$$\lambda = \frac{v_\perp^2}{2G} \to \lambda_{\text{apparent}} = \frac{v^2}{2G} = \frac{v_\perp^2}{2G\cos^2\theta} . \quad (34)$$

However, what would be observable is the long-term precession of the galactic plane that might give rise to interesting structures in stellar streams [25] or satellites.

## 5. The Tully–Fisher Relation

The renowned empirical Tully–Fisher relation [26] relates magnitude (light) and linewidth (velocity dispersion, a proxy for mass) was originally applied to assist with the cosmic distance ladder.

However, the striking feature is that the first depends on visible, ordinary, baryonic matter, and the second, however, on the total matter, whether dark or not. This strongly suggests that we should set the amount of dark matter to be proportional to that of luminous matter, a feature that, from the point of view of dark matter theories, is a complex dynamical effect without a very clear explanation. MOND, however, does predict this effect, as it modifies the effect of matter respecting the proportionality $a \propto M$, and it is the distance-dependence that is modified.

This relation between was later extended to the "Baryonic Tully–Fisher relation" closer to the discussion of this article, a power-law constraint between the rotation velocity $v$ and the luminous mass $M_L \propto v^\alpha$.

### 5.1. Luminous Matter Accretion on a Filamentary Overdensity

First, let us assume that the filaments or cylinders are simply overdensities of dark matter. Then, if ordinary matter can fall towards any two nearby ones, it will do so towards the one exerting the largest force (see Figure 7).

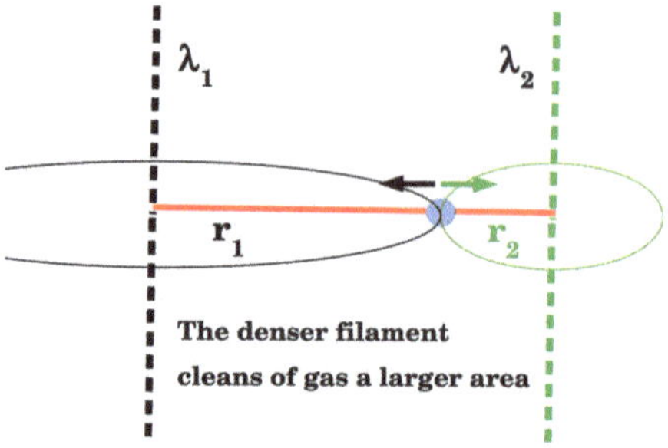


**Figure 7.** A denser dark matter filament cleans of luminous matter a larger area around it, with radius $r \propto \lambda$. The baryonic matter so accreted forms ordinary galaxies, so a dynamical (not exact) baryonic Tully–Fisher law follows, $M_{\rm luminous} \propto v^4$.

The force is proportional to the filament linear density and inversely proportional to the distance, $F \propto \frac{\lambda}{r}$, as per Equation (14). Therefore, the point at which the forces from two nearly parallel cylinders equilibrate is given by

$$\frac{r_1}{r_2} = \frac{\lambda_1}{\lambda_2} \, . \tag{35}$$

Thus, each dark filament cleans of gas an area extending out to $r \propto \lambda$. That area, taking a length $h$ along the $OZ$ axis, spans a volume $\pi r^2 h$; thus, it contains an amount of luminous matter given by

$$M_{\rm luminous} = \pi r^2 h \bar{\rho}_{\rm luminous} \, . \tag{36}$$

Thus, $M_{\rm luminous} \propto \lambda^2$ and, invoking Equation (17), that makes $\lambda \propto v^2$,

$$M_{\rm luminous} \propto v^4 \, . \tag{37}$$

Thus, the prediction of a cylindrically symmetric distribution of dark matter (or whatever gravitational source) coincides with that of Modified Newtonian Dynamics, that also yields an exponent of 4.

If we were to repeat the same reasoning for a spherical distribution, we would first have to argue for a density distribution $\rho \propto 1/r^2$ to yield a constant galactic rotation velocity (as in Equation (8)). A typical average density of dark matter $\bar{\rho}$ would follow from it, and $M \propto R^3$ would apply. Independently of that profile, taking $v_\infty$ beyond the end of the spherical distribution, $v_\infty \propto \sqrt{M}/\sqrt{R}$ (Kepler's third law), would then give $v_\infty \propto M^{1/3}$.

This proportionality would apply for all matter, luminous or otherwise. To convert it to a relation involving $M_{\rm luminous}$, we would need to consider that the (larger) volume cleaned in the accretion of luminous matter to the dark lump would have $R^2_{\rm accretion} \propto M$ from the force law from Equation (1). Since $M_{\rm luminous} \propto R^2_{\rm accretion}$, we would conclude that $M_{\rm luminous} \propto M^{3/2}$. Taking this to $v_\infty$ would finally yield

$$M_{\rm luminous} \propto v^{9/2} \quad \text{(sphere)}. \tag{38}$$

This is larger than and distinguishable from Equation (37). Obtaining other powers is possible with different assumptions, but the bottom line is that the sphere's relation has a larger exponent than the cylindrical one due to the different force law.

As typical data gives an exponent somewhere between 3 and 4 [27], it would perhaps suggest elongated geometry.

### *5.2. Scaling down to the Solar System*

In this subsection, alone, I discuss a point of view that is disfavored by mounting evidence from the bullet-cluster and galaxies devoid of dark matter, that the extra gravitation might still be due to a phenomenon attaching to ordinary matter (such as strings coupling to either of mass or its proxies, baryon or lepton number). This assumption elevates the Tully–Fisher relation from a dynamical effect to an actual law.

If that is the case, one could wonder how much would the effect be at solar system scales: could it be possible that a dark matter filament extended out of the solar poles and it had not been detected? This is actually not so easy to discard from planetary rotation measurements alone.

First, let us observe that the precision in the measurement of planet's distances $r$ ($a$), for example, Mercury, reaches $10^{-8}$ AU. Additionally, the measurement of their velocities is precise to $10^{-2}$ km/s. This yields a sensitivity floor on the $v(r)$ diagram below which no new effect would be visible yet (shaded band in Figure 8).

Because, under the assumption that the Tully–Fisher relation is exact and not a dynamical effect, $\lambda \propto M$, the known linear density of the filament associated to the entire galaxy can be rescaled to what would correspond to the solar system by means of $v \propto \sqrt{\lambda} \propto M$, so that, taking the ratio of the solar to the galactic mass,

$$v_{SS} = v_{\rm galaxy}\sqrt{\frac{1M_\odot}{(25.7 \pm 2.3) \times 10^{10} M_\odot}} \, . \tag{39}$$

Taking the resulting (dashed line) "flat velocity" to the solar system graph in Figure 8, we see that it comfortably lies two orders of magnitude below the precision achieved (which is already good enough to require isolation of much larger effects from conventional few-body classical mechanics).

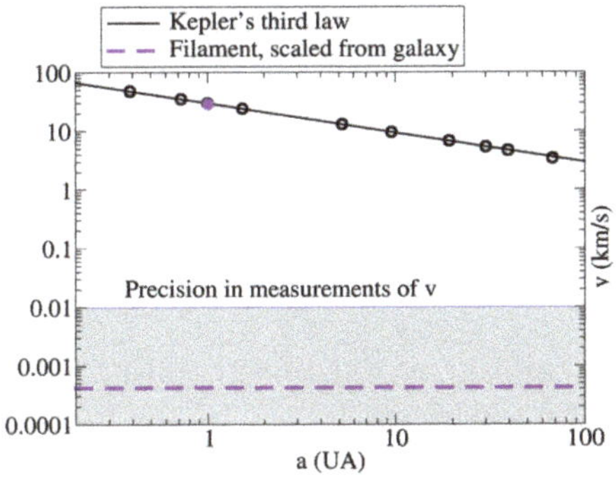


**Figure 8.** If the Tully–Fisher relation was an exact law and dark matter filaments were somehow attached to luminous matter, extrapolation of the flat rotation velocity (dashed line) from galaxy to solar mass would make the resulting velocity contribution too small to be detected: it lies well below Kepler's curve and the achieved precision in measuring planet velocities.

Of course, in conventional dark matter scenarios, there is no reason to believe any particular concentration of such material near the solar system, and no effect is expected here.

### *5.3. Inference by Stellar Scattering*

In this subsection, I turn to the detectability in our own galaxy via surveys, such as GAIA [28,29]. The idea is that, should filamentary overdensities of dark matter exist, even if they are not directly visible, unlike filamentary gas structures [30], they might still be inferable by the behavior of nearby objects.

The theory for the scattering by a Newtonian $1/r^2$ force is well-known [31], and the geometry is depicted in Figure 9.

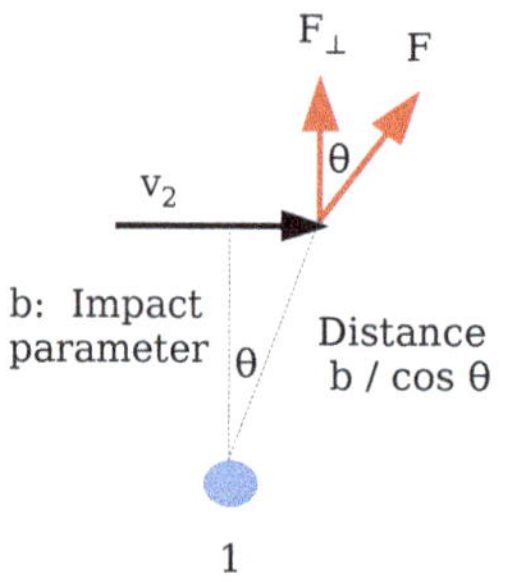


**Figure 9.** Geometry for the momentum transfer in a collision in the impact approximation [31] of a star (2) on either a spherical or a perpendicular cylindrical source (1), in the latter's reference frame. The trajectory along $v_2$ is practically straight and with constant velocity, with the transferred momentum approximately perpendicular to it.

Therein, the impact parameter is $b$, and the perpendicular force at a visual angle $\theta$ is

$$F_\perp = \cos\theta \frac{Gm_1m_2}{(b/\cos\theta)^2} . \tag{40}$$

If the scatterer is not a spherical body but, rather, a cylindrical one with linear mass density $\lambda_1$, the force law is modified to

$$F_\perp = \cos^2\theta \frac{2m_2\lambda_1 G}{b} . \tag{41}$$

The one less power of $1/r$ (see Equation (14)) entails here one less power of $\cos\theta$, that yields an inconsequential numeric factor but, more importantly, one less power of $b^{-1}$ in the denominator.

The momentum transfer to the projectile can be obtained by integrating the instantaneous impulse,

$$\Delta p_\perp = \int_{-\infty}^{+\infty} dt F_\perp ; \tag{42}$$

the integration time can be eliminated by the visual angle that is swiped along the (almost straight) scattered trajectory by

$$v_2 dt = d(b\tan\theta) . \tag{43}$$

Carrying the integration out with the $1/r^2$ or the $1/r$ forces just given yields

$$\Delta p_\perp = \frac{2Gm_1m_2}{bv_2} \text{ (spherical scatterer)}, \tag{44}$$

$$\Delta p_\perp = \frac{2\pi G\lambda_1 m_2}{v_2} \text{ (cylindrical scatterer)} . \tag{45}$$

The change from standard spherical scattering is the replacement of $m_1$ by $\pi\lambda b$. This entails that Equation (45) is independent of the impact parameter! That provides an interesting way of identifying such events: all stars in a small swarm or stellar stream change their velocity in the same amount (which is a feature that can be triggered on by Gaia's radial velocity measurements) and the ensemble of star's maintains its shape, as all its members slightly turn their velocities by the same amount.

As for the smallest filament so-detectable, solving for $\lambda$ and using $v_{2\perp} = \frac{p_{2\perp}}{m}$, we have

$$\lambda = \frac{v_2 \Delta v_{2\perp}}{2\pi G} ; \tag{46}$$

the quantity $v_2 \Delta v_{2\perp} / \pi$ can be reasonably measured by GAIA down to 10 $(\mathrm{km/s})^2$ (given typical peculiar velocities of 30 km/s and a measurement precision of 1 km/s, that limits the accessible $\Delta v_{2\perp}$).

Since this directly yields the $(2G\lambda)$ factor of the scatterer, that can be compared to a galaxy's $(2G\lambda)$ of order $(250\ \mathrm{km/s})^2$, we see that only scatterers by cylindrical overdensities of order $1\% - 0.1\%$ of the galactic ones will be conceivably detectable.

This discussion is relevant to distinguish whether the galactic dark matter halo, be it or not vertically elongated, can be composed of dark gas (WIMPS) or dark spherical bodies (MACHOS), for example, in which case this peculiar $b$-independent scattering will not be present, or whether there is a filamentary structure of dark matter at yet smaller scales than the galactic one. The peculiar motion of stars arises from random influences by stars and gas clouds (local overdensities above the average), so obviously it does not help with the global dark matter halo properties, but it would help with subhaloes or structures large enough, and in the context of this manuscript, with subfilaments or generally elongated overdensities.

A second handle to such potential substructure comes from the bound state problem instead of scattering. It falls off from the obvious observation that stars can orbit such subfilaments in an epicyclical fashion, with a velocity around the galactic center of order $\sqrt{2G\lambda}$ and a secondary velocity $\sqrt{2G\lambda'}$. Such bound stars perform a secondary oscillation that, crucially, is independent of the distance to the source. Thus, if such subfilaments exist, they are characterizable.

### 5.4. Direct Imaging

Galaxy catalogues, such as the Sloan Digital Sky Survey [32], clearly show that galaxies extend in filamentary structures forming a "cosmic web". At a scale of 40 Mpc, computer simulations do show a matching cosmic web of dark matter, where such linear structures are very prominent [33]. Zooming into smaller scales, it would appear that the filaments do extend, in the simulations, from galaxy to galaxy (see a beautiful illustration, last accessed on 10 September 2021, in https://skymaps.horizon-simulation.org/html/hz_AGN_lightcone.html).

It also appears that, looking back in time, one can also discern the filaments at a relatively smaller scale, directly linking galaxies, from observational data [34].

Further, though gravitational lensing has not been yet used to claim a filament at a galactic scale, a literature search reveals that a statistical stacking of galaxy pairs, with a rescaling performed so that all pairs sit on top of each others, shows evidence for dark matter filaments extending between neighboring galaxies [3], as mentioned above in Section 1. In addition to the imaged filament, these authors report that up to $1.5 \times 10^{13}$ Solar masses could be contained in such a filament, as per their lensing data. If this turns out to be statistically robust, it would eventually account for most of the dark matter, not leaving too much for spherical haloes. Further confirmation would entail that dark matter accretion has not evolved as much as usually assumed (from a homogeneous medium, to flat sheets, to filaments, to spherical structures: this last step would not be completed at today's $t_0$ cosmic time).

In the end, in spite of the many investigations addressing dark matter filaments, neither do those authors (nor many others) seem to have remarked the importance of the longitudinal structures that they were revealing for explaining galaxy rotation curves.

## 6. Further Consequences

### 6.1. Galaxy Plane—Galaxy Plane Correlations

If dark matter filaments extend between two or more galaxies, as revealed by both simulations and statistical stacking of galaxies in lensing studies, as discussed in Section 5.4, the two galaxy planes are correlated because both are preferentially perpendicular to the filament, as illustrated in Figure 10.

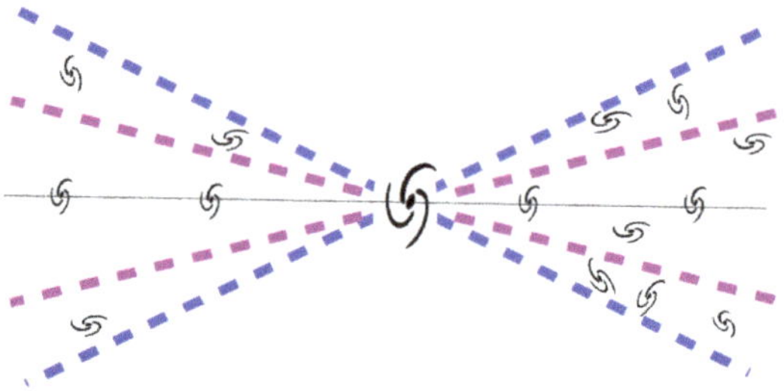

**Figure 10.** If a filament threads two or more galaxies before significantly bending, their rotation planes (perpendicular to the dark matter rope tying them) are parallel. Since the filaments are not visible in principle, one needs to correlate a distribution of galaxies. However, knowing that it is perpendicular to the spiral rotation plane, noise-reduction strategy is to not include all the space surrounding a given galaxy but, rather, to span only a cone given by a certain opening angle $\theta$ and then tighten that angle to improve the correlation.

As a measure of that correlation, one can take a sample of galaxies in a given volume and average the absolute value of their relative orientation cosine,

$$\xi = |\langle \hat{n}_1 \cdot \hat{n}_2 \rangle| \,. \tag{47}$$

In an infinite sample of randomly oriented galaxies, this number tends to zero. However, the approach to zero is slower if a few galaxies have oriented planes of rotation. To illustrate it, I have performed a simple calculation, shown in Figure 11. Spheres of increasing radius up to 10 Mpc are taken around a given galaxy, containing 1 galaxy/$\mathrm{Mpc}^3$ with its plane randomly oriented. The blue squares show that, indeed, the average over all pairs of their relative orientation cosine quickly vanishes upon averaging over a sphere with the radius $r$ indicated in the $OX$ axis.

A line of a few equidistant, parallel galaxies, is then added over the north pole and under the south pole (red circles). Finally, the average is limited not to the whole sphere out to $r$, but to a cone of polar angle

$$\theta \in [0, \theta_{\max}] \cup [\pi - \theta_{\max}, \pi], \tag{48}$$

where the $\theta_{\max}$ varies between plots. The resulting correlation is significantly larger for small $r$.

The observable so-constructed is clear, but its interpretation is more ambiguous, as it can also be obtained by tidal effects of a different type. It has, indeed, been shown in simulations, such as Illustris-1 [35] or Horizon [36]. Even observational evidence has been claimed for a while now [37] and looks reminiscent of Figure 11.

## 6.2. Virial Theorem for Small Galaxy Clusters

A further comment that deserves attention is related to the virial, often used to extract the mass of galaxy clusters. If the time scale characteristic of the motion, $\tau$, allows for filament-filament interaction to have virialized, because the filaments are extended, their interaction is closer to a 2-dimensional gas instead of a three-dimensional gas of spheres. In that case, the standard

$$\langle T \rangle = \frac{-1}{2} \sum \mathbf{F}_k \mathbf{r}_k \tag{49}$$

that yields, for Newtonian potentials,

$$\langle T \rangle = \frac{-1}{2} \langle V \rangle \tag{50}$$

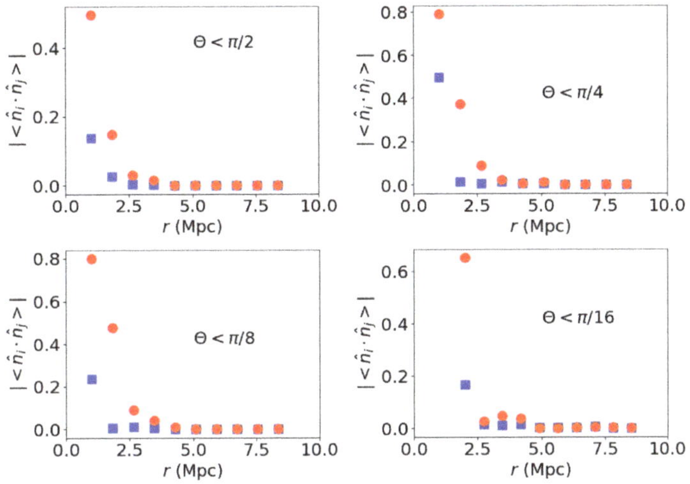


**Figure 11.** Toy simulations of a galaxy plane—galaxy plane correlation as function of the correlation distance. From top to bottom, the polar angle cut is tightened around the filament axis, so that the cone included features less random galaxies (but always the random ones along the filament). Blue squares: just the random galaxies. Red circles: the filament is now posited to thread perfectly oriented galaxies spaced at 1 Mpc, which are added to the sample from which the correlation is calculated.

is modified to its reduced-dimensional form with $F \propto 1/r \Rightarrow$,

$$\langle T \rangle \sim \text{constant}, \tag{51}$$

without a power dependence on the potential $V$. I have not studied whether $\tau$ is smaller enough than $1/H$ to have allowed such large structures to virialize.

### 6.3. Gravitational Lensing

The dark matter distribution of galactic haloes can be assessed with gravitational lensing, and, their shape is particularly amenable to study. The basic theory of lensing by an arbitrarily distorted mass distribution has recently been put forward by Turyshev [38], in terms of a spherical harmonic expansion. This allows studies of lensing with high distortion; in the extreme case of cylindrical distributions, one can use the geodesics of cylindrical solutions to Einstein's equations [39].

For smaller distortions, limited to an ellipticity in the dark matter halo of a localized population of galaxies, existing work has, indeed, extracted a significant deformation from Hubble space telescope data on gravitational lensing [40]. No specific analysis for spiral galaxies, where rotational curves have been measured, has been carried out.

This is an attractive venue for specialists in theoretical physics that will be revisited.

## 7. Discussion

Adopting the point of view that the source of the extra gravitational field driving galactic rotation curves is cylindrically distributed, or very elongated, their flatness is automatic (it is just Kepler's third law in one less dimension). No fine tuning of the dark matter distribution is needed; and the gravitational force remains the natural one in which the flux of the gravitational field is the same across concentric surfaces and the gravitational force just falls off because of its dilution (consistently with Gauss's law and Newtonian gravity). I believe this is a very educational exercise.

Whatever dark matter may fundamentally be, having it distributed with a spherical geometry is not a necessity. In fact, a cylindrically-symmetric distribution explains galactic rotation curves just as well as a halo and allows for disposing of a hypothesis, such as temperature equilibration across that halo.

There is ample evidence for a filamentary structure at large scales in the universe, so the tenet is not in contradiction with most of the literature. The point of view, that those filaments are relevant at the kpc galactic scale, has not been observed in the literature, at least not widely enough to call for a solution of the galaxy rotation problem, though investigations of "fuzzy dark matter" [41] seem to be favoring more filamentary structures.

The nature of such hypothetical filaments or elongated haloes remains, such as generally that of dark matter, unknown. Much work has been devoted to cosmic strings and their networks [42]. Alternatively, more conventional dark matter, thought of as unspecified gravitating "stuff", could be accreting and, still today, be organized in longitudinal structure rather than more spherical haloes. In that case, these flat rotation curves are a temporary effect: as accretion continues from cylinders into spherical haloes, they will look more "Keplerian" in another few Gyr.

In any case, this fun work shows that galactic rotation curves are natural in the analytic limit in which the gravitational source is cylindrical. Thus, simulations of dark matter haloes would improve the rotational-data fit quality if the outcome distributions were much more prolate [43] than usually considered in this context. Fuzzy dark matter simulations may be a worthwhile endeavor.

**Funding:** Work supported with funding by grant MINECO: FPA2016-75654-C2-1-P (Spain); MICINN grants PID2019-108655GB-I00, -106080GB-C21; and Univ. Complutense de Madrid under research group 910309 and the IPARCOS institute.

**Conflicts of Interest:** The author declares no conflict of interest.

## References

1. Rubin, V.C.; Ford, W.K., Jr. Rotation of the Andromeda Nebula from a Spectroscopic Survey of Emission Regions. *Astrophys. J.* **1970**, *159*, 379. [CrossRef]
2. Lelli, F.; McGaugh, S.S.; Schombert, J.M. SPARC: Mass Models for 175 Disk Galaxies with Spitzer Photometry and Accurate Rotation Curves. *Astron. J.* **2016**, *152*, 157. [CrossRef]
3. Epps, S.D.; Hudson, M.J. The Weak Lensing Masses of Filaments between Luminous Red Galaxies. *Mon. Not. R. Astron. Soc.* 2017, *468*, 2605. [CrossRef]
4. Weinberg, S. *Cosmology*; Oxford University Press: Oxford, UK, 2008; ISBN 10 0198526822.
5. Boveia, A.; Doglioni, C. Dark Matter Searches at Colliders. *Ann. Rev. Nucl. Part Sci.* **2018**, *68*, 429. [CrossRef]
6. Cebrián, S. Small scale direct dark matter search experiments. *arXiv* **2019**, arXiv:1910.13947.
7. Martínez, M. Dark Matter searches via direct detection. *PoS Proc. Sci.* **2019**, *2018*, 037. [CrossRef]
8. Hooper, D. TASI Lectures on Indirect Searches For Dark Matter. *PoS Proc. Sci.* **2019**, *2018*, 010. [CrossRef]
9. Monroy-Rodríguez, M.A.; Allen, C. The end of the MACHO era- revisited: New limits on MACHO masses from halo wide binaries. *Astrophys. J.* **2014**, *790*, 159. [CrossRef]
10. Garcia-Bellido, J.; Clesse, S.; Fleury, P. Primordial black holes survive SN lensing constraints. *Phys. Dark Univ.* 2018, *20*, 95–100. [CrossRef]
11. Natarajan, P.; Zhao, H. MOND plus classical neutrinos not enough for cluster lensing. *Mon. Not. Roy. Astron. Soc.* **2008**, *389*, 250. [CrossRef]
12. Milgrom, M. Gravitational waves in bimetric MOND. *Phys. Rev. D* **2014**, *89*, 024027. [CrossRef]
13. Varieschi, G.U. Newtonian Fractional-Dimension Gravity and MOND. *Found. Phys.* **2020**, *50*, 1608–1644. Erratum in **2021**, *51*, 41. [CrossRef]
14. Varieschi, G.U. Newtonian Fractional-Dimension Gravity and Disk Galaxies. *Eur. Phys. J. Plus* **2021**, *136*, 183. [CrossRef]
15. Varieschi, G.U. Newtonian Fractional-Dimension Gravity and Rotationally Supported Galaxies. *Mon. Not. R. Astron. Soc.* **2021**, *503*, 1915–1931. [CrossRef]
16. Giusti, A. MOND-like Fractional Laplacian Theory. *Phys. Rev. D* **2020**, *101*, 124029. [CrossRef]
17. Giusti, A.; Garrappa, R.; Vachon, G. On the Kuzmin model in fractional Newtonian gravity. *Eur. Phys. J. Plus* **2020**, *135*, 798. [CrossRef]
18. Dodelson, S. The Real Problem with MOND. *Int. J. Mod. Phys. D* **2011**, *20*, 2749. [CrossRef]
19. Pina, P.E.; Fraternali, F.; Adams, E.A.; Marasco, A.; Oosterloo, T.; Oman, K.A.; Leisman, L.; Di Teodoro, E.M.; Posti, L.; Battipaglia, M.; et al. Off the Baryonic Tully–Fisher Relation: A Population of Baryon-dominated Ultra-diffuse Galaxies. *Astrophys. J. Lett.* **2019**, *883*, L33. [CrossRef]

20. Clowe, D.; Gonzalez, A.; Markevitch, M. Weak lensing mass reconstruction of the interacting cluster 1E0657-558: Direct evidence for the existence of dark matter. *Astrophys. J.* **2004**, *604*, 596. [CrossRef]
21. Sofue, Y. Dark halos of M 31 and the Milky Way. *Publ. Astron. Soc. Jpn.* **2015**, *67*, 75. [CrossRef]
22. Bariego-Quintana, A.; Manzanilla, O.; Llanes-Estrada, F.J. Contribution to the EPS-HEP 2021 European Conference on High Energy Physics. Extended Work in Preparation. Available online: https://indico.desy.de/event/28202/contributions/105991/ (accessed on 10 September 2021).
23. Su, M.; Slatyer, T.R.; Finkbeiner, D.P. Giant Gamma-ray Bubbles from Fermi-LAT: AGN Activity or Bipolar Galactic Wind? *Astrophys. J.* **2010**, *724*, 1044. [CrossRef]
24. Pawlowski, M.S. The Planes of Satellite Galaxies Problem, Suggested Solutions, and Open Questions. *Mod. Phys. Lett. A* **2018**, *33*, 1830004. [CrossRef]
25. Gialluca, M.T.; Naidu, R.P.; Bonaca, A. Velocity Dispersion of the GD-1 Stellar Stream. *Astrophys. J. Lett.* **2021**, *911*, L32. [CrossRef]
26. Tully, R.B.; Fisher, J.R. A New method of determining distances to galaxies. *Astron. Astrophys.* **1977**, *54*, 661.
27. McGaugh, S. The Baryonic Tully-Fisher Relation of Gas Rich Galaxies as a Test of LCDM and MOND. *Astron. J.* **2012**, *143*, 40. [CrossRef]
28. Prusti, T.; De Bruijne, J.H.; Brown, A.G.; Vallenari, A.; Babusiaux, C.; Bailer-Jones, C.A.; Bastian, U.; Biermann, M.; Evans, D.W.; Eyer, L.; et al. The Gaia Mission. *Astron. Astrophys.* **2016**, *595*, A1. [CrossRef]
29. Brown, A.G.; Vallenari, A.; Prusti, T.; De Bruijne, J.H.; Babusiaux, C.; Bailer-Jones, C.A.; Biermann, M.; Evans, D.W.; Eyer, L.; Jansen, F.; et al. Gaia Data Release 2: Summary of the contents and survey properties. *Astron. Astrophys.* **2018**, *616*, A1. [CrossRef]
30. Alves, J.; Zucker, C.; Goodman, A.A.; Speagle, J.S.; Meingast, S.; Robitaille, T.; Finkbeiner, D.P.; Schlafly, E.F.; Green, G.M. A Galactic-scale gas wave in the solar neighbourhood. *Nature* **2020**, *578*, 237–239. [CrossRef]
31. Draine, B.T. *Physics of the Interstellar and Intergalactic Medium*; Princeton University Press: Princeton, NJ, USA, 2011.
32. Alam, S.; Albareti Franco, D.; Allende Prieto, C.; Anders, F.; Anderson Scott, F.; Anderton, T.; Andrews Brett, H.; Armengaud, E.; Aubourg, É.; Bailey, S.; et al. The Eleventh and Twelfth Data Releases of the Sloan Digital Sky Survey: Final Data from SDSS-III. *Astrophys. J.* **2015**, *219*, 12. [CrossRef]
33. Eckert, D.; Jauzac, M.; Shan, H.; Kneib, J.; Erben, T.; Israel, H.; Jullo, E.; Klein, M.; Massey, R.; Richard, J.; et al. Warm-hot baryons comprise 5–10 per cent of filaments in the cosmic web. *Nature* **2015**, *528*, 105–107. [CrossRef]
34. Umehata, H.; Fumagalli, M.; Smail, I.; Matsuda, Y.; Swinbank, A.M.; Cantalupo, S.; Sykes, C.; Ivison, R.J.; Steidel, C.C.; Shapley, A.E.; et al. Gas filaments of the cosmic web located around active galaxies in a protocluster. *Science* **2019**, *366*, 97–100. [CrossRef] [PubMed]
35. Wang, P.; Guo, Q.; Kang, X.; Libeskind, N.I. Illustris-1 simulation. *Astrophys. J.* **2018**, *866*, 138. [CrossRef]
36. Okabe, T.; Nishimichi, T.; Oguri, M.; Peirani, S.; Kitayama, T.; Sasaki, S.; Suto, Y. Projected alignment of non-sphericities of stellar, gas, and dark matter distributions in galaxy clusters: Analysis of the Horizon-AGN simulation. *Mon. Not. R. Astron. Soc.* **2018**, *478*, 1141. [CrossRef]
37. Pen, U.; Lee, J.; Seljak, U.; Tentative Detection of Galaxy Spin Correlations in the Tully Catalog. *Astrophys. J. Lett.* **2000**, *543*, L107–L110. [CrossRef]
38. Turyshev, S.G.; Toth, V.T. Multipole decomposition of gravitational lensing. *arXiv* **2021**, arXiv:2107.13126.
39. Trendafilova, C.S.; Fulling, S.A. Static solutions of Einstein's equations with cylindrical symmetry. *Eur. J. Phys.* **2011**, *32*, 1663–1677. [CrossRef]
40. Jauzac, M.; Harvey, D.; Massey, R. The shape of galaxy dark matter haloes in massive galaxy clusters: Insights from strong gravitational lensing. *Mon. Not. R. Astron. Soc.* **2018**, *477*, 4046–4051. [CrossRef]
41. Mocz, P.; Fialkov, A.; Vogelsberger, M.; Becerra, F.; Shen, X.; Robles, V.H.; Amin, M.A.; Zavala, J.; Boylan-Kolchin, M.; Bose, S.; et al. Galaxy formation with BECDM –II. Cosmic filaments and first galaxies. *Mon. Not. R. Astron. Soc.* **2020**, *494*, 2027–2044. [CrossRef]
42. Klaer, V.B.; Moore, G.D. Global cosmic string networks as a function of tension. *arXiv* **2020**, arXiv:1912.08058.
43. Schneider, M.D.; Frenk, C.S.; Cole, S. The Shapes and Alignments of Dark Matter Halos. *J. Cosmol. Astropart. Phys.* **2012**, *1205*, 030. [CrossRef]

universe

MDPI

Communication

# Scalar–Tensor–Vector Modified Gravity in Light of the Planck 2018 Data

John W. Moffat and Viktor Toth *

Perimeter Institute for Theoretical Physics, Waterloo, ON N2L 2Y5, Canada; jmoffat@perimeterinstitute.ca
* Correspondence: vttoth@vttoth.com

**Abstract:** The recent data release by the Planck satellite collaboration presents a renewed challenge for modified theories of gravitation. Such theories must be capable of reproducing the observed angular power spectrum of the cosmic microwave background radiation. For modified theories of gravity, an added challenge lies in the fact that standard computational tools do not readily accommodate the features of a theory with a variable gravitational coupling coefficient. An alternative is to use less accurate but more easily modifiable semianalytical approximations to reproduce at least the qualitative features of the angular power spectrum. We extend a calculation that was used previously to demonstrate compatibility between the Scalar–Tensor–Vector–Gravity (STVG) theory, also known by the acronym MOG, and data from the Wilkinson Microwave Anisotropy Probe (WMAP) to show the consistency between the theory and the newly released Planck 2018 data. We find that within the limits of this approximation, the theory accurately reproduces the features of the angular power spectrum.

**Keywords:** cosmology:theory; large-scale structure of universe; gravitation

**PACS:** 04.20.Cv; 04.50.Kd; 04.80.Cc; 45.20.D-; 45.50.-j; 98.80.-k

**Citation:** Moffat, J.W.; Toth, V. Scalar–Tensor–Vector Modified Gravity in Light of the Planck 2018 Data. *Universe* **2021**, *7*, 358. https://doi.org/10.3390/universe7100358

Academic Editors: Panayiotis Stavrinos and Emmanuel N. Saridakis

Received: 1 September 2021
Accepted: 23 September 2021
Published: 26 September 2021



## 1. Introduction

Though highly isotropic, the cosmic microwave background (CMB) shows small temperature fluctuations as a function of the sky direction. The magnitude of these fluctuations depends on the angular size. This location and size of these peaks is an important prediction of the standard model of cosmology, which has been confirmed by increasingly accurate experiments, such as the Boomerang experiment [1], the Wilkinson Microwave Anisotropy Probe (WMAP, [2]), and the Planck satellite [3].

The angular power spectrum of the CMB can be calculated in a variety of ways. The preferred method is to use numerical software, such as `CMBFAST` [4]. Unfortunately, such software packages cannot be easily adapted for use with a variable-$G$ theory of gravitation, such as the Scalar–Tensor–Vector–Gravity (STVG [5]) theory, also known as MOdified Gravity (MOG).

There are alternative methods of calculation, which, though somewhat less accurate, nonetheless capture the essential qualitative features of the CMB angular power spectrum. The advantage of such calculations is that the physics is transparent and not obscured by "black box" computer code; additionally, the calculations can be adapted with relative ease to accommodate a different theory. One such method is the semianalytical approximation presented in Ref. [6].

We have, in fact, used this approximation in the past showing the agreement between the predictions of the MOG theory and the WMAP results [7,8]. In light of the recently published Planck 2018 results, it is important to revisit and refine this computation and also extend it to high values of the multipole index $\ell$.

We begin in Section 2 with a brief introduction to the MOG theory and its acceleration law, which gives rise to the theory's effective gravitational coupling parameter. In

Section 3, we introduce the angular power spectrum and its semianalytical approximation, as presented in Ref. [6] (which the interested reader is advised to consult for details). We adapt the calculation to the MOG theory and show the results. We conclude by presenting our discussion and conclusions in Section 4.

## 2. The MOG Theory

Our MOG modified gravity theory, also known as Scalar–Tensor–Vector–Gravity (STVG [5]), is a relativistic theory of gravitation based on an action principle. In addition to the metrical field of gravitation, the theory introduces a repulsive vector field of finite range. The gravitational constant and the vector field range (mass) parameter are promoted to dynamical (massless) scalar fields. Within the range of the vector field, the theory replicates Newtonian gravitation; outside this range, in the absence of the repulsive force, gravitation is stronger. By this feature, the theory successfully accounts for galaxy rotation curves [9–13], the matter power spectrum [8], and other cosmological observations [14] while also remaining consistent with recent gravitational wave data [15].

In the weak field, low-velocity regime, the MOG theory yields a simple gravitational acceleration law [16]. For a point source of gravitation characterized by mass $M$ at the origin, the gravitational acceleration at position $\mathbf{r}$ is given by

$$\ddot{\mathbf{r}} = -\frac{G_{\rm eff}M}{r^3}\mathbf{r}, \tag{1}$$

with

$$G_{\rm eff} = G_N\left[1+\alpha-\alpha(1+\mu r)e^{-\mu r}\right], \tag{2}$$

where $G_N$ is Newton's constant of gravitation, the dimensionless quantity $\alpha = (G - G_N)/G_N$ (i.e., $G = (1+\alpha)G_N$) characterizes the difference between the theory's variable gravitational coupling coefficient $G$ and $G_N$, and $\mu$ is the mass of the vector field.

In an approximately homogeneous and isotropic universe, $\alpha$ and $\mu$ can be taken as constants. Consequently, at distance scales characterized by $\mu r \gg 1$, $G_{\rm eff} \sim G_N(1+\alpha)$ can be treated as constant as well.

The Friedmann equations that describe a homogeneous and isotropic universe remain valid in the MOG theory [7,8,17,18], with only trivial modifications, which is not surprising given that these equations can also be heuristically derived from the Newtonian theory [6,19]. The equations read (using $c = 1$):

$$\frac{\dot{a}^2}{a^2} + \frac{k}{a^2} = \frac{8\pi G_{\rm eff}\rho}{3} + \frac{\Lambda}{3}, \tag{3}$$

$$\frac{\ddot{a}}{a} = -\frac{4\pi G_{\rm eff}}{3}(\rho+3p) + \frac{\Lambda}{3}. \tag{4}$$

The critical density, characterized by $k = 0$, $\Lambda = 0$, is given by

$$\rho_{\rm crit}^{\rm MOG} = \frac{3H^2}{8\pi G_{\rm eff}}, \tag{5}$$

where $H = \dot{a}/a$.

Note the presence of a factor of $1/(1+\alpha)$ in this definition of $\rho_{\rm crit}$. Consequently, for a given baryon density $\rho_b$, the corresponding density parameter $\Omega_b$ is inflated by this same factor:

$$\Omega_b^{\rm MOG} = \frac{\rho_b}{\rho_{\rm crit}^{\rm MOG}} = (1+\alpha)\frac{8\pi G_N\rho_b}{3H^2} = (1+\alpha)\Omega_b. \tag{6}$$

Often, in cosmological calculations, $\Omega_b$ is used to represent the baryon density in equations describing both gravitational and nongravitational interactions. Clearly, this convenience is lost in the case of modified gravity in the presence of the $(1+\alpha)$ factor, which only applies to gravitational interactions.

## 3. Modeling the Cosmic Microwave Background (CMB)

It is surprisingly difficult to analyze high-quality Cosmic Microwave Background (CMB) data sets from the perspective of a modified gravity theory, such as MOG. The main reason for this difficulty lies in the fact that, as we alluded to above, the dimensionless density parameter $\Omega_b$ is used to represent baryonic matter in calculations that involve gravity as well as calculations that represent nongravitational physics.

Why is this a problem? Consider the definition:

$$\Omega_b = \frac{\rho_b}{\rho_{\rm crit}} = \frac{8\pi G\rho_b}{3H^2}. \tag{7}$$

In the standard theory, this expression will suffice. However, what about a theory, such as MOG, with a variable gravitational coefficient $G = G_{\rm eff} = (1+\alpha)G_N$? Clearly, when the context is gravitational, the product $G\rho_b$ accurately reflects the gravitational contribution of baryonic matter. However, when, e.g., the pressure of the medium is considered, $\Omega_b$ is not supposed to be scaled in this manner (pressure does not increase just because gravitation is stronger).

Disentangling these issues in computer codes that have been in use for years or decades, written or rewritten by multiple authors, perhaps even machine-translated from one programming language to another (e.g., from FORTRAN to C) is a daunting task.

Without access to a standard suite of computer programs that can reliably and provably deal with a variable-$G$ modified theory of gravity, we opted for another approach: use a semianalytical approximation that is sufficiently accurate to reproduce the key qualitative features of the CMB angular power spectrum and perhaps even allow us to make some cautious predictions.

Such an approximation method was published by Mukhanov [6]. We previously used this approximation method in the context of WMAP results, showing that MOG indeed fits the angular power spectrum well. In light of the recent release of Planck 2018 data, we found it imperative to revisit and, if necessary, refine this calculation and compare the Planck results against the MOG predictions.

### 3.1. Semi-Analytical Estimation of CMB Anisotropies

The general expression for the cosmic mean of the CMB temperature autocorrelation function, expressed in terms of multipoles $C_\ell$ (with the monopole and dipole components, $\ell = 0, 1$, excluded), can be written as (see Equation (9.38) in [6] and the discussion therein for details):

$$C_\ell = \frac{2}{\pi}\int\left|\left(\Phi_k(\eta_r) + \frac{\delta_k(\eta_r)}{4}\right)j_\ell(k\eta_0) - \frac{3\delta'_k(\eta_r)}{4k}\frac{dj_\ell(k\eta_0)}{d(k\eta_0)}\right|^2 k^2dk, \tag{8}$$

where $\Phi_k$ is the Fourier-decomposition of the gravitational potential $\Phi$ with respect to wavenumber $k$, $\eta_r$ is the conformal time at recombination, and $\eta_0$ corresponds to the present time. The quantity $\delta$ is the fractional energy fluctuation of radiation, defined using the 00-component of the radiation energy-momentum tensor before recombination as $T^0_0 = \epsilon(1+\delta)$, where $\epsilon$ is the radiation energy density, $\delta'$ is the derivative with respect to conformal time, and $j_\ell$ are the spherical Bessel functions.

For $k\eta_r \ll 1$, $\delta_k(\eta_r) \simeq -\frac{8}{3}\Phi_k(\eta_r)$, $\delta_k'(\eta_r) \simeq 0$; hence, we find that for $\ell \ll 200$, $\ell(\ell+1)C_\ell \simeq$ const. This observation is valid both in the standard $\Lambda$-CDM cosmology and the MOG theory, leaving us, for low $\ell$, with

$$C_l = \frac{2}{\pi}\int\left|\frac{1}{3}\Phi_k(\eta_r)j_l(k\eta_0)\right|^2 k^2 dk. \tag{9}$$

If $|\Phi_k|^2 = (9/10)^2 B/k^3$ (the extra factor $9/10$ corresponding to a drop of the potential on superhorizon scales after matter-radiation equality), we obtain

$$C_l = \frac{18B}{100\pi}\int j_l(k\eta_0)^2 k^{-1} dk. \tag{10}$$

Let $s = k\eta_0$, $ds/dk = \eta_0$, and then,

$$C_l = \frac{18B}{100\pi}\int j_l(s)^2 s^{-1} ds = \frac{9B}{100\pi l(l+1)}. \tag{11}$$

For large $\ell$, still following Ref. [6], we can then write

$$\frac{\ell(\ell+1)C_\ell}{[\ell(\ell+1)C_\ell]_{\text{low }\ell}} = \frac{100}{9}(O+N), \tag{12}$$

where we split the eventual solution into oscillatory ($O$) and non-oscillatory ($N$) parts.

Using the well-known trigonometric approximations of the spherical Bessel functions $j_\ell(s)$ for large real arguments, as well as other suitable numerical representations (for details, including the origin of the numerical factors in the equations that follow, consult [6]), we find the following expression for the oscillatory part:

$$O = e^{-(l/l_s)^2}\sqrt{\frac{\pi}{\bar{\rho}l}}\left[A_1\cos\left(\bar{\rho}l + \frac{\pi}{4}\right) + A_2\cos\left(2\bar{\rho}l + \frac{\pi}{4}\right)\right], \tag{13}$$

where

$$A_1 = 0.1\xi\frac{(P-0.78)^2 - 4.3}{(1+\xi)^{1/4}}e^{\frac{1}{2}(l_s^{-2}-l_f^{-2})l^2}, \tag{14}$$

and

$$A_2 = 0.14\frac{(0.5+0.36P)^2}{(1+\xi)^{1/2}}. \tag{15}$$

The non-oscillatory part, in turn, is split into a sum:

$$N = N_1 + N_2 + N_3\,, \tag{16}$$

where

$$N_1 = 0.063\xi^2\frac{[P-0.22(l/l_f)^{0.3}-2.6]^2}{1+0.65(l/l_f)^{1.4}}e^{-(l/l_f)^2}, \tag{17}$$

$$N_2 = \frac{0.037}{(1+\xi)^{1/2}}\frac{[P-0.22(l/l_s)^{0.3}+1.7]^2}{1+0.65(l/l_s)^{1.4}}e^{-(l/l_s)^2}, \tag{18}$$

$$N_3 = \frac{0.033}{(1+\xi)^{3/2}}\frac{[P-0.5(l/l_s)^{0.55}+2.2]^2}{1+2(l/l_s)^2}e^{-(l/l_s)^2}. \tag{19}$$

The parameters that occur in these expressions are as follows. First, the baryon density parameter:

$$\xi = 17\left(\Omega_b h_{75}^2\right), \tag{20}$$

where $\Omega_b \simeq 0.035$ is the baryon content of the universe at present relative to the critical density, and $h_{75} = H_0/(75\,\mathrm{km/s/Mpc})$, with $H_0$ being the Hubble parameter at the present epoch. The growth term of the transfer function is represented by

$$P = \ln \frac{\Omega_m^{-0.09} l}{200\sqrt{\Omega_m h_{75}^2}}, \tag{21}$$

where $\Omega_m \simeq 0.3$ is the total matter content (baryonic matter, neutrinos, and cold dark matter). The free-streaming and Silk damping scales are determined, respectively, by

$$l_f = 1600\left[1 + 7.8 \times 10^{-2}\left(\Omega_m h_{75}^2\right)^{-1}\right]^{1/2} \Omega_m^{0.09}, \tag{22}$$

$$l_s = \frac{0.7 l_f}{\sqrt{\frac{1+0.56\xi}{1+\xi} + \frac{0.8}{\xi(1+\xi)} \frac{\left(\Omega_m h_{75}^2\right)^{1/2}}{\left[1+\left(1+\frac{100}{7.8}\Omega_m h_{75}^2\right)^{-1/2}\right]^2}}}. \tag{23}$$

Lastly, the location of the acoustic peaks is determined by the parameter[1]

$$\bar{\rho} = 0.015(1 + 0.13\xi)^{-1}(\Omega_m h_{75}^{3.1})^{0.16}. \tag{24}$$

Finally, we note that the calculated result for $C_\ell$ assumes scale invariance. For small deviations from scale invariance characterized as usual by the parameter $n_s$ (with $|n_s - 1| \ll 1$), the result is scaled:

$$C_\ell \to \ell^{n_s - 1} C_\ell. \tag{25}$$

The quality of this approximation is demonstrated in Figure 1 (top left), which shows the estimated angular power spectrum using nominal parameters ($H_0 \sim 67.4\,\mathrm{km/s/Mpc}$, $h^2\Omega_b = 0.0224$, $\Omega_m = 0.315$, $n_s = 0.965$ with spatially flat cosmology, $\Omega_\Lambda = 1 - \Omega_m$) against Planck 2018 data[2] from http://pla.esac.esa.int/pla/#cosmology (accessed on 15 September 2021).

The quality of this fit improves significantly if we allow some of the parameters to vary. For instance, using a simple least squares fit, we obtain $h^2\Omega_b = 0.0187$, $n_s = 0.965$ (see Figure 1 top right).

### 3.2. The MOG CMB Spectrum

What are the key differences between the MOG theory and standard cosmology?

In the standard ΛCDM model in the early universe, there are two main sources of gravitation: baryonic matter and collisionless cold dark matter (CDM). The distribution of matter in the universe is still largely homogeneous, and the gravitational field is determined by the sum $\Omega_m = \Omega_b + \Omega_{\mathrm{DM}}$.

In the MOG theory, $\Omega_{\mathrm{DM}}$ is, of course, absent. However, the gravitational coupling parameter is no longer Newton's constant. In the late time universe, we expect the gravitational coupling parameter to vary from region to region (an essential feature of the MOG theory that accounts for its ability to model phenomena, such as galaxy rotation curves successfully.) In the early, mostly homogeneous universe, we expect little variation in the value of $G$; however, $G \neq G_N$.

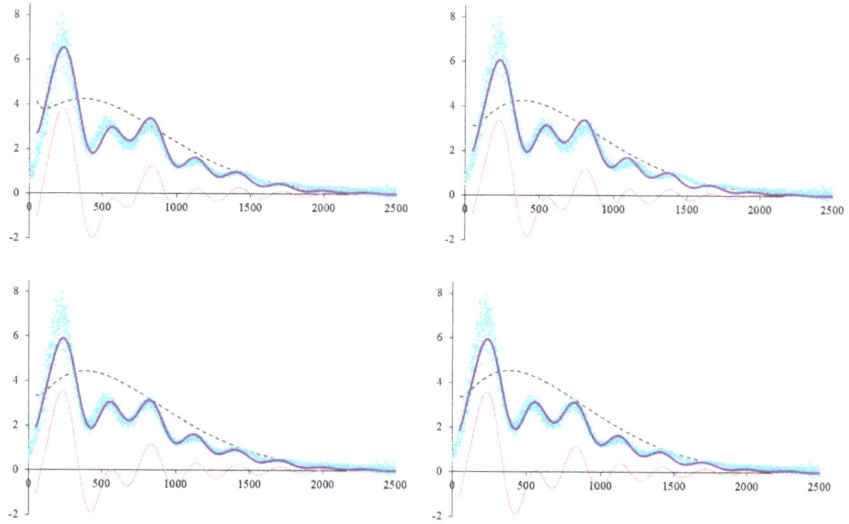


**Figure 1.** Mukhanov's approximation of the angular power spectrum in light of Planck 2018 data. Thick blue line: Mukhanov's approximation as a sum of an oscillatory part (thin dotted red line) and a nonoscillatory part (dashed green line). Planck 2018 data are shown in light blue with vertical error bars. Top row: standard cosmology, with nominal parameters (left) and least squares fitted values for $\Omega_b$ and $n_s$ (right). Bottom row: The MOG theory, with $\Omega_b$, $\alpha$ and $n_s$ fitted (left) and with the same 3-parameter fit but setting $H_0 = 73$ km/s/Mpc fitted (right).

This means that gravitational interactions are "enhanced" by the factor $1 + \alpha$, defined by the relationship $G = G_{\rm eff} = (1 + \alpha)G_N$. When computing the results, such as the angular power spectrum, this must be taken into account.

This actually leads to a fairly simple prescription. In the formulation presented in the previous subsection, the density parameter for matter, $\Omega_m$, must be replaced by $(1 + \alpha)\Omega_b$.

These changes are, of course, trivial. $\Omega_b$ only appears in Equation (20). For otherwise identical parameterization, we expect identical results.

Instead, we opted to relax the parameter space further as we investigate the MOG solution. Figure 1, bottom left, was obtained by fitting the values of $h^2\Omega_b = 0.0197$, $\alpha = 5.27$, and $n_s = 0.951$.

As we explored the parameter space, it became evident that there is significant degeneracy with respect to the value of $H_0$. Figure 1 (lower right) shows another fit, after setting $H_0 = 73$ km/s/Mpc, resulting in $h^2\Omega_b = 0.0199$, $\alpha = 4.75$, and $n_s = 0.949$. We believe that this degeneracy demonstrates the limit of the Mukhanov approximation.

## 4. Conclusions

Recently, the Planck collaboration released a data set characterizing the cosmic microwave background's angular power spectrum in more detail than anything previously published. This data release raises the bar for modified theories of gravitation that compete with the standard $\Lambda$CDM model as potentially viable representations of the evolution and structure formation in the universe.

We investigated, in particular, the behavior of Scalar–Tensor–Vector–Gravity, also known by the acronym MOG, in light of these new data. A key feature of the MOG theory is the presence of a variable gravitational coupling coefficient, which makes the task of adapting existing numerical models of the CMB or structure formation difficult. Large numerical code bases that are opaque and often use the dimensionless density parameters

$\Omega_b$, $\Omega_m$, etc., to model both gravitational and nongravitational interactions cannot be easily modified.

Instead, in this paper, we revived a model that we first employed in the wake of the WMAP data release. Extending the calculations to higher multipoles (up to $\ell = 2500$), we were able to demonstrate that the MOG theory correctly reproduces the qualitative features of the CMB and that within the limits of the approximation, it also produces good quantitative fits. At the same time, we also saw the limitations of the method, notably a degeneracy with respect to $H_0$. This leads us to conclude that, for instance, to decide whether or not the MOG theory can offer a better resolution to the Hubble tension (see [20] for an up-to-date review), more sophisticated methods will be required.

**Acknowledgments:** This research was supported in part by Perimeter Institute for Theoretical Physics. Research at Perimeter Institute is supported by the Government of Canada through the Department of Innovation, Science and Economic Development Canada and by the Province of Ontario through the Ministry of Research, Innovation and Science. V.T.T. acknowledges the generous support of Plamen Vasilev and other Patreon patrons.

**Conflicts of Interest:** The authors declare no conflict of interest.

## Notes

1. Note the slight changes in the coefficients in Equations (22) and (24) compared to the value published in [6]. We used best fit values for these coefficients from Mukhanov's approximation using the Planck collaboration's best estimates for the parameters of the standard ΛCDM cosmology.
2. For important explanations see https://wiki.cosmos.esa.int/planck-legacy-archive/index.php/CMB_spectrum_%26_Likelihood_Code (accessed on 15 September 2021).

## References

1. Jones, W.C.; Ade, P.A.R.; Bock, J.J.; Bond, J.R.; Borrill, J.; Boscaleri, A.; Cabella, P.; Contaldi, C.R.; Crill, B.P.; de Bernardis, P.; et al. A Measurement of the Angular Power Spectrum of the CMB Temperature Anisotropy from the 2003 Flight of BOOMERANG. *Astrophys. J.* **2006**, *647*, 823–832. [CrossRef]
2. Komatsu, E.; Dunkley, J.; Nolta, M.R.; Bennett, C.L.; Gold, B.; Hinshaw, G.; Jarosik, N.; Larson, D.; Limon, M.; Page, L.; et al. Five-Year Wilkinson Microwave Anisotropy Probe Observations: Cosmological Interpretation. *Astrophys. J. Suppl. Ser.* **2009**, *180*, 330–376. [CrossRef]
3. Planck, C.; Aghanim, N.; Akrami, Y.; Ashdown, M.; Aumont, J.; Baccigalupi, C.; Ballardini, M.; Banday, A.J.; Barreiro, R.B.; Bartolo, N.; et al. Planck 2018 results. VI. Cosmological parameters. *Astron. Astrophys.* **2020**, *641*, A6. [CrossRef]
4. Seljak, U.; Zaldarriaga, M. A Line-of-Sight Integration Approach to Cosmic Microwave Background Anisotropies. *Astrophys. J.* **1996**, *469*, 437. [CrossRef]
5. Moffat, J.W. Scalar-tensor-vector gravity theory. *J. Cosmol. Astropart. Phys.* **2006**, *2006*, 004. [CrossRef]
6. Mukhanov, V. *Physical Foundations of Cosmology*; Cambridge University Press: Cambridge, UK, 2005.
7. Moffat, J.W.; Toth, V.T. Modified Gravity: Cosmology without dark matter or a cosmological constant. *arXiv* **2007**, arXiv:0710.0364.
8. Moffat, J.W.; Toth, V.T. Cosmological Observations in a Modified Theory of Gravity (MOG). *Galaxies* **2013**, *1*, 65–82. [CrossRef]
9. Moffat, J.W.; Rahvar, S. The MOG weak field approximation and observational test of galaxy rotation curves. *Mon. Not. R. Astron. Soc.* **2013**, *436*, 1439–1451. [CrossRef]
10. Moffat, J.W.; Toth, V.T. Rotational Velocity Curves in the Milky Way as a Test of Modified Gravity. *Phys. Rev. D* **2015**, *91*, 043004. [CrossRef]
11. Green, M.A.; Moffat, J.W. Modified Gravity (MOG) fits to observed radial acceleration of SPARC galaxies. *Phys. Dark Universe* **2019**, *25*, 100323. [CrossRef]
12. Davari, Z.; Rahvar, S. Testing MOdified Gravity (MOG) theory and dark matter model in Milky Way using the local observables. *Mon. Not. R. Astron. Soc.* **2020**, *496*, 3502–3511. [CrossRef]
13. Moffat, J.W. Gravitational theory of cosmology, galaxies and galaxy clusters. *Eur. Phys. J. C* **2020**, *80*, 906. [CrossRef]
14. Davari, Z.; Rahvar, S. MOG cosmology without dark matter and the cosmological constant. *Mon. Not. R. Astron. Soc.* **2021**, *507*, 3387–3399. [CrossRef]
15. Green, M.A.; Moffat, J.W.; Toth, V.T. Modified Gravity (MOG), the speed of gravitational radiation and the event GW170817/GRB170817A. *Phys. Lett. B* **2018**, *780*, 300–302. [CrossRef]
16. Moffat, J.W.; Toth, V.T. Fundamental parameter-free solutions in Modified Gravity. *Class. Quant. Grav.* **2009**, *26*, 085002. [CrossRef]

17. Toth, V.T. Cosmological consequences of Modified Gravity (MOG). In Proceedings of the International Conference on Two Cosmological Models, Ciudad de Mexico, Mexico, 17–19 November 2010; Auping-Birch, J., Sandoval-Villalbazo, A., Eds.; Universidad Iberoamericana: Ciudad de Mexico, Mexico, 2012; pp. 385–398.
18. Moffat, J.W. Structure Growth and the CMB in Modified Gravity (MOG). *arXiv* **2014**, arXiv:1409.0853.
19. Weinberg, S. *Cosmology*; Oxford University Press: Oxford, UK, 2008.
20. Di Valentino, E.; Mena, O.; Pan, S.; Visinelli, L.; Yang, W.; Melchiorri, A.; Mota, D.F.; Riess, A.G.; Silk, J. In the Realm of the Hubble tension—A Review of Solutions. *arXiv* **2021**, arXiv:2103.01183.

*universe*

MDPI

*Article*

# Relativistic Fractional-Dimension Gravity

Gabriele U. Varieschi

Department of Physics, Loyola Marymount University, Los Angeles, CA 90045, USA; gvarieschi@lmu.edu

**Abstract:** This paper presents a relativistic version of Newtonian Fractional-Dimension Gravity (NFDG), an alternative gravitational model recently introduced and based on the theory of fractional-dimension spaces. This extended version—Relativistic Fractional-Dimension Gravity (RFDG)—is based on other existing theories in the literature and might be useful for astrophysical and cosmological applications. In particular, in this work, we review the mathematical theory for spaces with non-integer dimensions and its connections with the non-relativistic NFDG. The Euler–Lagrange equations for scalar fields can also be extended to spaces with fractional dimensions, by adding an appropriate weight factor, and then can be used to generalize the Laplacian operator for rectangular, spherical, and cylindrical coordinates. In addition, the same weight factor can be added to the standard Hilbert action in order to obtain the field equations, following methods used for scalar-tensor models of gravity, multi-scale spacetimes, and fractional gravity theories. We then apply the field equations to standard cosmology and to the Friedmann-Lemaître-Robertson-Walker metric. Using a suitable weight $v_t(t)$, depending on the synchronous time $t$ and on a single time-dimension parameter $\alpha_t$, we extend the Friedmann equations to the RFDG case. This allows for the computation of the scale factor $a(t)$ for different values of the fractional time-dimension $\alpha_t$ and the comparison with standard cosmology results. Future additional work on the subject, including studies of the cosmological late-time acceleration, type Ia supernovae data, and related dark energy theory will be needed to establish this model as a relativistic alternative theory of gravity.

**Keywords:** fractional-dimension gravity; modified gravity; dark matter; dark energy; cosmology

**Citation:** Varieschi, G.U. Relativistic Fractional-Dimension Gravity. *Universe* **2021**, *7*, 387. https://doi.org/10.3390/universe7100387

Academic Editors: Panayiotis Stavrinos and Emmanuel N. Saridakis

Received: 13 September 2021
Accepted: 13 October 2021
Published: 18 October 2021

**Publisher's Note:** MDPI stays neutral with regard to jurisdictional claims in published maps and institutional affiliations.



## 1. Introduction

This paper considers a possible relativistic generalization of Newtonian Fractional-Dimension Gravity (NFDG), which was previously introduced as a non-relativistic alternative gravity model ([1–3], papers I, II, and III in the following). The main goal of NFDG was to model galactic rotation curves without using the controversial Dark Matter (DM) component (see also [4] for a general overview of NFDG). This was done by assuming that galactic structures might behave like fractal media, with an effective spatial dimension which could be lower than the standard value $D = 3$, including possible fractional, i.e., non-integer values. Each galaxy was then characterized by a particular form of this varying dimension $D = D(r)$, which can be a function of the radial distance from the galactic center.

In paper I [1], it was shown how NFDG is a natural extension of standard Newtonian gravity to non-integer dimension spaces. Starting from a heuristic extension of Gauss's law for gravity to fractional-dimension spaces, we were able to generalize the gravitational field and potential for extended mass sources, the Laplace and Poisson equations, the multipole expansion, etc. Additionally, we modeled several types of spherically symmetric galactic structures, such as Plummer models and others, showing that flat rotation curves can be obtained in NFDG without resorting to DM.

In paper II [2], this analysis was extended to axially symmetric structures in order to model real galactic data from the Spitzer Photometry and Accurate Rotation Curves (SPARC) database [5]. In addition to exponential, Kuzmin, and other similar thin/thick disk mass distributions, the case of the disk-dominated dwarf spiral galaxy NGC 6503 was considered and it was shown that the rotation curve of this galaxy could be obtained by simply assuming $D(r) \approx 2$ over most of the radial range. In other words, if this galaxy were actually to behave like a fractal medium with (Hausdorff) dimension $D(r) \approx 2$, its dynamics would be fully explained by NFDG without any DM contribution.

In addition to NGC 6503, in paper III [3] we studied two additional galaxies with our methods: NGC 7814 (bulge-dominated spiral) and NGC 3741 (gas-dominated dwarf). Although these two galaxies seem to be characterized by different functions for the varying dimension $D = D(r)$, their rotation curves were also fully fitted with NFDG methods, again without any DM. In paper III, the use of a variable dimension $D(r)$ as a function of the field point was also discussed and justified in terms of other similar existing studies. In all these three papers, we pointed out that NFDG is only loosely based on the methods of fractional calculus and fractional mechanics (see [6] and references therein), but is not a fractional theory in the sense used by other gravitational models [7–20]. NFDG field equations are of integer order, therefore local, as opposed to non-local field equations based on fractional differential operators.

NFDG also shows possible connections with Modified Newtonian Dynamics (MOND) [21–23], as discussed in detail in our previous papers [1–3]. In particular, MOND phenomenology, including the recently reported Radial Acceleration Relation (RAR) [24–26], might be explained by our varying dimension $D = D(r)$, which provides the link between the inherently non-linear MOND theory and the linear NFDG.

In this paper, we focus our efforts instead on a relativistic version of our model, which will be called Relativistic Fractional-Dimension Gravity (RFDG). This extended version of NFDG is very similar to Calcagni's theory with ordinary derivatives [8,11], but uses the weight factors introduced in our previous papers I–III. Other more limited analyses of relativistic equations for non-integer dimension spaces are found in the literature [27,28], but they do not fully explore the subject. These relativistic approaches to non-integer, lower-dimension spaces should not be confused with past attempts to study General Relativity (GR) in two or three-dimensional spacetimes [29–31]: in NFDG (or RFDG) the spacetime is the usual $3 + 1$, while we consider possible subsets $X \subset \mathbb{R}^3$ of the standard tri-dimensional space, whose Hausdorff dimensions can be $D \neq 3$, and possibly also a fractional time dimension in RFDG.

Our RFDG model follows the lines of the many existing modified gravity theories in the literature (see [32] for a general review, or the more recent Ref. [33]) and their possible cosmological consequences. As in standard GR [34], an alternative model of gravity should be tested against experimental results of gravitational physics, or at least be consistent with General Relativity at scales where Einstein's theory is undisputed. For example, the MOND model is well established as an alternative gravitational theory (for general reviews see Refs. [35,36]) and its many implications for gravitation and cosmology have been studied for decades, determining the strong and weak points of the model. On the contrary, our NFDG and RFDG are very recent models with limited results and need to be analyzed in more detail through future work, in order to become viable alternatives to standard GR.

In Section 2, we will describe the mathematical theory for spaces with fractional dimension and review the fundamental NFDG results from our previous papers. In Section 3, we will review and expand the Euler–Lagrange equations for non-integer dimension spaces, while in Section 4 we will detail the relativistic equations and apply them to standard cosmology. Finally, in Section 5 conclusions are drawn and possible future work on the subject is outlined.

## 2. Mathematical Theory for Spaces with Non-Integer Dimension and NFDG

The dimensions of space and spacetime play an important role in determining the form of the physical laws and of the constants of nature. While we perceive space as three-dimensional (and time as one-dimensional), discussions on a possible explanation of the tri-dimensionality of space date back to Ptolemy and the early Greeks [37]. In modern times, Ehrenfest's famous article on the subject [38] explained how the tri-dimensionality of space is inherently connected with fundamental physical laws, such as those of stable planetary orbits, atoms and molecules stability, and several others. More recent discussions about the dimensionality of space can be found in the works by Barrow [37], Callender [39], and references therein.

With more recent advances in mathematical theories and fractal geometries, it also became possible to consider a continuous variation in the number of dimensions $D$ for space, i.e., not just positive integer dimensions, but any real (or even complex) spatial dimension $D$. Although this possibility emerged in several areas of physics, it became popular in dimensional regularization techniques commonly used in quantum field theory [40–42]. As part of these techniques (see also [43], page 249), the area of a unit hypersphere $S$ in $D$ dimensions was evaluated as $\int_S d\Omega_D = \frac{2\pi^{D/2}}{\Gamma(D/2)}$, which yields familiar results for integer values of $D$, such as 2 for $D = 1$, $2\pi$ for $D = 2$, $4\pi$ for $D = 3$, etc.

A more comprehensive theory for spaces with non-integer dimension was first introduced by Stillinger in 1977 [44]. Starting from quantities depending explicitly on a variable dimension $D$, such as the Gaussian integral $\int d\mathbf{r} \exp(-\alpha r^2) = (\pi/\alpha)^{D/2}$, or the radial Laplace operator $\frac{1}{r^{D-1}}\frac{d}{dr}\left(r^{D-1}\frac{d}{dr}\right) = \frac{d^2}{dr^2} + \frac{(D-1)}{r}\frac{d}{dr}$, an axiomatic theory for metric spaces of non-integer dimension was then introduced, based on weights, $W_n(\mathbf{x}_1, \ldots, \mathbf{x}_n | r_1, \ldots, r_n)$, for a fixed set of points $\mathbf{x}_1, \ldots, \mathbf{x}_n$ and distances $r_1, \ldots, r_n$ measured from them. The simplest of these weights, $W_1$, was computed as $W_1(r) = \sigma(D) r^{D-1} = \frac{2\pi^{D/2}}{\Gamma(D/2)} r^{D-1}$, with the radial distance $r$ measured from the origin.

This weight allows for the generalization of the integral of a spherically symmetric function $f = f(r)$ over a $D$-dimensional metric space as $\int_0^\infty f(r) W_1(r) dr = \frac{2\pi^{D/2}}{\Gamma(D/2)}$ $\int_0^\infty f(r) r^{D-1} dr$, and of the volume of the radius-R sphere as $V(R, D) = \int_0^R W_1(r) dr = \frac{\pi^{D/2} R^D}{\Gamma(1+D/2)}$.

In the same paper [44], Stillinger introduced a generalized Laplacian in polar coordinates: $\nabla^2 g = [\frac{1}{r^{D-1}}\frac{\partial}{\partial r}(r^{D-1}\frac{\partial}{\partial r}) + \frac{1}{r^2 \sin^{D-2}\theta}\frac{\partial}{\partial\theta}(\sin^{D-2}\theta\frac{\partial}{\partial\theta})]g = [\frac{\partial^2}{\partial r^2} + \frac{(D-1)}{r}\frac{\partial}{\partial r} + \frac{1}{r^2}(\frac{\partial^2}{\partial\theta^2} + \frac{(D-2)}{\tan\theta}\frac{\partial}{\partial\theta})]g$, and applied it to the solution of the generalized two-dimensional Schrödinger's equation, with the angular solution expressed in terms of Gegenbauer polynomials.

As for the physical meaning of a non-integer dimension $D$, Stillinger roughly estimated the possible uncertainty of the spatial dimension as $D \simeq 3 \pm 10^{-6}$ in our terrestrial locale and also explored the possibility of the role of $D$ as a field variable in geometric theories of gravity. In particular, he stated [44]: "However a more general class of spaces can also be generated within which $D$ varies continuously from point to point (integration weights $W_n$ would exhibit the change explicitly)". This seems to imply that the axiomatic bases for non-integer dimension spaces would still be valid for the weight $W_1$ generalized as $W_1(r) = \sigma[D(r)] r^{D(r)-1} = \frac{2\pi^{D(r)/2}}{\Gamma[D(r)/2]} r^{D(r)-1}$, with $D = D(r)$ an explicit function of the field point. This assumption was used as the rationale for a varying fractional dimension $D$ in all our three NFDG papers.

A similar but different approach was later introduced by Svozil [45], within the framework of the Hausdorff measure theory. This lead directly to the integral of a spherically symmetric function $f = f(r)$ over a $D$-dimensional metric space $\chi$ as follows:

$$\int_\chi f d\mu_H = \frac{2\pi^{D/2}}{\Gamma(D/2)} \int_0^\infty f(r) r^{D-1} dr, \tag{1}$$

where $\mu_H$ denotes an appropriate Hausdorff measure over the space. This result is the same obtained previously by Stillinger and was also connected by Svozil to the Weyl's fractional integral defined as $W^{-D} f(x) = \frac{1}{\Gamma(D)} \int_x^\infty (t - x)^{D-1} f(t) dt$, so that Equation (1) can also be written as $\int_\chi f d\mu_H = \frac{2\pi^{D/2}\Gamma(D)}{\Gamma(D/2)} W^{-D} f(0)$, thus connecting the theory of non-integer dimension spaces with fractional calculus.

In 2004, Palmer and Stavrinou [46] expanded the previous concepts into the theory of the equations of motion in a non-integer-dimensional space using Svozil's measure theory approach and multi-variable integration techniques. In particular, to integrate over a subset $X \subset \mathbb{R}^3$ they assumed that $X = X_1 \times X_2 \times X_3$, where each metric space $X_i$ $(i = 1, 2, 3)$ is equipped with a Hausdorff measure $\mu_i(X_i)$ and a dimension $\alpha_i$. When $\alpha_i = 1$, the Hausdorff measure simply becomes a Lebesgue measure. The Hausdorff measure for the product set $X$ can be defined as $\mu_H(X) = (\mu_1 \times \mu_2 \times \mu_3)(X_1 \times X_2 \times X_3) = \mu_1(X_1)\mu_2(X_2)\mu_3(X_3)$ and the overall Hausdorff spatial dimension is then $D = \alpha_1 + \alpha_2 + \alpha_3$.

Applying Fubini's theorem we have [46–50]:

$$\int_X f(x_1, x_2, x_3) d\mu_H = \int_{X_1} \int_{X_2} \int_{X_3} f(x_1, x_2, x_3) d\mu_1(x_1) d\mu_2(x_2) d\mu_3(x_3), \tag{2}$$
$$d\mu_i(x_i) = \frac{\pi^{\alpha_i/2}}{\Gamma(\alpha_i/2)} |x_i|^{\alpha_i - 1} dx_i,\ i = 1, 2, 3$$

where the infinitesimal measures $d\mu_i$ in the second line of the previous equations follow from the original Stillinger's weight $W_1$ described above, and used in the integral in Equation (1). The factor of two in the weight $W_1$ is now omitted, assuming integration between $-\infty$ and $+\infty$ in each sub-space $X_i$.

As was noted in paper I, it is easy to check that the integral in Equation (2) when applied to a function $f(x_1, x_2, x_3) = f(r)$ in spherical coordinates $(r, \theta, \varphi)$, yields the expression in Equation (1). This follows from the standard relations between rectangular and spherical coordinates and from the definitions for the differential measures in the second line of Equation (2): $d\mu_1 d\mu_2 d\mu_3 = \frac{\pi^{\alpha_1/2}}{\Gamma(\alpha_1/2)} \frac{\pi^{\alpha_2/2}}{\Gamma(\alpha_2/2)} \frac{\pi^{\alpha_3/2}}{\Gamma(\alpha_3/2)} r^{\alpha_1+\alpha_2+\alpha_3-1} dr |\sin\theta|^{\alpha_1+\alpha_2-1}$ $|\cos\theta|^{\alpha_3-1} d\theta |\sin\varphi|^{\alpha_2-1} |\cos\varphi|^{\alpha_1-1} d\varphi$. Performing the angular integrations, simplifying the results, and using $D = \alpha_1 + \alpha_2 + \alpha_3$, the result in Equation (1) is readily obtained.

While this result is independent of how the dimensions $\alpha_i$ arrange themselves to act on the orthogonal coordinates and depends only on the overall dimension $D$, Palmer and Stavrinou [46] also noted that in more general cases it is not clear if the non-integer dimension $D$ distributes itself over the $n$ space coordinates (example: $\alpha_1 = \alpha_2 = \cdots = \alpha_n = D/n$) or on only one coordinate (example: $\alpha_1 = \alpha_2 = \cdots = \alpha_{n-1} = 1$ and $\alpha_n = D - (n-1)$), eventually favoring the latter case in Ref. [46]. In these more general cases, the results of the integrations in Equation (2) will depend on how this choice for the $\alpha_i$ dimensions is made.

With all these assumptions, NFDG was developed in papers I–III [1–3] by extending Gauss's law for gravitation to lower-dimensional spacetime $D + 1$, with non-integer space dimension $0 < D \leq 3$. A scale length $l_0$ was needed for dimensional correctness of all expressions when $D \neq 3$, so that dimensionless coordinates were adopted in all formulas, such as the rescaled radial distance $w_r \equiv r/l_0$ or, in general, the dimensionless coordinates $\mathbf{w} \equiv \mathbf{x}/l_0$ for the field point and $\mathbf{w}' \equiv \mathbf{x}'/l_0$ for the source point. A rescaled mass "density" was also introduced: $\tilde{\rho}(\mathbf{w}') = \rho(\mathbf{w}' l_0) l_0^3 = \rho(\mathbf{x}') l_0^3$, where $\rho(\mathbf{x}')$ is the standard mass density in kg m$^{-3}$, and with $d\tilde{m}_{(D)} = \tilde{\rho}(\mathbf{w}') d^D \mathbf{w}'$ representing the infinitesimal source mass in a D-dimensional space[1].

The NFDG gravitational potential $\tilde{\phi}(\mathbf{w})$ was then obtained as:

$$\tilde{\phi}(\mathbf{w}) = -\frac{2\pi^{1-D/2}\Gamma(D/2)G}{(D-2)l_0} \int_{V_D} \frac{\tilde{\rho}(\mathbf{w}')}{|\mathbf{w} - \mathbf{w}'|^{D-2}} d^D \mathbf{w}';\ D \neq 2 \tag{3}$$
$$\tilde{\phi}(\mathbf{w}) = \frac{2G}{l_0} \int_{V_2} \tilde{\rho}(\mathbf{w}') \ln|\mathbf{w} - \mathbf{w}'| d^2 \mathbf{w}';\ D = 2$$

where the physical dimensions for the NFDG gravitational potential $\tilde{\phi}$ are the same as those of the standard Newtonian potential (i.e., measured in m$^2$ s$^{-2}$).

Assuming that $\widetilde{\phi}(\mathbf{w})$ and the NFDG gravitational field $\mathbf{g}(\mathbf{w})$ are connected by $\mathbf{g}(\mathbf{w}) = -\nabla_D\widetilde{\phi}(\mathbf{w})/l_0$, where the D-dimensional gradient $\nabla_D$ is equivalent to the standard one, but derivatives are taken with respect to the rescaled coordinates $\mathbf{w}$, we also obtained:

$$\mathbf{g}(\mathbf{w}) = -\frac{2\pi^{1-D/2}\Gamma(D/2)G}{l_0^2}\int_{V_D}\widetilde{\rho}(\mathbf{w}')\frac{\mathbf{w}-\mathbf{w}'}{|\mathbf{w}-\mathbf{w}'|^D}d^D\mathbf{w}'. \tag{4}$$

It is easy to check that the expressions in Equations (3) and (4) above correctly reduce to the standard Newtonian ones for $D = 3$. The gravitational potential and field in the last two equations were derived for a fixed value of the fractional dimension $D$, but it was argued that they could also be applicable to the case of a variable dimension $D(\mathbf{w})$, assuming a slow change of this dimension with the field point coordinates.

The scale length $l_0$ was related to the MOND acceleration constant $a_0$ (sometimes also denoted by $g_\dagger$ [24,25]):

$$a_0 \equiv g_\dagger = 1.20 \pm 0.02\,(\text{random}) \pm 0.24\,(\text{syst}) \times 10^{-10}\ \ \mathrm{m\,s^{-2}}, \tag{5}$$

which represents the acceleration scale below which MOND corrections are needed. In papers I–III, a possible connection between the scale length $l_0$ and the MOND acceleration $a_0$ was proposed as:

$$a_0 \approx \frac{GM}{l_0^2}, \tag{6}$$

where $M$ is the mass of the system being studied (or a suitable reference mass). The main consequences of the MOND theory (the flat rotation velocity $V_f \approx \sqrt[4]{GMa_0}$, the "baryonic" Tully–Fisher relation-BTFR $M_{bar} \sim V_f^4$, etc.) were recovered in NFDG by considering the MOND limit to be equivalent to a space dimension $D \approx 2$ [1].

The main NFDG Equations (3) and (4) were then adapted to spherically symmetric and axially symmetric cases of interest, then leading to detailed fits of galactic rotation curves for three notable cases (NGC 6503, NGC 7814, NGC 3741) as outlined in Section 1 above. It should be noted that the integrations over $D$-dimensional spaces were performed following the techniques based on Equations (1) and (2) and for different choices of how the individual dimensions $\alpha_1$, $\alpha_2$, $\alpha_3$ arrange themselves on the three spatial orthogonal coordinates (see papers I–III for full details).

## 3. Euler-Lagrange Equations for Spaces with Non-Integer Dimension

In this section, we will expand the treatment of the Euler–Lagrange equations for fields in non-integer-dimension spaces introduced by Palmer and Stavrinou [46], and use it as a starting point for the relativistic equations of motion. This approach has the obvious advantage of yielding the dynamics of the field for any number of degrees of freedom and in any coordinate basis.

We assume a Lagrangian density in four spacetime coordinates, $\mathcal{L} = \mathcal{L}(\phi, \partial_\mu\phi)$, where the field $\phi$ and $\partial_\mu\phi$ are functions of $(t, x^1, x^2, x^3)$ and with $\partial_\mu = (\partial_t, \partial_{x^1}, \partial_{x^2}, \partial_{x^3})$. The generalized action $S$ in a $D+1$ spacetime is [46][2]:

$$S = \int dt d^D x \mathcal{L}(\phi, \partial_\mu\phi) = \int dt \int d\mu_1\left(x^1\right)d\mu_2\left(x^2\right)d\mu_3\left(x^3\right)\mathcal{L}(\phi, \partial_\mu\phi) \tag{7}$$

$$d\mu_i\left(x^i\right) = W_1\left(x^i, \alpha_i\right)dx^i = \frac{\pi^{\alpha_i/2}}{\Gamma(\alpha_i/2)}\left|x^i\right|^{\alpha_i-1}dx^i,\ i = 1,2,3$$

where the measures $d\mu_i$ are those from Equation (2) and all the integrations now extend from $-\infty$ to $+\infty$, so that the measure weights are $W_1\left(x^i, \alpha_i\right) = \frac{\pi^{\alpha_i/2}}{\Gamma(\alpha_i/2)}\left|x^i\right|^{\alpha_i-1}$ (the factor of two in the original Stillinger's weight is now omitted)[3].

By taking variations and minimizing the action [46], it is straightforward to obtain the following Euler–Lagrange equations:

$$\prod_{i=1}^{3} W_1\left(x^i,\alpha_i\right)\frac{\partial\mathcal{L}(\phi,\partial_\mu\phi)}{\partial\phi} - \prod_{i=1}^{3} W_1\left(x^i,\alpha_i\right)\partial_\mu\frac{\partial\mathcal{L}(\phi,\partial_\mu\phi)}{\partial(\partial_\mu\phi)} - \frac{\partial\mathcal{L}(\phi,\partial_\mu\phi)}{\partial(\partial_\mu\phi)}\partial_\mu\prod_{i=1}^{3} W_1\left(x^i,\alpha_i\right)$$
$$= \prod_{i=1}^{3} W_1\left(x^i,\alpha_i\right)\frac{\partial\mathcal{L}(\phi,\partial_\mu\phi)}{\partial\phi} - \partial_\mu\left[\prod_{i=1}^{3} W_1\left(x^i,\alpha_i\right)\frac{\partial\mathcal{L}(\phi,\partial_\mu\phi)}{\partial(\partial_\mu\phi)}\right] = 0, \quad (8)$$

with the measure weights $W_1(x^i,\alpha_i)$ described above, or even for more general types of measures. Since for $D = 3$, and $\alpha_1 = \alpha_2 = \alpha_3 = 1$, we have $\prod_{i=1}^{3} W_1(x^i,\alpha_i) = 1$ and $\partial_\mu \prod_{i=1}^{3} W_1(x^i,\alpha_i) = 0$, Equation (8) reduces to standard Euler–Lagrange equations in $3+1$ spacetimes.

As noted in Ref. [46], the "flow" or "current" of the measure $\partial_\mu \prod_{i=1}^{3} W_1(x^i,\alpha_i)$, multiplied by the momentum density of the field $\frac{\partial\mathcal{L}(\phi,\partial_\mu\phi)}{\partial(\partial_\mu\phi)}$ in the third term of the first line in Equation (8), will alter the dynamics of the field $\phi$ in a non-integer-dimensional space, compared to the standard case. As a consequence, if the system is invariant under a symmetry transformation $\phi(x) \to \phi(x) + \delta\phi(x)$, the related conserved current density and conservation law in non-integer dimensions are [46]:

$$J^\mu = \prod_{i=1}^{3} W_1\left(x^i,\alpha_i\right)\frac{\partial\mathcal{L}(\phi,\partial_\mu\phi)}{\partial(\partial_\mu\phi)}\delta\phi \quad (9)$$
$$\partial_\mu J^\mu = 0.$$

This last equation, and the previous Equation (8), could have been also introduced from the standard equations by substituting $\mathcal{L} \to \prod_{i=1}^{3} W_1(x^i,\alpha_i)\mathcal{L}$ and $J^\mu \to \prod_{i=1}^{3} W_1(x^i,\alpha_i)J^\mu$, respectively. To conclude this general overview, we will outline in the following subsections the specific cases of rectangular, spherical, and cylindrical coordinates and the related $D$-dimensional Laplace operators.

### 3.1. Rectangular Coordinates

In rectangular coordinates, the generalized Euler–Lagrange equations can be obtained directly from Equation (8) with the weights in Equation (7) [46]:

$$\frac{\partial\mathcal{L}(\phi,\partial_\mu\phi)}{\partial\phi} - \partial_\mu\frac{\partial\mathcal{L}(\phi,\partial_\mu\phi)}{\partial(\partial_\mu\phi)} - \left(\alpha_{\mu\nu} - \delta_{\mu\nu}\right)\left(x^{(-1)}\right)^\nu\frac{\partial\mathcal{L}(\phi,\partial_\mu\phi)}{\partial(\partial_\mu\phi)} = 0, \quad (10)$$

where $\alpha_{\mu\nu} = diag(1,\alpha_1,\alpha_2,\alpha_3)$, $\delta_{\mu\nu}$ is the diagonal unit matrix, $x^{(-1)} = column\left(t^{-1},(x^1)^{-1},(x^2)^{-1},(x^3)^{-1}\right)$, with $\mu,\nu = 0,1,2,3$. The total spacetime dimension is $D_t = 1 + D = 1 + \alpha_1 + \alpha_2 + \alpha_3 = Tr(\alpha_{\mu\nu})$, where the time dimension is assumed to be integer.

As in the original treatment for the Schrödinger's Equation [46,51], we can consider $\phi$ and $\phi^*$ as separate fields which can be varied independently and then use the Lagrangian density $\mathcal{L} = \nabla\phi^* \cdot \nabla\phi = \partial_i\phi^*\partial_i\phi$ to obtain the generalized Laplace equation, using Equation (10) for the "mirror" field $\phi^*$. The Laplace equation becomes $\nabla^2_{\alpha_1,\alpha_2,\alpha_3}\phi(x,y,z) = 0$, where the generalized Laplacian operator written in standard rectangular coordinates $x$, $y$, $z$, is:

$$\nabla^2_{\alpha_1,\alpha_2,\alpha_3}\phi(x,y,z) = \left[\frac{1}{x^{\alpha_1-1}}\frac{\partial}{\partial x}\left(x^{\alpha_1-1}\frac{\partial}{\partial x}\right) + \frac{1}{y^{\alpha_2-1}}\frac{\partial}{\partial y}\left(y^{\alpha_2-1}\frac{\partial}{\partial y}\right) + \frac{1}{z^{\alpha_3-1}}\frac{\partial}{\partial z}\left(z^{\alpha_3-1}\frac{\partial}{\partial z}\right)\right]\phi$$
$$= \left[\frac{\partial^2}{\partial x^2} + \frac{(\alpha_1-1)}{x}\frac{\partial}{\partial x} + \frac{\partial^2}{\partial y^2} + \frac{(\alpha_2-1)}{y}\frac{\partial}{\partial y} + \frac{\partial^2}{\partial z^2} + \frac{(\alpha_3-1)}{z}\frac{\partial}{\partial z}\right]\phi. \quad (11)$$

The non-integer dimension can then be assigned to just one of the three coordinates (example: $\alpha_1 = \alpha_2 = 1$ and $\alpha_3 = D-2$), or distributed over the three coordinates (example: $\alpha_1 = \alpha_2 = \alpha_3 = D/3$).

*3.2. Spherical Coordinates*

To obtain similar results in spherical coordinates $r$, $\theta$, $\varphi$, we could transform directly Equations (10) and (11), or use the orthonormal basis $\partial_\mu = \left(\frac{\partial}{\partial t}, \frac{\partial}{\partial r}, \frac{1}{r}\frac{\partial}{\partial \theta}, \frac{1}{r\sin\theta}\frac{\partial}{\partial\varphi}\right)$. Following this latter option and using again a Lagrangian density $\mathcal{L} = \nabla\phi^* \cdot \nabla\phi = \partial_i\phi^*\partial_i\phi$ in Equation (8), we obtain:

$$\nabla^2_{\alpha_1,\alpha_2,\alpha_3}\phi(r,\theta,\varphi) = \left[\frac{\partial^2\phi}{\partial r^2} + \frac{(\alpha_1+\alpha_2+\alpha_3-1)}{r}\frac{\partial\phi}{\partial r}\right] \quad (12)$$
$$+\frac{1}{r^2}\left[\frac{\partial^2\phi}{\partial\theta^2} + \frac{(\alpha_1+\alpha_2-1)}{\tan\theta}\frac{\partial\phi}{\partial\theta} + \frac{(1-\alpha_3)}{\cot\theta}\frac{\partial\phi}{\partial\theta}\right] + \frac{1}{r^2\sin^2\theta}\left[\frac{\partial^2\phi}{\partial\varphi^2} + \frac{(\alpha_2-1)}{\tan\varphi}\frac{\partial\phi}{\partial\varphi} + \frac{(1-\alpha_1)}{\cot\varphi}\frac{\partial\phi}{\partial\varphi}\right].$$

The previous equation extends the results in Ref. [46], by providing the most general spherical Laplacian for $D = \alpha_1+\alpha_2+\alpha_3$ ($0 < \alpha_1,\alpha_2,\alpha_3 \leq 1$). For $\alpha_1 = \alpha_2 = \alpha_3 = 1$ ($D = 3$), the standard spherical Laplacian is recovered, while special cases are obtained if the non-integer dimension is assigned to just one of the three parameters.

If the non-integer parameter is the first one, that is $0 < \alpha_1 < 1$, $\alpha_2 = \alpha_3 = 1$, $D = \alpha_1 + 2$, we have:

$$\nabla^2_{D-2,1,1}\phi(r,\theta,\varphi) = \left[\frac{\partial^2\phi}{\partial r^2} + \frac{(D-1)}{r}\frac{\partial\phi}{\partial r}\right] \quad (13)$$
$$+\frac{1}{r^2}\left[\frac{\partial^2\phi}{\partial\theta^2} + \frac{(D-2)}{\tan\theta}\frac{\partial\phi}{\partial\theta}\right] + \frac{1}{r^2\sin^2\theta}\left[\frac{\partial^2\phi}{\partial\varphi^2} + \frac{(3-D)}{\cot\varphi}\frac{\partial\phi}{\partial\varphi}\right].$$

If instead, $0 < \alpha_2 < 1$, $\alpha_1 = \alpha_3 = 1$, $D = \alpha_2 + 2$, we have:

$$\nabla^2_{1,D-2,1}\phi(r,\theta,\varphi) = \left[\frac{\partial^2\phi}{\partial r^2} + \frac{(D-1)}{r}\frac{\partial\phi}{\partial r}\right] \quad (14)$$
$$+\frac{1}{r^2}\left[\frac{\partial^2\phi}{\partial\theta^2} + \frac{(D-2)}{\tan\theta}\frac{\partial\phi}{\partial\theta}\right] + \frac{1}{r^2\sin^2\theta}\left[\frac{\partial^2\phi}{\partial\varphi^2} + \frac{(D-3)}{\tan\varphi}\frac{\partial\phi}{\partial\varphi}\right].$$

Finally, if $0 < \alpha_3 < 1$, $\alpha_1 = \alpha_2 = 1$, $D = \alpha_3 + 2$, we obtain:

$$\nabla^2_{1,1,D-2}\phi(r,\theta,\varphi) = \left[\frac{\partial^2\phi}{\partial r^2} + \frac{(D-1)}{r}\frac{\partial\phi}{\partial r}\right] \quad (15)$$
$$+\frac{1}{r^2}\left[\frac{\partial^2\phi}{\partial\theta^2} + \frac{1}{\tan\theta}\frac{\partial\phi}{\partial\theta} + \frac{(3-D)}{\cot\theta}\frac{\partial\phi}{\partial\theta}\right] + \frac{1}{r^2\sin^2\theta}\left[\frac{\partial^2\phi}{\partial\varphi^2}\right].$$

In Ref. [46], Palmer and Stavrinou introduced the non-integer spherical Laplacian as the one in our Equation (14) above, but they stated that this form was obtained by assigning the non-integer dimension to $\alpha_3$, while it is in fact assigned to $\alpha_2$. In our paper, I, we used this same form of the spherical Laplacian to discuss the fractional-dimension solutions to the Laplace equation and the related multipole expansion (see Appendix A of Ref. [1]), but we could have used also the other forms of the Laplacian discussed in this section.

However, our main NFDG results in Equations (3) and (4) are independent of the choice of the fractional-dimension Laplace operator.

From the general Laplacian in Equation (12), other "mixed" forms of this operator are possible. For example, the non-integer dimension could be equally distributed over the three parameters by setting $\alpha_1 = \alpha_2 = \alpha_3 = D/3$, or in an unequal way, or over just two parameters, etc. Therefore, there is a certain ambiguity in how the non-integer dimension is acting over the three spatial coordinates, as we already remarked in Section 2 above. We also note that the order of the parameters, $\alpha_1$, $\alpha_2$, $\alpha_3$, refers to the original weights in Equation (2), which were related to rectangular coordinates and not to the spherical coordinates used in this section.

### 3.3. Cylindrical Coordinates

In cylindrical coordinates $R, \varphi, z$, we can use the orthonormal basis $\partial_\mu = \left(\frac{\partial}{\partial t}, \frac{\partial}{\partial R}, \frac{1}{R}\frac{\partial}{\partial \varphi}, \frac{\partial}{\partial z}\right)$ and the same Lagrangian density $\mathcal{L} = \nabla\phi^* \cdot \nabla\phi = \partial_i\phi^*\partial_i\phi$ in the main Equation (8). This time, we obtain:

$$\begin{aligned}\nabla^2_{\alpha_1,\alpha_2,\alpha_3}\phi(R,\varphi,z) &= \left[\frac{\partial^2\phi}{\partial R^2} + \frac{(\alpha_1+\alpha_2-1)}{R}\frac{\partial\phi}{\partial R}\right] \\ &+\frac{1}{R^2}\left[\frac{\partial^2\phi}{\partial\varphi^2} + \frac{(\alpha_2-1)}{\tan\varphi}\frac{\partial\phi}{\partial\varphi} + \frac{(1-\alpha_1)}{\cot\varphi}\frac{\partial\phi}{\partial\varphi}\right] + \left[\frac{\partial^2\phi}{\partial z^2} + \frac{(\alpha_3-1)}{z}\frac{\partial\phi}{\partial z}\right].\end{aligned} \tag{16}$$

This is the most general cylindrical Laplacian for $D = \alpha_1+\alpha_2+\alpha_3$ ($0 < \alpha_1, \alpha_2, \alpha_3 \leq 1$). For $\alpha_1 = \alpha_2 = \alpha_3 = 1$ ($D = 3$), the standard cylindrical Laplacian is recovered, while special cases are obtained if the non-integer dimension is assigned to just one of the three parameters, as for the spherical case studied in the previous subsection.

If the non-integer parameter is the first one, that is $0 < \alpha_1 < 1$, $\alpha_2 = \alpha_3 = 1$, $D = \alpha_1 + 2$, we have:

$$\begin{aligned}\nabla^2_{D-2,1,1}\phi(R,\varphi,z) &= \left[\frac{\partial^2\phi}{\partial R^2} + \frac{(D-2)}{R}\frac{\partial\phi}{\partial R}\right] \\ &+\frac{1}{R^2}\left[\frac{\partial^2\phi}{\partial\varphi^2} + \frac{(3-D)}{\cot\varphi}\frac{\partial\phi}{\partial\varphi}\right] + \left[\frac{\partial^2\phi}{\partial z^2}\right].\end{aligned} \tag{17}$$

If instead, $0 < \alpha_2 < 1$, $\alpha_1 = \alpha_3 = 1$, $D = \alpha_2 + 2$, we have:

$$\begin{aligned}\nabla^2_{1,D-2,1}\phi(R,\varphi,z) &= \left[\frac{\partial^2\phi}{\partial R^2} + \frac{(D-2)}{R}\frac{\partial\phi}{\partial R}\right] \\ &+\frac{1}{R^2}\left[\frac{\partial^2\phi}{\partial\varphi^2} + \frac{(D-3)}{\tan\varphi}\frac{\partial\phi}{\partial\varphi}\right] + \left[\frac{\partial^2\phi}{\partial z^2}\right].\end{aligned} \tag{18}$$

Finally, if $0 < \alpha_3 < 1$, $\alpha_1 = \alpha_2 = 1$, $D = \alpha_3 + 2$, we obtain:

$$\begin{aligned}\nabla^2_{1,1,D-2}\phi(R,\varphi,z) &= \left[\frac{\partial^2\phi}{\partial R^2} + \frac{1}{R}\frac{\partial\phi}{\partial R}\right] \\ &+\frac{1}{R^2}\left[\frac{\partial^2\phi}{\partial\varphi^2}\right] + \left[\frac{\partial^2\phi}{\partial z^2} + \frac{D-3}{z}\frac{\partial\phi}{\partial z}\right].\end{aligned} \tag{19}$$

From the general cylindrical Laplacian in Equation (16), other "mixed" forms of this operator are possible. Again, the non-integer dimension could be equally distributed over the three parameters by setting $\alpha_1 = \alpha_2 = \alpha_3 = D/3$, or in an unequal way, or over just two parameters, etc. In this cylindrical case, it is obvious that $\alpha_3$ refers directly to the $z$ coordinate, while it is not possible to assign $\alpha_1$ and $\alpha_2$ to the $R$, $\varphi$ coordinates. Therefore, a certain ambiguity remains in how to distribute the non-integer dimension over the three spatial coordinates also in this case.

## 4. Relativistic Equations for Spaces with Non-Integer Dimension

In Section 3, it was shown that the Euler–Lagrange equations for spaces with non-integer dimensions can be obtained by substituting $\mathcal{L} \to \prod_{i=1}^{3} W_1(x^i, \alpha_i)\mathcal{L}$, i.e., simply by multiplying the Lagrangian density by the product of the weights for the three spatial coordinates. This immediately suggests a possible procedure for the relativistic extension of NFDG: include the same weight factor $\prod_{i=1}^{3} W_1(x^i, \alpha_i)$ inside the standard Hilbert action $S_H = \int \sqrt{-g}\, R\, d^4x$ and then vary this modified action with respect to the inverse metric $g^{\mu\nu}$, as is usually done in standard GR.

This procedure is practically equivalent to the one used for scalar-tensor theories of gravity (see Ref. [52] for a general overview) and it has been used extensively by Calcagni in the context of multi-scale spacetimes and fractional gravity theories [7,8,10,11,15,17,18]. In the following subsections we will review these techniques and adapt them to our particular case.

### 4.1. RFDG Field Equations

In this section, we will obtain the field equations by following closely the methods used by Calcagni in their main paper on multi-scale gravity and cosmology [11] and the general procedure for field equations in alternative theories of gravity (see Section 4.8 in Ref. [52]). Following [8,11], the weight factor $\prod_{i=1}^{3} W_1(x^i, \alpha_i)$ introduced in Section 3, with the NFDG weights from Equation (2), is consistent with the general form of the weight $v(x)$, assumed to be factorizable in the coordinates and positive semi-definite [11]:

$$v(x) = \prod_{\mu=0}^{3} v_\mu(x^\mu),\ v_\mu(x^\mu) \geq 0 \tag{20}$$

$$q^\mu(x^\mu) = \int^{x^\mu} dx'^\mu\, v_\mu\left(x'^\mu\right)$$

as shown in the first line of the previous equation[4].

The action measure is assumed to be of the form $d\varrho(x) = d^4x\ v(x) = d^4q(x)$, where "geometric coordinates" $q(x)$, as defined in the second line of Equation (20), can be used formally to re-express the measure in a standard Lebesgue form. In this way [11], a multi-scale Minkowski spacetime is defined as the multiplet $\mathcal{M}^4 = (M^4, \varrho, \partial, \mathcal{K})$ based on an ordinary 4-dimensional Minkowski spacetime $M^4$, a Lebesgue-Stieltjes measure $\varrho$ for the action, a set of calculus rules with derivative operators $\partial$, and an appropriate Laplace-Beltrami operator $\mathcal{K}$.

Different multi-scale theories were then developed by Calcagni, with reference to the possible derivative operators $\partial$ being used: theory $T_1$ with ordinary derivatives, theory $T_v$ with weighted derivatives, and theory $T_q$ with q-derivatives (see [11,17] for full details). These models were then used in connection with the most general measure derived from first principles [13] and then applied to quantum field theories, quantum gravity, and cosmology [11,15–18].

For the purpose of deriving the RFDG field equations, we will consider the NFDG weight $v(x)$:

$$v(x) = \prod_{\mu=0}^{3} v_\mu(x^\mu) = \prod_{i=1}^{3} \frac{\pi^{\alpha_i/2}}{\Gamma(\alpha_i/2)} \left|x^i\right|^{\alpha_i - 1}, \tag{21}$$

consistent with Equations (2) and (7) and with the time weight assumed to be unity, i.e., $v_0(x^0) = 1$, but more general expressions can be used, including non-trivial time weights. As already noted in Appendix A of our paper III, using rescaled coordinates $w^i = x^i/l_0$, the NFDG weight $\frac{\pi^{\alpha_i/2}}{\Gamma(\alpha_i/2)} \left|\frac{x^i}{l_0}\right|^{\alpha_i-1}$ in Equation (21) is very similar to the binomial weight

$\left(1 + |\frac{x^i}{l_*}|^{\alpha_i - 1}\right)$ used by Calcagni [13]. However, in NFDG the transition from Newtonian to non-Newtonian behavior is achieved by varying continuously the fractional dimension parameters $\alpha_i$ from $\alpha_i = 1$ (Newtonian case, $v_i(x^i) = 1$) to $0 < \alpha_i < 1$ (non-Newtonian), with $l_0$ being an appropriate scale parameter linked to the MOND acceleration scale. In multifractional theories, the scale lengths $l_*$ represent the observation scales at which the spacetime dimension may change, with different behaviors for $x^i \ll l_*$ and $x^i \gg l_*$, and with a binomial weight which does not simply reduce to unity for $\alpha_i = 1$.

Apart from the different choice of weights, the RFDG field equations are obtained with the same procedure for the theory $T_1$ with ordinary derivatives [11]. The action for gravity can be taken as:

$$S_g = \frac{1}{16\pi G} \int d^4x \, \sqrt{-g} v(x) \left[ R - \omega \partial_\mu v \partial^\mu v - U(v) \right], \tag{22}$$

where $G$ is Newton's gravitational constant, $v(x)$ is the weight being considered, $g = |g_{\mu\nu}|$ is the determinant of the metric, $R = R^\mu_{\ \mu} = g^{\mu\nu} R_{\mu\nu}$ is the Ricci scalar, defined in terms of standard Ricci and Riemann tensors [52]. In scalar-tensor and multifractional theories, it is customary to include in the gravitational action a "kinetic" term $\omega \partial_\mu v \partial^\mu v$ and a "potential" term $U(v)$ (which can be set to $2\Lambda$, to include a cosmological constant $\Lambda$, or can be a function of the weight $v$). In general, these terms are not needed in RFDG, and we will set $\omega = 0$ and $U(v) = 0$ later.

Including also a matter action $S_m = \int d^4x \sqrt{-g} v(x) \mathcal{L}_m$, with $\mathcal{L}_m$ denoting an appropriate Lagrangian density, the energy-momentum tensor is now defined as:

$$T_{\mu\nu} = -\frac{2}{\sqrt{-g}\, v(x)} \frac{\delta S_m}{\delta g^{\mu\nu}}, \tag{23}$$

with the weight $v(x)$ added at the denominator. One can then obtain the field equations by varying the action with respect to the inverse metric $g^{\mu\nu}$, where additional terms are derived using the techniques used for scalar-tensor models [52]. The final result is [11]:

$$R_{\mu\nu} - \frac{1}{2} g_{\mu\nu} [R - U(v)] + g_{\mu\nu} \frac{\Box v}{v} - \frac{\nabla_\mu \nabla_\nu v}{v} + \omega \left( \frac{1}{2} g_{\mu\nu} \partial_\sigma v \partial^\sigma v - \partial_\mu v \partial_\nu v \right) = 8\pi G T_{\mu\nu} \tag{24}$$

where $\nabla_\mu$ indicates standard covariant differentiation, and the Laplace-Beltrami operator is defined as $\Box = \nabla^\mu \nabla_\mu = g^{\mu\nu} \nabla_\mu \nabla_\nu$. It is easy to check that standard GR field equations are recovered for $\omega = 0$ and $v(x) = 1$, including a cosmological constant term by setting $U = 2\Lambda$, or otherwise by simply setting $U = 0$.

The trace of Equation (24) yields:

$$-R + 2U(v) + 3\frac{\Box v}{v} + \omega \partial_\mu v \partial^\mu v = 8\pi G T_\mu^{\ \mu} \tag{25}$$

while variation of the total action $S = S_g + S_m$ with respect to the weight $v(x)$ gives:

$$R - U(v) = -16\pi G \mathcal{L}_m + v \frac{dU}{dv} - \omega (2v \Box v + \partial_\mu v \partial^\mu v). \tag{26}$$

Combining the last two equations, one can also obtain [11]:

$$R - 2v \frac{dU}{dv} + 3\frac{\Box v}{v} + \omega (4v \Box v + 3\partial_\mu v \partial^\mu v) = 8\pi G \left( T_\mu^{\ \mu} - 4\mathcal{L}_m \right) \tag{27}$$

which links directly the Ricci scalar $R$ with the weight $v(x)$.

An alternative version of the field Equation (24), can be obtained by taking the trace of this equation and then combining the result with the same Equation (24). The final result is:

$$R_{\mu\nu} = 8\pi G\left(T_{\mu\nu} - \frac{1}{2}g_{\mu\nu}T\right) + \frac{1}{2}g_{\mu\nu}U(v) + \frac{1}{2}g_{\mu\nu}\frac{\Box v}{v} + \frac{\nabla_\mu\nabla_\nu v}{v} + \omega\,\partial_\mu v\partial_\nu v, \tag{28}$$

where $T = T^\mu_{\ \mu}$ is the trace of the energy-momentum tensor.

The RFDG equations can be obtained from the previous general Equations (22)–(28) by setting $\omega = 0$, $U(v) = 0$, and using the NFDG weight $v(x)$ described in Equation (21), or any other appropriate weight. In particular, the field equation becomes:

$$R_{\mu\nu} - \frac{1}{2}g_{\mu\nu}R + g_{\mu\nu}\frac{\Box v}{v} - \frac{\nabla_\mu\nabla_\nu v}{v} = 8\pi G T_{\mu\nu} \tag{29}$$

where only the two additional terms $g_{\mu\nu}\frac{\Box v}{v} - \frac{\nabla_\mu\nabla_\nu v}{v}$ in the left-hand side of this equation need to be computed, in order to extend standard GR to RFDG. The alternative version, corresponding to Equation (28), is instead:

$$R_{\mu\nu} = 8\pi G\left(T_{\mu\nu} - \frac{1}{2}g_{\mu\nu}T\right) + \frac{1}{2}g_{\mu\nu}\frac{\Box v}{v} + \frac{\nabla_\mu\nabla_\nu v}{v}, \tag{30}$$

which will be used in the next section to derive the Friedmann equations of cosmology.

Following the discussion in Section 3.1 of Ref. [11], we note that the weight $v(x)$ can be treated as a scalar field in the derivation of the field equations [32,52], but it should be considered a "fixed coordinate profile" and not a Lorentz scalar. The derivation of the field equations is essentially equivalent to the one typically used in scalar-tensor theories [32,52], but the interpretation [11] of the scalar weight $v(x)$ differs from the one of the fields $\phi(x)$ used in modified gravity and in quintessence models of dark energy [53].

Although $v(x)$ does not represent a dynamical field, it affects the dynamics through the additional terms $g_{\mu\nu}\frac{\Box v}{v} - \frac{\nabla_\mu\nabla_\nu v}{v}$ in Equation (29) above. Since our weight $v(x)$ in Equation (21) is determined directly by our NFDG theory, we do not feel necessary, at least at this stage, to introduce kinetic and potential terms, $\omega\partial_\mu v\partial^\mu v$ and $U(v)$, as was done in multifractional gravitational theories [11].

Therefore, at least at this stage, RFDG is introduced in a phenomenological way by fixing from the beginning the coordinate profile or weight $v(x)$, which does not change while the system is evolving dynamically. The choice of the weight is suggested by those used in our previous NFDG papers, or by similar time-dependent weights which will be used in the next sub-section. As already mentioned above, $v(x)$ cannot be considered a scalar field, although the derivation of the field equations is equivalent to the one for scalar-tensor theories (see also Section 3.1 in Ref. [32]). The RFDG field Equations (29) and (30) obviously reduce to standard GR for $v(x) = 1$, i.e., for gravitational systems which do not possess any spatial or temporal fractional-dimension (for example, at the Solar System level). Therefore, RFDG and GR are fully consistent for structures whose Hausdorff dimension coincides with the topological one.

In the next subsection, we will apply the main field Equations (29) and (30) to the case of standard cosmology and to the Friedmann-Lemaître-Robertson-Walker metric.

### 4.2. Cosmology and RFDG

In standard cosmology [52,54], the Friedmann-Lemaître-Robertson-Walker (FLRW) metric is usually expressed as ($c = 1$):

$$ds^2 = -dt^2 + a^2(t)\left[\frac{dr^2}{1-\kappa r^2} + r^2 d\Omega^2\right], \tag{31}$$

where $a(t) = R(t)/R_0$ is the dimensionless scale factor ($R(t)$ is the scale factor, $R_0 = R(t_0)$, $t_0$ current time), $\kappa = k/R_0^2$ ($k = -1$ open universe; $k = 0$ flat universe; $k = 1$ closed universe), and $d\Omega^2 = d\theta^2 + \sin^2\theta d\varphi^2$. Following this choice for the FLRW metric, the

Christoffel symbols, the non-zero components of the Ricci tensor, and the Ricci scalar are readily computed [52] and are reported in Appendix A.

Matter and energy in the Universe are usually modeled as a perfect fluid with energy-momentum tensor:

$$T_{\mu\nu} = (\rho + p)U_\mu U_\nu + p g_{\mu\nu} \tag{32}$$

with the fluid at rest in comoving coordinates, so that the four-velocity is $U^\mu = (1, 0, 0, 0)$ and the energy-momentum tensor simply becomes

$$T_{\mu\nu} = \begin{pmatrix} \rho & 0 & 0 & 0 \\ 0 & & & \\ 0 & & g_{ij}p & \\ 0 & & & \end{pmatrix} \tag{33}$$

in terms of the energy density $\rho(t)$ and the pressure $p(t)$. This can also be written as $T^\mu_\nu = diag(-\rho, p, p, p)$ and with the trace given by $T = T^\mu_\mu = -\rho + 3p$.

In order to compute the additional terms $g_{\mu\nu}\frac{\Box v}{v}$, $\frac{\nabla_\mu \nabla_\nu v}{v}$ in Equations (29) and (30), we should express the NFDG weight of Equation (21) in terms of spherical coordinates $r$, $\theta$, $\varphi$. Using standard coordinate transformations between rectangular and spherical coordinates and assuming for example $\alpha_1 = \alpha_2 = \alpha_3 = D/3$, we obtain:

$$v(x) = \prod_{i=1}^{3} \frac{\pi^{\alpha_i/2}}{\Gamma(\alpha_i/2)} \left|x^i\right|^{\alpha_i - 1} = \frac{\pi^{D/2}}{[\Gamma(D/6)]^3} r^{D-3} |\sin\theta|^{\left(\frac{2}{3}D-2\right)} |\cos\theta|^{\left(\frac{D}{3}-1\right)} |\sin\varphi|^{\left(\frac{D}{3}-1\right)} |\cos\varphi|^{\left(\frac{D}{3}-1\right)} = v_r(r) v_\theta(\theta) v_\varphi(\varphi), \tag{34}$$

but this weight does not yield isotropic results for the Friedmann equations. Assuming instead a simpler radial weight $v_r(r) = \frac{\pi^{(D/2-1)}}{2\Gamma(D/2)} r^{D-3}$, which follows from the general fractional-dimension integral in Equation (1), divided by the standard factor of $4\pi r^2$ pertaining to the $D = 3$ case, still does not seem to yield isotropic results due to the presence of mixed $(t, r)$ components in the field tensors, which can be avoided only by adding a time weight $v_t(t) = a(t)$, equal to the scale factor[5].

As discussed in Appendix A, it might be more appropriate for cosmological applications to assume a purely temporal weight, similar to the spatial one in Equation (21):

$$v(x) \equiv v_t(t) = \frac{\pi^{\alpha_t/2}}{\Gamma(\alpha_t/2)} t^{\alpha_t - 1}, \tag{35}$$

where $t > 0$ and $0 < \alpha_t \leq 1$ is a time fractional dimension. This assumption is similar to the one used by Calcagni in their Ref. [8], but will yield different results in the context of RFDG.

With the particular weight in Equation (35), all quantities in the generalized field Equations (24) and (28) can be computed and the complete results are detailed in Appendix A. Using these results, the modified Friedmann equations are:

$$\begin{aligned} \left(\frac{\dot a}{a}\right)^2 + \frac{\dot a \dot v}{a v} - \frac{\omega \dot v^2}{6} - \frac{U(v)}{6} &= \frac{8\pi G}{3}\rho - \frac{\kappa}{a^2} \\ \frac{\ddot a}{a} + \frac{\dot a \dot v}{2 a v} + \frac{\ddot v}{2v} + \frac{\omega \dot v^2}{3} - \frac{U(v)}{6} &= -\frac{4\pi G}{3}(\rho + 3p) \end{aligned} \tag{36}$$

where we denoted the temporal weight simply as $v = v_t(t)$ and all time derivatives are shown using the over-dot notation.

These equations can be further simplified by taking $\omega = 0$ and by introducing a possible cosmological constant $\Lambda$ (setting $U(v) = 2\Lambda$), for comparison with standard $\Lambda CDM$ cosmology. Therefore, we obtain:

$$\left(\frac{\dot{a}}{a}\right)^2 + \frac{\dot{a}\dot{v}}{av} = \frac{8\pi G}{3}\rho - \frac{\kappa}{a^2} + \frac{\Lambda}{3} \tag{37}$$
$$\frac{\ddot{a}}{a} + \frac{\dot{a}\dot{v}}{2av} + \frac{\ddot{v}}{2v} = -\frac{4\pi G}{3}(\rho + 3p) + \frac{\Lambda}{3}$$

which can be compared directly with the standard Friedmann equations [52,54]. It is evident that both Equations (36) and (37) reduce to the standard ones for $v = 1$ ($\dot{v} = \ddot{v} = 0$).

The Hubble parameter $H$ characterizes the rate of expansion, as usual:

$$H = \frac{\dot{a}}{a} \tag{38}$$
$$\dot{H} = \frac{\ddot{a}}{a} - \left(\frac{\dot{a}}{a}\right)^2 = \frac{\ddot{a}}{a} - H^2$$

with the present epoch value as the Hubble constant $H_0 = 100$ h km s$^{-1}$ Mpc$^{-1}$ ($h \approx 0.7$). In a similar way, we can introduce a weight parameter $V$:

$$V = \frac{\dot{v}}{v} \tag{39}$$
$$\dot{V} = \frac{\ddot{v}}{v} - \left(\frac{\dot{v}}{v}\right)^2 = \frac{\ddot{v}}{v} - V^2$$

and rewrite the Friedmann Equations (37) in terms of the $H$ and $V$ parameters:

$$H^2 + HV = \frac{8\pi G}{3}\rho - \frac{\kappa}{a^2} + \frac{\Lambda}{3} \tag{40}$$
$$\dot{H} + H^2 + \frac{1}{2}\left(HV + V^2 + \dot{V}\right) = -\frac{4\pi G}{3}(\rho + 3p) + \frac{\Lambda}{3}.$$

We will assume that the standard components of the Universe have energy densities evolving as power laws, $\rho_i(t) = \rho_{i0}a^{-n_i}(t)$; each component will have equation of state $p_i(t) = w_i\rho_i(t)$, with parameters $w_i = \frac{1}{3}n_i - 1$. As in standard cosmology, we will include matter ($M$, $n_M = 3$, $w_M = 0$), radiation ($R$, $n_R = 4$, $w_R = \frac{1}{3}$), curvature ($C$, $n_C = 2$, $w_C = -\frac{1}{3}$), and vacuum ($\Lambda$, $n_\Lambda = 0$, $w_\Lambda = -1$) .

Generalizing the standard procedure used in $\Lambda CDM$ cosmology [52,54], we will still introduce the density parameter $\Omega$ and the critical density $\rho_{crit}$ as $\Omega = \frac{8\pi G}{3H^2}\rho = \frac{\rho}{\rho_{crit}}$ and $\rho_{crit} = \frac{3H^2}{8\pi G}$, respectively. These two equations assume that for each component the density parameter is defined as $\Omega_i = \frac{8\pi G}{3H^2}\rho_i = \frac{\rho_i}{\rho_{crit}}$, with the special cases for the curvature energy density $\rho_C \equiv -\frac{3\kappa}{8\pi G a^2}$ and the vacuum energy density $\rho_\Lambda \equiv \frac{\Lambda}{8\pi G}$. While the curvature density parameter $\Omega_C = -\frac{\kappa}{H^2a^2}$ is typically not included in the total $\Omega = \Omega_M + \Omega_R + \Omega_\Lambda$ introduced above, it is still possible to modify the first Friedmann Equation (40) and obtain:

$$1 + \beta = \Omega - \frac{\kappa}{H^2a^2} = \Omega_M + \Omega_R + \Omega_\Lambda + \Omega_C = \sum_i \Omega_i \tag{41}$$
$$\beta \equiv \frac{V}{H}$$

which extends the standard relation $\Omega - 1 = \frac{\kappa}{H^2a^2}$ and with the summation in the first line applied to all four components [6].

For the current time $t_0$, Equation (41) can be written as $\sum_i \Omega_{i0} = 1 + \beta_0$, with $\beta_0 = \frac{V_0}{H_0}$, and used to rewrite the first line in Equation (40) as:

$$H^2 + HV = \frac{8\pi G}{3}\sum_i \rho_i(t) = \frac{8\pi G}{3}\sum_i \rho_{i0}a^{-n_i}(t) = H_0^2 \sum_i \Omega_{i0}a^{-n_i}(t) \tag{42}$$
$$= H_0^2\{\Omega_{M0}a^{-3}(t) + \Omega_{R0}a^{-4}(t) + \Omega_{\Lambda 0} + [1 + \beta_0 - (\Omega_{M0} + \Omega_{R0} + \Omega_{\Lambda 0})]\, a^{-2}(t)\},$$

where the summation symbols include all four components of the energy density, the current-time curvature density parameter is expressed in terms of the other three, $\Omega_{C0} = 1 + \beta_0 - (\Omega_{M0} + \Omega_{R0} + \Omega_{\Lambda 0})$, and the explicit values of the integer parameters $n_i$ have also been used in the last line.

It is customary to use a dimensionless time $\bar{t} = H_0(t - t_0)$ when solving the previous differential equation, so we need to rewrite the RFDG weight in Equation (35) in terms of $t = t_0 + \frac{\bar{t}}{H_0}$ and then rescale this variable for dimensional correctness, dividing by a scale time $t_{sc}$ which can be simply taken as the current time, i.e., $t_{sc} \approx t_0$. Then, we have:

$$\frac{t}{t_{sc}} = \frac{t_0}{t_{sc}} + \frac{\bar{t}}{t_{sc}H_0} \approx 1 + \frac{\bar{t}}{t_0 H_0} = 1 + \delta_0 \bar{t} \tag{43}$$
$$v = v_t(\bar{t}) = \frac{\pi^{\alpha_t/2}}{\Gamma(\alpha_t/2)}\left(\frac{t}{t_{sc}}\right)^{\alpha_t - 1} \approx \frac{\pi^{\alpha_t/2}}{\Gamma(\alpha_t/2)}(1 + \delta_0\bar{t})^{\alpha_t - 1}$$

and the final weight $v_t(\bar{t})$ in the second line can be used with free parameters $\alpha_t > 0$ and $\delta_0 = \frac{1}{t_0 H_0} \sim 1$, since typically $t_0 \sim H_0^{-1}$. With these approximations, we also find $\beta_0 \approx (\alpha_t - 1)$ and the only free parameter remaining in our equations is the time dimension $\alpha_t$.

Using the definitions for $H$ and $V$ from Equations (38) and (39), the dimensionless time variable $\bar{t} = H_0(t - t_0)$ (with $d\bar{t} = H_0 dt$), and with some additional algebra the main Equation (42) can be recast as:

$$\dot{a} = -\frac{1}{2}\frac{a\dot{v}}{v} \pm a\sqrt{\left\{\Omega_{M0}a^{-3}(\bar{t}) + \Omega_{R0}a^{-4}(\bar{t}) + \Omega_{\Lambda 0} + [1 + \beta_0 - (\Omega_{M0} + \Omega_{R0} + \Omega_{\Lambda 0})]\, a^{-2}(\bar{t})\right\} + \frac{1}{4}\left(\frac{\dot{v}}{v}\right)^2}, \tag{44}$$

which becomes the RFDG differential equation for the scale factor $a(\bar{t})$ with the initial condition $a(0) = 1$ and time derivatives now taken with respect to $\bar{t}$. For an expanding universe at the current epoch, we will choose the positive sign in Equation (44), and then solve it numerically for any assumed values of $\Omega_{M0}$, $\Omega_{R0}$, $\Omega_{\Lambda 0}$ at the current time and for any given temporal weight $v = v_t(\bar{t})$. It should be noted that for $\alpha_t = 1$ and $\beta_0 = 0$ ($v = 1$, $\dot{v} = 0$, $\ddot{v} = 0$), Equation (44) correctly reduces to the $\Lambda CDM$ equivalent differential equation:

$$\dot{a} = a\sqrt{\{\Omega_{M0}a^{-3}(\bar{t}) + \Omega_{R0}a^{-4}(\bar{t}) + \Omega_{\Lambda 0} + [1 - (\Omega_{M0} + \Omega_{R0} + \Omega_{\Lambda 0})]\, a^{-2}(\bar{t})\}}, \tag{45}$$

which is commonly used in standard cosmology to obtain $a(\bar{t})$ from the initial $\Omega_{i0}$ values [52,54].

Using the RFDG Friedmann Equation (44), or the standard-cosmology equivalent (45) above, we plot in Figure 1 some results for different values of the parameters, using the temporal weight $v = v_t(\bar{t})$ as described in Equation (43) with $0 < \alpha_t \leq 1$ and $\delta_0 = \frac{1}{t_0 H_0} \sim 1$. The results do not appear to depend much on the value of this second parameter, so we simply set $\delta_0 = 1$ in the following.

In this figure, we plot three notable standard cosmology expansion histories, similar to those presented in Figure 8.3 of Ref. [52], or Figure 2 in Ref. [54]. These were obtained using Equation (45) above: the red-solid curve for $\Omega_{M0} = 0.3$, $\Omega_{\Lambda 0} = 0.7$ (and $\alpha_t = 1$, i.e., $v = 1$) represents the currently favored $\Lambda CDM$ expansion history for a universe dominated by about 70% of cosmological constant, Dark Energy (DE) component and only about 30% of matter component (baryonic and dark matter). The green-solid curve corresponds instead to a matter-dominated universe with $\Omega_{M0} = 1.0$ and no cosmological constant, while the blue-solid curve corresponds to a 30% matter component, without any cosmological constant. The radiation component at current epoch is assumed to be negligible ($\Omega_{R0} \approx 0$), while the curvature component is fixed by $\Omega_{C0} = 1 - (\Omega_{M0} + \Omega_{R0} + \Omega_{\Lambda 0})$.

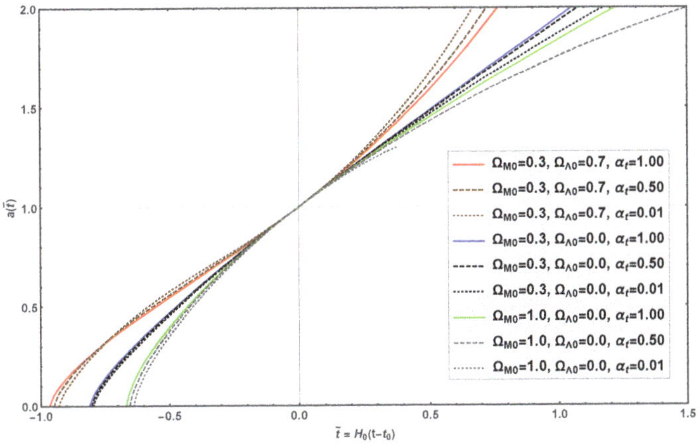


**Figure 1.** Expansion histories for different values of $\Omega_{M0}$, $\Omega_{\Lambda 0}$, and of the RFDG parameter $\alpha_t$. Three notable cases from standard cosmology (red, blue, and green solid curves) are compared with RFDG results for similar $\Omega_{M0}$, $\Omega_{\Lambda 0}$ parameters, but with variable $\alpha_t > 0$. RFDG curves for $\alpha_t = 0.01, 0.50$ (dotted and dashed curves) are only slightly different from their respective standard cosmology solid curves.

Using Equation (44), we also plotted RFDG expansion histories for the same values of the $\Omega_{M0}$, $\Omega_{\Lambda 0}$ parameters ($\Omega_{R0} = 0$), but for different values of the parameter $\alpha_t = 0.01$, 0.50 (dotted and dashed curves). This was done to show how the RFDG curves, with $\alpha_t \approx 0 - 1$, can modify the standard-cosmology histories by adding the temporal weight $v = v_t(\bar{t})$ from Equation (43). The goal of our original NFDG [1–3] was to show how the effect of adding a possible spatial fractional-dimension $D < 3$ could replace the DM component in astrophysical structures. Therefore, the goal of RFDG should be to show that also the DE component in the Universe might be explained by a fractional-dimension effect, possibly related to the temporal dimension parameter $\alpha_t < 1$.

However, as seen in the figure, the modified RFDG curves differ only slightly from the standard-cosmology curves, for the range of the $\alpha_t$ parameter being used. As a consequence, it seems unlikely that a RFDG curve with no cosmological constant ($\Omega_{\Lambda 0} = 0$) and $0 < \alpha_t < 1$ might be able to match the $\Lambda CDM$ red-solid curve, i.e., replacing DE with a fractional-dimension effect. Further analysis will be needed to check this possibility, by considering an extended range for the $\alpha_t$ parameter, using different approximations for $t_{SC}$ and $\delta_0$ in Equation (43), and possibly by also including the "kinetic" and "potential" terms in Equation (36) ($\omega \neq 0$ and $U(v) \neq 0$).

It is beyond the scope of this paper to expand these considerations any further, since the goal of this current work was just to introduce the main equations of Relativistic Fractional-Dimension Gravity, following the non-relativistic equations of our original NFDG. At the moment, RFDG is just a tentative modified gravity model which needs to be explored in more detail before it can be effectively applied to astrophysical objects or cosmological investigations. In the near future, we are planning to analyze measurements of the luminosity distance of type Ia supernovae with RFDG techniques, to see if our model can interpret these data without resorting to the DE component as in standard $\Lambda CDM$ cosmology. This would be a necessary condition for the viability of RFDG as an alternative model of gravity.

## 5. Conclusions

In this work, we outlined a relativistic extension of our Newtonian Fractional-Dimension Gravity, which was developed to model the dynamics of galaxies without using any dark matter component. While the analysis of the NFDG model is still ongoing with additional galaxies being studied with these methods, it was important to show that NFDG admits a possible relativistic version, although at the moment it is not sure if this Relativistic Fractional-Dimension Gravity will be useful to address astrophysical or cosmological problems.

In this paper, we showed that a relativistic version can be derived from the mathematical theory for spaces with non-integer dimensions, the extended Euler–Lagrange equations for scalar fields, and the existing methods for scalar-tensor models of gravity, multi-scale spacetimes, and fractional gravity theories. The key element in all these methods is to include an appropriate coordinate weight in the spacetime metric used in both NFDG and RFDG. These weights will include the fractional-dimension parameters which characterize these theories and should be considered to be different from the scalar functions used in other models.

As a first, tentative application of RFDG, we applied it to the FLRW metric of standard cosmology, using a simple time-dependent weight. We showed that it is straightforward to extend the standard Friedmann equations and to solve them numerically for different choices of the parameters. At this time, it is not possible to predict if these modified cosmological equations will be of any physical significance, in relation to the DE problem, or others.

Future work on the subject will be needed to test this model against the cosmological paradigm, considering other possible weights which might be relevant in astrophysics and cosmology, and also including the cosmic late-time acceleration, distance indicators, type Ia supernovae data, etc., before RFDG can be considered a viable alternative theory of gravity.

**Funding:** This research received no external funding.

**Institutional Review Board Statement:** Not applicable.

**Informed Consent Statement:** Not applicable.

**Data Availability Statement:** Not applicable.

**Acknowledgments:** This work was supported by the Department of Physics, Loyola Marymount University, Los Angeles. The author wishes to acknowledge G. Calcagni for very useful advice regarding multifractional theories as well as other topics, and the anonymous reviewers for helpful comments and suggestions.

**Conflicts of Interest:** The authors declare no conflict of interest.

## Appendix A. RFDG Tensors for the FLRW Metric

In this section, we will detail the RFDG tensors used for the study of the FLRW metric and related expansion histories discussed in Section 4.2. All these tensor quantities were computed using Mathematica code[7]. These programs were tested by checking them against results for known cases (standard GR and others) and then extended to include the additional tensors described in Section 4.1.

The FLRW metric was defined in Equation (31), in terms of the dimensionless scale factor $a(t)$ and using standard spherical coordinates $(r, \theta, \varphi)$; the energy-momentum tensor in Equations (32) and (33), where pressure $p(t)$ and energy density $\rho(t)$ depend on the synchronous time $t$. The only additional input is the factorizable weight $v(x) \equiv v_t(t)v_r(r)v_\theta(\theta)v_\varphi(\varphi)$, which in general can be a function of the four spacetime coordinates.

As already mentioned in Section 4.2, this general form of the weight does not seem to yield isotropic Friedmann equations, and even considering simplified weights, such as $v(x) \equiv v_t(t)v_r(r)$ or $v(x) \equiv v_r(r)$ does not seem to yield the required symmetry, although future studies might be needed to explore these weights in more detail. Therefore, we opted to use a purely time dependent weight, $v(x) \equiv v_t(t)$ and we computed all the tensors in terms of this general form for the weight, obtaining the following results.

Christoffel symbols, non-zero components of the Ricci tensor, and Ricci scalar (same as standard GR results [52]):

$$\begin{array}{ll} \Gamma^0_{11} = \frac{a\dot{a}}{1-\kappa r^2} & \Gamma^1_{11} = \frac{\kappa r}{1-\kappa r^2} \\ \Gamma^0_{22} = a\dot{a}r^2 & \Gamma^0_{33} = a\dot{a}r^2 \sin^2\theta \\ \Gamma^1_{01} = \Gamma^2_{02} = \frac{\dot{a}}{a} & \Gamma^3_{03} = \frac{\dot{a}}{a} \\ \Gamma^1_{22} = -r(1-\kappa r^2) & \Gamma^1_{33} = -r(1-\kappa r^2)\sin^2\theta \\ \Gamma^2_{12} = \frac{1}{r} & \Gamma^3_{13} = \frac{1}{r} \\ \Gamma^2_{33} = -\sin\theta\cos\theta & \Gamma^3_{23} = \cot\theta \end{array} \tag{A1}$$

$$\begin{aligned} R_{00} &= -3\frac{\ddot{a}}{a} \\ R_{11} &= \frac{a\ddot{a} + 2\dot{a}^2 + 2\kappa}{1-\kappa r^2} \\ R_{22} &= r^2\left(a\ddot{a} + 2\dot{a}^2 + 2\kappa\right) \\ R_{33} &= r^2\left(a\ddot{a} + 2\dot{a}^2 + 2\kappa\right)\sin^2\theta \\ R &= 6\left[\frac{\ddot{a}}{a} + \left(\frac{\dot{a}}{a}\right)^2 + \frac{\kappa}{a^2}\right] \end{aligned} \tag{A2}$$

where time derivatives are indicated by the over-dot notation.

The additional tensors in Equations (24) and (28) are computed as follows. The potential term $A_{\mu\nu} \equiv \frac{1}{2}g_{\mu\nu}U(v)$ is easily computed from the metric components:

$$\begin{aligned} A_{00} &= -\frac{1}{2}U(v) \\ A_{11} &= \frac{1}{2}\frac{a^2U(v)}{(1-\kappa r^2)} \\ A_{22} &= \frac{1}{2}r^2a^2U(v) \\ A_{33} &= \frac{1}{2}r^2a^2U(v)\sin^2\theta. \end{aligned} \tag{A3}$$

The components of the tensor $B_{\mu\nu} \equiv g_{\mu\nu}\frac{\Box v}{v}$, calculated using the Laplace-Beltrami operator $\Box = \nabla^\mu\nabla_\mu = g^{\mu\nu}\nabla_\mu\nabla_\nu$, are as follows:

$$\begin{aligned} B_{00} &= \frac{3\dot{a}\dot{v} + a\ddot{v}}{av} \\ B_{11} &= -\frac{a(3\dot{a}\dot{v} + a\ddot{v})}{v(1-\kappa r^2)} \\ B_{22} &= -\frac{r^2a(3\dot{a}\dot{v} + a\ddot{v})}{v} \\ B_{33} &= -\frac{r^2a(3\dot{a}\dot{v} + a\ddot{v})\sin^2\theta}{v} \end{aligned} \tag{A4}$$

where the weight $v_t(t)$ is simply denoted by $v$. The tensor $C_{\mu\nu} \equiv \frac{\nabla_\mu\nabla_\nu v}{v}$ has components:

$$C_{00} = \frac{\ddot{v}}{v} \tag{A5}$$
$$C_{11} = -\frac{a\dot{a}\dot{v}}{v(1-\kappa r^2)}$$
$$C_{22} = -\frac{r^2 a\dot{a}\dot{v}}{v}$$
$$C_{33} = -\frac{r^2 a\dot{a}\dot{v}\sin^2\theta}{v}$$

The tensor $D_{\mu\nu} \equiv \omega\left(\frac{1}{2}g_{\mu\nu}\partial_\sigma v\partial^\sigma v - \partial_\mu v\partial_\nu v\right)$ is computed as:

$$D_{00} = -\frac{1}{2}\omega\dot{v}^2 \tag{A6}$$
$$D_{11} = -\frac{1}{2}\frac{\omega a^2\dot{v}^2}{(1-\kappa r^2)}$$
$$D_{22} = -\frac{1}{2}r^2\omega a^2\dot{v}^2$$
$$D_{33} = -\frac{1}{2}r^2\omega a^2\dot{v}^2\sin^2\theta$$

while the simpler tensor $E_{\mu\nu} \equiv \omega\,\partial_\mu v\partial_\nu v$ has only one non-zero component:

$$E_{00} = \omega\dot{v}^2 \tag{A7}$$

From Equations (32) and (33), the components of the energy-momentum tensor are:

$$T_{00} = \rho(t) \tag{A8}$$
$$T_{11} = \frac{a^2 p(t)}{1-\kappa r^2}$$
$$T_{22} = r^2 a^2 p(t)$$
$$T_{33} = r^2 a^2 p(t)\sin^2\theta$$

with the trace given as $T = T^\mu_\mu = -\rho(t) + 3p(t)$.

Using all the above tensor components, the field Equation (24) can be written as:

$$R_{\mu\nu} - \frac{1}{2}g_{\mu\nu}R + A_{\mu\nu} + B_{\mu\nu} - C_{\mu\nu} + D_{\mu\nu} = 8\pi G T_{\mu\nu} \tag{A9}$$

while the alternative field Equation (28) can be computed as:

$$R_{\mu\nu} = 8\pi G\left(T_{\mu\nu} - \frac{1}{2}g_{\mu\nu}T\right) + A_{\mu\nu} + \frac{1}{2}B_{\mu\nu} + C_{\mu\nu} + E_{\mu\nu} \tag{A10}$$

It is usually easier to use this alternative field equation to derive the Friedmann equations. The $\mu\nu = 00$ equation from (A10), after some algebraic simplification, gives:

$$-3\frac{\ddot{a}}{a} - \frac{3}{2}\frac{\dot{a}\dot{v}}{av} - \frac{3}{2}\frac{\ddot{v}}{v} - \omega\dot{v}^2 + \frac{1}{2}U(v) = 4\pi G(\rho + 3p) \tag{A11}$$

while the $\mu\nu = ii$ equations ($i = 1,2,3$) from (A10) are all equivalent to each other and yield:

$$\frac{\ddot{a}}{a} + 2\left(\frac{\dot{a}}{a}\right)^2 + 2\frac{\kappa}{a^2} + \frac{5}{2}\frac{\dot{a}\dot{v}}{av} + \frac{1}{2}\frac{\ddot{v}}{v} - \frac{1}{2}U(v) = 4\pi G(\rho - p). \tag{A12}$$

Combining these last two equations together, after some simplifications, we obtain the modified Friedmann Equation (36) introduced in Section 4.2.

## Notes

1 SI units will be used throughout this paper, unless otherwise noted.

2 In Section 4, we will also include a possible time weight $v_t(t) = \frac{\pi^{\alpha_t/2}}{\Gamma(\alpha_t/2)}|t|^{\alpha_t-1}$ into the action. Following the original analysis in Ref. [46], we will not use this weight in this section.

3 Dimensionless coordinates, such as $w^i = x^i/l_0$, $w_r = r/l_0$, etc., should be used in most equations in this section and in the following ones. For simplicity's sake, in this paper we left standard coordinates ($x^i$, $r$, $R$, etc.) in most equations, without transforming them into dimensionless, rescaled ones.

4 We prefer to indicate explicitly the spacetime dimension (i.e., $D_{spacetime} = 4$, $\mu = 0, 1, 2, 3$), as opposed to using the symbol $D$ as in Ref. [11]. We will continue instead to denote with $D$ the variable NFDG space dimension, as was done in Sections 1–3.

5 Even using a combined weight, $v_t(t)v_r(r) = a(t)v_r(r)$, does not seem to yield fully isotropic Friedmann equations for the cosmological problem. A more detailed study of cosmological weights, including possible radial factors or even direct modifications to the FLRW metric in terms of variable space-time dimensions, will be done in a future publication.

6 In RFDG, the connection with open ($\kappa < 0$), flat ($\kappa = 0$), and closed ($\kappa > 0$) universes is not simply related to the density parameter $\Omega \lesseqgtr 1$ as in standard cosmology, due to the presence of the additional $\beta$ term in Equation (41).

7 Mathematica, Version 12.2.0.0, Wolfram Research Inc.

## References


1. Varieschi, G.U. Newtonian Fractional-Dimension Gravity and MOND. *Found. Phys.* **2020**, *50*, 1608–1644. [CrossRef]
2. Varieschi, G.U. Newtonian Fractional-Dimension Gravity and Disk Galaxies. *Eur. Phys. J. Plus* **2021**, *136*, 183. [CrossRef]
3. Varieschi, G.U. Newtonian fractional-dimension gravity and rotationally supported galaxies. *Mon. Not. R. Astron. Soc.* **2021**, *503*, 1915–1931. [CrossRef]
4. Varieschi, G.U. Newtonian Fractional-Dimension Gravity (NFDG). 2020. Available online: http://gvarieschi.lmu.build/NFDG2020.html (accessed on 16 October 2021).
5. Lelli, F.; McGaugh, S.S.; Schombert, J.M. SPARC: Mass Models for 175 Disk Galaxies with Spitzer Photometry and Accurate Rotation Curves. *Astron. J.* **2016**, *152*, 157. [CrossRef]
6. Varieschi, G.U. Applications of Fractional Calculus to Newtonian Mechanics. *J. Appl. Math. Phys.* **2018**, *6*, 1247–1257. [CrossRef]
7. Calcagni, G. Fractal universe and quantum gravity. *Phys. Rev. Lett.* **2010**, *104*, 251301. [CrossRef]
8. Calcagni, G. Quantum field theory, gravity and cosmology in a fractal universe. *JHEP* **2010**, *3*, 120. [CrossRef]
9. Calcagni, G. Geometry of fractional spaces. *Adv. Theor. Math. Phys.* **2012**, *16*, 549–644. [CrossRef]
10. Calcagni, G. Geometry and field theory in multi-fractional spacetime. *JHEP* **2012**, *1*, 65. [CrossRef]
11. Calcagni, G. Multi-scale gravity and cosmology. *JCAP* **2013**, *12*, 41. [CrossRef]
12. Calcagni, G. Multifractional theories: An unconventional review. *JHEP* **2017**, *3*, 138. [CrossRef]
13. Calcagni, G. Multiscale spacetimes from first principles. *Phys. Rev. D* **2017**, *95*, 064057. [CrossRef]
14. Calcagni, G. Towards multifractional calculus. *Front. Phys.* **2018**, *6*, 58. [CrossRef]
15. Calcagni, G.; De Felice, A. Dark energy in multifractional spacetimes. *Phys. Rev. D* **2020**, *102*, 103529. [CrossRef]
16. Calcagni, G. Quantum scalar field theories with fractional operators. *Class. Quant. Grav.* **2021**, *38*, 165006. [CrossRef]
17. Calcagni, G. Multifractional theories: An updated review. *Mod. Phys. Lett. A* **2021**, *36*, 2140006. [CrossRef]
18. Calcagni, G. Classical and quantum gravity with fractional operators. *Class. Quant. Grav.* **2021**, *38*, 165005; Erratum in **2021**, *38*, 169601. [CrossRef]
19. Giusti, A. MOND-like Fractional Laplacian Theory. *Phys. Rev. D* **2020**, *101*, 124029. [CrossRef]
20. Giusti, A.; Garrappa, R.; Vachon, G. On the Kuzmin model in fractional Newtonian gravity. *Eur. Phys. J. Plus* **2020**, *135*, 798. [CrossRef]
21. Milgrom, M. A Modification of the Newtonian dynamics as a possible alternative to the hidden mass hypothesis. *Astrophys. J.* **1983**, *270*, 365–370. [CrossRef]
22. Milgrom, M. A Modification of the Newtonian dynamics: Implications for galaxies. *Astrophys. J.* **1983**, *270*, 371–383. [CrossRef]
23. Milgrom, M. A modification of the Newtonian dynamics: Implications for galaxy systems. *Astrophys. J.* **1983**, *270*, 384–389. [CrossRef]
24. McGaugh, S.; Lelli, F.; Schombert, J. Radial Acceleration Relation in Rotationally Supported Galaxies. *Phys. Rev. Lett.* **2016**, *117*, 201101. [CrossRef]
25. Lelli, F.; McGaugh, S.S.; Schombert, J.M.; Pawlowski, M.S. One Law to Rule Them All: The Radial Acceleration Relation of Galaxies. *Astrophys. J.* **2017**, *836*, 152. [CrossRef]
26. Chae, K.H.; Lelli, F.; Desmond, H.; McGaugh, S.S.; Li, P.; Schombert, J.M. Testing the Strong Equivalence Principle: Detection of the External Field Effect in Rotationally Supported Galaxies. *Astrophys. J.* **2020**, *904*, 51; Erratum in **2021**, *81*, 910. [CrossRef]

27. Sadallah, M.; Muslih, S.I.; Baleanu, D. Equations of motion for Einstein's field in non-integer dimensional space. *Czechoslov. J. Phys.* **2006**, *56*, 323–328. [CrossRef]
28. Sadallah, M.; Muslih, S.I. Solution of the equations of motion for Einstein's field in fractional D dimensional space-time. *Int. J. Theor. Phys.* **2009**, *48*, 3312–3318. [CrossRef]
29. Collas, P. General relativity in two- and three-dimensional space-times. *Am. J. Phys.* **1977**, *45*, 833–837. [CrossRef]
30. Romero, C.; Dahia, F. Theories of gravity in (2+1)-dimensions. *Int. J. Theor. Phys.* **1994**, *33*, 2091–2098. [CrossRef]
31. Deser, S.; Jackiw, R.; 't Hooft, G. Three-dimensional Einstein gravity: Dynamics of flat space. *Ann. Phys.* **1984**, *152*, 220–235. [CrossRef]
32. Clifton, T.; Ferreira, P.G.; Padilla, A.; Skordis, C. Modified gravity and cosmology. *Phys. Rep.* **2012**, *513*, 1–189. [CrossRef]
33. Saridakis, E.N.; Lazkoz, R.; Salzano, V.; Moniz, P.V.; Capozziello, S.; Jiménez, J.B.; de Laurentis, M.; Olmo, G.J.; Akrami, Y.; Bahamonde, S.; et al. Modified Gravity and Cosmology: An Update by the CANTATA Network. *arXiv* **2021**, arXiv:2105.12582.
34. Will, C.M. The Confrontation between General Relativity and Experiment. *Living Rev. Rel.* **2014**, *17*, 4. [CrossRef]
35. Sanders, R.H.; McGaugh, S.S. Modified Newtonian dynamics as an alternative to dark matter. *Ann. Rev. Astron. Astrophys.* **2002**, *40*, 263–317. [CrossRef]
36. Famaey, B.; McGaugh, S. Modified Newtonian Dynamics (MOND): Observational Phenomenology and Relativistic Extensions. *Living Rev. Relat.* **2012**, *15*, 10. [CrossRef]
37. Barrow, J.D. Dimensionality. *Philos. Trans. R. Soc. Lond. Ser. A Math. Phys. Sci.* **1983**, *310*, 337–346.
38. Ehrenfest, P. Welche Rolle spielt die Dreidimensionalität des Raumes in den Grundgesetzen der Physik? *Ann. Phys.* **1920**, *366*, 440–446. [CrossRef]
39. Callender, C. Answers in search of a question: 'proofs' of the tri-dimensionality of space. *Stud. Hist. Philos. Mod. Phys.* **2005**, *36*, 113–136. [CrossRef]
40. Bollini, C.G.; Giambiagi, J.J. Dimensional Renormalization: The Number of Dimensions as a Regularizing Parameter. *Nuovo Cim.* **1972**, *B12*, 20–26. [CrossRef]
41. 't Hooft, G.; Veltman, M.J.G. Regularization and Renormalization of Gauge Fields. *Nucl. Phys.* **1972**, *B44*, 189–213. [CrossRef]
42. Wilson, K.G. Quantum field theory models in less than four-dimensions. *Phys. Rev.* **1973**, *D7*, 2911–2926. [CrossRef]
43. Peskin, M.E.; Schroeder, D.V. *An Introduction to Quantum Field Theory*; CRC Press: Boca Raton, FL, USA, 1995.
44. Stillinger, F.H. Axiomatic basis for spaces with noninteger dimension. *J. Math. Phys.* **1977**, *18*, 1224–1234. [CrossRef]
45. Svozil, K. Quantum field theory on fractal spacetime: A new regularisation method. *J. Phys. A Math. Gen.* **1987**, *20*, 3861–3875. [CrossRef]
46. Palmer, C.; Stavrinou, P.N. Equations of motion in a non-integer-dimensional space. *J. Phys. A Math. Gen.* **2004**, *37*, 6987–7003. [CrossRef]
47. Tarasov, V. *Fractional Dynamics: Application of Fractional Calculus to Dynamics of Particles, Fields and Media*; Springer Science & Business Media: Berlin, Germany, 2011.
48. Zubair, M.; Mughal, M.; Naqvi, Q. *Electromagnetic Fields and Waves in Fractional Dimensional Space*; Springer Science & Business Media: Berlin, Germany, 2012. [CrossRef]
49. Tarasov, V.E. Anisotropic fractal media by vector calculus in non-integer dimensional space. *J. Math. Phys.* **2014**, *55*, 083510. [CrossRef]
50. Tarasov, V.E. Vector calculus in non-integer dimensional space and its applications to fractal media. *Commun. Nonlinear Sci. Numer. Simul.* **2015**, *20*, 360–374. [CrossRef]
51. Morse, P.; Feshbach, H. *Methods of Theoretical Physics*; International Series in Pure and Applied Physics; McGraw-Hill: New York, NY, USA, 1953.
52. Carroll, S.M. *Spacetime and Geometry*; Cambridge University Press: Cambridge, UK, 2019.
53. Tsujikawa, S. Quintessence: A Review. *Class. Quant. Grav.* **2013**, *30*, 214003. [CrossRef]
54. Carroll, S.M. The Cosmological constant. *Living Rev. Relat.* **2001**, *4*, 1. [CrossRef] [PubMed]

universe MDPI

Article

# Dynamical Analysis and Cosmological Evolution in Weyl Integrable Gravity

Andronikos Paliathanasis [1,2]

[1] Institute of Systems Science, Durban University of Technology, P.O. Box 1334, Durban 4000, South Africa; anpaliat@phys.uoa.gr
[2] Instituto de Ciencias Físicas y Matemáticas, Universidad Austral de Chile, Valdivia 5090000, Chile

**Abstract:** We investigate the cosmological evolution for the physical parameters in Weyl integrable gravity in a Friedmann–Lemaître–Robertson–Walker universe with zero spatial curvature. For the matter component, we assume that it is an ideal gas, and of the Chaplygin gas, from the Weyl integrable gravity a scalar field is introduced by a geometric approach which provides an interaction with the matter component.We calculate the stationary points for the field equations and we study their stability properties. Furthermore, we solve the inverse problem for the case of an ideal gas and prove that the gravitational field equations can follow from the variation of a Lagrangian function. Finally, variational symmetries are applied for the construction of analytic and exact solutions.

**Keywords:** cosmological dynamics; Weyl integrable theory; scalar field; interaction

**Citation:** Paliathanasis, A. Dynamical Analysis and Cosmological Evolution in Weyl Integrable Gravity. *Universe* **2021**, *7*, 468. https://doi.org/10.3390/universe7120468

Academic Editor: Lorenzo Iorio

Received: 27 October 2021
Accepted: 29 November 2021
Published: 30 November 2021



## 1. Introduction

The cosmological constant component in the Einstein-Hilbert Action Integral is the simplest dark energy candidate to describe of the recent acceleration phase of the universe, as it is provided by the cosmological observations [1]. In the so-called ΛCDM cosmology the universe is considered to be homogeneous and isotropic, described by the Friedmann–Lemaître–Robertson–Walker (FLRW) geometry with spatially flat term, where the matter component consists of the cosmological constant and a pressureless fluid source which attributes the dark matter component of the universe. The gravitational field equations are of second-order and can be integrated explicitly. Indeed, the field equations can be reduced to that of the one-dimensional "hyperbolic oscillator". However, as the cosmological observations are improved, Λ-cosmology loses the important position in the "armoury" of cosmologists. For an interesting discussion on the subject we refer the reader to the recent review [2]. Furthermore, because of the simplicity of the field equations in Λ-cosmology, the cosmological constant term cannot provide a solution for the description of the complete cosmological evolution and history.

In order to solve these problems, cosmologists have introduced various solutions in the literature by introducing new degrees of freedom in the field equations. Time-varying Λ term, scalar fields and fluids with time-varying equation of state parameters, like the Chaplygin gases have been proposed to modify the energy-momentum tensor of the field equations [3–8]. On the other hand, a different approach is inspired by the modification of the Einstein-Hilbert Action integral, and leads to the family of theories known as alternative/modified theories of gravity [9–11]. Another interesting consideration is the interaction between the various components of the energy momentum tensor [12]. Interaction in the dark components of the cosmological model, that is, between, the dark energy and the dark matter terms, is supported by cosmological observations [13–16].

For a given proposed dark energy mode model, there are systematic methods for the investigation of the physical properties of the model. The derivation of exact and analytic solutions is an essential approach because analytic techniques can be used for the investigation of the cosmological viability of the model [17–20]. Furthermore, from the analysis of the asymptotic dynamics, that is, of the determination of the stationary points, the complete cosmological history can be constructed [21–23]. Indeed, constraints for the free parameters of a given model can be constructed through the analysis of the stationary points and the specific requirements for the stability of the stationary points [24–28].

In this piece of work, we study the evolution of the cosmological dynamics for the theory known as Weyl integrable gravity (WIG) [29–35]. In WIG a scalar field is introduced into the Einstein-Hilbert Action Integral by a geometric construction approach. Indeed, in Riemannian geometry the basic geometric object is the covariant derivative $\nabla_\mu$ and the metric tensor $g_{\mu\nu}$, such that it has no metricity component, i.e., $\nabla_\kappa g_{\mu\nu} = 0$ [36]. In Weyl geometry the fundamental geometric objects are the gauge vector field $\omega_\mu$ and the the metric tensor $g_{\mu\nu}$, such that $\tilde{\nabla}_\kappa g_{\mu\nu} = \omega_\kappa g_{\mu\nu}$, where now $\tilde{\nabla}_\mu$ notes the covariant derivative with respect to the affine connection $\tilde{\Gamma}^\kappa_{\mu\nu}$ which is defined as $\tilde{\Gamma}^\kappa_{\mu\nu} = \Gamma^\kappa_{\mu\nu} - \omega_{(\mu}\delta^\kappa_{\nu)} + \frac{1}{2}\omega^\kappa g_{\mu\nu}$. When $\omega_\mu$ is defined by a scalar field $\phi$, $\tilde{\Gamma}^\kappa_{\mu\nu}$ describes the affine connection for the conformal metric $\tilde{g}_{\mu\nu} = \phi g_{\mu\nu}$. The field equations of the WIG in the vacuum are equivalent to that of General Relativity with a massless scalar field, with positive or negative energy density. However, when a matter source is introduced, interaction terms appear as a natural consequence of the geometry of the theory [36]. In geometric terms of the interaction context, we investigate the dynamics of the cosmological field equations so that we construct the cosmological history and investigate the viability of the theory. Furthermore, the integrability property for the field equations is investigated by using the method of variational symmetries for the determination of conservation laws.

In Section 2 we present the basic elements for the WIG theory. Furthermore, we write the field equations for our cosmological model in a spatially flat FLRW background space. In Section 3 we present the main results of our analysis in which we discuss the asymptotic dynamics for the field equations in the cases for which the matter source is an ideal gas, or a Chaplygin gas. Moreover, we investigate the dynamics in the presence of the cosmological constant term. In Section 4 we show that the field equations have a minisuperspace description when the matter source is an ideal gas. Specifically, we solve the inverse problem and we construct a point-like Lagrangian which describes the cosmological field equations. With the use of the variational symmetries we determine a conservation law and we present the analytic solution for the field equations by using the Hamilton-Jacobi approach. Our results are summarized in Section 5.

## 2. Weyl Integrable Gravity

Consider the two conformal related metric tensors $g_{\mu\nu}$, $\tilde{g}_{\mu\nu}$ such that $\tilde{g}_{\mu\nu} = \phi g_{\mu\nu}$. The Christoffel symbols of the two conformal related metrics are related as

$$\tilde{\Gamma}^\kappa_{\mu\nu} = \Gamma^\kappa_{\mu\nu} - \phi_{,(\mu}\delta^\kappa_{\nu)} + \frac{1}{2}\phi^{,\kappa} g_{\mu\nu}. \tag{1}$$

In Weyl geometry the fundamental objects are the metric tensor $g_{\mu\nu}$ and the covariant derivative $\tilde{\nabla}_\mu$ defined by the Christoffel symbols $\tilde{\Gamma}^\kappa_{\mu\nu}$. Hence, the curvature tensor is defined

$$\tilde{\nabla}_\nu(\tilde{\nabla}_\mu u_\kappa) - \tilde{\nabla}_\mu(\tilde{\nabla}_\nu u_\kappa) = \tilde{R}_{\kappa\lambda\mu\nu} u^\lambda. \tag{2}$$

Consequently, the Ricci tensors of the two conformal metrics are related as follows:

$$\tilde{R}_{\mu\nu} = R_{\mu\nu} - \tilde{\nabla}_\nu(\tilde{\nabla}_\mu\phi) - \frac{1}{2}(\tilde{\nabla}_\mu\phi)(\tilde{\nabla}_\nu\phi) - \frac{1}{2}g_{\mu\nu}\left(\frac{1}{\sqrt{-g}}\tilde{\nabla}_\nu\tilde{\nabla}_\mu\left(g^{\mu\nu}\sqrt{-g}\phi\right) - g^{\mu\nu}(\tilde{\nabla}_\mu\phi)(\tilde{\nabla}_\nu\phi)\right), \tag{3}$$

thus the Ricci scalar

$$\tilde{R} = R - \frac{3}{\sqrt{-g}}\tilde{\nabla}_\nu\tilde{\nabla}_\mu\left(g^{\mu\nu}\sqrt{-g}\phi\right) + \frac{3}{2}(\tilde{\nabla}_\mu\phi)(\tilde{\nabla}_\nu\phi). \tag{4}$$

In WIG the the fundamental Action Integral is defined by using the Weyl Ricci scalar $\tilde{R}$ and the scalar field $\phi$ by the expression

$$S_W = \int dx^4 \sqrt{-g}(\tilde{R} + \xi(\tilde{\nabla}_\nu(\tilde{\nabla}_\mu\phi))g^{\mu\nu} - \Lambda), \tag{5}$$

where $\xi$ is a coupling constant. From (5) we observe that $\phi$ is a massless scalar field. However, more generally, a potential function may be considered.

From the Action Integral (5) the Weyl-Einstein equations are as [36]

$$\tilde{G}_{\mu\nu} + \tilde{\nabla}_\nu(\tilde{\nabla}_\mu\phi) - (2\xi - 1)(\tilde{\nabla}_\mu\phi)(\tilde{\nabla}_\nu\phi) + \xi g_{\mu\nu} g^{\kappa\lambda}(\tilde{\nabla}_\kappa\phi)(\tilde{\nabla}_\lambda\phi) - \Lambda g_{\mu\nu} = 0, \tag{6}$$

where $\tilde{G}_{\mu\nu}$ is the Weyl Einstein tensor. By using the Riemannian Einstein tensor $G_{\mu\nu}$, the Weyl-Einstein field Equations (6) become [36]

$$G_{\mu\nu} - \lambda\left(\phi_{,\mu}\phi_{,\nu} - \frac{1}{2}g_{\mu\nu}\phi^{,\kappa}\phi_{,\kappa}\right) - \Lambda g_{\mu\nu} = 0, \tag{7}$$

where $\lambda$ is defined as $2\lambda \equiv 4\xi - 3$. Equations (7) are nothing else than the field equations of Einstein's General Relativity with a massless scalar field. When $\lambda > 0$, the scalar field $\phi$ is a quintessence while, when $\lambda < 0$, $\phi$ is a phantom field [36]

Moreover, for the equation of motion of the scalar field $\phi$, the Klein-Gordon equation is [36]

$$(\tilde{\nabla}_\nu(\tilde{\nabla}_\mu\phi))g^{\mu\nu} + 2g^{\mu\nu}(\tilde{\nabla}_\mu\phi)(\tilde{\nabla}_\nu\phi) = 0, \tag{8}$$

or by using the Riemannian covariant derivative $\nabla_\mu$, expression (8) is written in the usual form $g^{\mu\nu}\nabla_\nu\nabla_\mu\phi = 0$.

As it was found in [36], the introduction of a perfect fluid in the gravitational model leads to the following set of gravitational field equations [36]

$$\tilde{G}_{\mu\nu} + \tilde{\nabla}_\nu(\tilde{\nabla}_\mu\phi) - (2\xi - 1)(\tilde{\nabla}_\mu\phi)(\tilde{\nabla}_\nu\phi) + \xi g_{\mu\nu} g^{\kappa\lambda}(\tilde{\nabla}_\kappa\phi)(\tilde{\nabla}_\lambda\phi) - \Lambda g_{\mu\nu} = e^{-\frac{\phi}{2}} T^{(m)}_{\mu\nu}, \tag{9}$$

that is,

$$G_{\mu\nu} - \lambda\left(\phi_{,\mu}\phi_{,\nu} - \frac{1}{2}g_{\mu\nu}\phi^{,\kappa}\phi_{,\kappa}\right) - \Lambda g_{\mu\nu} = e^{-\frac{\phi}{2}} T^{(m)}_{\mu\nu}, \tag{10}$$

where $T^{(m)}_{\mu\nu} = (\rho_m + p_m)u_\mu u_\nu + p_m g_{\mu\nu}$.

Moreover, the modified Klein-Gordon equation follows [36]

$$-g^{\mu\nu}\nabla_\nu\nabla_\mu\phi = \frac{1}{2\lambda}e^{-\frac{\phi}{2}}\rho_m. \tag{11}$$

Equation (11) follows from the identity $G^{\mu\nu}_{;\nu} = 0$, which provides the conserve of the effective energy-momentum tensor.

*FLRW Spacetime*

Following the cosmological principle, in very large scales the universe is considered to be isotropic and homogeneous. Hence, the physical space is described by the FLRW spacetime, where the three-dimensional surface is a maximally symmetric space and admits six isometries. However, from cosmological observations the spatial curvature is very small, which means that we can consider as background space the spatially flat FLRW metric

$$ds^2 = -dt^2 + a^2(t)\left(dr^2 + r^2\left(d\theta^2 + \sin^2\theta d\varphi^2\right)\right). \tag{12}$$

Moreover, we assume the co-moving observer $u_\mu = \delta^t_\mu$, with expansion rate $\theta = 3\frac{\dot{a}}{a}$, for the line element (12) and for a scalar field $\phi = \phi(t)$, the gravitational field equations are

$$\frac{\theta^2}{3} - \frac{\lambda}{2}\dot{\phi}^2 - \Lambda - e^{-\frac{\phi}{2}}\rho_m = 0, \tag{13}$$

$$\dot{\theta} + \frac{1}{3}\theta^2 + \frac{1}{2}e^{-\frac{\phi}{2}}(\rho_m + 3p_m) + \lambda\dot{\phi}^2 - \Lambda = 0, \tag{14}$$

$$\ddot{\phi} + \theta\dot{\phi} + \frac{1}{2\lambda}e^{-\frac{\phi}{2}}\rho_m = 0 \tag{15}$$

and

$$\dot{\rho}_m + \theta(\rho_m + p_m) - \rho_m\dot{\phi} = 0. \tag{16}$$

From the modified Friedmann equations we observe the existence of a non-zero interacting term for scalar field $\phi$ and the matter component $\rho_m$. When $\lambda > 0$, energy decays from scalar field to the $\rho_m$, while for $\lambda < 0$ energy decays from $\rho_m$ to the field $\phi$. Furthermore, the effective equation of state parameter for the effective cosmological matter is defined as $w_{eff} = -1 - 2\frac{\dot{\theta}}{\theta^2}$.

Finally, for the nature of the matter source $\rho_m$ in the following we consider that $\rho_m$ is an ideal gas, or a Chaplygin gas.

## 3. Cosmological Dynamics

We continue our analysis with the investigation of the stationary points for the cosmological field equations. In order to proceed with the study we define the new dimensionless variables in the context of $\theta$-normalization

$$x = \sqrt{\frac{3}{2}}\frac{\dot{\phi}}{\theta}, \; \Omega_\Lambda = \frac{3\Lambda}{\theta^2}, \; \Omega_m = \frac{3\rho_m}{\theta^2}e^{-\frac{\phi}{2}} \tag{17}$$

where for the equation of state parameter for the matter source we consider (i) ideal gas $p_m = (\gamma - 1)\rho_m, 0 \leq \gamma < 2$, and (ii) Chaplygin gas $p_m = \frac{A_0}{\rho_m^\alpha}, \alpha \geq 1$. Moreover, we define the new independent parameter to be $\tau = \ln(a)$, such that $x' = \frac{dx}{d\tau}$.

At the stationary points the effective equation of the state parameter is defined as $w_{eff} = w_{eff}(x, \Omega_\Lambda, \Omega_m)$, so that the asymptotic solution is described by the scale factor $a(t) = a_0 t^{\frac{2}{3(1+w_{eff})}}$, $w_{eff} \neq -1$ and $a(t) = a_0 e^{H_0 t}$, when $w_{eff} = -1$.

### 3.1. Ideal Gas with $\Lambda = 0$

Assume the equation of state of an ideal gas $p_m = (\gamma - 1)\rho_m$, without the cosmological constant term. Then in the new dimensionless variables (17) the field equations are

$$\Omega_m = 1 - \lambda x^2, \tag{18}$$

$$x' = -\frac{(1 - \lambda x^2)\left(\sqrt{6} - 6(\gamma - 2)\lambda x\right)}{12\lambda}. \tag{19}$$

Moreover, $\Omega_m$ is bounded as $0 \leq \Omega_m \leq 1$, such that the solution is physically acceptable, that is, from (18) it follows that there are physical stationary points only when $\lambda > 0$.

The stationary points of Equation (19) are

$$A_1^\pm : x_1^\pm = \frac{1}{\sqrt{\lambda}}, \; A_2 : x_2 = \frac{1}{\sqrt{6}(\gamma - 2)\lambda}. \tag{20}$$

Points $x_1^\pm$ describe asymptotic solutions where only the scalar field contributes to the cosmological fluid. The effective equation of state parameter is derived to be $w_{eff}(x_1^\pm) = 1$, from which we infer that the solution is that of a stiff fluid. On the other hand, the point $x_2$

is physically acceptable when $\lambda \geq \frac{1}{6(\gamma-2)^2}$, and the point describes a scaling solution with $w_{eff}(x_2) = -1+\gamma+\frac{1}{6\lambda(\gamma-2)}$. For $\gamma < \frac{2}{3}$, $\lambda > \frac{1}{8(1-2\gamma)+6\gamma^2}$ it follows that $w_{eff}(x_2) < -\frac{1}{3}$ which means that the asymptotic solution describes an accelerated universe, where in the limit $\lambda = \frac{1}{8(1-2\gamma)+6\gamma^2}$, the asymptotic solution is that of the de Sitter universe.

We proceed with the investigation of the stability properties for the stationary points. We linearize Equation (19) and we find the eigenvalues $e_1(x_1^{\pm}) = 2-\gamma\mp\frac{1}{\sqrt{6\lambda}}$, $e_1(x_2) = -1+\frac{\gamma}{2}+\frac{1}{12\lambda(2-\gamma)}$. Thus, point $x_1^-$ is always a source, $x_1^+$ is an attractor when $\lambda < \frac{1}{6(\gamma-2)^2}$, while $x_2$ is the unique attractor when it exists.

### 3.2. Ideal Gas with $\Lambda \neq 0$

In the presence of the cosmological constant, that is, $\Lambda \neq 0$, and when the matter term is that of the ideal gas, the field equations are written as follows

$$\Omega_m = 1-\lambda x^2 - \Omega_\Lambda\,, \tag{21}$$

$$\Omega'_\Lambda = -\Omega_\Lambda\Big((\gamma-2)\lambda x^2 + \gamma(\Omega_\Lambda - 1)\Big) \tag{22}$$

and

$$x' = \frac{1}{12\lambda}\Big(\Big(\lambda x^2-1\Big)\Big(\sqrt{6}-6(\gamma-2)\lambda x\Big)+\Big(\sqrt{6}-6\gamma\lambda x\Big)\Omega_\Lambda\Big)\,. \tag{23}$$

Furthermore, we assume that $|\Omega_\Lambda| \leq 1$, from which we infer that $x$ is also bounded, and we do not have to study the dynamical system for the existence of stationary points at infinity.

The stationary points of the dynamics system (22), (23) are defined in the plane $\{x,\Omega_\Lambda\}$, that is $B = (x(B),\Omega_\Lambda(B))$. The points are

$$B_1^{\pm} = \left(\pm\frac{1}{\sqrt{\lambda}},0\right)\,,\; B_2 = \left(\frac{1}{\sqrt{6}(\gamma-2)\lambda},0\right)\,, \tag{24}$$

$$B_3 = (0,1)\,,\; B_4 = \Big(\sqrt{6}\gamma, 1+6(2-\gamma)\gamma\lambda\Big)\,. \tag{25}$$

Points $B_1^{\pm}$, $B_2$ are actually the stationary points $A_1^{\pm}$ and $A_2$, respectively, for which the cosmological constant component is zero. The physical properties are the same as before. However, we should investigate the stability analysis.

For point $B_3$ we derive $w_{eff}(B_3) = -1$, $\Omega_m(B_3) = 0$. Thus point $B_3$ describes a de Sitter universe.

Furthermore, point $B_4$ provides $\Omega_m(B_4) = -12\gamma\lambda$, $w_{eff}(B_4) = -1$. The point is physically acceptable when $-\frac{1}{24} \leq \lambda < 0$, or $\lambda < -\frac{1}{24}$ with $\gamma \leq -\frac{1}{12\lambda}$ or $\gamma = 0$. The stationary point describes the de Sitter universe in which all the fluid components contribute in the cosmological solution.

We linearize the dynamical system (22), (23) around the stationary points and we derive the eigenvalues. For points $B_1^{\pm}$ the eigenvalues are $e_1(B_1^{\pm}) = 2-\gamma\mp\frac{1}{\sqrt{6\lambda}}$, $e_2(B_1^{\pm}) = 2$ from which we infer that $B_1^-$ is always a source, while $B_1^+$ is a saddle point when $\lambda < \frac{1}{6(\gamma-2)^2}$. Otherwise it is a source.

For point $B_2$ the two eigenvalues are $e_1(B_2) = -1+\frac{\gamma}{2}+\frac{1}{12\lambda(2-\gamma)}$, $e_2(B_2) = \gamma+\frac{1}{6\lambda(2-\gamma)}$. Thus, point is always a saddle point when it is physically acceptable because $e_1(B_2)$ is always negative while $e_2(B_2)$ is always positive.

The eigenvalues of the linearized system around the de Sitter point $B_3$ are calculated to be $e_1(B_3) = -1$ and $e_2(B_3) = -\gamma$, from which we infer that the point is always an attractor. Finally, for point $B_4$ we find the eigenvalues $e^{\pm}(B_4) = -\frac{1}{2}\pm\sqrt{1+4\gamma(1+6(2-\gamma)\lambda)}$. Consequently, point $B_4$ is always a saddle point.

### 3.3. Chaplygin Gas with $\Lambda = 0$

Consider now that the matter source satisfies the equation of the state parameter of a Chaplygin gas, $p_m = \frac{A_0}{\rho_m^\alpha}$, for which $\alpha \geq 1$, $A_0 = (-1)^\alpha 3^{-(1+\alpha)} A$ and $\rho_m \neq 0$. The field equations are written as follows

$$\Omega_m = 1 - \lambda x^2 , \tag{26}$$

$$x' = \frac{1}{12}\left(\frac{\left(\sqrt{6} + 6\lambda x\right)\left(\lambda x^2 - 1\right)}{\lambda} + 6x\left(\lambda x^2 - 1\right)^{-\alpha} Y\right) \tag{27}$$

and

$$Y' = \frac{1+\alpha}{6} Y\left(6 - \sqrt{6}x + 6\lambda x^2 + 6\left(\lambda x^2 - 1\right)^{-\alpha} Y\right), \tag{28}$$

where the new variable $Y$ is defined as $Y = Ae^{-\frac{1}{2}(1+\alpha)\phi}\theta^{-(2+\alpha)}$.

The stationary points $C = (x(C), Y(C)\,)$of the dynamical system (27), (28), with $\Omega_m > 0$ are

$$C_1 = \left(-\frac{1}{\sqrt{6}\lambda}, 0\right), \tag{29}$$

$$C_2 = \left(\sqrt{\frac{3}{2}} - \frac{\sqrt{\lambda(1+3\lambda)}}{\sqrt{2}\lambda}, \frac{\left(\sqrt{3\lambda(1+3\lambda)} + 6\lambda\left(1 + 3\lambda - \sqrt{3\lambda(1+3\lambda)}\right)\right)\left(-\frac{1}{2} - 3\lambda\sqrt{3\lambda(1+3\lambda)}\right)^\alpha}{6\lambda}\right) \tag{30}$$

and

$$C_3 = \left(\sqrt{\frac{3}{2}} + \frac{\sqrt{\lambda(1+3\lambda)}}{\sqrt{2}\lambda}, \frac{\left(\sqrt{3\lambda(1+3\lambda)} + 6\lambda\left(1 + 3\lambda + \sqrt{3\lambda(1+3\lambda)}\right)\right)\left(-\frac{1}{2} + 3\lambda\sqrt{3\lambda(1+3\lambda)}\right)^\alpha}{6\lambda}\right). \tag{31}$$

For point $C_1$ we derive $\Omega(C_1) = 1 - \frac{6}{\lambda}$, $w_{eff}(C_1) = \frac{1}{6\lambda}$. The point is physically acceptable when $\lambda \geq \frac{1}{6}$ while it always describes a universe without acceleration. For $\lambda = \frac{1}{6}$, the asymptotic solution is that of dust, while for $\lambda = \frac{1}{2}$ the asymptotic solution is that of radiation. The eigenvalues of the linearized system around the stationary point are calculated $e_1(C_1) = \frac{(1+\alpha)(1+3\lambda)}{3\lambda}$, $e_2(C_1) = \frac{1-6\lambda}{12\lambda}$, from which we can easily conclude that the stationary point is always a saddle point.

Point $C_2$ describes a universe for which $\Omega_m(C_2) = \frac{1}{2} - 3\lambda + \sqrt{3\lambda(1+3\lambda)}$ and $w_{eff}(C_2) = \lambda(x(C_2))^2 + \left(\lambda(x(C_2))^2 - 1\right)^{-\alpha} Y(C_2)$. The point is well defined when $\lambda > 0$, while for large values of $\lambda$ it follows that $w_{eff}(C_2; \lambda >> 1) \simeq -1$, which means that point $C_2$ can describe a solution near to the de Sitter point. On the other hand, point $C_3$ is physical acceptable for $0 < \lambda \leq \frac{1}{24}$, while we derive $\Omega_m = -3\lambda + \sqrt{3\lambda(1+3\lambda)}$ and $w_{eff}(C_3) = \lambda(x(C_3))^2 + \left(\lambda(x(C_3))^2 - 1\right)^{-\alpha} Y(C_3)$ in which $w_{eff}\left(C_3; \lambda = \frac{1}{24}\right) = 1$. Thus point $C_3$ does not describe any acceleration.

The eigenvalues of the linearized system near to the stationary points $C_2$ and $C_3$ are determined. Numerically we find that $e_1(C_2)$, $e_2(C_2)$ have always negative real parts for $\lambda > 0$ and $\alpha \geq 1$; on the other hand $\mathrm{Re}(e_1(C_3)) > 0$, $\mathrm{Re}(e_2(C_3)) > 0$ for $\alpha \geq 1$, $0 < \lambda \leq \frac{1}{24}$. Hence, point $C_2$ is always an attractor while point $C_3$ is always a source.

### 3.4. Chaplygin Gas with $\Lambda \neq 0$

In the presence of a non-zero cosmological constant term, the field equations are reduced to the following dynamical system

$$\Omega_m = 1 - \lambda x^2 - \Omega_\Lambda , \tag{32}$$

$$\Omega_\Lambda' = \Omega_\Lambda\left(1 + \lambda x^2 - \Omega_\Lambda + Y\left(\lambda x^2 + \Omega_\Lambda - 1\right)^{-\alpha}\right), \tag{33}$$

$$x' = \frac{1}{12}\left(x^2\left(\sqrt{6}+6\lambda\right) + \frac{\sqrt{6}}{\lambda}(\Omega_\Lambda - 1) + 6x\left(Y\left(\lambda x^2 + \Omega_\Lambda - 1\right)^{-\alpha} - 1 - \Omega_\Lambda\right)\right), \quad (34)$$

$$Y' = \frac{1+\alpha}{6}Y\left(6\left(1 + \lambda x^2 + \Omega_\Lambda + Y\left(\lambda x^2 + \Omega_\Lambda - 1\right)^{-\alpha}\right) - \sqrt{6}\lambda x\right). \quad (35)$$

The physically acceptable stationary points $D = (x(D), Y(D), \Omega_\Lambda(D))$ are

$$D_1 = (x(C_1), Y(C_1), 0)\ ,\ D_2 = (x(C_2), Y(C_2), 0)\ , \quad (36)$$

$$D_3 = (x(C_3), Y(C_3), 0)\ ,\ D_4 = \left(\sqrt{6}, 1+6\lambda, 0\right), \quad (37)$$

where $D_1$, $D_2$ and $D_3$ have the same physical properties as points $C_1$, $C_2$ and $C_3$, respectively.

For the point $D_4$ we find $\Omega_m(D_4) = -12\lambda$ and $w_{eff}(D_4) = -1$, which means that the asymptotic solution is physically acceptable when $-\frac{1}{12} \leq \lambda < 0$, while the asymptotic solution is that of the de Sitter universe.

The eigenvalues of the linearized system near $D_1$ are $e_1(D_1) = \frac{(1+\alpha)(1+3\lambda)}{3\lambda}$, $e_2(D_1) = \frac{1-6\lambda}{12\lambda}$ and $e_3(D_1) = \frac{1+6\lambda}{6\lambda}$, which means that point $D_1$ is always a saddle point. For the points $D_2$ and $D_3$ we find numerically that $D_2$ is always an attractor while $D_3$ is always a source. Finally, for the point $D_4$ we calculate $e_1(D_4) = -(1+\alpha), e_2^{\pm} = \frac{1}{2}\left(-1 \pm \sqrt{5+24\lambda}\right)$, from which it follows that the stationary point is always a saddle point.

## 4. Minisuperspace Description and Conservation Laws

For an ideal gas $p_m = (\gamma - 1)\rho_m$, from Equation (16) it follows $\rho_m(t) = \rho_{m0}a^{-3\gamma}e^{\phi}$ in which $\rho_{m0}$ is a constant of integration.

We substitute this into the rest of the field equations and we end with the following dynamical system

$$\frac{\theta^2}{3} - \frac{\lambda}{2}\dot{\phi}^2 - \Lambda - \rho_{m0}e^{\frac{\phi}{2}}a^{-3\gamma} = 0, \quad (38)$$

$$\dot{\theta} + \frac{1}{3}\theta^2 + \frac{(3\gamma-2)}{2}\rho_{m0}e^{\frac{\phi}{2}}a^{-3\gamma} + \lambda\dot{\phi}^2 - \Lambda = 0, \quad (39)$$

$$\ddot{\phi} + \theta\dot{\phi} + \frac{\rho_{m0}}{2\lambda}e^{\frac{\phi}{2}}a^{-3\gamma} = 0. \quad (40)$$

For the second-order differential Equations (39) and (40) in the space of variables $\{a, \phi\}$, the inverse problem for the determination of a Lagrangian function, provides that the function

$$L(a, \dot{a}, \phi, \dot{\phi}) = -3a\dot{a}^2 + \frac{\lambda}{2}a^3\dot{\phi}^2 - a^3\Lambda - \rho_{m0}e^{\frac{\phi}{2}}a^{3-3\gamma} \quad (41)$$

is an autonomous Lagrangian function for the field equations, while Equation (38) is conservation law of "energy", i.e., the Hamiltonian $\mathcal{H}$, constraint $\mathcal{H} = 0$.

In general, the field equations for the cosmological model in WIG theory with an ideal gas, for the metric

$$ds^2 = -N^2(t) + a^2(t)\left(dx^2 + dy^2 + dz^2\right), \quad (42)$$

follow from the singular point-like Lagrangian

$$\mathcal{L}(a, \dot{a}, \phi, \dot{\phi}) = \frac{1}{N}\left(-3a\dot{a}^2 + \frac{\lambda}{2}a^3\dot{\phi}^2\right) - N\left(a^3\Lambda + \rho_{m0}e^{\frac{\phi}{2}}a^{3-3\gamma}\right). \quad (43)$$

*Integrability Property and Analytic Solution*

Since the field equations admit a point-like Lagrangian various techniques inspired by analytic mechanics be applied for the study of the dynamical system. Indeed, variational symmetries and conservation laws can be determined by using Noether's theorems [37]. That approach has been widely used in various gravitational systems. New integrable cosmological models as also new analytic and exact solutions were found through the use of variational symmetries, see for instance [38].

We investigate for variational symmetries which have point transformations as generators and provide conservation laws linear in the velocities. Hence, for the Lagrangian function (41) and for $\rho_{m0} \neq 0$, we find that the variational symmetry $X = \frac{2}{3}a\partial_a + 4(\gamma-2)\partial_\phi$ exists for $\Lambda = 0$, and the corresponding conservation law is

$$F(a,\dot{a},\phi,\dot{\phi}) = 4a^2\dot{a} - 4(\gamma-2)\lambda a^3\dot{\phi} - F_0. \tag{44}$$

Function $F(a,\dot{a},\phi,\dot{\phi})$, $\frac{dF}{dt} = 0$, is the second-conservation law for the dynamical system, which means that the field equations form an integrable dynamical system.

In order to reduce the field equations and determine exact solutions, we apply the Hamilton-Jacobi approach. We define the momentum $p_a = -6a\dot{a}$, and $p_\phi = \lambda a^3\dot{\phi}$., thus the Hamiltonian function $\mathcal{H}(a,\phi,p_a,p_\phi) = 0$, reads

$$-\frac{p_a^2}{6a} + \frac{p_\phi^2}{\lambda a^3} + 2\left(a^3\Lambda + \rho_{m0}e^{\frac{\phi}{2}}a^{3-3\gamma}\right) = 0 \tag{45}$$

while the Hamilton-Jacobi equation is written in the following form

$$-\frac{1}{6a}\left(\frac{\partial}{\partial a}S(a,\phi)\right)^2 + \frac{1}{\lambda a^3}\left(\frac{\partial}{\partial\phi}S(a,\phi)\right)^2 + 2\rho_{m0}e^{\frac{\phi}{2}}a^{3-3\gamma} = 0, \tag{46}$$

where now $p_a = \frac{\partial S}{\partial a}$ and $p_\phi = \frac{\partial S}{\partial \phi}$.

Moreover, the conservation law (44) provides the constraint equation for the Action $S(a,\phi)$

$$\frac{2a}{3}\left(\frac{\partial}{\partial a}S(a,\phi)\right) + 4(\gamma-2)\frac{\partial}{\partial\phi}(S(a,\phi)) - F_0 = 0. \tag{47}$$

We define the new variable $\phi = 6(\gamma-2)\ln a + \Phi$, such that the constraint equation becomes

$$\frac{2}{3}a\frac{\partial}{\partial a}(S(a,\Phi)) - F_0 = 0. \tag{48}$$

This new set of variables $\{a,\Phi\}$ are the normal coordinates for the dynamical system.

Consequently, in the normal variables the analytic expression for the Action as provided by the Hamilton-Jacobi equation is

$$S(a,\Phi) = \frac{3}{2}F_0\ln a + \int \frac{\sqrt{2\lambda}\sqrt{16\rho_{m0}e^{\frac{\Phi}{2}}\left(6\lambda(\gamma-2)^2-1\right) + 3F_0} + 6\lambda(\gamma-2)F_0}{4\left(6\lambda(\gamma-2)^2-1\right)}d\Phi \tag{49}$$

for $\left(6\lambda(\gamma-2)^2-1\right) \neq 0$, or

$$S(a,\Phi) = \frac{3}{2}F_0\ln a + \frac{3F_0^2\Phi - 32\rho_0 e^{\frac{\Phi}{2}}}{24F_0(\gamma-2)}, \tag{50}$$

when $\left(6\lambda(\gamma-2)^2-1\right) = 0$.

However, in the new coordinates the momentum are defined as

$$p_a = -6a\left(\left(6\lambda(\gamma-2)^2-1\right)\dot{a} + (\gamma-2)\lambda a\dot{\Phi}\right), \tag{51}$$

$$p_\Phi = -\lambda a(6(\gamma-2)\dot{a} + a\dot{\Phi}), \tag{52}$$

which give the following expressions for the scale factor and the scalar field

$$6a^2\dot{a} = ap_a - 6(\gamma - 2)p_\Phi, \tag{53}$$

$$\lambda a^3\dot{\Phi} = -p_\Phi - \lambda(\gamma - 2)(Ap_A + 6(\gamma - 2)p_\Phi). \tag{54}$$

Hence, by using the Action (49) and expressions (53), (54), the cosmological field equations can be written into an equivalent system. We summarize the results in the following proposition.

**Proposition 1.** *The field equations in WIG for a FLRW background space with zero spatial curvature and an ideal gas form a Liouville integrable system when there is no cosmological constant term. The analytic solution for the Hamilton-Jacobi equation provides the Action (49), while the field equations can be written into an equivalent set of two first-order ordinary differential Equations (53) and (54).*

Assume now the simple case for which $\gamma = 1$ and $F_0 = 0$. Moreover, we define the new variable $T = T(t)$, such that $dT = \frac{\sqrt{(6\lambda-1)}}{A^3}dt$ and $\lambda \neq \frac{1}{6}$.
Thus, the field equations are

$$\frac{\dot{a}}{a} - \sqrt{2\lambda\rho_{m0}}e^{\frac{\Phi}{4}} = 0, \tag{55}$$

$$\dot{\Phi} - \sqrt{\frac{2}{\lambda}\rho_{m0}(6\lambda+1)}e^{\frac{\Phi}{4}} = 0,$$

with exact solution

$$a(t) = a_0 t^{\frac{4\lambda}{1+6\lambda}}\;,\; \Phi(t) = -2\ln\left(\frac{(6\lambda+1)\rho_{m0}}{8\lambda}t^2\right). \tag{56}$$

For this exact solution the background space is

$$ds^2 = -\frac{(6\lambda-1)}{a_0^6}t^{-\frac{24\lambda}{1+6\lambda}}dT^2 + a_0^2 t^{\frac{8\lambda}{1+6\lambda}}\left(dx^2+dy^2+dz^2\right). \tag{57}$$

The later solution describes a universe dominated by a perfect fluid source with constant equation of state parameter. This specific solution is described by the stationary points $A_2$, thus. the results are in agreement with the asymptotic analysis for the dynamics.

## 5. Conclusions

In this work we considered WIG to describe the cosmological evolution for the physical parameters in FLRW spacetime with zero spatial curvature. The gravitational field equations in WIG are of second-order and Einstein's theory, with the presence of the of a scalar field, is recovered. Scalar field plays the role for conformal factor which relates the connection of Weyl theory with the Levi-Civita connection of Riemannian geometry. However, the field equations differ when matter is introduced in the gravitational model. Indeed, in WIG the matter source interacts with the scalar field. The interaction term is introduced naturally from the geometric character of the theory.

In our study we considered the matter source to be described by that of an ideal gas, that is $p_m = (\gamma - 1)\rho_m$, or by the Chaplygin gas $p_m = -\frac{A_0}{\rho_m^\alpha}$. We defined new dimensionless variables based on the Hubble-normalization in order to write the field equations as a system of first-order algebraic differential system. In each model, we determined the stationary points for the latter system and we determined their dynamical properties as also the physical properties of the asymptotic solutions. In our analysis we also considered a non-zero cosmological constant.

For the ideal gas, we found that there exists an attractor with an asymptotic solution of an ideal gas, but with a different parameter for the equation of state. For instance, we can consider the matter source to be that of radiation while the attractor to describe an accelerated universe. In the presence of the cosmological constant, we find two asymptotic solutions which can describe the past acceleration phase of the universe known as inflation, as also the late time acceleration. The future attractor describes the de Sitter universe. When the matter component is that of a Chaplygin gas the stationary points as also the cosmological evolution are similar with the previous case.

Moreover, for the ideal gas case, we solved the inverse problem and determined a Lagrangian function, and a minisuperspace description, which generates the cosmological equations under a variation. We applied Noether's theorems for point transformations in order to construct a non-trivial conservation law when the cosmological constant term is zero. Hence, the cosmological field equations form a Liouville integrable dynamical system. The closed-form expression for the Hamilton-Jacobi equation derived. Finally, for specific values for the free parameters, we were able to construct an exact solution which is in agreement with the asymptotic analysis.

In a subsequent analysis we plan to investigate further the field equations as a Hamilton system and understand how a non-zero cosmological constant affects the integrability property of the field equations.

**Funding:** This research received no external funding.

**Institutional Review Board Statement:** Not applicable.

**Informed Consent Statement:** Not applicable.

**Data Availability Statement:** Not applicable.

**Conflicts of Interest:** The author declare no conflict of interest.

## References

1. Aghanim, N.; Akrami, Y.; Ashdown, M.; Aumont, J.; Baccigalupi, C.; Ballardini, M.; Banday, A.J.; Barreiro, R.B.; Bartolo, N.; Basak, S.; et al. Planck 2018 results. VI. Cosmological parameters. *Astron. Astrophys.* **2020**, *641*, A6.
2. Perivolaropoulos, L.; Skara, F. Challenges for ΛCDM: An update. *arXiv* **2021**, arXiv:2105.05208.
3. Ratra, B.; Peebles, P.J.E. Cosmological consequences of a rolling homogeneous scalar field. *Phys. Rev. D* **1988**, *37*, 3406. [CrossRef]
4. Armendariz-Picon, C.; Mukhanov, V.F.; Steinhardt, P.J. Essentials of k-essence.*Phys. Rev. D* **2001**, *63*, 103510. [CrossRef]
5. Faraoni, V. *Cosmology in Scalar-Tensor Gravity;* Kluwer Academic Publishers: Dordrecht, The Netherlands, 2004.
6. Bento, M.C.; Bertolami, O.; Sen, A.A. Generalized Chaplygin gas and CMBR constraints. *Phys. Rev. D* **2003**, *67*, 063003. [CrossRef]
7. Kamenshchik, A.; Moschella, U.; Pasquier, V. An alternative to quintessence. *Phys. Lett. B* **2001**, *511*, 265–268. [CrossRef]
8. Basilakos, S.; Mavromatos, N.E.; Solà Peracaula, J. Gravitational and chiral anomalies in the running vacuum universe and matter-antimatter asymmetry. *Phys. Rev. D* **2020**, *101*, 045001. [CrossRef]
9. Clifton, T.; Ferreira, P.G.; Padilla, A.; Skordis, C. Modified gravity and cosmology. *Phys. Rept.* **2012**, *513*, 1–189. [CrossRef]
10. Nojiri, S.I.; Odintsov, S.D. Introduction to modified gravity and gravitational alternative for dark energy. *IJGMMP* **2007**, *4*, 115–145. [CrossRef]
11. Valentino, E.D.; Mena, O.; Pan, S.; Visinelli, L.; Yang, W.; Melchiorri, A.; Mota, D.F.; Riess, A.G.; Silk, J. In the Realm of the Hubble tension a Review of Solutions. *Class. Quantum. Grav.* **2021**, *38*, 153001. [CrossRef]
12. Billyard, A.P.; Coley, A.A. Interactions in scalar field cosmology. *Phys Rev D* **2000**, *61*, 083503. [CrossRef]
13. Pan, S.; Sharov, G.S.; Yang, W. Field theoretic interpretations of interacting dark energy scenarios and recent observations. *Phys. Rev. D* **2020**, *101*, 103533. [CrossRef]
14. Yang, W.; Mukherjee, A.; Di Valentino, E.; Pan, S. Interacting dark energy with time varying equation of state and the H0 tension. *Phys. Rev. D* **2018**, *98*, 123527. [CrossRef]
15. Pan, S.; Sharov, G.S. A model with interaction of dark components and recent observational data. *MNRAS* **2017**, *472*, 4736–4749. [CrossRef]
16. Di Valentino, E.; Melchiorri, A.; Mena, O.; Vagnozzi, S. Interacting dark energy in the early 2020s: A promising solution to the H0 and cosmic shear tensions. *Phys. Dark Univ.* **2020**, *30*, 100666. [CrossRef]
17. Yu Vernov, S.; Pozdeeva, E. De Sitter Solutions in Einstein–Gauss–Bonnet Gravity. *Universe* **2021**, *7*, 149. [CrossRef]
18. Yu Kamenshchik, A.; Pozdeeva, E.O.; Venturi, G.; Yu Vernov, S. Integrable cosmological models in the Einstein and in the Jordan frames and Bianchi-I cosmology. *Phys. Part. Nucl.* **2018**, *49*, 1–4. [CrossRef]

19. Dimakis, N.; Paliathanasis, A.; Terzis, P.A.; Christodoulakis, T. Cosmological solutions in multiscalar field theory. *EPJC* **2019**, *79*, 618. [CrossRef]
20. Paliathanasis, A. De Sitter and scaling solutions in a higher-order modified teleparallel theory. *JCAP* **2017**, *8*, 027. [CrossRef]
21. Copeland, E.J.; Liddle, A.R.; Wands, D. Exponential potentials and cosmological scaling solution. *Phys. Rev. D* **1998**, *57*, 4686. [CrossRef]
22. Coley, A.; Leon, G. Static Spherically Symmetric Einstein-aether models I: Perfect fluids with a linear equation of state and scalar fields with an exponential self-interacting potential. *Gen. Rel. Grav.* **2019**, *51*, 115. [CrossRef]
23. Amendola, L.; Polarski, D.; Tsujikawa, S. Are f(R) dark energy models cosmologically viable? *Phys. Rev. Lett.* **2007**, *98*, 131302. [CrossRef] [PubMed]
24. Amendola, L.; Gannouji, R.; Polarski, D.; Tsujikawa, S. Conditions for the cosmological viability of f(R) dark energy models. *Phys. Rev. D* **2007**, *75*, 083504. [CrossRef]
25. Christodoulidis, P.; Roest, D.; Sfakianakis, E.I. Scaling attractors in multi-field inflation. *JCAP* **2019**, *12*, 059. [CrossRef]
26. Fadragas, C.R.; Cardenas, R.; Rodriguez-Ricard, M.; Rivero-Acosta, A.; Linares-Rodriguez, A. Detailed qualitative dynamical analysis of a cosmological Higgs field. *Gen. Rel. Gravit.* **2019**, *51*, 109. [CrossRef]
27. Gonzalez, T.; Leon, G.; Quiros, I. Dynamics of quintessence models of dark energy with exponential coupling to dark matter. *Class. Quantum Grav.* **2006**, *23*, 32165. [CrossRef]
28. Kerachia, M.; Acquaviva, G.; Lukes-Gerakopoulos, G. Dynamics of classes of barotropic fluids in spatially curved FRW spacetimes. *Phys. Rev. D* **2020**, *101*, 043535. [CrossRef]
29. Aguilar, J.E.M.; Romero, C. Inducing the cosmological constant from five-dimensional Weyl space. *Found. Phys.* **2009**, *39*, 1205–1216. [CrossRef]
30. Liu, Y.-X.; Yang, K.; Zhong, Y. de Sitter Thick Brane Solution in Weyl Geometry. *JHEP* **2010**, *10*, 069. [CrossRef]
31. Lobo, I.P.; Barreto, A.B.; Romero, C. Space-time singularities in Weyl manifolds. *EPJC* **2015**, *75*, 448. [CrossRef]
32. Paliathanasis, A.; Leon, G. Integrability and cosmological solutions in Einstein-æther-Weyl theory. *EPJC* **2021**, *81*, 255. [CrossRef]
33. Pucheu, M.L.; Alves, F.A.P., Jr.; Barreto, A.B.; Romero, C. Cosmological models in Weyl geometrical scalar-tensor theory. *Phys. Rev. D* **2016**, *94*, 064010. [CrossRef]
34. Miritzis, J. Isotropic cosmologies in Weyl geometry. *Class. Quantum Grav.* **2004**, *21*, 3043. [CrossRef]
35. Salim, J.M.; Sautú, S.L. Gravitational collapse in Weyl integrable space-times. *Class. Quantum Grav.* **1999**, *16*, 3281. [CrossRef]
36. Salim, J.M.; Sautú, S.L. Gravitational theory in Weyl integrable spacetime. *Class. Quantum Grav.* **1996**, *13*, 353. [CrossRef]
37. Halder, A.; Paliathanasis, A.; Leach, P.G.L. Noether's Theorem and Symmetry. *Symmetry* **2018**, *10*, 744. [CrossRef]
38. Tsampalis, M.; Paliathanasis, A. Symmetries of Differential Equations in Cosmology. *Symmetry* **2018**, *10*, 233. [CrossRef]

*universe*

MDPI

*Article*

# Killing Tensor and Carter Constant for Painlevé–Gullstrand Form of Lense–Thirring Spacetime

Joshua Baines [1,†], Thomas Berry [2,†], Alex Simpson [1,*,†] and Matt Visser [1,†]

1 School of Mathematics and Statistics, Victoria University of Wellington, P.O. Box 600, Wellington 6140, New Zealand; joshua.baines@sms.vuw.ac.nz (J.B.); matt.visser@sms.vuw.ac.nz (M.V.)
2 Robinson Research Institute, Victoria University of Wellington, P.O. Box 600, Wellington 6140, New Zealand; thomas.berry@vuw.ac.nz
* Correspondence: alex.simpson@sms.vuw.ac.nz
† These authors contributed equally to this work.

**Abstract:** Recently, the authors have formulated and explored a novel Painlevé–Gullstrand variant of the Lense–Thirring spacetime, which has some particularly elegant features, including unit-lapse, intrinsically flat spatial 3-slices, and some particularly simple geodesics—the "rain" geodesics. At the linear level in the rotation parameter, this spacetime is indistinguishable from the usual slow-rotation expansion of Kerr. Herein, we shall show that this spacetime possesses a nontrivial Killing tensor, implying separability of the Hamilton–Jacobi equation. Furthermore, we shall show that the Klein–Gordon equation is also separable on this spacetime. However, while the Killing tensor has a 2-form square root, we shall see that this 2-form square root of the Killing tensor is not a Killing–Yano tensor. Finally, the Killing-tensor-induced Carter constant is easily extracted, and now, with a fourth constant of motion, the geodesics become (in principle) explicitly integrable.

**Keywords:** Painlevé–Gullstrand metrics; Lense–Thirring metric; Killing tensor; Killing–Yano tensor; separability; Carter constant; geodesic integrability

**Citation:** Baines, J.; Berry, T.; Simpson, A.; Visser, M. Killing Tensor and Carter Constant for Painlevé–Gullstrand Form of Lense–Thirring Spacetime. *Universe* **2021**, *7*, 473. https://doi.org/10.3390/universe7120473

Academic Editors: Panayiotis Stavrinos and Emmanuel N. Saridakis

Received: 19 October 2021
Accepted: 1 December 2021
Published: 3 December 2021



## 1. Introduction

Recently, the current authors have introduced and explored a new variant of the Lense–Thirring spacetime [1], specified by the line element

$$\mathrm{d}s^2 = -\mathrm{d}t^2 + \left\{\mathrm{d}r + \sqrt{\frac{2m}{r}}\,\mathrm{d}t\right\}^2 + r^2\left\{\mathrm{d}\theta^2 + \sin^2\theta\left(\mathrm{d}\phi - \frac{2J}{r^3}\mathrm{d}t\right)^2\right\}. \tag{1}$$

The metric components are easily read off as

$$g_{ab} = \left[\begin{array}{c|ccc} -1 + \frac{2m}{r} + \frac{4J^2\sin^2\theta}{r^4} & \sqrt{\frac{2m}{r}} & 0 & -\frac{2J\sin^2\theta}{r} \\ \hline \sqrt{\frac{2m}{r}} & 1 & 0 & 0 \\ 0 & 0 & r^2 & 0 \\ -\frac{2J\sin^2\theta}{r} & 0 & 0 & r^2\sin^2\theta \end{array}\right]_{ab}. \tag{2}$$

It is easy to verify that $\det(g_{ab}) = -r^4\sin^2\theta$, and that the inverse metric is:

$$g^{ab} = \left[\begin{array}{c|ccc} -1 & \sqrt{\frac{2m}{r}} & 0 & -\frac{2J}{r^3} \\ \hline \sqrt{\frac{2m}{r}} & 1-\frac{2m}{r} & 0 & \sqrt{\frac{2m}{r}}\,\frac{2J}{r^3} \\ 0 & 0 & \frac{1}{r^2} & 0 \\ -\frac{2J}{r^3} & \sqrt{\frac{2m}{r}}\,\frac{2J}{r^3} & 0 & \frac{1}{r^2\sin^2\theta} - \frac{4J^2}{r^6} \end{array}\right]^{ab}. \tag{3}$$

This variant of the Lense–Thirring spacetime is rather useful since the metric is recast into the Painlevé–Gullstrand form [2–5]. Writing the metric in this form gives it two very useful properties: the first is the property of unit-lapse, characterised by $g^{tt} = -1$, and the second is the possession of a flat spatial 3-metric, notably

$$g_{ij}\, dx^i\, dx^j \longrightarrow dr^2 + r^2(d\theta^2 + \sin^2\theta\, d\phi^2). \tag{4}$$

A flat 3-metric allows for an almost trivial analysis of the constant-$t$ spatial hypersurfaces, while lapse unity permits straightforward calculation of particular geodesics of the spacetime. Specifically, the "rain" geodesics become almost trivial to calculate [6]. At the linear level in the rotation parameter, this spacetime is indistinguishable from the usual slow-rotation expansion of Kerr.

We also note the advantages of using this variant of the Lense–Thirring spacetime, as opposed to the exact Kerr solution, in some astrophysically interesting contexts. Firstly, since there is no analogue of the Birkhoff theorem for axisymmetric spacetimes in $(3+1)$ dimensions [7–11], the Kerr solution need not (and typically will not) perfectly model rotating horizonless astrophysical sources (such as stars, planets, etc.). This is due to the nontrivial mass multipole moments that these objects typically possess. Instead, the Kerr solution will model the gravitational field in the asymptotic regime, where Lense–Thirring serves as a valid approximation to Kerr [12–29]. Secondly, the Lense–Thirring metric is algebraically much simpler than the Kerr metric, making most calculations significantly easier to conduct. Furthermore, the Lense–Thirring metric can be recast into Painlevé–Gullstrand form, while the Kerr metric cannot [30–33].

Given that this variant of the Lense–Thirring metric is amenable to significantly more tractable mathematical analysis and is a valid approximation for the gravitational fields of rotating stars and planets in the same regime as the Kerr solution is appropriate, there is a compelling argument to use the Painlevé–Gullstrand form of Lense–Thirring to model various astrophysically interesting cases [34–36].

Supplementary to this, we will show below that this spacetime possesses a nontrivial Killing tensor, and we shall also present the 2-form square root of this Killing tensor, an object that acts as a "would-be" Killing–Yano tensor. We discuss precisely how this object does and does not satisfy the desiderata for being a genuine Killing–Yano tensor. We establish why this candidate spacetime does not possess the full Killing tower (consisting of principal tensor, Killing–Yano tensor, and Killing tensor). We also check that the Klein–Gordon equation is separable on this variant of Lense–Thirring spacetime.

Given only three constants of motion—the energy $E$, angular momentum $L$, and particle mass parameter $\epsilon$, the geodesic equations are not integrable. By finding a nontrivial Killing tensor for the spacetime, we generate a fourth constant of the motion, a generalization of the Carter constant $\mathcal{C}$.

The existence of this additional constant of motion then implies complete separability of the Hamilton–Jacobi equation, which makes the geodesic equations fully integrable, at least in principle.

## 2. Killing Tensor

Nontrivial Killing tensors are incredibly useful mathematical objects that are present in almost all (useful) candidate spacetimes and can be thought of as generalisations of Killing vectors. A Killing tensor is a completely symmetric tensor of type $(0, l)$ which satisfies the following equation:

$$\nabla_{(b}K_{a_1 \dots a_l)} = 0\,. \tag{5}$$

However, unlike Killing vectors, Killing tensors do not naturally arise from explicit symmetries present in the spacetime. Hence, finding nontrivial Killing tensors in a spacetime can be difficult in the abstract. However, in two recent papers by Papadopoulos and Kokkotas [37,38], which are in turn based on older results by Benenti and Francaviglia [39], it has been explicitly shown that if the inverse metric of a spacetime can be written in a particular form, then a nontrivial (contravariant) Killing tensor of rank 2 exists and can be easily calculated. (Here we make the distinction of requiring a nontrivial Killing tensor since the metric itself is always a trivial Killing tensor.)

To use this method, we first coordinate-transformed our Lense–Thirring metric variant into Boyer–Lindquist form [1]:

$$(ds^2)_{BL} = -(1-2m/r)dt^2 + \frac{dr^2}{1-2m/r} + r^2\left\{d\theta^2 + \sin^2\theta\left(d\phi - \frac{2J}{r^3}dt\right)^2\right\}. \tag{6}$$

Here

$$(g_{ab})_{BL} = \left[\begin{array}{c|cc|c} -1+\frac{2m}{r}+\frac{4J^2\sin^2\theta}{r^4} & 0 & 0 & -\frac{2J\sin^2\theta}{r} \\ \hline 0 & \frac{1}{1-2m/r} & 0 & 0 \\ 0 & 0 & r^2 & 0 \\ \hline -\frac{2J\sin^2\theta}{r} & 0 & 0 & r^2\sin^2\theta \end{array}\right]_{ab}, \tag{7}$$

and

$$(g^{ab})_{BL} = \left[\begin{array}{c|cc|c} -\frac{1}{1-2m/r} & 0 & 0 & -\frac{2J}{r^3(1-2m/r)} \\ \hline 0 & 1-\frac{2m}{r} & 0 & 0 \\ 0 & 0 & \frac{1}{r^2} & 0 \\ \hline -\frac{2J}{r^3(1-2m/r)} & 0 & 0 & \frac{1}{r^2\sin^2\theta} - \frac{4J^2}{r^6(1-2m/r)} \end{array}\right]^{ab}. \tag{8}$$

We then applied the Papadopoulos–Kokkotas algorithm [37,38] by first inverting the Boyer–Lindquist form of the metric (7) to obtain (8), then extracting the contravariant Killing tensor in these coordinates, and finally converting the result back to Painlevé–Gullstand coordinates.

After conversion back to Painlevé–Gullstand coordinates, where the line element is again (1), the Papadopoulos–Kokkotas algorithm [37,38] yields the particularly simple contravariant form of the Killing tensor:

$$K^{ab} = \begin{bmatrix} 0 & 0 & 0 & 0 \\ 0 & 0 & 0 & 0 \\ 0 & 0 & 1 & 0 \\ 0 & 0 & 0 & \frac{1}{\sin^2\theta} \end{bmatrix}^{ab}. \tag{9}$$

The corresponding covariant form of the Killing tensor, $K_{ab} = g_{ac}\, K^{cd}\, g_{db}$, is then

$$K_{ab} = \begin{bmatrix} \frac{4J^2\sin^2\theta}{r^2} & 0 & 0 & -2Jr\sin^2\theta \\ 0 & 0 & 0 & 0 \\ 0 & 0 & r^4 & 0 \\ -2Jr\sin^2\theta & 0 & 0 & r^4\sin^2\theta \end{bmatrix}_{ab}. \tag{10}$$

One can easily explicitly check that $\nabla_{(c}K_{ab)} = K_{(ab;c)} = 0$; hence, Equation (10) does indeed represent a Killing tensor. We can also compactly write:

$$K_{ab}\, dx^a\, dx^b = r^4\left\{d\theta^2 + \sin^2\theta\left(d\phi - \frac{2J}{r^3}dt\right)^2\right\}. \tag{11}$$

We now adopt an orthonormal basis, using the co-tetrad and tetrad developed in reference [1]. For the co-tetrad, we take

$$\begin{aligned} e^{\hat{t}}{}_a &= (1;0,0,0); \qquad e^{\hat{r}}{}_a = \left(\sqrt{\frac{2m}{r}};1,0,0\right); \\ e^{\hat{\theta}}{}_a &= r(0;0,1,0); \qquad e^{\hat{\phi}}{}_a = r\sin\theta\left(-\frac{2J}{r^3};0,0,1\right). \end{aligned} \tag{12}$$

The corresponding tetrad is then

$$e_{\hat{t}}{}^{a} = \left(1; -\sqrt{\frac{2m}{r}}, 0, \frac{2J}{r^3}\right); \qquad e_{\hat{r}}{}^{a} = (0; 1, 0, 0);$$
$$e_{\hat{\theta}}{}^{a} = \frac{1}{r}\,(0; 0, 1, 0); \qquad e_{\hat{\phi}}{}^{a} = \frac{1}{r\sin\theta}(0; 0, 0, 1). \tag{13}$$

For the tetrad components of the Killing tensor, we find

$$K_{\hat{a}\hat{b}} \longrightarrow r^2 \begin{bmatrix} 0 & 0 & 0 & 0 \\ 0 & 0 & 0 & 0 \\ 0 & 0 & 1 & 0 \\ 0 & 0 & 0 & 1 \end{bmatrix}_{\hat{a}\hat{b}} . \tag{14}$$

Since this is diagonal, and since we also know from reference [1] that the orthonormal form of the Ricci tensor $R_{\hat{a}\hat{b}}$ is diagonal, it follows that the Ricci tensor commutes with the Killing tensor: $R^{\hat{a}}{}_{\hat{b}}\, K^{\hat{b}}{}_{\hat{c}} = K^{\hat{a}}{}_{\hat{b}}\, R^{\hat{b}}{}_{\hat{c}}$. Indeed, even in a coordinate basis, it follows that $R^{a}{}_{b}\, K^{b}{}_{c} = K^{a}{}_{b}\, R^{b}{}_{c}$. Note that the commutator $[R, K]_{ab} = R_{ac} g^{cd} K_{db} - K_{ac} g^{cd} R_{db}$ can be viewed as a 2-form. It is also potentially useful to note that the trace of the Killing tensor is particularly simple; $K = K^{ab} g_{ab} = K_{ab} g^{ab} = 2r^2$.

If we now take the limit $J \to 0$, then the Lense–Thirring spacetime reduces to the spherically symmetric Schwarzschild spacetime. In this $J \to 0$ limit, the nontrivial (covariant) Killing tensor becomes

$$K_{ab} \longrightarrow \begin{bmatrix} 0 & 0 & 0 & 0 \\ 0 & 0 & 0 & 0 \\ 0 & 0 & r^4 & 0 \\ 0 & 0 & 0 & r^4 \sin^2\theta \end{bmatrix}_{ab} , \tag{15}$$

so that

$$K_{ab}\, dx^a\, dx^b \longrightarrow r^4 \left\{ d\theta^2 + \sin^2\theta\, d\phi^2 \right\}. \tag{16}$$

Indeed, it is easily verified that this is the appropriate Killing tensor in any arbitrary spherically symmetric spacetime, even if it is time-dependent. Furthermore, for any arbitrary (possibly time-dependent) spherically symmetric spacetime, one can always block-diagonalize the metric and Ricci tensors in the form

$$g_{ab} \longrightarrow \left[\begin{array}{cc|cc} * & * & 0 & 0 \\ * & * & 0 & 0 \\ \hline 0 & 0 & r^2 & 0 \\ 0 & 0 & 0 & r^2 \sin^2\theta \end{array}\right]_{ab} ; \qquad R_{ab} \longrightarrow \left[\begin{array}{cc|cc} * & * & 0 & 0 \\ * & * & 0 & 0 \\ \hline 0 & 0 & * & 0 \\ 0 & 0 & 0 & * \end{array}\right]_{ab} . \tag{17}$$

Hence, the Ricci tensor will algebraically commute with the Killing tensor via matrix multiplication: $R^{a}{}_{b} K^{b}{}_{c} = K^{a}{}_{b} R^{b}{}_{c}$.

These observations further reinforce the fact that this variant of the Lense–Thirring spacetime does indeed simplify to Schwarzschild spacetime in the appropriate limit. A quick ansatz for understanding the genesis of our variant of the Lense–Thirring spacetime is to simply take Schwarzschild spacetime and subject both the line element and Killing tensor to the replacement (not a coordinate transformation):

$$d\phi \longrightarrow \left( d\phi - \frac{2J}{r^3} dt \right). \tag{18}$$

We shall soon use this Killing tensor to construct a Carter constant for our variant of the Lense–Thirring spacetime, but we will first briefly digress to discuss Killing–Yano tensors.

## 3. Two-Form Square Root of the Killing Tensor

Interestingly, it is not too difficult to find a 2-form "square root" of this Killing tensor, in the sense of finding an antisymmetric tensor satisfying $K_{ab} = -f_{ac}\, g^{cd}\, f_{db}$. Explicitly, one finds

$$f_{ab} = \sin\theta \begin{bmatrix} 0 & 0 & 2J & 0 \\ 0 & 0 & 0 & 0 \\ -2J & 0 & 0 & r^3 \\ 0 & 0 & -r^3 & 0 \end{bmatrix}_{ab} . \tag{19}$$

We can also write this as

$$f_{ab}\, \mathrm{d}x^a \wedge \mathrm{d}x^b = r^3 \sin\theta \left\{ \mathrm{d}\theta \wedge \left( \mathrm{d}\phi - \frac{2J}{r^3}\mathrm{d}t \right) \right\} . \tag{20}$$

The contravariant components are even simpler:

$$f^{ab} = \frac{1}{r\sin\theta} \begin{bmatrix} 0 & 0 & 0 & 0 \\ 0 & 0 & 0 & 0 \\ 0 & 0 & 0 & 1 \\ 0 & 0 & -1 & 0 \end{bmatrix}_{ab} . \tag{21}$$

In the orthonormal basis, one finds

$$f_{\hat{a}\hat{b}} = r \begin{bmatrix} 0 & 0 & 0 & 0 \\ 0 & 0 & 0 & 0 \\ 0 & 0 & 0 & 1 \\ 0 & 0 & -1 & 0 \end{bmatrix}_{\hat{a}\hat{b}} . \tag{22}$$

Unfortunately, while the 2-form $f_{ab}$ is indeed a square root of the Killing tensor $K_{ab}$, it fails to be a Killing–Yano tensor; it is at best a "would-be" Killing–Yano tensor. Specifically, although the vector $g^{bc} f_{ab;c} = 0$, which in form notation can be written as $\delta f = 0$, the 3-index tensor $f_{a(b;c)}$ is nonzero:

$$f_{a(b;c)}\, \mathrm{d}x^a \mathrm{d}x^b \mathrm{d}x^c = \frac{3J\sin\theta}{2r}\{\mathrm{d}r \otimes (\mathrm{d}t \otimes \mathrm{d}\theta + \mathrm{d}\theta \otimes \mathrm{d}t) - \mathrm{d}t \otimes (\mathrm{d}r \otimes \mathrm{d}\theta + \mathrm{d}\theta \otimes \mathrm{d}r)\}. \tag{23}$$

Unfortunately, there does not seem to be any way to further simplify this result.

It is also potentially worthwhile to note

$$f_{[ab;c]} = \epsilon_{tabc}; \qquad \text{equivalently} \qquad \mathrm{d}f = 3\, \mathrm{d}r \wedge \mathrm{d}\theta \wedge \mathrm{d}\phi. \tag{24}$$

Indeed, one sees $\delta\, \mathrm{d}f \propto *\mathrm{d} * \mathrm{d}f = 3 * \mathrm{d} * (\mathrm{d}r \wedge \mathrm{d}\theta \wedge \mathrm{d}\phi) = 3 * \mathrm{d}(\mathrm{d}t) = 0$.

Consequently, since both $\delta \mathrm{d}f = 0$ and $\delta f = 0$, we see that the 2-form $f$ is harmonic: $\Delta f = (\delta\mathrm{d} + \mathrm{d}\delta) f = 0$. While the 2-form $f$ is not a Killing–Yano tensor, it certainly satisfies other interesting properties.

The non-existence of the Killing–Yano tensor in turn implies the non-existence of the full Killing tower. When possible to do so, one defines a principal tensor $h_{ab}$ as the foundation of the Killing tower by demanding the existence of a 2-form $h$ such that [40] (see discussion near page 47):

$$\nabla_a h_{bc} = \frac{1}{3}\left[ g_{ab} \nabla^d h_{dc} - g_{ac} \nabla^d h_{db} \right] . \tag{25}$$

The existence of such an object is dependent upon the satisfaction of a specific integrability condition, which directly implies the spacetime be of Petrov type D. However, in reference [1], the current authors found that the Painlevé–Gullstrand form of Lense–Thirring is Petrov type I, i.e., not algebraically special. It follows that no principal tensor can exist for this candidate spacetime, and hence there is no associated Killing–Yano tensor.

Similar oddities have also cropped up in other contexts. In references [41,42], those authors found that rotating black bounce spacetimes possess a nontrivial Killing tensor, and a 2-form square root thereof, but that this 2-form square root failed to be a Killing–Yano tensor.

One can also infer the non-existence of the Killing tower as a side effect of the fact that the Painlevé–Gullstrand form of Lense–Thirring does not mathematically fall into Carter's "off shell" 2-free-function distortion of the Kerr spacetime [40] (see discussion near page 42).

## 4. Separability of the Klein–Gordon Equation

Generally, the existence of a nontrivial Killing tensor is by itself not quite enough to guarantee separability of the Klein–Gordon equation. An explicit check needs to be carried out. There are two ways of proceeding—either via direct calculation, or indirectly by studying the commutativity properties of certain differential operators. We find it most illustrating to first perform a direct calculation, and then subsequently put the discussion into a more abstract framework.

We are interested in the behaviour of the massive or massless minimally coupled Klein–Gordon equation (wave equation with possibly a mass term):

$$\frac{1}{\sqrt{-g}}\partial_a\left(\sqrt{-g}\, g^{ab}\,\partial_b\Phi(t,r,\theta,\phi)\right) = \mu^2\Phi(t,r,\theta,\phi). \tag{26}$$

First, we note that $\sqrt{-g} = r^2\sin\theta$. Second, in view of the explicit Killing symmetries in the $t$ and $\phi$ coordinates, we can immediately write $\Phi(t,r,\theta,\phi) \longrightarrow \Phi(r,\theta)e^{-i\omega t}e^{in\phi}$.

Then we are reduced to considering

$$\partial_a\left(r^2\sin\theta\, g^{ab}\,\partial_b[\Phi(r,\theta)e^{-i\omega t}e^{in\phi}]\right) = \mu^2\, r^2\sin\theta\,\Phi(r,\theta)e^{-i\omega t}e^{in\phi}. \tag{27}$$

Now, going from the Painlevé–Gullstrand form of the metric to Boyer–Lindquist form involves a coordinate change: $t \longleftrightarrow t + f(r)$. Under such a coordinate change, $e^{-i\omega t} \longleftrightarrow e^{-i\omega[t+f(r)]} = e^{-i\omega f(r)}e^{-i\omega t}$. Thence, separability of the wave equation is unaffected by this coordinate transformation. Note also that the metric determinant, $\sqrt{-g} = r^2\sin\theta$, is the same in both coordinate systems.

Consequently, without loss of generality we may work in Boyer–Lindquist form, and for our current purposes it is advantageous to do so. The inverse metric is given by Equation (6):

$$(g^{ab})_{BL} = \left[\begin{array}{c|cc|c} -\frac{1}{1-2m/r} & 0 & 0 & -\frac{2J}{r^3(1-2m/r)} \\ \hline 0 & 1-\frac{2m}{r} & 0 & 0 \\ 0 & 0 & \frac{1}{r^2} & 0 \\ \hline -\frac{2J}{r^3(1-2m/r)} & 0 & 0 & \frac{1}{r^2\sin^2\theta} - \frac{4J^2}{r^6(1-2m/r)} \end{array}\right]^{ab}. \tag{28}$$

Then the Klein–Gordon Equation (27) reduces to

$$\begin{aligned} &\sin\theta\,\partial_r[r^2(1-2m/r)\partial_r\Phi] + \partial_\theta[\sin\theta\,\partial_\theta\Phi] \\ &+r^2\sin\theta\left(\frac{\omega^2}{1-2m/r} - \frac{4Jn\omega}{r^3(1-2m/r)} - n^2\left[\frac{1}{r^2\sin^2\theta} - \frac{4J^2}{r^6(1-2m/r)}\right]\right)\Phi \\ &= \mu^2 r^2\sin\theta\,\Phi. \end{aligned} \tag{29}$$

That is,

$$\partial_r[r^2(1-2m/r)\partial_r\Phi] + \frac{\partial_\theta[\sin\theta\,\partial_\theta\Phi]}{\sin\theta} - \frac{n^2}{\sin^2\theta}\Phi + r^2\left(\frac{(\omega-2Jn/r^3)^2}{1-2m/r}\right)\Phi$$
$$= \mu^2 r^2\Phi. \tag{30}$$

This is now manifestly separable:

$$\partial_r[r^2(1-2m/r)\,\partial_r\Phi] + r^2\,\frac{(\omega-2Jn/r^3)^2}{1-2m/r}\Phi - \mu^2 r^2\Phi$$
$$= -\frac{\partial_\theta[\sin\theta\,\partial_\theta\Phi]}{\sin\theta} + \frac{n^2}{\sin^2\theta}\Phi. \tag{31}$$

To be even more explicit about this, let us write $\Phi(r,\theta) = \mathcal{R}(r)\Theta(\theta)$, then:

$$\frac{1}{\mathcal{R}(r)}\left\{\partial_r[r^2(1-2m/r)\,\partial_r\mathcal{R}(r)] + r^2\,\frac{(\omega-2Jn/r^3)^2}{1-2m/r}\mathcal{R}(r) - \mu^2 r^2\mathcal{R}(r)\right\}$$
$$= \frac{1}{\Theta(\theta)}\left\{-\frac{\partial_\theta[\sin\theta\,\partial_\theta\Theta(\theta)]}{\sin\theta} + \frac{n^2}{\sin^2\theta}\Theta(\theta)\right\}. \tag{32}$$

(The left-hand side depends only on $r, \mathcal{R}(r)$, and its derivatives; the right-hand-side depends only on $\theta, \Theta(\theta)$, and its derivatives.) Thus, we have explicitly verified that the massive Klein–Gordon equation (the wave equation) does in fact separate on our variant of the Lense–Thirring spacetime.

A more abstract way of checking for separability of the wave equation is to consider the commutativity properties of appropriate differential operators. Assume one has a nontrivial Killing tensor $K_{ab}$, and define the Carter differential operator $\mathcal{K}$ and wave differential operator $\Box$ by:

$$\mathcal{K}\Phi = \nabla_a(K^{ab}\nabla_b\Phi); \qquad \Box\Phi = \nabla_a(g^{ab}\nabla_b\Phi)\,. \tag{33}$$

Then a brief (but somewhat messy) calculation yields:

$$[\mathcal{K},\Box]\Phi = \frac{2}{3}\left(\nabla_d[R,K]^d{}_b\right)\nabla^b\Phi\,. \tag{34}$$

(See proposition 1.3 of the recent reference [43], as modified in Appendix A below. See also the considerably older discussion presented in reference [44].)

Then a necessary and sufficient condition for the Carter operator to commute with the wave operator is that

$$\nabla_d[R,K]^d{}_b = 0\,. \tag{35}$$

Since, as we have already noted, $[R,K]$ can be viewed as 2-form, the condition $\nabla_d[R,K]^d{}_b = 0$ can be recast in the notation of differential forms as $\delta[R,K] = 0$. This condition is certainly satisfied for Ricci-flat and Einstein manifolds (such as Kerr and Kerr–de Sitter), but a weaker (yet still sufficient) condition is the vanishing of the commutator $[R,K]^d{}_b = 0$, and we have already seen that this commutator vanishes for our variant of Lense–Thirring spacetime.[1] This is enough to imply separability of the wave equation on our variant of Lense–Thirring spacetime.

## 5. Carter Constant and Other Conserved Quantities

Extraction of the (generalized) Carter constant is now straightforward:

$$\mathcal{C} = K_{ab}\frac{dx^a}{d\lambda}\frac{dx^b}{d\lambda} = r^4\left[\left(\frac{d\theta}{d\lambda}\right)^2 + \sin^2\theta\left(\frac{d\phi}{d\lambda} - \frac{2J}{r^3}\frac{dt}{d\lambda}\right)^2\right], \tag{36}$$

for any affine parameter $\lambda$. Without loss of generality, we may enforce that $\lambda$ be future-directed, as is conventional. Note that by construction, we have $\mathcal{C} \geq 0$.

In addition to the Carter constant, we have three other conserved quantities:

$$E = -\xi_a \frac{\mathrm{d}x^a}{\mathrm{d}\lambda} = \left(1 - \frac{2m}{r} - \frac{4J^2 \sin^2\theta}{r^4}\right)\frac{\mathrm{d}t}{\mathrm{d}\lambda} - \sqrt{\frac{2m}{r}}\frac{\mathrm{d}r}{\mathrm{d}\lambda} + \frac{2J\sin^2\theta}{r}\frac{\mathrm{d}\phi}{\mathrm{d}\lambda}; \tag{37}$$

$$L = \psi_a \frac{\mathrm{d}x^a}{\mathrm{d}\lambda} = r^2\sin^2\theta\frac{\mathrm{d}\phi}{\mathrm{d}\lambda} - \frac{2J\sin^2\theta}{r}\frac{\mathrm{d}t}{\mathrm{d}\lambda}; \tag{38}$$

and

$$\begin{aligned}\epsilon = g_{ab}\frac{\mathrm{d}x^a}{\mathrm{d}\lambda}\frac{\mathrm{d}x^b}{\mathrm{d}\lambda} = &-\left(\frac{\mathrm{d}t}{\mathrm{d}\lambda}\right)^2 + \left(\frac{\mathrm{d}r}{\mathrm{d}\lambda} + \sqrt{\frac{2m}{r}}\frac{\mathrm{d}t}{\mathrm{d}\lambda}\right)^2 \\ &+ r^2\left[\left(\frac{\mathrm{d}\theta}{\mathrm{d}\lambda}\right)^2 + \sin^2\theta\left(\frac{\mathrm{d}\phi}{\mathrm{d}\lambda} - \frac{2J}{r^3}\frac{\mathrm{d}t}{\mathrm{d}\lambda}\right)^2\right].\end{aligned} \tag{39}$$

The conserved quantities $E$ and $L$ arise from the time translation and azimuthal Killing vectors, respectively given by $\xi^a = (1;0,0,0)^a$ and $\psi^a = (0,0,0,1)^a$. In contrast, the conserved quantity $\epsilon$, with $\epsilon \in \{0,-1\}$ for null and timelike geodesics, respectively, arises from the trivial Killing tensor $g_{ab}$.

Note that if $\epsilon = 0$, then, without loss of generality, we can rescale the affine parameter $\lambda$ to set *one* of the constants $\{\mathcal{C}, E, L\} \to 1$. It is intuitive to set $E \to 1$. In contrast, if $\epsilon = -1$, then $\lambda = \tau$ is the proper time and there is no further freedom to rescale the affine parameter. $E$ then has real physical meaning, and the qualitative behaviour is governed by the sign of $E^2 + \epsilon$. Concretely: Is $E < 1$ (bound orbits), is $E = 1$ (marginal orbits), or is $E > 1$ (unbound orbits)?

We can now greatly simplify these four conserved quantities by rewriting them as follows:

$$L = r^2\sin^2\theta\left(\frac{\mathrm{d}\phi}{\mathrm{d}\lambda} - \frac{2J}{r^3}\frac{\mathrm{d}t}{\mathrm{d}\lambda}\right); \tag{40}$$

$$\mathcal{C} = r^4\left(\frac{\mathrm{d}\theta}{\mathrm{d}\lambda}\right)^2 + \frac{L^2}{\sin^2\theta}; \tag{41}$$

$$\epsilon = -\left(\frac{\mathrm{d}t}{\mathrm{d}\lambda}\right)^2 + \left(\frac{\mathrm{d}r}{\mathrm{d}\lambda} + \sqrt{\frac{2m}{r}}\frac{\mathrm{d}t}{\mathrm{d}\lambda}\right)^2 + \frac{\mathcal{C}}{r^2}; \tag{42}$$

$$E = \left(1 - \frac{2m}{r}\right)\frac{\mathrm{d}t}{\mathrm{d}\lambda} - \sqrt{\frac{2m}{r}}\frac{\mathrm{d}r}{\mathrm{d}\lambda} + \frac{2J}{r^3}L. \tag{43}$$

Notice that by construction, $\mathcal{C} \geq L^2$. Furthermore, the form of the Carter constant, Equation (41), gives a range of forbidden declination angles for any given non-zero values of $\mathcal{C}$ and $L$.

We require that $\mathrm{d}\theta/\mathrm{d}\lambda$ be real, and from Equation (41), this implies the following requirement:

$$\left(r^2\frac{\mathrm{d}\theta}{\mathrm{d}\lambda}\right)^2 = \mathcal{C} - \frac{L^2}{\sin^2\theta} \geq 0 \quad \Longrightarrow \quad \sin^2\theta \geq \frac{L^2}{\mathcal{C}}. \tag{44}$$

Then provided $\mathcal{C} \geq L^2$, which is automatic in view of (41), we can define $\theta_* \in [0, \pi/2]$ by setting

$$\theta_* = \sin^{-1}(|L|/\sqrt{\mathcal{C}}). \tag{45}$$

Then the allowed range for $\theta$ is the equatorial band

$$\theta \in \left[\theta_*, \pi - \theta_*\right]. \tag{46}$$

For $L^2 = \mathcal{C}$, we have $\theta = \pi/2$; the motion is restricted to the equatorial plane.
For $L = 0$ with $\mathcal{C} > 0$, the range of $\theta$ is a priori unconstrained; $\theta \in [0, \pi]$.
For $L = 0$ with $\mathcal{C} = 0$, the declination is fixed $\theta(\lambda) = \theta_0$, and the motion is restricted to a constant declination conical surface.

Using Equations (40)–(43), we can (at least in principle) analytically solve for the four unknown functions $\mathrm{d}t/\mathrm{d}\lambda$, $\mathrm{d}r/\mathrm{d}\lambda$, $\mathrm{d}\theta/\mathrm{d}\lambda$, and $\mathrm{d}\phi/\mathrm{d}\lambda$ as explicit functions of $r$ and $\theta$, parameterized by the four conserved quantities $\mathcal{C}$, $E$, $L$, and $\epsilon$, as well as the quantities $m$ and $J$ characterizing mass and angular momentum of the central object. The resulting formulae are quite tedious and will be reported elsewhere.

## 6. Conclusions

From the discussion above, we have seen that it is relatively straightforward to find a non-trivial Killing tensor for the Painlevé–Gullstrand version of the Lense–Thirring spacetime. We have also demonstrated separability of the Klein–Gordon equation and the non-existence of a Killing–Yano 2-form. Once we have found the non-trivial Killing tensor, we can easily extract the Carter constant—the fourth constant of the motion. Then the geodesic equations become integrable, which allows us (in principle) to solve for myriads of general geodesics.

**Author Contributions:** Conceptualization, J.B., T.B., A.S. and M.V.; methodology, J.B., T.B., A.S. and M.V.; validation, J.B., T.B., A.S. and M.V.; formal analysis, J.B., T.B., A.S. and M.V.; writing—original draft preparation, J.B., T.B., A.S. and M.V.; writing—review and editing, A.S. and M.V.; supervision, M.V.; project administration, M.V.; funding acquisition, M.V. All authors have read and agreed to the published version of the manuscript.

**Funding:** This research was primarily funded by the Marsden Fund administered by the Royal Society of New Zealand, and partially funded by the Victoria University of Wellington, New Zealand.

**Acknowledgments:** J.B. was supported by an MSc scholarship funded by the Marsden Fund, via a grant administered by the Royal Society of New Zealand. T.B. was supported by a Victoria University of Wellington MSc scholarship and was also indirectly supported by the Marsden Fund, via a grant administered by the Royal Society of New Zealand. A.S. was supported by a Victoria University of Wellington PhD Doctoral Scholarship and was also indirectly supported by the Marsden fund, via a grant administered by the Royal Society of New Zealand. M.V. was directly supported by the Marsden Fund, via a grant administered by the Royal Society of New Zealand.

**Conflicts of Interest:** The authors declare no conflict of interest.

## Appendix A. Wave Operators

In the recent reference [43] (page 9, proposition 1.3), the author demonstrated that

$$\begin{aligned} [\mathcal{K}, \Box]\Phi &= \Big\{ \Big( \nabla_c R - \frac{4}{3} \nabla_d R^d{}_c \Big) K^c{}_b \\ &\quad + \frac{2}{3} \Big( R^{dc} \nabla_d K_{cb} - R^c{}_b \nabla_d K^d{}_c - \{\nabla_c R^d{}_b\} K^c{}_d \Big) \Big\} \nabla^b \Phi\,. \end{aligned} \tag{A1}$$

Now use the (twice contracted) Bianchi identity, in the opposite direction from what one might expect, to temporarily make things more complicated:

$$\nabla_c R = 2 \nabla_d R^d{}_c\,. \tag{A2}$$

Then proposition 1.3 becomes

$$[\mathcal{K}, \Box]\Phi = \Big\{ \Big( +\frac{2}{3} \nabla_d R^d{}_c \Big) K^c{}_b + \frac{2}{3} \Big( R^d{}_c \nabla_d K^c{}_b - R^c{}_b \nabla_d K^d{}_c - \{\nabla_c R^d{}_b\} K^c{}_d \Big) \Big\} \nabla^b \Phi\,. \tag{A3}$$

That is,

$$[\mathcal{K},\Box]\Phi = \frac{2}{3}\Big\{R^d{}_c\nabla_d K^c{}_b - R^c{}_b\nabla_d K^d{}_c - (\nabla_c R^d{}_b)K^c{}_d + (\nabla_d R^d{}_c)K^c{}_b\Big\}\nabla^b\Phi\,. \tag{A4}$$

Relabelling some indices,

$$[\mathcal{K},\Box]\Phi = \frac{2}{3}\Big\{R^d{}_c\nabla_d K^c{}_b - R^c{}_b\nabla_d K^d{}_c - \{\nabla_d R^c{}_b\}K^d{}_c + \{\nabla_d R^d{}_c\}K^c{}_b\Big\}\nabla^b\Phi\,. \tag{A5}$$

That is,

$$[\mathcal{K},\Box]\Phi = \frac{2}{3}\nabla_d\Big\{R^d{}_c K^c{}_b - K^d{}_c R^c{}_b\Big\}\nabla^b\Phi\,. \tag{A6}$$

Finally, rewrite this as:

$$[\mathcal{K},\Box]\Phi = \frac{2}{3}\Big(\nabla_d[R,K]^d{}_b\Big)\nabla^b\Phi\,. \tag{A7}$$

(See also the considerably older discussion in reference [44], using somewhat different terminology.)

## Notes

1 This tensor commutator also vanishes for Kerr–Newman spacetimes and for the black-bounce modifications of Kerr and Kerr–Newman spacetimes studied in [41,42]. Thus, the wave equation is separable on all of these spacetimes.

## References


1. Baines, J.; Berry, T.; Simpson, A.; Visser, M. Painleve-Gullstrand form of the Lense-Thirring spacetime. *Universe* **2021**, *7*, 105. [CrossRef]
2. Painlevé, P. La mécanique classique et la théorie de la relativité. *Comptes Rendus de l'Académie des Sciences* **1921**, *173*, 677–680.
3. Painlevé, P. La gravitation dans la mécanique de Newton et dans la mécanique d'Einstein. *Comptes Rendus de l'Académie des Sciences* **1921**, *173*, 873–886.
4. Gullstrand, A. Allgemeine Lösung des statischen Einkörperproblems in der Einsteinschen Gravitationstheorie. *Arkiv för Matematik Astronomi och Fysik* **1922**, *16*, 1–15.
5. Martel, K.; Poisson, E. Regular coordinate systems for Schwarzschild and other spherical space-times. *Am. J. Phys.* **2001**, *69*, 476–480. [CrossRef]
6. Baines, J.; Berry, T.; Simpson, A.; Visser, M. Unit-lapse versions of the Kerr spacetime. *Class. Quant. Grav.* **2021**, *38*, 055001. [CrossRef]
7. Birkhoff, G. *Relativity and Modern Physics*; Harvard University Press: Cambridge, MA, USA, 1923.
8. Jebsen, J.T. Über die allgemeinen kugelsymmetrischen Lösungen der Einsteinschen Gravitationsgleichungen im Vakuum. *Arkiv för Matematik Astronomi och Fysik* **1921**, *15*, 18.
9. Deser, S.; Franklin, J. Schwarzschild and Birkhoff *a la* Weyl. *Am. J. Phys.* **2005**, *73*, 261. [CrossRef]
10. Johansen, N.V.; Ravndal, F. On the discovery of Birkhoff's theorem. *Gen. Rel. Grav.* **2006**, *38*, 537–540. [CrossRef]
11. Skakala, J.; Visser, M. Birkhoff-like theorem for rotating stars in (2+1) dimensions. *arXiv* **2009**, arXiv:0903.2128.
12. Thirring, H.; Lense, J. Über den Einfluss der Eigenrotation der Zentralkörperauf die Bewegung der Planeten und Monde nach der Einsteinschen Gravitationstheorie. *Phys. Z.* **1918**, *19*, 156–163.
13. Mashoon, B.; Hehl, F.W.; Theiss, D.S. On the influence of the proper rotations of central bodies on the motions of planets and moons in Einstein's theory of gravity. *Gen. Relativ. Gravit.* **1984**, *16*, 727–741.
14. Pfister, H. On the History of the So-Called Lense–Thirring Effect. Available online: http://philsci-archive.pitt.edu/archive/00002681/01/lense.pdf (accessed on 1 December 2021).
15. Adler, R.J.; Bazin, M.; Schiffer, M. *Introduction to General Relativity*, 2nd ed.; McGraw–Hill: New York, NY, USA, 1975.
16. Misner, C.; Thorne, K.; Wheeler, J.A. *Gravitation*; Freeman: San Francisco, CA, USA, 1973.
17. Wald, R. *General Relativity*; University of Chicago Press: Chicago, IL, USA, 1984.
18. Weinberg, S. *Gravitation and Cosmology: Principles and Applications of the General Theory of Relativity*; Wiley: Hoboken, NJ, USA, 1972.
19. Hobson, M.P.; Estathiou, G.P.; Lasenby, A.N. *General Relativity: An Introduction for Physicists*; Cambridge University Press: Cambridge, UK, 2006.
20. D'Inverno, R. *Introducing Einstein's Relativity*; Oxford University Press: Oxford, UK, 1992.
21. Hartle, J. *Gravity: An Introduction to Einstein's General Relativity*; Addison Wesley: San Francisco, CA, USA, 2003.
22. Carroll, S. *An Introduction to General Relativity: Spacetime and Geometry*; Addison Wesley: San Francisco, CA, USA, 2004.
23. Visser, M. The Kerr spacetime: A brief introduction. *arXiv* **2007**, arXiv:0706.0622.

4. Wiltshire, D.L.; Visser, M.; Scott, S.M. (Eds.) *The Kerr Spacetime: Rotating Black Holes in General Relativity*; Cambridge University Press: Cambridge, UK, 2009.
5. Kerr, R. Gravitational field of a spinning mass as an example of algebraically special metrics. *Phys. Rev. Lett.* **1963**, *11*, 237–238. [CrossRef]
6. Kerr, R. Gravitational collapse and rotation. In *Quasi-Stellar Sources and Gravitational Collapse, Proceedings of the First Texas Symposium on Relativistic Astrophysics*; Robinson, I., Schild, A., Schücking, E.L., Eds.; University of Chicago Press: Chicago, IL, USA, 1965; pp. 99–102.
7. Newman, E.; Couch, E.; Chinnapared, K.; Exton, A.; Prakash, A.; Torrence, R. Metric of a Rotating, Charged Mass. *J. Math. Phys.* **1965**, *6*, 918. [CrossRef]
8. O'Neill, B. *The Geometry of Kerr Black Holes*; Peters: Wellesley, MA, USA, 1995.
9. Hamilton, A.J.; Lisle, J.P. The River model of black holes. *Am. J. Phys.* **2008**, *76*, 519–532. [CrossRef]
0. Baines, J.; Berry, T.; Simpson, A.; Visser, M. Darboux diagonalization of the spatial 3-metric in Kerr spacetime. *Gen. Rel. Grav.* **2021**, *53*, 3. [CrossRef]
1. Kroon, J.A.V. On the nonexistence of conformally flat slices in the Kerr and other stationary space-times. *Phys. Rev. Lett.* **2004**, *92*, 041101. [CrossRef]
2. Kroon, J.A.V. Asymptotic expansions of the Cotton-York tensor on slices of stationary space-times. *Class. Quant. Grav.* **2004**, *21*, 3237–3250. [CrossRef]
3. Jaramillo, J.L.; Kroon, J.A.V.; Gourgoulhon, E. From geometry to numerics: Interdisciplinary aspects in mathematical and numerical relativity. *Class. Quant. Grav.* **2008**, *25*, 093001. [CrossRef]
4. Carballo-Rubio, R.; Filippo, F.D.; Liberati, S.; Visser, M. Phenomenological aspects of black holes beyond general relativity. *Phys. Rev. D* **2018**, *98*, 124009. [CrossRef]
5. Visser, M.; Barceló, C.; Liberati, S.; Sonego, S. Small, dark, and heavy: But is it a black hole? *arXiv* **2009**, arXiv:0902.0346.
6. Visser, M. Black holes in general relativity. *Commun. Math. Phys.* **2008**. [CrossRef]
7. Papadopoulos, G.O.; Kokkotas, K.D. On Kerr black hole deformations admitting a Carter constant and an invariant criterion for the separability of the wave equation. *Gen. Rel. Grav.* **2021**, *53*, 21. [CrossRef]
8. Papadopoulos, G.O.; Kokkotas, K.D. Preserving Kerr symmetries in deformed spacetimes. *Class. Quant. Grav.* **2018**, *35*, 185014. [CrossRef]
9. Benenti, S.; Francaviglia, M. Remarks on Certain Separability Structures and Their Applications to General Relativity. *Gen. Relativ. Gravit.* **1979**, *10*, 79–92. [CrossRef]
0. Frolov, V.; Krtous, P.; Kubiznak, D. Black holes, hidden symmetries, and complete integrability. *Living Rev. Rel.* **2017**, *20*, 6. [CrossRef] [PubMed]
1. Mazza, J.; Franzin, E.; Liberati, S. A novel family of rotating black hole mimickers. *JCAP* **2021**, *4*, 082. [CrossRef]
2. Franzin, E.; Liberati, S.; Mazza, J.; Simpson, A.; Visser, M. Charged black-bounce spacetimes. *JCAP* **2021**, *7*, 036. [CrossRef]
3. Giorgi, E. The Carter tensor and the physical-space analysis in perturbations of Kerr-Newman spacetime. *arXiv* **2021**, arXiv:2105.14379.
4. Benenti, S.; Chanu, C.; Rastelli, G. Remarks on the connection between the additive separation of the Hamilton–Jacobi equation and the multiplicative separation of the Schrödinger equation. II. First integrals and symmetry operators. *J. Math. Phys.* **2002**, *43*, 5223. [CrossRef]

universe

MDPI

Article

# Nontrivial Isometric Embeddings for Flat Spaces

Sergey Paston * and Taisiia Zaitseva

Department of High Energy and Elementary Particle Physics, Saint Petersburg State University, 199034 Saint Petersburg, Russia; taisiiazaitseva@gmail.com
* Correspondence: pastonsergey@gmail.com

**Abstract:** Nontrivial isometric embeddings for flat metrics (i.e., those which are not just planes in the ambient space) can serve as useful tools in the description of gravity in the embedding gravity approach. Such embeddings can additionally be required to have the same symmetry as the metric. On the other hand, it is possible to require the embedding to be unfolded so that the surface in the ambient space would occupy the subspace of the maximum possible dimension. In the weak gravitational field limit, such a requirement together with a large enough dimension of the ambient space makes embedding gravity equivalent to general relativity, while at lower dimensions it guarantees the linearizability of the equations of motion. We discuss symmetric embeddings for the metrics of flat Euclidean three-dimensional space and Minkowski space. We propose the method of sequential surface deformations for the construction of unfolded embeddings. We use it to construct such embeddings of flat Euclidean three-dimensional space and Minkowski space, which can be used to analyze the equations of motion of embedding gravity.

**Keywords:** isometric embeddings; symmetrical surfaces; free embedding; unfolded embedding; Regge–Teitelboim gravity; embedding theory

**Citation:** Paston, S.; Zaitseva, T. Nontrivial Isometric Embeddings for Flat Spaces. *Universe* **2021**, *7*, 477. https://doi.org/10.3390/universe7120477

Academic Editors: Panayiotis Stavrinos and Emmanuel N. Saridakis

Received: 10 November 2021
Accepted: 2 December 2021
Published: 4 December 2021



## 1. Introduction

According to the Janet–Cartan–Friedman (JCF) theorem [1], an arbitrary $n$-dimensional pseudo-Riemannian space can be locally isometrically embedded into the ambient flat space of dimension $N \geqslant n(n+1)/2$ with suitable signature. By isometric embedding we mean the surface described by the embedding function $y^a(x^\mu)$ in the ambient space for which the induced metric

$$g_{\mu\nu} = (\partial_\mu y^a)(\partial_\nu y^b)\eta_{ab} \tag{1}$$

coincides with the metric of the original pseudo-Riemannian space. Hereinafter, Greek indices $\mu, \nu, \ldots$ run over $n$ values; Latin indices $a, b, \ldots$ run over $N$ values; $\eta_{ab}$ is the flat metric of the ambient pseudo-Euclidean space. For specific pseudo-Riemannian spaces the required dimension of the ambient space can decrease. In particular, this happens if a space has a sufficiently large number of symmetries [2]. The difference $N - n$ is called the *class of the embedding*. We emphasize that the JCF theorem consider only *local* embeddings, and when passing to *global* embeddings, the required dimension of the ambient space increases sharply [3]. However, in specific cases, even for global embeddings, the class of the embedding can be smaller, see, for example, [4,5].

The interest in explicit isometric embeddings of physically meaningful pseudo-Riemannian spaces is due to several reasons. First of all, it provides an opportunity to understand the geometric structure of space-time better since this structure manifests itself in the presence of an explicit embedding. That is why a great interest in the construction of explicit embeddings has been shown by researchers in the case of various black hole metrics. For the Schwarzschild metric, the first embedding [6] was proposed just 5 years after its discovery. The only global embedding [7] turns out to be closely related to the maximum analytic extension of the Schwarzschild metric by the Kruskal–Shekeres coordinates (see the note at the end of [7]). In general, a lot of works have been devoted to the construction of explicit embeddings of various black holes, including charged and rotating ones; see, for example, the links in [5]. Other physically interesting metrics include various cosmological models, e.g., Friedmann–Robertson–Walker metric that describe the expanding universe. Explicit embedding of this metric [8] was also found a very long time ago. It should be noted that the problem of finding an embedding for a given metric usually has more than one solution since when solving differential equations, arbitrary parameters (numbers or functions) arise. A smooth surface deformation that does not alter the induced metric is called isometric bending; see, for example, the discussion of this question in [9] and references therein.

Other motivations for considering isometric embeddings include their use in the classification of exact solutions of the Einstein equations [2], as well as in the calculation of Hawking temperature of spacetimes with a horizon (see, for example, references in [10]). However, from the point of view of describing gravity, the main motivation is the possibility of obtaining a modified theory of gravity by variable substitution (1) in General Relativity (GR) action with matter contribution $\mathcal{L}_m$

$$S = \int d^4x \sqrt{-g}\left(-\frac{1}{2\varkappa}R + \mathcal{L}_m\right), \tag{2}$$

where $n = 4$. After such a substitution the theory might change (additional solutions appear, see [11] for a discussion of gravity modifications resulting from differential transformations of field variables). It happens even if the number of new variables $y^a(x)$, which is equal to the number of ambient space dimensions, corresponds to the JCF theorem value $N = 10$ and therefore does not differ from the number of the old metric variables $g_{\mu\nu}(x)$.

This string-inspired approach was first proposed in [12] and was subsequently studied in a number of works [13–20] under the names like embedding theory, geodetic brane gravity and embedding gravity. From variation of the action (2) with respect to the independent variable $y^a(x)$ the Regge–Teitelboim (RT) equations [12] arise:

$$(G^{\mu\nu} - \varkappa T^{\mu\nu})b^a_{\mu\nu} = 0. \tag{3}$$

Here $G^{\mu\nu}$ is the Einstein tensor, $T^{\mu\nu}$ is the energy-momentum tensor of matter, and

$$b^a_{\mu\nu} = D_\mu \partial_\nu y^a, \tag{4}$$

where $D_\mu$ is the covariant derivative, is called the second fundamental form of the surface described by the embedding function $y^a(x)$ (for example, see [21]).

It is easy to see that the RT equations (3) are more general than the Einstein equations: any solution to the Einstein equations is a solution to the RT equations, but not vice versa. In addition to Einstein's solutions, there are so-called "extra" solutions. As a result, the theory is not equivalent to GR. In [12], this was regarded as a problem since the goal of this paper was to obtain an equivalent reformulation of general relativity (mainly in the hope of advancing in the quantization of the theory) and not a transition to a more general theory. For this reason, additional conditions called Einstein constraints were imposed in [12] and several subsequent papers. However, at present, in connection with the modern cosmological mystery of dark matter and dark energy, the transition to modified theories of gravity which are more general than GR becomes more attractive. Along this path one can try to interpret *extra* solutions as effects associated with dark matter or dark energy within the framework of GR. The mimetic gravity [22–24] is the most famous approach of such kind, but the embedding theory approach is also possible [25–28].

In the analysis of solutions of the Equation (3) as the equation of modified gravity one usually starts from weak field limit when the metric $g_{\mu\nu}$ is close to the flat metric $\eta_{\mu\nu}$. Such a problem corresponds, for example, to the description of observations on the scale of the solar system or a galaxy. Then one should determine the form of explicit embedding of the flat metric which can serve as the background solution $\overset{(0)}{y}{}^a(x)$ in order to look for solutions of the Equation (3) corresponding to a weak gravitational field in the form:

$$y^a(x) = \overset{(0)}{y}{}^a(x) + \delta y^a(x). \tag{5}$$

The simplest option is to select a plane as the background surface:

$$\overset{(0)}{y}{}^a(x) = \delta^a_\mu x^\mu. \tag{6}$$

However, as noted in [13], when such a background is used, the equations of the embedding theory (3) turn out to be non-linearizable (non-linear with respect to variation $\delta y^a$). The easiest way to see it is to write down the Einstein tensor in the form (see, for example, [17])

$$G^{\mu\nu} = \frac{1}{2} g_{\xi\zeta} E^{\mu\xi\alpha\beta} E^{\nu\zeta\gamma\delta} b^b_{\alpha\gamma} \eta_{bc} b^c_{\beta\delta} \tag{7}$$

where $E^{\mu\xi\alpha\beta} = \varepsilon^{\mu\xi\alpha\beta} / \sqrt{|g|}$ is the covariant unit antisymmetric tensor. Then the RT equations (3) takes the form:

$$g_{\xi\zeta} E^{\mu\xi\alpha\beta} E^{\nu\zeta\gamma\delta} b^b_{\alpha\gamma} \eta_{bc} b^c_{\beta\delta} b^a_{\mu\nu} = 2\varkappa T^{\mu\nu} b^a_{\mu\nu} \tag{8}$$

where the left-hand side is cubic in $b^a_{\mu\nu}$, which according to (4) is linear in the small variation $\delta y^a$ when using the background (6).

Since for a weak gravitational field the principle of superposition must be satisfied, the non-linearity of the equation describing it seems unnatural. On the other hand, the Formula (6) is far from the only possible choice of the background embedding function for a weak gravitational field. As such, one can use any embedding of the flat metric $\eta_{\mu\nu}$ which can be quite nontrivial. This paper is devoted to the problem of constructing such nontrivial embeddings.

In the next section we discuss possible additional requirements that can be imposed on the sought nontrivial embeddings. The concept of "unfolded" embedding introduced here turns out to be close to the concept of "free" embedding introduced in [29]; Section 3 is devoted to their comparison. In Section 4, we discuss the construction of symmetric embeddings for flat metrics. We propose a nontrivial explicit symmetric embedding for the Minkowski metric. It turns out to be non-unfolded. As a result, if it is used as the background in the analysis of the RT equations solutions, linearization is only partial. In Section 5, we propose a method for constructing unfolded embeddings for flat metrics; we construct such explicit embeddings for flat 3-dimensional Euclidean space and Minkowski space.

## 2. Symmetrical and Unfolded Embeddings

When looking for nontrivial embeddings of a flat metric, some additional requirements can be imposed. It seems natural enough to assume that the surface resulting from the embedding must have the same symmetry as the embedded metric. For example, the metric $\eta_{\mu\nu}$ of Minkowski space $\mathbb{R}^{1,3}$ is symmetric with respect to the Poincare group $SO(1,3) \ltimes T^4$, and one can require the constructed surface to have the same symmetry. We say that a surface $\mathcal{M}$ is *symmetric* with respect to the group $G$ if $\mathcal{M}$ transforms into itself under the action of some subgroup of the group of motions $\mathcal{P}$ of the flat ambient space $\mathbb{R}^{n_+,n_-}$ when this subgroup is isomorphic to $G$. In [30], a method for constructing explicit embeddings with a given symmetry was proposed; it has recently been developed further in [31]. The idea is to consider all possible $N$-dimensional representations for a given symmetry group with the subsequent selection of those that have the form of transformations of group of motions $\mathcal{P}$ of the flat ambient space and lead to the correct surface dimension; see details in [30]. We discuss the construction of symmetric embeddings for flat metrics in Section 4.

Another interesting requirement that can be imposed when searching for a background embedding function for a weak gravitational field is, in a sense, the maximal non-degeneracy for the second fundamental form (4). Note that this object is symmetric with respect to the permutation of the indices $\mu$ and $\nu$, so this pair of indices can be replaced with a multi-index running through $n(n+1)/2$ values. On the other hand, for the second fundamental form $b^a_{\mu\nu}$ the following identity holds (see, for example, [21]):

$$b^a_{\mu\nu}\partial_\beta y_a = 0, \tag{9}$$

which means that the index $a$ of $b^a_{\mu\nu}$ is transverse. After the introduction of some basis in the space orthogonal to the surface at a given point, it is possible to replace the index $a$ of the object $b^a_{\mu\nu}$ with a new index running through $N-n$ values. As a result, this value can be interpreted as a matrix of size $n(n+1)/2$ by $(N-n)$. By the maximal non-degeneracy of $b^a_{\mu\nu}$ we mean that the rank of such a matrix is maximal, in other words, it coincides with its minimal dimension. A surface is called unfolded if its second fundamental form satisfies this requirement at all points except, perhaps, a set of zero measure. Violation of this requirement at some point geometrically means that in the neighborhood of this point the surface lies in some subspace of the ambient space the dimension of which is less than possible, i.e., one can additionally "unfold" the surface.

If, for example, for a 4-dimensional surface (i.e., $n=4$) we take the dimension of the ambient space $N=14$, then $b^a_{\mu\nu}$ turns out to be a square $10\times 10$ matrix in the indicated sense. If, in this case, the unfolded embedding of the flat metric is chosen as the background in the decomposition (5), then within the framework of the perturbation theory $b^a_{\mu\nu}$ (4) can be removed from the RT equations (3) as a non-singular matrix that is a factor in a homogeneous equation. As a result, in this case, the RT equations are completely equivalent to the Einstein equations. Thus, for $N=14$ and an unfolded embedding as a background the embedding theory becomes exactly equivalent to GR in the weak field limit. This creates relevance for the problem of constructing an explicit unfolded embedding of the flat metric with $N=14$. We propose a way to construct such an embedding in Section 5.

In the most frequently discussed $N=10$ case (which corresponds to the minimal dimension by the JCF theorem) $b^a_{\mu\nu}$ is a non-square matrix and it cannot be removed from the equation, which means that the theory contains *extra* solutions. In this case, the RT equations (3) can be rewritten [14] as the system of the equations:

$$G^{\mu\nu} = \varkappa(T^{\mu\nu} + \tau^{\mu\nu}), \tag{10}$$

$$\tau^{\mu\nu} b^a_{\mu\nu} = 0. \tag{11}$$

The first of them is the Einstein equation with an additional contribution $\tau^{\mu\nu}$ of some fictitious matter (the properties of which can be compared with the known properties of dark matter or energy), and the second plays the role of equations of motion of this matter, see details in [28]. This allows us to consider embedding theory as a possible way to explain the mystery of dark matter. The latter turns out to be a purely gravitational effect that arises when considering the solutions of the embedding theory equations from the Einsteinian point of view. When analyzing the properties of such matter in the non-relativistic limit, the embedding $y^a(x^\mu)$ in section $x^0 = const$ is an unfolded embedding of the flat three-dimensional Euclidean metric into the 9-dimensional ambient space [28].

In general, the zeroth-order embedding function $\overset{(0)}{y}{}^a(x)$ of a four-dimensional surface is an unfolded embedding of the metric of the Minkowski space into the 10-dimensional ambient space. To continue research in this direction, it is necessary to have an explicit form of such embeddings, and in this paper we find examples of these embeddings in Section 5.

## 3. The Relation between Unfolded and Free Embeddings

In the previous Section we introduced the notion of *unfolded* embedding, which is convenient when discussing *extra* solutions of the RT equations. It is closely related to the classification of embeddings introduced in [29], which includes so-called *free* embeddings, *q-free* embeddings and *spatially-free* embeddings. Let us discuss their relation.

Let us consider an embedding function of an $n$-dimensional surface $y^a(x)$. Let us investigate how its small variation $\delta y^a(x)$ affects the induced metric $g_{\mu\nu}$ in the lowest order. An arbitrary variation $\delta y^a(x)$ can be decomposed into longitudinal and transverse contributions:

$$\delta y^a = \xi^\mu \partial_\mu y^a + \delta y^a_\perp, \qquad \delta y^a_\perp \partial_\mu y_a = 0. \tag{12}$$

Then from (1) we find that:

$$\delta g_{\mu\nu} = (\partial_\mu y_a)(\partial_\nu \delta y^a) + (\partial_\nu y_a)(\partial_\mu \delta y^a) = D_\nu \xi_\mu + D_\mu \xi_\nu - 2b^a_{\mu\nu}\delta y_{a\perp}, \tag{13}$$

where (4) is used, as well as the properties of the covariant derivative in the embedding theory formalism, see details, for example, in [17].

In [29], an embedding for a $n$-dimensional metric is said to be "free" if the system of $n(n+1)/2$ equations (13) can be solved in the transverse variations $\delta y^a_\perp$ for any $\delta g_{\mu\nu}$ and $\xi^\mu$. Since $\delta y^a_\perp$ has $N-n$ independent components, a free embedding satisfies the relation

$$N - n \geqslant \frac{n(n+1)}{2} \quad \Rightarrow \quad N \geqslant \frac{n(n+3)}{2}. \tag{14}$$

In turn, an embedding is "$q$-free" if $q$ out of $n(n+1)/2$ equations can be solved in the transverse variations $\delta y^a_\perp$ for any $\xi^\mu$, and the $n(n+1)/2 - q$ remaining equations are constraints on $\xi^\mu$. It is easy to see that $q$ is the rank of the matrix constructed from the second fundamental form $b^a_{\mu\nu}$ in the manner described after (9). The definition of $q$-free embedding implies that:

$$N - n \geqslant q, \qquad q \leqslant \frac{n(n+1)}{2}, \qquad n \geqslant \frac{n(n+1)}{2} - q. \tag{15}$$

As a result, for a $q$-free embedding the following relations hold:

$$\frac{n(n-1)}{2} \leqslant q \leqslant \frac{n(n+1)}{2}, \qquad N \geqslant q + n, \tag{16}$$

moreover, for $q = n(n+1)/2$ a $q$-free embedding is a free embedding.

From the inequalities (15) it follows that for $q$-free embeddings (and, in particular, for free embeddings) $N \geqslant n(n+1)/2$. This corresponds to the fact that within the statement of the problem (13) we consider the perturbation of the metric $\delta g_{\mu\nu}$ to be arbitrary, and to embed an arbitrary metric, according to the JCF theorem, this restriction on the number of dimensions of the ambient space $N$ must be satisfied. Note that for a four-dimensional surface, i.e., for $n = 4$, $q$ lies in the interval $6 \leqslant q \leqslant 10$, and a free embedding is 10-free with $N \geqslant 14$.

Additionally, in [29] the concept of "spatially-free" embedding is introduced. A four-dimensional embedding is called spatially-free if one can choose a coordinate system $(x^0, x^i)$ such that 6 vector fields $b^a_{ij}$ (for $i, j = 1, 2, 3$) are linearly independent. Note that the type of a 10-dimensional unfolded embedding of the 4-dimensional Minkowski space metric described at the end of Section 2 (and used in the work [28]) is spatially free.

According to the definition (see after (9)) of an unfolded embedding introduced above, the matrix constructed from the second fundamental form $b^a_{\mu\nu}$ has the maximal possible rank. It is easy to see that for a free embedding, for which the requirement (14) is satisfied, the rank must also be subject to this condition, therefore, for:

$$N \geqslant n(n+3)/2 \tag{17}$$

the concepts of unfolded embedding and free embedding coincide. For smaller values of the dimensions of the ambient space $N$, namely, in the range $n(n+1)/2 \leqslant N \leqslant n(n+3)/2$, any unfolded embedding is a $(N-n)$-free embedding, but generally speaking, not vice versa. As mentioned above, for even smaller values of $N < n(n+1)/2$ the concept of $q$-free embedding is no longer applicable while the concept of unfolded embedding can still be used.

The concept of unfolded embedding is very important in the perturbative analysis of solutions of RT equations (3) based on the decomposition (5). If one takes an unfolded embedding as a background, then the equations acquire interesting properties. For $N \geqslant n(n+3)/2$, when the embedding is also free, the factor $b^a_{\mu\nu}$ (4) can be removed since for an unfolded embedding all vectors of the ambient space $b^a_{\mu\nu}$ are linearly independent for $\mu \geqslant \nu$. As a result, the RT equations reduce to the Einstein equations, and there will be no extra solutions in this case.

For smaller values of $N$, the usage of the unfolded embedding as a background guarantees the linearizability of the RT equations in the weak field limit. To see this, note that an arbitrary deformation of the surface can be defined by choosing the deformation $\delta y^a$ transverse to the surface in (5) so that an arbitrary deformation is defined by $N-n$ functions. In the case of a weak gravitational field in zeroth-order of perturbation theory the metric must be flat, therefore $\overset{(0)}{G}{}^{\mu\nu} = 0$. Thus, on the left-hand side of the RT Equation (8) the factor $b^a_{\mu\nu}$ should be taken to a zeroth-order. Linearization of the equations means that all $N-n$ functions defining an arbitrary deformation are solutions of linear equations, and for this the presence of $N-n$ independent equations is necessary. This is exactly what happens if there are $N-n$ linearly independent vectors among the ambient space vectors $\overset{(0)}{b}{}^a_{\mu\nu}$ for different $\mu,\nu$, which means that the embedding is unfolded for $N < n(n+3)/2$.

## 4. Explicit Symmetric Embeddings of Flat Metrics

Firstly, we will consider the explicit symmetric embedding of the flat Euclidian 3-dimensional (i.e., $n=3$) metric which has the $SO(3) \ltimes T^3$ symmetry. Such an embedding can be constructed by the method proposed in [30] which was discussed at the beginning of Section 2. This method is implemented in [32] for $N=5$ as an illustration of its application to the construction of embedding for a spatially flat FRW model since the sections $x^0 = \text{const}$ of spatially flat FRW spacetime have a flat Euclidean 3-dimensional metric. However, there is a simple alternative possibility of obtaining the same embedding.

Consider the 4-dimensional surface that is a hyperboloid of radius $R$ in the space $\mathbb{R}^{1,4}$ of signature $\{-++++\}$:

$$y^0 = \frac{1}{4t}(R^2 - x^i x^i) - t, \qquad y^1 = \frac{1}{4t}(R^2 - x^i x^i) + t, \qquad y^i = x^i, \tag{18}$$

where $i = 1,2,3$ and $t, x^i$ are the coordinates on the surface. It is easy to see that $y^a y^b \eta_{ab} = R^2$, i.e., it is indeed a hyperboloid. Note that (18) is an embedding of de Sitter space and the surface defined by this embedding is symmetric with respect to the group $SO(1,4)$. If we take the section $y^0 = \bar{y}^0 = const$ of the given surface at large values of $\bar{y}^0$, then the resulting 3-dimensional surface is a sphere of large radius which is locally indistinguishable from the 3-dimensional plane. Thus, in the limit, the symmetry of the section is the group $SO(3) \ltimes T^3$. If we make a hyperbolic rotation in the plane $y^0, y^1$ (which is an element of the group $SO(1,4)$) simultaneously with increasing $\bar{y}^0$, then in the limit $\bar{y}^0 \to \infty$ the section $y^0 = \bar{y}^0$ turns into the section:

$$y^1 - y^0 = 2\bar{t}, \tag{19}$$

where $\bar{t}$ is some constant, finite in the limit. Therefore we see that the 3-dimensional surface resulting from Formula (19) has the desired symmetry $SO(3) \ltimes T^3$. After an insignificant general translation of this surface its embedding function can be written as:

$$y^0 = y^1 = -\frac{1}{4t_0} x^i x^i, \qquad y^i = x^i, \tag{20}$$

corresponding to the symmetric 5-dimensional embedding of the flat Euclidean 3-dimensional metric (the fact that the resulting surface has the flat Euclidean induced metric can easily be checked directly by the Formula (1)).

We will use an analogous method to construct an embedding of the 4-dimensional Minkowski space metric with the Poincare group symmetry $SO(1,3) \ltimes T^4$, i.e., $n = 4$. Consider the 5-dimensional surface that is a hyperboloid of radius $R$ in the space $\mathbb{R}^{2,4}$ of signature $\{+----+\}$:

$$y^\mu = x^\mu, \qquad y^4 = \frac{1}{4t}(R^2 - x^\mu x^\nu \eta_{\mu\nu}) - t, \qquad y^5 = \frac{1}{4t}(R^2 - x^\mu x^\nu \eta_{\mu\nu}) + t, \tag{21}$$

where $\mu = 0,1,2,3$; $t, x^i$ are the coordinates on the surface, and $\eta_{\mu\nu}$ is the Minkowski metric of signature $\{+---\}$. It is easy to check that:

$$y^a y^b \eta_{ab} = R^2, \tag{22}$$

i.e., it is indeed a hyperboloid. Note that (21) is an embedding of 5-dimensional anti-de Sitter space $AdS_5$, and the surface is symmetric with respect to the group $SO(2,4)$. Take a section of the hyperboloid (21) by the plane:

$$y^4 = \bar{y}^4 = const. \tag{23}$$

The resulting 4-dimensional surface, according to (22), is described by the equation:

$$y^\mu y^\mu \eta_{ab} + \left(y^5\right)^2 = R^2 + \left(\bar{y}^4\right)^2, \tag{24}$$

hence, it is a 4-dimensional hyperboloid of radius $\sqrt{R^2 + \bar{y}^{4^2}}$. For $\bar{y}^4 \to \infty$ it is locally indistinguishable from the 4-dimensional plane of signature $\{+---\}$, so that in the limit the symmetry of section is the desired group $SO(1,3) \ltimes T^4$.

Let us find an explicit solution of Equation (23) (with $y^4$ from (21)) with respect to the coordinate $t$:

$$t = \frac{1}{2}\left(-\bar{y}^4 \pm \sqrt{\bar{y}^{4^2} + R^2 - x^\mu x^\nu \eta_{\mu\nu}}\right). \tag{25}$$

Each of the roots must be analysed separately. We will discuss the case of choosing the minus sign, and it is easy to show that the alternative choice leads to the same answer. When choosing the minus sign, at $\bar{y}^4 \to \infty$ the leading approximation is $t = -\bar{y}^4$. For the convenience of the analysis we pass to the light-like coordinates in the ambient space by introducing the coordinates:

$$y^+ = \frac{y^5 + y^4}{2}, \qquad y^- = \frac{y^5 - y^4}{2} \tag{26}$$

instead of the coordinates $y^4$ and $y^5$. Then the embedding (21) can be rewritten in a simpler form:

$$y^\mu = x^\mu, \qquad y^+ = \frac{1}{4t}(R^2 - x^\mu x^\nu \eta_{\mu\nu}), \qquad y^- = t. \tag{27}$$

Substituting the solution (23) found in the leading approximation for $\bar{y}^4 \to \infty$ we obtain the embedding:

$$y^\mu = x^\mu, \qquad y^+ = -\frac{1}{4\bar{y}^4}(R^2 - x^\mu x^\nu \eta_{\mu\nu}), \qquad y^- = -\bar{y}^4. \tag{28}$$

Now note that among the transformations $SO(2,4)$ from the symmetry group $AdS_5$ there are hyperbolic rotations in the plane $y^4, y^5$ which are reduced to the transformation:

$$y^+ \to ky^+, \qquad y^- \to \frac{1}{k}y^+ \tag{29}$$

in terms of light-like coordinates $y^+, y^-$. Here $k$ is an arbitrary transformation parameter. Making such a transformation with $k = \bar{y}^4/R$ (note that the parameter $k$ is dimensionless, so we used the existing dimensional quantity $R$ for dimensionlessness) we can exclude the infinite value $\bar{y}^4$ from the embedding function (28). As a result, after an insignificant general translation of the surface we finally obtain the embedding function as:

$$y^\mu = x^\mu, \qquad y^+ = \frac{1}{4R}x^\mu x^\nu \eta_{\mu\nu}, \qquad y^- = 0. \tag{30}$$

By construction, it is symmetric with respect to the Poincare group $SO(1,3) \ltimes T^4$. The fact that the resulting surface has the induced Minkowski metric is easy to check directly by the Formula (1).

Symmetric embedding (30) of the Minkowski metric constructed by considering a section, the use of which is justified by some transition to the limit, can be obtained directly as a result of using the [30] method which was mentioned at the beginning of Section 2. This approach was implemented by A. Trukhin in their bachelor's thesis.

Unfortunately, the symmetric embeddings (20) and (30) of flat metrics discussed in this section are not unfolded. This is easy to understand if we notice that both embeddings lie in some codimension 1 plains of the ambient space. It means that among the ambient space vectors $b^a_{\mu\nu}$ at $\mu \geqslant \nu$ there is no linearly independent set of $N - n$ vectors (in both considered cases $N - n = 2$), which means that there is no unfoldness at $N < n(n+3)/2$. In the next section, a method is proposed that allows one to construct unfolded embeddings of the Minkowski space, but this method does not provide embeddings with the Minkowski space symmetry. The resulting embeddings will be unfolded, but not symmetric. The problem of constructing a symmetric unfolded embedding of flat metrics is not yet amenable to the solution. A possible way is to find all symmetric embeddings of the Minkowski metric for a given dimension of the ambient space $N$ by the method already mentioned at the beginning of this section, proposed in [30], and then check unfoldness by direct computation. However, for sufficiently large $N$ (for example, for the interesting case $N = 10$) this problem is very difficult and its solution is beyond the scope of this work.

In connection with the resulting embedding (30) it should be noted that it can be easily generalized to the embedding:

$$y^\mu = x^\mu, \qquad y^+ = B(x^\mu), \qquad y^- = 0 \tag{31}$$

with a completely arbitrary function $B(x^\mu)$. It is easy to check that this embedding is also an embedding of the Minkowski space metric; however, it does not inherit its symmetry, and, like (30), it is not unfolded.

## 5. Explicit Unfolded Embeddings of Flat Metrics

We will look for embeddings of flat metrics (Euclidean and pseudo-Euclidean) which are unfolded by the definition given in Section 2.

### 5.1. Using q-Free Embeddings

As it was said in Section 3, unfolded embeddings are also $(N-n)$-free embeddings in the range of the ambient space dimension $n(n+1)/2 \leqslant N \leqslant n(n+3)/2$, therefore in the first place we will discuss the $q$-free embedding of the Minkowski metric proposed in [29]. Since the opposite is not true, one has to check whether this embedding is unfolded.

The $q$-free embeddings construction method which was proposed in [29] (authors limit themselves to the case $n = 4$) consists of splitting the ambient space into the direct sum of two flat subspaces:

1. the "base" ambient space of signature $\{- \ldots -\}$;

2. the "extra" space of signature $\{+-\ldots-\}$, i.e., it has one and only one time-like direction.

In the base ambient space *base embedding* is defined, with the embedding function $z^A(x^i)$ depending only on spatial coordinates and satisfying two requirements:

- the corresponding induced metric is the flat Euclidean metric;
- the set of the nine vectors $\{\partial_i z^A, \partial_j\partial_k z^A\}$ is linearly independent (which means that the base embedding is unfolded).

The authors of [29] propose the 11-dimensional base embedding, thus presenting an 11-dimensional unfolded embedding of the flat 3-dimensional Euclidean metric.

As for the extra space, it is proposed to construct an extra embedding $w^L(x^\mu)$. In contrast to a base embedding, an extra embedding depends on the time variable $x^0$. Consequently, the resulting induced metric of the 4-dimensional surface decomposes into:

$$g_{\mu\nu} = \eta_{LM}(\partial_\mu w^L)(\partial_\nu w^M) - \delta^i_\mu \delta^i_\nu. \quad (32)$$

In the construction of Minkowski metric embedding, the extra space is considered to be one-dimensional and the extra embedding has the simple form:

$$w = x^0. \quad (33)$$

The resulting 12-dimensional embedding is a 6-free embedding, but it is not unfolded, since the rank of the matrix constructed from $b^a_{\mu\nu}$ (in the manner described after (9)) is 6, while the maximum possible rank is $11+1-4=8$.

The situation can be improved by taking a 9-dimensional base embedding instead of an 11-dimensional one. Then the dimension of the transverse space, which in this case defines the maximal possible rank of the matrix constructed from $b^a_{\mu\nu}$ would equal $9+1-4=6$, thus, the rank would be the highest possible, and the embedding would be unfolded. We will implement this idea in Section 5.4.

### 5.2. Sequential Deformation Method

Consider the following method of unfolded embeddings construction for flat metrics of arbitrary dimension $n$:

1. We start from a simple $(2n)$-dimensional embedding in the form of the direct product of $n$ circles (pseudoeuclidean circles); note that it will not be unfolded;
2. We construct a trivial (in the form of a multidimensional plane) $N$-dimensional (with $N>2n$) embedding for the resulting $(2n)$-dimensional flat space;
3. On this $(2n)$-dimensional plane we choose $N-2n$ mutually orthogonal straight lines;
4. Using $N-2n$ transverse directions, we sequentially deform each of the $N-2n$ mentioned lines into a circle; such a deformation of the $2n$-dimensional plane is an isometric one;
5. We check whether the obtained embedding is unfolded.

### 5.3. 9-Dimensional Unfolded (and Free) Embedding of the Euclidean 3-Dimensional Metric

First, we will use the proposed method to construct an explicit unfolded embedding of the 3-dimensional flat Euclidean metric into the Euclidean 9-dimensional space, so $n=3$ and $N=9$. To simplify the formulas, we will not introduce dimensional coefficients. Thus, dimensional considerations will be inapplicable to the coordinates. In accordance with the first step of Section 5.2, we start from the embedding:

$$\begin{aligned} z^1(x^i) &= \sin x^1, & z^3(x^i) &= \sin x^2, & z^5(x^i) &= \sin x^3, \\ z^2(x^i) &= \cos x^1, & z^4(x^i) &= \cos x^2, & z^6(x^i) &= \cos x^3. \end{aligned} \quad (34)$$

It is easy to see that locally the metric induced by this embedding is the metric of the Euclidean space (see the Conclusion for a discussion of its global structure). In order to choose 3 straight lines in a nontrivial way in accordance with step 3 of Section 5.2, we perform a $SO(6)$ rotation:

$$z'^A(x^i) = O^{AB} z^B(x^i), \tag{35}$$

(where $A, B = 1, \dots, 6$), then we simply choose 3 coordinate axes $z'^4, z'^5, z'^6$. It is clear that the induced metric will not change after such a transformation. One can, for example, choose the matrix:

$$O = \exp \begin{pmatrix} 0 & 1 & 0 & -1 & 0 & 0 \\ -1 & 0 & 0 & 0 & 0 & 0 \\ 0 & 0 & 0 & -1 & 0 & -1 \\ 1 & 0 & 1 & 0 & 0 & 0 \\ 0 & 0 & 0 & 0 & 0 & 1 \\ 0 & 0 & 1 & 0 & -1 & 0 \end{pmatrix} \tag{36}$$

as an orthogonal matrix $O$, since the matrix exponent of an antisymmetric matrix is an orthogonal matrix. Depending on the choice of the matrix $O$, the embedding obtained by this method can be either unfolded or not. For example, one can check that if we take the identity matrix as the matrix $O$, then even after step 4 of Section 5.2 the resulting embedding will not be unfolded.

Now, in accordance with step 2 of Section 5.2, we add 3 trivial directions of the ambient space by introducing the 9-dimensional embedding function $\tilde{y}^a$:

$$\tilde{y}^A(x^i) = z'^A(x^i), \qquad \tilde{y}^7(x^i) = \tilde{y}^8(x^i) = \tilde{y}^9(x^i) = 0. \tag{37}$$

Obviously, this 9-dimensional embedding is not unfolded. Furthermore, finally, in accordance with step 4 of Section 5.2, we make an isometric deformation of the 6-dimensional plane $\tilde{y}^1, \dots, \tilde{y}^6$ in three transverse directions $\tilde{y}^7, \tilde{y}^8, \tilde{y}^9$ so that three coordinate lines $\tilde{y}^4, \tilde{y}^5, \tilde{y}^6$ turn into circles:

$$\begin{aligned} y^1(x^i) &= z'^1(x^i), & y^4(x^i) &= \cos z'^4(x^i), \\ y^2(x^i) &= z'^2(x^i), & y^5(x^i) &= \sin z'^4(x^i), \\ y^3(x^i) &= z'^3(x^i), & y^6(x^i) &= \cos z'^5(x^i), \\ & & y^7(x^i) &= \sin z'^5(x^i), \\ & & y^8(x^i) &= \cos z'^6(x^i), \\ & & y^9(x^i) &= \sin z'^6(x^i). \end{aligned} \tag{38}$$

Since after such a deformation the metric of the 6-dimensional plane does not change, the metric of the 3-surface defined by this embedding also remains flat. This can also be checked directly by substituting the embedding (38) into the induced metric Formula (1) considering (34)–(36). Further, following step 5 of Section 5.2, it is necessary to check whether the obtained embedding is unfolded.

According to the definition (see Section 2), an embedding is unfolded if the rank of the matrix composed from the second fundamental form $b^a_{ik}$ in the way described below (9) is the maximum possible one. In the given case this matrix is a square $6 \times 6$ matrix (the pair of symmetric indices $ik$ corresponds to the multi-index are running through 6 values, and there are the same number of transverse directions). Therefore, for this matrix the unfoldedness condition coincides with the non-singularity condition. Direct calculation shows that for the embedding (38) this matrix is indeed non-singular, thus the constructed embedding of the 3-dimensional flat Euclidean metric into the Euclidean 9-dimensional space is unfolded. It is also *free* due to the fulfillment of the condition (17).

### 5.4. 10-Dimensional Unfolded Embedding of the Minkowski Metric

The embedding obtained in the previous subsection can be easily applied to construct an unfolded embedding of the Minkowski metric. In terms of [29] for this one need to use it as a base embedding (see Section 5.1) with a simple extra embedding (33). As a result, we get the 10-dimensional embedding

$$\begin{array}{ll} y^0(x^\mu) = x^0, & y^4(x^\mu) = \cos z'^4(x^i), \\ y^1(x^\mu) = z'^1(x^i), & y^5(x^\mu) = \sin z'^4(x^i), \\ y^2(x^\mu) = z'^2(x^i), & y^6(x^\mu) = \cos z'^5(x^i), \\ y^3(x^\mu) = z'^3(x^i), & y^7(x^i) = \sin z'^5(x^i), \\ & y^8(x^\mu) = \cos z'^6(x^i), \\ & y^9(x^\mu) = \sin z'^6(x^i) \end{array} \tag{39}$$

into the ambient space of signature $\{+-\ldots-\}$. Since for this embedding the 3-dimensional components $b^a_{ik}$ of the second fundamental form $b^a_{\mu\nu}$ coincide with the ones corresponding to the embedding (38), the rank of the corresponding matrix is equal to the maximum possible value 6 (the number of transverse directions), which means that the embedding (39) is unfolded. Note that the condition (17) is not satisfied. Therefore, this embedding is not *free* but only *6-free*.

### 5.5. 14-Dimensional Unfolded (and Free) Embedding of the Minkowski Metric

Now we will apply the method described in Section 5.2 to the construction of an explicit unfolded embedding of Minkowski metric into a 14-dimensional space so that $n = 4$ and $N = 14$. Since the requirement (17) is satisfied, the resulting embedding will also be *free*.

Following the first step of Section 5.2, we start from the embedding:

$$\begin{array}{ll} z^0(x^\mu) = \sinh x^0, & z^4(x^\mu) = \sin x^2, \\ z^1(x^\mu) = \cosh x^0, & z^5(x^\mu) = \cos x^2, \\ z^2(x^\mu) = \sin x^1, & z^6(x^\mu) = \sin x^3, \\ z^3(x^\mu) = \cos x^1, & z^7(x^\mu) = \cos x^3 \end{array} \tag{40}$$

into the ambient space of signature $\{+-\ldots-\}$. Note that this embedding is the direct product of the pseudoeuclidean circle $z^{1^2} - z^{0^2} = 1$ and three circles. It is easy to check that the corresponding induced metric is the Minkowski metric. Next, we will proceed in the same way as in Section 5.3.

In order to select 6 straight lines in a nontrivial way in accordance with the third step of Section 5.2, we make a $SO(1,7)$ rotation:

$$z'^A(x^\mu) = \Lambda^A{}_B z^B(x^\mu), \tag{41}$$

(here $A, B = 0, \ldots, 7$), for example, using the orthogonal matrix:

$$\Lambda = \exp\begin{pmatrix} 0 & 0 & 0 & 0 & 0 & 0 & 0 & 0 \\ 0 & 0 & 1 & 0 & 0 & -1 & 0 & 0 \\ 0 & -1 & 0 & -1 & 0 & 0 & 0 & 0 \\ 0 & 0 & 1 & 0 & -1 & 0 & 0 & 0 \\ 0 & 0 & 0 & 1 & 0 & 0 & 1 & 0 \\ 0 & 1 & 0 & 0 & 0 & 0 & 0 & 1 \\ 0 & 0 & 0 & 0 & -1 & 0 & 0 & 0 \\ 0 & 0 & 0 & 0 & 0 & -1 & 0 & 0 \end{pmatrix}, \tag{42}$$

then we select 6 coordinate axes $z'^3, \ldots z'^8$.

In accordance with the second step of Section 5.2, we add 6 trivial space-like directions of the ambient space, introducing the 14-dimensional embedding function $\tilde{y}^a$ in which $\tilde{y}^A(x^i) = z'^A(x^i)$ while the other components with $a = 8, \ldots, 13$ are equal to zero. Further, in accordance with the fourth step of Section 5.2, we make an isometric deformation of the 8-dimensional plane corresponding to the directions $\tilde{y}^0, \ldots, \tilde{y}^7$ in six transverse directions $\tilde{y}^8, \ldots, \tilde{y}^{13}$ with 6 coordinate lines $\tilde{y}^2, \ldots, \tilde{y}^7$ turning into circles:

$$\begin{aligned} &y^0(x^\mu) = z'^0(x^\mu), && y^6(x^\mu) = \sin z'^4(x^\mu), \\ &y^1(x^\mu) = z'^1(x^\mu), && y^7(x^\mu) = \cos z'^4(x^\mu), \\ &y^2(x^\mu) = \sin z'^2(x^\mu), && y^8(x^\mu) = \sin z'^5(x^\mu), \\ &y^3(x^\mu) = \cos z'^2(x^\mu), && y^9(x^\mu) = \cos z'^5(x^\mu), \\ &y^4(x^\mu) = \sin z'^3(x^\mu), && y^{10}(x^\mu) = \sin z'^6(x^\mu), \\ &y^5(x^\mu) = \cos z'^3(x^\mu), && y^{11}(x^\mu) = \cos z'^6(x^\mu), \\ & && y^{12}(x^\mu) = \sin z'^7(x^\mu), \\ & && y^{13}(x^\mu) = \cos z'^7(x^\mu). \end{aligned} \tag{43}$$

By construction, for this embedding the induced metric (1) will locally coincide with the Minkowski metric (see the Conclusion for a discussion of its global structure). One can check that its second fundamental form $b^a_{\mu\nu}$, interpreted as a $10 \times 10$ matrix (see the explanation below the Formula (9)), turns out to be non-degenerate, so this embedding is unfolded.

## 6. Conclusions

Isometric embeddings of flat metrics can be nontrivial, i.e., different from a plane in the ambient space. Such nontrivial embeddings are of interest from the point of view of describing gravity within the framework of the embedding theory. We have discussed some possible additional requirements that may apply when searching for these embeddings. There is an obvious possibility to require the constructed surface to have the symmetry of the original metric. However, there is also an alternative requirement that turns out to be crucial from the point of view of the RT equations (3) analysis (in particular, when one tries to linearize them). This is the requirement of unfoldness. We call an isometric embedding of a given metric unfolded if the corresponding surface locally occupies a subspace of the maximum possible dimension almost everywhere. The introduced concept of unfoldness is closely related to the free embedding concept discussed in the work [29].

We have discussed symmetric embeddings of flat Euclidean three-dimensional space and Minkowski space. We have proposed the method of sequential deformation of the surface to construct unfolded (but not symmetric) embeddings, Using this method, we succeeded to construct an unfolded embedding (38) of the metric $\mathbb{R}^3$ into the ambient Euclidean space $\mathbb{R}^9$, as well as the unfolded embedding (43) of the Minkowski metric $\mathbb{R}^{1,3}$ into the ambient multidimensional Minkowski space $\mathbb{R}^{1,13}$. Based on the embedding (38) an unfolded embedding (39) of the Minkowski metric into $\mathbb{R}^{1,9}$ was also obtained. Note that the proposed method of sequential deformation can also be used to build new multidimensional embeddings based on already known embeddings with a small value of the embedding class. For example, this method can be applied to the known (see [30]) 6-dimensional black hole embeddings. However, whether it is possible to obtain unfolded embeddings of black holes in this way is the question that requires a separate study.

It should be noted that for all proposed embeddings (38), (39) and (43) the embedding functions are periodic in spatial coordinates by construction. This means that the surfaces defined by these embeddings are compact, thus their topology differs from the topology of the original metrics. From a physical point of view, within the framework of embedding gravity such a property of the background embedding function $\overset{(0)}{y}{}^a(x)$ does not agree well with observations. Indeed, even if the universe is compact in spatial directions (as, for example, within the framework of the closed FRW model), then the period has to be very large, no less than the size of the visible part of the universe $L$. We can provide such a value of the period by introducing the value $L$ into the Formulas (34) and (40). If we replace $x^1$ with $x^1/L$ and so on, then the coordinates become dimensional values, and the period becomes equal to $2\pi L$. However, then the part of the surface with a size of the order of the galaxy diameter will be practically indistinguishable from the plane, i.e., the unfoldness of the embedding will no longer be visible. This corresponds to the fact that the second fundamental form $b^a_{\mu\nu}$ will be of order $1/L$, i.e., it will be very small. Therefore, it is necessary to get rid of the periodic property of the embedding functions.

It turns out that for unfolded embeddings for $N = n(n+3)/2$ this can be easily done by an infinitesimal non-periodic isometric deformation of the surface (a deformation that does not change the metric locally). For this deformation, the left side of the Equation (13) is zero. We can take an arbitrary non-periodic function $\xi^{\mu}(x)$ which defines the longitudinal part of the deformation, and from the vanishing of the right-hand side of (13) we find the transverse part of the deformation $\delta y^a_{\perp}$, which will also be non-periodic. For $N = n(n+3)/2$ for an unfolded embedding this can always be done easily by inverting the value $b^a_{\mu\nu}$ interpreted as a matrix in the sense described below the Formula (9). This matrix will be a square matrix of size $n(n+1)/2$; its non-singularity follows from the definition of an unfolded embedding. The described periodicity elimination of the embedding is easiest to imagine by noting that it occurs in the same way as in the transition from a circle to a spiral. This procedure can be directly applied to unfolded embeddings (38) and (43) for which $N = n(n+3)/2$ in order to break the periodicity of them. A non-periodic analogue of the embedding (39) can be obtained by a procedure similar to the one described in Section 5.4, but taking the deformed embedding (38) as the base embedding the periodicity of which has already been eliminated. Note that the resulting non-periodic embeddings turn out to be global embeddings for the considered non-compact flat spaces.

The resulting embeddings and their deformations with broken periodicity can be used both in the analysis of the properties of extra matter in the non-relativistic limit of embedding gravity [28] and as a background in the study of more general solutions of the RT equations (3) in the limit of a weak gravitational field (5).

**Author Contributions:** Investigation, S.P. and T.Z.; writing, S.P. and T.Z. All authors have read and agreed to the published version of the manuscript.

**Funding:** The work was supported by RFBR Grant No. 20-01-00081.

**Institutional Review Board Statement:** Not applicable.

**Informed Consent Statement:** Not applicable.

**Data Availability Statement:** Not applicable.

**Acknowledgments:** The authors thank A. Trukhin who obtained the embedding (30) in an alternative way.

**Conflicts of Interest:** The authors declare no conflict of interest.

## References

1. Friedman, A. Local isometric embedding of Riemannian manifolds with indefinite metric. *J. Math. Mech.* **1961**, *10*, 625. [CrossRef]
2. Stephani, H.; Kramer, D.; Maccallum, M.; Hoenselaers, C.; Herlt, E. *Exact Solutions of Einstein's Field Equations*, 2nd ed.; Cambridge University Press: Cambridge, UK, 2003.
3. Kobayashi, S.; Nomizu, K. *Foundations of Differential Geometry*; Wiley: New York, NY, USA, 1963; Volumes 1 and 2.
4. Sheykin, A.A.; Paston, S.A. Classification of minimum global embeddings for nonrotating black holes. *Theor. Math. Phys.* **2015**, *185*, 1547–1556. [CrossRef]
5. Sheykin, A.A.; Solovyev, D.P.; Paston, S.A. Global Embeddings of BTZ and Schwarzschild-ADS Type Black Holes in a Flat Space. *Symmetry* **2019**, *11*, 841. [CrossRef]
6. Kasner, E. Finite Representation of the Solar Gravitational Field in Flat Space of Six Dimensions. *Am. J. Math.* **1921**, *43*, 130–133. [CrossRef]
7. Fronsdal, C. Completion and Embedding of the Schwarzschild Solution. *Phys. Rev.* **1959**, *116*, 778–781. [CrossRef]
8. Robertson, H.P. Relativistic Cosmology. *Rev. Mod. Phys.* **1933**, *5*, 62–90. [CrossRef]
9. Sheykin, A.; Markov, M.; Fedulov, Y.; Paston, S. Explicit isometric embeddings of pseudo-Riemannian manifolds: Ideas and applications. *J. Phys. Conf. Ser.* **2020**, *1697*, 012077. [CrossRef]
10. Paston, S.A. Hawking into Unruh mapping for embeddings of hyperbolic type. *Class. Quant. Grav.* **2015**, *32*, 145009. [CrossRef]
11. Sheykin, A.A.; Solovyev, D.P.; Sukhanov, V.V.; Paston, S.A. Modifications of gravity via differential transformations of field variables. *Symmetry* **2020**, *12*, 240. [CrossRef]
12. Regge, T.; Teitelboim, C. General relativity à la string: A progress report. In Proceedings of the First Marcel Grossmann Meeting, Trieste, Italy, 7–12 July 1975; Ruffini, R., Ed.; 1977; pp. 77–88.
13. Deser, S.; Pirani, F.A.E.; Robinson, D.C. New embedding model of general relativity. *Phys. Rev. D* **1976**, *14*, 3301–3303. [CrossRef]
14. Pavsic, M. Classical theory of a space-time sheet. *Phys. Lett. A* **1985**, *107*, 66–70. [CrossRef]

15. Maia, M.D. On the integrability conditions for extended objects. *Class. Quant. Grav.* **1989**, *6*, 173–183. [CrossRef]
16. Karasik, D.; Davidson, A. Geodetic Brane Gravity. *Phys. Rev. D* **2003**, *67*, 064012. [CrossRef]
17. Paston, S.A.; Franke, V.A. Canonical formulation of the embedded theory of gravity equivalent to Einstein's general relativity. *Theor. Math. Phys.* **2007**, *153*, 1582–1596. [CrossRef]
18. Estabrook, F.B. The Hilbert Lagrangian and Isometric Embedding: Tetrad Formulation of Regge–Teitelboim Gravity. *J. Math. Phys.* **2010**, *51*, 042502. [CrossRef]
19. Paston, S.A. Gravity as a field theory in flat space-time. *Theor. Math. Phys.* **2011**, *169*, 1611–1619. [CrossRef]
20. Faddeev, L.D. New dynamical variables in Einstein's theory of gravity. *Theor. Math. Phys.* **2011**, *166*, 279–290. [CrossRef]
21. Goenner, H. Local Isometric Embedding of Riemannian Manifolds and Einstein's Theory of Gravitation. In *General Relativity and Gravitation: One Hundred Years after the Birth of Albert Einstein*; Held, A., Ed.; Plenum Press: New York, NY, USA, 1980; Chapter 14, Volume 1, pp. 441–468.
22. Chamseddine, A.H.; Mukhanov, V. Mimetic dark matter. *J. High Energy Phys.* **2013**, *2013*, 135. [CrossRef]
23. Golovnev, A. On the recently proposed mimetic Dark Matter. *Phys. Lett. B* **2014**, *728*, 39–40. [CrossRef]
24. Sebastiani, L.; Vagnozzi, S.; Myrzakulov, R. Mimetic Gravity: A Review of Recent Developments and Applications to Cosmology and Astrophysics. *Adv. High Energy Phys.* **2017**, *2017*, 3156915. [CrossRef]
25. Davidson, A. $\Lambda = 0$ Cosmology of a Brane-like universe. *Class. Quant. Grav.* **1999**, *16*, 653. [CrossRef]
26. Davidson, A.; Karasik, D.; Lederer, Y. Cold Dark Matter from Dark Energy. *arXiv* **2001**, arXiv:0111107.
27. Paston, S.A.; Sheykin, A.A. Embedding theory as new geometrical mimetic gravity. *Eur. Phys. J. C* **2018**, *78*, 989. [CrossRef]
28. Paston, S.A. Non-relativistic limit of embedding gravity as general relativity with dark matter. *Universe* **2020**, *6*, 163. [CrossRef]
29. Bustamante, M.D.; Debbasch, F.; Brachet, M.E. Classical Gravitation as free Membrane Dynamics. *arXiv* **2005**, arXiv:0509090.
30. Paston, S.A.; Sheykin, A.A. Embeddings for Schwarzschild metric: Classification and new results. *Class. Quant. Grav.* **2012**, *29*, 095022. [CrossRef]
31. Sheykin, A.; Markov, M.; Paston, S. Global embedding of BTZ spacetime using generalized method of symmetric embeddings construction. *J. Math. Phys.* **2021**, *62*, 102502. [CrossRef]
32. Paston, S.A.; Sheykin, A.A. Embeddings for solutions of Einstein equations. *Theor. Math. Phys.* **2013**, *175*, 806–815. [CrossRef]

universe

MDPI

Article

# Charged Particle Motions near Non-Schwarzschild Black Holes with External Magnetic Fields in Modified Theories of Gravity

Hongxing Zhang [1,2], Naying Zhou [1,2], Wenfang Liu [1] and Xin Wu [1,2,3,*]

1 School of Mathematics, Physics and Statistics, Shanghai University of Engineering Science, Shanghai 201620, China; M130120111@sues.edu.cn (H.Z.); M130120101@sues.edu.cn (N.Z.); 21200007@sues.edu.cn (W.L.)
2 Center of Application and Research of Computational Physics, Shanghai University of Engineering Science, Shanghai 201620, China
3 Guangxi Key Laboratory for Relativistic Astrophysics, Guangxi University, Nanning 530004, China
* Correspondence: wuxin_1134@sina.com or xinwu@gxu.edu.cn

**Abstract:** A small deformation to the Schwarzschild metric controlled by four free parameters could be referred to as a nonspinning black hole solution in alternative theories of gravity. Since such a non-Schwarzschild metric can be changed into a Kerr-like black hole metric via a complex coordinate transformation, the recently proposed time-transformed, explicit symplectic integrators for the Kerr-type spacetimes are suitable for a Hamiltonian system describing the motion of charged particles around the non-Schwarzschild black hole surrounded with an external magnetic field. The obtained explicit symplectic methods are based on a time-transformed Hamiltonian split into seven parts, whose analytical solutions are explicit functions of new coordinate time. Numerical tests show that such explicit symplectic integrators for intermediate time steps perform well long-term when stabilizing Hamiltonian errors, regardless of regular or chaotic orbits. One of the explicit symplectic integrators with the techniques of Poincaré sections and fast Lyapunov indicators is applied to investigate the effects of the parameters, including the four free deformation parameters, on the orbital dynamical behavior. From the global phase-space structure, chaotic properties are typically strengthened under some circumstances, as the magnitude of the magnetic parameter or any one of the negative deformation parameters increases. However, they are weakened when the angular momentum or any one of the positive deformation parameters increases.

**Keywords:** modified gravity; black hole; magnetic field; chaos; symplectic integrator

**Citation:** Zhang, H.; Zhou, N.; Liu, W.; Wu, X. Charged Particle Motions near Non-Schwarzschild Black Holes with External Magnetic Fields in Modified Theories of Gravity. *Universe* **2021**, *7*, 488. https://doi.org/10.3390/universe7120488

Academic Editors: Panayiotis Stavrinos and Emmanuel N. Saridakis

Received: 8 November 2021
Accepted: 7 December 2021
Published: 10 December 2021



## 1. Introduction

A Schwarzschild solution describing a nonrotating black hole and a Kerr solution describing a rotating black hole are two exact solutions of Einstein's field equations of general relativity in a vacuum. According to the no-hair theorem, astrophysical (Kerr) black holes have their masses and spins as their unique characteristics. The theoretical prediction of the existence of black holes has been confirmed frequently by a wealth of observational evidence, such as X-ray binaries [1,2], detections of gravitational waves [3,4] and event-horizon-scale images of M87 [5,6].

Observational tests of strong-field gravity features cannot be based on an a priori hypothesis about the correctness of general relativity. Instead, such tests must allow ansatz metric solutions to deviate from the general relativistic black hole scenarios predicted by the no-hair theorem. These metric solutions often come from perturbations of the usual Schwarzschild (or Kerr) black hole or exact solutions in alternative (or modified) theories of gravity. A small deformation to the Schwarzschild metric describing a nonspinning black hole (i.e., a modified Schwarzschild metric) [7] could be required to satisfy the modified field equations in dynamical Chern–Simons modified gravity [8,9]. By applying the Newman–Janis algorithm and a complex coordinate transformation, Johannsen and Psaltis [10] transformed such a Schwarzschild-like metric with several free deformation parameters into a Kerr-like metric, including a set of free deformation parameters and mass and spin. This Kerr-like metric, which is a parametric deformation of the Kerr solution and is not a vacuum solution, is regular everywhere outside of the event horizon. These metric deformations away from the Schwarzschild or Kerr metric by one or more parameters contain modified multipole structures. Although the $\gamma$ metric (or Zipoy–Voorhees metric) describing a static and axially symmetric field [11,12] is also a parameterizing deviation from the Schwarzschild solution for $\gamma \neq 1$, it is an exact solution of Einstein's equations in a vacuum.

In addition to the above-mentioned simply modified theories of gravity, such as scalar-tensor gravity, many other forms of modified theories of gravity can be found in the literature. Some examples are scalar-tensor theories, such as the Brans–Dicke theory [13,14], general scalar-tensor theories [15–19], Einstein-ther theories [20], Bimetric theories [21,22], tensor-vector-scalar theories [23,24], Einstein–Cartan–Sciama–Kibble theory [25,26], scalar-tensor-vector theory [27], $f(R)$ theories [28–30], $f(G)$ theory [31,32], Hořava-Lifschitz gravity [33–35] and higher dimensional theories of gravity [36–38]. Researchers and students in cosmology and gravitational physics should also see review articles [29,30,39–41] for more information on these modified gravity theories. Black-hole solutions in modified theories of gravity are generally unlike those in general relativity, and include many additional free parameters and the parameters predicted by the no-hair theorem in general relativity. Although a solution in a modified gravity model can be mathematically equivalent to a scalar field model, this mathematical correspondence does not always mean physical equivalence. The two corresponding solutions may have different physical behaviors. Corrections to the classical Einsteinian black hole entropy are necessary so as to constrain the viability of modified gravity theories in the study of Schwarzschild–de Sitter black holes by the use of the Noether charge method [42]. However, not all black-hole solutions in modified theories of gravity must necessarily dissatisfy the Einstein field equations. For example, a stationary black-hole solution of the Brans–Dicke field equations must be that of the Einstein field equations [43]; this result is still present if no symmetries apart from stationarity are assumed [44]. The Kerr metric also remains a solution of certain $f(R)$ theories [45].

A deep understanding of the relevant properties of the standard general relativistic black hole solutions and particle motions in the vicinity of the black holes is important to study accretion disk structure, gravitational lensing, cosmology and gravitational wave theory. Observational data from the vicinity of the circular photon orbits or the innermost stable circular orbits could be used as tests of the no-hair theorem. The properties of the innermost stable circular orbits are useful for understanding the energetic processes of a black hole. For this reason, radial effective potentials and (innermost) stable circular orbits of charged particles in electromagnetic fields surrounding a black hole have been extensively investigated in a large variety of papers (see, e.g., [46–51]). The motions of charged particles in the equatorial plane sound simple, but off-equatorial motions of charged particles in the magnetic fields become very complicated. In a stationary and axisymmetric black hole solution, there are three conserved quantities, including the energy, angular momentum and rest mass of a charged particle. The fourth invariable quantity related to the azimuthal motion of the particle is destroyed in general when an electromagnetic field is included around the black hole. Thus, the particle motion in the spacetime background is not an integrable system. Chaos describing a dynamical system with sensitive dependence on initial conditions can occur in some circumstances. Various aspects of chaotic motions of charged particles around the standard general relativistic black holes perturbed by weak external sources, such as magnetic fields, are discussed in many references (see, e.g., [52–59]).

Thanks to the importance of the deformed (or modified) black hole solutions in tests of strong-field gravity features of general relativity, the motions of charged particles in the modified solutions with or without perturbations of weak external sources are naturally taken into account by some authors. The authors of [10] focused on the question of how the radii of the innermost stable circular orbits and circular photon orbits vary with increasing values of the spin and deviation parameters in a Kerr-like metric of a rapidly rotating black hole. They demonstrated that their Kerr-like metric is suitable for strong-field tests of the no-hair theorem in the electromagnetic spectrum. Charged particle motions around non-Schwarzschild or non-Kerr black hole immersed in an external uniform magnetic field were considered in [60–62]. The influence of a magnetic field on the radial motion of a charged test particle around a black hole surrounded with an external magnetic field in Hořava–Lifshitz gravity was investigated in [63–65]. The radial motions of charged particles in the $\gamma$ spacetime in the presence of an external magnetic field were studied in [66]. In fact, the $\gamma$ spacetime is nonintegrable and can allow for the onset of chaos if the external magnetic field is not included [67]. The authors of [68] gave some insights into the effect of one deformation parameter on the chaos of charged particles in the vicinity of a non-Schwarzschild black hole with an external magnetic field.

Numerical integration methods are vital to detecting the chaotic behavior of charged particles in the vicinity of the standard general-relativistic or modified black hole solutions with or without perturbations from weak external sources. They should have good stability and high precision so as to provide reliable results when detecting the chaotic behavior. The most appropriate long-term integration solvers for Hamiltonian systems constitute a class of symplectic integrators which respect the symplectic structures of Hamiltonian dynamics [69,70]. The motions of charged particles near the black holes with or without weak external sources can be described by Hamiltonian systems, and thus allow for the applicability of symplectic methods. If the Hamiltonian systems are split into two parts, explicit symplectic integration algorithms are not available in general. However, implicit symplectic integrators, such as the implicit midpoint rule [71,72] and implicit Gauss–Legendre Runge–Kutta symplectic schemes [54,73,74], are always suitable for their applications to these Hamiltonian systems that do not need any separable forms. When the Hamiltonians are separated into one group with explicit analytical solutions and another group with implicit solutions, explicit and implicit combined symplectic methods can be constructed [75–79]. The implicit algorithms are more computationally demanding than the explicit ones in general; therefore, the explicit symplectic integrations should be developed as much as possible. Recently, the authors of [80–82] successfully constructed the explicit symplectic integrators for the Schwarzschild-type black holes with or without external magnetic fields by splitting the corresponding Hamiltonians into several parts having analytical solutions as explicit functions of proper time. More recently, the time-transformed explicit symplectic integrators were designed for the Kerr family spacetimes [83–85].

The idea for constructing the time-transformed explicit symplectic integrators and the explicit symplectic integrators introduced in [80–83] allows for the applicability of many standard general-relativistic or modified black hole solutions with or without perturbations of weak external sources. In spite of this, there is no universal rule on how to construct explicit symplectic integrators for Hamiltonians corresponding to the spacetimes. Specific Hamiltonian problems have different separations, or different choices of time-transformed Hamiltonians and their splitting forms. As is claimed above, the non-Schwarzschild metric with four free deformation parameters could produce a Kerr-like metric through a complex coordinate transformation [10]. Now, there is the question of whether the time-transformed explicit symplectic integrators for the Kerr-type spacetimes [83] are applicable to such a deformed non-Schwarzschild black hole immersed in an external magnetic field. We address that question in this paper. In addition, we mainly pay attention to the effects of the four free deformation parameters on the chaotic behavior. The present work is unlike the study in [68], in which one deformation parameter is added to the non-Schwarzschild metric and no explicit symplectic integrators are considered.

The remainder of this paper is organized as follows. A metric deformation to the Schwarzschild spacetime is introduced in Section 2. Time-transformed explicit symplectic integrators are described in Section 3. Orbital dynamical properties are discussed in Section 4. Finally, the main results are presented in Section 5.

## 2. Deformed Schwarzschild Metric

In Schwarzschild coordinates $(t, r, \theta, \varphi)$, a Schwarzschild-like metric $ds^2 = g_{\alpha\beta}dx^\alpha dx^\beta$ is written in [7,10] as

$$\begin{aligned} ds^2 &= -f(1+h)dt^2 + f^{-1}(1+h)dr^2 + r^2 d\theta^2 + r^2 \sin^2\theta d\varphi^2, &(1)\\ f &= 1 - \frac{2M}{r}, \\ h &= k_0 + \frac{k_1 M}{r} + \frac{k_2 M^2}{r^2} + \frac{k_3 M^3}{r^3}. &(2) \end{aligned}$$

$M$ denotes a mass of the black hole. The speed of light $c$ and the gravitational constant $G$ are taken as geometric units; $c = G = 1$. Deformation function $h$ is a perturbation to the Schwarzschild metric, where $k_0$, $k_1$, $k_2$ and $k_3$ are deformation parameters. It comes from modified multipole structures related to spherical deformations of the star. When the action through algebraic, quadratic curvature invariants coupled to scalar fields is modified, such small deformations in the Schwarzschild metric are obtained from the modified field equations and the scalar field's equation in dynamical theory. Clearly, Equation (1) with $h = 0$ corresponds to the Schwarzschild metric. When $h \neq 0$, Equation (1) looks like the Schwarzschild metric but can be transformed into a Kerr-like black-hole metric by the Newman–Janis algorithm [86] and a complex coordinate transformation [10].

Suppose the black hole is immersed in an external electromagnetic field with a four-vector potential:

$$A_\mu = \frac{1}{2}\delta^\varphi_\mu B r^2 \sin^2\theta, \tag{3}$$

where $B$ is a constant strength of the uniform magnetic field. The motion of a test particle with mass $m$ and charge $q$ is described in the following Hamiltonian.

$$H = \frac{1}{2m} g^{\mu\nu}(p_\mu - qA_\mu)(p_v - qA_\nu). \tag{4}$$

where $p_\mu$ is a generalized momentum, which is determined by

$$\dot{x}^\mu = \frac{\partial H}{\partial p_\mu} = \frac{1}{m} g^{\mu\nu}(p_\nu - qA_\nu), \tag{5}$$

equivalently,

$$p_\mu = m\dot{x}^\nu g_{\mu\nu} + qA_\mu. \tag{6}$$

The 4-velocity $\dot{x}^\mu$ is a derivative of the coordinate $x^\mu$ with respect to proper time $\tau$. As the Hamiltonian equations satisfy Equation (5) and

$$\dot{p}_\mu = -\frac{\partial H}{\partial x^\mu}; \tag{7}$$

$p_t$ and $p_\varphi$ are two constants of motion:

$$\begin{aligned} p_t &= m\dot{t}g_{tt} = -m\dot{t}f(1+h) = -E, &(8)\\ p_\varphi &= m\dot{\varphi}g_{\varphi\varphi} + qA_\varphi = mr^2\dot{\varphi}\sin^2\theta + \frac{1}{2}qBr^2\sin^2\theta = L. &(9) \end{aligned}$$

$E$ is an energy of the particle, and $L$ is an angular momentum of the particle.

For simplicity, dimensionless operations are given to the related quantities as follows: $t \to tM$, $\tau \to \tau M$, $r \to rM$, $B \to B/M$, $E \to mE$, $p_r \to mp_r$, $L \to mML$, $p_\theta \to mMp_\theta$, $q \to mq$ and $H \to mH$. In this way, $M$ and $m$ in Equations (1)–(9) are taken as geometric units; $m = M = 1$. The Hamiltonian (4) has two degrees of freedom $(r, \theta)$ in a four-dimensional phase space $(r, \theta, p_r, p_\theta)$, and can be rewritten as a dimensionless form:

$$H = -\frac{E^2}{2f(1+h)} + \frac{1}{2r^2 \sin^2\theta}(L - \frac{1}{2}Qr^2 \sin^2\theta)^2 + \frac{fp_r^2}{2(1+h)} + \frac{p_\theta^2}{2r^2}, \tag{10}$$

where $Q = Bq$.

Besides the two constants (8) and (9), the conserved Hamiltonian quantity

$$H = -\frac{1}{2} \tag{11}$$

is a third constant of the system (10). The third constant of motion exists due to the invariance of the 4-velocity or the rest mass of the particle in the time-like spacetime (1). Given $Q = 0$, the system (10) holds a fourth constant of motion and therefore is integrable and nonchaotic. When $Q \neq 0$, the system (10) has no fourth constant and then becomes nonintegrable. In this case, analytical solutions cannot be given to the system (10), but numerical solutions can.

## 3. Explicit Symplectic Integrations

First, time-transformed explicit symplectic methods for the system (10) is introduced. Then, their performance is numerically evaluated.

### 3.1. Design of Algorithms

As is claimed above, the metric (1) seems to be the Schwarzschild metric, but the system (10) is not suitable for the application of the explicit symplectic methods suggested in [80–82] because the Hamiltonian (10) is unlike the Hamiltonians of the Schwarzschild-type spacetimes (including the Reissner-Nordström metric, the Reissner-Nordström-(anti)–de Sitter solution and these spacetimes perturbed by external magnetic fields), which can be separated into several parts having analytical solutions as explicit functions of proper time $\tau$. Since the Schwarzschild-like metric (1) can correspond to a Kerr-like metric via some coordinate transformation [12], the time-transformed explicit symplectic methods for the Kerr-type spacetimes proposed in [73] are guessed to be applicable to the system (10). The implementations of the algorithms are detailed below.

By extending the phase-space variables $(p_r, p_\theta; r, \theta)$ of the Hamiltonian (10) to $(p_r, p_\theta, p_0; r, \theta, q_0)$, where $\tau$ is viewed as a new coordinate $q_0 = \tau$ and its corresponding momentum is $p_0$ with $p_0 = -H = 1/2 \neq p_t$, we have an extended phase-space Hamiltonian:

$$J = H + p_0. \tag{12}$$

It is clear that $J$ is always identical to zero, $J = 0$. By taking a time transformation

$$d\tau = g(r)dw, \tag{13}$$

$$g(r) = 1 + h, \tag{14}$$

we get a new time transformation Hamiltonian:

$$\mathcal{H} = g(r)J = -\frac{E^2}{2f} + \frac{(1+h)(L - \frac{1}{2}Qr^2\sin^2\theta)^2}{2r^2\sin^2\theta} + \frac{p_r^2}{2} - \frac{p_r^2}{r} + \frac{(1+k_0)p_\theta^2}{2r^2} + \frac{k_1 p_\theta^2}{2r^3} + \frac{k_2 p_\theta^2}{2r^4} + \frac{k_3 p_\theta^2}{2r^5} + p_0 g(r). \tag{15}$$

The Hamiltonian $\mathcal{H}$ has new coordinate time variable $w$ and the phase-space variables $(p_r, p_\theta, p_0; r, \theta, q_0)$. As $J = 0$, $\mathcal{H} = 0$.

Similarly to the Hamiltonians of the Schwarzschild-type spacetimes in references [80–82], the time-transformed Hamiltonian $\mathcal{H}$ can be split in the following way:

$$\mathcal{H} = \mathcal{H}_1 + \mathcal{H}_2 + \mathcal{H}_3 + \mathcal{H}_4 + \mathcal{H}_5 + \mathcal{H}_6 + \mathcal{H}_7, \tag{16}$$

where sub-Hamiltonians read

$$\mathcal{H}_1 = -\frac{E^2}{2f} + \frac{(1+h)(L-\frac{1}{2}Qr^2\sin^2\theta)^2}{2r^2\sin^2\theta} + p_0(1+h), \tag{17}$$

$$\mathcal{H}_2 = \frac{p_r^2}{2}, \tag{18}$$

$$\mathcal{H}_3 = -\frac{p_r^2}{r}, \tag{19}$$

$$\mathcal{H}_4 = \frac{(1+k_0)p_\theta^2}{2r^2}, \tag{20}$$

$$\mathcal{H}_5 = \frac{k_1 p_\theta^2}{2r^3}, \tag{21}$$

$$\mathcal{H}_6 = \frac{k_2 p_\theta^2}{2r^4}, \tag{22}$$

$$\mathcal{H}_7 = \frac{k_3 p_\theta^2}{2r^5}. \tag{23}$$

Each of the seven sub-Hamiltonians is analytically solvable, and its solutions are explicit functions of the new coordinate time $w$. $\mathcal{A}$, $\mathcal{B}$, $\mathcal{C}$, $\mathcal{D}$, $\mathcal{E}$, $\mathcal{F}$ and $\mathcal{G}$ are differential operators, which correspond to $\mathcal{H}_1$, $\mathcal{H}_2$, $\mathcal{H}_3$, $\mathcal{H}_4$, $\mathcal{H}_5$, $\mathcal{H}_6$ and $\mathcal{H}_7$, respectively. These operators are written as

$$\begin{aligned}
\mathcal{A} &= -\frac{\partial \mathcal{H}_1}{\partial r}\frac{\partial}{\partial p_r} - \frac{\partial \mathcal{H}_1}{\partial \theta}\frac{\partial}{\partial p_\theta} + \frac{\partial \mathcal{H}_1}{\partial p_0}\frac{\partial}{\partial q_0} \\
&= f_1\frac{\partial}{\partial p_r} + f_2\frac{\partial}{\partial p_\theta} + (1+h)\frac{\partial}{\partial q_0}, \\
f_1 &= \frac{k_1}{2r^2} + \frac{k_2}{r^3} + \frac{3k_3}{2r^4} - \frac{E^2}{r^2(\frac{2}{r}-1)^2} \\
&\quad + \frac{(L-\frac{Qr^2\sin^2\theta}{2})^2(\frac{k_1}{r^2}+\frac{2k_2}{r^3}+\frac{3k_3}{r^4})}{2r^2\sin^2\theta} \\
&\quad + (L-\frac{Qr^2\sin^2\theta}{2})[Q+\frac{(L-\frac{Qr^2\sin^2\theta}{2})}{r^2\sin^2\theta}] \\
&\quad \cdot(\frac{k_0+1}{r} + \frac{k_1}{r^2} + \frac{k_2}{r^3} + \frac{k_3}{r^4}) - p_0\frac{\partial h}{\partial r}, \\
f_2 &= (L-\frac{Qr^2\sin^2\theta}{2})[Q+\frac{(L-\frac{Qr^2\sin^2\theta}{2})}{r^2\sin^2\theta}] \\
&\quad \cdot(k_0+1+\frac{k_1}{r}+\frac{k_2}{r^2}+\frac{k_3}{r^3})\cot\theta,
\end{aligned} \tag{24}$$

$$\mathcal{B} = p_r\frac{\partial}{\partial p_r}, \tag{25}$$

$$\mathcal{C} = -\frac{2}{r}p_r\frac{\partial}{\partial r} - \frac{p_r^2}{r^2}\frac{\partial}{\partial p_r}, \tag{26}$$

$$\mathcal{D} = \frac{(1+k_0)p_\theta}{r^2}\frac{\partial}{\partial\theta} - \frac{(1+k_0)p_\theta^2}{r^3}\frac{\partial}{\partial p_r}, \tag{27}$$

$$\mathcal{E} = \frac{k_1 p_\theta}{r^3}\frac{\partial}{\partial\theta} - \frac{3}{2}\frac{k_1 p_\theta^2}{r^4}\frac{\partial}{\partial p_r}, \tag{28}$$

$$\mathcal{F} = \frac{k_2 p_\theta}{r^4}\frac{\partial}{\partial\theta} - 2\frac{k_1 p_\theta^2}{r^5}\frac{\partial}{\partial p_r}, \tag{29}$$

$$\mathcal{G} = \frac{k_3 p_\theta}{r^5}\frac{\partial}{\partial\theta} - \frac{5}{2}\frac{k_3 p_\theta^2}{r^6}\frac{\partial}{\partial p_r}. \tag{30}$$

The solutions $\mathbf{z} = (r, \theta, q_0, p_r, p_\theta)^T$ for the time-transformed Hamiltonian $\mathcal{H}$ advancing a new coordinate time step $\Delta w = \sigma$ from the initial solutions $\mathbf{z}(0) = (r_0, \theta_0, q_{00}, p_{r0}, p_{\theta 0})^T$ can be given by

$$\mathbf{z} = S_2^{\mathcal{H}}(\sigma)\mathbf{z}(0), \tag{31}$$

where $S_2^{\mathcal{H}}$ represents symmetric products of exponents of the seven operators and has the expressional form

$$\begin{aligned} S_2^{\mathcal{H}}(\sigma) &= e^{\frac{\sigma}{2}\mathcal{G}} \times e^{\frac{\sigma}{2}\mathcal{F}} \times e^{\frac{\sigma}{2}\mathcal{E}} \times e^{\frac{\sigma}{2}\mathcal{D}} \times e^{\frac{\sigma}{2}\mathcal{C}} \times e^{\frac{\sigma}{2}\mathcal{B}} \times e^{\sigma\mathcal{A}} \times e^{\frac{\sigma}{2}\mathcal{B}} \\ &\quad \times e^{\frac{\sigma}{2}\mathcal{C}} \times e^{\frac{\sigma}{2}\mathcal{D}} \times e^{\frac{\sigma}{2}\mathcal{E}} \times e^{\frac{\sigma}{2}\mathcal{F}} \times e^{\frac{\sigma}{2}\mathcal{G}}. \end{aligned} \tag{32}$$

Such symmetric products are a component of symplectic operators of second order. The symplectic method $S_2$ is an extension to the works of [83–85] regarding the time-transformed explicit symplectic methods for the Kerr spacetimes. Of course, such symmetric products of order 2 easily yield a fourth-order construction of Yoshida [87]:

$$S_4^{\mathcal{H}} = S_2^{\mathcal{H}}(\gamma\sigma) \times S_2^{\mathcal{H}}(\delta\sigma) \times S_2^{\mathcal{H}}(\gamma\sigma), \tag{33}$$

where $\gamma = 1/(1-\sqrt[3]{2})$ and $\delta = 1 - 2\gamma$.

### 3.2. Numerical Evaluations

Let us choose parameters $E = 0.9965$, $L = 4$, $Q = 6 \times 10^{-4}$, $k_0 = 10^{-3}$, $k_1 = 10^{-2}$, $k_2 = 10^{-1}$ and $k_3 = 1$. The initial conditions are $p_r = 0$ and $\theta = \pi/2$. The initial value $r = 15$ for Orbit 1, and $r = 50$ for Orbit 2. The initial values $p_\theta > 0$ for the two orbits are determined by Equation (11).

Given the time step $\sigma = 1$, the errors of the Hamiltonian $J$ for the second-order method $S_2$ and the fourth-order method $S_4$ solving Orbit 1 have no secular drifts. The errors are three orders of magnitude smaller for $S_4$ than for $S_2$ before the integration time $w = 10^7$, as shown in Figure 1a. With the integration spanning this time and tending to $w = 10^8$, the errors still remain bounded for $S_2$, but exhibit long-term growths for $S_4$. The secular drifts of the Hamiltonian errors for $S_4$ are due to roundoff errors. When the number of integration steps is small, the truncation errors are more important than the roundoff errors. As the integration is long enough, the roundoff errors are dominant errors and cause the Hamiltonian errors to grow with time. However, such error drifts for $S_4$ lose when a larger time step $\sigma = 4$ is adopted. If Orbit 1 is replaced with Orbit 2, the Hamiltonian errors for each of the two methods are not explicitly altered.

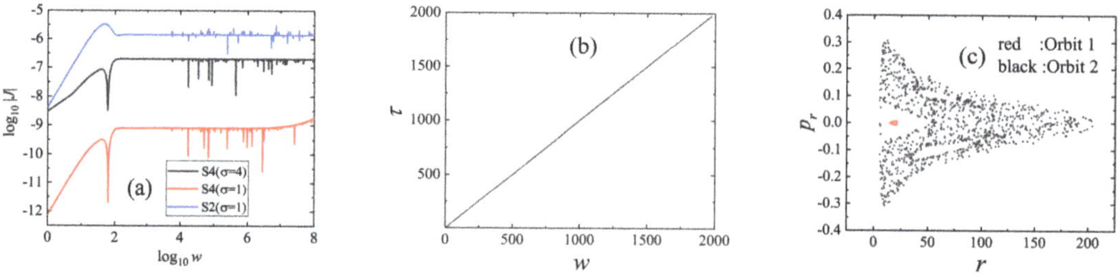


**Figure 1.** (**a**) Errors of the Hamiltonian $J$ in Equation (12). S2 ($\sigma = 1$) represents the second-order method S2 with time step $\sigma = 1$; S4 ($\sigma = 1$) means the fourth-order method S4 with new coordinate time step $\sigma = 1$, and S4 ($\sigma = 4$) stands for the fourth-order method S4 with time step $\sigma = 4$. Orbit 1 with the initial separation $r = 15$ is tested. Orbit 1 has the other initial conditions $p_r = 0$, $\theta = \pi/2$ and $p_\theta > 0$ determined by $J = 0$. The parameters are $E = 0.9965$, $L = 4$, $Q = 6 \times 10^{-4}$, $k_0 = 10^{-3}$, $k_1 = 10^{-2}$, $k_2 = 10^{-1}$ and $k_3 = 1$. The error for S4 ($\sigma = 1$) is three orders of magnitude smaller than for S2 ($\sigma = 1$). The error remains bounded for S2 ($\sigma = 1$), but it has a secular drift for S4 ($\sigma = 1$) due to roundoff errors. The secular drift in the error loses for S4 ($\sigma = 4$). (**b**) Relation between proper time $\tau$ and new coordinate time $w$. This shows that $\tau$ and $w$ are almost the same. (**c**) Poincaré sections at the plane $\theta = \pi/2$ with $p_\theta > 0$. Orbit 1 is ordered, whereas Orbit 2 with the initial separation $r = 50$ is chaotic. Panels (**b**,**c**) come from the results provided by the algorithm S4 ($\sigma = 4$).

In what follows, $S_4$ with the time step $\sigma = 4$ is used. Figure 1b describes the relationship between the proper time $\tau$ and the new coordinate time $w$ when Orbit 1 is tested. Clearly, $w$ is almost equal to $\tau$. This result coincides with the theoretical result $g \approx 1 + k_0 \approx 1$ when $r \gg 2$ and $k_0 \approx 0$. Therefore, the time transformation function $g$ in Equation (14) mainly plays an important role in implementing the desired separable form of the time-transformed Hamiltonian $\mathcal{H}$ rather than adaptive control to time steps.

## 4. Regular and Chaotic Dynamics of Orbits

The regularity of Orbit 1 and the chaoticity of Orbit 2 are clearly shown through the Poincaré section at the plane $\theta = \pi/2$ with $p_\theta > 0$ in Figure 1c. The phase-space of Orbit 1 is a Kolmogorov–Arnold–Moser (KAM) torus, which belongs to the characteristic of a regular quasi-periodic orbit. For Orbit 2, many discrete points are densely, randomly filled with an area and are regarded as the characteristic of a chaotic orbit. The Hamiltonian errors for $S_4$ acting on Orbit 1 are approximately same as those for $S_4$ acting on Orbit 2. This fact indicates that the algorithmic performance for the Hamiltonian error behavior is not related to the regularity or chaoticity of orbits.

Now, we continue to use the technique of Poincaré section to trace the orbital dynamical evolution. The parameters are the same as those in Figure 1; but $Q = 8 \times 10^{-4}$, $k_0 = 10^{-4}$ and different values $E$ are given. When $E = 0.991$ in Figure 2a, the plotted seven orbits are ordered. As the energy increases, e.g., $E = 0.9925$, three of the orbits are chaotic in Figure 2b. For $E = 0.9975$ in Figure 2c, chaos is present almost elsewhere in the whole phase space. These results indicate an increase in the energy enhances the strength of chaos from the global phase-space structure. However, the chaotic properties are weakened as the particle's angular momentum $L$ increasing, as shown in Figure 3.

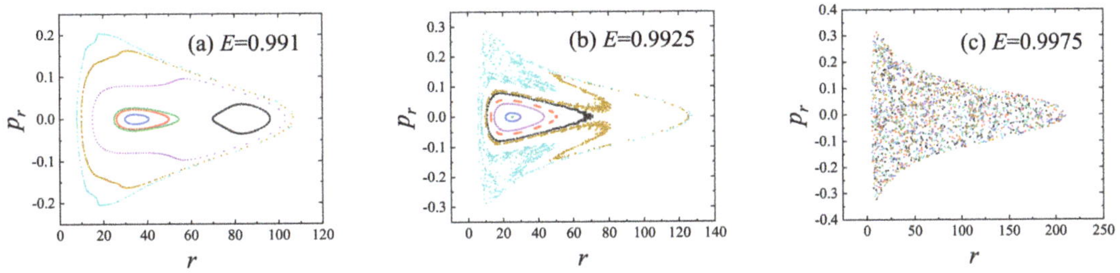


**Figure 2.** Poincaré sections. The parameters are the same as those in Figure 1c, but $Q = 8 \times 10^{-4}$, $k_0 = 10^{-4}$ and the energies $E$ are different. The energies are (**a**) $E = 0.991$, (**b**) $E = 0.9925$ and (**c**) $E = 0.9975$. The three sub-figures show that the chaoticity becomes strong as the energy increases.

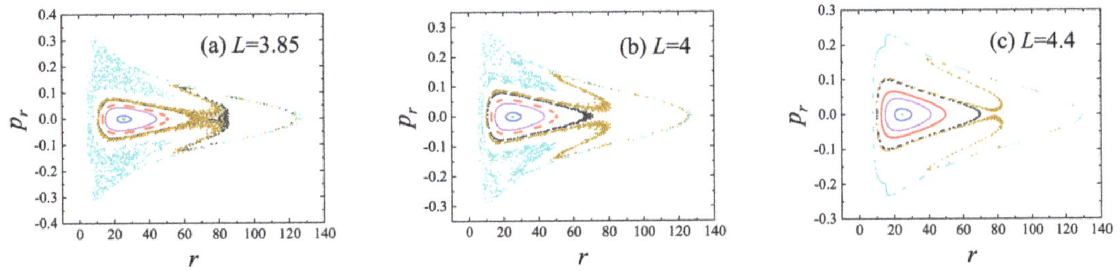


**Figure 3.** Poincaré sections. The parameters are $E = 0.9925$, $Q = 8 \times 10^{-4}$, $k_0 = 10^{-4}$, $k_1 = 10^{-2}$, $k_2 = 10^{-1}$ and $k_3 = 1$. The angular momenta are (**a**) $L = 3.85$, (**b**) $L = 4$ and (**c**) $L = 4.4$. It is clearly shown that chaos is gradually weakened as the angular momentum increases.

Besides the technique of Poincaré section, Lyapunov exponents for measuring an exponential rate of the separation between two nearby orbits with time are often used to distinguish chaos from order. The largest Lyapunov exponent is defined in [88] by

$$\lambda = \lim_{w \to \infty} \frac{1}{w} \ln \frac{d(w)}{d0}, \tag{34}$$

where $d0$ is the starting separation between the two nearby orbits and $d(w)$ is the distance between the two nearby orbits at time $w$. However, it takes long enough time to obtain stabilizing values of the Lyapunov exponents. Instead, a fast Lyapunov indicator (FLI), as a quicker method to distinguish between the ordered and chaotic two cases, is often used. It comes from a slightly modified version of the largest Lyapunov exponent, and is calculated in [88] by

$$FLI = \log_{10} \frac{d(w)}{d0}. \tag{35}$$

An exponential growth of FLI with time $\log_{10} w$ means that the bounded orbit is chaotic, whereas a power law growth of FLI shows the bounded orbit is regular. When the integration time arrives at $10^6$, the FLIs in Figure 4a can clearly identify the regular and chaotic properties of three energies corresponding to the orbits with the initial separation $r = 15$ in Figure 2. The regular and chaotic properties of three angular momenta corresponding to the orbits with the initial separation $r = 70$ in Figure 3 are also described the FLIs in Figure 4b. Clearly, the angular momentum $L = 4.4$ corresponds to the regularity, whereas the angular momenta $L = 3.85$ and $L = 4$ correspond to chaos. Chaos is stronger for $L = 3.85$ than for $L = 4$. As far as the Poincaré sections and FLIs are concerned, they are two popular methods to distinguish chaos from order. The technique of Poincaré sections can clearly, intuitively describe the global phase-space structure, but is mainly applicable to conservative systems with two degrees of freedom or four-dimensional phase spaces. The method of FLIs is suitable for any dimensions.

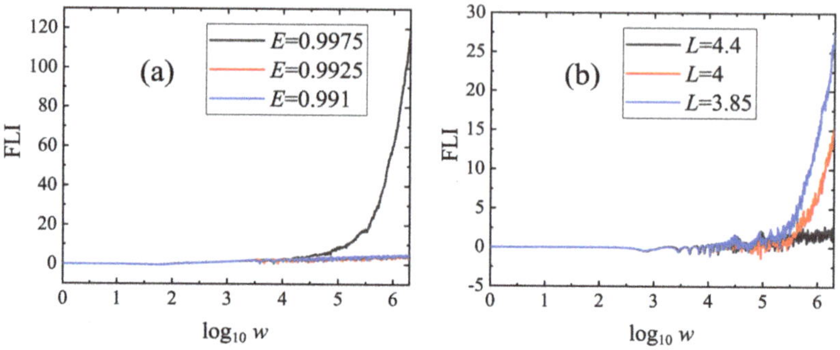


**Figure 4.** Fast Lyapunov indicators (FLIs). (**a**) The initial separation is $r = 15$; the other initial conditions and parameters are those of Figure 2. The FLIs for $E = 0.991$ and $E = 0.9925$ correspond to the regular behavior, but the FLI for $E = 0.9975$ shows the chaotic behavior. (**b**) The initial separation is $r = 70$; the other initial conditions and parameters are those of Figure 3. The FLI for $L = 4.4$ indicates the regularity. $L = 3.85$ corresponds to stronger chaos than $L = 4$.

Taking the parameters $L = 4$, $k_0 = 10^{-4}$, $k_1 = 10^{-2}$, $k_2 = 10^{-1}$ and $k_3 = 1$, we employ the technique of Poincaré sections to plot the global phase-space structures with $E = 0.9915$ for three positive values of the magnetic parameter $Q$ in Figure 5a–c. When $Q = 5 \times 10^{-4}$, all orbits are regular KAM tori in Figure 5a. Given $Q = 8 \times 10^{-4}$ in Figure 5b, many tori are twisted and a few orbits can be chaotic. When $Q = 10^{-3}$ in Figure 5c, the number of chaotic orbits increases and the strength of chaos is enhanced. In other words, an increase in the positive magnetic parameter is helpful to induce the occurrence of chaos. How does a negative magnetic parameter affect the chaotic behavior as the magnitude of the negative magnetic parameter increases? The key to this question can be found in Figure 5d–f with $E = 0.9975$. No chaos exists for $Q = -10^{-4}$ in Figure 5d. Three chaotic orbits are plotted for $Q = -8 \times 10^{-4}$ in Figure 5e. More orbits can be chaotic when $Q = -10^{-3}$ in Figure 5f. That is to say, the chaotic properties from the global phase-space structures are typically strengthened as the absolute value of the negative magnetic parameter increases. In short, chaos becomes stronger as the magnitude of the positive or negative magnetic parameter ($|Q|$) varies from small to large. This result is also supported by the FLIs in Figure 6. Here, the FLI for a given value of $Q$ is obtained after the integration time $w = 2 \times 10^6$. All FLIs that are not less than 6 correspond to the onset of chaos, and those that are less than this value turn out to indicate the regularity of orbits. When $Q > 8.5 \times 10^{-4}$ in Figure 6a or $Q < -7.5 \times 10^{-4}$ in Figure 6b, a dynamical transition from order to chaos occurs.

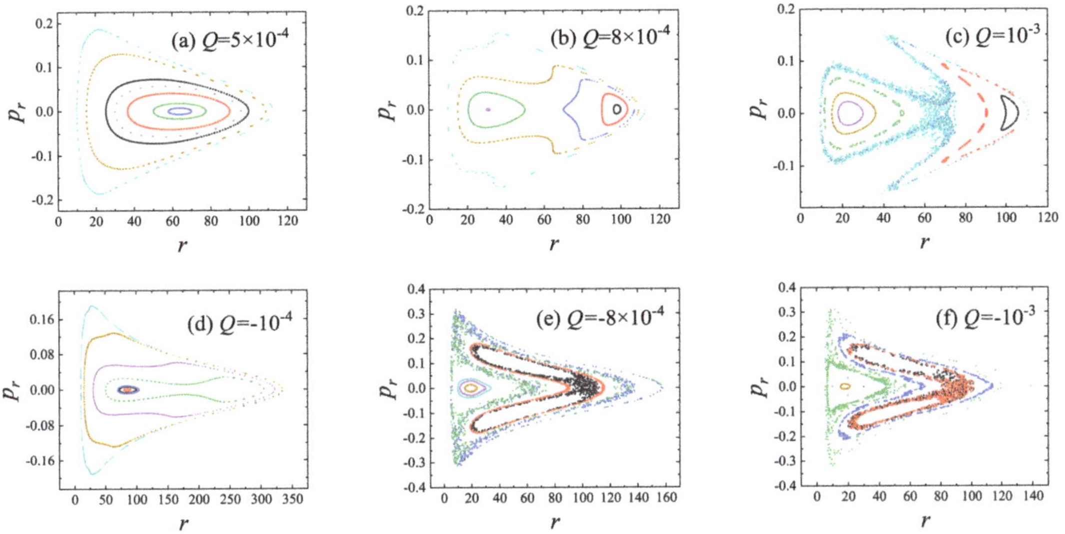


**Figure 5.** Poincaré sections for different values of the magnetic parameter $Q$. The other parameters are $L = 4$, $k_0 = 10^{-4}$, $k_1 = 10^{-2}$, $k_2 = 10^{-1}$ and $k_3 = 1$. (**a–c**): $E = 0.9915$ and $Q > 0$; the strength of chaos is enhanced with increasing $Q$. (**d–f**): $E = 0.9975$ and $Q < 0$; chaos is strong as $|Q|$ increases.

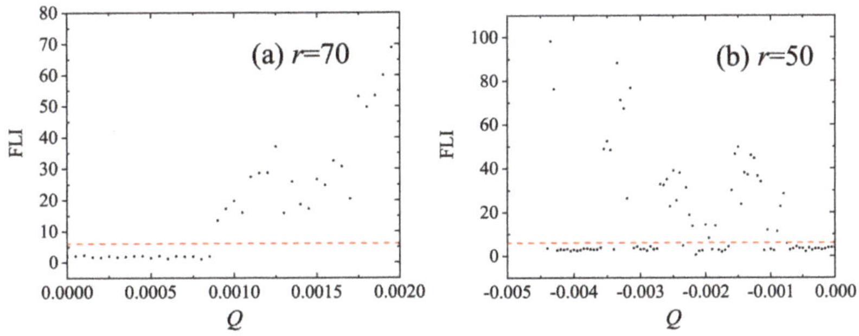


**Figure 6.** (**a**): Dependence of FLI on the positive magnetic parameter $Q$ in Figure 5a–c. The initial separation is $r = 70$. The FLI for each value of $Q$ is obtained after the integration time $w = 2 \times 10^6$. The FLIs $\geq 6$ mean chaos, and the FLIs $< 6$ show the regularity. When $Q > 8.5 \times 10^{-4}$, chaos begins to occur. (**b**): Dependence of FLI on the negative magnetic parameter $Q$ in Figure 5d–f. The initial radius is $r = 50$. When $Q < -7.5 \times 10^{-4}$, there is a dynamical transition from order to chaos.

Now, let us focus on the dependence of chaos on the deformation parameters. Chaos becomes weaker when the deformation parameter $k_0$ is positive and increases in Figure 7a–c. However, it gets stronger when the deformation parameter $k_0$ is negative and its magnitude increases in Figure 7d–f. The effects of the deformation parameter $k_0$ on chaos described by the technique of Poincaré sections are consistent with those described by the method of FLIs in Figure 8. The effects of the other deformation parameters on chaos are shown through the methods of Poincaré sections and FLIs in Figures 9–14. They are similar to the effect of the deformation parameter $k_0$ on chaos. Precisely speaking, an increase in any one of the positive deformation parameters $k_1$, $k_2$ and $k_3$ weakens the chaotic properties, and an increase in any of the magnitudes of the negative deformation parameters $k_1$, $k_2$ and $k_3$ strengthens the chaotic properties. The result regarding the effects of the four deformation parameters on the chaotic properties is similar to the result of [68] for describing the effect of deformation parameter $k_3$ on the chaotic properties.

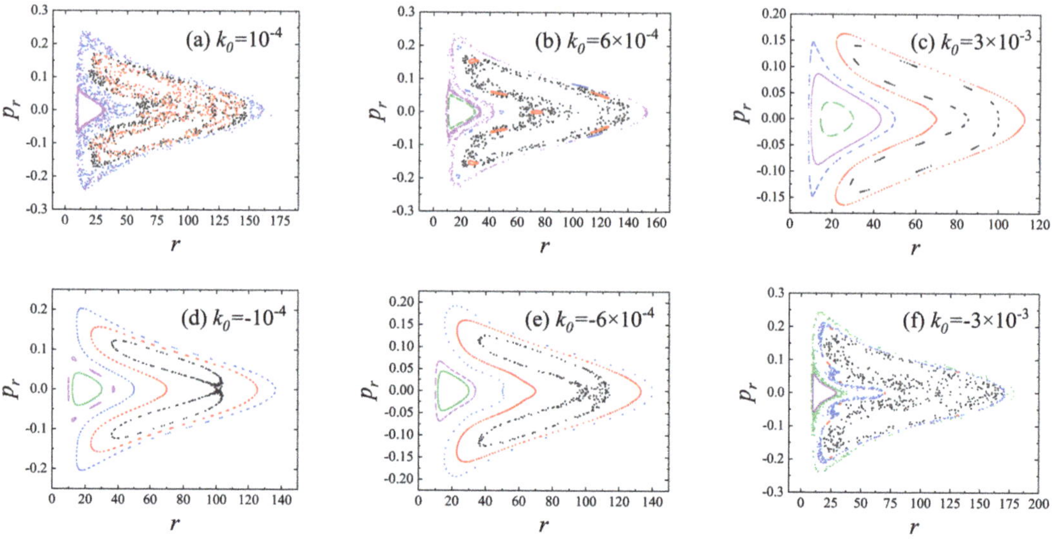


**Figure 7.** Poincaré sections for different values of the deformation parameter $k_0$. The parameters are $L = 4.6$, $Q = 8 \times 10^{-4}$, $k_1 = 10^{-2}$, $k_2 = 10^{-1}$ and $k_3 = 1$. (**a–c**): $E = 0.995$ and $k_0 > 0$. The strength of chaos is weakened with increasing $k_0$. (**d–f**): $E = 0.994$ and $k_0 < 0$. Chaos is enhanced as $|k_0|$ increases.

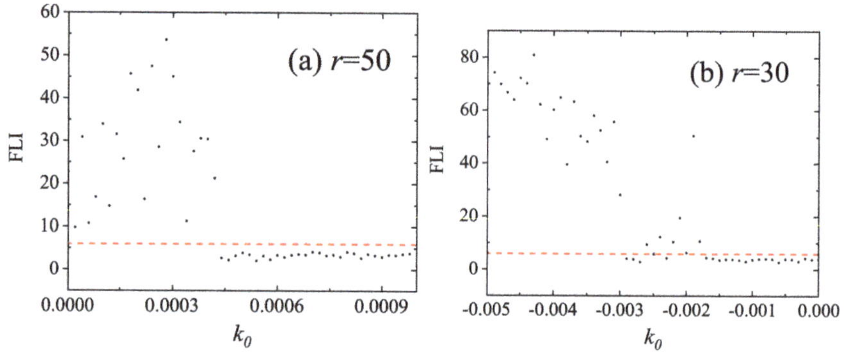


**Figure 8.** (**a**): Dependence of FLI on the positive deformation parameter $k_0$ in Figure 7a–c. The initial separation is $r = 50$. When $k_0 > 4.2 \times 10^{-4}$, chaos begins to lose. (**b**): Dependence of FLI on the negative deformation parameter $k_0$ in Figure 7d–f. The initial radius is $r = 30$. When $k_0 < 1.7 \times 10^{-3}$, the chaotic properties are strengthened.

The above demonstrations clearly show how small changes of these parameters affect the dynamical transitions from order to chaos. The main result is that chaos in the global phase space is strengthened the energy $E$, magnetic parameter $|Q|$ or an absolute value of one of the negative deformation parameters ($|k_0|$, $|k_1|$, $|k_2|$ and $|k_3|$) increases, but weakened when the angular momentum $L$ or any one of the positive deformation parameters $k_0$, $k_1$,

$k_2$ and $k_3$ increases. Here, an interpretation is given to the result. Expanding $1/f$ in the Taylor series, we rewrite Equation (17) at the equatorial plane $\theta = \pi/2$ as

$$\begin{aligned}\mathcal{H}_1 \approx\; & \frac{1}{2}[(1+k_0)(1-LQ) - E^2 + \frac{k_2}{4}Q^2] - \frac{E^2}{r} + \frac{Q^2}{8}(1+k_0)r^2 \\ & + \frac{L^2}{2r^2}(1+k_0) + \frac{L^2 k_1}{2r^3} + \frac{1-LQ}{2}(\frac{k_1}{r} + \frac{k_2}{r^2} + \frac{k_3}{r^3}) + \frac{k_3}{2r}Q^2. \end{aligned} \quad (36)$$

The second term corresponds to the black hole gravity acting on the particles. The third term yields an attractive force from a contribution of the magnetic field regardless of whether $Q > 0$ or $Q < 0$. The fourth term provides an inertial centrifugal force due to the particle's angular momentum. The fifth, sixth and seventh terms come from coupled interactions among the metric deformation perturbations, angular momentum and magnetic field. For $1 - LQ \approx 1$, they have repulsive force effects on the charged particles when $k_1 > 0$, $k_2 > 0$ and $k_3 > 0$, but attractive force effects when $k_1 < 0$, $k_2 < 0$ and $k_3 < 0$. A small increase in the energy $E$ or the magnetic field $|Q|$ means enhancing the attractive force effects, and therefore the motions of particles can become more chaotic in some circumstances. As the angular momentum $L$ increases, the repulsive force effects are strengthened and chaos is weakened. With a minor increase in relatively small positive deformation parameter $k_0$, the magnetic field attractive force and the centrifugal force will increase, but the centrifugal force has a larger increase than the magnetic field force for the parameters chosen in Figure 7. This leads to weakening the strength of chaos. However, as the absolute value $|k_0|$ with $k_0 < 0$ increases, the centrifugal force has a larger decrease than the magnetic field force, and chaos becomes stronger. Increases of the other positive deformation parameters $k_1$, $k_2$ and $k_3$ cause the repulsive forces to increase, and chaos to get weaker. However, the attractive force effects are enhanced and chaos gets stronger as the magnitudes of negative deformation parameters $k_1$, $k_2$ and $k_3$ increase.

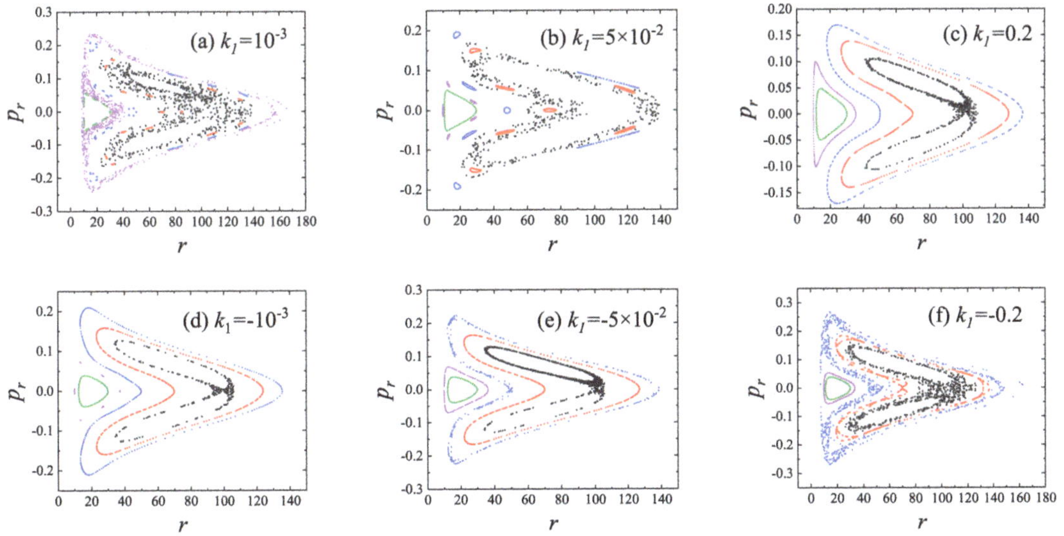


**Figure 9.** Same as Figure 7, but $k_0$ in Figure 7 is replaced with $k_1$. **(a–c)** : $k_0 = 5 \times 10^{-4}$. **(d–f)** : $k_0 = 10^{-4}$.

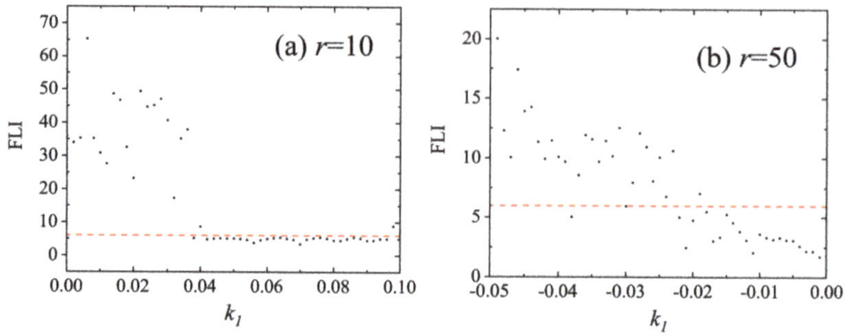


**Figure 10.** Same as Figure 8, but $k_0$ in Figure 8 is replaced with $k_1$. (**a**): $k_0 = 5 \times 10^{-4}$ and the initial radius is $r = 10$; chaos is ruled out as $k_1 > 0.042$. (**b**): $k_0 = 10^{-4}$ and the initial radius is $r = 50$; chaos is enhanced as $k_1 < -0.018$.

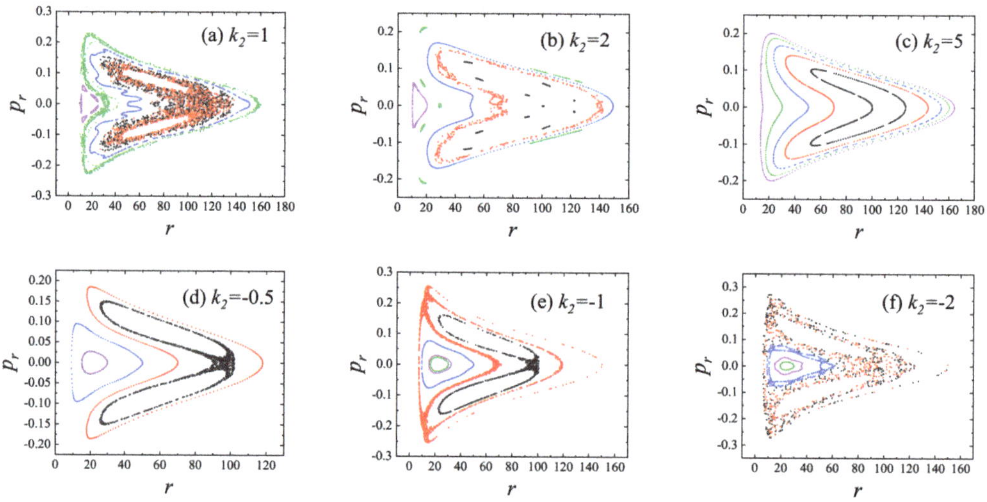


**Figure 11.** Poincaré sections for different values of the deformation parameter $k_2$. The parameters are $L = 4.6$, $Q = 8 \times 10^{-4}$, $k_0 = 5 \times 10^{-4}$, $k_1 = 5 \times 10^{-3}$ and $k_3 = 1$. (**a–c**): $E = 0.995$ and $k_2 > 0$. The strength of chaos is weakened with increasing $k_2$. (**d–f**): $E = 0.994$ and $k_2 < 0$. Chaos is enhanced as $|k_2|$ increases.

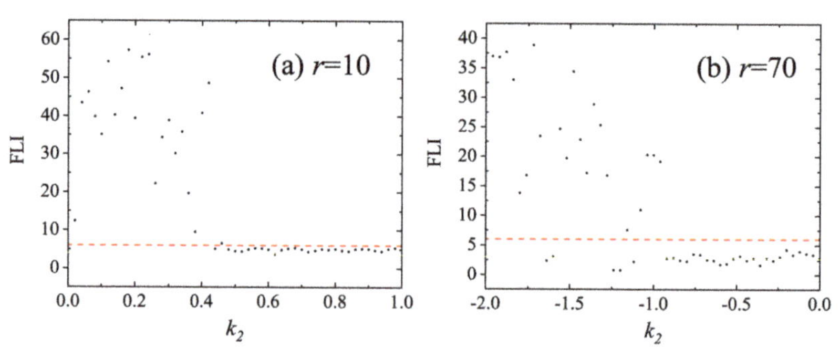


**Figure 12.** (**a**): Dependence of FLI on the positive deformation parameter $k_2$ in Figure 11a–c. The initial separation is $r = 10$. When $k_2 > 0.46$, chaos is absent. (**b**): Dependence of FLI on the negative deformation parameter $k_2$ in Figure 11d–f. The initial radius is $r = 70$. When $k_2 < -0.96$, the chaotic properties are strengthened.

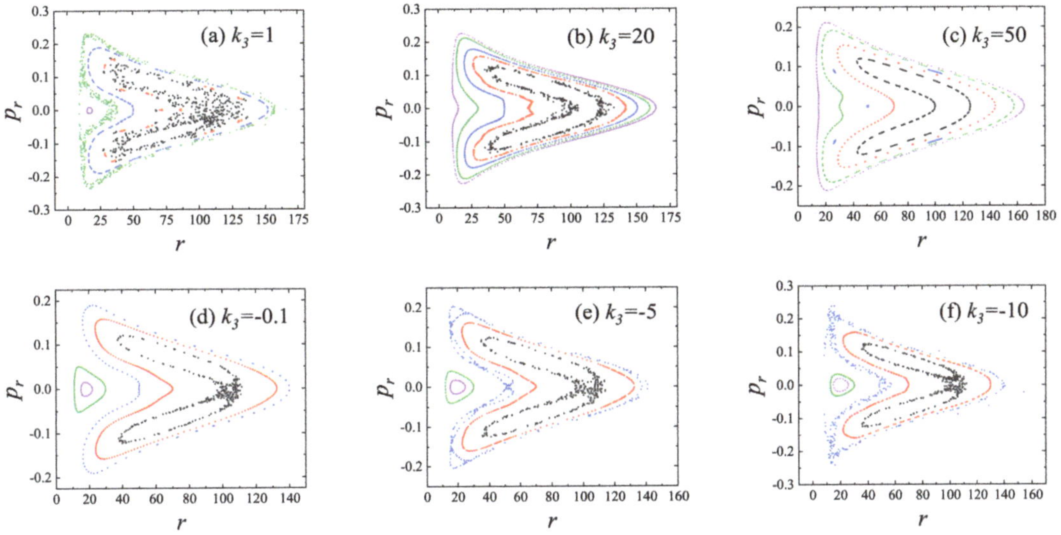


**Figure 13.** Similar to Figure 11, but $k_2$ in Figure 11 is replaced with $k_3$and energies $E$ are different. Here, $k_2 = 0.5$. (**a–c**): $E = 0.995$ and $k_3 > 0$. (**d–f**): $E = 0.9945$ and $k_3 < 0$.

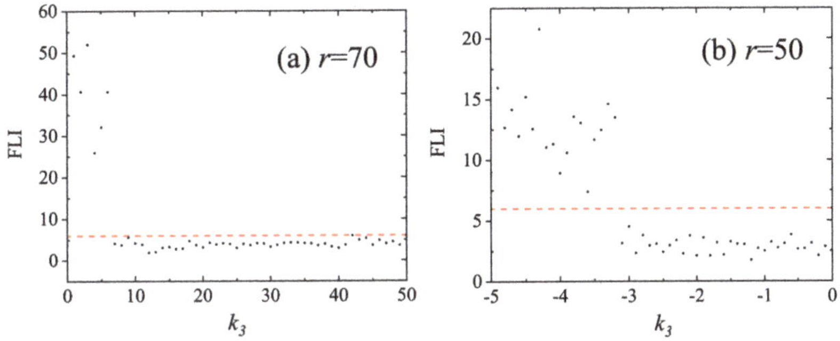


**Figure 14.** Dependence of FLI on the positive deformation parameter $k_3$. The other parameters are the same as those in Figure 13. (**a**): $E = 0.995$, $k_3 > 0$ and the initial separation $r = 70$; when $k_3 > 6$, chaos begins to disappear. (**b**): $E = 0.9945$, $k_3 < 0$ and the initial separation $r = 50$; when $k_3 < -3.2$, the chaotic properties are strengthened.

## 5. Conclusions

When a nonrotating compact object has spherical deformations, it has suffered from metric deformation perturbations. Such small deformation perturbations in the Schwarzschild metric could be regarded as a nonrotating black hole solution departure from the standard Schwarzschild spacetime in modified theories of gravity. The non-Schwarzschild spacetime with four free deformation parameters is integrable. However, the dynamics of charged particles moving around the Schwarzschild-like black hole is nonintegrable when the inclusion of an external asymptotically uniform magnetic field destroys the fourth invariable quantity related to the azimuthal motion of the particles.

Although the deformation perturbation metric looks like the Schwarzschild metric, it can be changed into a Kerr-like black hole metric via some appropriate coordinate transformation. Therefore, the time-transformed explicit symplectic integrators for the Kerr-type spacetimes introduced in [83] should be similarly applicable to the deformed Schwarzschild black hole surrounded with an external magnetic field. In fact, we can design explicit symplectic methods for a time-transformed Hamiltonian, which is split into seven parts with analytical solutions as explicit functions of new coordinate time. A main role for the time transformation function is the implementation of such desired separable form of the time-transformed Hamiltonian rather than that of adaptive time-step control. It was shown numerically that the obtained time-transformed explicit symplectic integrators perform well long-term in terms of stable error behavior regardless of regular or chaotic orbits when intermediate time steps are chosen.

One of the obtained time-transformed explicit symplectic integrators combined with the techniques of Poincaré sections and FLIs was used to show how small changes of the parameters affect the dynamical transitions from order to chaos. Chaos in the global phase space can be strengthened under some circumstances, if the energy or the absolute value of the (positive or negative) magnetic parameter or any of the negative deformation parameters increases. However, it is weakened as the angular momentum or any one of the positive deformation parameters increases.

**Author Contributions:** Conceptualization, methodology and supervision, X.W.; software and writing—original draft, H.Z.; software, N.Z. and W.L. All authors have read and agreed to the published version of the manuscript.

**Funding:** This research has been supported by the National Natural Science Foundation of China (Grant Nos. 11973020 and11533004) and the National Natural Science Foundation of Guangxi (No. 2019JJD110006).

**Institutional Review Board Statement:** Not applicable.

**Informed Consent Statement:** Not applicable.

**Data Availability Statement:** Not applicable.

**Acknowledgments:** The authors are very grateful to the four referees for the valuable comments and useful suggestions.

**Conflicts of Interest:** The authors declare no conflict of interest.

## References

1. Webster, B.L.; Murdin, P. Cygnus X-1—A Spectroscopic Binary with a Heavy Companion? *Nature* **1972**, *235*, 37–38. [CrossRef]
2. Remillard, R.A.; McClintock, J.E. X-ray Properties of Black-Hole Binaries. *Annu. Rev. Astron. Astrophys.* **2006**, *44*, 49–92. [CrossRef]
3. Abbott, B.P.; Abbott, R.; Abbott, T.D.; Abernathy, M.R.; Acernese, F.; Ackley, K.; Adams, C.; Adams, T.; Addesso, P.; Adhikari, R.X.; et al. Observation of Gravitational Waves from a Binary Black Hole Merger. *Phys. Rev. Lett.* **2016**, *116*, 061102. [CrossRef]
4. Abbott, R.; Abbott, T.D.; Abraham, S.; Acernese, F.; Ackley, K.; Adams, C.; Adhikari, R.X.; Adya, V.B.; Affeldt, C.; Agathos, M.; et al. Properties and Astrophysical Implications of the 150 $M_\odot$ Binary Black Hole Merger GW190521. *Astrophys. J. Lett.* **2020**, *900*, L13. [CrossRef]
5. Akiyama, K.; Alberdi, A.; Alef, W.; Asada, K.; Azulay, R.; Baczko, A.K.; Ball, D.; Baloković, M.; Barrett, J.; Bintley, D.; et al. First M87 Event Horizon Telescope Results. I. The Shadow of the Supermassive Black Hole. *Astrophys. J. Lett.* **2019**, *875*, L1.
6. Azulay, R.; Baczko, A.K.; Ball, D.; Baloković, M.; Barrett, J.; Bintley, D.; Blackburn, L.; Boland, W.; Bouman, K.L.; Bower, G.C.; et al. First M87 Event Horizon Telescope Results. VI. The Shadow and Mass of the Central Black Hole. *Astrophys. J. Lett.* **2019**, *875*, L6.
7. Yunes, N.; Stein, L.C. Nonspinning Black Holes in Alternative Theories of Gravity. *Phys. Rev. D* **2011**, *83*, 104002. [CrossRef]
8. Yunes, N.; Pretorius, F. Dynamical Chern-Simons Modified Gravity I: Spinning Black Holes in the Slow-Rotation Approximation. *Phys. Rev. D* **2009**, *79*, 084043. [CrossRef]
9. Molina, C.; Pani, P.; Cardoso, V.; Gualtieri, L. Gravitational signature of Schwarzschild black holes in dynamical Chern-Simons gravity. *Phys. Rev. D* **2010**, *81*, 124021. [CrossRef]
10. Johannsen, T.; Psaltis, D. Metric for rapidly spinning black holes suitable for strong-field tests of the no-hair theorem. *Phys. Rev. D* **2011**, *83*, 124015. [CrossRef]
11. Zipoy, D.M. Topology of Some Spheroidal Metrics. *J. Math. Phys.* **1966**, *7*, 1137–1143. [CrossRef]
12. Voorhees, B.H. Static Axially Symmetric Gravitational Fields. *Phys. Rev. D* **1970**, *2*, 2119. [CrossRef]
13. Brans, C.; Dicke, R.H. Mach's Principle and a Relativistic Theory of Gravitation. *Phys. Rev.* **1961**, *124*, 925. [CrossRef]
14. Brans, C. Mach's Principle and a Relativistic Theory of Gravitation. II. *Phys. Rev.* **1961**, *125*, 2194. [CrossRef]
15. Damour, T.; Nordtvedt, K. General relativity as a cosmological attractor of tensor-scalar theories. *Phys. Rev. Lett.* **1993**, *70*, 2217–2219. [CrossRef]
16. Stavrinos, P.C.; Ikeda, S. Some connections and variational principle to the Finslerian scalar-tensor theory of gravitation. *Rep. Math. Phys.* **1999**, *44*, 221–230. [CrossRef]

17. Minas, G.; Saridakis, E.N.; Stavrinos, P.C.; Triantafyllopoulos, A. Bounce Cosmology in Generalized Modified Gravities. *Universe* **2019**, *5*, 74. [CrossRef]
18. Ikeda, S.; Saridakis, E.N.; Stavrinos, P.C.; Triantafyllopoulos, A. Cosmology of Lorentz fiber-bundle induced scalar-tensor theories. *Phys. Rev. D* **2019**, *100*, 124035. [CrossRef]
19. Konitopoulos, S.; Saridakis, E.N.; Stavrinos, P.C.; Triantafyllopoulos, A. Dark gravitational sectors on a generalized scalar-tensor vector bundle model and cosmological applications. *Phys. Rev. D* **2021**, *104*, 064018. [CrossRef]
20. Jacobson, T. Einstein-aether gravity: A status report. *arXiv* **2008**, arXiv:0801.1547.
21. Rosen, N. General relativity and flat space. II. *Phys. Rev.* **1940**, *57*, 150–153. [CrossRef]
22. Rosen, N. A bi-metric theory of gravitation. *Gen. Relativ. Gravitation* **1973**, *4*, 435–447. [CrossRef]
23. Bekenstein, J.D. Relativistic gravitation theory for the MOND paradigm. *Phys. Rev. D* **2004**, *70*, 083509. [CrossRef]
24. Skordis, C. The tensor-vector-scalar theory and its cosmology. *Class. Quantum Grav.* **2009**, *26*, 143001. [CrossRef]
25. Hehl, F.W.; Von der Heyde, P.; Kerlick, G.D.; Nester, J.M. General relativity with spin and torsion: Foundations and prospects. *Rev. Mod. Phys.* **1976**, *48*, 393. [CrossRef]
26. Trautman, A. Einstein–Cartan theory. *Encycl. Math. Phys.* **2006**, *2*, 189–195.
27. Moffat, J.W. Scalar-tensor-vector gravity theory. *J. Cosmol. Astropart. Phys.* **2006**, *3*, 004. [CrossRef]
28. Sotiriou,T.P.; Faraoni, V. f(R) theories of gravity. *Rev. Mod. Phys.* **2010**, *82*, 451–497. [CrossRef]
29. Nojiri, S.I.; Odintsov, S.D. Unified cosmic history in modified gravity: From F(R) theory to Lorentz non-invariant models. *Phys. Rep.* **2011**, *505*, 59–144. [CrossRef]
30. De Felice, A.; Tsujikawa, S. f(R) Theories. *Living Rev. Relativ.* **2010**, *13*, 3. [CrossRef]
31. Silva, M.V.d.S.; Rodrigues, M.E. Regular black holes in f(G) gravity. *Eur. Phys. J. C* **2018**, *78*, 638. [CrossRef]
32. Nojiri, S.; Odintsov, S.D. Introduction to modified gravity and gravitational alternative for dark energy. *Int. J. Mod. Phys.* **2007**, *4*, 115–145. [CrossRef]
33. Horava, P. Membranes at quantum criticality. *J. High Energy Phys.* **2009**, *03*, 020. [CrossRef]
34. Horava, P. Quantum gravity at a Lifshitz point. *Phys. Rev. D* **2009**, *79*, 084008. [CrossRef]
35. Horava, P. Spectral dimension of the universe in quantum gravity at a Lifshitz point. *Phys. Rev. Lett.* **2009**, *102*, 161301. [CrossRef] [PubMed]
36. Overduin, J.M.; Wesson, P.S. Kaluza-Klein gravity. *Phys. Rep.* **1997**, *283*, 303–380. [CrossRef]
37. Polchinski, J. Dirichlet Branes and Ramond-Ramond charges. *Phys. Rev. Lett.* **1995**, *75*, 4724–4727. [CrossRef]
38. Charmousis, C. Higher order gravity theories and their black hole solutions. *Lect. Notes Phys.* **2009**, *769*, 299–346.
39. Nojiri, S.; Odintsov, S.D.; Oikonomou, V.K. Modified gravity theories on a nutshell: Inflation, bounce and late-time evolution. *Phys. Rep.* **2017**, *692*, 1–104. [CrossRef]
40. Capozziello, S.; De Laurentis, M. Extended Theories of Gravity. *Phys. Rep.* **2011**, *509*, 167–321. [CrossRef]
41. Clifton, T.; Ferreira, P.G.; Padilla, A.; Skordis, C. Modified gravity and cosmology. *Phys. Rep.* **2012**, *513*, 1–189. [CrossRef]
42. Briscese, F.; Elizalde, E. Black hole entropy in modifified-gravity models. *Phys. Rev. D* **2008**, *77*, 044009. [CrossRef]
43. Hawking, S.W. Black Holes in General Relativity. *Commun. Math. Phys.* **1972**, *25*, 152–166. [CrossRef]
44. Thomas, P. Sotiriou and Valerio Faraoni. Black Holes in Scalar-Tensor Gravity. *Phys. Rev. Lett.* **2012**, *108*, 081103.
45. Psaltis, D.; Perrodin, D.; Dienes, K.R.; Mocioiu, I. Kerr Black Holes Are Not Unique to General Relativity. *Phys. Rev. Lett.* **2008**, *100*, 091101. [CrossRef]
46. Esteban, E.P.; Medina, I.R. Accretion onto black holes in external magnetic fields. *Phys. Rev. D* **1990**, *42*, 307. [CrossRef] [PubMed]
47. de Felice, F.; Sorge, F. Magnetized orbits around a Schwarzschild black hole. *Class. Quantum Grav.* **2003**, *20*, 469–481. [CrossRef]
48. Abdujabbarov, A.; Ahmedov, B.; Rahimov, O.; Salikhbaev, U. Magnetized particle motion and acceleration around a Schwarzschild black hole in a magnetic field. *Phys. Scr.* **2014**, *89*, 084008. [CrossRef]
49. Kološ, M.; Stuchlík, Z.; Tursunov, A. Quasi-harmonic oscillatory motion of charged particles around a Schwarzschild black hole immersed in a uniform magnetic field. *Class. Quantum Grav.* **2015**, *32*, 165009. [CrossRef]
50. Shaymatov, S.; Patil, M.; Ahmedov, B.; Joshi, P.S. Destroying a near-extremal Kerr black hole with a charged particle: Can a test magnetic field serve as a cosmic censor? *Phys. Rev. D* **2015**, *91*, 064025. [CrossRef]
51. Tursunov, A.; Stuchlík, Z.; Kološ, M. Circular orbits and related quasiharmonic oscillatory motion of charged particles around weakly magnetized rotating black holes. *Phys. Rev. D* **2016**, *93*, 084012. [CrossRef]
52. Nakamura, Y.; Ishizuka, T. Motion of a Charged Particle Around a Black Hole Permeated by Magnetic Field and its Chaotic Characters. *Astrophys. Space Sci.* **1993**, *210*, 105–108. [CrossRef]
53. Takahashi, M.; Koyama, H. Chaotic Motion of Charged Particles in an Electromagnetic Field Surrounding a Rotating Black Hole. *Astrophys. J.* **2009**, *693*, 472. [CrossRef]
54. Kopáček, O.; Karas, V.; Kovář, J.; Stuchlík, Z. Transition from Regular to Chaotic Circulation in Magnetized Coronae near Compact Objects. *Astrophys. J.* **2010**, *722*, 1240. [CrossRef]
55. Kopáček, O.; Karas, V. Inducing Chaos by Breaking Axil Symmetry in a Black Hole Magenetosphere. *Astrophys. J.* **2014**, *787*, 117. [CrossRef]

56. Stuchlík, Z.; Kološ, M. Acceleration of the charged particles due to chaotic scattering in the combined black hole gravitational field and asymptotically uniform magnetic field. *Eur. Phys. J. C* **2016**, *76*, 32. [CrossRef]
57. Kopáček, O.; Karas, V. Near-horizon Structure of Escape Zones of Electrically Charged Particles around Weakly Magnetized Rotating Black Hole. *Astrophys. J.* **2018**, *853*, 53. [CrossRef]
58. Pánis, R.; Kološ, M.; Stuchlík, Z. Determination of chaotic behaviour in time series generated by charged particle motion around magnetized Schwarzschild black holes. *Eur. Phys. J. C* **2019**, *79*, 479. [CrossRef]
59. Stuchlík, Z.; Kološ, M.; Kovář, J.; Tursunov, A. Influence of Cosmic Repulsion and Magnetic Fields on Accretion Disks Rotating around Kerr Black Holes. *Univrse* **2020**, *6*, 26. [CrossRef]
60. Abdujabbarov, A.A.; Ahmedov, B.J.; Jurayeva, N.B. Charged-particle motion around a rotating non-Kerr black hole immersed in a uniform magnetic field. *Phys. Rev. D* **2016**, *87*, 064042. [CrossRef]
61. Rayimbaev, J.R. Magnetized particle motion around non-Schwarzschild black hole immersed in an external uniform magnetic field. *Astrophys. Space Sci.* **2016**, *361*, 288. [CrossRef]
62. Toshmatov, B.; Stuchlík, Z.; Ahmedov, B. Generic rotating regular black holes in general relativity coupled to nonlinear electrodynamics. *Phys. Rev. D* **2017**, *87*, 064042. [CrossRef]
63. Abdujabbarov, A.; Ahmedov, B.; Hakimov, A. Particle motion around black hole in Hořava-Lifshitz gravity. *Phys. Rev. D* **2011**, *8783*, 044053. [CrossRef]
64. Stuchlík, Z.; Abdujabbarov, A.; Schee, J. Ultra-high-energy collisions of particles in the field of near-extreme Kehagias-Sfetsos naked singularities and their appearance to distant observers. *Phys. Rev. D* **2014**, *89*, 104048. [CrossRef]
65. Toshmatov, B.; Abdujabbarov, A.; Ahmedov, B.; Stuchlík, Z. Motion and high energy collision of magnetized particles around a Hořava-Lifshitz black hole. *Astrophys. Space Sci.* **2015**, *360*, 19. [CrossRef]
66. Benavides-Gallego, C.A.; Abdujabbarov, A.; Malafarina, D.; Ahmedov, B.; Bambi, C. Charged particle motion and electromagnetic field in $\gamma$ spacetime. *Phys. Rev. D* **2019**, *99*, 044012. [CrossRef]
67. Lukes-Gerakopoulos, G. Nonintegrability of the Zipoy-Voorhees metric. *Phys. Rev. D* **2012**, *86*, 044013. [CrossRef]
68. Yi, M.; Wu, X. Dynamics of charged particles around a magnetically deformed Schwarzschild black hole. *Phys. Scr.* **2020**, *95*, 085008. [CrossRef]
69. Hairer, E.; Lubich, C.; Wanner, G. *Geometric Numerical Integration: Structure-Preserving Algorithms for Ordinary Differential Equations*, 2nd ed.; Springer: Berlin, Germany, 2006.
70. Feng, K.; Qin, M. *Symplectic Geometric Algorithms for Hamiltonian Systems*; Zhejiang Science and Technology Publishing House: Hangzhou, China; Springer: Berlin/Heidelberg, Germany, 2010.
71. Feng, K. Symplectic geometry and numerical methods in fluid dynamics. In *Proceedings of the Tenth International Conference on Numerical Methods in Fluid Dynamics, Beijing, China, 23–7 June 1986*; Lecture Notes in Physics; Springer: Berlin/Heidelberg, Germany, 1986; Volume 264, pp. 1–7.
72. Brown, J.D. Midpoint rule as a variational-symplectic integrator: Hamiltonian systems. *Phys. Rev. D* **2006**, *73*, 024001. [CrossRef]
73. Seyrich, J.; Lukes-Gerakopoulos, G. Symmetric integrator for nonintegrable Hamiltonian relativistic systems. *Phys. Rev. D* **2012**, *86*, 124013. [CrossRef]
74. Seyrich, J. Gauss collocation methods for efficient structure preserving integration of post-Newtonian equations of motion. *Phys. Rev. D* **2013**, *87*, 084064. [CrossRef]
75. Preto, M.; Saha, P. On post-Newtonian orbits and the Galactic-center stars. *Astrophys. J.* **2009**, *703*, 1743. [CrossRef]
76. Lubich, C.; Walther, B.; Brügmann, B. Symplectic integration of post-Newtonian equations of motion with spin. *Phys. Rev. D* **2010**, *81*, 104025. [CrossRef]
77. Zhong, S.Y.; Wu, X.; Liu, S.Q.; Deng, X.F. Global symplectic structure-preserving integrators for spinning compact binaries. *Phys. Rev. D* **2010**, *82*, 124040. [CrossRef]
78. Mei, L.; Ju, M.; Wu, X.; Liu, S. Dynamics of spin effects of compact binaries. *Mon. Not. R. Astron. Soc.* **2013**, *435*, 2246–2255. [CrossRef]
79. Mei, L.; Wu, X.; Liu, F. On preference of Yoshida construction over Forest-Ruth fourth-order symplectic algorithm. *Eur. Phys. J. C* **2013**, *73*, 2413. [CrossRef]
80. Wang, Y.; Sun, W.; Liu, F.; Wu, X. Construction of Explicit Symplectic Integrators in General Relativity. I. Schwarzschild Black Holes. *Astrophys. J.* **2021**, *907*, 66. [CrossRef]
81. Wang, Y.; Sun, W.; Liu, F.; Wu, X. Construction of Explicit Symplectic Integrators in General Relativity. II. Reissner-Nordström Black Holes. *Astrophys. J.* **2021**, *909*, 22. [CrossRef]
82. Wang, Y.; Sun, W.; Liu, F.; Wu, X. Construction of Explicit Symplectic Integrators in General Relativity. III. Reissner-Nordström-(anti)-de Sitter Black Holes. *Astrophys. J. Suppl. Ser.* **2021**, *254*, 8. [CrossRef]
83. Wu, X.; Wang, Y.; Sun, W.; Liu, F. Construction of Explicit Symplectic Integrators in General Relativity. IV. Kerr Black Holes. *Astrophys. J.* **2021**, *914*, 63. [CrossRef]
84. Sun, W.; Wang, Y.; Liu, F.; Wu, X. Applying explicit symplectic integrator to study chaos of charged particles around magnetized Kerr black hole. *Eur. Phys. J. C* **2021**, *81*, 785. [CrossRef]
85. Sun, X.; Wu, X.; Wang, Y.; Liu, B.; Liang, E. Dynamics of Charged Particles Moving around Kerr Black Hole with Inductive Charge and External Magnetic Field. *Universe* **2021**, *7*, 410. [CrossRef]
86. Newman, E.T.; Janis, A.I. Note on the Kerr Spinning-Particle *Metric. J. Math. Phys.* **1965**, *6*, 915. [CrossRef]

37. Yoshida, H. Construction of higher order symplectic integrators. *Phys. Lett. A* **1990**, *150*, 262. [CrossRef]
38. Wu, X.; Huang, T.Y.; Zhang H. Lyapunov indices with two nearby trajectories in a curved spacetime. *Phys. Rev. D* **2006**, *74*, 083001. [CrossRef]

universe MDPI

Article

# Gravity Models with Nonlinear Symmetry Realization

Stanislav Alexeyev [1,2,*], Daniil Krichevskiy [1,3,4] and Boris Latosh [5,6]

1 Sternberg Astronomical Institute, Lomonosov Moscow State University, 119991 Moscow, Russia; daniil.krichevskiy@mail.ru
2 Department of Quantum Theory and High Energy Physics, Faculty of Physics, Lomonosov Moscow State University, 119991 Moscow, Russia
3 Physics Department, Bauman Moscow State Technical University, 105005 Moscow, Russia
4 Faculty of Science, University of Bern, CH-3012 Bern, Switzerland
5 Bogoliubov Laboratory of Theoretical Physics, JINR, 141980 Dubna, Russia; latosh.boris@gmail.com
6 Department for Fundamental Problems of Microworld Physics, School of Physics and Engineering, Dubna State University, 141982 Dubna, Russia
* Correspondence: alexeyev@sai.msu.ru

**Abstract:** Validity of three gravity models with non-linear realization of conformal symmetry previously discussed in literature is addressed. Two models are found to be equivalent up to a change of coset coordinates. It was found that models contain ghost degrees of freedom that may be excluded by an introduction of an additional symmetry to the target space. One model found to be safe in early universe. The others found to lack spin-2 degrees of freedom and to have peculiar coupling to matter degrees of freedom.

**Keywords:** non-linear symmetry realization; modified gravity; conformal symmetry

**Citation:** Alexeyev, S.; Krichevskiy, D.; Latosh, S. Gravity Models with Nonlinear Symmetry Realization. *Universe* **2021**, *7*, 501. https://doi.org/10.3390/universe7120501

Academic Editors: Panayiotis Stavrinos and Emmanuel N. Saridakis

Received: 5 November 2021
Accepted: 14 December 2021
Published: 17 December 2021



## 1. Introduction

Conformal symmetry occupies a special place in gravity physics due to the well-known Ogievetsky theorem [1]. The theorem states that any generator of the infinitely-dimensional coordinate transformation group is presented as series of commutators of generators from the conformal group $C(1,3)$ and the affine one $A(4)$. Therefore, the conformal group is strongly related with coordinate transformations and should have a certain influence on the structure of a gravity theory.

Particular implementations of conformal symmetry for gravity models were studied in multiple papers, so we only mention a few key results. In paper [2], it was shown that any metric gravity theory can be viewed as a theory with a combined non-linear realization of conformal and affine symmetry (see also [3–6]). Explicit non-linear realization of the conformal symmetry within AdS/CFT correspondence was constructed in [7]. It also should be mentioned that there are models with a linear realization of the conformal symmetry [8,9], but their applicability is debatable [10–13].

There are a few physical reasons to study models with non-linear realizations of the conformal symmetry. Early Universe is naturally associated with the conformal symmetry. Firstly, it is reasonable to expect the early state of the Universe to have Planck scale temperature. Because of this all conceivable particles can be considered as massless and the conformal symmetry will emerge naturally. It is also possible to make a realistic case for a scenario with a conformal fixed point reached in the early Universe [14–16]. An alternative evidence supporting this reasoning comes from the inflation theory. If an inflation is driven by a scalar field potential then the potential has an area where it is approximately flat to be consistent with the slow-roll scenario. However, in this area the potential will admit a scalar field shift symmetry $\phi \to \phi + c$ which, in turn, excludes relevant dimensional parameters and enforces the conformal symmetry on the model.

During the universe evolution the conformal symmetry will inevitable be spontaneously broken down to the Poincare group. It is known that spontaneous symmetry breaking and non-linear symmetry realization are the same thing (except for a few very special cases that are irrelevant within the context of this paper). Therefore, it is natural to study models with non-linear realizations of the conformal symmetry that they are expected to appear natural in the context of a cosmological evolution originated from the conformal phase.

This framework points on an interesting opportunity to obtain a united description of both inflationary and post-inflationary expansion within a single model with a non-linear realized conformal symmetry. In full accordance with the Goldstone theorem, if the conformal symmetry is broken the corresponding model develops new massive and massless degrees of freedom (DoF). If the conformal symmetry is broken down to the Lorentz group of dimension ten one can try to associate ten corresponding massless Goldstone modes with ten components of the metric tensor. The massive components, in turn, can be associated with the inflation field. The corresponding mass, in turn, will define the inflation scale.

This reasoning highlights two perspective research direction. The first one is to search for models with a non-linear realization of the conformal symmetry which contain at least one scalar DoF and to verify its possibility to drive inflation. The other direction is to check if a given model with a non-linear symmetry realization has massless spin-2 degrees of freedom that could be associated with gravitons.

The main goal of this paper is to examine three particular models with the non-linear conformal symmetry realization presented in [17]. It must be noted that the manifold of models with a non-linear conformal symmetry realization is extremely wide [7,18–20]. The discussed models are chosen, firstly, for their simplicity and, secondly, because their scrutiny was already begun in [21].

In paper [17] three models were presented. The first one is defined by the Lagrangian:

$$\begin{aligned}\mathcal{L}_I = & \frac{1}{2}\left[1+\frac{\sigma^2}{\varepsilon^2}\left\{f_2\left(\frac{\psi}{\varepsilon}\right)\right\}^2\right]\eta^{\mu\nu}\,\partial_\mu\psi\,\partial_\nu\psi + \frac{1}{2}\left[f_1\left(\frac{\psi}{\varepsilon}\right)\right]^2\eta^{\mu\nu}\,\eta_{(\alpha)(\beta)}\,\partial_\mu\sigma^{(\alpha)}\,\partial_\nu\sigma^{(\beta)} \\ & -\frac{1}{\varepsilon}f_1\left(\frac{\psi}{\varepsilon}\right)f_2\left(\frac{\psi}{\varepsilon}\right)\eta^{\mu\nu}\,\partial_\mu\psi\,\sigma^{(\alpha)}\partial_\nu\sigma^{(\beta)}\,\eta_{(\alpha)(\beta)}.\end{aligned} \tag{1}$$

Here, $\psi$ and $\sigma^{(\alpha)}$ ($(\alpha) = 0,\cdots,4$) are scalar fields associated with target space coordinates on which the conformal symmetry acts non-linearly. Field indices $\sigma^{(\alpha)}$ taken in brackets should not be confused with Lorentz indices. All fields have the canonical mass dimension and $\varepsilon$ is a mass parameter corresponding to the conformal symmetry breaking scale. Finally, functions $f_i(x)$ are

$$\begin{aligned} f_1(x) &= \frac{e^x-1}{x}, \\ f_2(x) &= \frac{e^x-x-1}{x^2}. \end{aligned} \tag{2}$$

Therefore, the model (1) describes five scalar fields propagating in a flat space-time. Fields $\sigma^{(\alpha)}$ have the Minkowski space as the target space so their indices are contracted with the Minkowski target metric $\eta_{(\alpha)(\beta)}$.

A comment of a derivation of this model is due. Conformal group admits the following generators $L_{(\mu)(\nu)}$, $P_{(\mu)}$, $R_{(\mu)(\nu)}$, $K_{(\mu)}$, and $D$. The first two correspond to Lorentz transformations and coordinate shifts and constitute the Poincare algebra; the former three operators extend the Poincare algebra. Dynamical variables of model (1) are subjected to the following non-linear symmetry realization

$$\exp\left[\frac{i}{2}\theta^{(\mu)(\nu)}L_{(\mu)(\nu)}+i\,\theta D+i\theta^{(\mu)}K_{(\mu)}\right]\exp\left[i\phi D+i\sigma^{(\alpha)}K_{(\alpha)}\right] \tag{3}$$
$$=\exp\left[i\phi' D+i\sigma'^{(\alpha)}K_{(\alpha)}\right]\exp\left[\frac{i}{2}u^{(\mu)(\nu)}L_{(\mu)(\nu)}\right].$$

Here, $\phi$ is related with $\psi$ as $\psi=\varepsilon\phi$; $\theta^{(\mu)(\nu)}$, $\theta^{(\mu)}$, and $\theta$ are transformation parameters; $u^{(\mu)(\nu)}=u^{(\mu)(\nu)}(\theta,\theta^{(\alpha)},\theta^{(\alpha)(\beta)})$ are parameters of the associated Lorentz group transformations. In other words, this equitation defined a non-linear action of the conformal group on variables $\psi$ and $\sigma$ while $u^{(\mu)(\nu)}$ is responsible for a non-linear action of the conformal group on all objects subjected to the Lorentz group.

Let us put a special emphasis on the fact that the conformal symmetry acts on all objects subjected to Lorentz transformations, but its action is indistinguishable from the standard Lorentz group action. This allows one to include the regular matter in the model without an explicit violation of the conformal symmetry. This fact also holds for gravity. One of the cornerstones of gravitational theory is the equivalence between curved geometry and physical force. Usually this equivalence is used to justify a usage of geometric quantities, such as the Riemann tensor, for a description of gravity. However the equivalence works in both directions, so we can righteously consider gravity as a theory of a physical field $h_{\mu\nu}$ propagating about the flat spacetime. We will return to this issue in the next section and discuss it in more details.

In summary, (1) provides a model of five scalar fields subjected to a non-linear realization of the conformal symmetry. The model can be extended with the regular matter including gravity in a way consistent with the non-linear symmetry realization. The present scalar degrees of freedom serve as natural candidates for inflaton field and we will address this opportunity further. At the same time the model has no DoF that can be associated with gravitons, so we will discuss this model in the context of inflation only.

The second model has the following Lagrangian

$$\mathcal{L}=\eta^{\mu\nu}\nabla_\mu h^{(\alpha)(\beta)}\,\nabla_\nu h^{(\rho)(\sigma)}\,\eta_{(\alpha)(\rho)}\,\eta_{(\beta)(\sigma)}, \tag{4}$$

where the covariant derivatives are

$$\frac{i}{2}\nabla_\mu h^{(\alpha)(\beta)}=\frac{i}{2}\partial_\mu h^{(\alpha)(\beta)}+\sum_{n=1}^{\infty}\frac{i}{(2n+1)!}(\mathrm{ad}_h^{2n-1}\,h\partial_\mu h)^{(\alpha)(\beta)} \tag{5}$$
$$=\frac{i}{2}\left[\partial_\mu h^{(\alpha)(\beta)}-\eta_{(\nu)(\sigma)}\eta_{(\mu)(\lambda)}\left(\frac{1}{3}h^{(\alpha)(\nu)}\,h^{(\beta)(\lambda)}\partial_\mu h^{(\sigma)(\mu)}-\frac{1}{3}h^{(\alpha)(\nu)}\,h^{(\sigma)(\mu)}\partial_\mu h^{(\lambda)(\beta)}\right)\right. \tag{6}$$
$$\left.+\,\mathcal{O}(h^5)\right].$$

Here, all repeated bracket indices are contracted with the Minkowski metric of the target space and ad operator is defined as:

$$\left(\mathrm{ad}_h\,\partial_\mu h\right)^{(\mu)(\nu)}=[h,\partial_\mu h]^{(\mu)(\nu)}=h^{(\mu)(\rho)}\partial_\mu h^{(\sigma)(\nu)}\eta_{(\rho)(\sigma)}-\partial_\mu h^{(\mu)(\rho)}h^{(\sigma)(\nu)}\eta_{(\rho)(\sigma)}. \tag{7}$$

Degrees of freedom $h_{(\mu)(\nu)}$ are associated with the coset coordinates and their transformation under the non-linear conformal symmetry action is defined by the following formula:

$$\exp\left[\frac{i}{2}\theta^{(\mu)(\nu)}L_{(\mu)(\nu)}\right]\exp\left[\frac{i}{2}h^{(\mu)(\nu)}R_{(\mu)(\nu)}\right] = \exp\left[\frac{i}{2}h'^{(\mu)(\nu)}R_{(\mu)(\nu)}\right]\exp\left[\frac{i}{2}u^{(\mu)(\nu)}L_{(\mu)(\nu)}\right]. \tag{8}$$

Here, $\theta^{(\mu)(\nu)}$ are transformation parameters, and $u^{(\mu)(\nu)}$ realize a non-linear conformal group action on the Lorentz group.

Unlike the previous case the model has no natural candidates for an inflaton field, but $h_{(\mu)(\nu)}$ appear to be similar to small metric perturbations. In this paper, we consider such an equivalence and argue that despite their similarity they cannot be directly associated with gravitons.

Finally, the last model discussed in this paper in given by the following Lagrangian:

$$\mathcal{L} = \eta^{\mu\nu}\nabla_\mu h^{(\alpha)(\beta)}\,\nabla_\nu h^{(\rho)(\sigma)}\,\eta_{(\alpha)(\rho)}\,\eta_{(\beta)(\sigma)} + \eta^{\mu\nu}\partial_\mu\phi\partial_\nu\phi. \tag{9}$$

The same definition of covariant derivatives is used, and $\phi$ is a scalar. The model is similar to the previous one as it is constructed on the following non-linear realization:

$$\exp\left[\frac{i}{2}\theta^{(\mu)(\nu)}L_{(\mu)(\nu)}\right]\exp\left[\frac{i}{2}h^{(\mu)(\nu)}R_{(\mu)(\nu)} + i\phi D\right] = \exp\left[\frac{i}{2}h'^{(\mu)(\nu)}R_{(\mu)(\nu)} + i\phi' D\right]\exp\left[\frac{i}{2}u^{(\mu)(\nu)}L_{(\mu)(\nu)}\right]. \tag{10}$$

The formula shows that model (9) use a wider coset than (4). Coset of model (4) is founded on $R_{(\mu)(\nu)}$ operators while coset of (9) is founded on $R_{(\mu)(\nu)}$ and $D$ operators. As it was shown in the previous paper [17], the scalar $\phi$ has the trivial covariant derivative $\nabla_\mu\phi = \partial_\mu\phi$ so it does not require any coupling neither to the regular matter nor to $h_{(\mu)(\nu)}$. Note that such a coupling can be introduced in the model manually, but this case lies beyond the scope of this paper. In order to highlight the fact that $\phi$ does not require any coupling we will call it as a sterile scalar.

Similarly to the previous case, the model has no obvious candidates for an inflaton field. Therefore, we will only study an opportunity to associate $h^{(\mu)(\nu)}$ with the gravitational DoF. However, as we will show further, models (4) and (9) are equivalent. Because of this we will mainly focus on model (4).

The paper is split in two parts. In the first part we will discuss cosmological behavior of model (1) as it is the only model with a suitable candidates for inflatons. In the second part, we will study DoF of models (4) and (9) in order to establish if $h_{(\mu)(\nu)}$ can be associated with gravitons. Following this logic the paper is organized as follows. In Section 2, we discuss cosmological regimes described by the model (1) and show that scalar degrees of freedom are decoupled. Therefore, they do not influence the cosmological behavior in a meaningful way. We discuss a possible relation between this phenomenon and the conformal symmetry together with implications for realistic cosmological scenarios. In Section 3, we discuss the field content of models (4) and (9). It is shown that these models actually equivalent up to a coordinate redefinition on the target space. At the same time these models contain vector ghost degrees of freedom. We argue that these degrees of freedom can be excluded via an introduction of an additional symmetry to the target space. However, this symmetry should be agreed with the non-linear realization of the conformal symmetry which may influence the used non-linear realization in a meaningful way. Section 4 contains our conclusions which extend previous results [21]. Finally, in Appendix A we briefly show that DoF of the second model is also coupled to matter degrees of freedom in a peculiar way. We provide an expression for a covariant derivative of a vector field (A3) which defines such a coupling.

## 2. Cosmological Behavior

To study the cosmological behavior of the model (1) one has to introduce gravitational degrees of freedom because the number of DoF in (1) is not enough to describe gravitons. This can be consistently done because of the following.

Let us examine the non-linear realization of the conformal symmetry (3). The given formula defines transformations of $\phi$ and $\sigma^{(\mu)}$ under the non-linear symmetry action

$$\begin{aligned} \phi &\to \phi'(\phi,\theta,\theta^{(\mu)},\theta^{(\mu)(\nu)}), \\ \sigma^{(\alpha)} &\to \sigma^{(\alpha)}(\sigma,\theta^{(\mu)},\theta^{(\mu)(\nu)}). \end{aligned} \tag{11}$$

However, it also defines parameter of Lorentz transformations (i.e., linear action of the Lorentz group) through which the conformal symmetry acts on all objects subjected to the Lorentz transformations:

$$u^{(\alpha)(\beta)} = u^{(\alpha)(\beta)}(\theta,\theta^{(\mu)},\theta^{(\mu)(\nu)}). \tag{12}$$

This allows one to extend model (1) with arbitrary matter.

Gravity can be introduced this way and be consistent with the conformal symmetry. Due to the equivalence principle gravity can be considered either as a force (acting in a flat background spacetime) and as a geometry of a spacetime. This equivalence allows one to treat gravity as a gauge theory of symmetric tensor $h_{\mu\nu}$ in a flat spacetime. The gauge symmetry ensures that the corresponding action has an infinite number of terms and they can be rearranged in geometrical quantities such as the scalar curvature $R$. Such an approach to gravity description is more suitable for weak gravitational field when spacetime perturbations are weak and one can only account for a few leading terms in the action. However, it is also consistent with non-perturbative phenomena, such as the cosmological expansion. In that case the gravitational field $h_{\mu\nu}$ should be considered excited in all points of spacetime and one would be forced to deal with the whole infinite number of terms of the action. The geometric approach to gravity simply provides a tool to summarize this infinite series (to geometric quantities) and to obtain equations with a finite number of terms.

These reasons provide us with the following opportunity to introduce gravity consistent with the non-linear symmetry realization. One starts with general relativity given in a perturbative framework. This means that we consider general relativity action as an action with an infinite number of terms that describe gauge field $h_{\mu\nu}$ about a flat spacetime. Because of the equivalence principle this action is viewed only as a particular parameterization of general relativity. The gauge field $h_{\mu\nu}$ is subjected to the standard Lorentz transformations with parameters $u^{\mu\nu}$. In order to subject the theory to the non-linear conformal group action (3) one simply replace the standard Lorentz group parameters $u^{\mu\nu}$ with those obtained from (3). Therefore, each element of the conformal group is mapped on an element of the Lorentz group with the mapping given by (3). Hence, all quantities invariant with respect to the Lorentz group (including the scalar curvature $R$) are made to be invariant under the non-linear action of the conformal group. Finally, let us highlight that such a relation does take place only because the non-linear group action (3) also spawns a linear Lorentz group action through which it can act on the regular matter.

Because of the discussed reasons one can use the following model to study the cosmological expansions:

$$\mathcal{S} = \int d^4x\sqrt{-g}\Bigg\{ -\frac{2}{\kappa^2}R + \frac{1}{2}\left[1 + \frac{\sigma^2}{\varepsilon^2}\left\{f_2\left(\frac{\psi}{\varepsilon}\right)\right\}^2\right] g^{\mu\nu}\,\partial_\mu\psi\,\partial_\nu\psi \\ + \frac{1}{2}\left[f_1\left(\frac{\psi}{\varepsilon}\right)\right]^2 g^{\mu\nu}\,\eta_{(\alpha)(\beta)}\,\partial_\mu\sigma^{(\alpha)}\,\partial_\nu\sigma^{(\beta)} - \frac{1}{\varepsilon}f_1\left(\frac{\psi}{\varepsilon}\right)f_2\left(\frac{\psi}{\varepsilon}\right) g^{\mu\nu}\,\partial_\mu\psi\,\sigma^{(\alpha)}\partial_\nu\sigma^{(\beta)}\,\eta_{(\alpha)(\beta)}\Bigg\}, \tag{13}$$

where $\kappa$ is related with the Newton constant $G_N$ as $\kappa^2 = 32\pi G_N$. Fields $\psi$ and $\sigma^{(\alpha)}$ transform under the non-linear conformal group action with the target space remaining flat.

Let us consider the cosmological behavior of (13) with the open Friedmann space-time:

$$ds^2 = g_{\mu\nu}\,dx^\mu\,dx^\nu = dt^2 - a^2(t)\left(dx^2 + dy^2 + dz^2\right). \tag{14}$$

Here, $a(t)$ is the scale factor. The corresponding Einstein equations read

$$G_{\mu\nu} = \frac{\kappa^2}{4}C_{\mu\nu}{}^{\alpha\beta}\Bigg[\frac{1}{2}\left[1 + \frac{\sigma^2}{\varepsilon^2}\left\{f_2\left(\frac{\psi}{\varepsilon}\right)\right\}^2\right]\partial_\alpha\psi\,\partial_\beta\psi + \frac{1}{2}\left[f_1\left(\frac{\psi}{\varepsilon}\right)\right]^2\eta_{(\mu)(\nu)}\,\partial_\alpha\sigma^{(\mu)}\,\partial_\beta\sigma^{(\nu)} \\ -\frac{1}{\varepsilon}f_1\left(\frac{\psi}{\varepsilon}\right)f_2\left(\frac{\psi}{\varepsilon}\right)\partial_\alpha\psi\,\sigma^{(\mu)}\partial_\beta\sigma^{(\nu)}\,\eta_{(\mu)(\nu)}\Bigg] \tag{15}$$

where

$$C_{\mu\nu}{}^{\alpha\beta} \stackrel{\text{def}}{=} \delta^\alpha_\mu\delta^\beta_\nu + \delta^\beta_\mu\delta^\alpha_\nu - g_{\mu\nu}g^{\alpha\beta}. \tag{16}$$

These equations have two non-vanishing components which can be reduced to:

$$-3\frac{\ddot{a}}{a} = \frac{1}{4}\kappa^2\left(\frac{1}{2}\left[1 + \frac{\sigma^2}{\varepsilon^2}\left\{f_2\left(\frac{\psi}{\varepsilon}\right)\right\}^2\right]\dot{\psi}^2 + \left[f_1\left(\frac{\psi}{\varepsilon}\right)\right]^2\dot{\sigma}^{(\alpha)}\dot{\sigma}_{(\alpha)} - \frac{2}{\varepsilon}f_1\left(\frac{\psi}{\varepsilon}\right)f_2\left(\frac{\psi}{\varepsilon}\right)\dot{\psi}\,\dot{\sigma}_{(\alpha)}\sigma^{(\alpha)}\right), \\ 2\dot{a}^2 + a\ddot{a} = 0. \tag{17}$$

The second equation from (17) does not contain scalar fields and describes the behavior of the scalar factor by itself. It can be solved analytically with the result:

$$a(t) = c_2(c_1 + 3\,t)^{\frac{1}{3}}, \tag{18}$$

where $c_1$ and $c_2$ are the integration constants defined by the boundary conditions.

Now, we analyze the result (18). First of all we note that here the universe has only a decelerated expansion hence the model has no room for an inflationary phase.

Secondly, one can assume that the matter content of the model (i.e., the scalar fields) is described by the standard equation of state (EoS) $p = w\rho$. Here, $p$ is a pressure of scalar fields, $\rho$ is an energy density of the matter, and $w$ is the EoS parameter. Solutions with such EoS are well known [22,23], so one can easily restore $w$ from the form of asymptotic of (18). At large values of time the scale factor is proportional to $t^{\frac{1}{3}}$ corresponding to EoS parameter $w = 1$. That is why, despite the fact that scalar fields in this model admit vanishing masses, their behavior do not correspond to a relativistic matter one with EoS parameter $w = 1/3$. The reason is that the discussed scalar fields have a non-trivial interaction sector which influence their EoS.

Finally, the fact that the model admits a decelerating solution deserves a special attention as it has ghost degrees of freedom. These ghost degrees of freedom appear due to the metric on scalar field target space $\eta_{(\mu)(\nu)}$:

$$g^{\mu\nu}\,\eta_{(\alpha)(\beta)}\,\partial_\mu\sigma^{(\alpha)}\,\partial_\nu\sigma^{(\beta)} = \partial^\mu\sigma^{(0)}\,\partial_\mu\sigma^{(0)} - \sum_{i=1}^{3}\partial^\mu\sigma^{(i)}\,\partial_\mu\sigma^{(i)}\,. \tag{19}$$

Note that these ghost degrees of freedom do not manifest themselves at the level of cosmological solutions.

Despite the fact the analytical solution (18) can be obtained, there are no reasons to believe that it is stable. Equations (17) take a simple form due to a cancellation of the stress-energy tensor of scalar fields. This cancellation, in turn, is possible because both metric and scalar fields depend only on the time variable. As soon as one considers metric and scalar field perturbations propagating around the background a similar cancellation becomes impossible.

The existence of ghost degrees of freedom obstructs possible implementations of model (13). Let us discuss possible opportunities to exclude ghosts. The first opportunity is to use the inverse Higgs mechanism [24]. Unfortunately, this procedure is not applicable in the considered case because the discussed non-linear symmetry realization does no satisfy the necessary criteria. Another opportunity to exclude ghosts is to introduce an additional symmetry at the scalar field target space which would make $\sigma^{(1)} = \sigma^{(2)} = \sigma^{(3)} = 0$. Consequently, only a single massless sterile scalar field (i.e., it has neither self-interaction nor potential) $\psi$ remains and such a field can hardly be applied in realistic scenarios. The best opportunity would be to find a mechanism excluding ghost degrees of freedom from the model's physical spectrum, but allowing them to propagate only in loops. As it was shown in [25], for such a case the scalar field $\psi$ develops non-trivial interaction at the loop level. However, such a mechanism has yet to be found.

In summary, we conclude that the model (1) can be used for realistic scenarios after ghost degrees of freedom being excluded. For the time being it is possible to find a cosmological solutions (18) which shows that the scalar fields act as matter with EoS parameter $w = 1$ and cannot drive an inflation. This makes the model safe in the early Universe. It cannot drive inflation but it also cannot influence an inflationary scenario driven by another inflation field. Therefore the model should be extended in order to tame ghost degrees of freedom.

## 3. Field Content

Now we switch to a discussion of the field content of second (4) and third (9) models. Firstly, they have at least ten degrees of freedom from the symmetric matrix $h^{(\alpha)(\beta)}$, therefore they may describe spin-2 massless degrees of freedom associated with gravitons. Let us explain this feature in detail. Within the model discussed in the previous section there were non degrees of freedom that can be associated with gravitons (with small metric perturbations of a background spacetime). Because of this, one has no choice but to introduce gravity alongside the regular matter degrees of freedom. In turn, degrees of freedom present in the model can only be considered as generic scalar field that, at best, can drive an inflation. The models to be addressed in this sections, on the contrary, have degrees of freedom $h^{(\alpha)(\beta)}$ that do look like small metric perturbations. In order for them to actually be spin-2 massless degrees of freedom they must describe the correct number of DoF and be subjected to certain equations. Consequently, the main aim of this section is to examine if $h^{(\alpha)(\beta)}$ can in actuality be associated with gravity. Because of this we will not introduce any additional degrees of freedom and will only focus on $h^{(\alpha)(\beta)}$. The second issue we will address is the fact that $h^{(\alpha)(\beta)}$ may also contain two scalar degrees of freedom (associated with its determinant and trace) which could serve as inflatons. Finally, the third model (9) contains a sterile scalar appearing as a consequence of the properties of operator $D$ of the conformal group [17]. These issues are clarified further.

First and foremost, we shall address the issue related with the sterile scalar of model (9). In the original article [17] it was missed that the sterile scalar is related with the trace of $h^{(\alpha)(\beta)}$. The reason behind this is due to the relation between the conformal group generators. Namely, as degrees of freedom $h^{(\alpha)(\beta)}$ are associated with the coset coordinates along $R_{(\alpha)(\beta)}$ direction the sterile scalar $\phi$ is associated with the coset coordinates along $D$ direction also. However, operators $R_{(\alpha)(\beta)}$ are dependent and coupled as [1,2,17]:

$$\eta^{(\alpha)(\beta)} R_{(\alpha)(\beta)} = 2D\,, \tag{20}$$

which follows from definitions of generators $R_{(\alpha)(\beta)}$ and $D$:

$$\begin{aligned} D &= x^{\mu} P_{\mu}, \\ R_{(\mu)(\nu)} &= x_{\mu} P_{\nu} + x_{\nu} P_{\mu}, \end{aligned} \tag{21}$$

where $P_{\mu} = i\partial_{\mu}$ is the generator of translations.

Therefore, the corresponding coset coordinates are also dependent and the trace $\eta_{(\alpha)(\beta)} h^{(\alpha)(\beta)}$ should be associated with $\phi$. Hence, the trace component of $h^{(\alpha)(\beta)}$ acts as a sterile massless scalar and, therefore, cannot drive the inflation. Moreover, one can treat $h^{(\alpha)(\beta)}$ as a traceless matrix with 9 independent components reducing the number of valuable degrees of freedom in the model. On the other hand it guarantees the traceless of $h^{(\alpha)(\beta)}$ similar to GR degrees of freedom.

Finally, note that this result can be obtained independently via the direct verification. The definition $h^{(\alpha)(\beta)} = \frac{1}{4}\eta^{(\alpha)(\beta)}\, h$ with $h = \eta_{(\alpha)(\beta)} h^{(\alpha)(\beta)}$ causes the covariant derivative (5) to be completely reduced to the regular ones hence the Lagrangian (4) describes only a single massless sterile scalar.

Now, we switch to $\overline{h}^{(\alpha)(\beta)}$ as the traceless part of $h^{(\alpha)(\beta)}$ and start to study its Lagrangian. The corresponding covariant derivative (5) is:

$$\begin{aligned} &\frac{i}{2}\nabla_{\mu}\overline{h}^{(\alpha)(\beta)} \\ &= \frac{i}{2}\left[\partial_{\mu}\overline{h}^{(\alpha)(\beta)} - \eta_{(\nu)(\sigma)}\eta_{(\mu)(\lambda)}\left(\frac{1}{3}\overline{h}^{(\alpha)(\nu)}\,\overline{h}^{(\beta)(\lambda)}\partial_{\mu}\overline{h}^{(\sigma)(\mu)} - \frac{1}{3}\overline{h}^{(\alpha)(\nu)}\,\overline{h}^{(\sigma)(\mu)}\partial_{\mu}\overline{h}^{(\lambda)(\beta)}\right) + \mathcal{O}(h^5)\right]. \end{aligned} \tag{22}$$

This derivative matches the expression (5) because the trace component is contained only in $\partial_{\mu} h^{(\alpha)(\beta)}$. Therefore, the expression (4) determines the traceless part of $h^{(\alpha)(\beta)}$ without changing its form.

Further, as the target space metric is not positively defined the model may contain ghosts. Let us demonstrate this explicitly. The Lagrangian density $\mathcal{L}$ of (4) given up to $\mathcal{O}(h^3)$ reads:

$$\begin{aligned} \mathcal{L} &= \frac{1}{2}\eta_{(\alpha)(\rho)}\eta_{(\beta)(\sigma)}\,\partial_{\mu}\overline{h}^{(\alpha)(\beta)}\,\partial^{\mu}\overline{h}^{(\rho)(\sigma)} \\ &= \frac{1}{2}\partial_{\mu}\overline{h}^{(0)(0)}\partial^{\mu}\overline{h}^{(0)(0)} + \frac{1}{2}\sum_{a,b=1}^{3}\partial_{\mu}\overline{h}^{(a)(b)}\,\partial^{\mu}\overline{h}^{(a)(b)} - \sum_{s=1}^{3}\partial_{\mu}\overline{h}^{(0)(s)}\,\partial^{\mu}\overline{h}^{(0)(s)}. \end{aligned} \tag{23}$$

It is clearly seen that $\overline{h}^{(0)(s)}$ with $s = 1,2,3$ have the wrong sign kinetic term and describe ghost degrees of freedom. Because of the off-diagonal elements $h^{(0)(i)}$ the model cannot be considered realistic until these degrees of freedom are excluded. These ghosts cannot be excluded via the inverse Higgs mechanism as the corresponding generators do not satisfy the required conditions [24].

One can introduce an additional symmetry in the target space. The choice of the target space coordinates as $\zeta^{(\alpha)}$ causes the following form of the target space metric:

$$g = \eta_{(\alpha)(\beta)}\, d\zeta^{(\alpha)} \otimes d\zeta^{(\beta)} . \tag{24}$$

If one demands a symmetry with respect to $\zeta^{(0)}$ inversion ($\zeta^{(0)} \to -\zeta^{(0)}$) then the field $h^{(\alpha)(\beta)}$ must have the vanishing component $h^{(0)(i)}$ to be consistent with the considering symmetry. This symmetry condition should be considered independently from the particular choice of the non-linear conformal symmetry realization. However, it is unclear what physical reason can justify the introduction of such a symmetry. Therefore, for the time being we consider it as an ad hoc prescription.

With the discussed prescription the traceless part of $h^{(\alpha)(\beta)}$ includes six independent components which can fit one spin-2 degree of freedom and one spin-0 degree of freedom. To obtain the vanishing trace we set

$$\overline{h}^{(0)(0)} = \sum_{a=1}^{3} \overline{h}^{(a)(a)} . \tag{25}$$

In such a presentation, the only non-vanishing components are $h^{(a)(b)}$ where $a, b = 1, 2, 3$. Within such a setup the original Lagrangian (4) up to $\mathcal{O}(h^4)$ order looks as:

$$\begin{aligned} \mathcal{L} = &\; \partial_\mu h^{(1)(1)}\, \partial^\mu h^{(1)(1)} + \partial_\mu h^{(2)(2)}\, \partial^\mu h^{(2)(2)} + \partial_\mu h^{(3)(3)}\, \partial^\mu h^{(3)(3)} \\ &+ \partial_\mu h^{(1)(2)}\, \partial^\mu h^{(1)(2)} + \partial_\mu h^{(2)(3)}\, \partial^\mu h^{(2)(3)} + \partial_\mu h^{(3)(1)}\, \partial^\mu h^{(3)(1)} \\ &\partial_\mu h^{(1)(1)}\, \partial^\mu h^{(2)(2)} + \partial_\mu h^{(2)(2)}\, \partial^\mu h^{(3)(3)} + \partial_\mu h^{(3)(3)}\, \partial^\mu h^{(1)(1)} + \mathcal{O}(h^4) . \end{aligned} \tag{26}$$

Generically this Lagrangian is non-diagonal. It could be made diagonal in the following representation:

$$\begin{aligned} \zeta_1 &= \frac{1}{\sqrt{6}} \left[ h^{(1)(1)} + h^{(2)(2)} + h^{(3)(3)} \right], & \zeta_4 &= h^{(1)(2)} , \\ \zeta_2 &= h^{(1)(1)} - h^{(3)(3)} , & \zeta_5 &= h^{(2)(3)} , \\ \zeta_3 &= h^{(1)(1)} - h^{(2)(2)} , & \zeta_6 &= h^{(3)(1)} . \end{aligned} \tag{27}$$

The quadratic part of the diagonal Lagrangian reads

$$\mathcal{L} = \sum_{i=1}^{6} \partial_\mu \zeta_i\, \partial^\mu \zeta_i \tag{28}$$

so the corresponding field equations are reduced to the Klein–Gordon equation

$$\Box \zeta_i = 0 . \tag{29}$$

As a result the model describes massless degrees of freedom. However, one lacks a condition which can fix their chirality.

Mass and chirality of a particle are fixed by eigenvalues of the Poincare group Casimir operators [26,27]. The D'Alamber operator $\Box$ defined to the mass operator which is one of the two Poincare group Casimir operators. The second Casimir operator is the Pauli–Lubanski vector

$$W^\mu = \frac{1}{2} \varepsilon^{\mu\nu\alpha\beta}\, P_\nu\, M_{\alpha\beta} \tag{30}$$

where $M_{\alpha\beta}$ are Lorentz generators building Lorentz group action on a given degree of freedom. The degrees of freedom $h^{(\alpha)(\beta)}$ should be mixed to diagonalize the Lagrangian, therefore, they can be only scalars of the trivial Lorenz group action. Hence, the model has no room for spin-2 degrees of freedom.

This section could be summarized as follows: Both discussed models (4) and (9) really are equal because of the relations between the conformal group generators with the influence on the coset coordinates and the corresponding non-linear symmetry realization. Secondly, the model (4) contains ghost degrees of freedom that can be excluded from the model only with an ad hoc prescription of auxiliary symmetry of the model target space. Such a prescription makes the model to be not natural. Nonetheless, the model with the additional symmetry is healthy and describes massless degrees of freedom appearing to be scalar ones. All these factors make the considered model not realistic.

## 4. Discussion and Summary

Three models with particular non-linear conformal symmetry realizations [17] were studied. We extend the consideration started in [21] and demonstrate that the discussed models could become realistic only after significant modifications.

The first model (1) seems not to be realistic. Firstly, the original model contains five degrees of freedom propagating in a flat space-time. In [17], it was argued that an extension to a curved space-time case may realize a viable inflationary scenario. Following [21] we show that in this model a universe expands with a deceleration (EoS parameter $w = 1$) and, therefore, there is no inflation in it. Secondly, the model contains ghost degrees of freedom. Although they do not appear at the cosmological solution it is reasonable to expect that they make the solution unstable. Therefore, the model is not applicable unless ghosts are excluded from the perturbation spectrum.

Secondly, (4) and (9) were analyzed and found to be equivalent. This feature was missed both in [17,21]. The models are equivalent up to a parameterization of dynamical variables. As it is pointed in the previous section the trace component of coset coordinates $h^{(\alpha)(\beta)}$ present in model (4) is the coset coordinate $\phi$ present in model (9). The coset coordinate $\phi$ is associated with operator $D$ which is related with the trace of operators $R_{(\alpha)(\beta)}$ which, in turn, are associated with coordinated $h_{(\alpha)(\beta)}$ (see (20)). Therefore, models (4) and (9) merely provide different parameterization of the same model.

Finally, we analyzed the field content of model (4). The trace component of $h_{(\alpha)(\beta)}$ acts as a sterile massless scalar which excludes its practical application. The traceless part $\overline{h}_{(\alpha)(\beta)}$ contains nine degrees of freedom. They are three ghosts $\overline{h}^{(0)(s)}$ with $s = 1, 2, 3$ which cannot be excluded with the inverse Higgs mechanism [24]. An additional symmetry of the target space may exclude the ghosts. Therefore, an opportunity to introduce such a symmetry should be studied.

**Author Contributions:** The authors claim to have contributed equally and significantly in this paper. All authors have read and agreed to the published version of the manuscript.

**Funding:** The work (B.L.) was supported by the Foundation for the Advancement of Theoretical Physics and Mathematics "BASIS". The work (S.A.) was also supported by the Interdisciplinary Scientific and Educational School of Moscow University "Fundamental and Applied Space Research".

**Conflicts of Interest:** The authors declare no conflicts of interest. The funders had no role in the design of the study; in the collection, analyses, or interpretation of data; in the writing of the manuscript, or in the decision to publish the results.

## Abbreviations

The following abbreviations are used in this manuscript:

GR General relativity

## Appendix A

Here, it is necessary to demonstrate some features of an interaction between $h^{(\mu)(\nu)}$ and matter degrees of freedom within model (4). The issue provides an additional reason to believe that the model can hardly be considered realistic.

For the sake of simplicity we consider a single massless vector field (which can be associated with the electromagnetic field). Accordingly to [17] such a vector field is described by the standard Lagrangian

$$\mathcal{L}_{\text{vec}} = -\frac{1}{4} F_{\mu\nu} F^{\mu\nu} . \tag{A1}$$

However, a definition of the field tensor contains covariant derivatives:

$$F_{\mu\nu} = \nabla_\mu A_\nu - \nabla_\nu A_\mu . \tag{A2}$$

The covariant derivative, in turn, reads

$$\begin{aligned} \nabla_\mu A^\nu &= \partial_\mu A^\nu + \sum_{n=0}^{\infty} \frac{i}{(2n+2)!} (ad_h^{2n} h \partial_\mu h)^{(\alpha)(\beta)} (M_{(\alpha)(\beta)})^\nu_{\ \sigma} A^\sigma \\ &= \partial_\mu A^\nu + \frac{i}{2} \eta_{(\gamma)(\sigma)} h^{(\alpha)(\gamma)} \partial_\mu h^{(\beta)(\sigma)} (M_{(\alpha)(\beta)})^\nu_{\ \sigma} A^\sigma + \mathcal{O}(h^2) . \end{aligned} \tag{A3}$$

Here, $\left(M_{(\alpha)(\beta)}\right)_{\mu\nu} = i(\eta_{(\alpha)\mu}\eta_{(\beta)\nu} - \eta_{(\alpha)\nu}\eta_{(\beta)\mu})$ is the vector representation of Lorentz group generators.

The corresponding Lagrangian has a few peculiar features. First and foremost, at the leading order the model describes interaction between two modes $h^{(\mu)(\nu)}$ and two vectors $A^\mu$. Within GR, in contrast, the leading order interaction between gravity and a massless vector field is a cubic interaction describing an interaction between two vectors and a graviton. Secondly, in contrast with GR the interaction can contain only odd powers of $h^{(\mu)(\nu)}$.

Implications of these features lead to significant differences between GR and (4). The most interesting one is related with $2 \to 2$ scattering. Within GR there are tree-level amplitudes describing gravitational scattering of massless vectors. Within model (4) such a scattering appears only at the one-loop level.

It is necessary to point out that to pinpoint the exact difference in such scattering processes a more detailed analysis is required. However, even at the current level the model (4) appears to be inconsistent with GR.

## References


1. Ogievetsky, V.I. Infinite-dimensional algebra of general covariance group as the closure of finite-dimensional algebras of conformal and linear groups. *Lett. Nuovo Cim.* **1973**, *8*, 988–990. [CrossRef]
2. Borisov, A.B.; Ogievetsky, V.I. Theory of Dynamical Affine and Conformal Symmetries as Gravity Theory. *Theor. Math. Phys.* **1975**, *21*, 1179. [CrossRef]
3. Salam, A.; Strathdee, J.A. Nonlinear realizations. 1: The Role of Goldstone bosons. *Phys. Rev.* **1969**, *184*, 1750–1759. [CrossRef]
4. Salam, A.; Strathdee, J.A. Nonlinear realizations. 2. Conformal symmetry. *Phys. Rev.* **1969**, *184*, 1760–1768. [CrossRef]
5. Isham, C.J.; Salam, A.; Strathdee, J.A. Spontaneous breakdown of conformal symmetry. *Phys. Lett.* **1970**, *31B*, 300–302. [CrossRef]
6. Isham, C.J.; Salam, A.; Strathdee, J.A. Nonlinear realizations of space-time symmetries. Scalar and tensor gravity. *Ann. Phys.* **1971**, *62*, 98–119. [CrossRef]
7. Bellucci, S.; Ivanov, E.; Krivonos, S. AdS/CFT equivalence transformation. *Phys. Rev. D* **2002**, *66*, 086001. [CrossRef]
8. Mannheim, P.D. Making the Case for Conformal Gravity. *Found. Phys.* **2012**, *42*, 388–420. [CrossRef]
9. 't Hooft, G. A class of elementary particle models without any adjustable real parameters. *Found. Phys.* **2011**, *41*, 1829–1856. [CrossRef]
10. Riegert, R.J. The particle content of linearized conformal gravity. *Phys. Lett. A* **1984**, *105*, 110–112. [CrossRef]
11. Barabash, O.V.; Shtanov, Y.V. Newtonian limit of conformal gravity. *Phys. Rev. D* **1999**, *60*, 064008. [CrossRef]
12. Phillips, P.R. Schwarzschild and linear potentials in Mannheim's model of conformal gravity. *Mon. Not. R. Astron. Soc.* **2018**, *478*, 2827–2834. [CrossRef]

13. Caprini, C.; Hölscher, P.; Schwarz, D.J. Astrophysical Gravitational Waves in Conformal Gravity. *Phys. Rev. D* **2018**, *98*, 084002. [CrossRef]
14. Wetterich, C. Conformal fixed point, cosmological constant and quintessence. *Phys. Rev. Lett.* **2003**, *90*, 231302. [CrossRef] [PubMed]
15. Polyakov, A.M. Conformal fixed points of unidentified gauge theories. *Mod. Phys. Lett. A* **2004**, *19*, 1649–1660. [CrossRef]
16. Reuter, M.; Weyer, H. Conformal sector of Quantum Einstein Gravity in the local potential approximation: Non-Gaussian fixed point and a phase of unbroken diffeomorphism invariance. *Phys. Rev. D* **2009**, *80*, 025001. [CrossRef]
17. Arbuzov, A.B.; Latosh, B.N. Gravity and Nonlinear Symmetry Realization. *Universe* **2020**, *6*, 12. [CrossRef]
18. Ivanov, E.A. Gauge Fields, Nonlinear Realizations, Supersymmetry. *Phys. Part. Nucl.* **2016**, *47*, 508–539. [CrossRef]
19. Ivanov, E.A.; Krivonos, S.O. Nonlinear realization of the conformal group in two dimensions and the Liouville equation. *Theor. Math. Phys.* **1984**, *58*, 131–140. [CrossRef]
20. Creminelli, P.; Serone, M.; Trincherini, E. Non-linear Representations of the Conformal Group and Mapping of Galileons. *JHEP* **2013**, *10*, 040. [CrossRef]
21. Alexeyev, S.; Krichevskiy, D. Inflationary solutions in the simplest gravity model with conformal symmetry. *Phys. Part. Nucl. Lett.* **2021**, *18*, 128–130. [CrossRef]
22. Weinberg, S. *Cosmology*; Oxford University Press: New York, NY, USA, 2008.
23. Rubakov, V.A.; Gorbunov, D.S. *Introduction to the Theory of the Early Universe*; World Scientific: Singapore, 2017.
24. Ivanov, E.A.; Ogievetsky, V.I. The Inverse Higgs Phenomenon in Nonlinear Realizations. *Teor. Mat. Fiz.* **1975**, *25*, 164–177. [CrossRef]
25. Arbuzov, A.; Latosh, B. On anomalies in effective models with nonlinear symmetry realization. *Mod. Phys. Lett. A* **2020**, *35*, 2050294. [CrossRef]
26. Wigner, E.P. On Unitary Representations of the Inhomogeneous Lorentz Group. *Ann. Math.* **1939**, *40*, 149–204. [CrossRef]
27. Bilal, A. Introduction to supersymmetry. *arXiv* **2001**, arXiv:hep-th/0101055.

universe MDPI

rticle

# Palatini $f(R)$ Gravity and Variants of k-/Constant Roll/Warm Inflation within Variation of Strong Coupling Scenario

Mahmoud AlHallak [1,†], Amer AlRakik [1,†], Nidal Chamoun [2,*,†] and Moustafa Sayem El-Daher [3,4,†]

[1] Physics Department, Faculty of Sciences, Damascus University, Damascus, Syria; mahmoud.halag@unitedschool.ae (M.A.); amer.alrakik@univ-tlse3.fr (A.A.) ;
[2] Physics Department, Higher Institute for Applied Sciences & Technology (HIAST), P.O. Box 31983, Damascus, Syria
[3] Higher Institute of Laser Applications and Researches, Damascus University, Damascus, Syria; m-saemaldahr@aiu.edu.sy
[4] Faculty of Informatics and Communications, Arab International University, Daraa, Syria
* Correspondence: nchamoun@th.physik.uni-bonn.de
† These authors contributed equally to this work.

**Abstract:** We show that upon applying Palatini $f(R)$, characterized by an $\alpha R^2$ term, within a scenario motivated by a temporal variation of strong coupling constant, then one obtains a quadratic kinetic energy. We do not drop this term, but rather study two extreme cases: $\alpha << 1$ and $\alpha >> 1$. In both cases, one can generate a kinematically-induced inflationary paradigm. In order to fit the Planck 2018 data, the $\alpha >> 1$ case, called k-inflation, requires a fine tuning adjustment with nonvanishing nonminimal coupling to gravity parameter $\xi$, whereas the $\alpha << 1$ case, studied in the constant-roll regime, can fit the data for vanishing $\xi$. The varying strong coupling inflation scenario remains viable when implemented through a warm inflation scenario with or without $f(R)$ gravity.

**Keywords:** variation of constants; inflation; $f(R)$-gravity; k-inflation

**PACS:** 98.80Cq; 98.80-k

itation: AlHallak, M.; AlRakik, A.; hamoun, N.; El-Daher, M.S. Palatini $(R)$ Gravity and Variants of -/Constant Roll/Warm Inflation ithin Variation of Strong Coupling cenario. *Universe* **2022**, *8*, 126. ttps://doi.org/10.3390/ niverse8020126

cademic Editors: Panayiotis tavrinos and Emmanuel N. aridakis

eceived: 12 January 2022
ccepted: 11 February 2022
ublished: 15 February 2022



## 1. Introduction

In [1], we adopted a model of variations of constants in order to generate an inflationary scenario, where the strong coupling was assumed to vary in time encoded in a scalar field representing this variation. Although current geophysical and astronomical data preclude any variation of constants, be it strong coupling [2], or Higgs vev [3], or electric charge [4], no data preclude variation in very early times. In [5], a connection between variation of constants and inflation was suggested, whereas in [6], this idea was pursued further into a concrete model shown to be able to accommodate data in some variants involving multiple inflaton fields. Alternatively, the single inflaton model was shown in [1] to be viable provided one changes the gravitational sector and assumes $f(R)$ gravity.

Usually, any model of inflation is defined by the choice of the scalar fields involved, their kinetic terms, mutual couplings and potentials, and couplings to gravity. However, we likewise have to specify the gravitational action with the corresponding degrees of freedom. One example of the latter is the choice between the metric and the Palatini formulations. The simplest extended gravitational action is given by replacing the Einstein–Hilbert action of general relativity (GR) by a function $f(R)$ of the Ricci scalar. Whereas both formalisms agree in GR, they do differ in $f(R)$ gravity. $f(R)$ with metric formulation was studied extensively (see [7–10] and references therein), whereas $f(R)$ in Palatini formalism constitutes a current hot topic, studied, for example, in [11,12] and references therein.

In our inflationary model based on couplings time variation, the addition of an $\alpha R^2$ term in the pure gravity Lagrangian changed the potential into an effective one, but also led to a quadratic kinetic energy term which was dropped in [1] on the grounds that it involved an $\alpha$-coupling which could be argued to be small perturbatively, and this allowed us to derive formulae for the spectral index $n_s$ and the scalar-to-tensor ratio $r$ which contrasted with Planck data 2018 [13] separately or combined with other experiments [14]. In actuality, the model can be considered as a special case of [15] which treated the general case of an arbitrary potential leading also to a quadratic kinetic energy term. However, in our model the potential is not arbitrary but dictated from new physics linking the two concepts of "inflation" and "variation of constants". Thus, our setup models the variation of coupling by a scalar field with, according to Bekenstein arguments [2,4], self coupling, and, furthermore, we assume an additional conformal invariant nonminimal coupling of the scalar field to gravity, which in turn is given by $f(R)$ (classically equivalent to tensor-scalar model) and not by GR.

The aim of this work is twofold. First, we study the effect of the quadratic kinetic energy term. For this, we take two extreme cases. The first case corresponds to $\alpha >> 1$, which makes the scalar field noncanonical per excellence. Many studies were carried out to refine the inflationary scenario within the framework of scalar fields possessing a noncanonical kinetic term [16–23]. In actuality, such kinematically-induced inflationary scenarios go back to the Starobinsky model [24,25] more than four decades ago, which considered a geometrical modification to general relativity in order to explain inflation. Nonetheless, the Starobinsky model, when considered in the framework of the Palatini formalism, in contrast to the metric formulation, cannot represent a model for inflation, due to the absence of a propagating scalar degree of freedom that can play the inflaton role [26,27]. Here, we go beyond and consider a scalar field, motivated by a nongeometrical origin suggested by variation of constants *à* la Bekenstein, minimally or nonminimally coupled to gravity with a potential whose form is dictated by Bekenstein arguments [2,4]. We find that with a nonvanishing nonminimal coupling to gravity (non-MCtG), the model can fit the data. However, one cannot obtain closed forms of the "canonical" potential except in some cases which we illustrate in order to show the "plateau" form of the potential in terms of the "canonical" field which rolls slowly during inflation.

The second case corresponds to the perturbative regime where we restrict the analysis to first order in $\alpha$. Our model in this case parallels the well-known constant-roll k-inflation [28], and we prove that within a given limit corresponding to vanishing non-MCtG with $\alpha$ small and $\ell$ large, the model is viable, and we check this numerically for both small and large constant-roll parameter $\beta$.

Inflationary scenarios by variation of constants generically suffer from appealing to new physics for an exit scenario during reheating [6]. A solution to this problem is provided by warm inflation paradigm [29–31]. In this paradigm, the radiation era is accompanying the slow-roll regime, and no need for an exit scenario. For this, our second objective is to add the warm inflation ingredient into our varying coupling inflation scenario. We find that with no $f(R)$ gravity the solution is hardly viable, but with Palatini $f(R)$, which would correspond to new degrees of freedom, accommodation of data is easily met.

The paper is organized as follows. In Section 2, we introduce the model and illustrate how the quadratic kinetic energy appears. In Section 3, we study the case of large $\alpha$ computing the spectral parameters to be contrasted with data. Section 4 is devoted to the study of the "canonical" potential shape when $\alpha >> 1$. In Section 5, we analyze the perturbative regime where $\alpha$ is small, whereas in Section 6 we prove its viability. In Section 7, we treat the case of warm inflation in a certain weak limit. We end up with a summary and conclusion in Section 8.

## 2. Analysis of the Basic Model

Our starting point is the general four dimensional action:

$$S = S_\phi + S_g + S_{g\phi} \tag{1}$$

where $S_\phi$ is the varying strong coupling constant action given by [6]:

$$S_\phi \equiv \int d^4x\sqrt{-g}\mathcal{L}_\phi \;=\; \int d^4x\sqrt{-g}\{-\frac{1}{2}f(\phi)g^{\mu\nu}\partial_\mu\phi\partial_\nu\phi - V(\phi)\} \tag{2}$$

where $f(\phi) = \frac{1}{\ell^2\phi^2}$, and $V(\phi) = \frac{V_0}{\phi^2}$ with $\phi$ embodying the strong coupling constant variation $g^{st}(x) = g_0^{st}\phi(x)$; $\ell$ is the Bekenstein length scale, and $V_0 = \frac{\langle G^2\rangle_T}{4}$ encodes the gluon field strength vacuum expectation value (vev) at inflation temperature $T$, whereas $S_g$ is the pure gravity Lagrangian including the Einstein–Hilbert action to which is added an $f(R)$ gravity term, taken, in our case, as a quadratic function of the Ricci scalar $\alpha R^2$, and we include also a coupling term $S_{g\phi}$ between gravity and the field $\phi$. Adopting units where the Planck mass $M_{pl}$ is equal to one, we have:

$$S_g \;=\; \int d^4x\sqrt{-g}\left[\frac{1}{2}\left(R+\alpha R^2\right)\right] \tag{3}$$

$$S_{g\phi} \;=\; \int d^4x\sqrt{-g}\left[-\xi R\phi^2\right] \tag{4}$$

with $R$, the Ricci scalar, constructed from the metric $g_{\mu\nu}$. Note that the form of the potential in Equation (2) is not placed by hand, but rather is dictated by the physical assumption of a varying strong coupling constant, where gauge and Lorentz invariance impose this form originating from the gluon condensate [5,6].

We start by making a change of variable absorbing the function $f$ in order to obtain a "canonical" kinetic energy term. Thus, we introduce the field $h$ defined as $\phi = \exp(\ell h)$, so that we obtain the action:

$$S = \int d^4x\sqrt{-g}\left[\frac{1}{2}F(R) + \frac{1}{2}G(h)R - \frac{1}{2}g^{\alpha\beta}\partial_\alpha h\partial_\beta h - V(h)\right] \tag{5}$$

where

$$V(h) = V_0\exp(-2\ell h), G(h) = -\xi\exp(2\ell h), F(R) = R + \alpha R^2 \tag{6}$$

Instead of using at this stage the first-order cosmological perturbation theory, by perturbing the metric ($g_{\mu\nu} \to g_{\mu\nu} + \delta g_{\mu\nu}$) and keeping terms of first order in the perturbations, we anticipate that the $\alpha R^2$ would contribute involved terms upon this metric change, so we follow [15,32] and introduce an auxiliary field $\psi$ and an action:

$$S = \int d^4x\sqrt{-g}\left[\frac{1}{2}G(h)R + \frac{1}{2}\{F(\psi) + F'(\psi)(R-\psi)\} - \frac{1}{2}g^{\alpha\beta}\partial_\alpha h\partial_\beta h - V(h)\right] \tag{7}$$

The equation of motion of $\psi$ gives $R = \psi$, provided $F''(\psi) \neq 0$. We change variable again $\psi \to \lambda$ such that ($\lambda = F'(\psi) = 1 + 2\alpha\psi$), so we obtain

$$S = \int d^4x\sqrt{-g}\left[\frac{1}{2}\{\lambda + G(h)\}R - \frac{1}{2}\{\psi\lambda - F(\psi(\lambda))\} - \frac{1}{2}g^{\alpha\beta}\partial_\alpha h\partial_\beta h - V(h)\right] \tag{8}$$

We carry out a conformal transformation on the metric

$$g_{\alpha\beta} \to \Upsilon^2 g_{\alpha\beta} = \tilde{g}_{\alpha\beta} \;\;:\;\; \Upsilon^2 = \lambda + G(h) \tag{9}$$

then we obtain, in the "Metric" formulation, where the Christoffel symbols are defined in terms of the metric and thus are not independent, and the corresponding affine connection is defined to be the Levi–Civita one, the following [33]:

$$\begin{aligned} S^{\text{"Metric"}} &= \int d^4x\sqrt{-\tilde{g}}\left[\frac{1}{2}\tilde{R} - \frac{3}{4}\frac{\tilde{g}^{\mu\nu}}{(\lambda+G(h))^2}\nabla_\mu(\lambda+G(h))\nabla_\nu(\lambda+G(h))\right. \\ &\left. -\frac{1}{2}\frac{1}{\lambda+G(h)}\tilde{g}^{\alpha\beta}\partial_\alpha h\partial_\beta h - \tilde{V}(h,\lambda)\right] \qquad (10) \\ \tilde{V}(h,\lambda) &= \frac{V(h)+W(\lambda)}{(\lambda+G(h))^2} \qquad (11) \end{aligned}$$

where

$$W(\lambda) = \frac{1}{2}[\psi\lambda - F(\psi(\lambda))] = \frac{(\lambda-1)^2}{8\alpha} \qquad (12)$$

We see that in the "Metric" formulation, we obtain a kinetic energy term for $(\lambda + G(h))$, and the field $\lambda$ is dynamic, i.e., its equation of motion cannot be solved algebraically.

For simplicity, then, we restrict the study from now on to the "Palatini" formulation, where the Christoffel symbols are considered independent and are to be determined dynamically. Remembering here that the pure gravity is not represented by a simple $R$ term, the connection will be different from the Levi–Civita one. Under this formulation, we obtain (noting that $\sqrt{-g} = \Upsilon^{-4}\sqrt{-\tilde{g}}, g^{\alpha\beta} = \Upsilon^2\tilde{g}^{\alpha\beta}$ and $R = \Upsilon^2\tilde{R}$):

$$S^{\text{"Palatini"}} = \int d^4x\sqrt{-\tilde{g}}\left[\frac{1}{2}\tilde{R} - \frac{1}{2}\frac{1}{\lambda+G(h)}\tilde{g}^{\alpha\beta}\partial_\alpha h\partial_\beta h - \tilde{V}(h,\lambda)\right] \qquad (13)$$

where, again, $\tilde{V}(h,\lambda)$ is given by Equation (11), and where Equation (12) is again valid.

The equation of motion of $\lambda$ can be solved algebraically to give it in terms of the field $h$ and its derivatives, so $\lambda$ is not a new degree of freedom:

$$\lambda = \frac{1+G(h)+8\alpha V(h)+2\alpha G(h)(\partial h)^2}{1+G(h)-2\alpha(\partial h)^2} \qquad (14)$$

Substituting (Equation (14)) into (Equation (13)), we obtain (dropping the "Palatini" superscript and the $\sim$ over the metric):

$$\begin{aligned} S &= \int d^4x\sqrt{-g}\left[\frac{R}{2} - \frac{1}{2}\frac{1}{(1+G(h))(1+8\alpha\bar{U})}g^{\alpha\beta}\partial_\alpha h\partial_\beta h\right. \\ &\left. +\frac{\alpha}{2}\frac{1}{(1+G(h))^2(1+8\alpha\bar{U})}(\partial^\alpha h\partial_\alpha h)^2 - \frac{\bar{U}}{1+8\alpha\bar{U}}\right] \qquad (15) \end{aligned}$$

where

$$\bar{U} = \frac{V(h)}{(1+G(h))^2} = \frac{V_0\exp(-2\ell h)}{(1-\xi\exp(2\ell h))^2}. \qquad (16)$$

In order to obtain a "canonical" kinetic energy term, we again make the change of variable ($h \to \chi$) by

$$\frac{dh}{d\chi} = \pm\sqrt{(1+G(h))(1+8\alpha\bar{U})} \qquad (17)$$

to obtain finally

$$S = \int d^4x\sqrt{-g}\left[\frac{R}{2} - \frac{1}{2}g^{\alpha\beta}\partial_\alpha\chi\partial_\beta\chi + \frac{\alpha}{2}(1+8\alpha\bar{U})(\partial^\alpha\chi\partial_\alpha\chi)^2 - U\right] \qquad (18)$$

where

$$U = \frac{\bar{U}}{(1+8\alpha\bar{U})} = \frac{V_0}{8\alpha V_0 + \left(e^{\ell h} - \xi e^{3\ell h}\right)^2} \tag{19}$$

We see here that the effect of the $\alpha R^2$ term is manifested in two ways. First, it helps in obtaining a "flat" effective potential $U$. In actuality, regardless of the form of $\bar{U}$, we see that the $\alpha R^2$ term leads, say when $\bar{U}(V_0)$ increases in modulus indefinitely, to an effective potential with a flat portion ($U \sim (8\alpha)^{-1}$). Second, the $\alpha R^2$ term leads to the appearance of squared kinetic energy $(\partial^\alpha \chi \partial_\alpha \chi)^2$.

In [1], $\alpha$ was taken to be small in such a way to neglect the quadratic kinetic energy term. In fact, upon perturbing the metric, the $(\alpha\delta g)$ term would give higher-order terms, whereas the $\alpha(\partial^\beta \chi \partial_\beta \chi)^2$ would give, in the slow-roll inflationary era, contributions of order $\alpha\dot{\chi}^4$, which is subdominant compared to the $\alpha$-correction in $U$. Thus, in [1], one could apply the shortcut "potential method", using $U$ as an effective potential. We intend now to refine this analysis, and consider the effect of the quadratic kinetic energy, keeping first order in $\alpha$ when $\alpha$ is small, and studying, in addition, the case where $\alpha$ is large. We point out here that although we do not explicitly present the Einstein/$f(R)$ field equations, we use known formulae for the spectral observables $(n_S, r)$ in the different limits under consideration, which were derived using first-order cosmological perturbation theory in solving the field equations [1].

## 3. k-Inflation: Case $\alpha >> 1$

Under the assumption

$$1 \ll \alpha(1+8\alpha\bar{U})(\partial^\alpha \chi \partial_\alpha \chi) \tag{20}$$

our k-inflation model features a single scalar field with the action

$$S = \int d^4x \sqrt{-g}\left[\frac{R}{2} + \frac{\alpha}{2}(1+8\alpha\bar{U})(\partial^\alpha \chi \partial_\alpha \chi)^2 - U\right] \tag{21}$$

Introducing the "standard" field $\varphi$ defined by

$$\frac{\partial \varphi}{\partial \chi} = [2\alpha(1+8\alpha\bar{U})]^{\frac{1}{4}} \tag{22}$$

we obtain a "standard" form for the k-inflation Lagrangian

$$\mathcal{L} = \frac{R}{2} + p(\varphi, X) \quad : \quad p(\varphi, X) = X^2 - U(\varphi), X = \frac{1}{2}\partial^\alpha \varphi \partial_\alpha \varphi \tag{23}$$

$$S = \int d^4x \sqrt{-g}\left[\frac{R}{2} + (\frac{1}{2}\partial^\alpha \varphi \partial_\alpha \varphi)^2 - U\right] \tag{24}$$

The spectral index $n_S$ and the tensor-to-scalar ratio are given now by [34]:

$$n_s - 1 = \frac{1}{3}(4\eta - 16\epsilon) \quad , \quad r = 16 c_s \epsilon \tag{25}$$

where

$$\epsilon = \frac{1}{2} 3^{\frac{1}{5}} \frac{(U_{,\varphi})^{\frac{4}{3}}}{U^{\frac{5}{3}}} \quad , \quad \eta = 3^{\frac{1}{5}} \frac{(U_{,\varphi})_{,\varphi}}{U^{\frac{2}{3}} (U_{,\varphi})^{\frac{2}{3}}} \tag{26}$$

$$c_s^2 = \frac{p_{,X}}{2X(p_{,X})_{,X} + p_{,X}} = \frac{1}{3} \tag{27}$$

where the comma (,) means differentiation with respect to what follows it. However, one should note that in order to compute the derivative with respect to the "standard" field $\varphi$, one should differentiate $U$ with respect to $h$, which is known from Equation (19) and using Equations (17) and (22), to get

$$\frac{dh}{d\varphi} = \left(\frac{(1-\xi e^{2\ell h})^2 + 8\alpha V_0 e^{-2\ell h}}{2\alpha}\right)^{\frac{1}{4}} \tag{28}$$

$$U_{,\varphi} = \frac{dU}{dh}\frac{dh}{d\varphi}, \tag{29}$$

$$(U_{,\varphi})_{,\varphi} = \frac{d^2U}{dh^2}\left(\frac{dh}{d\varphi}\right)^2 + U_{,h}\frac{dh}{d\varphi}\frac{d}{dh}\left(\frac{dh}{d\varphi}\right) \tag{30}$$

The input parameters are $(V_0, \ell, \alpha, \xi)$ and the initial values of the "original" inflaton field $h$ at the start of inflation. However, one can show analytically that the model is able to fit the data for some regions in the parameter space. In actuality, we obtain the following analytic formulae:

$$1 - n_s = \frac{4\ell^{4/3}\left(3\xi e^{4\ell h}(44\alpha V_0\xi - 7) + e^{2\ell h}(2 - 112\alpha V_0\xi) + 12\alpha V_0 + 21\xi^4 e^{10\ell h} - 59\xi^3 e^{8\ell h} + 57\xi^2 e^{6\ell h}\right)}{\sqrt[3]{\alpha}\sqrt[3]{V_0}\left(\left(3 - 3\xi e^{2\ell h}\right)\left(3\xi e^{2\ell h} - 1\right)\right)^{2/3}\left(8\alpha V_0 + \xi^2 e^{6\ell h} - 2\xi e^{4\ell h} + e^{2\ell h}\right)^{2/3}} \tag{31}$$

$$\overset{y\,\equiv\,\xi e^{2\ell h}}{=} \frac{\ell^{4/3}\left(12 - 112y + 132y^2\right)}{\left(\left(3 - 3\xi e^{2\ell h}\right)\left(3\xi e^{2\ell h} - 1\right)\right)^{2/3}} + \mathcal{O}\left(\frac{1}{\alpha V_0}\right) \tag{32}$$

$$\overset{\xi\,=\,0}{=} \frac{8\ell^{4/3}\left(6\alpha V_0 + e^{2\ell h}\right)}{3^{2/3}\sqrt[3]{\alpha}\sqrt[3]{V_0}\left(8\alpha V_0 + e^{2\ell h}\right)^{2/3}} \tag{33}$$

$$r = \frac{16\ell^{4/3}e^{2\ell h}\left(1 - \xi e^{2\ell h}\right)^{4/3}\left(3\xi e^{2\ell h} - 1\right)^{4/3}}{\sqrt[6]{3}\sqrt[3]{\alpha}\sqrt[3]{V_0}\left(8\alpha V_0 + \xi^2 e^{6\ell h} - 2\xi e^{4\ell h} + e^{2\ell h}\right)^{2/3}} \tag{34}$$

$$\overset{\xi\,=\,0}{=} \frac{16\ell^{4/3}e^{2\ell h}}{\sqrt[6]{3}\sqrt[3]{\alpha}\sqrt[3]{V_0}\left(8\alpha V_0 + e^{2\ell h}\right)^{2/3}} \tag{35}$$

Thus, enforcing the Bekenstein hypothesis $\ell > 1$, which means in our adopted units the absence of any length scale shorter than Planck length, we see that for $(\xi = 0)$ one cannot accommodate the data requiring $(0 < 1 - n_s << 1$ and $0 < r << 1)$. However, in the limit $(\alpha V_0 >> 1)$, one can adjust the parameter $(y = \xi e^{2\ell h})$ around the roots of $(12 - 112 + 132y^2)$ and obtain the data fit. In actuality, the two roots $(0.125792, 0.722693)$ of the latter polynomial are less than one, which implies that $h$ at the start of inflation was negative. Physically, this means that the strong coupling $g^{st}$ was less than its current value $(\phi < 1)$.

Figure 1, indeed, shows that there are acceptable points, colored in blue, for the following scanning:

$$\ell \in [1,3], \alpha \in [10,20], e^{2\ell h} \in [0.723031, 0.723035], V_0 \in [0.5,2], \xi = 1. \tag{36}$$

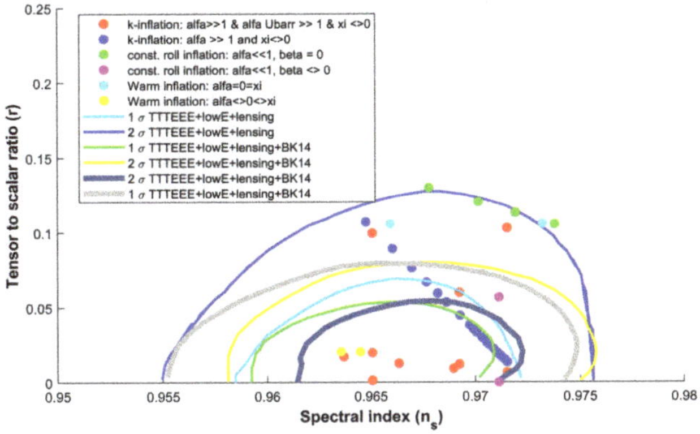


**Figure 1.** Kinematically derived inflation, in a model of varying strong coupling constant ($g^{st}(x) = g_0^{st}\phi(x)$), with $f(R)$ gravity via $\alpha R^2$ term and non-MCtG $-\xi R\phi^2$ term. The blue points correspond to the limit where $\alpha >> 1$, and we imposed $\xi = 1$. The red points correspond to the limit $\alpha >> 1$ and $\alpha\bar{U} >> 1$ with $\xi \neq 0$. The green (pink) points correspond to the limit $\alpha << 1$ with $\xi = 0$ and a vanishing (nonvanishing) constant-roll parameter $\beta$. The yellow (sky blue) points correspond to warm inflation scenario with (without) $f(R)$ gravity. The models are contrasted to Planck 2018, separately or combined with other experiments, contour levels of spectral parameters $(n_s, r)$. All acceptable points correspond to $\ell > 1$.

## 4. The "Plateau" Shape: Case $\alpha >> 1$

From Equation (19), we see that in the limit where

$$1 << 8\alpha\bar{U} \quad \Leftrightarrow \quad (1-\xi e^{2\ell h})^2 e^{2\ell h} << 8\alpha V_0 \tag{37}$$

the effective potential shows a "plateau" form ($U(h) \sim \frac{1}{8\alpha}$), and our objective in this section is to study the shape of this plateau in terms of the "canonical" field $\varphi$, which is the field to roll slowly along the effective potential.

In actuality, one would like, starting from the known potential $U(h)$ given in Equation (19), to find an analytic expression of the potential in terms of the "canonical" field $\varphi$. However, it is not possible in general to do this, as we cannot carry out analytically the following integral, originating from Equations (17) and (22), let alone invert it to express $h$ in terms of $\varphi$:

$$\varphi \;=\; (2\alpha)^{1/4} \int \frac{dh}{\left[(1-\xi e^{2\ell h})^2 + 8\alpha V_0 e^{2\ell h}\right]^{1/4}} \tag{38}$$

Even in the case of MCtG ($\xi = 0$), and although one can, in principle, carry out the above integration, the resulting expression involving hypergeometric functions is not invertible.

However, in the limit of Equation (37), one can carry out analytically the integration and obtain

$$e^{\ell h} \;=\; \frac{\sqrt{V_0}}{2}(\ell\varphi)^2 \tag{39}$$

and we see that the effective potential is given as

$$U(\varphi) \;=\; \left[8\alpha + \frac{\ell^4\varphi^4}{4}\left(1 - \xi\frac{V_0}{4}\ell^4\varphi^4\right)^2\right]^{-1} \tag{40}$$

In the left part (A) of Figure 2, we plot the shape of effective potential, and find that it has one local maximum (minimum) at $\varphi_0 = \sqrt[4]{4/(V_0\xi)}\ell^{-1}$ $(\varphi_0/\sqrt[4]{3})$. We see that the limit of Equation (37) is equivalent to

$$\ell^2\varphi^2\left|1-(\varphi/\varphi_0)^4\right| \quad << \quad \sqrt{32\alpha} \tag{41}$$

Thus, we see that as long as the field, during its slow rolling along the plateau from $\varphi = 0$, does not meet the local minimum, then the slow-roll condition is satisfied and the inflationary solution is consistent. In the right part (B) of Figure 2, we draw the same plateau in the case of MCtG. However, the solution is not viable for $\ell > 1$.

As a matter of fact, one can compute the observable parameters $(n_s, r)$ using the effective potential expression in this limit (Equation (40)), and we find with the combination $(z = \xi V_0\varphi^4\ell^4)$ the following

$$1-n_s \quad = \quad \ell^{4/3}3^{-2/3}\frac{48-112z+33z^2}{(8-8z+3z^2/2)^{2/3}} \tag{42}$$

$$r \quad = \quad 2^{2/3}3^{-1/6}8\ell^{16/3}\varphi^4\frac{(16-16z+3z^2)^{4/3}}{512\alpha+\ell^4\varphi^4(-4+z)^2} \tag{43}$$

We see here that for $\xi = 0$, one cannot meet $0 < 1-n_s \sim (12/\sqrt[3]{9})\ell^{4/3} << 1$ for $\ell > 1$, whereas for $z \sim 4/33(14 \pm \sqrt{97}$ (roots of the numerator of $(1-n_s)$) and having $\alpha$ quite large, one can satisfy $(0 < 1-n_s << 1, 0 < r << 1)$. The red points in Figure 1 represent acceptable points generated upon scanning the parameters as follows.

$$z \in [0.48, 0.52], \ell \in [1,2], \varphi \in [1,20], \alpha \in [400,500]. \tag{44}$$

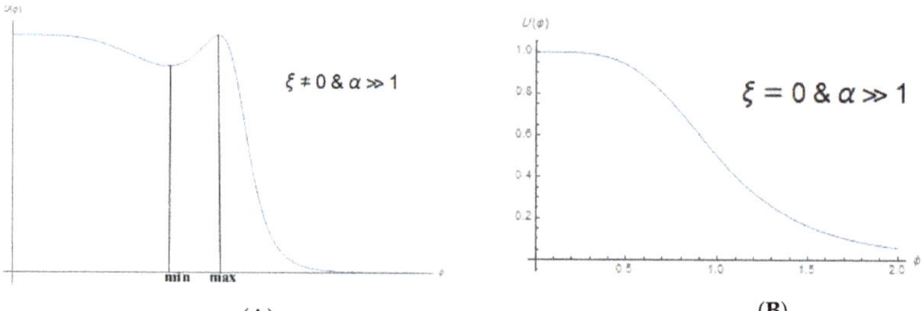


(A) (B)

**Figure 2.** Plateau shape in the limit of Equation (37). Scenario (B) with $\xi = 0$ fits data provided $\ell < 1$. (**A**) $max \equiv \varphi_0 = (\frac{4}{V_0\xi})^{1/4}\ell^{-1}$. $min \equiv \varphi_0 3^{-1/4}$; (**B**). $\xi = 0$.

### 5. Constant-Roll k-Inflation. Case $\alpha << 1$

In contrast to the preceding sections, we now take the perturbative limit $\alpha << 1$, and we work up to first order in $\alpha$. We shall consider a specific type of k-inflation called "constant-roll" inflation, where one slow-roll parameter ($\epsilon_2$) related to the time second derivative of the inflation is assumed constant, equaling $\beta$. Following [28], our model, which has the following action,

$$S \quad = \quad \int d^4x\sqrt{-g}/2f(R,\chi,X) \tag{45}$$

where

$$X = \frac{1}{2}\partial_\mu\chi\partial^\mu\chi = \frac{\dot{\chi}^2}{2} \quad , \quad f(R,\chi,X) = \left(R - 2X + 4\alpha X^2 - 2U\right) \tag{46}$$

will involve the slow-roll parameters defined as

$$\epsilon_1 \equiv \frac{\dot{H}}{H^2}, \epsilon_2 = \beta \equiv \frac{\ddot{\chi}}{H\dot{\chi}} \quad , \quad \epsilon_3 \equiv \frac{\dot{F}}{2HF} = 0, \epsilon_4 \equiv \frac{\dot{E}}{2HE} \tag{47}$$

where

$$F = f_{,R} = 1 \quad , \quad E \equiv -\frac{F}{2X}(Xf_{,X} + 2X^2 f_{,XX}) = 1 - 12\alpha X \tag{48}$$

At the horizon crossing time instance, we have

$$\epsilon_1 = -\frac{3}{4}\frac{\dot{\chi}^2 + \alpha\dot{\chi}^4}{U(\chi)} \quad , \quad \epsilon_4 = \frac{6\sqrt{3}\alpha\dot{\chi}\ddot{\chi}}{\sqrt{U}(1+6\alpha\dot{\chi}^2)} \tag{49}$$

with real solutions given by

$$\dot{\chi} = \frac{6(\beta+1)(\beta+3)4\alpha U - (81\Delta + 9\sqrt{S})^{2/3}}{3^{11/6}(\beta+1)4\alpha\sqrt{U}(81\Delta+9\sqrt{S})^{1/3}} \quad , \quad \ddot{\chi} = \beta\sqrt{\frac{U}{3}} \tag{50}$$

$$S = (\beta+1)^3(4\alpha)^3 U^2\left[81(\beta+1)4\alpha U_{,\chi}^2 + \frac{8}{3}(\beta+3)^3 U\right] \quad , \quad \Delta = 16(\beta+1)^2\alpha^2 U_{,\chi} U \tag{51}$$

The spectral parameters are given as

$$n_s = 1 + 2\frac{2\epsilon_1 - \epsilon_2 + \epsilon_3 - \epsilon_4}{1+\epsilon_1} = 1 + 2\frac{2\epsilon_1 - \beta - \epsilon_4}{1+\epsilon_1} \tag{52}$$

$$r = 4\left[\frac{\Gamma(3/2)}{\Gamma(3/2+\epsilon_2)2^{\epsilon_2}} c_A^{3/2+\epsilon_2}\frac{\sqrt{3}\dot{\chi}\sqrt{1+6\alpha\dot{\chi}^2}}{\sqrt{U}}\right]^2 \tag{53}$$

$$c_A^2 = \frac{f_{,X}}{f_{,X} + 2Xf_{,XX}} = \frac{-1+2\alpha\dot{\chi}^2}{-1+6\alpha\dot{\chi}^2} \tag{54}$$

The free input parameters here are $(\alpha, \xi, V_0)$ and $(\ell, h)$, which a priori determine $\chi$, and also $\beta$ of order unity expressing the constant-roll condition. However, note that we need to express $U_{,\chi}$ using Equations (17) and (19).

$$U_{,\chi} = \frac{dU}{dh}\frac{dh}{d\chi} \quad , \quad \frac{dh}{d\chi} = \pm\sqrt{1 - \xi e^{2\ell h} + \frac{8\alpha V_0 e^{-2\ell h}}{1 - \xi e^{2\ell h}}} \tag{55}$$

and even in the case of MCtG ($\xi = 0$), where we obtain an analytic expression of $\chi$ in terms of $h$:

$$\chi = \int \frac{dh}{\sqrt{1+8\alpha V_0 e^{-2\ell h}}} = \frac{e^{-\ell h}\sqrt{8\alpha V_0 + e^{2\ell h}}\log(e^{\ell h} + \sqrt{8\alpha V_0 + e^{2\ell h}})}{\ell\sqrt{1+8\alpha V_0 e^{-2\ell h}}} \tag{56}$$

one cannot invert it, so $U(\chi)$ is not obtained in a closed form.

## 6. Viability of the Constant-Roll k-Inflation: Case $\alpha << 1$

We show now the existence of viable points which fit the data. For this, we need a search strategy to reduce the number of input parameters, since our objective is limited to a proof of existence with no claim to exhaustive covering of all acceptable points; otherwise, scanning over the formulae of Equations (49)–(54), which are far from simple analytical formulae, is not a trivial task.

Let us take the case of MCtG ($\xi = 0$) which, with our limit case ($\alpha << 1$), leads to

$$\chi \simeq h, \bar{U} = V \simeq U, U_{,\chi} \sim \ell U \tag{57}$$

For the sake of showing the existence of acceptable solutions, if we assume that the constant slow-roll parameter $\epsilon_2 = \beta$ is quite small, to imply dropping of $\ddot{\chi}$, then $\epsilon_4$ is negligible as well. In order to meet the requirements ($\alpha << 1, \ell > 1$), we shall scan over the one-dimensional sub-parameter space parameterized as

$$\alpha = \Lambda^{-n}, \ell = \Lambda^{m}, V_0 = \Lambda, \chi \sim h = \ell^{-1} = \Lambda^{-m} \tag{58}$$

with ($n, m > 0$). Noting that $e^{\ell h}$ is of order $\mathcal{O}(1)$, we obtain for $\Lambda$ large

$$\dot{\chi} = \frac{\mathcal{O}(\Lambda^{1-n}) - \left(\mathcal{O}(\Lambda^{-2n+m+2}) + \mathcal{O}(\Lambda^{1-3n/2})\sqrt{\mathcal{O}(\Lambda^{2+2m-n}) + \mathcal{O}(\Lambda)}\right)^{2/3}}{\mathcal{O}(\Lambda^{1/2-n})\left(\mathcal{O}(\Lambda^{2+m-2n}) + \mathcal{O}(\Lambda^{1-3n/2})\sqrt{\mathcal{O}(\Lambda^{2+2m-n}) + \mathcal{O}(\Lambda)}\right)^{1/3}} \tag{59}$$

Then, in order to obtain the following quantities small

$$1 - n_s \approx -\frac{4\epsilon_1}{1+\epsilon_1} \quad , \epsilon_1 = -\tfrac{3}{4}\tfrac{\dot{\chi}^2 + \alpha\dot{\chi}^4}{U}, \quad r \approx \frac{12\dot{\chi}^2}{U} \tag{60}$$

we need to enforce

$$0 < n < 1 \quad , \quad 0 < m < \frac{1-n}{4} \tag{61}$$

Numerically, we checked the viability of the model for vanishing and nonvanishing $\beta$ parameter. By taking the following six choices, the obtained points for the upper four (lower two) choices corresponding to vanishing (nonvanishing) constant-roll parameters, represented in Figure 1 by green (pink) dots, do fit the data:

$$\beta = 0, \Lambda = 10^{6}, n = 0.5, m = 0.1 \quad \Rightarrow \quad (1 - n_s, r) = (0.0280827, 0.112981), \tag{62}$$
$$\beta = 0, \Lambda = 10^{5.8}, n = 0.5, m = 0.1 \quad \Rightarrow \quad (1 - n_s, r) = (0.032229, 0.12977), \tag{63}$$
$$\beta = 0, \Lambda = 10^{6.1}, n = 0.5, m = 0.1 \quad \Rightarrow \quad (1 - n_s, r) = (0.0262134, 0.10542), \tag{64}$$
$$\beta = 0, \Lambda = 10^{4.44}, n = 0.6, m = 0.001 \quad \Rightarrow \quad (1 - n_s, r) = (0.0298586, 0.120145) \tag{65}$$
$$\beta = 1, \Lambda = 10^{4.44}, n = 0.6, m = 0.1 \quad \Rightarrow \quad (1 - n_s, r) = (0.0288759, 0.0566994) \tag{66}$$
$$\beta = 10, \Lambda = 3 \times 10^{4}, n = 0.6, m = 0.1 \quad \Rightarrow \quad (1 - n_s, r) = (0.0288759, 0) \tag{67}$$

which proves the viability of the model.

## 7. Warm Inflation Variant

As mentioned earlier, the varying coupling inflation variants generally call for new physics in order to treat the reheating process and to provide for an exit scenario. This problem can be addressed in the warm inflation paradigm where the perturbations are generated thermally from a dissipative term characterized by a decay rate parameter $\Gamma$, which is sufficiently strong compared to Hubble parameter $H$ characterized by the ratio:

$$Q = \frac{\Gamma}{3H} \tag{68}$$

Here, the radiation is close to thermal equilibrium, and both the particle production rate and dissipation rate are controlled by $\Gamma$. The radiation takes place in parallel to the slow-roll regime, and there is no need for a specific exit scenario.

We readdress our Bekenstein-like scenario within the warm inflation paradigm assuming non-MCtG and $f(R)$ gravity embodied in the potential of Equation (19), whereupon placing $\alpha = 0 = \xi$, we switch back to the original scenario of [6]. We shall also restrict our study to the weak dissipative regime $Q << 1$, remembering that $Q = 0$ corresponds to the cold inflation.

The temperature during inflation is given by [35,36]

$$T = \left(\frac{\Gamma_0 U_\varphi^2}{36H^3 C_\gamma}\right)^{1/3} \tag{69}$$

where

$$\Gamma = \Gamma_0 T \quad , \quad C_\gamma = \frac{\pi^2}{30} g_* \tag{70}$$

with $\varphi$ as the canonical inflaton field, and we shall always take $g_* = 228.75$, representing the number of relativistic degrees of freedom of radiation of created massless modes, evaluated within minimal supersymmetric standard model at temperatures higher than the electroweak phase transition. In order to compute the derivatives with respect to $\varphi$ in terms of the derivatives with respect to $h$, we, as usual, use Equation (28).

Using the approximation

$$H = \sqrt{\frac{U}{3}}, \tag{71}$$

we have the slow-roll parameters given by

$$\epsilon_V = \frac{1}{2}\left(\frac{U_\varphi}{U}\right)^2 \quad , \beta_V = \left(\frac{\Gamma_\varphi U_\varphi}{\Gamma U}\right), \quad \eta_V = \left(\frac{U_{\varphi\varphi}}{U}\right), \tag{72}$$

Two parameters interfere to represent corrections due to the nontrivial occupation number ($n_*$) and to thermal effects ($\omega$) given by:

$$n_* = \frac{1}{e^{\frac{H}{T}} - 1} \quad , \quad \omega = \frac{2\pi\Gamma_0 T^2}{3H^2} \tag{73}$$

and, finally, we obtain, in the limit $\omega << 1$, the expressions for the observables:

$$n_s - 1 = -6\epsilon_V + 2\eta_V + \omega\left(\frac{15\epsilon_V - 2\eta_V - 9\beta_V}{4}\right) \quad , \quad r = \frac{16\epsilon_V}{(1+Q)^2(1+2n_* + \omega)} \tag{74}$$

Numerically, we find that upon switching off modification of gravity (i.e., $\alpha = 0 = \xi$), the value of $r$ is generically large, and one needs to fine-tune and adjust the parameters in order to find acceptable points, whereas switching on $\alpha$ helps generically to reduce $r$ and one can fit the data easier. In Figure 1, we designate two points in yellow and the other two ones in sky blue fitting the data corresponding to $\alpha = 0$ and $\alpha \neq 0$, respectively, with the following choice of parameters.

$$\alpha = 0, \xi = 0, \Gamma_0 = 41.02 \times 10^{10^{-7}}, V_0 = 2, \ell = 1.5, h = 11 \Rightarrow (n_s, r) = (0.965929, 0.105719), \tag{75}$$

$$\alpha = 0, \xi = 0, \Gamma_0 = 41.04 \times 10^{10^{-7}}, V_0 = 2, \ell = 1.5, h = 11 \Rightarrow (n_s, r) = (0.973216, 0.105702), \tag{76}$$

$$\alpha = 1000, \xi = 0, \Gamma_0 = 1, V_0 = 1, \ell = 1, h = 1.05 \Rightarrow (n_s, r) = (0.964472, 0.0202682), \tag{77}$$

$$\alpha = 1000, \xi = -0.002, \Gamma_0 = 1, V_0 = 1, \ell = 1, h = 1 \Rightarrow (n_s, r) = (0.963546, 0.0202916), \tag{78}$$

## 8. Summary and Conclusions

We continued in this letter the work of [1] on the inflationary model generated by varying strong coupling constant, and studied here the effect of the quadratic kinetic energy term which appears upon introducing an $f(R)$ gravity, represented by an $\alpha R^2$ term in the pure gravity Lagrangian. We investigated in Palatini formalism two extreme cases corresponding first to ($\alpha >> 1$), which represents thus a highly noncanonical k-inflation, and second to ($\alpha << 1$), where we kept terms to first order in $\alpha$ and examined a specific type of the k-inflation, namely the constant-roll inflation. In both cases, we showed the viability of the model for some choices of the free parameters in regards to the spectral parameters $(n_s, r)$ when compared to the results of Planck 2018 separately and combined with other experiments. However, the k-inflation required a non-MCtG and fine-tuned adjustment in order to accommodate data, whereas the constant-roll is able to accommodate data even in the MCtG situation, irrespective of the value of the constant-roll parameter $\beta$. This amendment of inflationary models, which were thought before not to fit the data, by assuming $f(R)$ gravity and/or nonminimal coupling to gravity, is a strong hint that this may be applicable to inflationary models other than the one studied in this work.

Finally, we readdressed the same model, *à* la Bekenstein within warm inflation scenario, which potentially is devoid of the exit scenario complications. In a specific limit, the weak limit corresponding to small parameters $Q$ and $\omega$, the model is able to accommodate data especially when supplemented with $f(R)$ gravity.

**Author Contributions:** All authors contributed equally to this work. All authors have read and agreed to the published version of the manuscript.

**Funding:** This research received no external funding.

**Institutional Review Board Statement:** Not applicable.

**Informed Consent Statement:** Informed consent was obtained from all subjects involved in the study.

**Acknowledgments:** N.C. acknowledges support from ICTP-Associate program, and from the Alexander von Humboldt Foundation, and is grateful for the hospitality of the Bethe Center for Theoretical Physics at Bonn University.

**Conflicts of Interest:** The authors declare no conflict of interest.

## References


1. AlHallak, M.; AlRakik, A.; Bitar, S.; Chamoun, N.; Eldaher, M.S. Inflation by Variation of the Strong Coupling Constant: update for Planck 2018. *Int. J. Mod. Phys. A* **2021**, 30, 2150226. [CrossRef]
2. Chamoun, N.; Landau, S.J.; Vucetich, H. Bekenstein model and the time variation of the strong coupling constant. *Phys. Lett. B* **2001**, *504*, 1–5. [CrossRef]
3. Chamoun, N.; Landau, S.J.; Mosquera, M.E.; Vucetich, H. Helium and deuterium abundances as a test for the time variation of the fine structure constant and the Higgs vacuum expectation value. *J. Phys. G* **2007**, *34*, 163. [CrossRef]
4. Bekenstein, J. Fine-structure constant: Is it really a constant? *Phys. Rev. D* **1982**, *25*, 1527. [CrossRef]
5. Chamoun, N.; Landau, S.J.; Vucetich, H. On inflation and variation of the strong coupling constant. *Int. J. Mod. Phys. D* **2007**, *16*, 1043. [CrossRef]
6. AlHallak, M.; Chamoun, N. Realization of Power-Law Inflation & Variants via Variation of the Strong Coupling Constant. *J. Cosmol. Astropart. Phys.* **2016**, *9*, 6.
7. Simon, J.Z. Higher Derivative Lagrangians, Nonlocality, Problems and Solutions. *Phys. Rev. D* **1990**, *41*, 3720. [CrossRef]
8. Woodard, R.P. Avoiding dark energy with $1/r$ modifications of gravity. *Lect. Notes Phys.* **2007**, *720*, 403–433.
9. Barbon, J.L.F.; Casas, J.A.; Elias-Miro, J.; Espinosa, J.R. Higgs Inflation as a Mirage. *J. High Energy Phys.* **2015**, *9*, 27. [CrossRef]
10. Salvio, A. Initial Conditions for Critical Higgs Inflation. *Phys. Lett. B* **2018**, *780*, 111–117. [CrossRef]
11. Sotiriou, T.P.; Liberati, S. Metric-affine $f(R)$ theories of gravity. *Ann. Phys.* **2007**, *322*, 935–966. [CrossRef]
12. Olmo, G.J. Palatini Approach to Modified Gravity: $f(R)$ Theories and Beyond. *Int. J. Mod. Phys. D* **2011**, *20*, 413–462. [CrossRef]
13. Akrami, Y.; Arroja, F.; Ashdown, M.; Aumont, J.; Baccigalupi, C.; Ballardini, M.; Banday, A.J.; Barreiro, R.B.; Bartolo, N.; Basak, S.; et al. Planck 2018 results-X. Constraints on inflation. *Astron. Astrophys.* **2020**, *641*, A10.
14. Ade, P.A.; Aghanim, N.; Ahmed, Z.; Aikin, R.W.; Alexer K.D.; Arnaud, M.; Aumont, J.; Baccigalupi, C.; Bay, A.J.; Barkats, D.; et al. Joint analysis of BICEP2/Keck Array and Planck data. *Phys. Rev. Lett.* **2015**, *114*, 101301. [CrossRef]
15. Enckell, V.-M.; Enqvist, K.; Rasanen, S.; Wahlman, L.-P. Inflation with $R^2$ term in the Palatini formalism. *J. Cosmol. Astropart. Phys.* **2019**, *2*, 22. [CrossRef]
16. Unnikrishnan, S.; Sahni, V.; Toporensky, A. Refining inflation using non-canonical scalars. *J. Cosmol. Astropart. Phys.* **2012**, *1208*, 18. [CrossRef]
17. Nojiri, S.; Odintsov, S.D.; Oikonomou, V.K. Modified gravity theories on a nutshell: Inflation, bounce and late-time evolution. *Phys. Rep.* **2017**, *692*, 1–104. [CrossRef]
18. Nojiri, S.; Odintsov, S.D.; Oikonomou, V.K. k-essence $f(R)$ Gravity Inflation. *Nucl. Phys. B* **2019**, *941*, 11. [CrossRef]
19. Odintsov, S.D.; Oikonomou, V.K. $f(R)$ gravity inflation with string-corrected axion dark matter. *Phys. Rev. D* **2019**, *99*, 064049. [CrossRef]
20. Allemandi, G.; Borowiec, A.; Francaviglia, M.; Odintsov, S.D. Dark energy dominance and cosmic acceleration in first-order formalism. *Phys. Rev. D* **2005**, *72*, 063505. [CrossRef]
21. Gialamas, I.D.; Karam, A.; Pappas, T.D.; Spanos, V.C. Scale-invariant quadratic gravity and inflation in the Palatini formalism. *Phys. Rev. D* **2021**, *104*, 023521. [CrossRef]

2. Gialamas, I.D.; Karam, A.; Racioppi, A. Dynamically induced Planck scale and inflation in the Palatini formulation. *J. Cosmol. Astropart. Phys.* **2020**, *11*, 14. [CrossRef]
3. Karam, A.; Tomberg, E.; Veermae, H. Tachyonic preheating in Palatini $R^2$ inflation. *J. Cosmol. Astropart. Phys.* **2021**, *6*, 23. [CrossRef]
4. Starobinsky, A.A. Spectrum Of Relict Gravitational Radiation And The Early State of the Universe. *J. Exp. Theor. Phys. Lett.* **1979**, *30*, 682.
5. Starobinskii, A.A. Spectrum of relict gravitational radiation and the early state of the universe. *Sov. J. Exp. Theor. Phys. Lett.* **1979**, *30*, 719.
6. Antoniadis, I.; Karam, A.; Lykkas, A.; Pappas, T.; Tamvakis, K. Rescuing quartic and natural inflation in the Palatini formalism. *J. Cosmol. Astropart. Phys.* **2019**, *3*, 5. [CrossRef]
7. Antoniadis, I.; Karam, A.; Lykkas, A.; Tamvakis, K. Palatini inflation in models with an $R^2$ term. *J. Cosmol. Astropart. Phys.* **2018**, *11*, 28. [CrossRef]
8. Odintsov, S.D.; Oikonomou, V.K. Constant-roll k-inflation dynamics. *Class. Quantum Grav.* **2020**, *37*, 025003. [CrossRef]
9. Berera, A.; Fang, L.Z. Thermally Induced Density Perturbations in the Inflation Era. *Phys. Rev. Lett.* **1995**, *74*, 1912. [CrossRef]
0. Berera, A. Warm Inflation. *Phys. Rev. Lett.* **1995**, *75*, 3218. [CrossRef]
1. Berera, A.; Moss, I.G.; Ramos, R.O. Warm Inflation and its Microphysical Basis. *Rep. Prog. Phys.* **2009**, *72*, 026901. [CrossRef]
2. Sotiriou, T.P.; Faraoni, V. $f(R)$ Theories of Gravity. *Rev. Mod. Phys.* **2010**, *82*, 451–497. [CrossRef]
3. Budhi, R.H.S. Inflation due to non-minimal coupling of $f(R)$ gravity to a scalar field. *J. Phys. Conf. Ser.* **2019**, *1127*, 012018. [CrossRef]
4. Li, S.; Liddle, A.R. Observational constraints on k-inflation models. *J. Cosmol. Astropart. Phys.* **2012**, *10*, 11. [CrossRef]
5. Visinelli, L. Observational Constraints on Monomial Warm INflation. *J. Cosmol. Astropart. Phys.* **2016**, *1607*, 54. [CrossRef]
6. Kamali, V. Non-minimal Higgs inflation in the context of warm scenario in the light of Planck data. *Eur. Phys. J. C* **2018**, *78*, 975. [CrossRef]

*universe*

MDPI

*Article*

# Interiors of Terrestrial Planets in Metric-Affine Gravity

**Aleksander Kozak [1,†] and Aneta Wojnar [2,*,†]**

1 Institute of Theoretical Physics, University of Wroclaw, pl. Maxa Borna 9, 50-206 Wroclaw, Poland; aleksander.kozak@uwr.edu.pl

2 Laboratory of Theoretical Physics, Institute of Physics, University of Tartu, W. Ostwaldi 1, 50411 Tartu, Estonia

* Correspondence: aneta.magdalena.wojnar@ut.ee

† These authors contributed equally to this work.

**Abstract:** Using a semiempirical approach, we show that modified gravity affects the internal properties of terrestrial planets, such as their physical characteristics of a core, mantle, and core–mantle boundary. We also apply these findings for modeling a two-layer exoplanet in Palatini $f(R)$ gravity.

**Keywords:** modified gravity; Ricci-based gravity; Palatini gravity; exoplanets; planet's interior

**Citation:** Kozak, A.; Wojnar, A. Interiors of Terrestrial Planets in Metric-Affine Gravity. *Universe* **2022**, *8*, 3. https://doi.org/10.3390/universe8010003

Academic Editors: Panayiotis Stavrinos and Emmanuel N. Saridakis

Received: 23 November 2021
Accepted: 17 December 2021
Published: 22 December 2021



## 1. Introduction

Discoveries of exoplanets in the Milky Way Galaxy [1,2] and in the Whirlpool Galaxy [3], as well as growing observational datasets of those objects provided by the current and future missions [4–8], have increased the need for theoretical tools which allow us to describe the planets' interiors and eventual habitable properties on the basis of those data. A common approach is to extrapolate the Preliminary Reference Earth Model (PREM) [9] and its later improvements [10–12] (see more at [13]). Therefore, although an Earth-like planet should have at least six differently composed layers, one usually considers two [14]: iron core and silicate mantle, as they have the biggest impact on the observed properties, such as the planet's mass, radius, and polar moment of inertia. However, a very different composition of the rocky planets may also be possible, as argued in [15], such as quartz-rich mantles, in comparison to the Solar System ones, whose mantles are mainly made of silicates. Clearly, such findings call for more research in planetary physics, not only from an observational point of view, but also in theoretical modeling.

Regarding the planet's modeling based on PREM, we are still improving our knowledge on the deepest zones of the Earth, as well as the instrumentation and methods used becoming ameliorated, allowing us to obtain more accurate data regarding the planet's interior. For instance, recent seismic observation [16] has revealed the existence of a liquid/mushy region of the inner core instead of the solid one, as has been believed so far. On the other hand, a new generation of the neutrino telescopes will be settled to provide information on matter density inside the planet, and on characteristics and abundances of light elements in the outer core [17–20]. In addition, in laboratories, with the use of lasers [21], the high pressures and temperatures, that is, the extreme conditions of the Earth's core, are recreated in order to understand the properties and behavior of iron, which is the main element of planets' cores. All those revelations make the research regarding planets' modeling relevant, especially agreeing with the fact that various models of gravity predict different layers' structure in comparison to the Newtonian model [22], commonly used in planetary science. Therefore, knowing the planet's profile with high accuracy, that is, the number of differently composed layers and their thicknesses, might be another tool to test theories of gravity (see the details on the method in [23]).

As already mentioned, some extensions of Einstein's theory of gravity may impact the internal structure of the rocky planets, as well as their properties [22–24]. This is so, as such theories modify the nonrelativistic hydrostatic equilibrium equations [25] and others, crucial for stellar and planetary modeling. For instance, in the Schwarzschild criterion, which is used to constitute a type of the energy transport through an astrophysical object, there appears an additional term making the star more or less stable with respect to convective processes [26]; energy production in a stellar core is also affected [27–30], as well as stars' evolution [31], or cooling processes of substellar objects [32]. Therefore, modified gravity theories proposed to provide some explanations of dark matter and dark energy phenomena [33–38], spacetime singularities [39], extreme masses of compact objects [40–45], or to unify all four interactions into a single theory [46,47], also impact modeling of gravitational systems for which full relativistic description is not necessary.

One of such theories we are interested in is a subclass of the so-called Ricci-based theories [48], that is, Palatini $f(R)$ gravity. The main geometric property of these theories is that the metric and connection are considered as independent objects in comparison to most extensions of Einstein's theory. In Ricci-based gravities, the connection is not coupled to the matter fields, assuming that we are dealing with metric theories, that is, the particles are moving along geodesics distinguished by the metric; moreover, in such a formulation, the connection is not dynamical. However, their most important feature is related to their vacuum dynamics, as it provides the same dynamical equations as general relativity ones with a cosmological constant [49–51], providing that those proposals pass the Solar System tests [52] and gravitational waves' observations as the waves are moving with the speed of light in those theories. However, the difference is clear when one deals with matter fields—Ricci-based gravities then introduce terms which depend on energy density, modifying the structural equations [53].

In this work, we focus on a gravitational model which introduces a quadratic Ricci scalar term, and it is considered in the Palatini approach. Since those terms contribute to the structural equations of spherical symmetric low-temperature spheres, such a modification will have an influence on internal properties of the planet. Therefore, using an analytical method allowing us to obtain the core and core–mantle boundary values of pressure from given masses and radii of transiting exoplanets, we demonstrate that those values will differ in modified gravity. Moreover, we also use them to model an exoplanet interior.

## 2. Simple Model of Small Rocky Planets in Palatini Gravity

In this section, we recall the hydrostatic equilibrium equations for a cold, low-mass spherical symmetric object. Our terrestrial planets, with masses from the range $M_p \in (0.1-10)M_\oplus$, where $M_\oplus$ is the Earth's mass, and core mass fraction (CMF), defined as

$$\mathrm{CMF} = \frac{M_{\mathrm{core}}}{M_p}, \tag{1}$$

not exceeding $\sim$0.4 of the total planet's mass[1], will be modeled as a two-layer planet, that is, consisting of an iron core and a silicate mantle. Then, using the semiempirical expression relating the CMF with the radius and mass of a transiting exoplanet, we derive the planet's internal characteristics, such as core pressure and density, their boundary values between the core and mantle, and the mantle's ones.

### 2.1. Planets' Structure Equations

Nonrelativistic hydrostatic equilibrium equations for the quadratic Starobinski model[2]

$$f(\mathcal{R}) = \mathcal{R} + \beta\mathcal{R}^2 \tag{2}$$

considered in the Palatini approach are given by [53,56]

$$p'(r) = -\frac{Gm\rho}{r^2}\Big(1 - \beta c^2\kappa^2(5\rho - 2r\rho')\Big), \tag{3}$$

$$m(r) = \int_0^r 4\pi\tilde{r}^2\rho(\tilde{r})d\tilde{r}, \tag{4}$$

where prime denotes the derivative with respect to the radial coordinate. The matter part of the full relativistic field equation is described as a perfect fluid in this approach, $T_{\mu\nu} = (\rho + p)u_\mu u_\nu + pg_{\mu\nu}$, where $p = p(r)$ and $\rho = \rho(r)$ are pressure and energy density, respectively, while $u^\mu$ is a normalized 4-vector, representing an observer comoving with the fluid. Let us notice that the different numerical factors appearing in the modification term in Equation (3) are the results of the considered assumptions; for example, in [56], the equations were obtained by assuming the conformal invariance of the standard polytropic equation of state for the quadratic model demonstrated in [57], while the equations derived in [53] are more general, without adopting any equation of state. In this work, we also use some polytropic equations of state, however it differs slightly with respect to the common one, as explained later in the text.

Our small rocky exoplanet is modeled as a cold sphere consisting of two different layers. As already mentioned, the material they are made of is iron in the core and silicate in the mantle, whose equations of state are given by the Birch equation of state [58,59], working well when temperatures can be considered uniform but less than 2000 K, and when pressure is below 200 GPa. However, in order to be able to consider more massive objects than the terrestrial planets of the Solar System, one has to take into account the electron degeneracy, as the internal pressure can be $p \gtrsim 10^4$ GPa. The usual procedure is to match this equation of state with the Thomas–Fermi–Dirac one [60–63], which also qualifies to describe density-dependent correlation energy [64] which appears because of the interactions between electrons when they obey the Pauli exclusion principle and move in the Coulomb field of the nuclei. Such a hybrid equation of state is very well approximated by a modified polytropic equation of state (SKHM) of the form [14]

$$\rho(p) = \rho_0 + cp^n, \tag{5}$$

whose best-fit parameters $\rho_0$, $c$, and $n$ for iron and silicate (Mg, Fe)$SiO_3$ are provided in Table 1. Because solids and liquids are incompressible at the low-pressure regimes, the additional term $\rho_0$ is present to include this effect. Equation of state constructed in such a way is valid up to $p = 10^7$ GPa, giving the maximal value of the central pressure possible in our analysis.

**Table 1.** Best-fit parameters for the SKHM equation of state (Equation (5)) obtained in [14].

| **Material** | $\rho_0$ **(kg m$^{-3}$)** | $c$ **(kg m$^{-3}$ Pa$^{-n}$)** | $n$ |
|---|---|---|---|
| Fe($\alpha$) | 8300 | 0.00349 | 0.528 |
| (Mg, Fe)$SiO_3$ | 4260 | 0.00127 | 0.549 |

Moreover, to explore the model with the described features, one needs to establish the initial and boundary conditions. In previous works, we have used the shooting method in order to find the initial values of the core's densities as well as between the layers' ones [22,23]. This demonstrated that modified gravity can have a significant impact on those values, and this is a result of different physical assumptions to, for example, Newtonian physics. Therefore, even slight modification to the standard hydrostatic equilibrium equation will have an effect on the internal structure. Keeping this in mind, we have restudied a simple but reasonable method [65] used to obtain the internal characteristic of a distant planet, whose mass and radius can be found by the use of the transit observation techniques [66]. Therefore, for the given total mass of the planet and its radius, we derive the central pressure, its value on the core–mantle boundary (CMB), and the mantle one. This will show that modified gravity indeed affects them.

## 2.2. Internal Structure of Palatini Planets

There is only one planet whose interior structure and materials, that is, equations of state, are known: Earth[3]. The many-layers structure, their thickness, and equations of state are given by seismic data, that is, PREM [9]. Since some planets of our Solar

System and exoplanets are alike dense and possess similar other characteristics, one usually extrapolates the Earth's model to describe them. Therefore, extrapolating the Earth's model, one may derive the semiempirical expression for the core mass fraction (CMF) which carries the information on the core–mantle boundary, often used in numerical procedures and simulations of very distant planets, whose mass $M_p$ and radius $R_p$ are given by the transit Such a relation between CMF and observed radius and mass was given in [68]:

$$\mathrm{CMF} = \frac{1}{0.21}\left[1.07 - \left(\frac{R_p}{R_\oplus}\right) / \left(\frac{M_p}{M_\oplus}\right)^{0.27}\right], \tag{6}$$

where $R_\oplus$ and $M_\oplus$ are Earth's radius and mass, respectively. Furthermore, CMF can be also used to obtain the approximated value for the core radius fraction (CRF), defined as

$$\mathrm{CRF} = \frac{R_{\mathrm{core}}}{R_p}, \tag{7}$$

which is also suitable for numerical analysis [65]:

$$\mathrm{CRF} \approx \sqrt{\mathrm{CMF}}. \tag{8}$$

Using these two values, that is, CMF and CRF, we derive the core's and mantle's pressure, as well as its boundary value, for an exoplanet of the mass $M_p$ and radius $R_p$.

Let us firstly use the definition of local gravity, usually defined as

$$g = \frac{Gm(r)}{r^2}, \tag{9}$$

to rewrite Equation (3) in a more suitable form for further purposes:

$$p'(r) = -g\rho\left(1 - \alpha\left[\frac{14g + g'r - 2g''r^2}{4\pi Gr}\right]\right), \tag{10}$$

where we have defined a new parameter $\alpha = \kappa^2 c^2 \beta$ for the further convenience. Using the mass equation (Equation (4)), together with the expression for the local gravity (9), it can be transformed into

$$\frac{dp}{dm} = -\frac{g^2}{4\pi G}\frac{d\ln(m)}{dm}\sigma, \tag{11}$$

where $\sigma = 1 - \alpha\left[\frac{14g+g'r-2g''r^2}{4\pi Gr}\right]$ while $\ln(m)$ is the natural logarithm of $m$. Assuming that the surface pressure is zero, we integrate the above equation from the surface inward, such that

$$\int_{\mathrm{surface}}^{\mathrm{interior}} dp = -\frac{1}{4\pi G}\int_{M_p}^{\text{mass enclosed inside}} g^2 d\ln(m)\sigma. \tag{12}$$

Before proceeding further, let us define the surface gravity $g_s$ as a local gravity on the planet's surface with mass $M_p$ and radius $R_p$

$$g_s := \frac{GM_p}{R_p^2}, \tag{13}$$

while the so-called typical pressure $p_{\mathrm{typ}}$ is defined as

$$p_{\mathrm{typ}} := \frac{g_s^2}{4\pi G} = \frac{GM_p^2}{4\pi R_p^4}. \tag{14}$$

As the local gravity of the mantle can be assumed to be a constant [65], we may integrate Equation (12) to obtain the pressure of the mantle:

$$p_{\rm mantle} = 2p_{\rm typ}\ln\left(\frac{R_p}{r}\right)\left[1+\alpha\frac{7g_s}{\pi G}\frac{M_p}{R_p}\left(\frac{1}{\sqrt{M_p}}-\frac{1}{\sqrt{m}}\right)\right], \tag{15}$$

where we use the planet's characteristics defined before. In particular, the pressure on the core–mass boundary (CMB) can be obtained by inserting $r \to R_{\rm core}$ and $m \to M_{\rm core}$ such that

$$p_{\rm CMB} = p_{\rm typ}\ln\left(\frac{1}{\rm CMF}\right)\left[1+\alpha\frac{7g_s\sqrt{M_p}}{\pi G R_p}\left(1-\frac{1}{\sqrt{\rm CMF}}\right)\right], \tag{16}$$

where we have used Equations (7) and (8).

On the other hand, since in our model the core density $\rho_{\rm core}$ can be assumed to be a constant value, the core mass is given as $M_{\rm core} = \frac{4}{3}\pi R_{\rm core}^3\rho_{\rm core}$. Therefore, the hydrostatic equilibrium Equation (3) can be written with the use of Equation (4) as

$$\frac{dp_{\rm core}}{dr} = -g\rho_{\rm core}\left(1-\alpha\left[\frac{9m'}{4\pi r^2}-\frac{m''}{2\pi r}\right]\right) = -\frac{3rp_{\rm typ}}{R_{\rm core}^2}\left[1-\alpha\frac{15g_s}{4\pi G R_{\rm core}}\right]. \tag{17}$$

Integrating the above equation results in

$$p_{\rm core}(r) = p_0 - \frac{3}{2}p_{\rm typ}\left(\frac{r}{R_{\rm core}}\right)^2\left(1-15\alpha\frac{g_s}{4\pi G R_{\rm core}}\right), \tag{18}$$

where $p_0$ is the central pressure which can be determined by matching the above $p_{\rm core}$ at CMB with the pressure on the boundary (Equation (16)):

$$\begin{aligned} p_0 &= p_{\rm CMB} + \frac{3}{2}p_{\rm typ}\left(1-15\alpha\frac{g_s}{4\pi G R_{\rm core}}\right) \\ &= p_{\rm typ}\left(\frac{3}{2}\left[1-15\alpha\frac{g_s}{4\pi G R_{\rm core}}\right]+\ln\left(\frac{1}{\rm CMF}\right)\left[1+\alpha\frac{7g_s\sqrt{M_p}}{\pi G R_p}\left(1-\frac{1}{\sqrt{\rm CMF}}\right)\right]\right). \end{aligned} \tag{19}$$

The above result allows us to find an approximated value of the central pressure for a given terrestrial exoplanet whose mass and radius are provided by the transit observations. The effect of modified gravity is clearly present; therefore, in the next section, we numerically solve the structural equations with the use of those findings.

## 3. Numerical Solutions

In order to compare models of different values of the Starobinsky parameter $\beta$, we have introduced earlier a dimension-full parameter $\alpha = c^2\kappa^2\beta$, which allows one to write the formulas in a more convenient way. We chose four values of the parameter, $\alpha \in \{0, 10^{-15}, 10^{-14}, 10^{-13}\} \times \mathrm{m^3/kg}$, that is, $\beta \in \{0, 10^{11}, 10^{12}, 10^{13}\} \times \mathrm{m^2}$, neglecting the possibility of negative values of the parameter[4]. Let us comment that with the current experiments performed in the Solar System, one is not able to distinguish between Palatini $f(R)$ gravity and GR [52]. Upper bounds on the absolute value of the parameter $\beta$ in the Palatini approach have been determined to be $\beta \sim 10^{12}$ cm$^2$, when one investigates weak-field limit of the theory [69], or $\beta \sim 10^9$ cm$^2$, if gravitational forces become as strong as electric forces [70]. It must be noted that the absolute bounds differ from the ones obtained for metric counterpart of the theory [69]. Another issue concerns the critical value of the parameter. It can be shown that, when $\beta$ takes negative values, there also exists an upper bound on the value of the parameter depending on the energy density of matter; any values above the critical one lead to unphysical results [23].

Having established the range of the parameter, we focus on numerically solving Equations (3) and (4), supplemented with the equation of state, Equation (5). In order to determine the exact density profile for a planet of given mass and radius, and chemical composition, one needs to use the shooting method, i.e., find a value of internal density such that, at the surface of the planet, the radius and the mass coincide with the desired values (the surface, if defined by $p(R_p) = 0$). The fact that the masses and radii of the planets we examine are fixed by the transit observations provides the possibility to determine the core density and core size with its mass, as well as to plot the density profiles. As one can see in Figure 1, all curves denoting solutions for different values of $\alpha$ end at the same point; what changes is the size of the core. This allows us to compare CMFs and CRFs obtained from the quasi-empirical Formula (6) (which is constant once the mass and the radius of the planet are given) to the numerical findings.

As far as the pressure is concerned, we simply calculate it for one planet, Kepler-78 b[5], using Formulas (15) and (18), as well as the exact value of $R_{\rm core}$ determined in the previous numerical step. The results are shown in Figure 2, illustrating the effects of modified gravity on pressure within the exoplanet. The analytical solutions are then compared with numerical ones, to determine how good the approximations are. The results are shown in Figure 3 for two values of $\alpha$.

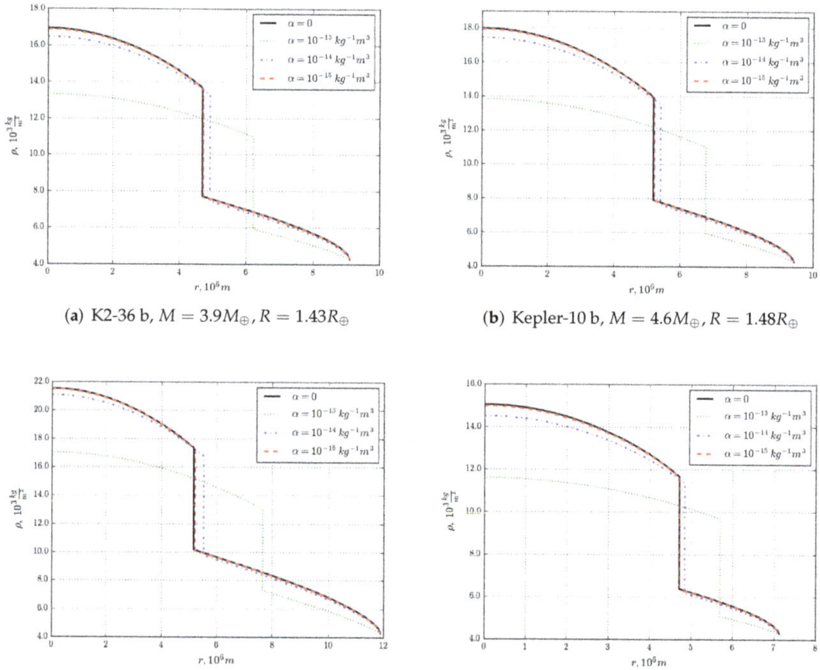


(**a**) K2-36 b, $M = 3.9M_\oplus, R = 1.43R_\oplus$

(**b**) Kepler-10 b, $M = 4.6M_\oplus, R = 1.48R_\oplus$

(**c**) Kepler-20 b, $M = 9.7M_\oplus, R = 1.87R_\oplus$

(**d**) Kepler-78 b, $M = 1.97M_\oplus, R = 1.12R_\oplus$

**Figure 1.** Density profiles for four different Earth-like exoplanets, for different values of the parameter $\alpha = c^2\kappa^2\beta$. The planets are assumed to be composed of two layers: iron core, and mantle made of (Fe, Mg)$SiO_3$.

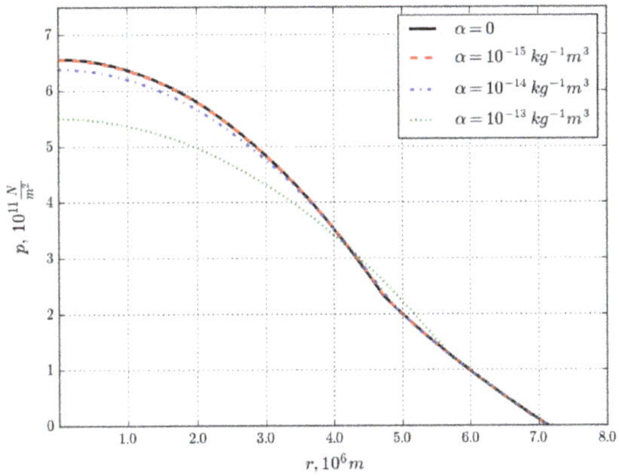


**Figure 2.** Relation between pressure and radius for Kepler-78 b exoplanet calculated analytically using the formulas derived in this work. The curves are plotted for four different values of the parameter $\alpha = c^2\kappa^2\beta$. The planet is assumed to be composed of two layers.

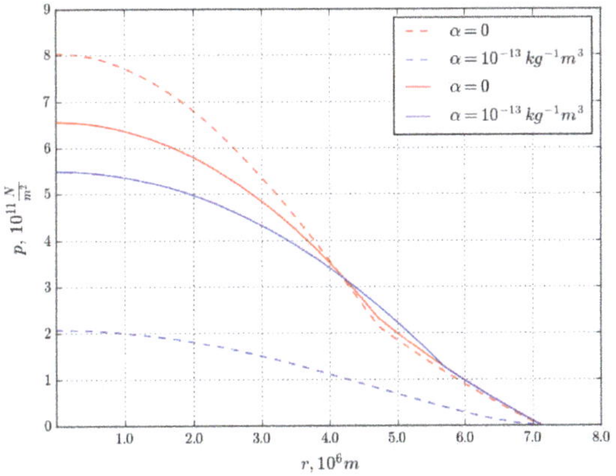


**Figure 3.** Relation between pressure and radius for Kepler-78 b exoplanet calculated analytically and numerically. The dashed line represents the numerical solution, whereas the solid line—analytical one. The curves are plotted for two different values of the parameter $\alpha = c^2\kappa^2\beta$.

## 4. Conclusions

Previous studies regarding terrestrial planets in modified gravity [22] revealed that extensions of Einstein's gravity alter the internal structure of those objects, providing a possibility to test such theories with the use of seismic data [23]. Therefore, the physical quantities, such as core pressure and energy density, as well as their boundary values between layers, should also be affected, which would have an impact on the way we model distant planets, where seismology cannot be applied. This fact forces us to look for methods allowing us to find those values, when only the observed characteristics, such as mass and radius of a transiting exoplanet, are available. In this work, we wanted to check if such methods are model-independent.

As clearly demonstrated, the methods can indeed depend on the applied theory of gravity. For this analysis, we considered quadratic modification to the general relativity's Lagrangian Equation (2), considered in the Palatini approach; however, our conclusions are valid for other theories of gravity which modify the nonrelativistic limits of their field equations.

- Density profiles, as already noticed in our previous works, can significantly differ in modified gravity with respect to the Newtonian model. We observe not only lower values of central density and on the core–mantle boundary, but also the cores of the given exoplanets are bigger; that is, the cores are less dense in the case of Palatini gravity. Therefore, the observed transiting planets can have different structure for the same masses and radii than the one predicted in the usual way, and can affect the planet's polar moment of inertia. The fact that internal structure of planets is affected by modifications of gravitational interaction is to be expected, since Equations (3) and (4), allowing one to compute the density profiles, change. This entails the fact that modifications of gravity introduce additional degeneracy when trying to determine planets internal composition by looking at the mass–radius relationship [23]. The values of internal pressure and core radius, giving the same total mass and radius, depend on the parameter $\alpha$. Therefore, this fact alone does not allow us to constrain alternative gravity models. What actually could help in distinguishing between different models would be collecting seismic data from Solar System planets, and investigating their density profiles. For example, Earth's mass and radius are well known, as well as its internal composition, so, after having developed a more realistic model taking into account modifications of gravity, it will be possible to place a stringent constraint on values of $\alpha$.
- A similar situation happens when we plot the pressure curves obtained in this work: its central values decrease in modified gravity; however, when we approach the planet's surface, the mantles do not differ much. This result derives from the fact that the additional term in Equation (15) for the pressure in the mantle is small, and smaller than the extra term appearing in the analogous equation for the core (Equation (18)).
- We also compared the numerical solutions for the pressure obtained from Equations (3) and (4) to the ones resulting from the analytical approach (which are approximated solutions). As one can see, the pressure drops roughly, similar to $-r^2$ in the core, and then changes in a linear way in the mantle in the case of both numerical and analytical solution (although it is less pronounced for larger values of the parameter $\alpha$). One notices that in the case of Newtonian gravity ($\alpha = 0$), analytical (approximated) solution tends to provide smaller values than the numerical one. However, in the case of modified gravity, the effect is the reverse—approximated analytical solution provides larger values than the numerical one. This can be explained in the following way: the analytical approximation does not take into account the effect of modification of gravity in the CMF Formula (6), so it stays constant for various values of the parameter $\alpha$ (as it depends of the mass and radius of the planet only, and these values do not change). On the other hand, the numerical method suggests that the size of the core and its mass grow in modified gravity, and hence the CMF must change. This combined effect of change in $\alpha$ and CMF/CRF results in a bigger drop in internal pressure.
- Moreover, as already mentioned in the previous point, our numerical analysis revealed that the equation for the semiempirical CMF used in that work also depends on modified gravity. This is not a surprise, remembering the fact that for finding that relation, one uses the PREM model, which is based on Newtonian gravity.

Although our studies presented in this paper are based on crude methods and assumptions, such as spherical symmetric, nonrotating planets, their two-layers structure, and constant values for the mantle's characteristics, it is evident that alternative theories of gravity do impact the planets' descriptions and modeling. Improving our analytical and numerical methods, that is, taking into account the missing ingredients mainly related to more realistic planet's geometry, should also manifest similar results. The work along these lines is currently underway.

**Author Contributions:** Conceptualization, A.W.; methodology, A.W.; software, A.K.; validation, A.W. and A.K.; formal analysis, A.W. and A.K.; writing—original draft preparation, A.W.; writing—review and editing, A.W. and A.K.; visualization, A.K.; supervision, A.W.; project administration, A.W.; funding acquisition, A.W. and A.K. All authors have read and agreed to the published version of the manuscript.

**Funding:** This work was supported by the EU through the European Regional Development Fund CoE program TK133 "The Dark Side of the Universe". A.K. is a beneficiary of the Dora Plus Program, organized by the University of Tartu.

**Institutional Review Board Statement:** Not applicable.

**Informed Consent Statement:** Not applicable.

**Data Availability Statement:** Not applicable.

**Conflicts of Interest:** The authors declare no conflict of interest.

## Notes

1. The exoplanets of Mercury's type, having cores with masses $\sim$0.7 of the total mass [14], are excluded from such an analysis.
2. For full relativistic equations in Palatini gravity, see [54,55].
3. However, we will be equipped with the Mars ones, too, thanks to the Seismic Experiment for Interior Structure from NASA's MARS InSight Mission's seismometer [67].
4. We do so in order to avoid reaching nonphysical solutions being a fact of the conformal transformation, for which there exists a singular value of $\alpha < 0$. To learn more about that feature, see [55,56].
5. But the results are similar for the other ones, too, with the more significant differences for larger planet's masses with respect to the Newtonian solutions.

## References


1. Wolszczan, A.; Frail, D.A. A planetary system around the millisecond pulsar PSR1257 + 12. *Nature* **1992**, *355*, 145–147. [CrossRef]
2. Available online: http://exoplanet.eu/catalog/ (accessed on 20 December 2021).
3. Di Stefano, R.; Berndtsson, J.; Urquhart, R.; Soria, R.; Kashyap, V.L.; Carmichael, T.W.; Imara, N. A possible planet candidate in an external galaxy detected through X-ray transit. *Nat. Astron.* **2021**, *5*, 1–11. [CrossRef]
4. Available online: https://www.nasa.gov/mission_pages/webb/about/index.html (accessed on 20 December 2021).
5. Available online: https://www.nasa.gov/feature/goddard/2021/nasa-s-roman-mission-will-probe-galaxy-s-core-for-hot-jupiters-brown-dwarfs (accessed on 20 December 2021).
6. Available online: https://heasarc.gsfc.nasa.gov/docs/tess/ (accessed on 20 December 2021).
7. Available online: https://www.spitzer.caltech.edu/ (accessed on 20 December 2021).
8. Available online: https://exoplanets.nasa.gov/exep/NNExplore/ (accessed on 20 December 2021).
9. Dziewonski, A.M.; Anderso, D.L. Preliminary reference Earth model. *Phys. Earth Plan. Int.* **1981**, *25*, 297. [CrossRef]
10. Kustowski, B.; Ekström, G.; Dziewoński, A.M. Anisotropic shear-wave velocity structure of the Earth's mantle: A global model. *J. Geophys. Res. Solid Earth* **2008**, *113*, B6. [CrossRef]
11. Kennett, B.L.N.; Engdahl, E.R. Traveltimes for global earthquake location and phase identification. *Geophys. J. Int.* **1991**, *105*, 429–465. [CrossRef]
12. Kennett, B.L.N.; Engdahl, E.R.; Buland, R. Article Navigation Constraints on seismic velocities in the Earth from traveltimes. *Geophys. J. Int.* **1995**, *122*, 108–124. [CrossRef]
13. Available online: https://ds.iris.edu/ds/products/emc-referencemodels/ (accessed on 20 December 2021).
14. Seager, S.; Kuchner, M.; Hier-Majumder, C.A.; Militzer, B. Mass-Radius Relationships for Solid Exoplanets. *Astrophys. J.* **2007**, *669*, 1279. [CrossRef]
15. Putirka, K.D.; Xu, S. Polluted white dwarfs reveal exotic mantle rock types on exoplanets in our solar neighborhood. *Nat. Commun.* **2021**, *12*, 6168. [CrossRef]
16. Butler, R.; Tsuboi, S. Antipodal seismic reflections upon shear wave velocity structures within Earth's inner core. *Phys. Earth Planet. Inter.* **2021**, *321*, 106802. [CrossRef]
17. Winter, W. *Walter, Neutrino Geophysics: Proceedings of Neutrino Sciences 2005*; Springer: New York, NY, USA, 2006; pp. 285–307.
18. Donini, A.; Palomares-Ruiz, S.; Salvado, J. Neutrino tomography of Earth. *Nat. Phys.* **2019**, *15*, 37–40. [CrossRef]
19. Bourret, S.; van Elewyck, V. Earth tomography with neutrinos in KM3NeT-ORCA. *EPJ Web Conf.* **2019**, *207*, 04008. [CrossRef]
20. van Elewyck, V.; Coelho, J.; Kaminski, E.; Maderer, L. Probing the Earth's interior with neutrinos. *Europhys. News* **2021**, *52*, 19–21. [CrossRef]

21. Merkel, S.; Hok, S.; Bolme, C.; Rittman, D.; Ramos, K.J.; Morrow, B.; Lee, H.J.; Nagler, B.; Galtier, E.; Granados, E.; et al. Femtosecond Visualization of hcp-Iron Strength and Plasticity under Shock Compression. *Phys. Rev. Lett.* **2021**, *127*, 205501. [CrossRef]
22. Kozak, A.; Wojnar, A. Non-homogeneous exoplanets in metric-affine gravity. *arXiv* **2021**, arXiv:2110.15139.
23. Kozak, A.; Wojnar, A. Metric-affine gravity effects on terrestrial exoplanet profiles. *Phys. Rev. D* **2021**, *104*, 084097. [CrossRef]
24. Wojnar, A. Jupiter and jovian exoplanets in Palatini $f(\bar{R})$ gravity. *Phys. Rev. D* **2021**, *104*, 104058. [CrossRef]
25. Olmo, G.J.; Rubiera-Garcia, D.; Wojnar, A. Stellar structure models in modified theories of gravity: Lessons and challenges. *Phys. Rep.* **2020**, *876*, 1. [CrossRef]
26. Wojnar, A. Early evolutionary tracks of low-mass stellar objects in modified gravity. *Phys. Rev. D* **2020**, *102*, 124045. [CrossRef]
27. Sakstein, J. Hydrogen Burning in Low Mass Stars Constrains Scalar-Tensor Theories of Gravity. *Phys. Rev. Lett.* **2015**, *115*, 201101. [CrossRef]
28. Olmo, G.J.; Rubiera-Garcia, D.; Wojnar, A. Minimum main sequence mass in quadratic Palatini $f(R)$ gravity. *Phys. Rev. D* **2019**, *100*, 044020. [CrossRef]
29. Wojnar, A. Lithium abundance is a gravitational model dependent quantity. *Phys. Rev. D* **2021**, *103*, 044037. [CrossRef]
30. Rosyadi, A.S.; Sulaksono, A.; Kassim, H.A.; Yusof, N. Brown dwarfs in Eddington-inspired Born-Infeld and beyond Horndeski theories. *Eur. Phys. J. C* **2019**, *79*, 1030. [CrossRef]
31. Chowdhury, S.; Sarkar, T. Modified gravity in the interior of population II stars. *J. Cosmol. Astropart. Phys.* **2021**, *2021*, 040. [CrossRef]
32. Benito, M.; Wojnar, A. Cooling process of brown dwarfs in Palatini $f(R)$ gravity. *Phys. Rev. D* **2021**, *103*, 064032. [CrossRef]
33. Copeland, E.J.; Sami, M.; Tsujikawa, S. Dynamics of dark energy. *Int. J. Mod. Phys. D* **2006**, *15*, 1753. [CrossRef]
34. Nojiri, S.; Odintsov, S.D. Introduction to Modified Gravity and Gravitational Alternative for Dark Energy. *Int. J. Geom. Meth. Mod. Phys.* **2007**, *4*, 115. [CrossRef]
35. Nojiri, S.; Odintsov, S.D.; Oikonomou, V.K. Modified Gravity Theories on a Nutshell: Inflation, Bounce and Late-time Evolution. *Phys. Rep.* **2017**, *692*, 7. [CrossRef]
36. Nojiri, S.; Odintsov, S.D. Unified Cosmic History in Modified Gravity: From $F(R)$ Theory to Lorentz Non-Invariant Models. *Phys. Rep.* **2011**, *505*, 59-144. [CrossRef]
37. Capozziello, S.; Francaviglia, M. Extended Theories of Gravity and their Cosmological and Astrophysical Applications. *Gen. Rel. Grav.* **2008**, *40*, 357. [CrossRef]
38. Carroll, S.M.; De Felice, A.; Duvvuri, V.; Easson, D.A.; Trodden, M.; Turner, M.S. Cosmology of generalized modified gravity models. *Phys. Rev. D* **2005**, *71*, 063513. [CrossRef]
39. Senovilla, J.; Garfinkle, D. The 1965 Penrose singularity theorem. *Class. Quantum Gravity* **2015**, *32*, 124008. [CrossRef]
40. Linares, M.; Shahbaz, T.; Casares, J. Peering into the dark side: Magnesium lines establish a massive neutron star in PSR J2215+5135. *Astrophys. J.* **2018**, *859*, 54. [CrossRef]
41. Antoniadis, J.; Freire, P.; Wex, N.; Tauris, T.M.; Lynch, R.S.; van Kerkwijk, M.H.; Kramer, M.; Bassa, C.; Dhillon, V.S.; Driebe, T.; et al. A Massive Pulsar in a Compact Relativistic Binary. *Science* **2012**, *340*, 6131.
42. Crawford, F.; Roberts, M.S.E.; Hessels, J.W.T.; Ransom, S.M.; Livingstone, M.; Tam, C.R.; Kaspi, V.M. A Survey of 56 Mid-latitude EGRET Error Boxes for Radio Pulsars. *Astrophys. J.* **2006**, *652*, 1499. [CrossRef]
43. Abbott, R.; Abbott, T.D.; Abraham, S.; Acernese, F.; Ackley, F.; Adams, C.; Adhikari, R.X.; Adya, V.B.; Affeldt, C.; Agathos, M. GW190814: Gravitational Waves from the Coalescence of a 23 Solar Mass Black Hole with a 2.6 Solar Mass Compact Object. *Astrophys. J.* **2020**, *896*, L44. [CrossRef]
44. Abbott, R.; Abbott, T.D.; Abraham, S.; Acernese, F.; Ackley, F.; Adams, C.; Adhikari, R.X.; Adya, V.B.; Affeldt, C.; Agathos, M.; et al. GW190521: A Binary Black Hole Merger with a Total Mass of 150 $M_{\odot}$. *Phys. Rev. Lett.* **2020**, *125*, 101102. [CrossRef]
45. Croon, D.; McDermott, S.D.; Straight, M.C.; Baxter, E.J. Beyond the Standard Model Explanations of GW190521. *Phys. Rev. Lett.* **2020**, *125*, 261105.
46. Parker, L.; Toms, D.J. *Quantum Field Theory in Curved Spacetime: Quantized Fields and Gravity*; Cambridge University Press: Cambridge, UK, 2009.
47. Birrel, N.D.; Davies, P.C.W. *Quantum Fields in Curved Space*; Cambridge University Press: Cambridge, UK, 1982.
48. Afonso, V.I.; Olmo, G.J.; Rubiera-Garcia, D. Mapping Ricci-based theories of gravity into general relativity. *Phys. Rev. D* **2018**, *97*, 021503. [CrossRef]
49. Ferraris, M.; Francaviglia, M.; Volovich, I. The Universality of Einstein Equations. *Class. Quantum Gravity* **1994**, *11*, 1505. [CrossRef]
50. Borowiec, A.; Ferraris, M.; Francaviglia, M.; Volovich, I. Universality of the Einstein equations for Ricci squared Lagrangians. *Class. Quantum Gravity* **1998**, *15*, 43. [CrossRef]
51. Sotiriou, T.P. $f(R)$ gravity and scalar–tensor theory. *Class. Quantum Gravity* **2006**, *23*, 5117. [CrossRef]
52. Toniato, J.D.; Rodrigues, D.C.; Wojnar, A. Palatini $f(R)$ gravity in the solar system: Post-Newtonian equations of motion and complete PPN parameters. *Phys. Rev. D* **2020**, *101*, 064050. [CrossRef]
53. Olmo, G.; Rubiera-Garcia, D.; Wojnar, A. Parameterized nonrelativistic limit of stellar structure equations in Ricci-based gravity theories. *Phys. Rev. D* **2021**, *104*, 024045. [CrossRef]
54. Wojnar, A. On stability of a neutron star system in Palatini gravity. *Eur. Phys. J. C* **2018**, *78*, 421. [CrossRef]
55. Kozak, A.; Wojnar, A. Invariant quantities of scalar–tensor theories for stellar structure. *Eur. Phys. J. C* **2021**, *81*, 492. [CrossRef]

6. Wojnar, A. Polytropic stars in Palatini gravity. *Eur. Phys. J. C* **2019**, *79*, 51. [CrossRef]
7. Mana, A.; Fatibene, L.; Ferraris, M. Extended Cosmology in Palatini f(R)-theories. *J. Cosmol. Astropart. Phys.* **2015**, *2015*, 040. [CrossRef]
8. Birch, F. Finite Elastic Strain of Cubic Crystals. *Phys. Rev.* **1947**, *71*, 809. [CrossRef]
9. Poirier, J.-P. *Introduction to the Physics of the Earth's Interior*; Cambridge University Press (Virtual Publishing): Cambridge, UK, 2000.
0. Thomas, L.H. The calculation of atomic fields. *Proc. Cam. Phil. Soc.* **1927**, *23*, 542. [CrossRef]
1. Fermi, E. Eine statistische Methode zur Bestimmung einiger Eigenschaften des Atoms und ihre Anwendung auf die Theorie des periodischen Systems der Elemente. *Z. Phys.* **1928**, *48*, 73. [CrossRef]
2. Dirac, P.A.M. Note on Exchange Phenomena in the Thomas Atom. *Proc. Cam. Phil. Soc.* **1930**, *26*, 376. [CrossRef]
3. Feynman, R.P.; Metropolis, S.; Teller, E. Equations of State of Elements Based on the Generalized Fermi-Thomas Theory. *Phys. Rev.* **1949**, *75*, 1561. [CrossRef]
4. Salpeter, E.E.; Zapolsky, H.S. Theoretical High-Pressure Equations of State including Correlation Energy. *Phys. Rev.* **1967**, *158*, 876. [CrossRef]
5. Zeng, L.; Jacobsen, S.B. A Simple Analytical Model for Rocky Planet Interiors. *Astrophys. J.* **2017**, *837*, 164. [CrossRef]
6. Available online: https://exoplanets.nasa.gov/ (accessed on 20 December 2021).
7. Available online: https://mars.nasa.gov/insight/spacecraft/instruments/seis/ (accessed on 20 December 2021).
8. Zeng, L.; Sasselov, D.D.; Jacobsen, S.B. Mass-Radius Relation for Rocky Planets based on PREM. *Astrophys. J.* **2016**, *819*, 127. [CrossRef]
9. Masó-Ferrando, A.; Sanchis-Gual, N.; Font, J.A.; Olmo, G.J. Boson stars in Palatini $f(\mathcal{R})$ gravity. *Class. Quan. Grav.* **2021**, *38*, 194003. [CrossRef]
0. Beltrán Jiménez, J.; Heisenberg, L.; Olmo, G.J.; Rubiera-Garcia, D. Born-Infeld inspired modifications of gravity. *Phys. Rep.* **2018**, *727*, 1–129. [CrossRef]

universe

MDPI

*Article*

# On Maxwell Electrodynamics in Multi-Dimensional Spaces

Alexei M. Frolov

Department of Applied Mathematics, University of Western Ontario, London, ON N6H 5B7, Canada;
alex1975frol@gmail.com

**Abstract:** The governing equations of Maxwell electrodynamics in multi-dimensional spaces are derived from the variational principle of least action, which is applied to the action function of the electromagnetic field. The Hamiltonian approach for the electromagnetic field in multi-dimensional pseudo-Euclidean (flat) spaces has also been developed and investigated. Based on the two arising first-class constraints, we have generalized to multi-dimensional spaces a number of different gauges known for the three-dimensional electromagnetic field. For multi-dimensional spaces of non-zero curvature the governing equations for the multi-dimensional electromagnetic field are written in a manifestly covariant form. Multi-dimensional Einstein's equations of metric gravity in the presence of an electromagnetic field have been re-written in the true tensor form. Methods of scalar electrodynamics are applied to analyze Maxwell equations in the two and one-dimensional spaces.

**Keywords:** electromagnetic; covariant; field; constraints; curved space

**Citation:** Frolov, A.M. On Maxwell Electrodynamics in Multi-Dimensional Spaces. *Universe* **2022**, *8*, 20. https://doi.org/10.3390/universe8010020

Academic Editors: Panayiotis Stavrinos, Emmanuel N. Saridakis and Xue-Mei Deng

Received: 22 November 2021
Accepted: 24 December 2021
Published: 30 December 2021



## 1. Introduction

The main goal of this communication is to develop the logically closed and non-contradictory version of electrodynamics in the multi-dimensional (or $n$-dimensional) space. Right now, such a development can be considered as a pure theoretical (or model) task, but originally, our plan was to include the multi-dimensional electromagnetic fields in our Hamiltonian analysis of the metric gravity [1]. Note that all Hamiltonian approaches that are based on the $\Gamma - \Gamma$ Lagrangian (see, e.g., [1] and earlier references therein) have been derived in the manifestly covariant form and can be applied to multi-dimensional (or $n$-dimensional, where $n$ ($\geq$3) is an arbitrary integer) Riemannian spaces without any modification. On the other hand, our current Maxwell theory of electromagnetic fields and corresponding Hamiltonian approach can be used only for three-dimensional (geometrical) spaces. This contradiction creates numerous problems for the development of any united theory of the coupled electromagnetic and gravitational fields. Furthermore, it is hard to believe that in reality one can smoothly combine two theories that have different properties with respect to their extensions on multi-dimensional spaces.

After our investigations began, it did not take long to understand that such a theory of the free electromagnetic fields in multi-dimensions simply does not exist even in the first-order approximation (in contrast with metric gravity). There are quite a few reasons why a similar generalization of the classical electrodynamics to multi-dimensional spaces has not been developed earlier. For instance, the explicit expression for the action integral and therefore for the Lagrangian of the electromagnetic field in multi-dimensions is unknown. However, if we do not know the Lagrangian of the multi-dimensional electromagnetic field, then it is impossible to construct any valuable Hamiltonian. There have been a number of smaller problems which have substantially complicated any direct generalization of Maxwell theory to $n$-dimensional spaces. One of them is the lack of a reliable and practically valuable definition of a *curl*−operator (or *rot*-operator) in multi-dimensional spaces, where $n \geq 4$. In general, it is difficult to develop multi-dimensional electrodynamics without such an operator. Finally, we have decided to investigate this problem and derive some useful results which are of great interest for the Hamiltonian formulation of the metric gravity combined with electromagnetic field(s) in multi-dimensional spaces.

First, let us briefly discuss the classical Maxwell equations known for the three-dimensional electromagnetic fields. The Maxwell equations were first written by J.C. Maxwell in 1862 (published in 1865 [2] (see also [3,4])) for the intensities of electric **E** and magnetic **H** fields (or for the electric and magnetic field strengths):

$$\begin{aligned} div\mathbf{E} &= 4\pi\rho,\ curl\mathbf{E} = -\frac{1}{c}\frac{\partial\mathbf{H}}{\partial t}, \\ div\mathbf{H} &= 0,\ curl\mathbf{H} = \frac{1}{c}\frac{\partial\mathbf{E}}{\partial t} + \frac{4\pi}{c}\mathbf{j}, \end{aligned} \tag{1}$$

where $\rho$ and $\mathbf{j} = \rho\mathbf{v}$ are the electric charge density (scalar) and electric current density (vector), respectively. In this study, the charge density and current are defined exactly as in \$ 29 from [5]. Later, it was noticed by Hertz and others that these four equations from Equation (1) can be re-written in a simple form if we can introduce the four-dimensional potential $\bar{A} = (\varphi, \mathbf{A})$, where $\varphi$ is the scalar potential and $\mathbf{A}$ is the vector potential of the electromagnetic field. Note that the scalar potential $\varphi$ can equally be considered as the 0-component ($A_0$) of the four-dimensional vector potential $\bar{A}$ of the electromagnetic field. The $\varphi$ and $\mathbf{A}$ potentials are simply related to the intensities of electric **E** and magnetic **H** fields: $\mathbf{H} = curl\mathbf{A}$ and $\mathbf{E} = -\frac{\partial\mathbf{A}}{\partial t} - grad\varphi$. By using these relations between the potentials $(\varphi, \mathbf{A})$ and intensities $(\mathbf{E}, \mathbf{H})$ of electromagnetic field, one finds that the second equation in the first line and first equation in the second line of Equation (1) hold identically. The two remaining equations from Equation (1) lead to the following non-homogeneous equations:

$$\frac{1}{c^2}\frac{\partial^2\mathbf{A}}{\partial t^2} - \Delta\mathbf{A} + grad\Big(div\mathbf{A} + \frac{1}{c}\frac{\partial\varphi}{\partial t}\Big) = \frac{4\pi}{c}\mathbf{j} \tag{2}$$

$$-\quad \Delta\varphi - \frac{1}{c}div\Big(\frac{\partial\mathbf{A}}{\partial t}\Big) = 4\pi\rho \tag{3}$$

where $\Delta = \frac{\partial^2}{\partial x^2} + \frac{\partial^2}{\partial y^2} + \frac{\partial^2}{\partial z^2}$ is the three-dimensional Laplace operator. By applying the "gauge condition" $\frac{\partial\varphi}{\partial t} + div\mathbf{A} = 0$ for the four-dimensional potential, one reduces the two last equations to the form

$$\frac{1}{c^2}\frac{\partial^2\mathbf{A}}{\partial t^2} - \Delta\mathbf{A} = \frac{4\pi}{c}\rho\mathbf{v}, \tag{4}$$

$$\frac{1}{c^2}\frac{\partial^2\varphi}{\partial t^2} - \Delta\varphi = 4\pi\rho, \tag{5}$$

where the operator $\frac{1}{c^2}\frac{\partial^2}{\partial t^2} - \Delta$ is the four-dimensional Laplace operator in pseudo-Euclidean space, which is often called the d'Alembertian operator.

It is interesting that all equations mentioned above can be derived by varying the action functional $S$ which is written for a system of particles and electromagnetic fields interacting with these particles. In Gauss units, the explicit form of this action function (or action, for short) $S$ is

$$S = S_p + S_{fp} + S_f = -\sum_k \int m_k c ds_k - \sum_k \int \frac{e_k}{c} A_\alpha(k) dx^\alpha - \frac{1}{16\pi}\int F_{\alpha\beta}F^{\alpha\beta} d\Omega, \tag{6}$$

where the two sums are taken over particles, $s = \sqrt{x_\mu x^\mu} = \sqrt{g_{\mu\nu} x^\mu x^\mu}$ is the interval, $S_p$ is the action for the particles ($k = 1, 2, \ldots$), and $S_{fp}$ is the action which describes the interaction between particles and electromagnetic field, while $S_f$ is the action for the electromagnetic field itself. The notation $e_k$ stands for the electric charge of the $k$-th particle, while $m_k$ means the mass of the same particle, and $A_\alpha$ is the covariant component of the four-dimensional vector potential $\bar{A}$ of the electromagnetic field. This formula, Equation (6), is written for the four-dimensional pseudo-Euclidean (flat) space-time. This fact drastically simplifies the analysis and derivation of the Maxwell and other equations in classical three-dimensional electrodynamics.

In this study, we discuss a possibility to generalize the usual (or three-dimensional) Maxwell equations to spaces of larger dimensions. In respect to this, below, we shall consider $n$-dimensional, pure geometrical spaces and $(n+1)$-dimensional space-time manifolds. Our main goal is to derive the correct form of multi-dimensional Maxwell equations and investigate their basic properties. In particular, we want to understand how many and what kind of changes we can expect in the multi-dimensional Hamiltonian of the free electromagnetic field and in a number of arising first-class constraints. A separate but closely related problem is the gauge invariance of the free electromagnetic field. Another interesting problem is to investigate the explicit form of multi-dimensional Maxwell equations in the presence of multi-dimensional gravitational fields. A brief discussion of scalar electrodynamics can be found in Appendix A. All new results obtained in the course of our current analysis will be used later to develop the modern united theory of electromagnetic and gravitational fields.

## 2. Scalar and Vector Potentials of the Electromagnetic Field

Let us derive the closed system of Maxwell equations for the $n$-dimensional (geometrical) space, where $n \geq 3$. The time $t$ is always considered as an independent scalar and special $(n+1)$-st variable. This means that we are dealing with manifolds of variables defined in $(n+1)$-dimensional space-time. First, we need to define the vector potential $\bar{A}$ in this $(n+1)$-dimensional space-time. Based on experimental facts known for actual electromagnetic systems considered in one, two, and three dimensions, below, we assume that the interaction of a point particle with the electromagnetic field is determined by a single, scalar parameter $e$, which is the electric charge of this particle. The parameter $e$ can be positive, negative, or equal to zero. The properties of the electromagnetic field are described by the $(n+1)$-dimensional vector potential $\bar{A}$. The notation $A_\mu$ (or $\bar{A}_\mu$) stands for the covariant $\mu-$component of this $(n+1)$-dimensional vector potential $\bar{A}$. In this study, we also deal with the $n$-dimensional space-like vector potential $\mathbf{A}$. Co- and contravariant components of this vector are designated by Latin indexes; e.g., $A_k$ and $A^k$, where $k = 1, 2, \ldots, n$. The same rule is applied to all vectors and tensors mentioned in this study: components of $(n+1)$-vectors are labeled by Greek indices (each of which varies between 0 and $n$), while spatial components of these $n$-dimensional vectors (each varying between 1 and $n$) are denoted by Latin indices. The generalization of this rule to the tensors of arbitrary ranks is straightforward and simple. Note also that in all formulas below, the following "summation rule" is applied: a repeated suffix (or index) in any formula means summations over all values of this suffix (or index).

In general, the vector potential $\bar{A}$ can be written in the form $\bar{A} = (\varphi, \mathbf{A})$, which includes the scalar potential $\varphi(= A_0)$ and $n$-dimensional vector potential $\mathbf{A} = (A_1, A_2, \ldots, A_n)$. For arbitrary scalar $\Phi$ and vector $\mathbf{V}$ functions in $n$-dimensional space, we can determine the first-order differential operators: the (a) gradient operator $\nabla$ (or *grad*) and (b) divergence operator *div*. They are defined as follows:

$$\nabla\Phi = grad\ \Phi = \Big(\frac{\partial\Phi}{\partial x_1}, \frac{\partial\Phi}{\partial x_2}, \ldots, \frac{\partial\Phi}{\partial x_n}\Big) \text{ and } div\ \mathbf{V} = \frac{\partial V_1}{\partial x_1} + \frac{\partial V_2}{\partial x_2} + \ldots + \frac{\partial V_n}{\partial x_1} \quad (7)$$

Analogous definitions of these two operators can easily be generalized and applied to the scalar and vector functions defined in $(n+1)$-dimensional space. By using these definitions, we can discuss the gradient of the scalar potential $\nabla\varphi(= \nabla A_0)$ (vector) and divergence of vector potential $div\mathbf{A}$ (scalar) in the $n$-dimensional space.

The $(n+1)$-dimensional vector potential $\bar{A} = (A_0, A_1, \ldots, A_n)$ allows us to define the truly antisymmetric $(n+1) \times (n+1)$ electromagnetic field tensor $F_{\alpha\beta}(= -F_{\beta\alpha})$ by using the relation

$$F_{\alpha\beta} = \frac{\partial A_\beta}{\partial x^\alpha} - \frac{\partial A_\alpha}{\partial x^\beta} = -F_{\beta\alpha}, \text{ and } F^{\alpha\beta} = \frac{\partial A^\beta}{\partial x_\alpha} - \frac{\partial A^\alpha}{\partial x_\beta} = -F^{\beta\alpha}, \tag{8}$$

which formally coincides with the analogous definition of this tensor known in the four-dimensional space-time. For the $(n+1)$-dimensional space-time manifold, this tensor has zero-diagonal matrix elements (or components); i.e., $F_{\alpha\alpha} = 0$. Therefore, in $n$-dimensional space, each of the antisymmetric $F^{\alpha\beta}$ and $F_{\alpha\beta}$ tensors have $\frac{n(n-1)}{2}$ different and independent components. The double sum $F_{\alpha\beta}F^{\alpha\beta}$ is the first (or main) invariant of the electromagnetic field defined in the $(n+1)$-dimensional space. Now, let us write the following explicit formula for the action $S$ for the system, which includes the particles and electromagnetic field itself. This action takes the following form (see, e.g., [5]):

$$S = S_p + S_{fp} + S_f = -\sum_k \int m_k c ds - \sum_k \int \frac{e_k}{c} A_\alpha(k) dx^\alpha - a \int F_{\alpha\beta}F^{\alpha\beta} d\Omega, \tag{9}$$

where $s = \sqrt{x_\mu x^\mu} = \sqrt{g_{\mu\nu}x^\mu x^\mu}$ is the interval, $S_p$ is the action function for the particles, $S_{fp}$ is the action function which describes the interaction between particles and the electromagnetic field, and $S_f$ is the action function for the electromagnetic field itself. In this equation, the summation is performed over all particles (index $k$). The notation $A_\alpha(k)$ shows that the $\alpha-$component of the vector potential must be determined at the point of location of $k-$th particle. Note that the formula, Equation (9), is applicable in the flat pseudo-Euclidean and/or Euclidean spaces only. Its generalization to multi-dimensional Riemannian spaces (spaces of non-zero curvature) is considered below. In the next step, we need to determine the constant $a$ in Equation (9). This can be achieved by considering Coulomb's law in multi-dimensions (see the next section).

As a conclusion of this section, we want to emphasize the fact that our action function, which is chosen in the form of Equation (9), allows one to derive the equations of motion for a system of electrically charged, point particles which move in the electromagnetic field. For instance, for one electrically charged particle, by varying the coordinates of this particle (i.e., the $x^\mu$ and $x^\alpha$ variables) in the action function, Equation (9), one finds the following equation of motion for one electrically charged, point particle which moves in the non-flat multi-dimensional space:

$$\frac{d^2x^\alpha}{ds^2} + \Gamma^\alpha_{\beta\gamma}\frac{dx^\beta}{ds}\frac{dx^\gamma}{ds} - \frac{e}{c}F^{\alpha\beta}g_{\beta\gamma}\frac{dx^\gamma}{ds} = 0, \text{ or } \frac{d^2x^\alpha}{ds^2} + \Gamma^\alpha_{\beta\gamma}\frac{dx^\beta}{ds}\frac{dx^\gamma}{ds} - \frac{e}{mc^2}F^\alpha_\beta\frac{dx^\beta}{ds} = 0, \tag{10}$$

where $\Gamma^\alpha_{\beta\gamma}$ are the Cristoffel symbols of the second kind [6,7] which equal zero identically in any flat space. It is clear that the last term in the action function $S$ is not varied, and we do not know the exact numerical value of the constant $a$ in Equation (9). In addition, for the non-flat spaces, in the last term, we have to replace $d\Omega \rightarrow \sqrt{-g}d\Omega$.

## 3. Coulomb's Law in Multi-Dimensions

The explicit form of the Coulomb interaction between two point, electrically charged particles is of crucial importance for our present purposes. In Gauss units, which are used almost everywhere in this study, the Coulomb's law for three-dimensional space has a very simple form: $V(r_{21}) = \frac{q_1q_2}{r_{21}}$, where $V(r_{21})$ is the Coulomb potential, $q_1$ and $q_2$ are the electric charges of the two point particles (1 and 2), and $r_{21}$ is the interparticle distance, which equals $r = \sqrt{(x_2-x_1)^2 + (y_2-y_1)^2 + (z_2-z_1)^2}$, where $(x_1, y_1, z_1)$ and $(x_2, y_2, z_2)$ are the Cartesian coordinates of the two interacting particles. Note that the Coulomb interaction potential does not contain the factor $4\pi$. Furthermore, the Coulomb potential essentially coincides with the singular part of the Green's function for the three-dimensional Laplace operator; i.e., $V(r_{21}) = q_1q_2G(\mathbf{r}_1, \mathbf{r}_2) = q_1q_2G(|\ \mathbf{r}_1 - \mathbf{r}_2\ |) = \frac{q_1q_2}{|\mathbf{r}_2-\mathbf{r}_1|}$ and $\Delta\left(\frac{1}{|\mathbf{r}_2-\mathbf{r}_1|}\right) = \nabla^2\left(\frac{1}{|\mathbf{r}_2-\mathbf{r}_1|}\right) = \nabla\left(\frac{\mathbf{r}_1-\mathbf{r}_2}{|\mathbf{r}_2-\mathbf{r}_1|^3}\right) = -4\pi\delta(\mathbf{r}_2 - \mathbf{r}_1)$. The last equation can also be re-written for the intensity of electric field **E**, which is the negative gradient of the potential $\varphi$. This equation takes the familiar form $div\mathbf{E} = -\nabla\left[\left(\frac{q_1q_2}{r_21}\right)\right] = q_1q_2\nabla\left(\frac{\mathbf{r}_{21}}{r_{21}^3}\right) = 4\pi\rho(\mathbf{r}_{21})$, where $\rho(\mathbf{x})$ is a continuous charge density. The derived expression coincides with the well-known differential form of Gauss's law of electrostatic and one of the Maxwell equations. These two properties (or two criteria) of three-dimensional Coulomb potential plays a crucial role in our definition of the multi-dimensional Coulomb potential (see below).

Now, we need to define the Coulomb potential in multi-dimensional (or $n$-dimensional) space. This is a crucial moment for the Maxwell electrodynamics in multi-dimensional spaces which we try to develop in this study. Any mistake in such a definition will cost too much for our present purposes. In this sense, this section was the most difficult part of our analysis and it was re-written quite a few times. Indeed, we cannot send someone to the four-dimensional (geometrical) space to repeat the well known Coulomb and Cavendish experiments; therefore, we need to find a way to make an analytical generalization of the Coulomb potential to multi-dimensional spaces. In respect to our first criterion formulated above, the Coulomb potential in the $n$-dimensional space must coincide with the singular part of the Green's function defined for the multi-dimensional (or $n$-dimensional) Laplace operator $\Delta = \Delta_n = \frac{\partial^2}{\partial x_1^2} + \frac{\partial^2}{\partial x_2^2} + \ldots + \frac{\partial^2}{\partial x_n^2}$. This leads [8] to the following general expression for the Coulomb potential in $n$-dimensional space: $V(r) = b\frac{q_1q_2}{r_{21}^{n-2}} = b\frac{q_1q_2}{r^{n-2}}$, where $b$ is some numerical factor, $n \geq 3$, and the explicit expression for the interparticle distance $r_{21} = r$ takes the multi-dimensional form $r = \sqrt{[x_2^{(1)} - x_1^{(1)}]^2 + [x_2^{(2)} - x_1^{(2)}]^2 + \ldots + [x_2^{(n)} - x_1^{(n)}]^2}$. Here $(x_1^{(1)}, x_1^{(2)}, \ldots, x_1^{(n)})$ and $(x_2^{(1)}, x_2^{(2)}, \ldots, x_2^{(n)})$ are the Cartesian coordinates of the two interacting particles in $n$-dimensional Euclidean space. The $n$-dimensional radius $r = \sqrt{[x^{(1)}]^2 + [x^{(2)}]^2 + \ldots + [x^{(n)}]^2}$ is, in fact, the hyper-radius of this point particle. To derive the explicit formula for the Coulomb potential in $n$-dimensional space, we have applied the method developed by A. Sokolov (see, e.g., [8,9] and earlier references therein) which allows one to determine the Green's functions for an arbitrary linear differential operator.

In order to determine the factor $b(n)$, we apply the second criterion (see above), which states that Gauss's law must be written in the form $\nabla\mathbf{E} = f(n)q_1q_2$, where $f(n)$ is a pure angular (or hyper-angular for $n \geq 4$) factor. From here, one finds that $b = \frac{1}{n-2}$ and the explicit formula for Coulomb's law in $n$-dimensional space takes the final form $V(r) = \frac{q_1q_2}{(n-2)r_{21}^{n-2}}$. Now, let us consider a slightly different problem. Suppose that we have to determine the static multi-dimensional Coulomb potential $\varphi(r)$ and the corresponding intensity of electric field **E**, which are generated by a point particle with the electric charge $Q$. For this problem, we write the following formulas for the potential $\varphi$ and for the field strength **E**: $\varphi = \frac{Q}{(n-2)r^{n-2}}$ and $\mathbf{E} = -\nabla\varphi = \frac{Q\mathbf{n}_r}{r^{n-1}}$, where $\mathbf{n}_r$ is the unit vector $\mathbf{n}_r = \frac{\mathbf{r}}{r}$ which is directed from the electric charge $Q$ to an observation point. To write Gauss's law in multi-dimensional space, let us assume that a point electrical charge $Q$ is located inside (and outside) of a closed $(n-1)$ dimensional hyper-surface. In this case, $r$ is the distance from the charge to a point on the hyper-surface, **n** is outwardly directed normal $\mathbf{n} = \frac{\mathbf{r}}{r}$ to the surface at that point, and $da$ is the element of the surface area. Then, for the normal component of **E** times the area element, we can write

$$(\mathbf{E} \cdot \mathbf{n})da = Q\ \frac{cos\Theta}{r^{n-1}}\ da = Q\ \frac{r^{n-1}d\Omega}{r^{n-1}} = Qd\Omega, \tag{11}$$

where $d\Omega$ is the element of the solid hyper-angle (in $n$-dimensional space) subtended by $da$ at the position of the charge. It is important here that the **E** is directed along the line from the hyper-surface element to the charge $Q$. This means that we have found no contradiction here between out two criteria and and Equation (11), since the following hyper-angular integration over $\Omega$ produces only an additional pure hyper-angular factor $f(n)$.

Now, by integrating the normal component of $\mathbf{E}$ over the whole hyper-surface, it is easy to find that

$$\oint(\mathbf{E}\cdot\mathbf{n})da = Q\oint d\Omega = Q\;\frac{n\pi^{\left(\frac{n}{2}\right)}}{\Gamma\left(1+\frac{n}{2}\right)} = f(n)Q, \tag{12}$$

where $f(n) = \frac{n\pi^{\left(\frac{n}{2}\right)}}{\Gamma\left(1+\frac{n}{2}\right)}$ is the geometrical (or hyper-angular) factor. In this equation, the symbol $\Gamma(x)$ stands for the Euler's gamma function (or Euler's integral of the second kind). It can be shown (see, e.g., [10]) that $\Gamma(1+x) = x\Gamma(x)$ and $\Gamma\left(\frac{1}{2}\right) = \sqrt{\pi}$. The formula, Equation (12), is true if the charge $Q$ lies inside of the $n$-dimensional hyper-surface. However, if this charge lies outside of this hyper-surface, the expression on the right-hand side of Equation (12) equals zero identically. Thus, we have reproduced Gauss's law in multi-dimensional spaces for a single point charge $Q$. For a discrete set of point charges and for a continuous charge density $\rho(\mathbf{r})$, Gauss's law becomes

$$\oint(\mathbf{E}\cdot\mathbf{n})da = \frac{n\pi^{\left(\frac{n}{2}\right)}}{\Gamma\left(1+\frac{n}{2}\right)}\;\sum_{k=1}^{K}Q_k\; = f(n)\;\sum_{k=1}^{K}Q_k \tag{13}$$

and

$$\oint(\mathbf{E}\cdot\mathbf{n})da = \frac{n\pi^{\left(\frac{n}{2}\right)}}{\Gamma\left(1+\frac{n}{2}\right)}\;\int_V\rho(\mathbf{r})d^n\mathbf{r}\; = f(n)\;\int_V\rho(\mathbf{r})d^n\mathbf{r} \tag{14}$$

respectively. In Equation (13), the sum is over only those charges inside of the hyper-surface $S$, while in Equation (14), the sum is over the volume (or hyper-volume) enclosed by $S$.

The differential form of these equations in $n$-dimensional Euclidean space is

$$div\mathbf{E} = -div\left(grad\;\varphi\right) = -\Delta\varphi = \frac{n\pi^{\left(\frac{n}{2}\right)}}{\Gamma\left(1+\frac{n}{2}\right)}\rho(\mathbf{r}) = f(n)\rho(\mathbf{r}), \tag{15}$$

where $f(n) = \frac{n\pi^{\left(\frac{n}{2}\right)}}{\Gamma\left(1+\frac{n}{2}\right)}$ is the geometrical (or hyper-angular) factor, which is the volume $V_n$ of the $n$-dimensional unit ball times the dimension $n$ of geometrical space. In other words, the factor $f(n)$ is the surface area $S_n$ of the $n$-dimensional unit ball, since the equality $S_n = nV_n$ is always obeyed for the $n$-dimensional unit ball [11] and $n$ is an integer positive number. The physical sense of this factor $f(n)$ is simple: it is the total hyper-angle defined for a single point (central) particle located in the $n$-dimensional space. For a system of a few discrete charges, one has to replace $\rho(\mathbf{r}) \rightarrow \sum_{k=1}^{K} Q_k$, etc.

The $n$-dimensional hyper-angular factor $f(n)$ from Equation (12) plays a central role in our development of Maxwell electrodynamics in multi-dimensional spaces. In particular, the knowledge of this factor allows one to write the explicit formula for the action function (or action integral) of the electrically charged particles that move in the multi-dimensional (or $n$-dimensional) electromagnetic field. This problem is considered below.

## 4. Action Function and Maxwell Equations in Multi-Dimensional Flat Spaces

In this section, we consider Maxwell's equation in multi-dimensional flat spaces; e.g., in pseudo-Euclidean spaces. The results derived below are extensively used in the following sections of this study. First of all, by using the factor $f(n)$ obtained in Equation (12), we can write the final expression for the action function $S$ in Gauss units:

$$S = S_p + S_{fp} + S_f = -\sum_k \int m_k c ds - \frac{1}{c^2} \int A_\alpha j^\alpha dx^\alpha - \frac{1}{4cf(n)} \int F_{\alpha\beta} F^{\alpha\beta} d\Omega, \tag{16}$$

where $\frac{1}{4}$ (or $-\frac{1}{4}$) is the Heaviside constant, $c$ is the speed of light in a vacuum, while $j^\alpha$ is the electric current (or simply, current) in $(n+1)$-dimensional space. By varying all components of the $\bar{A}$ vector in this action integral, Equation (16), we derive the second group of Maxwell's equations, Equation (19), which contains, in the general case, the non-homogeneous differential equations. By omitting some obvious details, we can write the complete set of Maxwell's equations in the following tensor form:

$$\frac{\partial F_{\gamma\lambda}}{\partial x^\beta} + \frac{\partial F_{\lambda\beta}}{\partial x^\gamma} + \frac{\partial F_{\beta\gamma}}{\partial x^\lambda} = 0 \tag{17}$$

and

$$\frac{\partial F^{\alpha\beta}}{\partial x^\beta} = -\frac{n\pi^{\left(\frac{n}{2}\right)}}{c\Gamma\left(1+\frac{n}{2}\right)} j^\alpha = -\frac{f(n)}{c} j^\alpha, \tag{18}$$

where $j^\alpha$ is the $(n+1)$-dimensional current-vector (or current, for short) defined above. All equations from the both groups of these equations, Equations (17)–(19), are the first-order differential equations upon spatial coordinates and time $t$ (or temporal coordinate). From Equation (17) one finds the following condition for the current:

$$\frac{\partial^2 F^{\alpha\beta}}{\partial x^\alpha \partial x^\beta} = -\frac{f(n)}{c} \frac{\partial j^\alpha}{\partial x^\alpha} = 0\,. \tag{19}$$

This result is obvious, since the application of any symmetric operator (upon $\alpha \leftrightarrow \beta$ permutation)—e.g., the $\frac{\partial^2}{\partial x^\alpha \partial x^\beta}$ operator—to the truly antisymmetric $F^{\alpha\beta}$ tensor always gives zero. Thus, the equality $\frac{\partial j^\alpha}{\partial x^\alpha} = 0$ derived here is a necessary condition for any actual electric current. Note also that this equation is written in the form of $(n+1)$-dimensional divergence. In respect to Noether's second theorem, this equation $\frac{\partial j^\alpha}{\partial x^\alpha} = 0$ means some conservation law. It is easy to understand that this law describes the conservation of the total electric charge.

A very close similarity between the Maxwell equations derived for multi-dimensional spaces, where $n \geq 3$, and analogous Maxwell equations known in three-dimensional space is obvious. However, in some cases, this leads to fundamental mistakes, and most of such mistakes originate from Equation (17). Note here that in $n$-dimensional geometrical space, we have exactly $n$ components of the intensity of electric field **E** and $\frac{n(n+1)}{2}$ intensities of magnetic field **H**. For $n = 3$ (and only in this case), we have equal numbers of components in both **E** and **H** vectors. This leads to the well-known vector form of Maxwell electrodynamics. However, even for $n = 4$, the electric field has four components, while the magnetic field has six components. When $n$ increases, then the total number of components of the magnetic field grows rapidly (quadratically) and significantly exceeds the analogous number of components of the electric field. This fact substantially complicates the derivation of Maxwell equations written in terms of the intensities of electric and magnetic fields in multi-dimensional spaces. Plus, we have a certain problem with the general definition of the *curl* (or *rot*) operator in such cases.

Another interesting result follows from the analysis of tensor equations, Equation (17) If one of the indexes in this equation equals zero, then this group of equations gives us Faraday's law in multi-dimensional space, which describes the time-evolution of the magnetic field and is written in the form of $n$ equations. This is good, but what about other $\frac{n(n-1)(n-2)}{6}$ equations that are also included in tensor equations Equation (17)? After some transformations, one finds that these additional equations are written in a form whereby three-dimensional divergences of some three-dimensional pure-magnetic vectors equal zero By pure magnetic vectors, we mean vectors assembled from the space-like components of the field tensor $F^{pq}$ (or $F_{pq}$) only (for flat spaces, it is always possible). Based on ideas by Dirac [12], we can formulate this result in the following form: *the magnetic field can have sources neither in our three-dimensional space nor in any three-dimensional subspace of multi-dimensional spaces*. This fundamental statement is directly and very closely related to the discrete nature of electric charge. Furthermore, the correctness of Maxwell electrodynamics (in any space) is essentially based on this statement. By taking into account arguments from [13], we can re-formulate our statement in the followingform: *the existence of magnetic monopoles in our three-dimensional space and, in general, in any three-dimensional subspace of multi-dimensional spaces is strictly prohibited*. Otherwise, the Maxwell electrodynamics will not be correct and must be replaced by a different approach.

To conclude this section, let us present the explicit formula for the energy momentum tensor in multi-dimensional space. The definition of this tensor and all details of its calculations are well described in [5]. Therefore, we can only present a few basic formulas here, which will be used below in Section 6. The explicit formula for the non-symmetrized energy momentum tensor is

$$T_{\alpha}^{\beta} = \frac{1}{f(n)}\Big(\frac{\partial A_{\gamma}}{\partial x_{\alpha}} F^{\gamma\beta} + \frac{1}{4} g_{\alpha}^{\beta} F_{\gamma\rho} F^{\gamma\rho}\Big), \tag{20}$$

where the factor $f(n)$ is the hyper-angular (or geometrical) factor mentioned above. After symmetrization, this tensor takes the form

$$T_{\alpha}^{\beta} = \frac{1}{f(n)}\Big(F_{\alpha\gamma} F^{\beta\gamma} + \frac{1}{4} g_{\alpha}^{\beta} F_{\gamma\rho} F^{\gamma\rho}\Big), \tag{21}$$

where $g_{\alpha}^{\beta} = \delta_{\alpha}^{\beta}$ is the substitution tensor [6]. The corresponding co- and contravariant tensors are

$$T_{\alpha\beta} = \frac{1}{f(n)}\Big(F_{\alpha\gamma} F_{\beta}^{\gamma} + \frac{1}{4} g_{\alpha\beta} F_{\gamma\rho} F^{\gamma\rho}\Big) \quad \text{and} \quad T^{\alpha\beta} = \frac{1}{f(n)}\Big(g_{\gamma}^{\alpha} F_{\beta\gamma} F^{\beta\gamma} + \frac{1}{4} g^{\alpha\beta} F_{\gamma\rho} F^{\gamma\rho}\Big), \tag{22}$$

where $f(n) = \frac{n\pi^{\frac{n}{2}}}{\Gamma\left(1+\frac{n}{2}\right)}$ is the geometrical (or hyper-angular) factor.

## 5. Hamiltonian of the Electromagnetic Field in Multi-Dimensional Flat Spaces

The second goal of this study is to develop the Hamiltonian formulation of the multi-dimensional electrodynamics. First, let us obtain the explicit formula for the Hamiltonian $H$ of the free electromagnetic field in multi-dimensional flat spaces. By using the formula, Equation (16), for the action integral, we can write the Lagrangian $L$ of the free electromagnetic field in multi-dimensional pseudo-Euclidean space (in Heaviside units)

$$L = -\frac{1}{4}\int F_{\alpha\beta} F^{\alpha\beta}\, d^n\mathbf{x} = -\frac{1}{4}\int F^{\alpha\beta} F_{\alpha\beta}\, d^n\mathbf{x}\,, \tag{23}$$

where $F_{\mu\nu} = A_{\nu,\mu} - A_{\mu,\nu}$ is the electromagnetic field tensor which is antisymmetric $F_{\mu\nu} = -F_{\nu\mu}$. From here, one finds the following equality $A_{\mu,\nu} = -F_{\mu\nu} + A_{\nu,\mu} = F_{\nu\mu} + A_{\nu,\mu}$. Variations of this Lagrangian are written in the following general form:

$$\delta L = -\frac{1}{2}\int F_{\alpha\beta}\delta F^{\alpha\beta} d^n\mathbf{x} = -\frac{1}{2}\int F^{\alpha\beta}\delta F_{\alpha\beta} d^n\mathbf{x}, \tag{24}$$

where $d^n\mathbf{x}$ means $dx^1 dx^2 \dots dx^n$ and the integration is over $n$-dimensional space. Note that all integrals considered in this section are the spatial integrals that contain no integration over the temporal (or time) variable. Furthermore, in this section, we shall apply only the Heaviside units. The use of Gauss units complicates all formulas below, including the expressions for the momenta.

In order to develop the Hamiltonian approach for the electromagnetic field, we need to consider all variations of the velocities for each component of the $(n+1)$-dimensional vector potential $\bar{A}$. In other words, below, we deal with variations of the $A_{\mu,0}$ derivatives only, where $\mu = 0, 1, \dots, n$. In other words, in our Hamiltonian formulation, all components of the $(n+1)$-dimensional vector potential $\bar{A}$—i.e., $A_0, A_1, \dots, A_n$ components—are the generalized coordinates of our problem. For variations of the velocities $A_{\mu,0}$, our formula, Equation (24), for $\delta L$ is written in the form

$$\delta L = \int F^{\alpha 0}\delta A_{\alpha,0}\, d^n\mathbf{x} = \int B^{\alpha}\delta A_{\alpha,0}\, d^n\mathbf{x}, \tag{25}$$

where $B^{\alpha} = F^{\alpha 0}$ are the contravariant components of the $(n+1)$-dimensional vector momenta $\bar{B}$. In fact, this equation must be considered as the explicit definition of momenta. However, from this definition and the antisymmetry of the electromagnetic field tensor, one finds $B^0 = F^{00} = 0$. This means that the 0-component of momenta $\bar{B}$ of the electromagnetic field—i.e., $B^0$—must be equal to zero at all times. According to Dirac [14], all similar equations derived at this stage of the Hamiltonian procedure are the primary constraints. In our current case, this constraint is better to write in the form of a weak identity $B^0 \approx 0$.

By using our momenta $B^{\alpha}$, we can introduce the Hamiltonian of the free electromagnetic field in multi-dimensional pseudo-Euclidean (flat) space:

$$\begin{aligned} H &= \int B^{\alpha} A_{\alpha,0}\, d^n\mathbf{x} - L = \int \Big(F^{q0}A_{q,0} + \frac{1}{4}F^{pq}F_{pq} + \frac{1}{4}F^{p0}F_{p0} + \frac{1}{4}F^{0p}F_{0p}\Big) d^n\mathbf{x} \\ &= \int \Big(F^{q0}A_{q,0} + \frac{1}{4}F^{pq}F_{pq} + \frac{1}{2}F^{p0}F_{p0}\Big) d^n\mathbf{x} = \int \mathcal{H} d^n\mathbf{x}, \end{aligned} \tag{26}$$

where $\mathcal{H}$ is the Hamiltonian space-like density (scalar), which is

$$\mathcal{H} = F^{q0}A_{q,0} + \frac{1}{4}F^{pq}F_{pq} + \frac{1}{2}F^{p0}F_{p0} \tag{27}$$

For the $A_{q,0}$ derivative, we substitute its equivalent expression $A_{q,0} = -F_{q0} + A_{0,q}$ (see above) and obtain

$$H = \int \Big(\frac{1}{4}F^{pq}F_{pq} - \frac{1}{2}F^{p0}F_{p0} + F^{q0}A_{0,q}\Big) d^n\mathbf{x} = \int \Big(\frac{1}{4}F^{pq}F_{pq} + \frac{1}{2}B^pB^p + B^qA_{0,q}\Big) d^n\mathbf{x}. \tag{28}$$

In the last term of this Hamiltonian, we can perform a partial integration, which actually leads to the following replacement: $F^{q0}A_{0,q} \rightarrow -A_0\frac{\partial F^{q0}}{\partial x_q} = -A_0(B^q)_q = -A_0B^p_{,p}$. This reduces our Hamiltonian, Equation (28), to the form

$$H = \int \Big(\frac{1}{4}F^{pq}F_{pq} - \frac{1}{2}F^{p0}F_{p0} + F^{q0}A_{0,q}\Big) d^n\mathbf{x} = \int \Big(\frac{1}{4}F^{pq}F_{pq} + \frac{1}{2}B^pB^p - A_0B^p_{,p}\Big) d^n\mathbf{x}\ . \tag{29}$$

This is the Hamiltonian of the free electromagnetic field written in the closed analytical form. The corresponding Hamiltonian space-like density takes the form

$$\mathcal{H} = \frac{1}{4}F^{pq}F_{pq} + \frac{1}{2}B^pB^p - A_0B^p_{,p}. \tag{30}$$

Note that by performing these transformations and deriving the Hamiltonian, Equation (29), we have gained even more than we wanted at the beginning of our procedure. In fact, the development of any Hamiltonian approach means that we have a simplectic structure, which is defined by the Poisson brackets between basic dynamical (Hamiltonian) variables: $(n+1)$ coordinates $A_\mu$ and $(n+1)$ momenta $B^\mu$. These Poisson brackets are defined as follows:

$$[A_\mu(\bar{x}_1), B^\nu(\bar{x}_2)] = g^\nu_\mu \delta^{(n)}(\mathbf{x}_1 - \mathbf{x}_2), \; [A_\mu(\mathbf{x}_1), A_\nu(\mathbf{x}_2)] = 0, \; [B^\mu(\mathbf{x}_1), B^\nu(\mathbf{x}_2)] = 0, \tag{31}$$

where $g^\nu_\mu = \delta^\nu_\mu$ is the Kronecker delta-function, while $\mu = 0, 1, \ldots, n$, and $\nu = 0, 1, \ldots, n$.

In general, the Poisson brackets are used as the main working tool in any Hamiltonian approach developed for a given physical system. Moreover, these brackets allow one to introduce a simplectic $(2n+2)$-dimensional phase space of the Hamiltonian variables $\{A_\alpha, B^\beta\}$ which are defined in each point $\bar{x}$ of the $(n+1)$-dimensional space-time manifold. The original configuration space of this problem is the direct sum of the $(n+1)$-dimensional subspace of $A_\mu-$coordinates and $(n+1)$-dimensional subspace of $A_{\mu,0}-$velocities. In turn, this allows one to consider and apply various canonical transformations of the Hamiltonian canonical variables. Furthermore, by using the Poisson brackets in Equation (31), we can complete our Hamiltonian approach for the classical electrodynamics and perform its quantization.

To illustrate this fact, let us go back to the primary constraint $B^0 \approx 0$ mentioned above. This constraint must remain satisfied at all times. This means that its time derivative $\frac{dB^0}{dt}$, which in our Hamiltonian approach equals the Poisson bracket $[B^0, H]$, must be zero at all times. This Poisson bracket is easily determined, since in the Hamiltonian, Equation (29), there is only one term (the last term) that does not commute with the momentum (or primary constraint) $B^0$:

$$[B^0, \frac{1}{4}F^{pq}F_{pq} - \frac{1}{2}F^{p0}F_{p0} - A_0B^q_q] = -[B^0, A_0]B^p_{,p} = [A_0, B^0]B^p_{,p} = B^p_{,p} \tag{32}$$

In other words, we have found another weak equality $B^p_{,p} \approx 0$ that must be obeyed at all times. According to Dirac [14,15], this condition is the secondary constraint of our Hamiltonian formulation of the multi-dimensional Maxwell theory of radiation. The next Poisson bracket $[B^p_{,p}, H]$ (or $[B^p_{,p}, \mathcal{H}]$) equals zero identically, which indicates clearly that the chain of first-class constraints is closed, and our Hamiltonian formulation does not lead to any tertiary and/or other constraints of higher order. Briefly, this means the complete closure (or Dirac closure) of the Hamiltonian procedure for the free electromagnetic field in multi-dimensional space.

### 5.1. Further Transformations of the Hamiltonian

The first term in the Hamiltonian of the free electromagnetic field in multi-dimensional space, Equation (29), includes a number of different terms, but it does not contain any of the canonical variables. It is difficult to use such a Hamiltonian for the analysis and solution of actual problems in classical and/or quantum electrodynamics. Therefore, we have to transform this Hamiltonian to a form that explicitly contains canonical variables in each term. Then, our newly derived Hamiltonian $H$ and/or the corresponding Hamiltonian density $\mathcal{H}$ can be applied for the solution of many actual problems. For convenience, below, we shall deal with the Hamiltonian density $\mathcal{H}$. The partial integration of the first term in the Hamiltonian, Equation (29), leads to the following expression for the Hamiltonian density Equation (30):

$$\mathcal{H} = \left(F^{qp}\right)_{q} A_p + \frac{1}{2}B^p B^p - A_0 B^p_{,p} = \left(\frac{\partial^2 A^p}{\partial x_q \partial x^q} - \frac{\partial^2 A^q}{\partial x_q \partial x_p}\right) A_p + \frac{1}{2}B^p B^p - A_0 B^p_{,p}, \qquad (33)$$

where $p = 1, 2, \dots, n$ and $q = 1, 2, \dots, n$. For this Hamiltonian density, we can write the following system of canonical equations:

$$\frac{dA_p}{dt} = [A_p, \mathcal{H}] = \frac{1}{2}\left(2B^p\right) = B^p \qquad (34)$$

and

$$\frac{dB^p}{dt} = [B^p, \mathcal{H}] = -\left(\frac{\partial^2 A^p}{\partial x_q \partial x^q} - \frac{\partial^2 A^q}{\partial x_q \partial x_p}\right) = \frac{\partial^2 A_p}{\partial x_q \partial x^q} - \frac{\partial^2 A_q}{\partial x_q \partial x_p}. \qquad (35)$$

Combining these two equations, one finds

$$\frac{d^2 A_p}{dt^2} = \frac{\partial^2 A_p}{\partial x_q \partial x^q} - \frac{\partial^2 A_q}{\partial x_q \partial x_p}. \qquad (36)$$

Taking into account the gauge condition $\frac{\partial A_q}{\partial x_q} = 0$ (see below), we reduce the last equation to the form

$$\frac{\partial^2 A_p}{\partial t^2} - \frac{\partial^2 A_p}{\partial x_q \partial x^q} = 0, \text{ or } \frac{\partial^2 \mathbf{A}}{\partial t^2} - \Delta \mathbf{A} = 0, \qquad (37)$$

which is the wave equations written in the $(n+1)$-dimensional space-time. The $n$-dimensional Laplace operator $\Delta$ in this equation is

$$\Delta = \frac{\partial^2}{\partial x_q \partial x^q} = g^{qr}\frac{\partial^2}{\partial x^q \partial x^r} = g_{qr}\frac{\partial^2}{\partial x_q \partial x_r}. \qquad (38)$$

Thus, in our Hamiltonian approach, the multi-dimensional wave equation for the free electromagnetic field is derived as a direct consequence of the canonical Hamilton equations obtained for this field. Such a derivation of the wave equation for a free electromagnetic field described here is, probably, the most direct, fast, and logically clear of all known (alternative) methods. In addition to this, we have rigorously derived the two additional conditions for the momenta of the free electromagnetic filed: $B^0 \approx 0$ and $B^p_{,p} \approx 0$. In our Hamiltonian formulation, these two weak equations are called the primary and secondary constraints, respectively. It is easy to show that these two constraints are first-class [14]. In the four-dimensional case, Dirac has suggested [14] that these two constraints are the generators (or generating functions) for infinitesimal contact transformations which do not change the actual physical state of the free electromagnetic field; i.e., they are two independent generators of internal symmetry. Twenty years later, this statement has rigorously been proven by L. Castellani [16]. All these results are the great and obvious advantages of the Dirac's (Hamiltonian) formulation of the Maxwell theory. Now, by using all first-class constraints that have been derived during the Hamiltonian formulation, one can determine the true symmetry of any given physical field. For the free electromagnetic field, such a symmetry group coincides with the Lorentz $SO(3,1)$-group. In general, by operating with the first-class constraints only, it is impossible to restore the so-called hidden (or additional) symmetries of the free electromagnetic field. For instance, for the free electromagnetic field considered in three-dimensional space, the complete group of point symmetry is the $SO(4,2)$-group, which has 15 generators [17], while the Lorentz $SO(3,1)$-group has only 6 generators. The powerful method of Bessel–Hagen [17] is based on applications of Noether's second theorem, which is applied to the Lagrangian of the free electromagnetic field. In this short paper, we cannot discuss all details of this interesting problem.

*5.2. First-Class Constraints and Gauge Invariance*

In this section, we consider a different symmetry (or invariance) of Maxwell equations that is directly and closely related to the primary and secondary first-class constraints. This invariance is the well-known gauge invariance (or symmetry) of the Maxwell equations The gauge invariance of three-dimensional Maxwell equations has been studied by many famous authors, including Heitler [18], Jackson [19,20], Gelfand and Fomin [21], and others (see, e.g., [22]). Briefly, the gauge invariance means that we can impose some additional conditions upon the physical fields, or some of their components, and these additional conditions do not change solutions of the original problem (but they can change equations) The gauge conditions are often used to simplify the Hamiltonian equations of motion, either by reducing the total number of variable fields or by vanishing some terms (or combinations of terms) in these equations. Let us discuss the gauge invariance of the free electromagnetic field (or "pure radiation field" [18]) by using the two first-class constraints which we have derived above: $B^0 \approx 0$ and $B^p_{,p} \approx 0$. By re-writing these two constraints in terms of the components of the $(d+1)$-dimensional vector potential $\bar{A} = (\varphi, \mathbf{A})$ and their temporal derivatives, one finds

$$B^0 \approx 0 \Rightarrow \frac{\partial \varphi}{\partial t} = 0 \;\; \text{and} \;\; B^p_{,p} \approx 0 \Rightarrow \frac{\partial}{\partial t}\Big(div\mathbf{A}\Big) = 0 \tag{39}$$

where we gave used the traditional sign of actual equality "=" instead of the weak equality "≈", which has been used above in the Dirac's Hamiltonian approach. The two equalities in the right-hand side of Equation (39) lead us to the two following equations: $\varphi = \varphi(\mathbf{r})$ and $div\mathbf{A} = C(\mathbf{r})$, where the scalars $\varphi(\mathbf{r})$ and $C(\mathbf{r})$ are the functions of $n$ spatial coordinates only, and they do not change with time; i.e., they are time-independent scalar functions. It is clear that these two time-independent scalars are not related in any way to the Hamiltonian formulation of the Maxwell theory of electromagnetic fields. Indeed, the Hamiltonian approaches describe only the time-evolution of the Hamiltonian dynamical variables. For static problems, there are other different methods. Therefore, without loss of generality, we can assume that these time-independent scalars $\varphi(\mathbf{r})$ and $C(\mathbf{r})$ equal zero identically at all times.

Based on these arguments, we can write the four following equations for the field dynamical variables (or Hamiltonian variables):

$$\varphi = 0, \;\; \frac{\partial \varphi}{\partial t} = 0, \;\; div\mathbf{A} = 0 \;\; \text{and} \;\; \frac{\partial}{\partial t}\Big(div\mathbf{A}\Big) = 0, \tag{40}$$

which can be considered as the four independent "basis vectors". In general, the set of $N_g$ gauge conditions $\psi_i$ is represented as a linear combination of the four basis vectors from Equation (40):

$$\psi_i = \alpha_i \varphi + \beta_i \frac{\partial \varphi}{\partial t} + \gamma_i \; div\mathbf{A} + \delta_i \frac{\partial}{\partial t}\Big(div\mathbf{A}\Big) = 0, \tag{41}$$

where $i = 1, 2, 3, 4$, while $\alpha_i, \beta_i, \gamma_i$, and $\delta_i$ are some numerical constants. Let us discuss the principal question about the number $N_g$, which is the number of sufficient (or essential) gauge equations. For the free electromagnetic field, $N_g$ equals two, since exactly this number of conditions has been found in the Hamiltonian formulation of electrodynamics developed by Dirac (see above). The two equations $\frac{\partial \varphi}{\partial t} = 0$ and $\frac{\partial}{\partial t}\Big(div\mathbf{A}\Big) = 0$ define the so-called Dirac gauge, which is discussed above. Formally, for the Dirac gauge, we can introduce the third gauge condition $\varphi = 0$ and completely exclude the pair of variables $\left(\varphi, \frac{\partial \varphi}{\partial t}\right)$ from the list of our dynamical variables. However, this follows not from some general principle but from the explicit form of Dirac's Hamiltonian density, Equation (30), for the pure radiation field (see above), where the only term that includes the scalar potential $\varphi$ is written as a product of $\varphi$ (or $A_0$) and secondary constraint $B^p_{,p}$. This term equals zero on the shell of the first-class constraints.

An alternative choice of two gauge equations $\frac{\partial \varphi}{\partial t} = 0$ and $div\mathbf{A} = 0$ corresponds to the famous Coulomb gauge, which provides the best choice for many three-dimensional QED problems in atomic and molecular physics. In the Coulomb gauge, the scalar potential $\varphi(= A_0)$ is always a static potential, while the $n$-dimensional vector potential $\mathbf{A}$ is always transverse. The Coulomb gauge and other gauges discussed here are easily generalized for $n$-dimensional spaces. Another choice of the basic gauge equations defines the Lorentz gauge. Formally, this gauge is defined by one (Fermi's) equation $\frac{\partial \varphi}{\partial t} + div\mathbf{A} = 0$. In respect to the Dirac theory, this set of gauge conditions is not complete and a second gauge equation can be added. For instance, one can choose the second condition in the form $\frac{\partial \varphi}{\partial t} - div\mathbf{A} = 0$, which is a relativistic invariant for the electromagnetic wave that propagates from the present to the past. A different choice of the second equation for the Lorentz gauge corresponds to the so-called Heitler's gauge, which is based on the two equations $\frac{\partial \varphi}{\partial t} + div\mathbf{A} = 0$ and $\frac{\partial}{\partial t}\left(div\mathbf{A}\right) = 0$ for the free electromagnetic field [18]. The advantage of this useful gauge is obvious: if these equations hold at $t = 0$, then the equation $\frac{\partial \varphi}{\partial t} + div\mathbf{A} = 0$ is always satisfied. These simple examples of different gauges are mentioned here only to illustrate the ultimate power of Dirac's approach, which simplifies the internal analysis of various gauges.

Let us discuss the general source of gauges which often arise in different field theories; e.g., in Maxwell theory of radiation, metric gravity, tetrad gravity, etc. Here, we want to investigate this problem from the Hamiltonian point of view. First, let us assume that we have imposed all four conditions from Equation (40) on our dynamical variables. What does this mean for these variables? The first two equations $\varphi = 0$ and $\frac{\partial \varphi}{\partial t} = 0$ mean that the variable $\varphi$ and corresponding momentum $B^0$ (or velocity $\frac{\partial \varphi}{\partial t}$) are not dynamic (Lagrange) variables of our problem. In other words, we have to exclude these two variables before the application of our Hamiltonian procedure. The same statement is true for the two equations $div\mathbf{A} = 0$ and $\frac{\partial}{\partial t}\left(div\mathbf{A}\right) = 0$, but $div\mathbf{A}$ is not a regular dynamic variable of the original problem. In reality, the function $div\mathbf{A}$ appears in the secondary constraint in Dirac's Hamiltonian formulation developed for the pure radiation filed. This function is a linear combination of the first-order derivatives of covariant components of the multi-dimensional vector potential $\mathbf{A}$. The Hamiltonian canonical variables do not include any sum of the space-like derivatives of this potential. Therefore, it is not clear how we can exclude the scalar $div\mathbf{A}$ and its time-derivative from the list of our canonical variables. However, the main obstacle to the exclusion of the four variables, Equation (40), follows from the fact that we have only two gauge equations (not four). This means that we cannot correctly exclude all four variables and have to keep them in our procedure. These "extra" variables survive our Hamiltonian procedure only in the form of additional equations for the Hamiltonian dynamical variables. In other words, the gauge conditions are the integral parts of any Hamiltonian approach developed for an arbitrary physical field. This is the general principle that explains why different field theories with first-class constraints always have some number of non-trivial gauge conditions (or equations).

However, this is not the end of the story. Let us look at the constraints in multi-dimensional electrodynamics from a different point of view. Consider the following two-parametric $(\alpha, \beta)$-family of the Hamiltonian densities:

$$\mathcal{H}(\alpha, \beta) = \frac{1}{4} F^{pq} F_{pq} + \frac{1}{2} B^p B^p - A_0 B^p_{,p} + \left(\alpha B^0 + \beta B^p_{,p}\right)^2. \tag{42}$$

where $B^0$ and $B^p_{,p}$ are the functions of the canonical variables of the problem. At this moment, we cannot assume that there are some restrictions on these two quantities. In other words, for now, the $B^0$ and $B^p_{,p}$ values are not yet constraints.

In general, to operate with the two-parametric family of Hamiltonian densities $\mathcal{H}(\alpha,\beta)$ in some constructive way, we have to formulate the following variational principle: the actual (or true) Hamiltonian density coincides with the minimal Hamiltonian density $\mathcal{H}(\alpha,\beta)$, Equation (42), in respect to possible variations of the two numerical parameters $\alpha$ and $\beta$. This principle immediately leads to the two following weak identities:

$$\left(\alpha B^0 + \beta B^p_{,p}\right) B^0 \approx 0 \quad \text{and} \quad \left(\alpha B^0 + \beta B^p_{,p}\right) B^p_{,p} \approx 0. \tag{43}$$

One obvious solution of this system gives us the two Dirac's constraints $B^0 \approx 0$ and $B^p_{,p} \approx 0$ which have been derived above. In general, there are other solutions of the system Equation (43), and one of them can be written in the form

$$\alpha_1 B^0 + \beta_1 B^p_{,p} \approx 0 \quad \text{and} \quad \alpha_2 B^0 + \beta_2 B^p_{,p} \approx 0. \tag{44}$$

where the coefficients $\alpha_1, \beta_1, \alpha_2$ and $\beta_2$ form a regular (i.e., invertible) $2 \times 2$ matrix. The principle formulated above is called the optimal principle for the constrained motions, since in actual physical systems, the motion along first-class constraints is optimal, or it can be considered as optimal.

## 6. Multi-Dimensional Maxwell Equations in Non-Flat Spaces

The Maxwell equations can be written in the covariant form, which is more appropriate in applications to the metric gravity (or general relativity) in multi-dimensional Riemannian spaces. In this and the next sections, we deal with the multi-dimensional Riemannian spaces only. These spaces are not flat, and they are often called the spaces of non-zero curvature. Indeed, the corresponding equations, Equations (17) and (19), for the flat multi-dimensional spaces have already been written in the tensor (or covariant) form. Furthermore, the electromagnetic field tensor $F_{\alpha\beta}$, which has been defined by Equation (8), is truly skew-symmetric with respect to permutations of its indexes; i.e., $F_{\alpha\beta} = -F_{\beta\alpha}$ and $F^{\alpha\beta} = -F^{\beta\alpha}$. These two facts simplify the process of derivation of the Maxwell equations in the covariant form. In fact, to derive the covariant form of Maxwell equations, one needs to replace all usual derivatives written in Cartesian coordinates by the tensor derivatives. After such a replacement, the first group of Maxwell equations in multi-dimensional Riemannian spaces takes the form

$$\nabla_\beta F_{\gamma\lambda} + \nabla_\lambda F_{\beta\gamma} + \nabla_\gamma F_{\lambda\beta} = 0 \quad (\text{or } \nabla_\beta F_{\gamma\lambda} = \nabla_\gamma F_{\beta\lambda} - \nabla_\lambda F_{\beta\gamma}), \tag{45}$$

where $\nabla_\beta$ is the tensor (or covariant) derivative; i.e.,

$$\nabla_\beta F_{\gamma\lambda} = \frac{\partial F_{\gamma\lambda}}{\partial x^\beta} - \Gamma^\mu_{\gamma\beta} F_{\mu\lambda} - \Gamma^\mu_{\lambda\beta} F_{\gamma\mu} \tag{46}$$

where $\Gamma^\gamma_{\alpha\beta} = \frac{1}{2}\left(\frac{\partial g_{\gamma\beta}}{\partial x^\alpha} + \frac{\partial g_{\alpha\gamma}}{\partial x^\gamma} - \frac{\partial g_{\alpha\beta}}{\partial x^\gamma}\right) = \Gamma^\gamma_{\beta\alpha}$ are the Cristoffel symbols of the second kind. It is interesting to note that the form of Equation (45) does not depend explicitly upon the parameter $n$, which defines the dimension of Riemann space. By performing a few simple transformations, we can reduce the formula, Equation (46), to a form that exactly coincides with Equation (17). This has been noticed in many textbooks on three-dimensional electrodynamics (see, e.g., [5]).

The second group of Maxwell equations for multi-dimensional spaces of non-zero curvature is written in the form (in Gauss units)

$$\nabla_\beta F^{\alpha\beta} = \frac{1}{\sqrt{-g}} \frac{\left(\partial\sqrt{-g}F^{\alpha\beta}\right)}{\partial x^\beta} = -\frac{n\pi^{\left(\frac{n}{2}\right)}}{c\Gamma\left(1+\frac{n}{2}\right)} j^\alpha = -\frac{f(n)}{c} j^\alpha, \tag{47}$$

since the tensor $F^{\alpha\beta}$ is antisymmetric. In this equation, $g$ is the determinant of the fundamental tensor, which is always negative in the metric gravity. By applying the operator $\nabla_\alpha$ to the last formula, one finds

$$\nabla_\alpha \nabla_\beta F^{\alpha\beta} = -\frac{f(n)}{c} \nabla_\alpha j^\alpha \implies -\frac{f(n)}{c} \nabla_\beta j^\beta = \nabla_\beta \nabla_\alpha F^{\beta\alpha} = -\nabla_\beta \nabla_\alpha F^{\alpha\beta}. \tag{48}$$

In other words, the expression on the left-hand side of these equations can be re-written in the following form:

$$\frac{1}{2}\Big(\nabla_\alpha \nabla_\beta + \nabla_\beta \nabla_\alpha\Big) F^{\alpha\beta}. \tag{49}$$

which equals zero identically, since here the truly symmetric tensor operator (upon $\alpha \leftrightarrow \beta$ permutation) is applied to an antisymmetric tensor (upon the same permutations). Finally, one finds that $\nabla_\alpha j^\alpha = 0$; i.e., the conservation law for electric charge written in the $(n+1)$-dimensional Riemannian space.

In many books and textbooks, the electrodynamic derivation of Maxwell equations in the manifestly covariant form is traditionally considered as the final step. A similar approach, however, ignores an additional group of governing equations that is obeyed for the electromagnetic field in the presence of actual gravitational fields. These additional equations determine the general properties, time evolution, and propagation of electromagnetic fields in the metric gravitational fields. The explicit derivation of these additional governing equations for the electromagnetic field tensor is straightforward. Indeed, if the electromagnetic field tensor $F_{\alpha\beta}$ is considered in the metric gravity, then the following equations must be obeyed:

$$\nabla_\lambda \nabla_\sigma F^\beta_\alpha - \nabla_\sigma \nabla_\lambda F^\beta_\alpha = F^\mu_\alpha R^\beta_{\sigma\lambda\mu} - F^\beta_\mu R^\mu_{\sigma\lambda\alpha}, \tag{50}$$

or in a slightly different form:

$$\nabla_\lambda \nabla_\sigma F_{\alpha\beta} - \nabla_\sigma \nabla_\lambda F_{\alpha\beta} = -F_{\mu\beta} R^\mu_{\sigma\lambda\alpha} - F_{\alpha\mu} R^\mu_{\sigma\lambda\beta} = F_{\alpha\mu} R^\mu_{\lambda\sigma\beta} + F_{\mu\beta} R^\mu_{\lambda\sigma\alpha}, \tag{51}$$

where the notation $R^\sigma_{\alpha\beta\gamma} = g^{\sigma\mu} R_{\alpha\beta\gamma\mu}$ is the Riemann-.Cristoffel tensor of the fourth rank, which is three times covariant and once contravariant (see, e.g., [6,7]). In turn, the $R_{\alpha\beta\gamma\sigma}$ is the Riemann curvature tensor (or Riemann–Cristoffel tensor):

$$R_{\alpha\beta\gamma\sigma} = \frac{1}{2}\Big[\frac{\partial^2 g_{\alpha\sigma}}{\partial x^\beta \partial x^\gamma} + \frac{\partial^2 g_{\beta\gamma}}{\partial x^\alpha \partial x^\sigma} - \frac{\partial^2 g_{\alpha\gamma}}{\partial x^\beta \partial x^\sigma} - \frac{\partial^2 g_{\beta\sigma}}{\partial x^\alpha \partial x^\gamma}\Big] + \Gamma_{\rho,\alpha\sigma}\Gamma^\rho_{\beta\gamma} - \Gamma_{\rho,\beta\sigma}\Gamma^\rho_{\alpha\gamma}\,, \tag{52}$$

where $\Gamma_{\gamma,\mu\nu} = \frac{1}{2}\Big(\frac{\partial g_{\gamma\alpha}}{\partial x^\beta} + \frac{\partial g_{\gamma\beta}}{\partial x^\alpha} - \frac{\partial g_{\alpha\beta}}{\partial x^\gamma}\Big)$ are the Cristoffel symbols of the first kind. The Riemann–Cristoffel tensor defined in Equation (52) is a covariant tensor of the fourth rank. Note that similar problems have been extensively studied since the 1920s in numerous papers and books on General Relativity (see, e.g., [23,24] and references therein). As follows from these equations, Equations (50) and (51), the propagation and other properties of the "free" electromagnetic fields in multi-dimensional spaces of non-zero curvature (or in non-flat spaces) are always affected by the gravitational fields. For relatively small gravitational fields, Equations (50) and (51) can be considered as small perturbations to the Maxwell equations. However, in strong gravitational fields, where some of the $|\frac{\partial g_{\alpha\beta}}{\partial x^\gamma}|$ derivatives are very large, the laws of propagation and other properties of the electromagnetic fields can significantly be changed by the gravity. Briefly, we can say say that in similar non-flat spaces, the actual properties of electromagnetic fields cannot be described by the Maxwell equations only. Furthermore, in more complex "combined" theories of gravity and radiation—e.g., in the well known Born–Infeld theory (see, e.g., [25])—the total fundamental tensor is represented as a function—e.g., as a sum—of the gravitational $g_{\alpha\beta}$ and electromagnetic $F_{\alpha\beta}$

tensors, while the time-evolution and propagation of electromagnetic fields is described by the non-linear, well-coupled equations.

### 6.1. Multi-Dimensional Electromagnetic Field in Metric Gravity

Now, we are ready to vary the sum of action integrals for the gravitational $S_g$ and electromagnetic $S_f$ fields; i.e., to vary the $\delta(S_g + S_f)$ action. The both fields are considered as free; i.e., there are no masses, no free electric charges and no electric currents in the area of our interest. Our goal in this section is to derive (variationally) the governing Einstein equations (in multi-dimensions) in the presence of electromagnetic fields. To achieve this goal, we have to vary the gravitational field only; i.e., the components of the metric tensor $g_{\alpha\beta}$ (or $g^{\alpha\beta}$). The variation of the gravitational action $S_g$ is written in the form (see, e.g., [5,24]):

$$\delta S_g = -\frac{c}{f(n)\mathcal{K}} \int \Big( R_{\alpha\beta} - \frac{1}{2} g_{\alpha\beta} R \Big) \delta g^{\alpha\beta} \sqrt{-g} d\Omega, \tag{53}$$

where $R_{\alpha\beta}$ is the Ricci tensor. In older works [6], authors used the the Einstein tensor, which is $G_{\alpha\beta} = -R_{\alpha\beta}$. The explicit form of the Ricci tensor is

$$R_{\alpha\beta} = \frac{\partial \Gamma^{\gamma}_{\alpha\beta}}{\partial x^{\gamma}} - \frac{\partial \Gamma^{\gamma}_{\alpha\gamma}}{\partial x^{\beta}} + \Gamma^{\gamma}_{\alpha\beta}\Gamma^{\lambda}_{\gamma\lambda} - \Gamma^{\lambda}_{\alpha\gamma}\Gamma^{\gamma}_{\beta\lambda}, \text{ or } R_{\alpha\beta} = g^{\mu\nu} R_{\mu\alpha\beta\nu} = g^{\nu\mu} R_{\nu\beta\alpha\mu} = R_{\beta\alpha} \tag{54}$$

and $R = g^{\alpha\beta} R_{\alpha\beta}$ is the scalar (or Gauss) curvature of space. In addition, in this equation, the notation $\mathcal{K} = \frac{k}{c^2} = 7.4259155 \times 10^{-29}$ cm $\cdot$ s$^{-1}$ denotes the universal (or $n$-independent) gravitational constant. A similar variation of the electromagnetic action $S_f$ is

$$\delta S_f = \frac{2}{c} \int T_{\alpha\beta} \delta g^{\alpha\beta} \sqrt{-g} d\Omega = \frac{2}{c f(n)} \int \Big( F_{\alpha\gamma} F^{\gamma}_{\beta} + \frac{1}{4} g_{\alpha\beta} F_{\gamma\rho} F^{\gamma\rho} \Big) \delta g^{\alpha\beta} \sqrt{-g} d\Omega. \tag{55}$$

Therefore, for the variation of the sum of these two actions, we can write

$$\delta(S_g + S_f) = \frac{c}{f(n)\mathcal{K}} \int \Big( -R_{\alpha\beta} + \frac{1}{2} g_{\alpha\beta} R + \frac{2 f(n) \mathcal{K}}{c^2} T_{\alpha\beta} \Big) \delta g^{\alpha\beta} \sqrt{-g} d\Omega. \tag{56}$$

Since variations of the gravitational field are arbitrary, then from this equation, one finds

$$R_{\alpha\beta} - \frac{1}{2} g_{\alpha\beta} R = \frac{2\mathcal{K}}{c^2} \Big( F_{\alpha\gamma} F^{\gamma}_{\beta} + \frac{1}{4} g_{\alpha\beta} F_{\gamma\rho} F^{\gamma\rho} \Big) = \frac{2\mathcal{K}}{c^2} \tilde{T}_{\alpha\beta}, \tag{57}$$

where $\tilde{T}_{\alpha\beta} = F_{\alpha\gamma} F^{\gamma}_{\beta} + \frac{1}{4} g_{\alpha\beta} F_{\gamma\rho} F^{\gamma\rho}$ is the reduced (or universal) energy–momentum tensor of the electromagnetic field, which does not include the hyper-angular $f(n)$ factor. The last equation, Equation (57), is the well known Einstein equation for the gravitational and electromagnetic field. This equation is a true tensor equation, since both parts of this equation do not include the geometrical (or hyper-angular) factor $f(n)$. In other words, by looking at this equation, one cannot say what the actual dimension of our working space is. For this reason, Flanders [11] and others have criticized classical tensor analysis: "In classical tensor analysis, one never knows what the range of applicability is simply because one is never told what the space is". However, for the purposes of this study, this fact is an obvious advantage. Any of the true tensor equations that appear in fundamental physics cannot include factors that explicitly depend upon the dimension $n$ (or $n + 1$) of the working Riemann space. Moreover, this is a simple criterion that can be used to separate the true (also universal, or absolute) tensor equations from similar tensor-like equations that can be correct only for some selected Riemannian spaces. As follows from the arguments presented above, both Einstein equations of the metric gravity for the free gravitational field, when $\tilde{T}_{\alpha\beta} = 0$ in Equation (57), and Einstein equations of metric gravity in the presence of electromagnetic field, Equation (57), are the true tensor equations.

*6.2. Radiation from a Rapidly Moving Electric Charge*

As is well known (see, e.g., [5,19]), any electric charge that accelerates in the electromagnetic field always emits EM radiation. Nowadays, this statement is repeated so often that a large number of students and researchers sincerely believe that EM radiation can only be emitted in the presence of an electromagnetic field. In general, this is not an absolute truth, and the emission of EM radiation is also possible in the presence of a strong (or rapidly varying) gravitational field. Below, we want to prove this statement and, for simplicity, here we restrict our analysis to the three-dimensional space only. However, all our formulas are written in the explicitly covariant form. This means that all these formulas can be generalized to describe the actual situation in multi-dimensional spaces as well. In General Relativity, the formula for the radiated four-momentum $dP^{\kappa}$ is written in the form (see, e.g., [5]):

$$dP^{\kappa} = -\frac{2e^2}{3c} g_{\alpha\mu} \Big(\frac{d^2 x^{\alpha}}{ds^2}\Big)\Big(\frac{d^2 x^{\mu}}{ds^2}\Big) dx^{\kappa} = -\frac{2e^2}{3c} g_{\alpha\mu} \Big(\frac{du^{\alpha}}{ds}\Big)\Big(\frac{du^{\mu}}{ds}\Big) u^{\kappa} ds, \quad (58)$$

where $u^{\beta} = \frac{dx^{\beta}}{ds}$ is the corresponding "velocity". Now, by taking the expression for the acceleration from Equation (10), one finds

$$\begin{aligned} dP^{\kappa} &= -\frac{2e^2}{3c} g_{\alpha\mu} \Big(\Gamma^{\alpha}_{\beta\gamma} u^{\beta} u^{\gamma} - \frac{e}{mc^2} F^{\alpha}_{\beta} u^{\beta}\Big)\Big(\Gamma^{\mu}_{\lambda\sigma} u^{\lambda} u^{\sigma} - \frac{e}{mc^2} F^{\mu}_{\sigma} u^{\sigma}\Big) u^{\kappa} ds = -\frac{2e^2}{3c} \times \\ &\Big(g_{\alpha\mu} \Gamma^{\alpha}_{\beta\gamma} \Gamma^{\mu}_{\lambda\sigma} u^{\beta} u^{\gamma} u^{\lambda} u^{\sigma} u^{\kappa} - \frac{2e}{mc^2} g_{\alpha\mu} \Gamma^{\alpha}_{\beta\gamma} F^{\mu}_{\sigma} u^{\beta} u^{\gamma} u^{\sigma} u^{\kappa} + \frac{e^2}{m^2 c^4} g_{\alpha\mu} F^{\alpha}_{\beta} F^{\mu}_{\sigma} u^{\beta} u^{\sigma} u^{\kappa}\Big) \\ &= T^{\kappa}_{2} + T^{\kappa}_{2} + T^{\kappa}_{3} = -\frac{2e^2}{3c} \Gamma^{\alpha}_{\beta\gamma} \Gamma_{\alpha,\lambda\sigma} u^{\beta} u^{\gamma} u^{\lambda} u^{\sigma} u^{\kappa} + \frac{4e^3}{3mc^3} \Gamma^{\alpha}_{\beta\gamma} F_{\alpha\sigma} u^{\beta} u^{\gamma} u^{\sigma} u^{\kappa} \\ &- \frac{2e^4}{3m^2 c^5} F^{\alpha}_{\beta} F_{\alpha\sigma} u^{\beta} u^{\sigma} u^{\kappa}, \end{aligned} \quad (59)$$

where the last term (vector) $T^{\kappa}_{3} = -\frac{2e^4}{3m^2c^5} F^{\alpha}_{\beta} F_{\alpha\sigma} u^{\beta} u^{\sigma} u^{\kappa}$. This term describes the emission of EM radiation by a single electrical charge that is rapidly moving in some electromagnetic field. This was extensively discussed in numerous books on classical electrodynamics (see, e.g., [5,19]), and we do not want to repeat these discussions below. The first term in Equation (59) $T^{\kappa}_{1} = -\frac{2e^2}{3c} \Gamma^{\alpha}_{\beta\gamma} \Gamma_{\alpha,\lambda\sigma} u^{\beta} u^{\gamma} u^{\lambda} u^{\sigma} u^{\kappa}$ is also a vector. This vector represents the emission of EM radiation by a point electric charge that rapidly moves in the gravitational field. The second term (vector) in Equation (59) describes the interference between gravitational and electromagnetic emissions of the EM field. The explicit formula for this term is $T^{\kappa}_{2} = \frac{4e^3}{3mc^3} \Gamma^{\alpha}_{\beta\gamma} F_{\alpha\sigma} u^{\beta} u^{\gamma} u^{\sigma} u^{\kappa}$.

There are a number of interesting observations that directly follow from the three formulas for the $T^{\kappa}_{1}$, $T^{\kappa}_{2}$, and $T^{\kappa}_{3}$ terms in Equation (59). First, let us note that the $T^{\kappa}_{1}$ term does not contain any particle mass. This means that one fast electron and/or one fast proton, which move with the equal velocities in a pure gravitational field, will always emit an equal amount of radiation. This the main distinguishing feature of the gravitation emission of EM radiation. Second, this term is a fifth-order power function of the velocities. Therefore, it is clear that overall contribution of this term will rapidly increase for relativistic particles that move with velocities close to the speed of light in a vacuum $c$. It is also clear that usually in Equation (59), the third term $T^{\kappa}_{3}$ is substantially larger than two other terms. In other words, the gravitational emission of EM radiation is hard to observe at "normal" gravitational conditions. However, in strong gravitational fields, where the absolute values of Cristoffel symbols are very large (or the $|\frac{\partial g_{\alpha\beta}}{\partial x^{\gamma}}|$ derivatives are very large), the situation can be different. The second condition is simple: the rapidly moving particle must be truly relativistic; i.e., it must move with a velocity which is close to the speed of light $v \geq 0.9\,c$ with respect to the system where the rapidly changing gravitational field originated. If these two conditions are obeyed, then one can see a relatively intense gravitational EM radiation which is emitted by a single relativistic particle which has non-zero electric charge $e$.

## 7. Conclusions

We have generalized the three-dimensional Maxwell theory of radiation to multi-dimensional flat and curved spaces. Some equations derived in three-dimensional Maxwell electrodynamics do not change their form in multi-dimensional space. In other equations, we have to make a number of changes. In fact, all properties of the electromagnetic field are described by the $(n+1)$-dimensional vector potential $\bar{A} = (\phi, \mathbf{A})$, while the interaction between any particle and electromagnetic field is described by one experimental parameter, which is the electric charge $e$ of this particle. The governing Maxwell equations for the multi-dimensional electromagnetic field have been derived and written in the covariant (or tensor) form. These equations include the geometrical (or hyper-angular) factor $f(n) = \frac{n\pi^{\frac{n}{2}}}{\Gamma\left(1+\frac{n}{2}\right)}$, which explicitly depend upon the dimension of space $n$.

The Hamiltonian formulation of the Maxwell radiation field in multi-dimensional spaces is developed and investigated. We have found that the total number of first-class constraints in this Hamiltonian formulation equals two (one primary and one secondary constraints). This number exactly coincides with the number of first-class constraints in the analogous Hamiltonian formulation developed earlier by Dirac [14] for the pure radiation field in three-dimensional space. In other words, the total number of first-class constraints in any Hamiltonian formulation developed for the free radiation field does not depend upon the dimension of space $n$. To understand how lucky we are with the Hamiltonian formulations of electrodynamics, let us note that in the $(n+1)$-dimensional metric gravity, we always have $(n+1)$ primary and $(n+1)$ secondary first-class constraints. In addition to this, in many sets of canonical variables, the explicit form of all arising secondary constraints are very cumbersome (see, e.g., [26–29]), and this substantially complicates all operations with these values. By using these primary and secondary first-class constraints, we have investigated the gauge conditions in multi-dimensional electrodynamics.

In addition, in the last section, the Maxwell equations in multi-dimensional non-flat spaces are written in the manifestly covariant form. It is shown that any gravitation field changes the actual properties, time-evolution and space-time propagation of electromagnetic fields. For gravitation fields with large and very large connectivity coefficients $\Gamma^{\alpha}_{\beta\gamma}$, the "pure" radiation field cannot be described by the Maxwell equations only. Additional equations for the antisymmetric tensor of the electromagnetic field $F_{\alpha\beta}$ (and $F^{\beta}_{\alpha}$) have been derived in this study (see Equations (50) and (51)). An analogous equation for the reduced energy-momentum tensor of electromagnetic field is now written in the true tensor form (see Equation (57)), which does not contain any $n$-dependent factor.

In conclusion, we wish to note that the investigation of multi-dimensional Maxwell equations is not a purely academic problem. In fact, there are a number of advantages that one can gain by performing such an investigation. First, it helps to clarify additional and interesting features of Maxwell's equations in the usual three-dimensional space (or in four-dimensional space-time). By working only with the three-dimensional Maxwell equations in our everyday life, we simply do not pay attention to some fundamental and amazing facts. Second, if we have a complete and correct formulation for Maxwell's electrodynamics in multi-dimensional spaces, then it possible to develop the so-called unified theories of various fields, which include the electromagnetic field. In particular, the correct unified theory of the gravitational and electromagnetic fields in multi-dimensional spaces is of great interest in modern theoretical physics. Third, in experiments in high-energy physics, it has recently been noted that at very high collision energies, many results can be represented to very good numerical accuracy and with higher symmetry if we introduce multi-dimensional spaces at the intermediate stages of calculations. This fact is not completely unexpected, but we need to understand the internal nature of such a phenomenon. If multi-dimensional spaces do play a significant role during such processes, then this can change a great deal in modern physics and natural philosophy. Note that some of the problems mentioned in this study have been considered earlier (see, e.g., [30–33]).

**Funding:** No funding has been used for this research.

**Institutional Review Board Statement:** Not applicable.

**Informed Consent Statement:** Not applicable.

**Data Availability Statement:** Not applicable.

**Conflicts of Interest:** The author declares no conflict of interest.

## Appendix A. Scalar Electrodynamics

In this study, our analysis of electrodynamics in multi-dimensional spaces was restricted to spaces which have geometrical dimension $n \geq 3$. For the sake of completeness, we now want to consider the one and two-dimensional spaces. To investigate these small-dimensional cases, we shall apply one effective method which is based on the so-called scalar electrodynamics. This "pre-Maxwell" method was described and briefly discussed in [4]. Scalar electrodynamics can be introduced in three-dimensional space, where one can compare the arising equations with the usual Maxwell equations. The foundation of scalar electrodynamics is the well-known theorem from vector calculus (see, e.g., [6]) which states that an arbitrary vector **B** in three-dimensional space can be represented in the following *two − gradient* form:

$$\mathbf{B} = \Psi_1 \nabla \Psi_2 + \nabla \Psi_3, \tag{A1}$$

where $\Psi_1, \Psi_2$, and $\Psi_3$ are three arbitrary analytical functions of three spatial coordinates and one temporal coordinate. In general, each of these functions can be real or complex. This formula can directly be applied to the vector potential of the electromagnetic field **A**. The four-dimensional vector potential $(\varphi, \mathbf{A})$ and intensities of electric **E** and magnetic **H** field are also represented in terms of the four $\Psi_1, \Psi_2, \Psi_3$, and $\varphi$ scalar functions. For two and one-dimensional (geometrical) spaces, the total numbers of such scalar functions equal three and two, respectively.

To derive the explicit expressions and obtain the governing equations of electrodynamics, one needs to use the two following formulas which play a central role in scalar electrodynamics:

$$curl\mathbf{A} = \nabla \Psi_1 \times \nabla \Psi_2 \quad \text{and} \quad div\mathbf{A} = \Psi_1 \Delta \Psi_2 + \nabla \Psi_1 \cdot \nabla \Psi_2 + \Delta \Psi_3 \tag{A2}$$

As follows from Equation (A2), in scalar electrodynamics, there are a number of advantages to choose some of the $\Psi_1, \Psi_2$ and $\Psi_3$ functions (where it is possible) as harmonic functions for which $\Delta \Psi_k = 0$, where $k$ = 1, 2, 3. Such a choice of functions reduces the total number of terms in Maxwell equations and gauge conditions. In turn, this simplifies the analysis and solutions of many problems in scalar electrodynamics. In fact, in three-dimensional spaces, the scalar electrodynamics cannot compete with the traditional vector approach. The main reason is obvious, since the regular Maxwell equations are linear for all components of the electromagnetic field. However, some selected three-dimensional problems can be solved (completely and accurately) if we apply the method of scalar electrodynamics.

The equation for two-dimensional spaces, Equation (A1), takes the form $\mathbf{A} = \Psi_1 \nabla \Psi_2$, since in this case we can assume that $\Psi_3 = 0$. The equality $\mathbf{A} \cdot curl\mathbf{A} = 0$ is a necessary and sufficient condition to represent the vector **A** in such a form [6] (it does obey in this case). This leads to the following equations:

$$\mathbf{H} = curl\mathbf{A} = \nabla \Psi_1 \times \nabla \Psi_2 \quad \text{and} \quad div\mathbf{A} = \Psi_1 \Delta \Psi_2 + \nabla \Psi_1 \cdot \nabla \Psi_2. \tag{A3}$$

We also need the explicit expression for the $curl\mathbf{H}$

$$curl\mathbf{H} = \nabla\Psi_1\Delta\Psi_2 - \nabla\Psi_2\Delta\Psi_1 + (\nabla\Psi_1 \cdot \nabla)\Psi_2 - (\nabla\Psi_2 \cdot \nabla)\Psi_1 = \nabla\Psi_1\Delta\Psi_2 - \nabla\Psi_2\Delta\Psi_1$$

One should also note that if $\Psi_2$ is chosen as a harmonic function—i.e., $\Delta\Psi_2 = 0$, and $\nabla\Psi_1 \perp \nabla\Psi_2$—then the gauge condition is obeyed automatically, and solutions of a large number of problems known in two-dimensional electrodynamics are simplified significantly. In general, it can be shown that the both two-dimensional electrodynamics and two-dimensional electrostatics include a number of operations with the harmonic functions (see, e.g., [34–36]. In turn, this leads to numerous successful applications of conformal mapping methods to describe the two-dimensional electromagnetic waves and determine solutions of numerous problems in two-dimensional electrostatics.

In the equation for the one-dimensional case, Equation (A1), one finds $\mathbf{A} = \nabla\Psi_2 = \nabla\Psi$. Therefore, the *curl* of the vector potential equals zero identically. This means that there is no classical magnetic field in one-dimensional space. Moreover, any time-variations of the electric field cannot generate any magnetic field; i.e., we have no Faraday's law in one-dimensional (geometrical) space. In other words, the one-dimensional electrodynamics does not exist. On the other hand, many one-dimensional electrostatic problems that include the potential and intensity of the electric field only can still be formulated and solved correctly.

## References


1. Frolov, A.M. General Principles of Hamiltonian Formulations of the Metric Gravity. *Phys. Atomic Nuclei (Yad. Fiz.)* **2021**, *84*, 750–722. [CrossRef]
2. Maxwell, J.C. A dynamical theory of the electromagnetic field. *Phil. Trans. R. Soc. Lond.* **1865**, *155*, 489–512.
3. Maxwell, J.C. *A Treatise on Electricity and Magnetism*; Oxford University Press: Oxford, UK, 1873; Volume 2.
4. Frolov, A.M. On the 150th anniversary of Maxwell equations. *J. Multidiscip. Eng. Sci. Technol. (JMEST)* **2015**, *2*, 361–369.
5. Landau, L.D.; Lifshitz, E.M. *The Classical Theory of Fields*, 4th ed.; Pergamon Press Ltd.: London, UK, 1975.
6. Kochin, N.E. *Vector Calculus and the Principles of Tensor Calculus*, 9th ed.; USSR Acad. of Sciences Publishing: Moscow, Russia, 1965.
7. Dashevskii, P.K. *Riemannian Geometry and Tensor Analysis*, 3rd ed.; Nauka (Science): Moscow, Russia, 1967.
8. Sokolov, A.A. *Introduction in Quantum Electrodynamics*; Fizmatgiz: Moscow, Russia, 1958. (In Russian)
9. Sokolov, A.A.; Ternov, I.M. *Relativistic Electron*, 2nd ed.; Nauka (Science): Moscow, Russia, 1983; Chapters 1 and 2. (In Russian)
10. Gradstein, I.S.; Ryzhik, I.M. *Tables of Integrals, Series and Products*, 6th ed.; Academic Press: New York, NY, USA, 2000.
11. Flanders, H. *Differential Forms with Applications to the Physical Sciences*; Dover Publications, Inc.: Mineola, NY, USA, 1989.
12. Dirac, P.A.M. The Theory of Magnetic Poles The Theory of Magnetic Poles. *Phys. Rev.* **1948**, *817*, 74.
13. Amaldi, E. On the Dirac Magnetic Poles. In *Old and New Problems in Elementary Particles*; Puppi, G., Ed.; Academic Press: New York, NY, USA, 1968.
14. Dirac, P.A.M. *Lectures on Quantum Mechanics*; Befler Graduate School of Sciences, Yeshiva University: New York, NY, USA, 1964.
15. Dirac, P.A.M. Generalized Hamiltonian dynamics. *Can. J. Math.* **1950**, *2*, 129–148. [CrossRef]
16. Castellani, L. Symmetries in constrained Hamiltonian systems. *Ann. Phys.* **1982**, *143*, 357–371. [CrossRef]
17. Bessel-Hagen, E. Über die Erhaltungssätze der Elektrodynamik. *Math. Ann.* **1921**, *84*, 258–276. [CrossRef]
18. Heitler, W. *The Quantum Theory of Radiation*, 3rd ed.; Oxford University Press: London, UK, 1954.
19. Jackson, J.D. *Classical Electrodynamics*, 2nd ed.; J. Wiley & Sons Inc.: New York, NY, USA, 1975; Section 6.5.
20. Jackson, J.D. From Lorenz to Coulomb and other explicit gauge transformations. *Am. J. Phys.* **2002**, *70*, 917–928. [CrossRef]
21. Gelfand, I.M.; Fomin, S.V. *Calculus of Variations*; Dover Publ., Inc.: Mineola, NY, USA, 1990; Chapter 7.
22. Engelhardt, W. Gauge Invariance in Classical Electrodynamics. *Annal. Fond. Louis Broglie* **2005**, *30*, 157.
23. Tolmen, R.C. *Relativity, Thermodynamics and Cosmology*, 3rd ed.; Oxford at the Clarendon Press: Oxford, UK, 1969; Chapter VIII.
24. Carmeli, M. *Classical Fields: General Relativity and Gauge Theory*; World Scientific Publ. Co.: Singapore, 2002.
25. Rafelski, J.; Greiner, W.; Fulcher, L.P. Superheavy elements and nonlinear electrodynamics. *Nuovo C* **1973**, *13B*, 135–160. [CrossRef]
26. Dirac, P.A.M. The theory of gravitation in Hamiltonian form. *Proc. R. Soc.* **1958**, *246*, 333–343.
27. Kiriushcheva, N.; Kuzmin, S.V.; Racnkor, C.; Valluri, S.R. Diffeomorphism Invariance in the Hamiltonian formulation of General Relativity. *Phys. Lett. A* **2008**, *372*, 5101–5105. [CrossRef]
28. Frolov, A.M.; Kiriushcheva, N.; Kuzmin, S.V. On canonical transformations between equivalent Hamiltonian formulations of General Relativity. *Gravit. Cosmol.* **2011**, *17*, 314–323. [CrossRef]
29. Frolov, A.M. On the Hamiltonian and Hamilton–Jacobi equations for metric gravity. *Can. J. Phys.* **2020**, *98*, 405–412. [CrossRef]
30. Lemos, P.; Quinta, G.M.; Zaslavskii, O.B. Entropy of a self-gravitating electrically charged thin shell and the black hole limit. *Phys. Rev. D* **2015**, *91*, 104027. [CrossRef]

31. Kratovich, P.V.; Ju,V. Tchemarina. *arXiv* **2018**, arXiv:1805.02698.
32. Yousaf, Z.; Bamba, K.; Bhatti, M.Z.; Ghafoor, U. Charged gravastars in modified gravity. *Phys. Rev. D* **2019**, *100*, 024062. [CrossRef]
33. Pugliese, D.; Valiente Kroon, J.A. On the evolution equations for a self-gravitating charged scalar field. *Relat. Gravit.* **2013**, *45*, 1247–1269. [CrossRef]
34. Tikhonov, A.N.; Samarskii, A.A. *Equations of Mathematical Physics*; Dover Publ., Inc., New York, USA: 1990; Chapter IV.
35. Smythe, W.R. *Static and Dynamic Electricity*; McGraw-HIll, Inc.: New York, NY, USA, 1950.
36. Landau, L.D.; Lifshitz, E.M. *Electrodynamics of Continuous Media*, 2nd ed.; Pergamon Press Ltd.: London, UK, 1984.

universe
MDPI

Article

# On the Conformal Frames in $f(R)$ Gravity

Yuri Shtanov [1,2]

1 Bogolyubov Institute for Theoretical Physics, Metrologichna St. 14-b, 03143 Kiev, Ukraine; shtanov@bitp.kiev.ua
2 Department of Physics, Taras Shevchenko National University of Kiev, Volodymyrska St. 60, 01033 Kiev, Ukraine

**Abstract:** We discuss gravitational physics in the Jordan and Einstein frames of $f(R)$ gravity coupled to the Standard Model. We elucidate the way in which the observed gravitational coupling arises in the Einstein frame for generic $f(R)$. We point out that the effect of "running units" in the Einstein frame is related to the fact that the explicit and implicit quantum parameters of the Standard Model, such as the Higgs vacuum expectation value and the parameter $\Lambda_{\mathrm{QCD}}$, are modified by the conformal transformation of the metric and matter fields and become scalaron-dependent. Considering the scalaron of $f(R)$ gravity describing dark matter, we show that the effect of running units in this case is extremely weak, making two frames practically equivalent.

**Keyword:** modified gravity

**Citation:** Shtanov, Y. On the Conformal Frames in $f(R)$ Gravity. *Universe* **2022**, *8*, 69. https://doi.org/10.3390/universe8020069

Academic Editor: Panayiotis Stavrinos

Received: 16 December 2021
Accepted: 21 January 2022
Published: 23 January 2022



## 1. Introduction

Modification of the general relativity theory by considering the Lagrangian in the form of a nonlinear function $f(R)$ of the scalar curvature $R$ is, perhaps, the simplest one and has long been the subject of numerous studies and applications (see [1–3] for reviews). Compared to the general relativity theory, such $f(R)$ gravity contains one extra degree of freedom, which can be used for modelling a wide variety of phenomena, from the inflationary regime in the early universe [4] to dark matter at later epochs [5–11].

The extra degree of freedom is most conveniently identified in the so-called Einstein frame of fields, where it becomes a separate scalar field, called the scalaron, while the remaining gravitational degrees of freedom are described by the general-relativistic action. The existence of different conformal frames has long ago raised the issue of their physical equivalence [12]. After some debates, this question, in principle, appears to have been resolved (see [13]). The conformal frames are physically equivalent and describe the same observable phenomena if one carefully takes into account conformal transformation of all masses. Thus, in the Einstein frame, one then deals with so-called "running units", with all physical masses becoming scalaron-dependent in a universal way.

Although the relation between the conformal frames has been understood in general, it is, perhaps, worth giving it a closer look in the concrete theory of fundamental interactions we are working with. This is the main subject of the present paper, in which we consider the Standard Model minimally coupled to $f(R)$ theory of gravity. In addition, working in the Einstein frame, we are going to estimate potential observable effects of $f(R)$ gravity in a late-time universe in which the oscillating scalaron plays the role of dark matter [6,11].

The Lagrangian of the Standard Model explicitly contains only one dimensionful parameter (in the units $\hbar = c = 1$), the vacuum expectation value $\eta_0$ of the Higgs field. However, according to our current understanding, this Lagrangian is to be regarded as an asymptotic local limit of the renormalisation-group flow. The physics that this theory describes at finite energy scales is characterised also by physical constants arising from the phenomenon known as dimensional transmutation. Most important of these is the parameter $\Lambda_{\mathrm{QCD}}$, which enters the law of renormalisation of the coupling constant of strong interactions. Simplifying things by disregarding other gauge groups, we may take that $\Lambda_{\text{QCD}}$ and $\eta_0$ determine the masses of all observable particles: hadrons, leptons, and gauge bosons.

We will see that the scalaron in the Einstein frame couples to the Higgs field, in particular, through the scalaron-dependence of the new vacuum expectation value $\tilde{\eta}(\phi)$ In this sense, the Einstein frame becomes the frame with transformed, or running mass units (in the terminology of [12,13]) for all bare masses of elementary particles, which arise due to the Higgs mechanism. As regards the masses of bound states such as hadrons, they depend in a non-trivial way also on the implicit dimensionful quantum parameters such as $\Lambda_{\text{QCD}}$. This opens up two possibilities of interpreting the theory in the Einstein frame: as a theory with running implicit parameters (which then becomes the frame with running mass units), equivalent to the theory in the original Jordan frame, or as a theory with fixed implicit parameters. Although the two interpretations, in general, differ in their observable predictions, they become equivalent in situations with a completely stabilised or weakly excited scalaron. The last situation arises in a late-time universe in which the excited scalaron plays the role of dark matter [6,11], and we will show that the difference between these interpretations is practically negligible in this case.

## 2. Gravitational Constant in the Einstein Frame

In this section, we review the well-known transition from the Jordan frame to the Einstein frame in the gravity sector. Our attention will be focused on the origin of the gravitational constant (Planck mass) in this frame.

Adopting the metric signature $(-,+,+,+)$, we write the gravitational action in the form:

$$S_g = \int d^4x\sqrt{-g}\, f(R)\,. \tag{1}$$

Note that the function $f(R)$ of the scalar curvature has mass dimension four in the unit system $\hbar = c = 1$. In general relativity, we have:

$$f_{\text{GR}}(R) = \frac{M_{\text{P}}^2}{3}(R - 2\Lambda)\,, \tag{2}$$

where $M_{\text{P}} = \sqrt{3/16\pi G} \approx 3 \times 10^{18}$ GeV is a conveniently normalised Planck mass (the reason for our choice of this normalisation will become clear below). It is customary to explicitly introduce the factor $M_{\text{P}}^2/3$ in $f(R)$. This can be done without loss of generality, but we will not do this here for better clarity. The point is that any other constant of the same dimension can be factored out here, while our aim is to trace the origin of the physical Planck mass in the Einstein frame.

Proceeding to the Einstein frame, as a first step, one writes action (1) in the form

$$S_g = \int d^4x\sqrt{-g}\left[\Omega R - h(\Omega)\right], \tag{3}$$

where $\Omega$ is a new field with mass dimension two, and $h(\Omega)$ is the Legendre transform of $f(R)$. It is defined by the following equations:

$$f'(R) = \Omega \quad \Rightarrow \quad R = R(\Omega)\,, \tag{4}$$

$$h(\Omega) = \left[\Omega R - f(R)\right]_{R=R(\Omega)}\,. \tag{5}$$

The inverse transform allows one to calculate $f(R)$ given $h(\Omega)$; it is obtained by variation of (3) with respect to $\Omega$:

$$h'(\Omega) = R \quad \Rightarrow \quad \Omega = \Omega(R)\,, \tag{6}$$

$$f(R) = \left[\Omega R - h(\Omega)\right]_{\Omega=\Omega(R)}\,. \tag{7}$$

These transformations may involve subtleties as to which solution is to be chosen in (4) and (6). Solutions of these equations are unique for convex functions, e.g., if $f''(R) > 0$ everywhere in the domain of validity. In what follows, we will assume $\Omega$ to be positive; therefore, in view of (4), we also require[1] $f'(R) > 0$.

Our next step is to transform action (3) so that its linear term in $R$ takes the Einstein form. For this purpose, we perform a conformal transformation of the metric:

$$g_{\mu\nu} = \frac{M^2}{3\Omega}\widetilde{g}_{\mu\nu}\,. \tag{8}$$

Here, we explicitly introduced an arbitrary mass parameter $M$, compensating for the dimension of $\Omega$ so that the conformal transformation parameter is dimensionless (leaving the dimension of the metric intact). With this transformation, we have:

$$\sqrt{-g}\,\Omega R = \frac{M^2}{3}\sqrt{-g}\,\frac{3\Omega}{M^2}R = \frac{M^2}{3}\sqrt{-\widetilde{g}}\left[\widetilde{R} - \frac{3}{2}\left(\widetilde{\nabla}\ln\Omega\right)^2 + 3\widetilde{\Box}\ln\Omega\right], \tag{9}$$

in which all objects related to the new metric $\widetilde{g}_{\mu\nu}$ are denoted by tildes. The last term is the total derivative and can be dropped. The transformed action (3) then becomes:

$$S_g = \int d^4x\sqrt{-\widetilde{g}}\left[\frac{M^2}{3}\widetilde{R} - \frac{M^2}{2}\left(\widetilde{\nabla}\ln\Omega\right)^2 - W(\Omega)\right], \tag{10}$$

where

$$W(\Omega) = \frac{M^4}{9}\frac{h(\Omega)}{\Omega^2}\,. \tag{11}$$

We have obtained an Einstein theory of gravity with a minimally coupled scalar field and with a Planck mass $M$. The theory is stable only if the potential $W(\Omega)$ has a minimum at $\Omega = \Omega_0$. In view of system (4)–(7), this condition is equivalent to the existence of $R_0$, such that:

$$R_0 f'(R_0) = 2f(R_0)\,, \qquad \frac{1}{f''(R_0)} - \frac{R_0^2}{2f(R_0)} > 0\,. \tag{12}$$

Then, $\Omega_0 = f'(R_0)$. From these relations, it is clear that the values of $\Omega_0$ and $R_0$ are independent of $M$ introduced in (8). This is also evident from the fact that the parameter $M$ enters only as an overall scaling in potential (11).

We then introduce a scalar field (scalaron) $\phi$ with a canonical kinetic term and with a minimum of potential at $\phi = 0$ by setting:[2]

$$\Omega = \Omega(\phi) = \Omega_0 e^{\phi/M}\,. \tag{13}$$

Action (10), eventually, becomes:

$$S_g = \int d^4x\sqrt{-\widetilde{g}}\left[\frac{M^2}{3}\widetilde{R} - \frac{1}{2}\left(\widetilde{\nabla}\phi\right)^2 - V(\phi)\right], \tag{14}$$

where the scalaron potential $V(\phi)$ is calculated by using (5), (11) and (13):

$$V(\phi) \equiv W(\Omega(\phi)) = \frac{M^4}{9}\left[\frac{R}{\Omega} - \frac{f(R)}{\Omega^2}\right]_{\substack{R=R(\Omega)\\ \Omega=\Omega(\phi)}}\,. \tag{15}$$

We note that the mass parameter $M$ has appeared as the Planck mass in action (14), and as an overall scaling in potential (15).[3] However, this parameter was introduced in (8) quite arbitrarily. This might appear paradoxical, as if $f(R)$ gravity does not predict a specific value for the gravitational constant in the Einstein frame. This paradox is resolved by examining the matter part of the action, which is done in the following section.

## 3. Coupling of Gravity to Matter

As regards the matter action in the Jordan frame, we take it to be that of the Standard Model minimally coupled to gravity. Proceeding to the Einstein frame via (8) affects this action as well. Note, however, that most of the Standard Model action is classically conformally invariant (with proper conformal transformation of the matter fields), and, therefore, will retain its original form after transformation (8). The only part that breaks conformal invariance is the Higgs sector, with the action:

$$S_{\rm H} = -\int d^4x\sqrt{-g}\left[g^{\mu\nu}\left(D_\mu\Phi\right)^\dagger D_\nu\Phi + \lambda\left(\Phi^\dagger\Phi - \frac{\eta_0^2}{2}\right)^2\right]. \tag{16}$$

Here, $D_\mu$ is the gauge covariant derivative involving the SU(2) and U(1) electroweak gauge fields and acting on the Higgs doublet $\Phi$, and $\eta_0$ is the symmetry-breaking parameter in the Jordan frame. After the conformal transformation (8), (13) is accompanied by the transformation of the Higgs scalar field:

$$\Phi = \frac{\sqrt{3\Omega}}{M}\,\widetilde{\Phi}\,, \tag{17}$$

and this action becomes:[4]

$$S_{\rm H} = -\int d^4x\sqrt{-\widetilde{g}}\,\widetilde{g}^{\mu\nu}\left[\left(D_\mu\widetilde{\Phi}\right)^\dagger D_\nu\widetilde{\Phi} + \frac{1}{2M}\widetilde{\nabla}_\mu\left(\widetilde{\Phi}^\dagger\widetilde{\Phi}\right)\widetilde{\nabla}_\nu\phi + \frac{1}{4M^2}\widetilde{\Phi}^\dagger\widetilde{\Phi}\,\widetilde{\nabla}_\mu\phi\widetilde{\nabla}_\nu\phi\right]$$
$$-\lambda\int d^4x\sqrt{-\widetilde{g}}\left(\widetilde{\Phi}^\dagger\widetilde{\Phi} - \beta e^{-\phi/M}\frac{\eta_0^2}{2}\right)^2, \tag{18}$$

where

$$\beta = \frac{M^2}{3\Omega_0} > 0 \tag{19}$$

is a dimensionless constant. We observe the appearance of non-renormalisable interactions of the scalaron $\phi$ with the Higgs field in (18), which, however, are all suppressed by inverse powers of the Planck mass $M$.

From (18), one observes that the Higgs vacuum expectation value in the Einstein frame is:

$$\widetilde{\eta}(\phi) = \sqrt{\beta}\,e^{-\phi/2M}\eta_0\,. \tag{20}$$

It is this parameter that will determine the bare masses of all fermions and gauge bosons in the model, which are all proportional to it. Now, in the scalaron vacuum $\phi = 0$, the ratio of $\widetilde{\eta}_0 = \widetilde{\eta}(0) = \sqrt{\beta}\eta_0$ to the Planck mass $M$ in (14) is:

$$\frac{\widetilde{\eta}_0}{M} = \frac{\eta_0}{\sqrt{3\,\Omega_0}}\,. \tag{21}$$

This ratio is independent of the chosen scale $M$ in (8), and is uniquely determined by the original Jordan-frame actions (1) and (16). Only this ratio makes sense and is physically measurable. This explains the freedom of choosing $M$ arbitrarily in (8). Assigning the observed value $\widetilde{\eta}_0 \approx 246$ GeV, we should then equate $M$ to the Planck mass $M_{\rm P} = \sqrt{3/16\pi G} \approx 3\times10^{18}$ GeV.

The same reasoning applies to the issue of cosmological constant in the Einstein frame. We observe that its purely gravitational contribution $\widetilde{\Lambda}$ in this frame is given by the minimum of the scalaron potential (15):

$$\widetilde{\Lambda} = \frac{M^2}{24}\frac{R_0^2}{f(R_0)}\,, \tag{22}$$

where we have used equation (12). We see that the observed ratio $\widetilde{\Lambda}/M^2$ is also independent of the chosen scale $M$ in (8). The mass hierarchy problem of modern cosmology can be expressed as:

$$\frac{\widetilde{\Lambda}}{M^2} \ll \frac{\widetilde{\eta}_0^2}{M^2} \ll 1 \quad \Rightarrow \quad \frac{R_0^2}{f(R_0)} \ll \frac{R_0\eta_0^2}{f(R_0)} \ll 1\,, \tag{23}$$

where, we remember, $R_0$ is a solution of (12). The last set of inequalities are written in terms of the action in the original Jordan frame.

This analysis would be the whole story for a world described by classical fields. However, the fields in the Standard Model Lagrangian are quantum, and their quantum dynamics are non-trivial.

The Lagrangian of the Standard Model in the Jordan frame contains only one explicit dimensionful parameter, the vacuum expectation value $\eta_0$ of the Higgs field. However, according to modern understanding, this Lagrangian is to be regarded as the relevant part of the low-energy (or large-scale) action of some renormalisation-group flow (see, e.g., [18]). The physics that this theory describes at finite energy scales is also characterised by implicit dimensionful parameters arising in what is known as dimensional transmutation. Such is the QCD parameter $\Lambda_{\rm QCD}$ that enters the law of renormalisation-group flow of the coupling constant of strong interactions and determines the masses of hadrons (see, e.g., [19,20]). Simplifying the situation by disregarding other gauge interactions, we may take that two dimensionful parameters, $\Lambda_{\rm QCD}$ and $\eta_0$, control the masses of all particles and bound states, including hadrons, in the Jordan frame. With this simplification, we will have, for the $i$th particle mass:

$$m_i = \Lambda_{\rm QCD}\, f_i\left(\frac{\eta_0}{\Lambda_{\rm QCD}}\right), \tag{24}$$

where $f_i(x)$ are some dimensionless functions.

This consideration opens up two possibilities of interpreting the theory in the Einstein frame.

### *3.1. Einstein Frame with Running Implicit Parameters*

In the matter Lagrangian density, we can proceed to the Einstein frame by the conformal transformation (8) of the metric, scaling the Higgs field and the fermionic fields $\psi$ accordingly:

$$\mathcal{L} = \mathcal{L}\left(\beta e^{-\phi/M}\widetilde{g}_{\mu\nu},\, \beta^{-1/2}e^{\phi/2M}\widetilde{\Phi},\, \beta^{-3/4}e^{3\phi/4M}\widetilde{\psi}\right) \equiv \widetilde{\mathcal{L}}\left(\widetilde{g}_{\mu\nu},\, \widetilde{\Phi},\, \widetilde{\psi},\, \phi\right). \tag{25}$$

Here, by virtue of an almost perfect conformal invariance of the action, the last expression differs from the Lagrangian density $\mathcal{L}\left(\widetilde{g}_{\mu\nu},\, \widetilde{\Phi},\, \widetilde{\psi}\right)$ only in the Higgs part (18). However, the scalaron-dependent scaling of quantum fields, together with (8), lead us to a quantum theory with accordingly scaled, implicit quantum dimensionful parameters. In particular, the QCD parameter in the Einstein frame is locally scaled as:

$$\widetilde{\Lambda}_{\rm QCD}(\phi) = \frac{M}{\sqrt{3\Omega}}\Lambda_{\rm QCD} = \sqrt{\beta}\, e^{-\phi/2M}\Lambda_{\rm QCD}\,, \tag{26}$$

similarly to the scaling (20) of the parameter $\eta_0$ in (18). Replacing $\Lambda_{\rm QCD}$ and $\eta_0$ in (24) with their scaled values $\widetilde{\Lambda}_{\rm QCD}(\phi)$ and $\widetilde{\eta}(\phi)$ in the Einstein frame, we observe that all masses are scaled in the same way:

$$\widetilde{m}_i = \sqrt{\beta}\, e^{-\phi/2M} m_i\,. \tag{27}$$

Their ratios to the Planck mass $M$ at the scalaron vacuum $\phi = 0$ are, again, independent of our choice of $M$ in (8).

Scaling (27) describes the situation of an *Einstein frame with running units*, an option first discussed in [12] and further elucidated in [13]. Here, the scalaron, in addition to the interaction with the Higgs field through the explicit mass parameter $\widetilde{\eta}(\phi)$ in (18), also interacts with matter implicitly via (26) and, therefore, (27). One can arrive at the same picture by considering the matter Lagrangian density in the Einstein frame with transformed metric field only, i.e.,

$$\mathcal{L} = \mathcal{L}\left(\beta e^{-\phi/M}\tilde{g}_{\mu\nu}, \Phi, \psi\right), \tag{28}$$

and treating $\Lambda_{\text{QCD}}$ and related quantum condensates of the $\psi$ fields as quantities coinciding with their values in the Jordan frame. In this case, one obtains the usual relation between the stress–energy tensors in two frames:

$$\tilde{T}_{\mu\nu} = \beta e^{-\phi/M} T_{\mu\nu} . \tag{29}$$

An expression for the mass of a static localised object is:

$$m_i = \int_\Sigma T_{\mu\nu} n^\mu \xi^\nu d\mu_\Sigma , \tag{30}$$

where the integral is taken over a hypersurface $\Sigma$, with $n^\mu$ being the vector field of unit normal to this hypersurface; $\xi^\mu$ is the timelike killing vector field such that $\xi^\mu \xi_\mu = -1$ at spatial infinity, and $d\mu_\Sigma$ is the volume measure determined by the induced metric on $\Sigma$. Using the conformal transformation laws of these quantities, we again arrive at the transformation law (27) for the mass.

The two (Jordan and Einstein) frames in this interpretation are equivalent; it is a matter of convenience in regards to which frame one chooses to work with, as long as one keeps track of scaling (26) and (27). In particular, all objects (massive as well as massless) move along the geodesics of the Jordan-frame metric $g_{\mu\nu} = \beta e^{-\phi/M}\tilde{g}_{\mu\nu}$, which is the "observable" metric in all respects [12,13].[5]

### 3.2. *Einstein Frame with Fixed Implicit Parameters*

Treating the fields in the Lagrangian $\tilde{\mathcal{L}}\left(\tilde{g}_{\mu\nu}, \tilde{\Phi}, \tilde{\psi}, \phi\right)$ of (25) as given, and "forgetting" about their Jordan-frame origin, one can specify their quantum theory by a $\phi$-independent implicit quantum parameter $\Lambda_{\text{QCD}}$ in the Einstein frame. This will create a situation quite different from that of Section 3.1, since now, the bare masses of quarks, leptons, and gauge fields will depend on the scalaron, as before, through the Higgs expectation-value parameter (20), while the hadron masses will be given by:

$$\tilde{m}_i = \Lambda_{\text{QCD}} f_i\left(\frac{\tilde{\eta}(\phi)}{\Lambda_{\text{QCD}}}\right), \tag{31}$$

depending on the scalaron in a way that is more complicated than (27). We see that, in our framework and strictly speaking, there is no conformal frame with completely fixed units. Particle masses in this frame depend on the scalaron field in a different manner.

For the scalaron in the vacuum, this difference between frames will not be revealed, but it will exist in situations where the scalaron is dynamically excited. One such situation is considered in Section 4.

### 3.3. *Conformal Anomaly*

The quantum loop corrections to the classical action lead to the effect that the extra degree of freedom present in $f(R)$ gravity couples to matter also due to the conformal anomaly. This is most easily seen in the Einstein frame, in which couplings between the scalaron and gauge fields with strength tensor $F_{\mu\nu}$, for small values of $|\phi|/M$, are proportional to [6,8]:

$$\alpha_g \frac{\phi}{M} \operatorname{tr} F_{\mu\nu} F^{\mu\nu} , \tag{32}$$

where $\alpha_g = e_g^2/4\pi$, and $e_g$ is the relevant gauge-coupling parameter.

## 4. Light Scalaron as Dark Matter

Since the original value of $M$ can be fixed arbitrarily (as was shown Section 3), we fix it in what follows so that $\beta = 1$ (this constant is defined in (19)).

The $\phi$-dependence of the particle masses, such as (27) or (31), might be potentially interesting in the case of a classically evolving scalaron. This may lead to important phenomena in the early universe, where the scalaron can be highly excited. For example, if the scalaron plays the role of an inflaton, when proceeding to the Einstein frame, it may be necessary to take into account the dependence (27) of the masses of fundamental particles on the scalaron field during inflation. The same dependence is responsible for particle creation during preheating in such an inflationary theory [14,23].

In this paper, however, we will focus on the situation that arises in a late-time universe in which the oscillating scalaron plays the role of dark matter [6,11]. In this case, the scalaron oscillations might lead to potentially observable effects. Such effects are determined by the small ratio:[6]

$$\frac{|\phi|}{M} \simeq \frac{\sqrt{2\rho_s}}{M^2}\frac{M}{m} \simeq 10^{-33}\left(\frac{\rho_s}{\overline{\rho}_s}\right)^{1/2}(1+z)^{3/2}\,\frac{\text{eV}}{m}\,, \tag{33}$$

where $z$ is the cosmological redshift, $\rho_s$ is the local scalaron energy density, $\overline{\rho}_s$ is its spatial average in the universe, and $m$ is the scalaron mass. The effects are very small because the scalaron mass in the interpretation of the Einstein frame with running units is bounded from below by non-observation [25,26] of the additional Yukawa forces [27] between non-relativistic masses (see also [6,28]):

$$m \geq 2.7 \times 10^{-3}\,\text{eV} \quad \text{at 95\% C.L.} \tag{34}$$

As regards the Einstein frame with constant implicit parameter $\Lambda_{\text{QCD}}$, the $\phi$-dependence in (31) will have additional smallness because the contribution of the bare quark masses to the masses of hadrons constitute only a tiny fraction of the total mass [19].

Let us examine this in more detail for the late-time universe. The effect is most prominent in the interpretation of the Einstein frame with running units, where the observable metric will be that of the Jordan frame. Then, in the Einstein frame, all masses scale with the scalaron as (27). This produces second-order effects in the small gravitational potential because of the smallness of the ratio (33). However, in the observable metric, this gives an effect of the first order because of the scaling $g_{\mu\nu} = e^{-\phi/M}\widetilde{g}_{\mu\nu}$. This will not affect null geodesics apart from additional redshift, but will produce an effective Newtonian potential,

$$\varphi_{\text{eff}} = \varphi - \frac{\phi}{2M}, \tag{35}$$

for non-relativistic matter. Here, $\varphi$ is the Newtonian potential in the Einstein-frame metric $\widetilde{g}_{\mu\nu}$, which is determined by the distribution of the usual matter and dark matter in the form of scalaron. In the Newtonian approximation to gravity, which is of relevance here, it is described by the Poisson equation $\nabla^2\varphi = 3\rho/4M^2$, where $\rho$ is the total energy density of matter, including the scalaron field.

The scalaron field $\phi$ of mass $m$ is oscillating in time with the following period:

$$t = \frac{2\pi}{m} \approx 4.1 \times 10^{-15}\left(\frac{\text{eV}}{m}\right)\text{s}\,. \tag{36}$$

Therefore, the last term in the effective Newtonian potential (35) is rapidly oscillating in time with space-dependent amplitude. Since one is interested in the motion of astrophysical bodies on time scales much longer than (36), one should perform time averaging of their dynamics in such a rapidly oscillating potential. The solution to this classical problem is well known (see §30 in [29]). The average long-term effective potential acting on test bodies is given by:

$$\overline{\varphi}_{\rm eff} = \varphi + \frac{\overline{(\nabla\phi)^2}}{8m^2M^2} = \varphi + \frac{(\nabla\phi_0)^2}{16m^2M^2}\,, \tag{37}$$

where overline denotes averaging over a period of oscillations of $\phi$, and $\phi_0$ is the space-dependent amplitude of its oscillations. Since the scalaron energy density $\rho_{\rm s} = \frac{1}{2}m^2\phi_0^2$, we have:

$$\overline{\varphi}_{\rm eff} = \varphi + \frac{(\nabla\rho_{\rm s})^2}{32m^4M^2\rho_{\rm s}} = \varphi + \frac{\left(\nabla\nabla^2\varphi_{\rm s}\right)^2}{24m^4\nabla^2\varphi_{\rm s}}\,, \tag{38}$$

where we have used the Poisson equation $\rho_{\rm s} = \frac{4}{3}M^2\nabla^2\varphi_{\rm s}$ for the scalaron contribution $\varphi_{\rm s}$ to the total gravitational potential $\varphi$.

The scalaron energy density, and the gravitational potential $\varphi_{\rm s}$, hence, varies on the spatial scale of the de Broglie wavelength (see [30] for a review on such wave dark matter):

$$\lambda_{\rm dB} \simeq \frac{2\pi}{mv} = 124\left(\frac{10^{-3}\,{\rm eV}}{m}\right)\left(\frac{10^{-3}}{v}\right)\,{\rm cm}\,, \tag{39}$$

where $v$ is the velocity dispersion in a virialised dark-matter halo (in units of the speed of light). For the last term in (38), this gives an estimate:

$$\frac{\left(\nabla\nabla^2\varphi_{\rm s}\right)^2}{24m^4\nabla^2\varphi_{\rm s}} \sim \frac{|\varphi_{\rm s}|}{24m^4\lambda_{\rm dB}^4} \sim 10^{-4}v^4|\varphi_{\rm s}|\,. \tag{40}$$

Here, we have replaced all spatial gradients by the characteristic inverse length $\lambda_{\rm dB}^{-1}$. For typical velocity dispersions $v \sim 10^{-2}$–$10^{-3}$, this is many orders of magnitude smaller than $|\varphi_{\rm s}|$. The de Broglie wavelength scale (39) and time scale $t_{\rm dB} = \lambda_{\rm dB}/v$ themselves are rather small for masses $m \gtrsim 10^{-3}\,$eV allowable in this theory. The direct effects of the scalaron oscillations are, thus, quite negligible, and the Jordan and Einstein conformal frames are practically indistinguishable in this case.

Couplings (32) due to the conformal anomaly lead to the scalaron decay into photons, with lifetime $\tau \sim M^2/\alpha^2m^3 \sim 10^{36}\,({\rm eV}/m)^3\,$yr, exceeding the age of the universe ($1.4\times10^{10}\,$yr) for $m \ll 10^8\,$eV. (Here, $\alpha$ is the fine-structure constant.) For the scalaron masses of order $m \sim 10^{-3}\,$eV, as in the scenario of [11], such a light scalaron dark matter appears to be quite "sterile" and hard to detect by means other than gravitationally. The smallness of the specific gravitational manifestations in the scenario under consideration would make it very difficult to establish that we are dealing with $f(R)$ gravity. Perhaps, this could be done only by detecting a specific Yukawa contribution to gravitational forces at submillimetre spatial scales [25–28].

## 5. Discussion

A generic gravity theory with action (1) has a stable point if there exists a solution to (12). In this case, it is conformally transformed by (8) to a general-relativistic theory (14) with a minimally coupled scalar field with potential (15) that has minimum at $\phi = 0$. The gravitational coupling at this stage is introduced arbitrarily in (8). However, its physical value in the Einstein frame is uniquely determined by the function $f(R)$, together with the matter action in the Jordan frame. This was demonstrated in Section 3, where we considered the action of the Standard Model minimally coupled to gravity in the Jordan frame.

We reviewed and further elucidated two possible interpretations of this model in the Einstein frame, namely, as the frame with either running or constant implicit quantum parameters. The Standard Model contains at least one such implicit parameter $\Lambda_{\rm QCD}$, which transforms under conformal transformation of the metric. The difference between these two interpretations, however, is practically insignificant in situations where the scalaron field is weakly excited. We verified this for the case of cosmology in which a light scalaron plays the role of dark matter. In such a scenario, the fact that we are dealing with $f(R)$ gravity could be observationally verified, perhaps, only by detecting a specific Yukawa contribution to gravitational forces at submillimetre spatial scales [25–28].

**Funding:** This research was funded by the National Academy of Sciences of Ukraine project number 0121U109612.

**Institutional Review Board Statement:** Not applicable.

**Informed Consent Statement:** Not applicable.

**Data Availability Statement:** No new data were created or analysed in this study. Data sharing is not applicable to this article.

**Acknowledgments:** The author is grateful to Maria Khelashvili and Anton Rudakovskyi for discussion.

**Conflicts of Interest:** The author declares no conflict of interest. The funders had no role in the design of the study; in the collection, analyses, or interpretation of data; in the writing of the manuscript, or in the decision to publish the results.

## Abbreviations

The following abbreviations are used in this manuscript:

| | |
|---|---|
| C.L. | Confidence Level |
| GR | General Relativity |
| QCD | Quantum Chromodynamics |

## Notes

1. This requirement ensures that the effective gravitational coupling is positive in the Jordan frame, see [1–3] for reviews.
2. If $W(\Omega)$ does not have a minimum, we still can write (13) by choosing $\Omega_0$ arbitrarily. In this case, however, the theory will not have a stable point.
3. The appearance of a simple expression $\phi/M$ (without numerical factor) in the exponent (13) and in all subsequent exponents of this type is the reason why we have chosen the particular normalisation constant in (8) and in (2).
4. A similar result of the conformal transformation of fields was under consideration, e.g., in [14–16]. In passing, we note that conformal transformation, in our theory, where the Higgs scalar field is minimally coupled to gravity, looks much simpler compared to the case of its non-minimal coupling, as is the case, e.g., in the model of Higgs inflation [17].
5. In the context of scalar-tensor theories, such an equivalence between frames on the tree level was recently demonstrated in [16]. On the one-loop level, on-shell equivalence between conformal frames was demonstrated previously in [21,22].
6. For the solar neighbourhood, the dark-matter density is $\rho_{\rm dm} \simeq 10^{-2} M_\odot/\mathrm{pc}^3$ [24], which gives $(\rho_s/\bar{\rho}_s)^{1/2} \simeq 500$.

## References

1. Sotiriou, T.P.; Faraoni, V. $f(R)$ theories of gravity. *Rev. Mod. Phys.* **2010**, *82*, 451–497. [CrossRef]
2. De Felice, A.; Tsujikawa, S. $f(R)$ Theories. *Living Rev. Rel.* **2010**, *13*, 3. [CrossRef]
3. Nojiri, S.; Odintsov, S.D.; Oikonomou, V.K. Modified Gravity Theories on a Nutshell: Inflation, Bounce and Late-time Evolution. *Phys. Rept.* **2017**, *692*, 1–104. [CrossRef]
4. Starobinsky, A.A. A new type of isotropic cosmological models without singularity. *Phys. Lett. B* **1980**, *91*, 99–102. [CrossRef]
5. Nojiri, S.; Odintsov, S.D. Dark energy, inflation and dark matter from modified F(R) gravity. *TSPU Bull.* **2011**, *N8*, 7–19. arXiv:0807.0685.
6. Cembranos, J.A.R. Dark Matter from $R^2$ Gravity. *Phys. Rev. Lett.* **2009**, *102*, 141301. [CrossRef] [PubMed]
7. Corda, C.; Mosquera Cuesta, H.J.; Lorduy Gómez, R. High-energy scalarons in $R^2$ gravity as a model for Dark Matter in galaxies. *Astropart. Phys.* **2012**, *35*, 362–370. [CrossRef]
8. Katsuragawa, T.; Matsuzaki, S. Dark matter in modified gravity? *Phys. Rev. D* **2017**, *95*, 044040. [CrossRef]
9. Yadav, B.K.; Verma, M.M. Dark matter as scalaron in $f(R)$ gravity models. *J. Cosmol. Astropart. Phys.* **2019**, *10*, 052. [CrossRef]
10. Parbin, N.; Goswami, U.D. Scalarons mimicking dark matter in the Hu–Sawicki model of $f(R)$ gravity. *Mod. Phys. Lett. A* **2021**, *36*, 2150265. [CrossRef]
11. Shtanov, Y. Light scalaron as dark matter. *Phys. Lett. B* **2021**, *820*, 136469. [CrossRef]

12. Dicke, R.H. Mach's principle and invariance under transformation of units. *Phys. Rev.* **1962**, *125*, 2163–2167. [CrossRef]
13. Faraoni, V.; Nadeau, S. The (pseudo)issue of the conformal frame revisited. *Phys. Rev. D* **2007**, *75*, 023501. [CrossRef]
14. Rudenok, I.; Shtanov, Y.; Vilchinskii, S. Post-inflationary preheating with weak coupling. *Phys. Lett. B* **2014**, *733*, 193–197. [CrossRef]
15. Burrage, C.; Copeland, E.J.; Millington, P.; Spannowsky, M. Fifth forces, Higgs portals and broken scale invariance. *J. Cosmol. Astropart. Phys.* **2018**, *11*, 036. [CrossRef]
16. Copeland, E.J.; Millington, P.; Muñoz, S.S. Fifth forces and broken scale symmetries in the Jordan frame. *arXiv* **2021**, arXiv:2111.06357.
17. Bezrukov, F.L.; Shaposhnikov, M. The Standard Model Higgs boson as the inflaton. *Phys. Lett. B* **2008**, *659*, 703–706. [CrossRef]
18. Costello, K. *Renormalization and Effective Field Theory*; Mathematical Surveys and Monographs 170; American Mathematical Society: Providence, RI, USA, 2011; 251p.
19. Chivukula, R.S. The Origin of mass in QCD. *eConf* **2004**, *C040802*, L010.
20. Deur, A.; Brodsky, S.J.; de Teramond, G.F. Connecting the hadron mass scale to the fundamental mass scale of quantum chromodynamics. *Phys. Lett. B* **2015**, *750*, 528–532. [CrossRef]
21. Kamenshchik, A.Y.; Steinwachs, C.F. Question of quantum equivalence between Jordan frame and Einstein frame. *Phys. Rev. D* **2015**, *91*, 084033. [CrossRef]
22. Ruf, M.S.; Steinwachs, C.F. Quantum equivalence of $f(R)$ gravity and scalar-tensor theories. *Phys. Rev. D* **2018**, *97*, 044050. [CrossRef]
23. Gorbunov, D.S.; Panin, A.G. Scalaron the mighty: Producing dark matter and baryon asymmetry at reheating. *Phys. Lett. B* **2011**, *700*, 157–162. [CrossRef]
24. Read, J.I. The local dark matter density. *J. Phys. G* **2014**, *41*, 063101. [CrossRef]
25. Kapner, D.J.; Cook, T.S.; Adelberger, E.G.; Gundlach, J.H.; Heckel, B.R.; Hoyle, C.D.; Swanson, H.E. Tests of the gravitational inverse-square law below the dark-energy length scale. *Phys. Rev. Lett.* **2007**, *98*, 021101. [CrossRef]
26. Adelberger, E.G.; Heckel, B.R.; Hoedl, S.A.; Hoyle, C.D.; Kapner, D.J.; Upadhye, A. Particle-physics implications of a recent test of the gravitational inverse-square law. *Phys. Rev. Lett.* **2007**, *98*, 131104. [CrossRef]
27. Stelle, K.S. Classical gravity with higher derivatives. *Gen. Rel. Grav.* **1978**, *9*, 353–371. [CrossRef]
28. Perivolaropoulos, L.; Kazantzidis, L. Hints of modified gravity in cosmos and in the lab? *Int. J. Mod. Phys. D* **2019**, *28*, 1942001. [CrossRef]
29. Landau, L.D.; Lifshitz, E.M. *Mechanics. Course of Theoretical Physics*; Butterworth-Heinemann: Oxford, UK, 1976; Volume 1.
30. Hui, L. Wave Dark Matter. *Annu. Rev. Astron. Astrophys.* **2021**, *59*, 247–289. [CrossRef]

universe MDPI

Article

# Estimating the Parameters of the Hybrid Palatini Gravity Model with the Schwarzschild Precession of S2, S38 and S55 Stars: Case of Bulk Mass Distribution

Duško Borka [1,*], Vesna Borka Jovanović [1], Violeta N. Nikolić [1], Nenad Đ. Lazarov [1] and Predrag Jovanović [2]

1 Department of Theoretical Physics and Condensed Matter Physics (020), Vinča Institute of Nuclear Sciences-National Institute of the Republic of Serbia, University of Belgrade, P.O. Box 522, 11001 Belgrade, Serbia; vborka@vinca.rs (V.B.J.); violeta@vinca.rs (V.N.N.); lazarov@vinca.rs (N.Đ.L.)
2 Astronomical Observatory, Volgina 7, P.O. Box 74, 11060 Belgrade, Serbia; pjovanovic@aob.rs
* Correspondence: dusborka@vinca.rs

**Abstract:** We estimate the parameters of the Hybrid Palatini gravity model with the Schwarzschild precession of S-stars, specifically of the S2, S38 and S55 stars. We also take into account the case of bulk mass distribution near the Galactic Center. We assume that the Schwarzschild orbital precession of mentioned S-stars is the same as in General Relativity (GR) in all studied cases. In 2020, the GRAVITY Collaboration detected the orbital precession of the S2 star around the supermassive black hole (SMBH) at the Galactic Center and showed that it is close to the GR prediction. The astronomical data analysis of S38 and S55 orbits showed that, also in these cases, the orbital precession is close to the GR prediction. Based on this observational fact, we evaluated the parameters of the Hybrid Palatini Gravity model with the Schwarzschild precession of the S2, S38 and S55 stars, and we estimated the range of parameters of the Hybrid Palatini gravity model for which the orbital precession is as in GR for all three stars. We also evaluated the parameters of the Hybrid Palatini Gravity model in the case of different values of bulk mass density distribution of extended matter. We believe that proposed method is a useful tool to evaluate parameters of the gravitational potential at the Galactic Center.

**Keywords:** alternative theories of gravity; supermassive black hole; stellar dynamics

**Citation:** Borka, D.; Borka Jovanović, V.; Nikolić, V.N.; Lazarov, N.Đ.; Jovanović, P. Estimating the Parameters of the Hybrid Palatini Gravity Model with the Schwarzschild Precession of S2, S38 and S55 Stars: Case of Bulk Mass Distribution. *Universe* **2022**, *70*, 915. https://doi.org/10.3390/universe8020070

Academic Editors: Panayiotis Stavrinos and Emmanuel N. Saridakis

Received: 27 December 2021
Accepted: 17 January 2022
Published: 24 January 2022



## 1. Introduction

In recent decades, various modified gravity theories have appeared as potential extensions of Einstein's gravity theory [1]. One of the reasons for a postulation of the mentioned theories is the possibility to exclude the concept of dark energy and dark matter and to explain cosmological and astrophysical data collected at different scales considering further degrees of freedom of the gravitational field. This occurs as a consequence of geometric corrections [2]. Modified gravity theories have to resolve different observations concerning, starting from the Solar system, neutron stars, binary pulsars, spiral and elliptical galaxies and clusters of galaxies, up to the large-scale structure of the Universe [3–7]. In Ref. [3] a cosmological reconstruction (characterized by a very general character) of various modified gravity is given, and, in [4] various formalisms of representatives $(F(R), F(G), F(T))$ of standard modified gravity are presented, as well as alternative theoretical approaches. Ref. [5] described stars and cluster of galaxies (spiral and elliptical galaxies), beyond the scope of dark matter, by extending the Hilbert–Einstein action to $f(R)$ gravity, and, in [6], the authors discussed observations and experiments, which depicted the fact that GR and the standard model of elementary particles are unable to explain the phenomena behind the dark matter concept. In [7], the chosen cosmological parameters were determined (as accurate cosmological solutions) within the framework of the represented nonlocal gravitational model, which showed satisfactory agreement with experimental observations.

*Some Alternative Theories of Gravity.*

Let us recall that numerous alternative gravity theories have been proposed (see, e.g., [8–18]). For example, the alternative theories of gravity are discussed in [8]. In [9], the authors introduced extension of the post-Newtonian relativistic theory by additionally considering all relativistic effects, which originated from the presumable existence of a scalar field. Ref. [10] presents a review article, in which the authors discussed specific aspects of 4D massive gravities. In Ref. [11] a numerical solution of the nonlinear Pauli–Fierz theory is given. The proposed solution represents an improvement of the existing solution of GR, which was achieved by including the Vainshtein mechanism. In [12], extended theories of gravity were discussed by taking into account $f(R)$ and scalar-tensor gravity in metric and Palatini approaches; the issues, such as inflation, large scale structure, dark energy, dark matter and quantum gravity, were discussed also. Ref. [13] is a review of modified theories of gravity and models of extra dimensions, such as Scalar-Tensor, Einstein–Aether, Bimetric theories, TeVeS, $F(R)$, Horava–Lifschitz gravity, Galileons, Ghost Condensates, Kaluza–Klein, Randall–Sundrum, DGP, higher co-dimension braneworlds as well as the construction of the Parametrized Post-Friedmannian formalism. In the paper [14], the Dvali–Gabadadze–Porrati model (DGP), cascading gravity, ghost-free massive gravity, new mass gravity, Lorentz-violating massive gravity and non-local massive gravity are discussed. The $f(R)$ modifications of general relativity, considering galaxy clusters, cosmological perturbations, and N-body simulations, are discussed in [15]. A few observational mass bounds have been established, and among them, the mass bounds from the effects of the Yukawa potential in Ref. [16]. Ref. [17] presents monograph in which the mathematical background is given (for example, conservation laws and symmetries for different theories of gravity), necessary for comparison of methods of perturbations in general relativity; this mathematical introduction enables the building of different modified-gravity theories. In the paper [18], the method for the evaluation of the parameters of the gravitational potential at the Galactic Center, based on the extended gravity models (power-law $f(R)$, general Yukawa-like corrections, scalar-tensor gravity and non-local gravity theories formulated in both metric and Palatini formalism) is given.

*Some Alternative Approaches for the Weak Field Limit of Theories of Gravity.*

Noteworthy, different alternative approaches for the weak field limit (starting from fourth-order theories of gravity, such as $f(R)$), have been proposed and considered [19–32]. For example, in Ref. [19] the gravitational microlensing is discussed, considered from the aspect of the weak field limit of fourth-order gravity theory, and, in [20], determination of the mass and the size of dark matter sphere is discussed, based on the $\gamma$-ray emission from the Galactic Center region. Ref. [21] examined the consequences of modified $f(R)$ gravity (power-law $f(R)$) on galactic scales, by performing an analysis of rotational curves. In Ref. [22], the authors discuss the search for general relativistic periastronic shifts, which is limited by the existence of clusters around black hole, which could modify orbits due to classical effects that mask the general relativistic effect. Ref. [23] represents a discussion of solving the problem of dark matter and dark energy (which could be done by considering changing the fundamental law of gravity). Ref. [24] showed that the metric approach of any analytic $f(R)$-gravity model presents a weak field limit (the standard Newtonian potential is corrected by a Yukawa-like term), and [25] considered the limitations of the range parameters $\lambda$ that are described by modifications of Newton's inverse square law of the gravity similar to Yukawa; the results of this study could affect all modified theories of gravity, which include Yukawa-type terms (which are characterized by a range of parameters much larger than the size of the solar system). In [26], a Yukawa-like long-range modified model of gravity (MOG) is discussed. Ref. [27] considered the Modified Newtonian Dynamics, introducing the integration of the equations of motion of Magellanic clouds in a numerical manner. In the paper [28], the limitation of the $R^n$ gravity at Galactic scales, based on the simulation of the S2-like stars orbits, is discussed; it was shown that $R^n$ gravity impacts the simulated orbits in a qualitatively similar way as a bulk distribution of matter in Newton's gravity. In Ref. [29], an analytic fourth-order theory of gravity (which is non-minimally coupled with a massive scalar field) is applied, to explain deviations of S2 star orbit, by using gravitational potentials derived from modified gravity models in the absence of dark matter. Refs. [30,31] considered an analytical expression for the precession angle (with assumption of a power-law profile of the dark matter density); they calculated the mass of the dark matter in the vicinity of a SMBH at the galaxy center, based on the observations of nonrelativistic precession of the orbits of S0 stars. While, in [32], the authors discuss the physical processes that occurred at the center of the galaxy; the results of this study revealed the mass of the SMBH Sgr A*.

*Experimental Limits Related to Extended Theories of Gravity.*

Also, literature review revealed the presence of some experimental limits related to extended theories of gravity [33–41]. In Ref. [33], the authors used cosmography to examine the kinematics of the Universe by a combination of theoretical derivation of cosmological distances and numerical data fitting, while in [34], the authors investigated whether cosmography could be used to ensure information on the cosmological expansion history and discussed the limits of experimentally probing of cosmographic expansion. In Ref. [35], the authors performed cosmographic analyses and discussed the cosmological consequences of $f(R)$ and $f(T)$ gravities as well as their influence on the cosmography framework. They depicted to the unfavorable degeneracy problem (cosmographic constraints on $f(R)$ and $f(T)$ cannot be distinguished by theories of GR extensions and dark energy models). In [36], the differences between the Newtonian and relativistic approaches are described, and it is revealed that the relativistic approach presents a more suitable strategy for further probing of modified theories of gravity. In Ref. [37] the generalization of the gravitational action to a function $f(R)$ is investigated, as an alternative to the dark matter and dark energy, and the weak field limit of the $f(R)$-gravity is discussed. In [38], the analytical $f(R)$-gravity model is considered, which is characterized by a Yukawa-like modification of the Newtonian potential, and this leads to a modification of particle dynamics. In the paper [39], the authors performed a comparison between the $\Lambda CDM$ cosmological model and $f(R)$ and $f(T)$ models; they presented a new approach to breaking degeneration among dark energy models, which was introduced to overcome the limits of standard cosmography. The reference [40] discussed the usage of S-stars observations to constrain a Yukawa-like gravitational potential and considered the fact that deviations from GR are parametrized by the strength of the potential, $\delta$, and its length scale, $\lambda$. In [41], it is shown that the observing stars orbiting closer to the central gravitational source could allow distinguishing between the black hole and wormhole nature of this object (by observing S2 and S62 stars).

*Gravitational Potentials and the Stellar Dynamics.*

In this study, the gravitational potentials of self-gravitating structures were investigated by considering the stellar dynamics. Recall that S-stars are the bright stars that move around the Galactic Center [42–57] where Sgr A* (which presents a compact massive object) is located. The conventional model, used to describe the Galactic Center, considers the SMBH with mass around $4.3 \times 10^6 M_\odot$ and an extended mass distribution formed with stellar cluster and dark matter. A spherical shell, where trajectories of bright stars are located, should be characterized by a total mass of bulk distribution, which is significantly smaller compared to the black hole mass. In Ref. [42] measurements of the accelerations for three stars located $\sim$0.005 pc from the central radio source Sgr A* are discussed; the obtained data revealed the localization of the dark mass to within $0.05 \pm 0.04$ arcsec of the nominal position of Sgr A*. In [43], astrometric and radial velocity measurements, performed by the Keck telescopes, are discussed, as well as the estimated distance ($R0$) and the galaxy's local rotation speed. They noticed that increased black hole mass depicted a longer period for the innermost stable orbit and longer resonant relaxation timescales for stars in the vicinity of the black hole. The authors of paper [44] discussed a moderate improvement of the statistical errors of mass and distance to Sgr A*, and, in [45], the orbits of 38 stars (among them, the orbit of the S2 star) were determined; all stellar orbits were fitted satisfactorily by a single point mass potential. In Ref. [46], the high resolution astrometric imaging is discussed, which is used to investigate two thirds of the orbit of the star currently closest to the massive black hole candidate SgrA*; they authors found that the star was on a bound, highly elliptical Keplerian orbit around SgrA*, with an orbital period of 15.2 years and a pericentre distance of only 17 light hours. The authors in [47] considered a massive black hole in the Galactic Center and a nuclear star cluster, by analyzing the size and motion measurements of the radio source Sgr A*, which is understood as a massive black hole surrounded by a dense nuclear star cluster. In Ref. [48], the authors examined the behavior of a SMBH by investigating stars with short orbital periods at the center of our galaxy; measurements from the Keck Observatory discovered the star S0-102 orbiting a black hole with a period of less than 15 years. Ref. [49] represents an update of the main conclusions regarding the measurement of mass and distance to Sgr A*, derived from data obtained by monitoring stellar orbits in the Galactic Center. In Ref. [50], it is shown that short-period stars orbiting around the SMBH in our Galactic Center can successfully be used to probe the gravitational theory in a strong regime. In [51], the behavior of the star S2, which orbits a SMBH in a short period of time (less than 20 years) is considered; the authors reported on the first binarity limits of S0-2, observed from radial velocity monitoring. The GRAVITY Collaboration [52] discussed the orbit of the S2 star around the massive black hole Sgr A*, which is used as probe of the gravitational field in the center of the galaxy; by using different statistical analysis methods, the authors detected the combined gravitational redshift and relativistic transverse Doppler effect for the S2 star and found that the S2 data were not consistent with pure Newtonian dynamics. In [53], they presented the results of the measurement of the $R0$ (the geometric distance to the Galactic Center), by probing the S2 star, which is orbiting around the SMBH Sgr A*. In Ref. [54], the authors examined the prediction of GR (that a star passing near a SMBH shows a relativistic redshift), by using observations of the Galactic Center star S2; a combination of special relativistic- and gravitational-redshift was discovered, which confirms the model of GR and excludes Newtonian's model. Ref. [55] considered the assumption of the presence of a scalar field structure associated with a black hole at the center of our galaxy. The authors used the results of the orbital perturbation theory to compute the extent to which the orbital parameters of the S2 star change during the orbital period. Ref. [56] introduced a new ways of probing fundamental physics, tracking stars in the Galactic Center; a new way of looking for changes in the fine structure constant was proposed, by using measurements of late-type evolved giant stars from the S-star cluster orbiting a SMBH in our Galactic Center. Ref. [57] reported the first detection of the GR Schwarzschild precession in S2's orbit.

Ruffini, Argüelles & Rueda [58] discussed a dark matter distribution and proposed that it consists of a dense core and a diluted halo. The dark matter distribution was named as the RAR-model. In 2021, Becerra-Vergara et al. [59] commented this model and concluded that the mentioned model ensures a better fit of bright star trajectories compared to the SMBH model. The properties of bright star trajectories in the gravitational field of a dense core, described by the RAR-model, were discussed in [60]. In such a case, trajectories of stars are ellipses as in Kepler's two-body problem but with one big difference: instead of their foci, the centers of the ellipses coincide with a Galactic Center, and their orbital periods do not depend on their semi-major axes. Therefore, these properties are not consistent with existing observational data [60]. The orbital precession occurs as a consequence of relativistic effects, as well as due to extended mass distribution, because both effects could cause perturbation of the Newtonian potential. In the first case, the precession induces a prograde pericentre shift, while, in the second case, retrograde shift occurs [61]. In both cases, as a final result, rosette-shaped orbits are obtained [62,63].

In addition to Schwarzschild precession, relativistic frame-dragging due to the spin of SMBH, also known as the Lense-Thirring (LT) effect, could cause orbital precession. The LT precession in the case of several S-stars was studied in references [18,64–67], and it was found that it is much smaller than Schwarzschild precession [18,65]. The spin of Sgr A* was estimated to $\chi_g < 0.1$ by the observed distribution of the orbital planes of the S-stars [68]. In this paper, we considered only the solutions of the Hybrid Palatini gravity model for a spherically symmetric and stationary gravitational field, which do not include the SMBH spin. Having this in mind, we did not take into account the LT precession in our calculations for S-stars precession.

In our previous studies, we considered various extended gravity theories and compared theoretical models with astronomical data for different astrophysical scales: the S2 star orbit [28,69–77], fundamental plane of elliptical galaxies [78–80] and barionic Tully–Fischer relation of spiral galaxies [81]. In this study, as a continuation of our previous paper [18], the parameters of the Hybrid Palatini gravity model will be evaluated by Schwarzschild precession of the S2, S38 and S55 stars. Here, we will also take into account the bulk mass density distribution of extended matter in the Galactic Center and assume that the orbital precession of the S2, S38 and S55 stars are equal to the corresponding GR predictions of $0^\circ.18$, $0^\circ.11$ and $0^\circ.10$ per orbital period, respectively. We use this assumption because the GRAVITY Collaboration detected the orbital precession of the S2 star around the SMBH [57] and showed that it is close to the corresponding prediction of GR. According to data analysis in the framework of Yukawa gravity model in the paper [40], the orbital precessions of the S38 and S55 stars are close to the corresponding prediction of GR for these stars.

The paper is organized in the following way. In Section 2, we present the basics of the Hybrid Palatini theoretical model as well as the model for bulk mass density distribution of extended matter. In Section 3, we evaluate the parameters of the Hybrid Palatini theoretical model by Schwarzschild precession of the S2, S38 and S55 stars and discuss the obtained results. Our concluding remarks are given in Section 4, while Appendix A contains the detailed derivation of gravitational potential in the weak field limit for this gravity model.

## 2. Theory

In this article, we found constraints on the parameters of the Hybrid Palatini gravity model with request that the obtained values of orbital precession angles are the same as in GR but for different values of mass density of matter. We used a weak field limit for the Hybrid Palatini gravitation potential. A straightforward extension of GR is $f(R)$ gravity, which, instead of the Einstein–Hilbert action (linear in the Ricci scalar $R$), considers a generic function of $R$ [19–21,82–85].

### 2.1. Modified Hybrid Palatini Gravity Model

There are two variational principles that one can apply to the Einstein–Hilbert action in order to derive Einstein's equations: the standard metric variation and the Palatini variation [85–87]. The choice of the variational principle is usually referred to as a formalism, and thus one can use the terms metric or second-order formalism and Palatini or first-order formalism. In the Palatini variation, the metric and the connection are assumed to be independent variables, and one varies the action with respect to both of them. This variation leads to Einstein's equations, under the important assumption that the matter action does not depend on the connection. Both variational principles lead to the same field equation for an action whose Lagrangian is linear in $R$, for example in the context of GR, but not for a more general action, for example in extended gravities. $f(R)$ gravity in the metric formalism is called metric $f(R)$ gravity, and $f(R)$ gravity in the Palatini formalism is called Palatini $f(R)$ gravity. The Palatini variational approach leads to second-order differential field equations, while the resulting field equations in the metric approach are fourth-order coupled differential equations [85–87]. There is also a novel approach, the hybrid variation of these theories. It consists of adding, to the metric Einstein–Hilbert Lagrangian, an $f(R)$ term constructed within the framework of the Palatini formalism, i.e., purely metric Einstein–Hilbert action is supplemented with metric-affine correction terms constructed as Palatini [88–91]. The $f(R)$ theories are the special limits of the one-parameter class of theories where the scalar field depends solely on the stress energy trace $T$ (Palatini version) or solely on the Ricci curvature $R$ (metric version). Here, we consider the hybrid metric-Palatini gravitational theory. In the general case, the field equations are fourth-order both in the matter and in the metric derivatives. Hybrid metric-Palatini theory provides a unique interpolation between the two *a priori* completely distinct classes of gravity theories. The aim of this formulation has two-fold benefits: from one side, one wants to describe the extra gravitational budget in a metric-affine formalism; on the other side, one wants to cure the shortcomings emerging in $f(R)$ gravity both in metric and Palatini formulations. In particular, hybrid gravity allows to disentangle the metric and the geodesic structures pointing out that further degrees of freedom coming from $f(R)$ can be recast as an auxiliary scalar field. An interesting aspect of metric-Palatini theories is the possibility to generate long-range forces without entering into conflict with local tests of gravity. The possibility of expressing these hybrid $f(R)$ metric-Palatini theories using a scalar-tensor representation simplifies the analysis of the field equations and the construction of solutions. To obtain deeper insights, see [86,88–93].

The Palatini formalism and the metric one are completely different both from a qualitative and from a quantitative viewpoint. In the Palatini formalism, field equations are easily solvable [94]. In this sense, the Palatini formalism is easier to handle and simpler to analyze compared with the corresponding metric formalism. It is clear that any reasonable model of gravity should satisfy the standard solar system tests. It has been shown that, in principle, the Palatini formalism provides a good Newtonian approximation. It is known that on-shell formulation of Palatini gravity coincides with that of same metric gravity [94]. In the paper [95], a class of scalar-tensor theories was proposed including a non-metricity that unifies the metric, Palatini and hybrid metric-Palatini gravitational actions with non-minimal interaction. The authors presented a new approach to scalar-tensor theories of gravity that unifies metric, Palatini and hybrid. Such an approach will encompass, within one family of theories, not only metric but also Palatini scalar-tensor theories of gravity and will be a natural extension of the hybrid metric-Palatini gravity. It is shown that every such theory can be represented on-shell by a purely metric scalar-tensor theories possessing the same solutions for a metric and a scalar field.

Recall that, in the weak field limit (see the Appendix A for detailed explanation), the scalar field behaves as $\phi(r) \approx \phi_0 + \frac{2G\phi_0 M}{3rc^2}e^{-m_\phi r}$, where $M$ is the mass of the system and $r$ is the interaction length. The leading parameters for Hybrid Palatini gravity are $m_\phi$ and $\phi_0$. The aim of this study was to evaluate these parameters. We can write the modified gravitational potential in the following form [71,89]:

$$\Phi(r) = -\frac{G}{1+\phi_0}\left[1-(\phi_0/3)e^{-m_\phi r}\right]M/r. \tag{1}$$

The parameter $m_\phi$ represents a scaling parameter for gravity interaction and $[m_\phi] = [Length]^{-1}$. We measured the parameter in $\mathrm{AU}^{-1}$ (AU is the astronomical unit). The parameter $\phi_0$ represents the amplitude of the background value of the scalar field $\phi$ and it is dimensionless. Non-zero values of these two parameters, if obtained, would indicate a potential deviation from GR.

### 2.2. Orbital Precession in Case of Bulk Mass Distribution

In this study, we investigated S2, S38 and S55 stars. Orbital precession of investigated stars is influenced by other stars, gas and dark matter. It is expected that the stars represent the dominant component of the extended galactic mass distribution near the central SMBH. To investigate orbital precession of S-stars, we made two assumptions. First, we suppose the presence of the Hybrid Palatini gravitational potential [71]. The second assumption is a bulk distribution of mass around SMBH in the central regions of our galaxy [77]:

$$M(r) = M_{SMBH} + M_{ext}(r). \tag{2}$$

A bulk mass distribution $M(r)$ consists of the central black hole of mass $M_{SMBH} = 4.3 \times 10^6 M_\odot$ [44] and extended mass distribution $M_{ext}(r)$ enclosed within some radius $r$. $M_{ext}(r)$ is the total mass, including the stellar cluster, interstellar gas and dark matter. To describe the mass density distribution of extended matter, we adopted a double power-law mass density profile [55,96,97]:

$$\rho(r) = \rho_0 \left(\frac{r}{r_0}\right)^{-\alpha}, \; \alpha = \begin{cases} 2.0 \pm 0.1, & r \geq r_0 \\ 1.4 \pm 0.1, & r < r_0 \end{cases} \quad (3)$$

where $\rho_0$ is varied from 2 to 8 $\times 10^8\ M_\odot \cdot \mathrm{pc}^{-3}$ and $r_0 = 10''$.

In the case of S-stars throughout the whole region, which we investigated, we can choose only one value of power-law exponent: $\alpha = 1.4$.

A combination of the above mentioned formulas enabled us to obtain the following expression for the extended mass distribution:

$$M_{ext}(r) = \frac{4\pi\rho_0 r_0^\alpha}{3-\alpha} r^{3-\alpha}. \quad (4)$$

Note that, in [30,31], the authors used a similar method for estimation of the total dark matter mass near the SMBH at the Galactic Center based on observations of orbital precession of S-stars and derived an analytical expression for the precession angle in the case of a power-law profile of the dark matter density.

The gravitational potential for the extended mass model can be evaluated as [20]:

$$\begin{aligned} \Phi_{ext}(r) &= -G \int_r^{r_\infty} \frac{M_{ext}(r')}{r'^2} dr' = \\ &= \frac{-4\pi\rho_0 r_0^\alpha G}{(3-\alpha)(2-\alpha)} \left({r_\infty}^{2-\alpha} - r^{2-\alpha}\right), \end{aligned} \quad (5)$$

where $r_\infty$ is the outer radius for an extended mass distribution of matter. The total gravitational potential is obtained as a sum of the Hybrid Palatini potential for SMBH with mass $M_{SMBH}$ and potential for extended matter with mass $M_{ext}(r)$:

$$\Phi_{total}(r) = \Phi(r) + \Phi_{ext}(r). \quad (6)$$

Modified gravity potential, similarly to GR, gives precession around SMBH. At the center of the galaxy, around the SMBH, there are invisible sources of mass (clouds of gas, stars and their remnants and a distributed mass in the form of the diffuse dark matter). This additional invisible sources of mass would cause deviation of the total Newtonian gravitational potential [30–32]. As a result of both effects, the orbits of S-stars would be unclosed and would precess. If it is assumed that the total potential $\Phi_{total}(r)$ does not differ significantly from the Newtonian potential, the perturbed potential has the following form:

$$V_p(r) = \Phi_{total}(r) - \Phi_N(r) \; ; \quad \Phi_N(r) = -\frac{GM}{r} \; . \quad (7)$$

## 3. Results and Discussion

In this section, we give the estimation of parameters of the Hybrid Palatini gravity model by Schwarzschild precession of the S2, S38 and S55 stars, with and without taking into account the bulk mass density distribution of extended matter in the Galactic Center. We assume that the orbital precession of the S2, S38 and S55 stars is equal to the GR value. The main reason is that the GRAVITY Collaboration detected the orbital precession of the S2 star and showed that it is close to the GR prediction and that the direction is the same as in GR [57]. The second reason is that, according to astronomical data fitting in Yukawa gravity model, which are presented in the paper [40], the orbital precessions of the S38 and S55 stars are also close to the corresponding prediction of GR for these stars.

*Calculation of Orbital Precession of S-Stars*

A general expression for apocenter shifts for Newtonian potential and small perturbing potential is given as a solution (in Section III Integration of the equations of motion, Chapter 15 Kepler's problem) of problem 3, page 40, Equation (1) in the Landau and Lifshitz book [98]. Assuming that a particle moves in slightly perturbed Newtonian potential, Adkins and McDonnell [62] derived an expression that is equivalent to the above mentioned relation from the Landau and Lifshitz book [98] but in an alternative way. It was shown that the expressions are equivalent, and, after that, they calculated apocenter shifts for several examples of perturbing functions.

According to [62], the orbital precession $\Delta\theta$ per orbital period, induced by small perturbations to the Newtonian gravitational potential $\Phi_N(r) = -\dfrac{GM}{r}$ could be evaluated as:

$$\Delta\theta = \frac{-2L}{GMe^2}\int_{-1}^{1}\frac{z \cdot dz}{\sqrt{1-z^2}}\frac{dV_p(z)}{dz}, \tag{8}$$

while, in the textbook [98], it was given in the form

$$\Delta\theta = \frac{2}{GMe}\int_{0}^{\pi}\cos\varphi r^2\frac{\partial V_p(r)}{\partial r}d\varphi, \tag{9}$$

where $V_p(z)$ is the perturbing potential, $r$ is related to $z$ via: $r = \dfrac{L}{1+ez}$ in Equation (8) (and $r = \dfrac{L}{1+e\cos\varphi}$ in Equation (9)), and $L$ is the semilatus rectum of the orbital ellipse with semi-major axis $a$ and eccentricity $e$:

$$L = a\left(1-e^2\right). \tag{10}$$

Equations (8) and (9) are equivalent, i.e., Equation (8) can be obtained from Equation (9) after substitution: $z = cos\varphi$.

Dokuchaev and Eroshenko [30–32] evaluated relativistic precessions around SMBH in the case of an additional potential due to the presence of dark matter. The precession angle per orbital period is expressed analytically using the hypergeometric function [30–32]:

$$\delta\theta = -\frac{4\pi^2\rho_0 r_0^\alpha L^{3-\alpha}}{(1-e)^{4-\alpha}M_{SMBH}}\,{}_2F_1\left(4-\alpha, \frac{3}{2}; 3; -\frac{2e}{1-e}\right), \tag{11}$$

where ${}_2F_1$ is the hypergeometric function. This expression is in good agreement with the corresponding expression given in the Landau and Lifshitz book [98]. More details are given in the references [30–32]. If one takes the expressions for precession from the books by Danby [99] (Chapter 11 equation 11.5.13) and by Murray and Dermott [100] (Chapter 2, equation 2.165.), one can obtain the same equations as the above Equation (8).

To calculate the precession of the S2, S38 and S55 stars in Hybrid Palatini modified gravity, we assumed that the perturbed potential is of the form:

$$V_p(r) = \Phi(r) + \Phi_{ext}(r) - \Phi_N(r); \quad \Phi_N(r) = -\frac{GM}{r}, \tag{12}$$

and it can be used to calculate the precession angle according to Equation (8):

In order to investigate the parameters of the Hybrid Palatini gravity, which, in the case of the extended mass distribution, give the same orbital precession as GR, we graphically presented Equation (8) by adopting different values of the extended mass density $\rho_0$ and for three different S-stars. In that way, we created the below Figures 1–6 showing the dependence of orbital precession angle $\Delta\theta$ on the gravity parameters $\phi_0$ and $m_\phi$ for several extended mass densities $\rho_0$ and for the following three S-stars: S2, S38 and S55. The observed quantities that are used in this paper are the parameters of the central SMBH in our galaxy as well as the orbital elements for the mentioned stars.

For our calculations, we used the results presented in [49], according to which, the mass of the SMBH of the Milky Way is $M_{SMBH} = 4.3 \times 10^6\ M_\odot$; the semi-major axis of the S2 star orbit is $a = 0.''1255$, and its eccentricity is $e = 0.8839$; the semi-major axis of the S38 star orbit is $a = 0.''1416$, and its eccentricity is $e = 0.8201$; and the semi-major axis of the S55 star orbit is $a = 0.''1078$, and its eccentricity is $e = 0.7209$.

Figure 1 shows the precession per orbital period for the $\phi_0$ - $m_\phi$ parameter space in the case of the Hybrid Palatini gravity potential with extended mass distribution in the case of the S2 star. The mass density distribution of extended matter is $\rho_0 = 2 \times 10^8 M_\odot \mathrm{pc}^{-3}$. The white dashed line depicts the locations in the parameter space where the precession angle has the same value as in GR for the S2 star ($0^\circ.18$). It can be shown that precession of the orbit in the Hybrid Palatini potential is in the same direction as in GR [71], but extended mass distribution produces a contribution to precession in the opposite direction [77].

According to Figure 1 and the formulas for potential in Modified Hybrid Palatini gravity (see denominator in Equation (1)), parameter $\phi_0$ is between $-1$ (vertical asymptote) and 0. If $\phi_0 = 0$ the Hybrid Palatini potential reduces to the Newtonian one. The maximal value for $m_\phi$ is about 0.075 $\mathrm{AU}^{-1}$ and for $m_\phi$ near 0.005 $\mathrm{AU}^{-1}$, a maximal value for $\phi_0$ is obtained, and it is around $-0.1$ (see left panel). We can see from the right panel that $m_\phi$ can also take negative values, but when $m_\phi$ become less than $-0.0001$, the $\mathrm{AU}^{-1}$ parameter $\phi_0$ becomes very near 0, and the Hybrid Palatini potential reduces to the Newtonian one. Figure 2 represents the same as Figure 1 but for the values of the mass density distribution of extended matter $\rho_0 = 4 \times 10^8 M_\odot \mathrm{pc}^{-3}$. We notice a similar tendency as in previous cases regarding dependence of shape of dashed curve with respect to the values of parameters $m_\phi$ and $\phi_0$. The maximal value for $m_\phi$ is about 0.065 $\mathrm{AU}^{-1}$, and for $m_\phi$ near 0.005 $\mathrm{AU}^{-1}$, a maximal value for $\phi_0$ is obtained, and it is around $-0.17$. If we compare Figures 1 and 2 with the corresponding Figure 4 from paper [18] where we did not take into account the extended mass distribution (maximal value for $m_\phi$ is about 0.10 $\mathrm{AU}^{-1}$ and for $m_\phi$ near 0.005 $\mathrm{AU}^{-1}$, a maximal value for $\phi_0$ is obtained, and it is around $-0.01$), then we can conclude that the mass density distribution of extended matter $\rho_0$ has a strong influence on the gravity parameter $m_\phi$ and value of the precession angle per orbital period for S2 star. If we increase the value of $\rho_0$, we obtain a decrease of the corresponding values of parameters $m_\phi$ and $\phi_0$.

Figure 3 shows the precession per orbital period for the $\phi_0$ - $m_\phi$ parameter space in the case of the Hybrid Palatini gravity potential without extended mass distribution in the case of the S38 star. The white dashed line depicts the locations in the parameter space where the precession angle has the same value as in GR for the S38 star ($0^\circ.11$). The maximal value for $m_\phi$ is about 0.06 $\mathrm{AU}^{-1}$, and for $m_\phi$ near 0.005 $\mathrm{AU}^{-1}$, a maximal value for $\phi_0$ is obtained, and it is around $-0.01$. According to the right panel, we can see that $m_\phi$ can also take negative values. Figure 4 represent sthe same as Figure 3 but for the mass density distribution $\rho_0 = 4 \times 10^8 M_\odot \mathrm{pc}^{-3}$. The maximal value for $m_\phi$ is less than 0.04 $\mathrm{AU}^{-1}$, and for $m_\phi$ near 0.005 $\mathrm{AU}^{-1}$, a maximal value for $\phi_0$ is obtained, and it is less than $-0.2$.

Figures 5 and 6 represent the same as Figures 3 and 4 but for the S55 star (precession angle in GR is $0^\circ.10$). If we compare the the estimated parameters of the Hybrid Palatini gravity model of the S2 star with the S38 and S55 stars for the same value of $\rho_0$, it can be seen that results are slightly different, i.e., the obtained values for the parameters $\phi_0$ and $m_\phi$ are not the same, but they are very close. It appears that parameters of the Hybrid Palatini gravity depend on the scale (the values of the semi-major axes).

According to Figures 1–6, the mass density distribution of extended matter has significant influence on the values of the precession angle and of the parameters $\phi_0$ and $m_\phi$. We notice that it is not possible to evaluate $\phi_0$ and $m_\phi$ in a unique way, if we consider only following two conditions: (1) the orbital precession is prograde as in GR and (2) the value of the precession angle is as in GR. We obtained lines in the $\phi_0$ - $m_\phi$ parameter space, and the points of these lines have the coordinates $\phi_0$ and $m_\phi$, which fulfill the above mentioned two requests. If we want to obtain only one unique value of parameters $\phi_0$ and $m_\phi$, we need an additional independent set of observations to combine with these obtained sets of points ($\phi_0$, $m_\phi$).

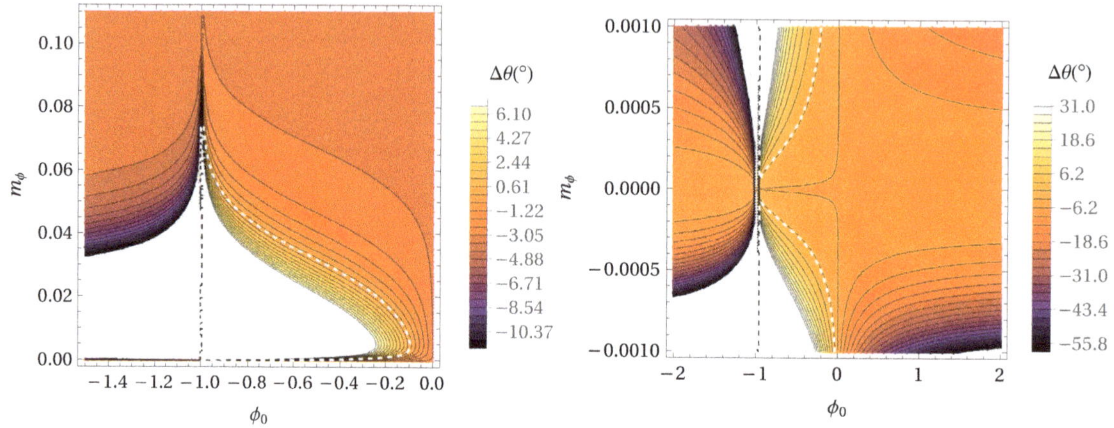


**Figure 1.** The precession per orbital period for the $\phi_0$ - $m_\phi$ parameter space in the case of the Hybrid Palatini gravity potential with extended mass distribution in the case of the S2 star. The mass density distribution of extended matter is $\rho_0 = 2 \times 10^8 M_\odot \text{pc}^{-3}$. With a decreasing value of the precession angle, the colors are darker. Parameter $m_\phi$ is expressed in $\text{AU}^{-1}$. The white dashed line depicts the locations in the parameter space where the precession angle has the same value as in GR (0°.18). The right panel represents the same as the left panel but for smaller values of the $m_\phi$ parameter.

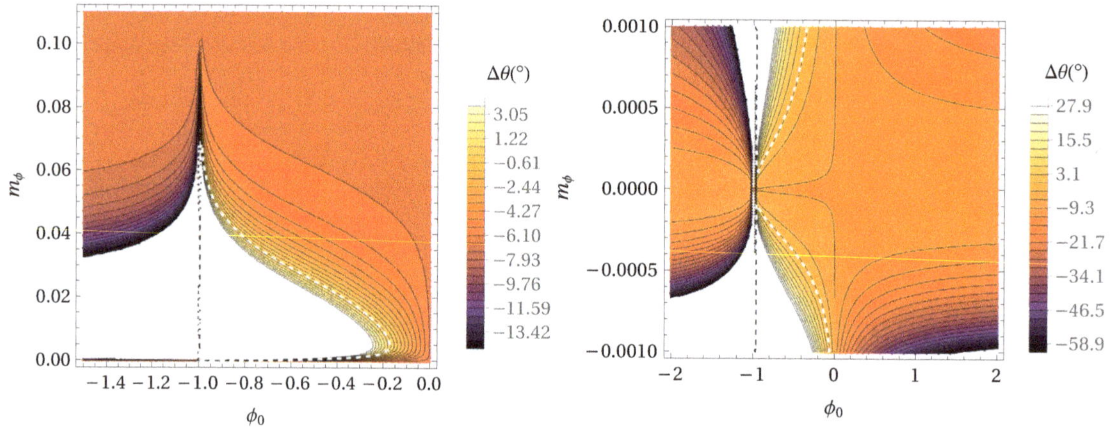


**Figure 2.** The same as in Figure 1 but for the values of the mass density distribution of extended matter $\rho_0 = 4 \times 10^8 M_\odot \text{pc}^{-3}$. The right panel represents the same as the left panel but for smaller values of the $m_\phi$ parameter.

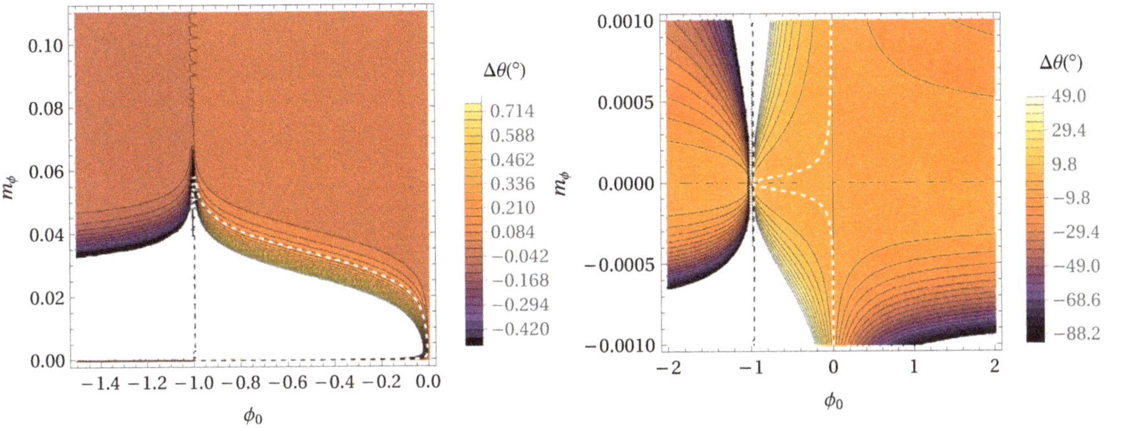


**Figure 3.** The precession per orbital period for the $\phi_0$ - $m_\phi$ parameter space in the case of the Hybrid Palatini gravity potential without extended mass distribution in the case of the S38 star. With a decreasing value of the precession angle, the colors are darker. Parameter $m_\phi$ is expressed in $AU^{-1}$. The white dashed line depicts the locations in the parameter space where the precession angle has the same value as in GR ($0^\circ.11$). The right panel represents the same as the left panel but for smaller values of the $m_\phi$ parameter.

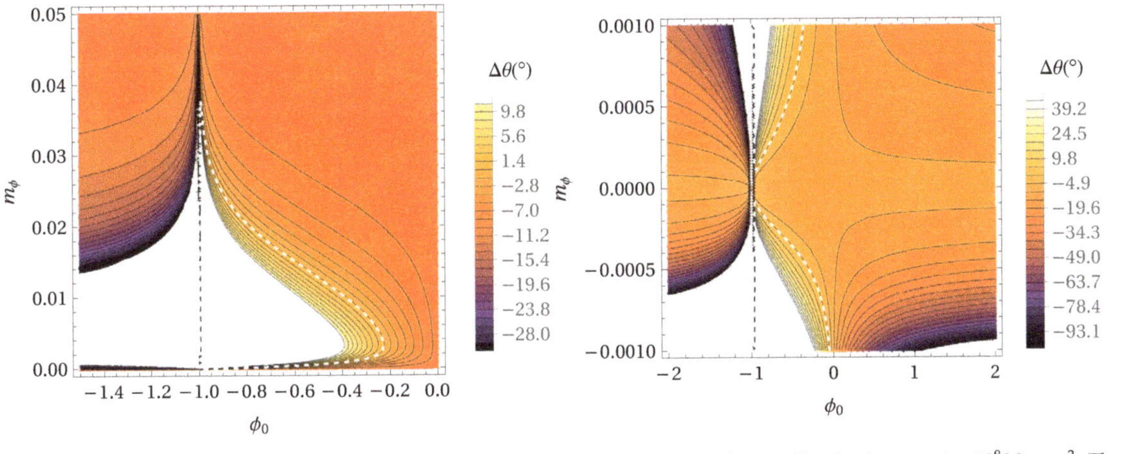


**Figure 4.** The same as in Figure 3, but for the mass density distribution $\rho_0 = 4 \times 10^8 M_\odot pc^{-3}$. The right panel represents the same as the left panel but for smaller values of the $m_\phi$ parameter.

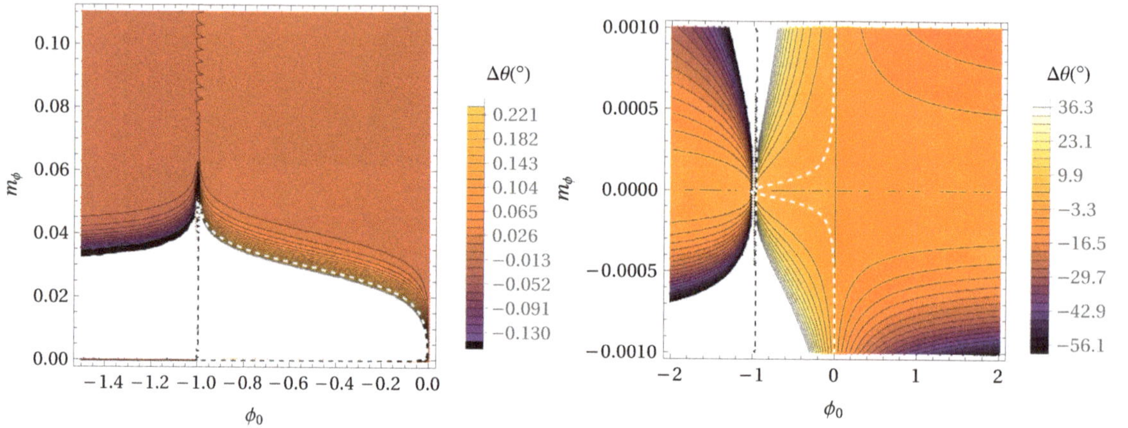


**Figure 5.** The precession per orbital period for the $\phi_0$ - $m_\phi$ parameter space in the case of the Hybrid Palatini gravity potential without extended mass distribution in the case of the S55 star. With a decreasing value of the precession angle, the colors are darker. Parameter $m_\phi$ is expressed in $AU^{-1}$. The white dashed line depicts the locations in the parameter space where the precession angle has the same value as in GR (0°.10). The right panel represents the same as the left panel but for smaller values of the $m_\phi$ parameter.

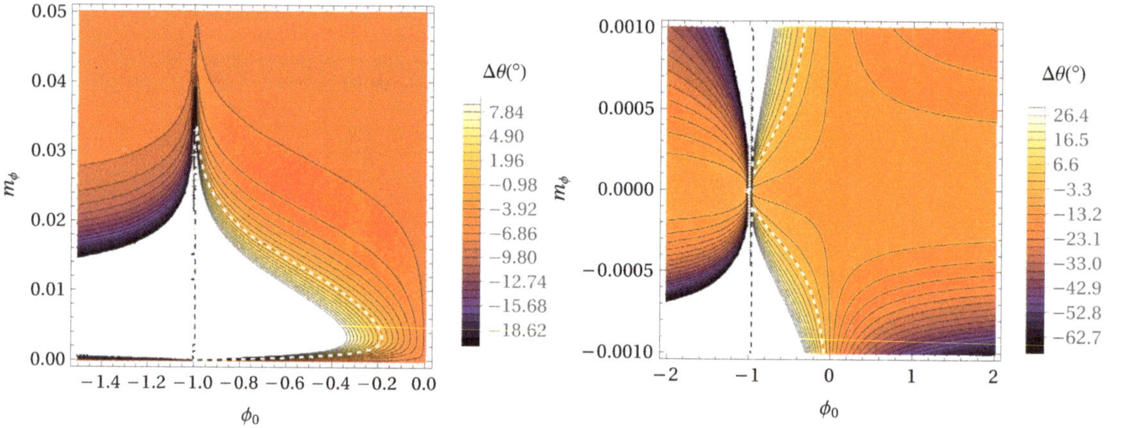


**Figure 6.** The same as in Figure 5, but for the mass density distribution $\rho_0 = 4 \times 10^8 M_\odot pc^{-3}$. The right panel represents the same as the left panel but for smaller values of the $m_\phi$ parameter.

This paper is a continuation of our previous research [80], but we extended our research on the following points:

(i) In this study, we estimated the parameters of the Hybrid Palatini gravity model with the Schwarzschild precession of S-stars. In addition to the S2 star, here, for the first time, we took into account the S38 and S55 stars also. If we compare the estimated parameters of the Hybrid Palatini gravity model of the S2 star with the S38 and S55 stars, it can be seen that the parameters of the Hybrid Palatini gravity depend on the scale of a gravitational system, which, in this case, is the semi-major axis of a stellar orbit.

(ii) In this paper, we considered the orbital precession of the mentioned stars due to additional contributions to the gravitational potential from a bulk distribution of matter. We took into account the different values of bulk mass density distribution of extended matter in the Galactic Center and analyzed their influence on values of parameters $m_\phi$ and $\phi_0$ of the Hybrid Palatini gravity model. We concluded that the mass density distribution of extended matter had significant influence on the values of precession angle and of modified gravity parameters. For higher values of $\rho_0$, we obtained lower values of gravity parameters $m_\phi$ and $\phi_0$. This paper is also an extension of our previous paper where we investigated the gravity parameters of Yukawa theory and how they change under different values of bulk mass density distribution of extended matter [77]. In this paper, we applied the same procedure but for parameters of the Hybrid Palatini gravity model and we extended it to the S38 and S55 stars.

(iii) We believe that in addition to the most often used S2 star, the S38 and S55 stars are also excellent candidates for probing the gravitational potential around central SMBH and could be also very useful for evaluating accurate parameters of different alternative gravity models.

(iv) In our previous paper [71], where we constrained the parameters of Hybrid Palatini gravity, we used observational data from the VLT and Keck collaborations. The results were obtained by fitting the simulated orbits of S2 star to its observed astrometric positions. Observational data were obtained with relatively large errors, especially at the first stage of monitoring (data were collected for decades). In this paper, we did not fit the observational data but instead we only assumed that the orbital precession of S2 star is equal to the corresponding value predicted by GR because recently the GRAVITY Collaboration claimed that they detected the orbital precession of the S2 star and showed that it is close to the GR prediction [57]. We extended our analysis to the stars S38 and S55 stars because astronomical data analysis of their orbits showed that, also in these cases, orbital precession is close to the GR prediction [40].

## 4. Conclusions

In this study, we estimated the parameters of the Hybrid Palatini gravity model with the Schwarzschild precession of the S2, S38 and S55 stars. We estimated the parameters with and without taking into account case of bulk mass distribution near Galactic Center. In this study, we were not fitting observation data, but instead we assumed that the Schwarzschild orbital precessions of the S2, S38 and S55 stars are the same as in of GR, i.e., $0^\circ.18$, $0^\circ.11$ and $0^\circ.10$ per orbital period, respectively. We introduced this approximation, since the observed precession angle of S2 star is very close to the GR prediction [57] and according the paper [40] where the authors analyzed observation data in the framework of Yukawa gravity and concluded that the orbital precessions of the S38 and S55 stars were in good agreement to the corresponding prediction of GR for these stars. We had a second reason, i.e., that we should recover the prograde orbital precession of S-stars, as in GR. Our findings indicate that:

1. The Modified Hybrid Palatini gravity parameter $\phi_0$ is between $-1$ (vertical asymptote) and 0. If $\phi_0 = 0$, the Hybrid Palatini gravity potential reduces to the Newtonian one.
2. For the Hybrid Palatini gravity model (described with two parameters), it is not possible to evaluate both parameters in a unique way, if we consider only the conditions that orbital precession is prograde as in GR and that the value of the precession angle is as in GR. Instead of that, we obtained lines in the $\phi_0$ - $m_\phi$ parameter space. The points of these lines have the coordinates $\phi_0$ and $m_\phi$, which fulfilled our two requests (the value of precession as in GR and the precession is prograde as in GR). The white dashed line depicts the locations in the parameter space of these points. If we want to obtain only one value of the parameters $\phi_0$ and $m_\phi$, we need to combine the obtained sets of ($\phi_0$, $m_\phi$) with an additional independent set of observations.
3. The mass density distribution of extended matter has a significant influence on the values of precession angle and of the modified gravity parameters. Higher values of $\rho_0$ decrease the corresponding values of parameters $m_\phi$ and $\phi_0$.

4. Our analysis shows that the precession of orbit in Hybrid Palatini potential is in the same direction as in GR, but the extended mass distribution produces a contribution to precession in the opposite direction. This means that, for higher mass densities, in order to obtain the same orbital precession as in GR, one has to take the significantly different values of the Hybrid Palatini gravity parameters. In the case when $\phi_0 = 0$, the Hybrid Palatini gravitational potential reduces to the Newtonian one. However, in order to compensate the effects of extended mass distribution on orbital precession and to obtain the same precession as in GR, $\phi_0$ has to be larger by an absolute value, thus, causing the larger deviation of the Hybrid Palatini gravitational potential with respect to the Newtonian one.
5. If we compare the estimated parameters of the Hybrid Palatini gravity model of the S2 star with the S38 and S55 stars, it can be seen that results are slightly different, i.e., the obtained values for the parameters of the gravity models are not the same, but they are very close. It appears that the parameters of the Hybrid Palatini gravity depend on the scale of a gravitational system, which, in this case, is the semi-major axis of a stellar orbit, in contrast to GR, which is the scale-invariant theory of gravitation. Therefore, we believe that this behavior originates from the deviation of modified gravity from GR.

It is crucial to investigate gravity in the vicinity of very massive compact objects, such as Sgr A*, because the environment around these objects is drastically different from that in the Solar System framework or at extragalactic and cosmological scales. The precession of the S stars is a unique opportunity to test gravity at the sub-parsec scale of a few thousand AU because these stars are bright stars and the periods of these stars are relatively short. We believe that it is useful to evaluate the parameters of different alternative modified gravity theories in the vicinity of SMBH with and without extended mass distribution in the metric and Palatini approach. There are various approaches to the construction of the modified gravity theories. In general, one can classify most efforts as modified gravity or introducing exotic matter, such as dark matter and dark energy. The truth, as usual, may lie in between [94].

We hope that using this method and more precise astronomical data will help to evaluate accurate parameters of different alternative gravity models and to obtain gravitational potentials at the Galactic Center.

**Author Contributions:** All coauthors participated in writing, calculation and discussion of obtained results. All authors have read and agreed to the published version of the manuscript.

**Funding:** This research received no external funding.

**Acknowledgments:** This work is supported by Ministry of Education, Science and Technological Development of the Republic of Serbia. PJ wishes to acknowledge the support by this Ministry through the project contract No. 451-03-9/2021-14/200002. The authors also wish to thank the Center for mathematical modeling and computer simulations in physics and astrophysics of Vinča Institute of Nuclear Sciences.

**Conflicts of Interest:** The authors declare no conflict of interest.

## Abbreviations

The following abbreviations are used in this manuscript:

| | |
|---|---|
| GR | General Relativity |
| LT | Lense-Thirring |
| SMBH | Supermassive black hole |

## Appendix A. Hybrid Palatini Gravity Model

It is important to note that theoretical studies in this field commonly assume $c = G = 1$ units. However, for practical purposes, i.e., for comparisons with the astronomical observations, it is necessary to recast gravitation potential in appropriate units. Thus, here we derive gravitation potential in weak field limit of the Hybrid Palatini gravity in a form convenient for this purpose.

The action, proposed in the papers by Capozziello et al. (2012,2013) [89,93], Harko et al. (2012) [88] and Borka et al. (2016) [71], is given by:

$$S = \frac{1}{2\kappa}\int d^4x\sqrt{-g}[R + \phi\mathcal{R} - V(\phi) + 2\kappa L_m], \tag{A1}$$

where $\kappa = \dfrac{8\pi G}{c^4}$, $R$ is the Ricci scalar, $\mathcal{R} = g^{\mu\nu}\mathcal{R}_{\mu\nu}$ presents the Palatini curvature with the independent connection $\widetilde{\Gamma}^{\lambda}_{\mu\nu}$, $L_m$ is the density Lagrangian, and $g$ is the determinant of $g_{\mu\nu}$.

The Palatini curvature is given by the following equations, with the scalar field $\phi$ and potential $V(\phi)$:

$$\mathcal{R}_{\mu\nu} \equiv \widetilde{\Gamma}^{\alpha}_{\mu\nu,\alpha} - \widetilde{\Gamma}^{\alpha}_{\mu\alpha,\nu} + \widetilde{\Gamma}^{\alpha}_{\alpha\lambda}\widetilde{\Gamma}^{\lambda}_{\mu\nu} - \widetilde{\Gamma}^{\alpha}_{\mu\lambda}\widetilde{\Gamma}^{\lambda}_{\alpha\nu} \tag{A2}$$

$$\widetilde{\Gamma}^{\lambda}_{\mu\nu} = \frac{1}{2}\widetilde{g}^{\lambda\sigma}(\widetilde{g}_{\mu\sigma,\nu} + \widetilde{g}_{\nu\sigma,\mu} - \widetilde{g}_{\mu\nu,\sigma}) \tag{A3}$$

$$\widetilde{g}_{\lambda\sigma} = g_{\lambda\sigma}F(\mathcal{R}). \tag{A4}$$

Combination of the Equations (A2)–(A4) resulted in the equation:

$$\begin{aligned}\widetilde{\Gamma}^{\lambda}_{\mu\nu} \quad = \quad & \frac{g^{\lambda\sigma}}{2F(\mathcal{R})}\Big(g_{\mu\sigma,\nu}F(\mathcal{R}) + g_{\nu\sigma,\mu}F(\mathcal{R}) - g_{\mu\nu,\sigma}F(\mathcal{R}) + \\ & + g_{\mu\sigma}F(\mathcal{R})_{,\nu} + g_{\nu\sigma}F(\mathcal{R})_{,\mu} - g_{\mu\nu}F(\mathcal{R})_{,\sigma}\Big).\end{aligned} \tag{A5}$$

Substitution of Equation (A5) into Equation (A2) enabled obtaining the expression for Palatini curvature:

$$\mathcal{R}_{\mu\nu} = R_{\mu\nu} + \frac{3\nabla_\mu F(\mathcal{R})\nabla_\nu F(\mathcal{R})}{2F(\mathcal{R})^2} - \frac{\nabla_\mu\nabla_\nu F(\mathcal{R})}{F(\mathcal{R})} - \frac{g_{\mu\nu}}{2}\frac{\Box F(\mathcal{R})}{F(\mathcal{R})}. \tag{A6}$$

The action is varied respectively to the metric $g_{\mu\nu}$, scalar field $\phi$ and connection $\widetilde{\Gamma}^{\lambda}_{\mu\nu}$, which leads to the following equations:

$$R_{\mu\nu} + \phi\mathcal{R}_{\mu\nu} - \frac{1}{2}g_{\mu\nu}[R + \phi\mathcal{R} - V(\phi)] = \kappa T_{\mu\nu} \tag{A7}$$

$$\mathcal{R} - V'(\phi) = 0 \tag{A8}$$

$$\widetilde{\nabla}_\alpha(\sqrt{-g}\phi g^{\mu\nu}) = 0. \tag{A9}$$

The Palatini connection is represented by Equation (A9) [101], which is obtained by varied action with respect to the relation $\widetilde{\Gamma}^{\lambda}_{\mu\nu}$, by keeping the metric constant $g^{\mu\nu}$. Equation (A9) implied that the function $F(R) = \phi$, and thus the Palatini Tensor and Palatini scalars are given by the following equations:

$$\mathcal{R}_{\mu\nu} = R_{\mu\nu} + \frac{3\partial_\mu\phi\partial_\nu\phi}{2\phi^2} - \frac{\nabla_\mu\nabla_\nu\phi}{\phi} - \frac{g_{\mu\nu}}{2}\frac{\Box\phi}{\phi}, \tag{A10}$$

$$\mathcal{R} = R + \frac{3\partial_\mu\phi\partial^\mu\phi}{2\phi^2} - \frac{3\,\Box\phi}{\phi}. \tag{A11}$$

The trace of Equation (A7) is given in the next relation:

$$R + \kappa T = 2V(\phi) - \phi V_\phi, \quad V'(\phi) = V_\phi. \tag{A12}$$

Combination of Equations (A7), (A8), (A10) and (A12), enabled obtaining the metric field equations:

$$(1+\phi)R_{\mu\nu} = \kappa(T_{\mu\nu} - \frac{1}{2}g_{\mu\nu}T) + \frac{1}{2}g_{\mu\nu}(V(\phi) + \Box\phi) + \nabla_\mu\nabla_\nu\phi - \frac{3\partial_\mu\phi\partial_\nu\phi}{2\phi}. \quad \text{(A13)}$$

and the trace of Equation (A13) is:

$$(1+\phi)R = -\kappa T + 2(V(\phi) + \Box\phi) + \Box\phi - \frac{3\partial_\mu\phi\partial^\mu\phi}{2\phi}. \quad \text{(A14)}$$

The scalar field equation is obtained by combination of the Equations (A12) and (A14):

$$-\Box\phi + \frac{\partial_\mu\phi\partial^\mu\phi}{2\phi} + \frac{\phi}{3}(2V(\phi) - (1+\phi)V_\phi) = \frac{\phi\kappa T}{3}. \quad \text{(A15)}$$

We can see that scalar field is governed by the second-order evolution equation, which is an effective Klein–Gordon equation.

*Equations for Newtonian Limit*

In order to derive the Newtonian limit, it is common to write metric $g_{\mu\nu}$ as a sum of Minkowski metric $\eta_{\mu\nu}$ and perturbation metric $h_{\mu\nu}$: $g_{\mu\nu} = \eta_{\mu\nu} + h_{\mu\nu}$, $|h_{\mu\nu}| \ll 1$, $T_{00} = -\rho c^2$, $T_{ij} = 0$, $\eta_{00} = -1$ [87,101], where $c$ is the speed of light. The paper [87] reviewed the formulation of hybrid metric-Palatini approach and its main achievements in passing the local tests and in applications to astrophysics and cosmology, and, in [101], the gravitational field equations for the modified gravity $f(R,T)$ theory are considered in the framework of the Palatini formalism.

The basic properties of Newtonian limit are: $\phi = \phi_0 + \psi$, $\phi \gg \psi$, $\frac{3\partial_\mu\phi\partial_\nu\phi}{2\phi} = \frac{3\partial_\mu\psi\partial_\nu\psi}{2\phi} \ll 1$. We denote the asymptotic of $\phi$ as $\phi_0$ and the local perturbation as $\psi$. Accordingly, Equation (A15) obtained the following shape of linear order:

$$-\Box\psi + (2V(\phi) - (1+\phi)V_\phi)\frac{\psi}{3} = \frac{\phi_0\kappa T}{3} \quad \text{(A16)}$$

We neglected the time derivatives of $\psi$, and thus Equation (A16) can be written in the following way:

$$\Delta\psi - m_\phi^2\psi = -\frac{\phi_0\kappa M\delta(r)c^2}{3}, \quad \text{(A17)}$$

where $m_\phi^2 = \frac{1}{3}(2V(\phi) - (1+\phi)V_\phi)|_{\phi=\phi_0}$ and $T = \rho c^2 = Mc^2\delta(r)$. It can be shown that the effective mass can be expressed in the form: $m_\phi^2 = (2V - V_\phi - \phi(1+\phi)V_{\phi\phi})|_{\phi=\phi_0}$, where $V$, $V_\phi$ and $V_{\phi\phi}$ are the potential and its first and second derivatives with respect to $\phi$, respectively. Solving the equation (A17), we obtained:

$$\phi = \phi_0 + \psi = \phi_0 + \frac{2G\phi_0 M}{3c^2}\frac{e^{-m_\phi r}}{r}. \quad \text{(A18)}$$

Since the background is Minkowskian, the perturbed Ricci tensor is given by $\delta R_{\mu\nu} = \frac{1}{2}(\partial_\sigma\partial_\mu h_\nu^\sigma + \partial_\sigma\partial_\nu h_\mu^\sigma - \partial_\mu\partial_\nu h - \Box h_{\mu\nu}) \approx -\frac{1}{2}\Delta h_{\mu\nu}$ and $\frac{\partial^2 h}{\partial t^2} \approx 0$, $\frac{\partial^2\psi}{\partial t^2} \approx 0$ (slow motion) [87,101]. Using the following gauge conditions: $\partial_\lambda\widetilde{h}_\mu^\lambda - \frac{1}{1+\phi_0}\partial_\mu\psi = 0$, where $\widetilde{h}_\nu^\lambda \equiv h_\nu^\lambda - \frac{1}{2}\delta_\nu^\lambda h_\alpha^\alpha$ [87], Equation (A13) becomes:

$$-\frac{1}{2}\Delta h_{\mu\nu}(1+\phi_0) = \kappa(T_{\mu\nu} - \frac{1}{2}\eta_{\mu\nu}T) + \frac{1}{2}\eta_{\mu\nu}(V(\phi) + \Delta\phi), \quad \text{(A19)}$$

and from this, we obtain:

$$\Delta h_{00} = -\frac{2\kappa}{1+\phi_0}(T_{00} - \frac{1}{2}\eta_{00}T) + \frac{-2\eta_{00}}{2(1+\phi_0)}(V_0 + \Delta\psi), \quad \text{(A20)}$$

where $V_0$ is the minimum of potential $V$ [71], and then

$$h_{00} = -\frac{\kappa M c^2}{1+\phi_0}\frac{1}{4\pi r} + \frac{V_0}{1+\phi_0}\frac{r^2}{6l_c^2} + \frac{\psi}{1+\phi_0}, \quad \text{(A21)}$$

where $l_c$ is a characteristic length scale, corresponding to the cosmological background.

By equating $2\Phi(r)/c^2 = h_{00}$, we have:

$$\begin{aligned} 2\Phi(r)/c^2 &= -\frac{2GM}{1+\phi_0}\frac{1}{c^2 r} + \frac{V_0}{1+\phi_0}\frac{r^2}{6l_c^2} + \frac{2G\phi_0 M}{3(1+\phi_0)c^2}\frac{e^{-m_\phi r}}{r} \\ &= -\frac{2G_{eff}M}{c^2 r} + \frac{V_0}{1+\phi_0}\frac{r^2}{6l_c^2}, \end{aligned} \quad \text{(A22)}$$

with an effective potential introduced $G_{eff} = \frac{G}{1+\phi_0}\left(1 - \frac{\phi_0}{3}e^{-m_\phi r}\right)$. The term in Equation (A22) proportional to $r^2$ corresponds to the cosmological background, and it can be neglected on a galactic level [87].

The modified gravitation potential of the Newtonian limit is:

$$\Phi(r) \approx -\frac{G_{eff}M}{r} = -\frac{G}{1+\phi_0}\left(1 - \frac{\phi_0}{3}e^{-m_\phi r}\right)\frac{M}{r}. \quad \text{(A23)}$$

## References


1. Fischbach, E.; Talmadge, C.L. *The Search for Non–Newtonian Gravity*; Springer: Berlin/Heidelberg, Germany; New York, NY, USA, 1999; 305p.
2. Capozziello, S.; Faraoni, V. *Beyond Einstein Gravity: A Survey of Gravitational Theories for Cosmology and Astrophysics*; Fundamental Theories of Physics; Springer: Berlin/Heidelberg, Germany, 2011; Volume 170.
3. Nojiri, S.; Odintsov, S.D. Unified cosmic history in modified gravity: From $F(R)$ theory to Lorentz non-invariant models. *Phys. Rept.* **2011**, *505*, 59. [CrossRef]
4. Nojiri, S.; Odintsov, S.D.; Oikonomou, V.K. Modified Gravity Theories on a Nutshell: Inflation, Bounce and Late-time Evolution. *Phys. Rept.* **2017**, *692*, 1. [CrossRef]
5. Capozziello, S.; De Laurentis, M. The dark matter problem from $f(R)$ gravity viewpoint. *Ann. Phys.* **2012**, *524*, 545. [CrossRef]
6. Salucci, P.; Esposito, G.; Lambiase, G.; Battista, E.; Benetti, M.; Bini, D.; Boco, L.; Sharma, G.; Bozza, V.; Buoninfante, L.; et al. Einstein, Planck and Vera Rubin: Relevant encounters between the Cosmological and the Quantum Worlds. *Front. Phys.* **2021**, *8*, 603190. [CrossRef]
7. Dimitrijević, I.; Dragović, B.; Koshelev, A.S.; Rakić, Z.; Stanković, J. Cosmological solutions of a nonlocal square root gravity. *Phys. Lett. B* **2019**, *797*, 134848. [CrossRef]
8. Clifton, T. *Alternative Theories of Gravity*; University of Cambridge: Cambridge, UK, 2006.
9. Kopeikin, S.; Vlasov, I. Parametrized post-Newtonian theory of reference frames, multipolar expansions and equations of motion in the N-body problem. *Phys. Rep.* **2004**, *400*, 209. [CrossRef]
10. Rubakov, V.A.; Tinyakov, P.G. Infrared-modified gravities and massive gravitons. *Phys. Usp.* **2008**, *51*, 759. [CrossRef]
11. Babichev, E.; Deffayet, C.; Ziour, R. Recovery of general relativity in massive gravity via the Vainshtein mechanism. *Phys. Rev. D* **2010**, *82*, 104008. [CrossRef]
12. Capozziello, S.; De Laurentis, M. Extended Theories of Gravity. *Phys. Rep.* **2011**, *509*, 167. [CrossRef]
13. Clifton, T.; Ferreira, P.G.; Padilla, A.; Skordis, C. Modified gravity and cosmology. *Phys. Rep.* **2012**, *513*, 1. [CrossRef]
14. De Rham, C. Massive Gravity. *Living Rev. Relativ.* **2014**, *17*, 7. [CrossRef] [PubMed]
15. De Martino, I.; De Laurentis, M.; Capozziello, S. Constraining $f(R)$ Gravity by the Large-Scale Structure. *Universe* **2015**, *1*, 123–157. [CrossRef]
16. De Rham, C.; Deskins, J.T.; Tolley, A.J.; Zhou, S.-Y. Massive Gravity. *Rev. Mod. Phys.* **2017**, *89*, 025004. [CrossRef]
17. Petrov, A.N.; Kopeikin, S.M.; Lompay, R.R.; Tekin, B. *Metric Theories of Gravity: Perturbations and Conservation Laws*; De Gruyter Studies in Mathematical Physics; De Gruyter: Berlin, Germany, 2017; ISBN 9783110351781.
18. Borka, D.; Borka Jovanović, V.; Capozziello, S.; Zakharov, A.F.; Jovanović, P. Estimating the Parameters of Extended Gravity Theories with the Schwarzschild Precession of S2 Star. *Universe* **2021**, *7*, 407. [CrossRef]

19. Zakharov, A.F.; Nucita, A.A.; Paolis, F.D.; Ingrosso, G. Solar system constraints on $R^n$ gravity. *Phys. Rev. D* **2006**, *74*, 107101. [CrossRef]
20. Zakharov, A.F.; Nucita, A.A.; Paolis, F.D.; Ingrosso, G. Apoastron shift constraints on dark matter distribution at the Galactic Center. *Phys. Rev. D* **2007**, *76*, 062001. [CrossRef]
21. Martins, C.F.; Salucci, P. Analysis of rotation curves in the framework of $R^n$ gravity. *Mon. Not. R. Astron. Soc.* **2007**, *381*, 1103. [CrossRef]
22. Nucita, A.A.; Paolis, F.D.; Ingrosso, G.; Qadir, A.; Zakharov, A.F. Sgr A*: A laboratory to measure the central black hole and stellar cluster parameters. *Publ. Astron. Soc. Pac.* **2007**, *119*, 349. [CrossRef]
23. Zakharov, A.F.; Capozziello, S.; Paolis, F.D.; Ingrosso, G.; Nucita, A.A. The Role of Dark Matter and Dark Energy in Cosmological Models: Theoretical Overview. *Space Sci. Rev.* **2009**, *148*, 301. [CrossRef]
24. Capozziello, S.; Stabile, A.; Troisi, A. A general solution in the Newtonian limit of $f(R)$-gravity. *Mod. Phys. Lett. A* **2009**, *24*, 659. [CrossRef]
25. Iorio, L. Constraints on the range $\Lambda$ of Yukawa-like modifications to the Newtonian inverse-square law of gravitation from Solar System planetary motions. *JHEP* **2007**, *10*, 041. [CrossRef]
26. Iorio, L. Putting Yukawa-like Modified Gravity (MOG) on the test in the Solar System. *Sch. Res. Exch.* **2008**, *2008*, 238385. [CrossRef]
27. Iorio, L. Galactic orbital motions in the dark matter, modified Newtonian dynamics and modified gravity scenarios. *Mon. Not. R. Astron. Soc.* **2010**, *401*, 2012. [CrossRef]
28. Borka, D.; Jovanović, P.; Borka Jovanović, V.; Zakharov, A.F. Constraints on $R^n$ gravity from precession of orbits S2-like stars. *Phys. Rev. D* **2012**, *85*, 124004. [CrossRef]
29. Capozziello, S.; Borka, D.; Jovanović, P.; Borka Jovanović, V. Constraining Extended Gravity Models by S2 star orbits around the Galactic Centre. *Phys. Rev. D* **2014**, *90*, 044052. [CrossRef]
30. Dokuchaev, V.I.; Eroshenko, Y.N. Weighing of the Dark Matter at the Center of the Galaxy. *JETP Lett.* **2015**, *101*, 777. [CrossRef]
31. Dokuchaev, V.I.; Eroshenko, Y.N. Weighing of Dark Matter in the Galactic Center: Proceedings of the Seventeenth Lomonosov Conference on Elementary Particle Physics. In *Particle Physics at the Year of Light*; WSPC: Singapore, 2017; pp. 335–339.
32. Dokuchaev, V.I.; Eroshenko, Y.N. Physical laboratory at the center of the Galaxy. *Phys. Uspekhi* **2015**, *58*, 772. [CrossRef]
33. Aviles, A.; Gruber, C.; Luongo, O.; Quevedo, H. Cosmography and constraints on the equation of state of the Universe in various parametrizations. *Phys. Rev. D* **2012**, *86*, 123516. [CrossRef]
34. Dunsby, P.K.S.; Luongo, O. On the theory and applications of modern cosmography. *Int. J. Geom. Meth. Mod. Phys.* **2016**, *13*, 1630002. [CrossRef]
35. Capozziello, S.; De Laurentis, M.; Luongo, O.; Ruggeri, A.C. Cosmographic Constraints and Cosmic Fluids. *Galaxies* **2013**, *1*, 216–260. [CrossRef]
36. De Laurentis, M.; De Martino, I.; Lazkoz, R. Modified gravity revealed along geodesic tracks. *Eur. Phys. J. C* **2018**, *78*, 916. [CrossRef] [PubMed]
37. De Martino, I.; Lazkoz, R.; De Laurentis, M. Analysis of the Yukawa gravitational potential in $f(R)$ gravity I: Semiclassical periastron advance. *Phys. Rev. D* **2018**, *97*, 104067. [CrossRef]
38. De Laurentis, M.; De Martino, I.; Lazkoz, R. Analysis of the Yukawa gravitational potential in $f(R)$ gravity II: Relativistic periastron advance. *Phys. Rev. D* **2018**, *97*, 104068. [CrossRef]
39. Capozziello, S.; D'Agostino, R.; Luongo, O. Extended gravity cosmography. *Int. J. Mod. Phys.* **2019**, *28*, 1930016. [CrossRef]
40. D'addio, A. S-star dynamics through a Yukawa-like gravitational potential. *Phys. Dark Universe* **2021**, *33*, 100871. [CrossRef]
41. De Martino, I.; Della Monica, R. Unveiling the nature of Sgr A* with the geodesic motion of S-stars. *arXiv* **2021**, arXiv:2112.01888.
42. Ghez, A.M.; Morris, M.; Becklin, E.E.; Tanner, A.; Kremenek, T. The accelerations of stars orbiting the Milky Way's central black hole. *Nature* **2000**, *407*, 349. [CrossRef]
43. Ghez, A.M.; Salim, S.; Weinberg, N.N.; Lu, J.R.; Do, T.; Dunn, J.K.; Matthews, K.; Morris, M.R.; Yelda, S.; Becklin, E.E.; et al. Measuring distance and properties of the Milky Way's central supermassive black hole with stellar orbits. *Astrophys. J.* **2008**, *689*, 1044. [CrossRef]
44. Gillessen, S.; Eisenhauer, F.; Fritz, T.K.; Bartko, H.; Dodds-Eden, K.; Pfuhl, O.; Ott, T.; Genzel, R. The orbit of the star S2 around SGR A* from very large telescope and Keck data. *Astrophys. J.* **2009**, *707*, L114. [CrossRef]
45. Gillessen, S.; Eisenhauer, F.; Trippe, S.; Alexander, T.; Genzel, R.; Martins, F.; Ott, T. Monitoring stellar orbits around the massive black hole in the Galactic Center. *Astrophys. J.* **2009**, *692*, 1075. [CrossRef]
46. Schodel, R.; Ott, T.; Genzel, R.; Hofmann, R.; Lehnert, M.; Eckart, A.; Mouawad, N.; Alexander, T.; Reid, M.J.; Lenzen, R.; et al. Closest star seen orbiting the supermassive black hole at the Centre of the Milky Way. *Nature* **2002**, *419*, 694. [CrossRef] [PubMed]
47. Genzel, R.; Eisenhauer, F.; Gillessen, S. The Galactic Center massive black hole and nuclear star cluster. *Rev. Mod. Phys.* **2010**, *82*, 3121. [CrossRef]
48. Meyer, L.; Ghez, A.M.; Schödel, R.; Yelda, S.; Boehle, A.; Lu, J.R.; Do, T.; Morris, M.R.; Becklin, E.E.; Matthews, K. The Shortest-Known-Period Star Orbiting Our Galaxy's Supermassive Black Hole. *Science* **2012**, *338*, 84. [CrossRef] [PubMed]
49. Gillessen, S.; Plewa, P.M.; Eisenhauer, F.; Sari, R.E.; Waisberg, I.; Habibi, M.; Pfuhl, O.; George, E.; Dexter, J.; von Fellenberg, S.; et al. An Update on Monitoring Stellar Orbits in the Galactic Center. *Astrophys. J.* **2017**, *837*, 30. [CrossRef]

50. Hees, A.; Do, T.; Ghez, A.M.; Martinez, G.D.; Naoz, S.; Becklin, E.E.; Boehle, A.; Chappell, S.; Chu, D.; Dehghanfar, A.; et al. Testing General Relativity with Stellar Orbits around the Supermassive Black Hole in Our Galactic Center. *Phys. Rev. Lett.* **2017**, *118*, 211101. [CrossRef]
51. Chu, D.S.; Do, T.; Hees, A.; Ghez, A.; Naoz, S.; Witzel, G.; Sakai, S.; Chappell, S.; Gautam, A.K.; Lu, J.R.; et al. Investigating the Binarity of S0-2: Implications for Its Origins and Robustness as a Probe of the Laws of Gravity around a Supermassive Black Hole. *Astrophys. J.* **2018**, *854*, 12. [CrossRef]
52. GRAVITY Collaboration; Abuter, R.; Amorim, A.; Anugu, N.; Bauböck, M.; Benisty, M.; Berger, J.P.; Blind, N.; Bonnet, Brandner, W.; et al. Detection of the gravitational redshift in the orbit of the star S2 near the Galactic centre massive black hole. *Astron. Astrophys.* **2018**, *615*, L15. [CrossRef]
53. GRAVITY Collaboration; Abuter, R.; Amorim, A.; Bauböck, M.; Berger, J.P.; Bonnet, H.; Brandner, W.; Clénet, Y.; Du Foresto, V.C.; et al. A geometric distance measurement to the Galactic center black hole with 0.3% uncertainty. *Astron. Astrophys.* **2019**, *625*, L10.
54. Do, T.; Hees, A.; Ghez, A.; Martinez, G.D.; Chu, D.S.; Jia, S.; Sakai, S.; Lu, J.R.; Gautam, A.K.; O'neil, K.K.; et al. Relativistic redshift of the star S0-2 orbiting the Galactic Center supermassive black hole. *Science* **2019**, *365*, 664. [CrossRef]
55. GRAVITY Collaboration; Amorim, A.; Bauböck, M.; Benisty, M.; Berger, J.P.; Clénet, Y.; Forest, V.C.d.; de Zeeuw, T.; Dexter, J.; Duvert, G.; et al. Scalar field effects on the orbit of S2 star. *Mon. Not. R. Astron. Soc.* **2019**, *489*, 4606.
56. Hees, A.; Do, T.; Roberts, B.M.; Ghez, A.M.; Nishiyama, S.; Bentley, R.O.; Gautam, A.K.; Jia, S.; Kara, T.; Lu, J.R.; et al. Search for a Variation of the Fine Structure Constant around the Supermassive Black Hole in Our Galactic Center. *Phys. Rev. Lett.* **2020**, *124*, 081101. [CrossRef] [PubMed]
57. GRAVITY Collaboration; Abuter, R.; Amorim, A.; Bauböck, M.; Berger, J.P.; Bonnet, H.; Brandner, W.; Cardoso, V.; Clénet, Y.; de Zeeuw, P.T.; et al. Detection of the Schwarzschild precession in the orbit of the star S2 near the Galactic centre massive black hole. *Astron. Astrophys.* **2020**, *636*, L5. [CrossRef]
58. Ruffini, R.; Argüelles, C.R.; Rueda, J.A. On the core-halo distribution of dark matter in galaxies. *Mon. Not. R. Astron. Soc.* **2015**, *451*, 622. [CrossRef]
59. Becerra-Vergara, E.A.; Argüelles, C.R.; Krut, A.; Rueda, J.A.; Ruffini, R. Hinting a dark matter nature of Sgr A* via the S-stars. *Mon. Not. R. Astron. Soc.* **2021**, *505*, L64. [CrossRef]
60. Zakharov, A.F. Testing the Galactic Centre potential with S-stars. *Mon. Not. R. Astron. Soc. Lett.* **2021**. [CrossRef]
61. Rubilar, G.F.; Eckart, A. Periastron shifts of stellar orbits near the Galactic Center. *Astron. Astrophys.* **2001**, *374*, 95. [CrossRef]
62. Adkins, G.S.; McDonnell, J. Orbital precession due to central-force perturbations. *Phys. Rev. D* **2007**, *75*, 082001. [CrossRef]
63. Weinberg, N.N.; Milosavljević, M.; Ghez, A.M. Stellar dynamics at the Galactic Center with an extremely large telescope. *Astrophys. J.* **2005**, *622*, 878. [CrossRef]
64. Peißker, F.; Eckart, A.; Zajaček, M.; Michal, A.; Ali, B.; Parsa, M. S62 and S4711: Indications of a Population of Faint Fast-moving Stars inside the S2 Orbit-S4711 on a 7.6 yr Orbit around Sgr A*. *Astrophys. J.* **2020**, *899*, 50. [CrossRef]
65. Iorio, L. The Short-period S-stars S4711, S62, S4714 and the Lense-Thirring Effect due to the Spin of Sgr A*. *Astrophys. J.* **2020**, *904*, 186. [CrossRef]
66. Iorio, L. On the 2PN Pericentre Precession in the General Theory of Relativity and the Recently Discovered Fast-Orbiting S-Stars in Sgr A*. *Universe* **2021**, *7*, 37. [CrossRef]
67. Gainutdinov, R.; Baryshev, Y. Relativistic Effects in Orbital Motion of the S-Stars at the Galactic Center. *Universe* **2020**, *6*, 177. [CrossRef]
68. Fragione, G.; Loeb, A. An Upper Limit on the Spin of Sgr A* Based on Stellar Orbits in Its Vicinity. *Astrophys. J. Lett.* **2020**, *901*, L32. [CrossRef]
69. Borka, D.; Jovanović, P.; Borka Jovanović, V.; Zakharov, A.F. Constraining the range of Yukawa gravity interaction from S2 star orbits. *J. Cosmol. Astropart. Phys.* **2013**, *11*, 081101. [CrossRef]
70. Zakharov, A.F.; Borka, D.; Borka Jovanović, V.; Jovanović, P. Constraints on $R^n$ gravity from precession of orbits of S2-like stars: A case of a bulk distribution of mass. *Adv. Space Res.* **2014**, *54*, 1108. [CrossRef]
71. Borka, D.; Capozziello, S.; Jovanović, P.; Borka Jovanović, V. Probing hybrid modified gravity by stellar motion around Galactic Center. *Astropart. Phys.* **2016**, *79*, 41. [CrossRef]
72. Zakharov, A.F.; Jovanović, P.; Borka, D.; Borka Jovanović, V. Constraining the range of Yukawa gravity interaction from S2 star orbits II: Bounds on graviton mass. *J. Cosmol. Astropart. Phys.* **2016**, *5*, 45. [CrossRef]
73. Zakharov, A.F.; Jovanović, P.; Borka, D.; Borka Jovanović, V. Constraining the range of Yukawa gravity interaction from S2 star orbits III: Improvement expectations for graviton mass bounds. *J. Cosmol. Astropart. Phys.* **2018**, *2018*, 50. [CrossRef]
74. Zakharov, A.F.; Jovanović, P.; Borka, D.; Borka Jovanović, V. Different Ways to Estimate Graviton Mass. *Int. J. Mod. Phys. Conf. Ser.* **2018**, *47*, 1860096. [CrossRef]
75. Dialektopoulos, K.F.; Borka, D.; Capozziello, S.; Borka Jovanović, V.; Jovanović, P. Constraining nonlocal gravity by S2 star orbits. *Phys. Rev. D* **2019**, *99*, 044053. [CrossRef]
76. Borka Jovanović, V.; Jovanović, P.; Borka, D.; Capozziello, S.; Gravina, S.; D'Addio, A. Constraining scalar-tensor gravity models by S2 star orbits around the Galactic Center. *Facta Univ. Ser. Phys. Chem. Tech.* **2019**, *17*, 11–20. [CrossRef]
77. Jovanović, P.; Borka, D.; Borka Jovanović, V.; Zakharov, A.F. Influence of bulk mass distribution on orbital precession of S2 star in Yukawa gravity. *Eur. Phys. J. D* **2021**, *75*, 145. [CrossRef]
78. Borka Jovanović, V.; Capozziello, S.; Jovanović, P.; Borka, D. Recovering the fundamental plane of galaxies by $f(R)$ gravity. *Phys. Dark Universe* **2016**, *14*, 73. [CrossRef]

79. Capozziello, S.; Borka Jovanović, V.; Borka, D.; Jovanović, P. Constraining theories of gravity by fundamental plane of elliptical galaxies. *Phys. Dark Universe* **2020**, *29*, 100573. [CrossRef]
80. Borka Jovanović, V.; Borka, D.; Jovanović, P.; Capozziello, S. Possible effects of hybrid gravity on stellar kinematics in elliptical galaxies. *Eur. Phys. J. D* **2021**, *75*, 149. [CrossRef]
81. Capozziello, S.; Jovanović, P.; Borka Jovanović, V.; Borka, D. Addressing the missing matter problem in galaxies through a new fundamental gravitational radius. *J. Cosmol. Astropart. Phys.* **2017**, *6*, 44. [CrossRef]
82. Clifton, T.; Barrow, J.D. The power of general relativity. *Phys. Rev. D* **2005**, *72*, 103005. [CrossRef]
83. Capozziello, S.; Cardone, V.F.; Troisi, A. Gravitational lensing in fourth-order gravity. *Phys. Rev. D* **2006**, *73*, 104019. [CrossRef]
84. Capozziello, S.; Cardone, V.F.; Troisi, A. Low surface brightness galaxy rotation curves in the low energy limit of $R^n$ gravity: No need for dark matter? *Mon. Not. R. Astron. Soc.* **2007**, *375*, 1423. [CrossRef]
85. Sotiriou, T.P.; Faraoni, V. $f(R)$ theories of gravity. *Rev. Mod. Phys.* **2010**, *82*, 451. [CrossRef]
86. Olmo, G.J. Palatini Approach to Modified Gravity: $f(R)$ Theories and Beyond. *Int. J. Mod. Phys. D* **2011**, *20*, 413. [CrossRef]
87. Capozziello, S.; Harko, T.; Koivisto, T.S.; Lobo, F.S.N.; Olmo, G.J. Hybrid Metric-Palatini Gravity. *Universe* **2015**, *1*, 199–238. [CrossRef]
88. Harko, T.; Koivisto, T.S.; Lobo, F.S.N.; Olmo, G.J. Metric-Palatini gravity unifying local constraints and late-time cosmic acceleration. *Phys. Rev. D* **2012**, *85*, 084016. [CrossRef]
89. Capozziello, S.; Harko, T.; Koivisto, T.S.; Lobo, F.S.N.; Olmo, G.J. Galactic rotation curves in hybrid metric-Palatini gravity. *Astropart. Phys.* **2013**, *35*, 65. [CrossRef]
90. Capozziello, S.; Harko, T.; Koivisto, T.S.; Lobo, F.S.N.; Olmo, G.J. Cosmology of hybrid metric-Palatini $f(X)$-gravity. *JCAP* **2013**, *1304*, 011. [CrossRef]
91. Capozziello, S.; Harko, T.; Lobo, F.S.N.; Olmo, G.J. Hybrid modified gravity unifying local tests, galactic dynamics and late-time cosmic acceleration. *Int. J. Mod. Phys. D* **2013**, *22*, 1342006. [CrossRef]
92. Koivisto, T.S. Cosmology of modified (but second order) gravity. *AIP Conf. Proc.* **2010**, *1206*, 79.
93. Capozziello, S.; Harko, T.; Koivisto, T.S.; Lobo, F.S.N.; Olmo, G.J. Wormholes supported by hybrid metric-Palatini gravity. *Phys. Rev. D* **2012**, *86*, 127504. [CrossRef]
94. Allemandi, G.; Borowiec, A.; Francaviglia, M.; Odintsov, S.D. Dark energy dominance and cosmic acceleration in first-order formalism. *Phys. Rev. D* **2005**, *72*, 063505. [CrossRef]
95. Borowiec, A.; Kozak, A. New class of hybrid metric-Palatini scalar-tensor theories of gravity. *J. Cosmol. Astropart. Phys.* **2020**, *07*, 003. [CrossRef]
96. Genzel, R.; Ott, T.; Eisenhauer, F.; Hofmann, R.; Alexander, T.; Sternberg, A.; Lenzen, R.; Lacombe, F.; Rouan, D.; Renzini, A.; et al. The Stellar Cusp Around the Supermassive Black Hole in the Galactic Center. *Astrophys. J.* **2003**, *594*, 812. [CrossRef]
97. Preto, M.; Saha, P. On Post-Newtonian Orbits and the Galactic-Center Stars. *Astrophys. J.* **2009**, *703*, 1743. [CrossRef]
98. Landau, L.D.; Lifshitz, E.M. *Mechanics*; Butterworth-Heinemann: Oxford, UK, 1976.
99. Danby, J.M.A. *Fundamental of Celestial Mechanics*; Macmillan: New York, NY, USA, 1962.
100. Murray, C.D.; Dermott, S.F. *Solar System Dynamics*; Cambridge University Press: Cambridge, UK, 2000.
101. Wu, J.; Li, G.; Harko, T.; Liang, S.D. Palatini formulation of $f(R, T)$ gravity theory, and its cosmological implications. *Eur. Phys. J. C* **2018**, *78*, 430. [CrossRef]

MDPI
St. Alban-Anlage 66
4052 Basel
Switzerland
Tel. +41 61 683 77 34
Fax +41 61 302 89 18
www.mdpi.com

*Universe* Editorial Office
E-mail: universe@mdpi.com
www.mdpi.com/journal/universe

www.ingramcontent.com/pod-product-compliance
Lightning Source LLC
LaVergne TN
LVHW070206100526
838202LV00015B/2001